Y0-BUB-674

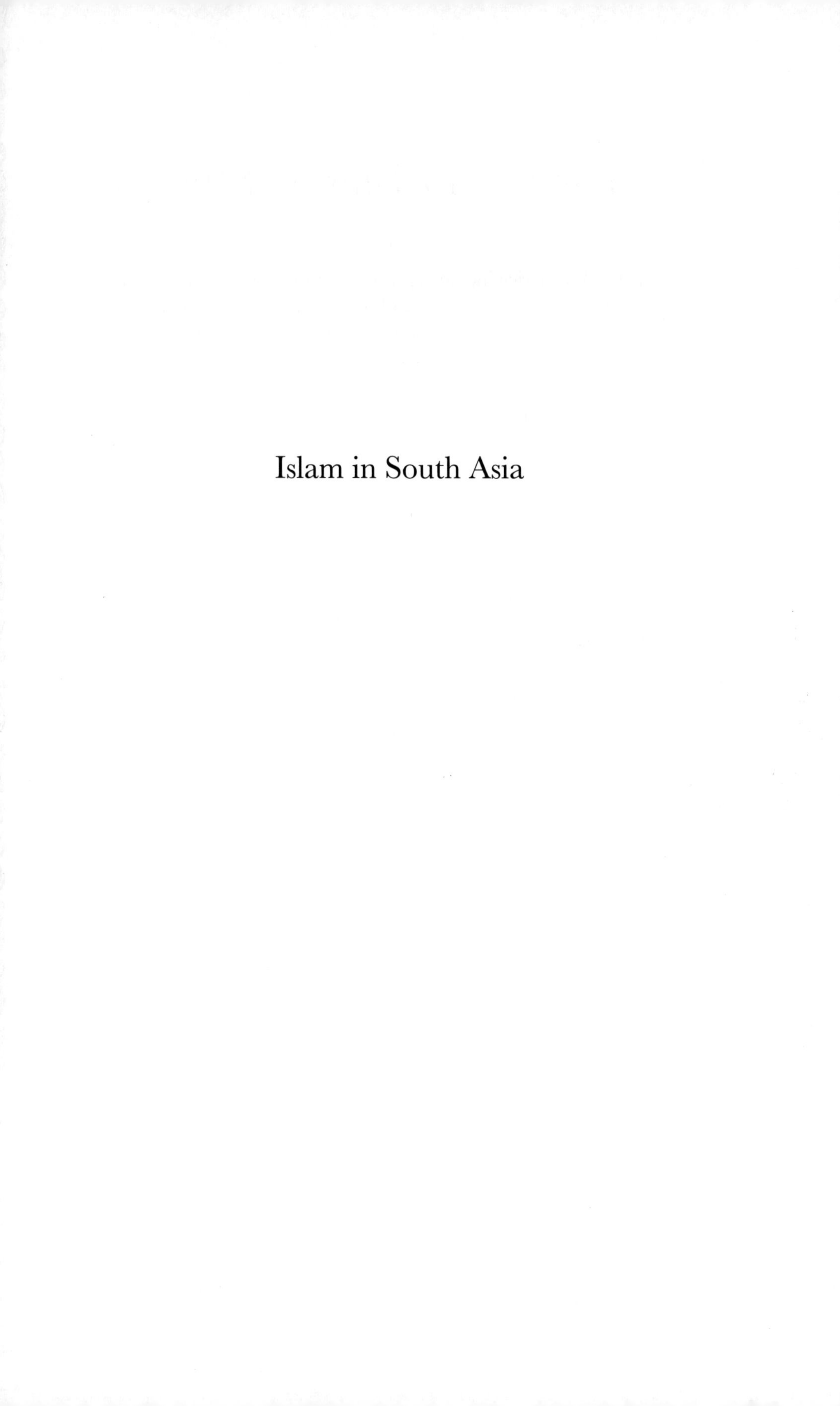

Islam in South Asia

Themes in Islamic Studies

A (new) Brill Series including short histories and concise surveys of appealing themes in the field of Islamic and Arabic Studies. The various titles give an accessible overview of a specific aspect or topic. Scholars and graduate students find in this series easy reference tools to current subjects in Islamic history and culture. Several titles are edited compilations of articles from the Encyclopaedia of Islam (second edition).

VOLUME 4

Islam in South Asia

A Short History

By

Jamal Malik

BRILL

LEIDEN • BOSTON
2008

Cover illustration: Faisal Mosque, Islamabad (personal archive), pierced carved stone-screen of Madrasa Ghazial-Din, outside Kashmiri Gate, Delhi (personal archive) and Minaret of Baba Lulu'i's mosque, photograph by Dinesh Mehta, in George Michell and Snehal Shah (eds.), Ahmadabad, Mumbai, Marq 2003 (reprint), p. 101. Courtesy Snehal Shah.

This book is printed on acid-free paper.

Library of Congress Cataloging-in-Publication Data

Malik, Jamal.
Islam in South Asia : a short history / By Jamal Malik.
p. cm. — (Themes in Islamic studies, ISSN 1389-823X ; v. 4)
Includes bibliographical references and index.
ISBN 978-90-04-16859-6 (hardback : alk. paper) 1. Islam—South Asia—History. 2. Muslims—South Asia—History. 3. South Asia—History. I. Title. II. Series.

BP63.A37M35 2008
297.0954—dc22

2008021190

ISSN 1389-823X
ISBN 978 90 04 16859 6

PRINTED IN THE NETHERLANDS

CONTENTS

ACKNOWLEDGEMENTS

Attempting a Short History of Islam in South Asia is an ambitious project, not the least because the contestation of Muslims in South Asia has become a major feature in media, academics and religious self-presentation. There is a rising curiosity about the region's Muslim cultures, not only in terms of quantity, which are virtually unlimited, but specifically in terms of quality, calling for an overview that would make plausible major trends which can provide some sort of comprehension for the immense complexity of Muslims in the sub-continent and so to improve the understanding of the current situation. Thus, the idea of the book was conceived against the backdrop of 9/11 when the world was still under shock and attention was shifted to South Asia and its many Muslim cultures. Indeed, writing such a challenging volume in the "Themes in Islamic Studies" book series has its drawbacks. This is so because all of the many voices actually involved in this composition can hardly be heeded even to some degree.

I would like to thank Brill for providing me such an opportunity; Trudy Kamperveen's patient collaboration in handling the problems of publication were indispensable for the outcome. I am thankful to Murshirul Hasan for his never ending hospitality and to Imtiaz Ahmad for his exciting intellectual stimulus. Adam Nayyar, Zafar Ahmad Ansari and Muhammad Khalid Masud always were important discussion partners. Many thanks go to members—current and former—of the Department of Religious Studies, University of Erfurt, such as Arshad Alam, Hasnain Bokhari, Moez Khalfaoui, Jan-Peter Hartung, and Margrit Pernau. They all took pains to critically read and make revisions of parts of the manuscript, in their capacities as scholars of South Asian Islam, in spite of their own academic preoccupations. Seema Alavi, Monica Juneja, Marcia Hermansen, and Yohannan Friedmann focussed on specific chapters; they shared their expertise. Muzaffar Alam, Carl Ernst and his students carefully read major parts of the manuscript and offered suggestions, both minor and major, which have been accommodated as far as possible. To all these colleagues, peers, students and friends I am greatly thankful; their expertise and comments were important additions to my own perspective. Thanks also go to the Max Weber Center for Advanced Cultural and Social

Studies, University of Erfurt, to have given me the chance to finalise the draft during a sabbatical. Stefan Hoffmann arranged for the maps. I am also grateful to Lelah Ferguson and Timothy Bell for correcting the manuscript.

My wife's constant interest and attendance during different phases of the work were as important as Benjamin's and Momin's rather realistic approach to my writing desk. How could the book have been finished without their abiding encouragement and love?

So it is my privilege to submit the final script with all its ups and downs, for which I am happy to take responsibility. However, this book is far from being a definitive contribution to what is *bahr-e zakhkhar*, a rising ocean, and one can look forward to further studies hoping that this work can provide a helpful perspective on the state of the field and will stimulate further interest in the area.

As far as the system of transliteration is concerned, Urdu, Arabic, Persian, Turkish, Hindi, and Sanskrit words have been written without diacritical marks, using a slightly altered version of the format in The Encyclopaedia of Islam (New Edition), unless otherwise noted. It should be emphasised that the lack of diacriticals and the use of the Christian calendar are aimed at making this study accessible to a wider audience in comparative studies of religion, history, and cultural and social sciences.

Erfurt, March 2008 Jamal Malik

ABBREVIATIONS

A.D.	Anno Domini
AIMMM	All India Muslim Majlis-e Mushawarat
AIMPLB	All-India Muslim Personal Law Board
Approx	Approximately
B.C.	Before Christ
BJP	Bharatiyya Janata Party
BNP	Bangladesh National Party
BSOAS	*Bulletin of the School of Oriental and African Studies*
C.E.	Christian Era
CII	Council of Islamic Ideology
COP	Combined Opposition Party
CUP	Cambridge University Press
EI(2)	*The Encyclopaedia of Islam*, new edition
EIC	East India Company
EnI	*Encyclopaedia Iranica*
h.	Hijra
IC	*Islamic Culture*
IESHR	*The Indian Economic and Social History Review*
IHC	*Indian History Congress*
IHR	*The Indian Historical Review*
IJMES	*International Journal of Middle Eastern Studies*
IL	*Indian Literature*
INC	Indian National Congress
IQ	*Islamic Quarterly*
IS	*Islamic Studies*
JAH	*Journal of Asian History*
JAOS	*Journal of the American Oriental Society*
JAS	*Journal of Asian Studies*
JASB	*Journal of the Asiatic Society of Bombay*
JASP	*Journal of the Asiatic Society of Pakistan*
JESHO	*Journal of the Economic and Social History of the Orient*
JIH	*Journal of Indian History*
JIS	*Journal of Islamic Studies*
JKLF	Jammu and Kashmir Liberation Front
JPHS	*Journal of the Pakistan Historical Society*

JRAS	*Journal of the Royal Asiatic Society*
JSAL	*Journal of South Asian Literature*
JSS	*Journal of Semitic Studies*
JUH	Jamʿiyyat al-ʿUlama-ye Hind
JUI	Jamʿiyyat-e ʿUlama-ye Islam
JUP	Jamʿiyyat-e ʿUlama-ye Pakistan
MAS	*Modern Asian Studies*
MW	*Muslim World*
n.d.	no date
N.W.	North Western
NWFP	Northwest Frontier Province
NWP	Northwestern Provinces
OUP	Oxford University Press
PPP	Pakistan People's Party
PUP	Princeton University Press
RSS	Rashtriyya Serayamsevah Sangh
S.	Sayyid
s.l.	no place
s.t.	no date
SI	*Studia Islamica*
U.P.	United Provinces
UCP	University of California Press
VHP	Vishwa Hindu Parishad
VOC	Vereenigde Oostindische Compagnie
WI	*Die Welt des Islams*

LIST OF ILLUSTRATIONS

Maps

Pictures

Pie chart

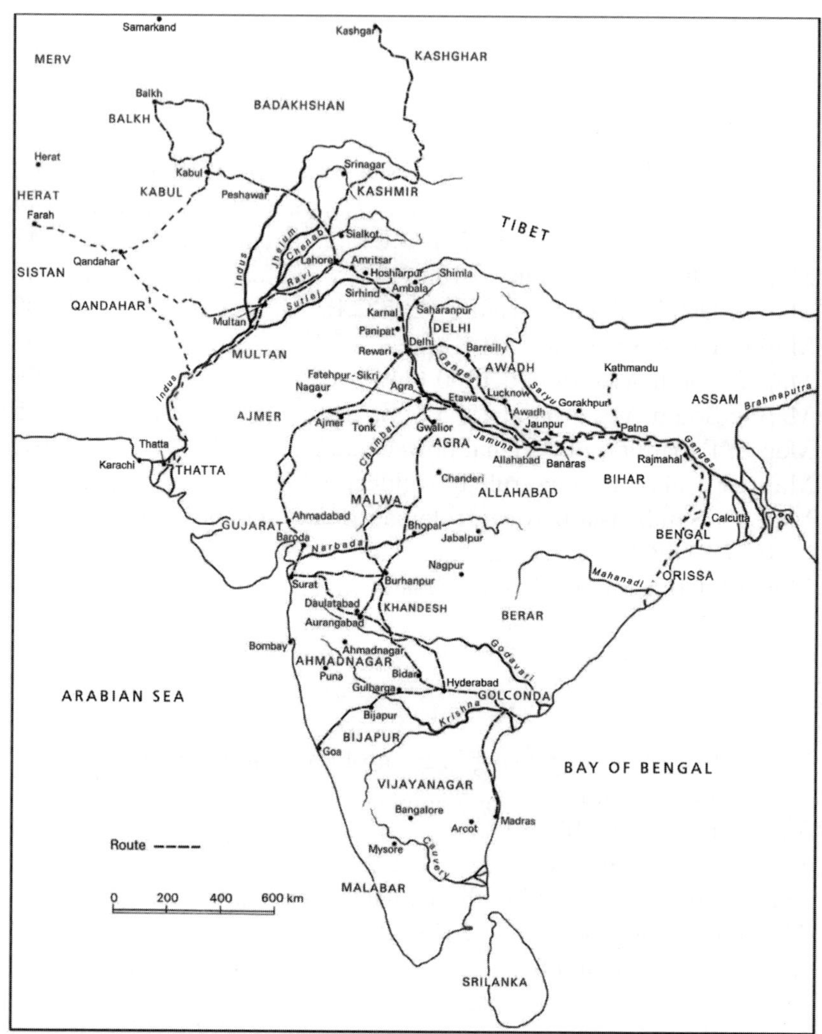

Map 1: Cities and central lines of communication in early modern South Asia

INTRODUCTION

South Asia comprises a vast geographical area, half the size of Europe. A geographical unit harbouring many cultures influenced by Hindu traditions, it has been the topic of many descriptions, whether academic, fictional or as travelogue. This region has—due to its wealth of mineral and natural resources, cultural variety and propensity to integrate different cultures—provided enough space for projections, yearnings, dreams and even traumata. Many books have been written on Muslims in South Asia, and many contributions penned recently, have tried in part, successfully to work their way through the religious vitality and breadth of ethnic, linguistic and political plurality of the sub-continent. Much more has to be communicated on South Asian Muslims in future; after all, they make up a sizable population: in 1901 approx. 63 million and 1941 some 94 million Muslims, increasing to 243 million in 1981, their number climbed to approx. 300 million in 1991,[1] and to approx. 430 million in 2000, including two Muslim majority countries, Pakistan with 150 million and Bangladesh with some 140 million Muslims. India with approx. 140 million harbours the largest Muslim minority world-wide. The region with currently nearly one third of the Muslim world population and an annual increase of more than 2% has always been a hub of Muslim theological, intellectual, and political as well as literary activities, representing incredibly multifaceted dynamics, at times affecting wider circles of the Muslim world through travel and communication and becoming increasingly virtual. Yet, it is problematic to speak of a monolithic South Asian Islam and an Indian Muslim minority, given the extent of diversity and distinction in the formations of religious communities—or religious communalisation or communitarisation,[2] on a scale ranging from pure to hybrid that has evolved over time and space. There are even stark cultural and climatic

[1] See Raymond Delval (ed.): *A Map of the Muslims in the World*, Leiden: Brill 1984, pp. 18f.; Raghuraj Gupta: "Changing Role and Status of the Muslim Minority in India: A Point of View", in: *Journal; Institute of Muslim Minority Affairs* 5/1 (1984), p. 182.

[2] It is difficult in English to convey *construction processes of new religious communities* in the sense of Max Weber's "religiöse Vergemeinschaftung"; see Max Weber: "Religionssoziologie, Typen religiöser Vergemeinschaftung", in: *Wirtschaft und Gesellschaft, Grundriss der verstehenden Soziologie*, Tübingen 1980(5), pp. 245–381.

differences between North and South India, the borderline being the Narmada River. These differences have historically affected politics and economy. While in the first case Islam was introduced by land, military conquest and forced migration, in South India it was introduced basically by sea, trade and commerce.

Yet, the questions legitimate to pose are, as to where Muslims came from and how they settled down in their interaction with local Hindu cultures. Which channels were operative that made possible political manoeuvring in a predominantly Hindu environment, and what discourses were helpful in that project? What of Muslim cultures that strove for public acceptance or for a place in the respective master narrative and could be challenged by a narrative of a dominant normative history developed on stark dichotimisations? Over a process of time, how did the monotheistically inclined theology of Islam lead to a process of regularisation, in which alternative options were hereticised by the respective 'meta narrative'? Similarly, was there a specific Muslim tradition in terms of a firm and authoritative part of religious and cultural identity, or were there cultural and discursive limitations to what was negotiated as tradition? What were the cultural overlappings that blurred religious and religiously legitimised boundaries to the extent that Islamic became what Marshall Hodgson has called Islamicated?[3] What made Muslim traditions flexible and adaptable to local variations of life on the one hand yet exclusivist in terms of sticking to what was perceived to be the essentials on the other? How was this tussle or tension between identity and alterity negotiated in a pluralist context and eventually used for the establishment of Muslim empires? And what lay beneath dynastic structures that operated as significant residuals powerful enough to outlive dynasties? Who were the actors?

This pantheon of questions is further complicated when in the process of cultural interaction, both Hindu and Muslim communities—diverse as they are in their construction processes—encountered European colonial power. Was this subjugation a unilateral process in the rationale of colonial encounter, or can forces of reciprocity be traced between Indians, both Hindus and Muslims, and colonial elites? Did colonial power—in analogy to the term Islamicated—become colonialicated?

[3] See Marshall Hodgson: *Venture of Islam. Conscience and History in a World Civilization*, Chicago 1975, Vol. 1, p. 59.

After all, both sides have been benefiting from the process of cultural encounter, albeit with the major difference that while Europeans strengthened their native countries, Muslims settled down in South Asia. What kind of colonial policies were envisaged and to what end? And, finally, why was the disintegration of British India inevitable for the creation of a separate Muslim homeland?

As the narrative goes, in the course of political manoeuvring toward a separate Muslim homeland, religion played a major mobilising force, endowing both sides—Muslims and Hindus—with identity and solidarity, ushering in imagined communities, which were probably more effective than any use of identity politics have ever been from 711 up to 1947. Religious communalisation or formation of religious communities were meant to integrate large and fragmented societies into perceptibly homogenous nations but did not succeed in the end. Why? Finally, how do Muslims or those who call themselves Muslims conceive of their destinies in different political contexts which range from singular coercive-dictatorial contexts to pluralist democratic ones?

There are indeed many more pertinent questions to pose than plausible answers available. The book in hand shall not and cannot, of course, satisfactorily answer even a fraction of all of these appropriate queries, nor can it present all of the manifold Muslim identities evolving in South Asia in the process of cultural encounter, even in part, satisfactorily. It is true that many studies have been written on different aspects of the history of Muslims and Islam in South Asia, from diachronic and synchronic perspectives. Yet, because of the sheer diversity of cultural articulations it has been hard to produce a systematic and synthesising approach, which can bring together some of the precious results of the vast research available, in a plausible narrative and help illustrate a few important gestating tracks over a long time: from Arab conquests starting even before 711 through to the rule of Turkic and Afghan-based dynasties from the thirteenth century onwards and the experience of European colonialism, up to state formation in the twentieth century and the following waves of Islamisation.

Due to the long expanding time-frame and the sheer complex polyvocality of the sources, a comprehensive narrative is hard to sustain. What is even more bewildering is the fact that most of the literature available is—to paraphrase Bruce Lawrence—characterised by "sweeping narratives", mostly focusing on dynastic history, teleologically oriented with a beginning and usually ending with a grim scenario. This image usually envisions an Islamic Golden age, followed by a decline, followed by a revival,[4] or by an increasingly militant Islam. It is also in line with long standing Orientalist[5] perceptions which see a gradually improving Islamic high culture swept away by the Mongols in 1258, followed by a long dark-age and stagnation culminating by around 1750 when enlightenment came to flourish in Europe while barbarism and despotism reigned in the Orient.[6] This mirror image is complemented by the idea of a deep colonial kiss to awaken the sleeping beauty resulting in an Islamic revival in the nineteenth century. This effective and memorable image is unfortunately also believed by many a Muslim. The underlying essentialism[7] is based on "orientalist empiricism"[8] and was continuously pursued in colonial and nationalist historiography, producing quite a number of orientalist studies.

Readers may find themselves perplexed at the attempts of this book to shake off these stereotypes. And if epistemological compatibility with European historiography is attempted, then the charge of being

---

[4] Bruce Lawrence: "Islam; South Asia", in: J.L. Esposito et al. (eds.): *The Oxford Encyclopedia of the Modern Islamic World*, Vols. I–IV, New York and Oxford: OUP 1995, Vol. II, p. 284.

[5] Orientalist in the sense of Edward S. Said: *Orientalism*, London 1978. Said has been criticised severely but has opened up new vistas for research in history and cultural and literary studies; see *JAS* 39 (1980); Sadik Jalal al-ʿAzm: "Orientalism and Orientalism in Reverse", in: *Khamsin: Journal of Revolutionary Socialists of the Middle East* 8 (1981), pp. 5–26; Carol A. Breckenridge and Peter van der Veer (eds.): *Orientalism and the Postcolonial Predicament*, Philadelphia 1993; Timothy Mitchell: *Colonising Egypt*, Cambridge 1988.

[6] In how far the construction of a backward Orient was immanently important for European enlightenment, is discussed by Urs Bitterli in his study: *Die "Wilden" und die "Zivilisierten"; Grundzüge einer Geistes- und Kulturgeschichte der europäischen-überseeischen Begegnung*, München: Beck 1991. See also Jürgen Osterhammel: *Die Entzauberung Asiens. Europa und die asiatischen Reiche*, München: Beck 1998.

[7] Even the German philosopher G.W.F. Hegel (1770–1831), basing his information on contemporary Jesuit standard works and reports of British ambassadors, distinguished that Far East was in the actual state of lawlessness, without spiritual reality. "The whole history of India... is full of perpetuate disgust, killings and local wars..." where the subjective was not yet recognised, and government is based on the arbitrary will of a single man. See G.F.W. Hegel: *Vorlesungen über die Weltgeschichte*, ed. Georg Lasson (*Sämtliche Werke*, VIII–IX, Leipzig 1919), II: "Die orientalische Welt", pp. 275–342. For Hegel's perceptions see Ernst Schulin: *Die weltgeschichtliche Erfassung des Orients bei Hegel und Ranke*, Göttingen 1958; Wilhelm Halbfass: *Indien und Europa: Perspektiven ihrer geistigen Begegnung*, Basel/Stuttgart 1981, pp. 104ff., and the stimulating contributions by R. Inden: "Orientalist Constructions of India", in: *MAS* 20 (1986), pp. 401–446, and Thierry Hentsch: *Imagining the Middle East*, transl. by Fred A. Reed, Montréal and New York 1992, pp. 139ff.

[8] See David Ludden: "Orientalist Empiricism: Transformations of Colonial Knowledge", in: Breckenridge et al. (eds.): *Orientalism*, pp. 314–340.

heuristically and perhaps also normatively euro-centric will be rapidly at hand. Finally, if things are supposed to speak for themselves, then some voices have to be disclaimed. And one is left arbitrarily to one's own liabilities. So one "risks being reductive rather than representative."[9] Despite this conceptual danger looming, in comparison to other works on South Asian Muslim history, this book tries to focus precisely on the destructive and constructive sides of diversity, and on processes of reciprocity. It attempts to cover some ground, both at the level of social and cultural history and the history of ideas, over a period of thirteen hundred years taking into account different contesting as well as overlapping voices deemed to be important for the narrative. In the face of the complex historical developments, the history of events is also followed up, playing out sometimes consciously or unconsciously the dynastic card.

The reader will realise before long that not all voices—important as they may have been for a specific context—have been made accessible. This silencing is crucial and cannot be compensated for, such as for the Muslims in Nepal and Ceylon.[10] The initial, rather too ambitious plan to write a history of Islam in South Asia specifically from the margins—in terms of geography as well as of institutional and societal formations and ideas—could be realised only in parts. Firstly, detailed analyses are available for the political centres—Delhi, Hyaderabad and Lucknow. By nature, centripetal narratives are more easily accessible and due to their enduring symbolic efficacy and historical plausibility are not easy to destruct and deconstruct. Secondly, political but not necessarily socio-cultural peripheries, not to mention the marginal or subaltern groups, are for the most part still waiting for academic discussions, especially when it comes to early modernity and before. Thirdly, linguistic barriers in a region harbouring hundreds of languages were always looming on the heuristic horizon. Therefore, the composition of a typology of the transfer of ideas and institution-building processes over so many centuries was hardly possible.

[9] Lawrence: "Islam; South Asia", p. 278.

[10] See Dennis B. McGilvray: "Arabs, Moors and Muslims: Sri Lankan Muslim ethnicity in regional perspective", in: *Contributions to Indian Sociology* 32 (1998), pp. 433–483; Sudhindra Sharma: "Lived Islam in Nepal", in: Imtiaz Ahmad and Helmut Reifeld (eds.): *Lived Islam in South Asia. Adaptation, Accommodation and Conflict*, New Delhi: Social Science Press 2004.

Leaving these apologies aside, this Short History covers some wealth of detail; it is assumed that the reader has some acquaintance with the subject. The reading audience addressed would include students of South Asian history from different academic backgrounds such as religious studies, theology, Indology, history, social and cultural studies as well as political science. Researchers from Area Studies as well as those from systematic traditions might find the book useful. An attempt is made to give voice to preconditions for the evolution of new political or religious formations operating below the level of rule and lordship trespassing and crossing dynastic rule. Attempt has also been made to elaborate on social themes such as market and garrison towns (*qasbahs*) and urban organisation over the centuries. Critical perspectives on the study of South Asian Islam to Orientalism and European imperialism have been employed following the latest academic discourses. As such this book is a modest attempt to identify some of the major trajectories that seem to be characteristic of Islamic or Islamicated cultures in this vast region over time. It also tries to find a remedy for some academic desiderata by unfolding and juxtaposing political, religious and cultural references floating between different dynamic societal formations, some of which are forgotten, collecting dust under sustained and lasting colonial and nationalist narratives. In this respect, the book ties in with *Islam in the Indian Subcontinent* (Leiden 1980) by the late Annemarie Schimmel, but transcends it critically in terms of diachrony with a focus on modern times and modifies the problem through the methodological approach in the above-mentioned sense. In doing so, the narrative is orientated towards contemporary Anglo-American historical and cultural scientific research and also towards subaltern studies. Attempt is made to confront contributions to the sociology of religion with an extensive body of empirical material which has not been easy to tame.

The religious history of South Asia with special reference to Muslims and their sometimes deeply differing or dramatically similar Islamic and Islamicated forms of cultural articulation has been traced through the processes of institution-building—such as religious schools and endowments, mystical orders, religious reforms, but also through empire- and nation-building—with the help of a rich literature, both primary and secondary sources in many forms, such as mystical texts, imperial edicts, formal legal opinions, literary contributions, polemics, the mirrors of princes, colonial and post-colonial correspondence and also cultural artefacts. These largely normative texts—broadly defined in oral, written, and visual terms—reveal negotiations over religious and religiously legitimised boundaries not only between protagonists of different religions, but also between those of the same religious tradition, making a point that differences within one religion can be as severe as those between different religions. At the same time, interesting cultural syntheses between seemingly contradictory religions come to the fore contributing substantially to the creativity of South Asian Muslim composite culture. One may add that contemporary Indian historiography, both liberal and Marxist in contradistinction to the conservative-reactionary, has treated the notion of composite culture and composite secular nationalism as a powerful resource in Indian society to combat communalism and other forms of sectarian strife. Thus historical narrative is functionally equipped, for it would be naïve to consider that there was no interaction between academic description and religious practice. The relationship of religion and the academic study of religion is endemic, and in most cases academic description has actually created or established religion.

By the same token, most narratives so far have been focusing on and presupposing the building of empires towards the present day situation. A reading concentrating on dynastic history is easy going for it reduces a complex reading of the sources to specific ruling houses. In contrast, more recent works on South Asian Islamic history and overlapping South Asian history, such as David Gilmartin and Bruce Lawrence, Richard Eaton and Carl Ernst, Muzaffar Alam and Sanjay Subrahmanyam, Barbara Metcalf and Thomas Metcalf, Catherine Asher and Cynthia Talbot, examine at a quite deep level specific regions, eras and disciplines, societal formations and ideologies, enhancing our knowledge of the dynamics of social and cultural history, cultural artefacts and religion to a very considerable degree. The book builds on the expertise of these and other important monographs to a large extent.

The particular thesis which goes along with the narrative is the extremely complex and difficult negotiation of the implicit tension between the notion of Muslims as rulers and Islamic rule as such, in different historical and societal dimensions, when ideals are re-negotiated. This tension unfolds precisely in the dynamics in and between world religions, which by definition are not limited to a specific region but go far beyond their actual culture of origin. Here one might look at the functionality and flexibility of religious repertory which can be by all means a reflection of any given cultural environment. In the process of negotiation over normativity and agency, religious boundaries, identity and alterity, the religious actors are highly important variables determined by constant changes and thereby constantly expanding the semantics of the religious. Therefore, it must be the task of academic inquiry to carefully focus on the actors and to disclose and comprehend those specific and complicated interpretation processes that unfold their meaning in context. The importance of the significance of such a hermeneutic twist also increases in the face of the fact that the Quran revised some of the pre-Islamic customary laws which pertained to individual issues and were considered as gravely un-Islamic, such as in the field of personal law and law of succession. Barely more than eighty verses in the Quran (of approx. 6,240 verses) refer to questions of society and have—in a narrower sense—any relevance for legal matters. Thus, the Quran can neither serve as a constitution nor as a civil code, but instead must be read and understood in the context of a particular period of time and space. After all, Islamic theology is not the word of God but it is—first and foremost—based on the fallible human interpretation of God's word. It is precisely in this context that the study of Prophetic tradition and Islamic law has been taken into account by Muslim scholars during the course of history. Therefore, if the question arises as to how Islam refers to certain cardinal terms such as protection and dues, minority law and human rights, military rule and democracy, both aspects must be taken into consideration: the Islamic scholastic belief which is based on certain normative texts and the interpretations of these texts by various Muslims who are always embedded in different contexts. Muslims as well as non-Muslims can no longer hide behind the image of an ideal Islam. Instead we need to appreciate cultural diversity and contextuality in the world of Islam. Thus our aim is to elaborate on the trends within Muslim cultural articulations, in their different manifestations in situations of Muslim majority and minority regions.

The issues

To this end several core issues—some of them already mentioned—may be highlighted, the less contentious ones being discourses of and on Islamic scholarship and mysticism, and the processes of their institutionalisation; it is important to state right away that the realm of Islamic scholarship and mysticism grew over time. These systems of knowledge were marked by certain stages of development reflecting the incremental complexity of social systems; and they changed their nature in relation to the social formations or groups concerned, such as scholars, students, mystics and their followers, and the holders of political power. Scholars and mystics oscillated between patronage and loyalty on the one hand, and rebellion and subalternity on the other, depending on the degree and nature of their political integration, on their theological rationalisations, and on the products they offered. They contested, marginalised but also influenced each other. Rationality and discipline, bureaucratisation and centralisation, as well as functional differentiation eventually changed the character of religion, ultimately ushering in contestant religious communities who began to bargain as actors of civil society in the public sphere.

Similarly important are ambivalences in the field of identity and alterity, raising questions, as to how far self-perceptions and perceptions of the others are delimiting and restricting, but at the same time require and account for each other, to such an extent that reflexive self-perceptions bring to light the formation-process of new religious communities. Thus, identity is understood as a procedural event, as situational, corporate or multiple, rather than a given entity. Identity is a mode of being, not a property. Consequently, it is the notion of multiple and embedded identities that makes it possible to argue for social constructions of the self and the other that lie beyond assumptions of primordialism. In fact, the setting of criteria of difference unfolds its impact only when endowed with meaning, when identity must not only be defined by alterity or otherness alone but also by a mediating pluralising space—the creative and meaningful subset, when the "me" becomes "me" through the other. Thus, multiplicity of identity not only implies, but rather presupposes ambivalence. Therefore, the other can be perceived as part of the self, and transcend fixed, confessionalised discourses. In short, identity matters in context.

Yet the problem is based in instrumentally endowed constructions of enemy images with enormous lasting power. They confine the other to specific central, culturalist features, which easily can be distilled from the poly-vocality and plurality of human identity which at the same time silences the other, contextual markers of a lived religion. Thus, the essentialised other can serve as a folio to project native fears. It can serve as a locus in which to banish the negative aspects of one's own culture. This imagination of another world provides for the important segregation between us and the other, which must not be blurred. Cultural similarities would hamper the self-image and destroy the contours of the self. The enemy has to be *different*. In times of crisis this othering becomes even more pronounced. Therefore, it is important to hermeneutically understand the context of this process, before, during and after colonial rule.

Obviously, religious symbols have an important role to play with regard to awareness and understanding the staging of discourses on identity and alterity. Thus, confessional boundaries must be negotiated, crossed, shifted, and transgressed in pluralist contexts. However, this should not be read as a statement in favour of post-modern romanticism. Learned interventions, the media and discourses of religious specialists and politicians vehemently opposing religious pluralism through identity-politics are equally discussed and placed in the context of everyday life. Thus, religion is understood in terms of cultural dynamics, being integrated in and affiliated to specific networks of change and exchange also within the area of non-religion. In this dynamic the actors are crucial, because they shape cultures and religions, and are thereby contextually dependent and exposed to perpetual change. Religion is considered as a process of appropriation of a metaphysical world, a system through which human beings appropriate the world. Instead of establishing and fostering essentialised positions—which is often being done not only by, say, Non-Muslims regarding Islam but also by Muslims themselves, when some of them claim that Islamic practice and confession are not subject to historical change—culture and religion can be grasped as a repertory of references that enables people to interpret—and hence make meaningful—their complex lifeworlds. Contextualisation is as important as the media (forms, script, orality, music, architecture) which changes religious experience and mental mapping. It is doubted that religion is the prime force for Muslim, Christian or Hindu rationality. One needs to recognise the active role played by different religious actors rather than calling for an essentialised religious tradition which would regularise religious dynamics through epistemologies endowed with political power. Religion is thus conceived as one of many identity markers in a disputed and competitive discursive field, in contrast to mainstream colonial and post-colonial nationalistic narratives which consider religion to be the prime marker.

Another issue is that of processes that question the definition and creation of religious and religiously legitimated boundaries. The perspective on and from the border is a view from the edge—in contrast to the one from an historically constructed centre—which makes the border itself into the main topic of academic inquiry: who constructed which boundary and why, and how is it transcended? Dealing with boundaries focuses on mutual relations and processes of reciprocal perception of the self and the other. Constructions of identities have a prominent role to play in border discourses. It is in the context of boundaries that conflicts can evolve from competitive situations and can occasionally be misused for political ends. This is especially the case for ethnic-religious conflicts, when religious systems of belief assist the eruption of irrational violence. The collapse of law and order can also induce and authorise communities to a religious legitimisation of acts of violence. However, religion cannot be looked upon as the sole source of violence and conflicts. Indeed, accepted borders are conducive to peace; recognised conflicts are in general the condition for tolerance. The transition from accepted and theologically digested differences to the active force of violence or use of violence is therefore crucial, and has to be taken into account, such as those arising from deviations and "heresies". Yet, conflicts are not only signs of social pathologies but can also contribute decisively to the stability and cohesion of societies and to religious pluralism.

Finally, the issue of pluralism is differentiated from plurality as it is an active and reflexive perception of the other. It implies more than co-existence of two or more communities at the same time and in the same space. It presumes that co-existence was made into an issue either by those who were or are politically in charge, and/or by the religious communities themselves. Such traditions can be considered self-reflexive, having been discussed and legitimised within the religious traditions as well as in academia. All religions have developed and defined themselves by mutual reference. So it was not distance but proximity which persuaded religious communities to draw up boundaries, boundaries that were important for the construction of the self and of the other. Pluralism does not displace or eliminate deep religious commitments; rather it is the encounter of commitments. Islam has a variety of manifestations in different regions all over the world; there is no single reading of the holy text, the Prophetic tradition or the shariʿa. There have always been different and contesting readings. Islam has no common religious authority, comparable to the Pope, but an interpretative religion invested by pluralism; it has mingled with local religious forms in many different contexts which have resulted in diverse forms. It is clear that any Muslim if asked would not necessarily consider religion to be the prime marker of their identity. This plurality and pluralism actually endow Islam with dynamic power which, however, has through the centuries been taken advantage of by different players.

Thus, the project aims at an understanding of the complex images of Islam as they evolved over time and space by analysing the tensions between religiously advanced identification and other societally important identity markers, such as political, social and ethnic affiliation on the one hand and the dynamics of religious and political arrangements of the secular on the other. The analysis of how these shared traditions, no matter how normative they are, have been partly transformed into exclusivist religious discourses and practices is an important part of the narrative. For it can be argued that in specific historical contexts selective discourses endowed with particular meaning came to become the core elements of the exclusivist identity-politics that led to religiously legitimised conflict, ultimately to the emergence of new independent nation-states in South Asia, and subsequently created a scenario for the largest wave of mass migration in modern time. These identity-politics construct antagonist or agonistic relations of the self and the other and usually do not interrogate hegemonic concepts of social order. Yet, they did not cease to exist once these new religiously defined spaces were established. Rather they developed critical velocity and intensity. Let me briefly introduce the organisation of the book in its clusters and the individual chapters, so as to let the issues speak for themselves.

The Chapters

The book has been organised in a way interleafing topical subjects such as historiography, caste, conversion and gender between chronological arrangements of chapters which occasionally overlap in terms of dates. There are four main clusters to it. The first two chapters cover early Muslim expansion and the formative phase with its constituencies in context of early cultural encounter, after Arab traders had landed at Malabar and Kerala and produced a unique blend of Islamicated culture (approx. 700–1300). In the second cluster the narrative deals with the establishment of Muslim empire cultures oscillating between Islamic and Islamicate, between centralised and regionalised power (approx. 1300–1700). The third cluster is composed in the backdrop of territorial states and colonial rule, the accommodation and processes of integration and differentiation of Muslim cultures in colonial setting (approx. 1700–1930). Finally, tensions between Muslim pluralism and singularity as they are articulated by different actors in public sphere make up for the fourth cluster (approx. 1930–2002). These clusters can be explicated as follows.

The *first cluster* opens with a broad description of South Asia, before embarking on the early Arabs who slowly began to penetrate into a politically fragmented South Asia partly by force but basically by contract—from the south-west, that is Sind (precisely along the river Indus) which was located on major trade routes connecting West Asia with South East Asia (Chap. 1). There they stayed for a couple of hundred years, consolidating Muslim Shafiʿi power through trade, military and forced migration. In doing so they made use of Islamic semantics, which they expanded intelligently, particularly since the rationale for expansion was not so much religious zeal but economic opportunities. The Eastern market was so extremely lucrative for Arab traders that locally conquered non-Muslims, Hindus in particular, came to be appreciated as people of the covenant, *dhimmis*. Thus, the theoretical basis was laid for an administrative necessity, in an environment overwhelmingly Hindu. Muslim jurisprudence displayed flexibility. Mercantile Buddhists converted to Islam to take part in Muslim cultural and symbolic capital. Conversion functionally provided possibility to participate in a global horizon, and at the same time guaranteed coherence and continuity to a large extent. Yet, there were also trends of minoritising Hindus and segregating Muslims. Thus, tensions between Islamisation and Islamicatisation were characteristic right from the beginning, the latter being the *conditio sine qua non* for Muslim expansion into al-Hind when the Islamic mingled with local populations. The first referred to critical Muslim discourses on the question of Islamicity, as the discussions between the people of hadith, e.g., those who considered sayings attributed to the Prophet Muhammad to be of normative character, and other Muslim scholars showed. Similarly, the marginalised and the dissidents, free thinkers and atheists, the Ismailis and Sufis found their ways to India to establish their realm. Eventually Sind became area of proxy wars between different Muslim Arab dynasties. Thus, there was no one single Islamic, let alone Islamicate voice but many overlapping and contesting voices. Yet, Islamic historiography has always tried to establish a normative master narrative that is biased towards Prophetic tradition and linked to *adab* literature, as discussed in the excursus on historiography.

When Arabic Shafiʿi forces faded away after 300 years, particularly due to the intra-Arab-Muslim disputes such as those between Sunnite Abbasids and Shiʿite Fatimids, another force intervened from the north-west: Turkic Hanafites slave dynasties who ruled major parts of South Asia for quite some time. In doing so they were pragmatic enough to introduce Persianate rules of comportment informed by *akhlaqi* norms, liberal sufi discourses and flexible Islamic law that would fit to the new environment at the expense of Prophetic tradition and its relevance as an ethical ideal. Specific constituents for the new system were the transferable revenue assignment in lieu of salary for service (*iqta*ʿ). This included the Islamicatedly evolving spaces such as the *qasbah*, the shrine (*dargah*), religious school (*madrasa*) and endowment (*waqf*) while Muslim mystics and sufi orders as well as scholars flocked to this region. As outlined in Chapter 2, they did so not only for patronage but also to escape Mongol onslaughts. In the wake of these developments, two major contesting Sufi orders emerged sharing some sort of division of labour. Thus, India's Islamicate traditions were to become more versatile and inclusive, as the immigrant Muslim communities adapted to Indian environments as the bearers of a different civilisation and faith. They increasingly expressed their concerns in shared cultural symbols and local languages rather than in the high cultural icons and language of the elite. Arabic continued to be the language of orthodox scholars while Persian became the language of the court, administration and mystical lore. Mechanisms of assimilation and refraction in the field of material culture were also discernable: the integration of local architectural forms by the new political leaders was to sustain the grandeur of local dynasties in popular memory. These were some of the constituent channels used by Muslims during their expansion in order to manage the new areas initially. They were used by later dynasties which were wise and at times also pragmatic enough to accommodate their policy and symbolic use of authority to the local environment. After all, the appropriation of South Asia was not possible without local acknowledgement and support. This appropriation occurred gradually, at times through war but also through peaceful transfers of power.

The *second cluster* focuses on processes of empire building: the provision of ideas and structures on the one hand and an increasingly fragmenting Hindu environment gave way to Ghaznawids and Ghorids, culminating in the establishment of the Delhi Sultanate, a sultanate that seemed to be—at least in the cultural memory of South Asian Muslims—the only guarantor of Sunni territory after the sack of Baghdad by the Mongols in 1258. These military slave governors from Central Asia represented an amalgamation of Islamic and Turkic cultures with a strong Iranian underpinning, as outlined in Chapter 3. By extending their power as far as Western Persia and the Ganges valley, these slave dynasties Persianised cultures in South Asia. Both, Islamisation and Islamicatisation, that is coercive Islamic politics and pragmatic indigenous realpolitik were used in the quest to establish, confirm and legitimise power. Interestingly, coercion and the symbolic affiliation to the Islamic mainland through caliphal investiture and accommodation through political and social indigenisation went hand in hand with their power over land and people: the more the Muslim power holders fell behind, the more they tended towards Islamisation which provided them a basis for centralisation; the more they flourished, the more they turned to local expertise and thus to accommodationism. In their political actions they made use of the discourses and institutions of religious scholars and divines, who not only were cooperative but also critical of assimilation, depending upon their own interests. Notorious, were the contentions between rulers who issued profane edicts and orthodox scholars or mystics who produced their own contesting discursive texts. While some Muslim thinkers and politicians strove to establish universal and exclusivistic Islamic identity in the broadest sense, others seemed to work for inclusivistic and plural Muslim identities, using historical memories and religious symbols to their advantage. Yet, we cannot speak of one common or monolithic body of rulers, nor was there any one body of Muslim functionaries. Both contested among and with each other. Both, exclusivism and inclusivism can be traced through cultural, and numismatic artefacts. Even Mahmud, the archetypical Islamic warrior of al-Barani, issued a Sanskrit version of the Islamic profession of faith, describing the Prophet as the *avatar* of God. Thus the numismatic continuity did not correspond to the normative values of textual rhetoric but symbolised reassurance for the indigenous population for their economic and administrative participation. As such, alliances were not based on the identities of Muslim and Hindu, but on the identities and requirements of smaller communities. Similarly, the rational sciences (*maʿqulat*), focusing on law, ousted the transmitted sciences (*manqulat*) concentrating on theology. In settling the Sultanate, however, major land grants were issued to loyal service elites who eventually became virtually independent and challenged Sultanic authority; this group also included the Shiʿites. An important but perhaps unintended consequence of this loss of central authority was the growth of several independent centres of Islamic learning and culture under the patronage of local rulers, the Mongol invasion on the offing. The versatile relations between Sunnis and Shiʿites and the internal diversification of this Muslim minority have been traced in the following excursus.

The dismantling of the Delhi Sultanate was the acculturative result of successive administrative, economic, ethnic and cultural restructuring.

Chapter 4 argues that these Islamicating tendencies produced a context in which different traditions interacted and contested over Muslim hegemony, thereby adding to the religious and societal complexity of South Asia. In this emerging and often fluid context, the dialectic between the social location of Muslim identities and its cultural articulation played a crucial role. On a higher plane, it was embedded within the greater dialectics between indigenous and Islamic cosmology. The complex, sacral geography resulting from such an interplay of cosmologies considerably weakened the centre-periphery relations if not altogether dissolving them, leading to different, contestant, sometimes also complementary regional entities, such as Kashmir, Bengal, Deccan, and the South. Sufi orders were particularly important in a process of trickle-down, for they informed the high culture of the elite with the local, and regional symbols, thereby making it accessible to the masses within their own subaltern matrix, and at times becoming agents of high culture themselves. Needless to say, these processes of universalisation and parochialisation provided the basis for a variety of exclusive, inclusive and liminal religious identities. This was even more important, since annexation of larger parts of al-Hind was basically driven by the search for new cultivation areas and the revenue income attached to them. Through sedentarisation an agrarian population was integrated into religious institutions organised around charismatic figures. Reception, appropriation and obliteration of autochthonous ideas and institutions marked the process of Muslim expansion. Mutual encounters and interaction between Muslims migrating from the North, or having been settled there for many centuries, gave these regions their peculiar Indian Muslim traditions. As evident in the local architecture, in the practice of religion as well as Sanskrit epigraphic and literary sources, religiosity was not the prime marker of identity, distancing or exclusivism. The coalescence of different interest groups opened numerous fissures which found their theological rationalisation in different schools of thought. In this context the rational sciences that focused on law seem to play a major role, outnumbering the transmitted sciences characterised by the study of hadith. The first sciences went back to the Persian-Shiʿite immigration to provide legitimation for the settlement of a powerful state, the latter took recourse to Prophetic ethics often based in Arab culture. Here, the old tensions between *ʿarab* and *ʿajam* became crucial and went hand in hand with the substitution of the liturgical language Arabic by the more profane Persian. This gradually caused an accretion of the *shariʿa* in a non-Arab culture of eastern Islam. Due to these developments, tensions emerged between immigrants, the older settlers and natives that were part of the social fabric. The societal distinctions between different social actors and their meaningfulness for the South Asian Muslim context are traced in an excursus on caste.

The tensions accruing in and between these many independent states were taken advantage of by the Mughals from Central Asia. Networks of loyalty were extended through patronage. Chapter 5 shows that administrative and fiscal reforms were paralleled by a vast network of small garrison posts and market places, having not only military significance but also linking the economy of Bengal to that of Northern India. Through further Persianisation Mughals could effectively negotiate the diversities of Indian society. Political tactics of conquest, annexation and matrimonial alliance, as well as patronage particularly of the Sufi orders, all focused on the person of the Mughal emperor. Social and religious policies towards universal dominion which championed the equality of all people were never bereft of political motives however: securing authority internally and extending power externally through expansion. These successes of appropriating authority depended on those very Hindu landlords who had been variously subjugated. Initial contacts with European traders created an interesting cultural symbiosis. Renaissance traditions supported further developments of a humanist worldview, shifting from the framework of an Islamic community to that of humanity as a whole. The emperor's imperial construction reflected this transference of divine benediction. "Pax Mughalica" was based on wide-ranging fiscal, administrative, military and land reforms, as well as the mixture of rational sciences and monistic mysticism, supported by *akhlaq* literature, which perceived political organisation in terms of cooperation achieved through justice. This system of universal dominion gave way to what has been called patrimonialism, which again produced millennial revolts that increasingly questioned imperial power, competing for the establishment of their faith more firmly by enforcing stricter rules and as a consequence, creating distinctive confessional identities. So again, different forms of Islamic and Islamicated articulation can be delineated: from most orthodox ones to most inclusive ones, leaving a broad belt of discourses and practices for the new formations of religious communities and thinkers as different as Rawshaniyya, Mahdawiyya, Sirhindi or Dara. The dynamics of religious "communalisation" are discussed in terms of conversion and mission in the following excursus.

Problems occurring mainly on the margins of the empire resulted in a policy towards a strong monarchy compatible with orthodox Islamic principles pursued with the help of landowners, religious scholars and orthodox sufis mostly from Turani stock. A shift from Islamicatisation to Islamisation can be traced, as documented in Chapter 6; yet, the implicit religious iconoclasm has been exposed as a portrayal of an essentialised Islam which has been especially supported by later colonialist historiography. The system had however seen the day: the Maratha war cost immense sums which could only be raised by giving land rights to the extent that land became hereditary. In the attempt to impose a clearly defined and homogenised legal system the emperor commissioned an authoritative *fatwa*-collection. Thus, the patronage of Hanafi scholars and institutions strengthened Muslim orthodoxy vis-à-vis Shiʿites in particular. Yet, the collection also reproduced Hindu social stratification.

A juridical codification and collective endeavour conceived in this way however was new, and probably anticipated the first steps towards a modern state legislation. This codification stressed the tradition of what has been called the rational sciences which on the eve of the political collapse of Mughal rule made a crucial advance when it came to be institutionalised in a syllabus called *dars-e nizami*, designed for "scribal groups", able to develop new administrative techniques. Thus this system sought to legitimise the evolving regional powers at the expense of the decaying central political power. At the same time pietist formations evolved for the most part inspired by Arab influence. Hadith and Sufism became political and social utopia, challenging the authority of received legal authority. While Prophetic *sunna* was considered a model for social and political reform, Muhammad was humanised. Confessional trends increased—between Sunni and Shia as well as among confessions themselves. At the same time, new audiences and fora emerged to provide for the articulation of new ideas. In what was a remarkable but true development, the central control of the provinces in the seventeenth century turned into a provincial control of the centre in the eighteenth century. While the Mughal Empire had tried to integrate different cultures into an imperial unity and world economy, the evolving national markets in new princely states sought the regionalisation of imperial culture. Thus, ironically enough, the territorial disintegration of the Empire resulted in various levels of regional and local integration.

These developments are discussed in the *third cluster*: by the end of seventeenth century the feebleness of the Mughal fiscal system ultimately led to autonomy movements initiated by many chiefs who had been high officials in the Mughal administration (Chapter 7). They considered their former fiefs as home provinces, and were closely affiliated with wealthy merchants and bankers. They introduced various land and administrative measures throughout these national markets wherein Muslim communities were now perceived as cultural unities in specific territories, with local patriotisms and devotional religions, centralised revenue systems, and standardised language. Every principality boasted its own religious-cultural "variety" cum "verity". Externally they struggled with Delhi; while internally they pursued centralisation on the regional level which eventually resulted in "regional centralisation". These national markets also provided space for Europeans who were competing materially and politically to control the new world economy. Thus colonialism did not expand into traditional and primitive societies but into closed political entities, which had replaced the Mughal Empire. The British East India Company gradually integrated these national markets into a colonial economy with the help of local informants using indirect rule. But since these cultural translators could insert their own personal information, acquiring local knowledge became important for the Europeans. Colonial educational institutions were established and English translations of Hindu and Muslim law texts produced. A new land revenue system was introduced by the end of the eighteenth century which created a new class of landowners, but also fuelled Hindu and Muslim animosities which had already been in the making due to Hindu affluence. Under subsidiary alliances local rulers protected themselves from external aggression by using British troops, whom they had to maintain financially. This was economically viable and saved energies for different fields. It was legitimised through the reproduction of Mughal nominalism. In this process, India gradually became a supplier of raw materials; this exploitation resulted among others in the decline of the *qasbah*s. European economic liberalism was introduced. The misery was compounded due to fragmentation of land holdings, which was the inevitable result of above factors. By 1820 the Company had nearly established its all-India rule thereby converting trade monopoly into a monopoly of territorial domination. The importance of religious endowments for purposes of sedentarisation, education and politics, from early Muslim times to the colonial period and well into the policy of nationalisation by contemporary Muslim states times will be outlined in the excursus on *waqf*.

The increasing colonial influence was paralleled by changes that were reflected in normative terms underlying the colonial process

(Chapter 8). A cultural technique for self-affirmation and demarcation was cultural projection: ontological fixation and valorisation of differences as congenital and inherent helped maximise disparities. A strategy of plausibilisation was provided by colonial historiography backed by the establishment of colonial academies. The construction of the cultural other followed by "purification"-discourses eventually culminated in the idea that the Indian Orient was chaotic, caste-ridden and governable only by indirect rule: by a policy of subsidiary alliances or coercive intervention. Yet, at the same time agents of colonial power were very clearly emulating Mughal culture, to the point of cultural mimicry, appropriating, appreciating and absorbing local reformist discourses which helped create their own identities. The "eccentrics" of European identity[11] lay in these processes of reciprocity, gradually turning into discourses of distinction, especially with the increasing influx of Christian missionaries after 1813. In this context, evolving Muslim religious communities, associations and societies began to act as agents of contesting publics, increasingly using local media, providing space for reformed discourses. Emulation of the sunna as symbol of Prophetic authority and source of continuity with the past was deemed necessary to guide Muslims in what they perceived to be a situation of increasing depravity. Some of these movements even humanised the Prophet while others stuck to his inviolability, all adhering to same aims: mobilising against unjust rule and offering alternative remedies in line with Prophetic ethics. This complex process of evolution of different religious publics enabled colonial encounters to take place on the same reformed discursive level and could allow for a great deal of emancipation.

This prompted the colonialists to move towards the semantics of "tradionalising" the colony, thereby introducing a policy of civilising mission and modernisation. "Modernising" the colony required vast and detailed information about the subject and its processing (Chapter 9). In doing so, Indian societies came to be communalised, Hindu and Muslim communities becoming two monolithic actors in colonial memory. Different reforms and juridical changes had repercussions on post-Mughal societies, when Muslim space, Muslim education and its institutions were relegated to the private realm. The pace of colonial encroachment eventually led to the revolt of 1857. In the cultural

[11] See Rémi Brague: *Europa. Eine exzentrische Identität*, Frankfurt am Main 1993.

memories of both the colonialists and the colonialised this bloody event made history in different ways. From a war of independence to rebellion, from an attempt to establish a reformed agenda to an attempt to re-establish traditional Mughal rule. The policy of civilising mission served the policy of homogenisation and official nationalism. This provided legitimacy for the colonial sector as it was expanding gradually with the help of influential loyal actors and religious endowments alimenting Muslim education coming under colonial control. However, the massive restructuring of society produced new societal formations with new social needs and new forms of articulation and discontent caused by the lack of opportunities to participate in the colonial project. Language has always played a major role in the making of homogeneous and coherent entities as was the case in the context of eighteenth century growing regional powers and then again with the growing communal scenario by the end of the nineteenth century. Some of these issues are discussed in the excursus on Urdu.

The embracing colonial situation ushered in a new phase of formation and institutionalisation of Muslim communities. As contesting actors in a plural religious field they varied from "traditionalist" to "modernist"[12] reshaping and rendering local the new situation in a colonial environment in different ways (Chap. 10). In their quests for "civility" their Islamicities went public, keeping alive Prophet Muhammad as the normative example, either by emulating his tradition or criticising its historical viability. Iconoclastic hadith-based reformists next to educational reformists with their focus on theology and the study of traditional sciences emerged next to sufi groups, safeguarding Hanafite tradition or rejecting it. Based in different social and regional groups their actors focused on law, Prophetic tradition, on Sufism and folk-religious practices, and differed in issues of doctrine such as following a school of law, mysticism or the definition of innovation. In contrast

[12] To be sure, this bipolar distinction in modern(ist) and traditional(ist) is reductionist and is reminiscent of theories of modernisation. However, since we are concerned with the societal dynamics between these two poles, the notion of tradition is understood as being value-free, very consciously in contrast to the semantics of colonialism which sees therein some sort of backwardness. Often Muslim intellectuals have adopted the notion of tradition in the colonial sense, used it for their reforms and aimed their reforms teleologically at "modernity", which was considered inherent to colonialism. That traditionalisms can have a dynamic and innovative side has been shown by Dietmar Rothermund: "Der Traditionalismus als Forschungsgegenstand für Historiker und Orientalisten", in: *Saeculum* 40/2 (1989), pp. 142–148.

to these more inwardly looking movements, others sought a more outwardly looking approach taking up issues of colonial critique such as the one on the authenticity of hadith. In making this fruitful for their own Muslim tradition they also adopted colonial categories of religious minorities and majorities thereby reproducing a Muslim angst-discourse in a Hindu dominated context. Yet others tried to strike a balance by reforming the traditional syllabus which had evolved in the context of the evolution of princely territorial states in the eighteenth century. In the quest for civility and to meet colonial demands, all these groups tried to bring the *religious* (that had been rendered *private* since colonial intervention) back to the *public*. They ended up politicising and also masculinising Islam which met yet another wave of colonial constrains. While these movements failed in organising Indians on a common platform to voice their concern about colonial policy, other secular organisations evolved led by middle-class and landlords of Hindu and Muslim origin. Their "moderate" argument for greater participation and representation in British-Indian politics eventually made much use of identity-politics which led to the evolution of religious monolithic blocs on the eve of political independence. It is at this time that a specific notion about Muslim women evolved, some of them based on Islamic tradition, but most of them referring to colonial encounter and the processes of reciprocating with European ideals of chastity. This is discussed in the excursus on gender.

While discontent grew, nationalist movements raised their heads against the colonial rule leading to temporary compromises which could not prevent the masses from going to the streets. When colonial policy accelerated the pace of communalisation, Muslim loyalists were swift to form institutional bodies (Chap. 11). In the shadow of colonial shelter they hoped for safeguarding their socio-economic positions from Hindu majority that was rallying behind slogans of Hindu identity-politics. Thus, both Hindu and Muslim identity-politics arose simultaneously under conditions of colonial modernity. Several policies and reforms followed to negotiate these polarising religious boundaries, but to no avail. In an attempt to overcome this communal aporia both Hindu and Muslim pan-Indian nationalists came together in a unique entente in the first quarter of the twentieth century. Yet, the Khilafat movement had different meanings for different players. Its collapse eventually ushered in much more communal blood-shedding, providing a basis for political mass mobilisation until then unknown in this part of the world. While some Muslim nationalists played out the card of identity-politics for a separate Muslim homeland, other Muslim nationalists were apprehensive to join the movement. After the idea of an independent Muslim nation was openly voiced, the shaping of a sovereign state took another decade and a half to materialise. The semantics of Islamic symbolism was expanded, while colonial politics oscillated between coercion and appeasement. Finally, British India was divided into an independent India and Pakistan into an Eastern and Western wing, causing the largest migration movement and human displacement in recent history. How communal violence emerged and what role it played in the context of identity-politics, both positively as well as negatively, is elaborated in the excursus on communalism.

This complex history is complemented by the *fourth* and last *cluster*. While the Muslim public had diversified into a plethora of communities, some of them participating in the struggle for an independent state for Muslims, most of them were reluctant to see secular leaders represent Islamic agency. Again the issue was the agency to represent the singularity of prophetic tradition. Messianic, missionary, quasi-fascist, Islamist, modernist and secular groups, some of them were very tightly held together by institutional patterns and normative ideas; others loosely organised leaving much individual space for political manoeuvring (Chap. 12). Some were confined to South Asia and interior discourses, others became global due to their sheer flexible organisational structures and universal postulates. Yet others became the vanguards of an Islamic revolution. Muslim mystical culture and shared religion did play some role in the making of such movements, even if their leaders formulated their resentment over these traditional patterns of social and religious organisation, yet they took recourse to them considerably in terms of semantics and institutionalisation. Increasingly Sufis had been contested by emerging urban Islamic reform movements, pan-Islamic and Salafi endeavours and eventually by Islamist organisations. The latter used the language of colonial and colonialised urban culture to which they had access via media and their social embeddedness. In different discourses—polemic as well as academic—they tried to render themselves into the sole agents of Islam, regardless of their contesting opinions, calling mystical ideas and folk-religious practices unlawful innovations. Thus, this side of Islamicated traditions was relegated to the private, and thereby feminised. Yet these forms of shared religion are very much prevalent in South Asia and are relevant for the limited success of reformist and politicised movements vis-à-vis this complex and vital side of lived Islam which is practiced virtually everywhere.

Given the various competing religious and secular formations evolving, establishing and disappearing over times—effective in carving master narratives or challenging them successfully—the story of South Asian Muslims seems to provide the best examples for teleological trends which are so characteristic for the sweeping narratives of this part of the world (Chap. 13). As if the Arab commander Muhammad ibn Qasim had laid the foundation stone for the establishment of an independent Muslim nation some thirteen centuries ago! The narrative power of these stories can however, not be belittled, let alone ignored. It determines the political cultures of independent states in their daily politics and current affairs, informed by identity-politics impelling the states to fight armed hostilities, especially over Kashmir, and even drive them to the brink of atomic destruction. The division was created for Muslims rather than Islam in the first place, but was adjured as such in the laborious and extensive dramaturgy underlying the speeches of religious politicians. And since the Muslim state was separated into two wings by its alleged adversary, a productive form of cultural and national integration could not develop. Instead, one-sided dependencies developed, which as was to be expected led to resentments on both sides. The political leaders who themselves stood in the colonial tradition, emerged as authoritarian potentates who would seek coalitions to keep their positions stable. The controversial debates about the Islamicity of the new state carried weight, but they did not suffice to integrate the particular concerns in these regions, nor did it bring the issues in two culturally and linguistically different wings, into a homogenous national ideology. Coercive politics did not succeed to establish the extremely necessary, but lacking infrastructural preconditions for that process of national integration. Moreover, still functioning patterns of social organisation which had long and deep roots in society, were dissolved by the policy of nationalisation without providing adequate alternatives. Modernisation-policy had negative consequences for the majority of rural population, discourses on modernisation revolved around the authenticity and the normative meaning of hadith, whose guardians the ulama (*'ulama'*) considered themselves to be. Thus, it was only a matter of time that the country would split apart. Here and there repressive policies continued which led to eruptions of massive violence—eruptions that represent the distressed attempts of masses of pauperised and marginalised citizens to liberate themselves from the yoke of post-colonial domination rather than the nihilistic excesses of some marginal groups. How far Islamic fundamentalism can prosper in this sort of a soil and how it articulates itself to offer ways towards a self-proclaimed salvation is shown in the following excursus on Islamic fundamentalism.

These tensions became even more apparent after the establishment of the third new state in South Asia in 1971. On the whole, one must assert that Islam's repertory provided ways of ingenious interpretation in the use of religious semantics to serve political purposes, especially in the face of the growing number of religiously articulated social forms of civil society made up as it was of Islamic scholars and Sufis, intellectuals and politicians alike (Chap. 14). Religious schools relegated to the private sphere since colonial times provided shelter and support for the destitute, and came to play some role in mobilising and fuelling their sentiments of despair. This was a resulting conflict against state power arrayed against marginalised citizens, and one may add, a systemic one. Moreover, the homogenising language of the policy of Islamisation met with similar attempts of homogenisation among different schools of thought competing each other from below. While these developments certainly have indigenous roots, they were much supported by foreign interests using the net-work of these institutions to design and carry out even proxy wars which literally led the Muslim majority countries in South Asia to the verge of collapse and civil war. Yet, this does not mean that we are teleologically heading towards a bleak destiny as the media and also much of recent political analysis have been making us believe. In fact, there are many gleaming examples of flourishing Muslim cultures on different societal levels which—in conjunction with the floating discourses on Islam and power—can be made fertile for a political culture in which at least the majority of participants can find their destinies. Whether the imposed politics of "enlightened moderation" has enough semantic coverage to provide for these developments is doubtful, even though this policy wants to ostensibly make use of the integrative potential of Sufism. What seems to be more important is the empowerment of the people. The tool for empowerment is more democratisation of all institutions in which all citizens can seek their benefits and assert their rights. Here ideas of reform and democratisation pertaining to Islamic discourses might be helpful, because it is this religiously connoted and socio-culturally embedded language that most people understand and appreciate.

The same is true as much for Muslims in independent India who are divided into several contesting groups (in every aspect of the term) and whose structural heterogeneity is discussed in the excursus on the social structure of Muslims in India. Similar to Pakistan and Bangladesh the situation of the majority of Indian Muslims is a state of distress, if not desolation, while the Indian nation is still haunted by the challenges of communalism and religious fundamentalism, possibly in its worst and most aggressive form (Chap. 15). The narrative of monolithic but powerful Indian Hindu and powerless Muslim communities unfolds its remarkable energies in those areas pertinent to language, gender, space and law. These are instrumentalised by religious and identity-politicians on both the Hindu and Muslim side, in order to consolidate their own positions. Up until now this narrative has flared up in communal riots which again petrify the religious and religiously legitimated boundaries between these communities. Here as well, Muslim institutions such as the madrasas and endowments are subject to attempts at civility disguised as state reforms which are usually resented. Again, it is the formations of religious communities which constitute, in a de-privatised manner, the pattern of civil society and in this way have the potential to offer feasible, practicable and promising alternatives. Whether they are really able, in the current situation which is heavily determined by global actors, to consolidate civil society for the sake of a nationally integrated unity with the help of religiously connoted postulates is debatable. This is particularly the case when the gulf between the rapidly increasingly number of those living below the poverty line and a seemingly increasing (in absolute terms) yet decreasing (in relation to population) middle-class, is widening day by day.

The discussions on Islamic identity and normativity, the degree of orthodoxy and the following of Prophetic tradition are constitutive for scholarly Islam which again is informed by superiority complexes. The semantics of the diaspora, the notion of exile and the myth of return are celebrated, and a backward-looking nostalgic diasporic memory suggested. Religion as a cultural resource is supposed to mobilise specific and particular interests. Yet, South Asia is rich, not only in terms of imaginaries but also in terms of spaces for religious pluralism which can and do accommodate multiple identities and boundary-work in the best sense of the words. As long as we consider the fuzzy and non-ideological potential of everyday lived religious reality as something viable for the process of cultural integration, we may be on the safe side. Lived Islam offers a broad panoply of internal arrangements, beyond any dogmas and debates about normativity. On the level of everyday Islam there is hardly any questioning of Islamicity but it provides a basis of identity and source of morality. In contrast, it seems to be the learned discourse of Islam that reformulates the frustrations of Muslims into generalising Muslim problems. How then did Islam and its actors evolve in their different Islamicated and Islamic manifestations in such a context informed by religious pluralism?

PART ONE

EARLY MUSLIM EXPANSION, CULTURAL ENCOUNTER AND ITS CONSTITUENCIES

CHAPTER ONE

MUSLIM EXPANSION. TRADE, MILITARY AND THE QUEST FOR POLITICAL AUTHORITY IN SOUTH ASIA (APPROX. 700–1300)

South Asia, made up of present day India, Pakistan, Bangladesh and Sri Lanka was at one time a separate continent. Millions of years ago, the Indian tectonic plate then drifted northwards to hit the Asian supercontinent. The impact created the Himalayas. India is still pressing northwards, lifting the mountain range even higher. This tectonic phenomenon accounts for the huge differences between both the Himalayas, the valley of the Ganges in the north and the rugged peninsula in the south as well as between the two sides of the Himalayas—between South Asia on the one hand and China, Mongolia and Central Asia on the other. The climate over the region is dictated by the monsoon, the rain season, although it is exceedingly variegated across the subcontinent. The productivity and population density of all cities and regions have always been dependent on a sufficiently heavy rain season, and the lack of rainfall in some years inevitably signalled a decline.[1]

The triangle that is South Asia, although bounded by the sea on two sides and the world's highest mountain range on the third, has never been an isolated region. As far as one can trace back, there have been continuous relations between the people of the subcontinent and their neighbours. However in many aspects, until the advent of Islam, the contacts between North and South India were less pronounced than those with its neighbours.[2]

Thus, the differences between Northern and Southern India are immense. In geographical terms, the large valleys of the Ganges and Yamuna Rivers in the North provided very fertile soils and constitute a relatively dense system of communication. The coastal regions in the South, on the other hand, though relatively well connected with each

[1] See Francis Robinson (ed.): *Cambridge Encyclopaedia of India, Pakistan, Bangladesh, Sri Lanka, Nepal, Bhutan and the Maldives*, Cambridge: CUP 1989, pp. 12–19; Burton Stein: *A history of India*, Oxford: Blackwell 1998, pp. 7–8.

[2] Stein: *A history of India*, pp. 6–7, 100.

other, had difficulties communicating with the mountainous inland. There was extensive trade and intermingling between coastal India and Africa in the West and South East Asia in the East, however. The dividing line between the North and the South is conventionally drawn along the Narmada or Narbada River. The political and cultural developments differ extensively between these two regions. The North-west, which is now Pakistan does have a mountainous profile and lacks substantial tributaries to the Indus River, yet many of the important traces of civilisation such as the Harappa and Ghandhara civilisations have been found along the Indus River.[3]

India before the Arab-Muslim advent was divided into numerous small states, each controlling a core area, usually fertile lands of relatively smooth terrain. The earliest Indian state formations seem to date back to 2500 B.C. However, these early communities were rather complex social formations persisting over an extended period of time and space than actual states. From about 800 B.C., there existed so-called *janapadas* in the North, which have been variously conceived as 'clan territories' or 'proto-republics.' The *janapadas* were not monarchical, but their governance was carried out by sophisticated and religiously legitimated collegial institutions. The first Indian documentary records date from about 270 B.C., and were issued by the Buddhist King Ashoka (died 232 B.C.). The Mauryan kingdom of Northern India over which he ruled seems to have had a monarchical structure. However, although it covered about two thirds of the Indian subcontinent, it seemed to have had little influence on the structures of later Indian state formations.[4]

It was with the Gupta Empire, founded around 320 C.E. that the basis was first laid for later Indian imperial structures. The period between the two Empires has often been dismissed as the Dark Ages. However, it was characterised by impressive cultural, political and economic developments. The so-called 'Gupta golden age' then continued many of these developments. In the political sphere, the Gupta kings developed a system of vassal organisation, in which the kings could keep close control over temples and other religious institutions while leaving judicial and economic powers in the hands of various local institutions. In the area of religious practices, a new type of worship

---

[3] Robinson (ed.): *Cambridge Encyclopaedia*, pp. 44–48, Stein: *A history of India*, pp. 10–11; David Ludden: *An Agrarian History of South Asia*, Cambridge: CUP 1999, pp. 48–55.

[4] Stein: *A history of India*, pp. 15–23, 73–79; Robinson (ed.): *Cambridge Encyclopaedia*, pp. 73–83.

appeared during the Gupta golden age. Instead of the ritual rigidity that had dominated Hindu religious practices up until then, devotional aspects were emphasised. This development initiated the spread of a rich tradition of demotic poetry, singing the praises of Vishnu and Shiva in the different Indian languages. It also engendered a revalorisation of the occupations of merchants, artisans and scribes, improving the social standing of these groups.[5]

In the early sixth century C.E., the so-called golden age of Northern India came to an end, just as was the case with the Roman Empire in Europe. Invasions by horsemen from Central Asia signalled an end to the expansion of the Gupta Kingdom. However, unlike in Europe, the extensive developments in the political, social and economic spheres that had been achieved by the sixth century were not lost, and persisted until the decline of the Mughal Empire in the eighteenth century. In the centuries that followed, the Indian subcontinent was again divided into numerous smaller state formations, contesting one another for political dominance. The last emperor to rule an extensive part of India before the advent of Islam was Harsha, ruling from 606–647 C.E. However, his nominal territory was far larger than what he actually controlled, which was confined to a compact landscape between the Ganges and Yamuna rivers.[6]

The political situation in the South was somewhat different as the North was much easier to integrate in ancient times, because of its relatively homogeneous riverine environment. The three Tamil dynasties of the Cholas, the Cheras, and the Pandyas dominated in the South from the first century C.E. until the Pallava kingdom rose in the sixth century. The Pallava kings were the first to exercise sovereign power over the whole of Southern India, and even occasionally intruded into the politics of Northern India. The Pallava, Chola and other southern kings managed their own affairs from seventh to twelfth century without taking note of the Arab Muslim conquests of the Northwest.[7]

From some early Indian religious texts, especially the Mahabharata (ca. 200 B.C.), Manu Smriti (ca. 200–100 B.C.) and the Bhagavad Gita (ca. 100 B.C.–100 C.E.) one can draw a picture of the Indians before

---

[5] Ludden: *An Agrarian History*, pp. 67ff.; Stein: *A history of India*, pp. 79–83, 90–92, 96–100.

[6] Robinson (ed.): *Cambridge Encyclopaedia*, pp. 83–85; Stein: *A history of India*, pp. 111, 116–120.

[7] Stein: *A history of India*, pp. 23–25, 100–103.

Islam. These texts indicate that the notion of private property and a system of taxation already existed in the Indian society. By the eighth century, the social division of labour also had become quite complex evolving into a widely accepted multilayered caste hierarchy.[8]

During the Gupta era, an interesting tradition developed which later spread across the subcontinent, whereby dynastic authorities used to endow certain piece of land on *Brahmans* to administer and develop it. Such endowments were a gauge of the royalty; the more religiously attractive such sites were the more prestigious were their royal patrons. From the sixth century onwards, these centres of production where *Brahmans* recorded, created and propagated agricultural knowledge sprang up all over India. Between these agrarian centres in the vast plains, mountainous regions and tropical jungles with hunters, gatherers and nomads were scattered the settlements of half-nomadic farming communities. For the early Indian dynasties, the claim to land almost exclusively concentrated on the agrarian centres, whose control determined the overall political power of an empire. The state formations were thus characterised by an agrarian base, unlike the Roman and Chinese empires, which were based on an urban, ethnically homogeneous elite.[9]

Between the royal dynasties and the agrarian base were the *Brahmans*, who constituted something like an agrarian gentry. The dynasties and the agrarian gentry comprised a mutually beneficial relationship. For the *Brahmans*, their royal patron provided protection while the king was legitimised and sanctified by the *Brahmans*. In many cases, however, the *Brahmans* did not shy away from establishing their own dynasties at a lower level, and sometimes even growing more powerful than their former royal patrons and overthrowing them. In any case, many of these families of agrarian gentry remained in dominant power in their regions for centuries to come.[10] One such Brahmin, Chach, had conquered Sind (which included parts of Punjab to the delta, Makran and Turan) around 622 to expand into Multan and parts of Baluchistan. His successor Raja Dahir (died 712 C.E.) had some initial encounters along the south coast with the expanding Arabs who were thriving towards the east. How did Muslim expansion occur initially?

---

[8] Peter Robb: *A History of India*, Basingstoke: Palgrave, 2002, pp. 28–38.

[9] Ludden: *An Agrarian History*, pp. 76–85; Stein: *A history of India*, p. 131.

[10] Stein: *A history of India*, p. 99.

Arab encroachment and the role of Islamic semantics

In negotiating Muslim expansion one usually is confronted with powerful perceptions that Islam expanded by force and coercion alone. Explanations such as an "eruption of (hungry) tribal elemental forces from arid environments of Arabia" or the "expansion of Islam with fire and sword through fanaticised holy warriors" are not well afforded. These perceptions spread by the travel of ideas and the reciprocity of relations, however, helped establish master narratives that are difficult to deconstruct and counteract. There is no doubt that the fulminate wave of expansion in the first century *hijra* shaped—as a collective experience—the self-image and the development of Muslims. The concept of *futuh* (from the Arab root *fataha*, to open) played an important role, as the early successes were called "the opening of non-Muslim lands for Muslims with the help of God". Al-Baladuri (died approx. 892) refers to a similar concept of *futuh* when he quotes the Prophet who is reported to have said that every city or village which will be opened with force can be considered as having been opened by the Quran. However, strategy of Muslim conquests (*futuh*) can be adumbrated only: as the late Albrecht Noth has pointed out, they were quick and constant but hardly centrally planned and managed by the caliphs. For the most part different Muslim units operated autonomously. They favoured only a few but major battles (*ayyam*) and the caliphs could hardly interfere, particularly when it came to the division of booty.[11]

The spectacularly swift spread of Islamic belief did have its reasons. It is right that the conquest (*fath*) was a unique experience of collective identity of the Muslim *umma*. Yet, it was too complex a phenomenon to be explained by the simple illustrations such as those mentioned above.[12] For our purpose it is sufficient to point out that religion was not the prime and only factor for this mobilisation. In fact, there have been other hard to ignore factors, for example the surrounding Byzantine and Sasanian Empires exhaustion fighting each other, the local populations desire to rid themselves the yoke of these two Empires;

---

[11] See Albrecht Noth: "Früher Islam", in: Ulrich Haarmann (ed.): *Geschichte der arabischen Welt*, München 1991, pp. 11–100; the division of booty was stipulated by Quranic injunctions (8:41 and 59:7) in reference to the tribal customs of the time.

[12] See A. Noth: *The Early Arabic Historical Tradition. A source-critical study*, 2nd. ed. in collaboration with Lawrence I. Conrad. Transl. from the German by Michael Bonner, Princeton 1994 (= Studies in Late Antiquity and Islam 3); F.M. Donner: *The Early Muslim Conquest*, Princeton 1981.

and the ability of Muslims to accommodate both themselves and their new subjects as well as their ability to adopt to new environments with a fair amount of pragmatism and flexibility. Hence the *futuh* can be considered as a series of contracts which in many cases helped the conquered non-Muslims to secure status quo. These contracts seemed to follow a specific scheme: protection (*dhimma*) of body, life, property and cultus against variable dues—eventually *jizya* for non-Muslims. During this wave the gestating administrative, judicial and political structures of "Islamic" rule and society gradually developed.

There is evidence that the early Muslim Arabs made use of the concepts of *jihad*, *fitna* and *hijra* for their politics of conquest, the semantics of which were expanded gradually, as can also be gauged from the term *futuh*. The starting points for the *futuh*-activities and first collecting posts for the incoming booty as well as the contractually arranged booty were the early settlements and garrison towns, the *amsar* (pl. of *misr*) or *ajnad* (pl. of *jund*) or *qasabat*.

During the expansion (*futuh*), the idea of the second class citizenship (*dhimmi*) not only further developed but was also perpetuated: early *futuh*-warrior groups had segregated themselves from later Arabs, as well as, from New-Muslims of non-Arab descent leading to an *ʿarab*—*ʿajam*-divide, *ʿajam* literally meaning "having no voice". These non-Arab Muslims, *mawalis*, were looked down upon,[13] although they were compensated later by the fact that they became leading scientists and administrators. Therefore, discrimination proliferated to other strata such as the imported groups of soldiers of Turkish origin (slaves), or Indians,[14] who, however, advanced to become the torchbearers of Muslim culture and politics after the fall of Bagdad 1258.

By the same token, the semantic of migration (*hijra*) was expanded, now also implying to help Muslim troops against the enemy. It was considered necessary, in fact obligatory, to make *hijra* into one of the new garrison posts (*amsar*). Hence, the seizure of Medina to be the

---

[13] *Mawalis* were discriminated also through the new legal position concerning taxation. This legal position was implemented in order to prevent mass conversion and the decrease of levying land revenue (*kharaj*) at one tenth, e.g., the amount of *sadaqa/zakat*. The position determined that converts too had to pay the original tax: only persons could become Muslims, the land, however, could not "convert". See Noth: "Früher Islam", here p. 95.

[14] Albrecht Noth: "Schichten und Gruppen innerhalb der 'Umma'", in: Albrecht Noth and Jürgen Paul (eds.): *Der islamische Orient—Grundzüge seiner Geschichte*, Würzburg 1998, pp. 135–150, here p. 145.

only *dar al-hijra*, the place to migrate to.[15] Apparently, expansion and political stability as well as conquest were more important than religious zeal; the emigration of Muslim troops into *amsar* was supported; the return of the *muhajirun* from the *amsar* became as severely punishable as apostasy. Thus a Muslim could claim his booty only after he had been sedentarised.[16]

This fostered sedentarisation gave emotional, economic and political strength: ideas and metaphors became informed by new meanings, e.g., movement ultimately meant settlement and spiritual retreat. It is in this context that soldiers on the borders developed their own ideas of the world and in this way emancipated themselves from the central power of the caliphate. They undertook razzias (*ghazawat*) and established their own spiritual and social centres, as had been the case in *ribat*s, outposts of Islamic territories, and, later the warrior-sufis.[17]

It is in this context that treachery, sedition, an illegitimate "civil war" among Muslims (*fitna*), between Muslims and their protected non-Muslim subjects or allies were of major importance for legitimising the expansion and the Islamic political order. For, with the expansion of the frontier, the outside enemy became the internal agent of *fitna*. Thus, *fitna* was closely connected to *jihad*. The notion of *jihad*, actually the fight against non-Muslims, was also expanded. The Quran when speaking of the fight against the People of the Book (*ahl al-kitab*), such as in Sura 9:29–35, uses the word *qital* rather than *jihad*. But now *jihad* also implied the struggle and fight on the way to God at the border. Accordingly, the concepts of "House of Islam" (*dar al-Islam*), "House of War" (*dar al-harb*) and "House of Truce" (*dar al-sulh*) were gradually developed,[18] but most of the conquests were made on treaties, i.e., through *sulh*. This indeed corresponded to the proven practice of *futuh*.

Actually, the religious rhetoric of *jihad* became necessary due to the Arab *fitna* which was plaguing the early Umayyads, though Muslim

---

[15] Already, after the conquest of Mecca, it was declared by the Prophet that henceforth the call for migration to Medina stood abrogated.

[16] Compare Khalil Athamina: "*A'râb* and *Muhâjirûn* in the Environment of *Amsâr*", in: *Studia Islamica* 66 (1987), pp. 5–26; Donner: *The Early Islamic Conquests*, pp. 79f.

[17] For the warrior-sufis in 14th century Deccan see R.M. Eaton: *Sufis of Bijapur 1300–1700*, Princeton University Press 1978.

[18] "These distinctions are classical, clearly reverting to Roman categories of conquest which distinguished between an *Ager Romanus* ('House of Islam'), *Ager Hostis* ('House of War') and the *Foederati* ('House of Truce')." Andre Wink: *Al-Hind. The Making of the Indo-Islamic World; Early Medieval India and the Expansion of Islam, Seventh to Eleventh Centuries*, Vol. I, Delhi: OUP 1990, p. 197.

expansion had already occurred during the rule of first four caliphs. Now, the external trope of *jihad* served to control the internal *fitan* and painted both the internal (to the Umayyad dynasty) and external (the fledgling empire) challengers with the same brush, i.e. considering and treating them equally as enemies of Islam. Hence, the interrelationship of *jihad* and *fitna*.

Muslim expansion into the East was also facilitated by the perception that India was a fabled land of dreams and legends and abandoned gods, as had been the case in early "European" cultural constructions such as the writings of the Greek traveller and geographer Megasthenes (died 290 B.C.).[19] It seems that the Arabs were informed by these perceptions which had taken roots in this region during the Byzantine and Sasanian Empires.[20] The carriers of these perceptions were Arab tribes moving on the traditional trade routes through the Arabian Peninsula permitting trans-regional trade. This was possible only due to the complex relationships among nomads, peasants and trading communities on the peninsula that maintained contacts between neighbours. The two Empires, the Byzantine, which claimed agency for the universality of Christianity, and the Persian Sasanians, who were particularly interested in the control of trade, however, were not able to subdue Arabia. But both Empires disposed of different Arab tributary tribes, who were in constant contact with the imperial worlds, opportunistically changing their loyalties and thereby acquiring and exchanging knowledge of high cultures.[21] The Islamic master narrative around *Jahiliyya* as a pre-Islamic condition of ignorance and barbarianism is difficult to sustain, unless it is understood purely as a metaphor for the breach of tradition and history carried over from pagan Arab society, in order to provide identity and enhance solidarity among the emerging monotheistic Muslim community.

Arab Muslims seemed to have some notion about India because of their consistent, albeit limited trade-contacts and interaction with this region and even beyond. They conceptualised South Asia as a civilisa-

---

[19] Cf. J.W. McCrindle (transl. and ed.): *Ancient India as Described by Megasthenes and Arrian*, Calcutta and Bombay: Thacker, Spink 1877.

[20] There is a rich Muslim literature on Arab—Indian cultural and trade relations. The voluminous works on history show that Muslim Arabs displayed the signs of historical consciousness quite early. Quite a number of these seminal works have been consulted in a most impressive way by Wink: *al-Hind*, I.

[21] Walter Dostal: "Die Araber in vorislamischer Zeit", in: Noth and Paul (eds.): *Der islamische Orient*, pp. 25–44, here pp. 29f.

tion and drew its boundaries up in a geo-political sense and called it *al-Sind wa al-Hind*, adopting a pre-existing Persian term. In this constrution the contours of al-Hind extended from Sind and Makran to the Indonesian Archipelago and mainland of Southeast Asia.[22] In a way, the Arab Muslims provided South Asia with a distinct cultural and collective identity that has never lost its significance.

Rationale for expansion

Expansion towards the East was primarily informed by geo-political, economic and later by manorial considerations. Thus between the seventh and eleventh centuries, Arabo-Persian Muslims tried to establish economic power through new connections between the Mediterranean and Indian Ocean with their vast natural resources. According to Andre Wink, the economic and geo-strategic importance of South Asia increased by virtue of its natural geographic location as the centre between the two dynamic poles, West Asia (the Middle East) and East Asia (China). He maintains that the Muslim conquest was able to integrate different regions into a greater economic power by fusing Byzantine gold and Sasanian silver into one unified currency. By bringing two contesting and separate cultural and commercial worlds closer together, Muslims integrated the conquered regions into a wider pattern. In other words: Islamisation stood for integration.[23] This Arabo-centric view has been challenged by Sanjay Subrahmanyam on the grounds that neither did Muslims act *en bloc* nor were they the only groups participating in this trade.[24] Arab Muslims had to pragmatically accommodate and flexibly negotiate their positions in context and time. This ventured into what Marshall Hodgson has called Islamicated culture, one that does not refer to religion in the first place, "but to the social and cultural complex historically associated with Islam and

[22] In fact, Ibn Khaldun calls it "al-Hind wa al-Sind", translated as "Eastern and Western India" by Franz Rosenthal. See Ibn Khaldûn: *The Muqaddimah. An introduction to History*, translated by F. Rosenthal, in three volumes, London: PUP 1967(2), here Vol. 1, p. 99.

[23] See the path-breaking work of Wink: *Al-Hind*, I, p. 4; similarly Richard M. Eaton: *The Rise of Islam and the Bengal Frontier, 1204–1760*, Berkeley: UCP 1993, passim.

[24] For a critique on Wink's thesis see Sanjay Subrahmanyam: *Explorations in Connected History. From the Tagus to the Ganges*, New Delhi: OUP 2005, Chap. 3: "Persianization and 'Mercantilism' in Bay of Bengal History, 1400–1700", pp. 51–52.

the Muslims, both among Muslims themselves and even when found among non-Muslims."[25]

Arab expansion made use of existing local cultural and social structures as a base and as bridgeheads. It was preceded by Muslim settlements on the western seaboard of India. In fact, pagan Arab traders had known the region long before Arab Muslims came to South Asia, due to their contacts with coastal trade diasporas of Christians, Jews, and Parsis. For example, Ceylon had accommodated settlers from Yemen and Hadhramaut since the first century C.E.[26] For the seafaring Arabs Ceylon was an important commercial junction, where profitable trade in pearls, gems, spices and other valuable articles could be made, and the tolerant and friendly attitude of the rulers and people of the island is said to have encouraged settlement.[27]

Similarly, contemporaneous Arab navigational texts indicate that ocean-going vessels generally touched at Malabar[28] where ports were most numerous. It seems as if Malabar was the site of the earliest Muslim community to have been established on the South Asian subcontinent (see Chap. 3).[29] Likewise the Coromandal Coast, called al-Maʿbar, "the place of crossing", was also known since it was from here that the boats of the Arabs sailed or crossed over from India to China. The expansion of southern India's wide-ranging trading networks brought Arab traders and navigators to this region in the eighth and ninth centuries, where soon the Muslim mystical (Sufi) tradition became a natural bridge between the Muslim faith and the beliefs of native non-Muslims. Later, the Sufis used their power to attract devotees and disciples and aligned themselves with the dynamic elements in the south Indian religious culture (see Chap. 2). In the course of

---

[25] See Marshall Hodgson: *Venture of Islam. Conscience and History in a World Civilization*, Vols. 1–3, Chicago 1975, Vol. 1, p. 59; also David Gilmartin and Bruce B. Lawrence (eds.): *Beyond Turk and Hindu: Rethinking Religious Identities in Islamicate South Asia*, New Delhi: Research Press 2002.

[26] Wink: *al-Hind*, I, p. 80; Geneviève Bouchon: "Quelques aspects de l'Islamisation des régions maritimes de l'Inde à l'époque médiévale (XIIe–XVIe siècles)", in: Marc Gaboriau (ed.): *Islam et Société en Asie du Sud*, Paris 1986, pp. 29–36; for the Hadhrami diaspora see Ulrike Freitag and William G. Clarence-Smith (eds.): *Hadhrami Traders, Scholars and Statesmen in the Indian Ocean 1750s–1960s*, Leiden: Brill 1997.

[27] A.M.A. Azeez: "Ceylon", in: *The Encyclopaedia of Islam. New Edition.* Edited by P.J. Bearman, Th. Bianquis, C.E. Bosworth, E. van Donzel, W.P. Heinrichs et alii., Leiden: Brill 1954–ff., II, pp. 26ff.; henceforth EI(2).

[28] A.D.W. Forbes: "Maʿbar", in: EI(2), V, pp. 937f.

[29] A.D.W. Forbes: "Malabar", in: EI(2), VI, pp. 206f; Stephen F. Dale: *The Mappillas of Malabar, 1498–1922*, Oxford 1980, Chap. 1.

time and due to the steadily modified trading network, the formally small Muslim enclaves in cities along the coast expanded considerably. Arab Muslims settling down married locally and consequently observed local customs sharing cultures.[30] Until the beginning of the fourteenth century, relations between Maʿbar and the Arab Muslim world were generally those of peaceful trading contacts.[31] In these coastal areas and Ceylon, incoming Muslims in the eighth and ninth centuries adhered to Shafiʿi school of law (*madhhab*), pointing to an Arab origin based in the continuing contacts with Baghdad and the towns of the Persian Gulf, as well as with Arabia, Yemen and Hadhramaut. In contrast, when the Muslims entered Northern India much later, the Hanafi school of law became dominant there because of its Turkish-Persianate tradition which evolved some centuries later.[32]

But it was not only Malabar, Maʿbar and Ceylon which were known to Arabs before Islam. Pre-Muslim Gujarat was also part of the Arab landscape due to its natural resources, its piracy and maritime trade, local Hindu[33] and Jain practices, as well as religious pluralism.[34] Moreover, Makran, the frontier of India, had been frequented by Arabs almost three-quarters of a century before Muhammad b. al-Qasim al-Thaqafi invaded Sind in 711, which occurred less than a hundred years after the death of Prophet Muhammad (632) and which was paralleled by the Muslim conquest of Spain. As a connecting link between *al-Hind* and Persia, the Makran route was more vital than the route running through the Kabul river valley further north. Along these two highways flowed virtually all of India's overland trade with the West. Makran was thus widely known because its people carried on much traffic by sea and land in different directions.[35] Similarly, the

---

[30] Cf. Wink: *al-Hind*, I, pp. 68ff.; see Susan Bayly: *Saints, Goddesses and Kings—Muslims and Christians in South Indian society 1700–1900*, Cambridge 1989.

[31] A.D.W. Forbes: "Maʿbar", in: EI(2), V, pp. 937f.

[32] Cf. Wink: *al-Hind*, I, p. 69. For the evolution of Islamic law see, for example, the contributions in *Islamic Law and Society* (Leiden), particularly Vol. 10/2 (2003): *The Madhhab.*

[33] As many authors have pointed out, the very word Hindu does not occur in the classical "Hindu" texts. Originally, the term *al-Hind* was used in a geographical, rather than a religious context by the ancient Persians and later by Muslim Arab and Persian invaders, to denote all non-Muslims living to the east of the Indus river, thus all those inhabitants of the region who were not Muslims, or later, not Jews and Christians as well. See, for example, Dominique Sila Khan: *Crossing the Threshold: Understanding Religious Identities in South Asia*, London: IB Tauris 2004.

[34] J. Burton-Page: "Gudjarât", in: EI(2), II: pp. 1123ff.

[35] Wink: *al-Hind*, I, pp. 139f.

major ports of Oman were frequented by the merchants who dealt with Sind, India and China. They were ruled by a Persian governor in collaboration with an Arab client king who also became an important bridgehead for the Arab conquest in Sind.

Indian trade became the main external source of wealth for Islam, not the least because of non-Muslim Asian merchant groups. The first Muslim-built city, the garrison town of Basra (635), benefited so much from these trade relations that it became a centre of the Indian trade, to such an extent that Ubulla, a part of Basra, was called "the land of India" (*wa kanat al-Ubulla tusamma ard al-hind*)[36] and "a part of al-Hind" (*juz'an min al-Hind*) and a "harbor of Sind and Hind" (*marsan al-hind wa sind*).[37] Al-Ya'qubi (died 897) considered Basra, Oman, Hind and Sind a common geographical area.[38] In the cultural memory of contemporary scientific research, the Indian Ocean gradually developed into the domain of Islam or better, of Muslims, an 'Arabic-speaking Mediterranean' as it were, connecting the Persian Gulf with China. And Sind was the borderland between the kingdom of Islam and al-Hind,[39] its sizeable mercantile Buddhist population connected Central Asia and China. Sind was therefore, the hub of the Indian trade and the overland passage, and its invasion can be seen as part of a larger Arab expansion towards the east (China).[40] At the same time Sind could be an important safeguard from piracy. Thus it was a matter of time before it was conquered.

Sind's majority population followed Hindu traditions[41] but a substantial minority was Buddhist. Rural Hindu population pertained

---

[36] See Yaqut al-Hamawi: *Mu'jam al-buldan*, Vol. 1, ed. Ferdnand Wüstenfeld, Leipzig 1866, pp. 620–621.

[37] See Ibn Battuta: *Rihlat*, ed. Talal Harb, Beirut: Dar al-Kutub al-'Ilmiyya 2002, p. 206; also Wink: *al-Hind*, I, p. 54.

[38] See Ahmad ibn Abi Ya'qub Ya'qubi: *Kitab al-Buldan*, ed. Leiden 1892, p. 320.

[39] Wink: *al-Hind*, I, pp. 25, 4.

[40] D.N. Mac Lean: *Religion and Society in Arab Sind*, Leiden: Brill 1989, pp. 61–63, 67–71.

[41] Hinduism displays enormous heterogeneity in terms of doctrinal differences and in terms of fundamentally different types of religion. Heinrich von Stietencron, therefore, tends to speak of Hinduism as a "civilisation", in which these very different religions co-exist in a historically evolved and extraordinarily tolerant way. See Heinrich von Stietencron: "Religious Configurations in Pre-Muslim India and the Modern Concept of Hinduism", in: Vasudha Dalmia & Heinrich von Stietencron (eds.): *Representing Hinduism. The Construction of Religious Traditions and National Identity*, New Delhi: Sage 1995, pp. 51–81; see also the interesting discussion by Dwijendra Narayan Jha: "Looking for a Hindu Identity", in: http://www.sacw.net/India_History/dnj_Jan06.pdf (accessed 2.12.2007).

to Pashupata Shaivanism which was deistic in nature, believing in a supreme unborn and eternal lord, Ishwara. The centre of their heliolatry cult with some 300 temples in Sind was the sun temple in Multan. In contrast, the Buddhists of Sind belonged to the anti-intellectual and populist Sammitiyya school of thought postulating "the actual existence of a readily comprehensible...self which transmigrated." They had a mercantile orientation through their monasteries set up along the major trade routes and had not been very happy with their socio-economic situation under the Brahman dynasty.[42]

Sind's major city, Dewal or Daybul (at the site of today's Karachi), a junction of several trade routes, was inhabited mostly by Buddhist merchants and craftsmen. Ships sailing between India and the Persian Gulf called here and vessels were loaded and unloaded. The town had a large population with abundant wealth. Its control meant the control of seaports and maritime routes in this part of the world, but it also implied the control of the pastoral-nomadic activity following the sedentarisation of such Hindu tribes, as the Med and Jat, the two major groups inhabiting Sind.[43] The Med were known for their piracy, and in Arab accounts were considered robbers and infidels. Their raids extended as far as Makran and sometimes even to Alor (near modern Sukkur in Upper Sind) on the river Indus.[44] Initially, they successfully encountered early Arab incursions on Sind. As a pastoral or semi-pastoral population of a very low status, the Jat (arab. Zutt) were barely integrated into Hindu society. Though conquest initiated an enforced sedentary lifestyle, the Jats' shift to settled agriculture took place only much later—as the Persian wheel improved irrigation in the fourteenth century.

Sind becoming Arabic Muslim

The first Muslim naval expedition took place at the end of the caliphate of ʿUmar b. al-Khattab (died 644), most probably in the year 636 or 644,[45] though without caliphal consent, as reported by al-Baladhuri,

[42] Mac Lean: *Religion and Society*, pp. 7–10, 13–19, 57–60, 66, quotation, p. 108.

[43] Wink: *al-Hind*, I, pp. 182, 51f.

[44] Y. Friedmann, D. Shulman: "Mêd", in EI(2), VI, 967a.

[45] See also Mohammad Ishaq: "A peep into the first Arab expedition to India under the companions of the Prophet", in: *Islamic Culture* 19 (1945), pp. 109–114.

the oldest Arabic source on Muslim expansion into the East available to us.[46] On the other hand, 'Umar, the second caliph, is said to have asked the Hindu rulers of Sind to accept Islam and his supremacy. It is stated that several of them did so and took on Arab names.[47] Qandabil (popularly known as such from the sixteenth century and now Gandava in Baluchistan), a town connecting different important market towns, such as Multan, was initially captured, but the Arab armies withdrew after receiving the news of Caliph 'Umar's death which ushered in the Arab-Muslim frictions (*fitna*). While these raids did not permanently occupy the areas in India proper, further expansions must be seen in the background of the intra-Muslim struggles occurring in eastern Iraq and Khurasan.

In order to facilitate expansion, the Arabs pragmatically made use of primordial ties of ethnicity, caste and kinship, the forces of al-Hajjaj (died 714) being instrumental in expanding the Islamic Empire.[48] Al-Hajjaj, who had been able to consolidate Syrian military rule, sent several commanders to Makran, when in 710 an Arab ship carrying precious gifts from the ruler of Maldives to Caliph al-Walid I (ruled 705–15), and (Muslim) women were captured by the pirates of Daybul.[49] The Brahmin king Dahir, the powerful Med ruler of Sind, who had occupied Qandabil (704–11),[50] denied any involvement upon al-Hajjaj's demand to release the prisoners. The Muslim governor swore to take revenge, but the area was successfully defended by the Jats[51] leaving several Arab commanders dead.

This story, though told in several ways, serves as the *casus belli* and a powerful master narrative for the first attack on India with proclaimed caliphal backing. However, the punishment of the Med can also be

[46] Ahmad b. Yahya ibn Jabir al-Baladhuri: *Kitab Futuh al-Buldan*, ed. M.J. de Goeje, Leiden 1866, p. 432. Another source is Buzurg b. Shahriyar, a Persian ships'-captain (first half of the tenth century) and author of *Kitab 'aja'ib al-Hind* (approx. 953). This is a compilation of stories and anecdotes gathered from ships'-captains, pilots, traders who used to sail the Indian Ocean.

[47] Cf. al-Baladhuri: *Kitab Futuh al-Buldan*, p. 441.

[48] Wink: *al-Hind*, I, pp. 51, 136.

[49] In fact, it was good Arab tradition that Abyssinian male and female slaves accompanied Muslim women in the early eighth century from Ceylon to Mecca, implying that the Arabs sold black slaves in Asia. The most visible among them is the Siddhi tribe still living in southern Gujarat in India. For this interesting group see Helene Basu: *Habshi Sklaven, Sidi-Fakire: Muslimische Heiligenverehrung im westlichen Indien*, Berlin: Das Arabische Buch 1994.

[50] N.A. Baloch: "Kandâbîl", in: EI(2), IV, pp. 534ff.

[51] A.S. Bazmee Ansari: "Djât", in: EI(2), II, pp. 488f.

taken as pretext to expand Muslim power into the eastern direction. Al-Hajjaj sent his 17-year-old nephew Muhammad b. al-Qasim al-Thaqafi against Daybul in 711–12.[52] Some 6,000 Syrian cavalry and another 6,000 troops embarked for the Indus delta through the arid region of the Makran coastland. Supplies and ammunition such as siege implements were sent by sea. Officially it was a war (*ghazwa*) against an area mostly occupied by chieftains, usurpers, *mutaghalliba*—a term not found with reference to Umayyad times.[53] The use of *ghazwa* and *jihad* rhetoric was interchangeable[54] and had an enormous mobilising effect, but the object was not only to propagate Islam or take revenge but also to get rid of the piracy along the Makran coast and to open up new markets and consolidate the economy.

In Daybul, Muslims made use of catapults powered by 500 men—equivalent to a counterweight of three metric tons and a calculated range of several hundred meters.[55] The locals submitted under a peace treaty in 712, except for Dahir who was in Alor. The Jats were captured in large numbers and shipped to al-Hajjaj as slaves. While Sind and Makran supplied the Arabs with slaves, most of the Jats soon converted to Islam.[56] Eventually Muhammad b. al-Qasim also subdued the Med, pirates of the sea. He is reported to have written to Dahir that he considered this fight a *jihad*—which was similar to *ghazwa*. This is the only mention of *jihad* in this early context, given the thirteenth century Persian chronicle named after Dahir's father Chach, the famous *Chachnama*.[57] Subsequently, Muhammad conquered several important

---

[52] A. Dietrich: "al-Hadjdjâdj", in: EI(2), III, pp. 39ff.; A.S. Bazmee Ansari: "Daybul", in: EI(2), II, pp. 188f.

[53] Wink: *al-Hind*, I, pp. 131, 212; al-Baladhuri: *Kitab Futuh al-Buldan*, p. 445.

[54] See E.C. Sachau: *Alberuni's India*, I–II, Lahore: Muhammad Ashraf 1962, I, p. 26.

[55] See Michael Farnworth: *Inventive Steps in Trebuchet Evolution*, www.thehurl.org/tiki-download_file.php?fileId=66 (accessed 8 Feb. 2008)

[56] Jats (Zutts) were also settled in Basra, Syria and Iraq and Antioch even before the time of al-Muʿawiya, but apparently were segregated and only marginally integrated, as in the Arab accounts Zutts are portrayed as ignorant and uncultured, living as brigands (al-Baladhuri: *Kitab Futuh al-Buldan*, pp. 445f). But in fact, Zutts have produced a number of well known people, among them scholars such as Abu Hanifa (699–767), the founder of the Hanafite school of law, who was of Zutt stock, most probably descending from those early prisoners sent to Iraq; cf. A.S. Bazmee Ansari: "Djât", in: EI(2), II, p. 488b. See also Charles Pellat: *Le milieu Basrien et la formation de Jahiz*, Paris 1953, pp. 37–40, who describes the relations between Basra and India in the context of the Zutts, whom he calls the contemporary Bohemians.

[57] The chronicle is a translation from a lost near-contemporary account in Arabic referred to by later Arab historians; its authenticity can, however, be doubted because

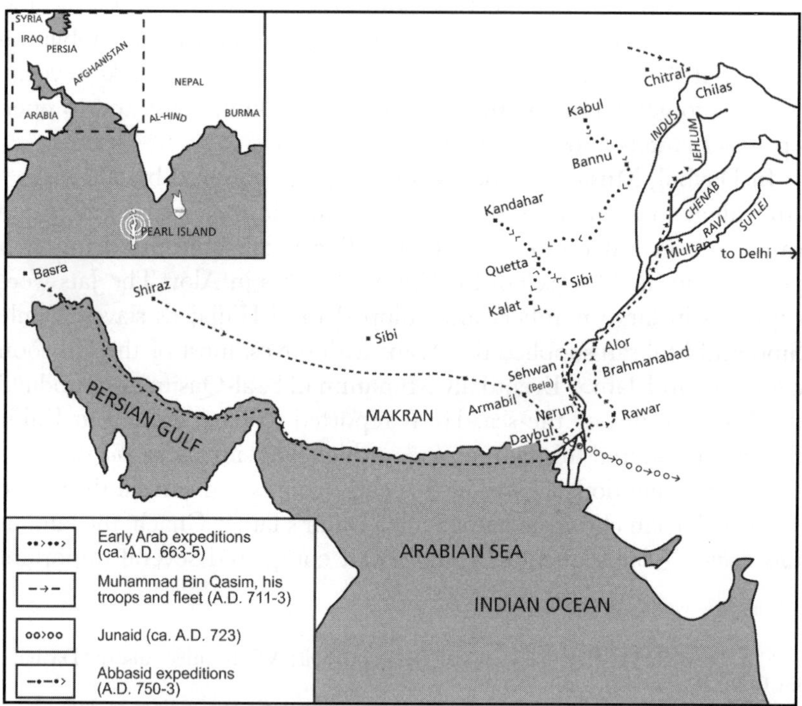

Map 2: Arab Expeditions in the Western parts of al-Hind 663–820 C.E.

cities along the Indus such as Nerunkot near the site of present-day Haydarabad, Sehwan, Rawar, Brahmanabad, Alor. Multan, a rich city benefiting from overland trade, and harbouring the great idol of the sun-temple, the House of Gold, was conquered in 713. Muhammad however, left the Temple of the Sun intact and established a mosque, for obvious reasons. The conquest extended Arab power to upper Sind.[58]

From the inadequate records available on this period it seems there was hardly any forced conversion of the locals nor was there any "invitation" by the Buddhist "traitors" to come to Sind to usurp the power of the Brahmins. In fact both collaborated with the Muslim invaders. "Treaties, the scramble for immunities, alliances and declarations of loyalty were opportunistically motivated, without moral scruples, the product of rational reflection rather than religious faith."[59] The population comprised mostly of Buddhists and Hindus converted voluntarily. In fact, Buddhists tended to collaborate more easily than Hindus since their economic capital was at stake while suffering from the Islamic turn: when Muslim internal trade came to be controlled by Muslim merchants, who traditionally had been the moral pillars of the community (as can be gleaned from the prophetic tradition), and Buddhists were displaced by Muslims in mercantile and industrial sectors, Buddhists started to participate in this larger cosmopolitan society by taking up Muslim symbols. Thus sharing Muslim cultural and symbolic capital and thereby solving the problem of their gradual social and economic marginalisation and debasement became a plausible option for the Buddhists.[60] Moreover, there were also ideological reasons, as Derryl N. MacLean has plausibly argued (see below).

In contrast, the vast non-mercantile agrarian Hindu population was less confronted with and challenged by Islamic urbanism and mercantilism; either the Arabs did not alter their position substantially, or/and they were flexible enough to accommodate and Islamicate. This process

---

it incorporates meagre authentic material of the lost Arabic tradition. See Peter Hardy: "Is the Chach Nama Intelligible as Political Theory?", in: Hamida Khuro (ed.): *Sind Through the Centuries*, Karachi: OUP 1982, pp. 111–117; Y. Friedmann: "The Origins and Significance of the Chach Nama", in: *Islam in Asia*, Vol. I: South Asia, Jerusalem 1984, pp. 23–37; Wink: *al-Hind*, I, pp. 192–196.

[58] For details see Wink: *Al-Hind*, I, pp. 192ff., and Mac Lean: *Religion and Society*; for the conquest of Multan see also Yohanan Friedmann: "The temple of Multân", in: *Israel Oriental Studies* 2 (1972), pp. 176–182.

[59] Wink: *al-Hind*, I, p. 151.

[60] Mac Lean: *Religion and Society*, pp. 52, 72–76.

is in contrast to the popular understanding that conversion to Islam occurred among the Hindus because Islam provided vertical, social and religious mobility apparently not otherwise possible due to a rigid and hierarchical Hindu social structure. It seems more plausible that Islam as a liberating theology appealed to relatively few; otherwise the proportion of Muslims in India should have been much larger (see Excursus: Conversion and Mission). It is said that the Arabs gave peace, *aman*, to poor and common people, artisans, traders and cultivators, who were encouraged to continue their occupations,[61] while the traditional Brahmin elite were given high posts.[62]

Thus, the Arabs were able to assimilate important elements of the defeated opponents in their civil and military administrations. Certainly, this cooption and reproduction of Buddhist hierarchy and Hindu social stratification were necessary, not only to finally settle treaties with local people but also to get access to major markets and to settle taxes and tributes. Because Arab Islam was indifferent to conversion, Hinduism persisted here. In this way a financially viable Sind could be secured.

This pragmatic Islamicating approach found its initial climax in Muhammad b. al-Qasim accepting the native Hindus as people of the covenant: at Alor he is said to have stated that "to us the (Hindu) temples shall be like the churches of the Christians, the synagogues of the Jews, and the fire temples of the Magians".[63] Apparently, the city was willing to surrender provided that its people were not killed and their temples not attacked. So the famous statement of Muhammad b. al-Qasim which had some precedence in caliph ʿUmar's *dhimmi-isation* of Sabians back in Medina considerably expanded the semantics of *dhimmi*-status. The statement thus became "the theoretical basis for an administrative necessity: for reasons of state, the Hindûs had to be considered *ahl al-dhimma*."[64] By analogy, Buddhists and Hindus were to be levied a variable poll tax (*jizya*, as stipulated in Quran 9:29). In fact, to allow retaining local traditions was the only way to govern a majority of idolatrous population, and it soon became clear that in this way the non-Muslims financed Muslim power and domination.

---

[61] al-Baladhuri: *Kitab Futuh al-Buldan*, pp. 426f; Mac Lean: *Religion and Society*, p. 38.

[62] Mac Lean: *Religion and Society*, p. 43; Yohanan Friedmann: "A Contribution to the early History of Islam in India" in: M. Rosen-Ayalon (ed.): *Studies in Memory of Gaston Wiet*, Jerusalem 1977.

[63] See al-Baladhuri: *Kitab Futuh al-Buldan*, p. 439.

[64] See Yohanan Friedmann: *Tolerance and Coercion in Islam*, Cambridge: CUP 2003, pp. 84f.

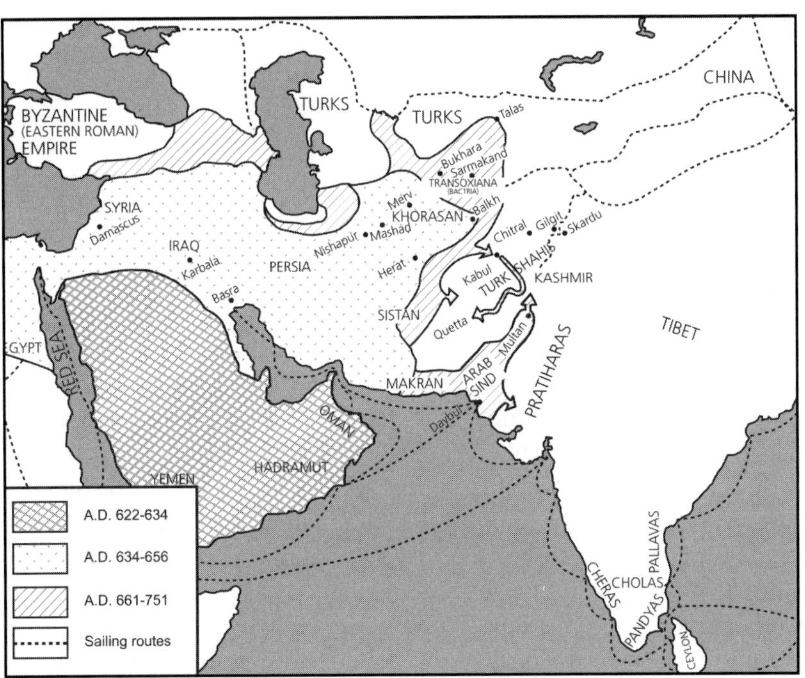

Map 3: Arab conquests until 751 C.E.

Therefore, conversion on a larger scale was not appreciated. As Yohanan Friedmann has pointed out, Muhammad b. al-Qasim's policy towards non-Muslims varied from place to place, but many modern Muslim writers see in him a champion of early Islamic tolerance.[65]

The minoritisation of Hindu majority—through the Muslim institutional instrument of *dhimma*—did become prominent among the Hanafi school that came to dominate the North Indian Islamic discourse. Beneath the rhetoric of Islamic egalitarianism and tolerance, caste system and social inequality were continued by Muslim rulers in agreement with native elite.[66] It is true though, that a top-down intervention in the caste system, which is one of the pillars of Hindu religious orthodoxy, could have been considered by the Hindu as coercion. Thus, one might argue that the notions of egalitarianism and tolerance were in dialectical relationship with each other and difficult to be combined with one another.

At the level of elites there was some intermingling,[67] yet, the theoretical status of *ahl al-dhimma* did not necessarily imply the rights that were given to *dhimmis* in practice later, as is shown in a passage by al-Baladhuri: ʿImran b. Musa (835–41), who was deputed by Abbasid caliph al-Muʿtasim (reigned 833–842) to look after this region,[68] is said to have ordered (while drunken) *jizya*-paying Zutts (Jats) to walk with dogs.[69] Since a dog in Islam as well as in the Hindu tradition is considered an impure animal, the humiliation seems to be obvious, similar not only to discriminatory regulations pertaining to Hindu outcaste *candela*,[70] but also to some regulations against *dhimmis* in Arab lands, such as the notorious ʿUmar's pact, which was however, hardly put into practice.[71] According to al-Baladhuri the obligation of the Jat

---

[65] Compare Friedmann: "A Contribution to the early History", p. 313, Fn 25; C.E. Bosworth: "Muhammad b. Mahmûd", in: EI(2), VII, pp. 406f.

[66] Mac Lean: *Religion and Society*, pp. 31, 48.

[67] For example, Jaysinha, the son of Dahir, and other princes who even took on Arab names, or ʿUsayfan who got the Hindu priests killed and invited Muslim merchants to his kingdom. See al-Baladhuri: *Kitab Futuh al-Buldan*, pp. 441, 446; other examples are given by Mac Lean: *Religion and Society*.

[68] ʿImran fought against the Zutt, won and built a city which he called al-Baydaʾ, and used it as a garrison post (*askanaha al-jund*). After coming to al-Mansura he preceded for mountainous Qandabil to put down rebel (*mutaghallib*), and following that, ʿImran killed several hundred Meds; see al-Baladhuri: *Kitab Futuh al-Buldan*, p. 445.

[69] Al-Baladhuri: *Kitab Futuh al-Buldan*, pp. 445–446.

[70] Mac Lean: *Religion and Society*, pp. 47f.

[71] See A. Noth: "Abgrenzungsprobleme zwischen Muslimen und Nicht-Muslimen. Die 'Bedingungen ʿUmars (*ash-shurût al-ʿUmariyya*)' unter einem anderen Aspekt gelesen", in: *Jerusalem Studies in Arabic and Islam* 9 (1987), pp. 290–315.

to walk with dogs seems to have increased the price of dogs rather than discourage the practise. It implies that this had become an actual practice rather than simply a case of an individual's uttering an insult while drunk. It is yet another question from where these dogs came and who the dog-traders were.

Be it as it may, Muslims did not change the caste-ridden structure of Indian society.[72] This assertion can be made considering the privileges and high social standing given to the Brahmins and later to the Rajputs. Meanwhile, the degraded status of lower castes such as Zutts and others continued. The appreciation of the caste system is also confirmed in the tendentious *Chachnama*, which seems to project *sharʿī* injunctions into the past, in an asserted confirmation through Muhammad b. al-Qasim.[73] On the other hand, the well read al-Biruni (973–1050) opines in his travelogue that the greatest obstacle preventing any rapprochement between Hindus and Muslims was the caste system, thereby identifying Hindus as a distinct religious group from Muslims perhaps for the first time. Most probably he was referring to the Brahmanical discourse of purity, or he perceived himself as outsider, *mleccha*. Al-Biruni also qualified the Hindu idolatry (*shirk*) of idol worship, stating that this type of worship was designed for the benefit of the uneducated, who needed pictorial representations, while the elites of all communities, including the Hindus, worshipped Allah alone.[74] Certainly, he was writing in and for the court.

Settling down

However, with the establishment of *Muslim rule*,[75] different ideological groups influenced India to integrate it into the Islamic cosmos. Certainly, there is no mentioning of Hindus and Indians in the Quran.

[72] Friedmann: "A Contribution to the early History", p. 332; Mac Lean: *Religion and Society*.

[73] See Friedmann: "The Origins and Significance of the Chach Nama", pp. 23–37.

[74] Cf. E.C. Sachau: *Alberuni's India*, I, pp. 22f., II, p. 185; also Friedmann: "Islamic thought in relation to the Indian context", pp. 81f.

[75] It has been convincingly argued that it is quite problematic to speak of 'Muslim rule' "since much more was involved than the religion of the ruling class..." Romila Thapar: *Somanatha. The Many Voices of a History*, New Delhi: Penguin 2004, p. 170. Moreover, different policies were pursued by the conquerors, f.e., Arab Sind entered into alliances with Hindu states to respond to Muslim Ghaznawid forces (Mac Lean *Religion and Society*, p. 27). Yet, the term will be used out of convenience.

But we find several *ahadith* in which Prophet Muhammad prophesied the *ghazwa al-Hind*, the land of Adam's descent to earth after his expulsion from paradise, and promised a special reward for the participants of that battle. The most popular, however, is the weak hadith: "God saved two groups of my community from hell-fire: a group which will attack India and a group which will be (at the end of the day) with ʿIsa b. Maryam".[76] Much later, the celebrated poet of the Delhi Sultanate, Amir Khusraw (1253–1325), would refer to similar concepts in order to demonstrate that India was indeed a paradise on earth.[77]

Islamisation of this kind prevailed in this coastal region for some time, in the seventh to thirteenth century idol-temples were still in use, such as in Daybul.[78] The building of a mosque and the settlement of some 6,000 Syrian Arabs and 6,000 troops in new quarters, according to ethnic and religious segregation,[79] pointed however, to some kind of Muslim permanency. Some founded dynasties survived down to the thirteenth century.[80]

Unfortunately no further information about these Arab settlers is available but most probably they were (male) soldiers of different tribes from Iraq and Syria who eventually got married to local (Hindu) women. It is probable, that like in many Arab cities such as Basra and Kufa, land was divided among tribal groups along *khitat*, appropriating virgin land which was marked and then settled, with each tribal leader additionally assigned a piece of land outside the city as fief (*qataʾiʿ*). As will be seen below, the system of *iqtaʿ*, i.e., the transferable revenue assignment in lieu of salary for service, provided the necessary device to settle the regions hitherto Muslim rule did not have.

One can discern that the Arab expansion to the East was not a glorious holy war but rather a contract between different parties with political and economic interests. This is also suggested by the *Chachnama*, which is of the view that al-Hajjaj ordered his commander Muhammad b. al-Qasim to provide the conquered with money, rewards, promotions and immunity (*aman*) and to try to grant every request made by the

---

[76] Al-Nasaʾi: *al-Sunan al-Sughra*, Cairo n.d., VI, 43; Friedmann: "A Contribution to the early History", pp. 318f.

[77] Cf. Yohanan Friedmann: "Islamic thought in relation to the Indian context", in: Marc Gaboriau (ed.): *Islam et Société en Asie du Sud*, Paris 1986, pp. 79–92, here pp. 82f., 85.

[78] A.S. Bazmee Ansari: "Daybul", in: EI(2), II, p. 188.

[79] al-Baladhuri: *Kitab Futuh al-Buldan*.

[80] Mac Lean: *Religion and Society*, pp. 99, 123.

princes and to please them by giving them bonds for the fulfilment of mutual promises.[81] Moreover, the *Chachnama* alludes to four ways of acquiring a kingdom as referred to by Hindu thinkers: conciliation, bribery, dissension and finally force,[82] and hastens to add that al-Hajjaj followed these Indian tactics of political conquest.

Upon the accession of Sulaiman b. ʿAbd al-Malik (ruled 715–717) the Muslim impact in Sind weakened, because sections of the army loyal to al-Hajjaj did not receive caliphal backing, and also because Muhammad b. al-Qasim was alleged to have been disloyal and was killed in 714. Under these circumstances some Indian princes who had submitted to Muhammad b. al-Qasim, regained independence. By the end of the Umayyad rule many Arab Muslims started to leave al-Hind.[83]

During the reign of the Abbasids (750–1258),[84] caliph al-Mansur (died 775) had to take quite a few steps to restore caliphal authority. Though many expeditions followed, the Arab rule over Sind stayed unstable due to fast changes in governorship, inter-tribal feuds among the Arabs[85] and the threat of conflict with local forces, who were contesting the rule of the caliphs. True, Islam had vast expansionist power but was still in its formative phase, and certainly at the beginning of proclaiming a normative order. Arab Muslims could learn a lot from those they conquered. In fact, Muslims received such precious sciences as astronomy, and received the Hindu numerical and decimal systems. Thus it was a classic case of dominance without hegemony.

Though the conquered region was continuously expanding, the intra-Muslim conflicts in Syria and the war of succession influenced Muslim presence in Sind. It was only under the Abbasids that a further wave of expansion occurred, though between Muhammad b. al-Qasim's death and the establishment of Abbasid rule in 750, expeditions were despatched from time to time as far as Kashmir and Malwa.[86] The early

---

[81] Wink: *al-Hind*, I, p. 200.

[82] U.N. Goshal: *A History of Indian Political Ideas*, Madras 1966, p. 182.

[83] Al-Baladhuri: *Kitab Futuh al-Buldan*, pp. 443f.; Friedmann: "A Contribution to the early History", p. 314.

[84] For the Abbasids see M.Q. Zaman: *Religion and Politics Under the Early Abbasids*, Leiden: Brill 1997.

[85] Cf. al-Baladhuri: *Kitab Futuh al-Buldan*, pp. 444, 446; Friedmann: "A Contribution to the early History", p. 315.

[86] See J. Richards: "The Islamic frontier in the east: expansion into South Asia", in: *South Asia* 4 (1974), pp. 94ff.

eastern expansion of Muslims was stopped basically by the powerful Gurjara-Pratihara dynasty with its capital at Kannauj.

At the same time the foundation of new mosques stabilised and widened commercial networks that became important for the Muslim newcomers. These institutions were partly founded in old existing cities but were also extended to newly built cities such as al-Mahfuza and al-Mansura ('the victorious'), the Arab capital in Sind founded by Muhammad b. al-Qasim's son ʿAmr, in approx. 738. The name might point to the Abbasid caliph al-Mansur, but then, numerous cities were named al-Mansura as an omen for victory and durability. Al-Mansura was a garrison post or *misr* (border, or demarcation of two distinct regions, see Chap. 2), similar to al-Mahfuza,[87] but built on the remains of Brahmanabad.[88]

Al-Mansura and also al-Mahfuza were to provide a secure base in the hostile Hindu environment from which the invaders could attempt to expand their rule.[89] Being located on fertile land al-Mansura flourished, serving as a centre for a number of smaller towns. The city's ruler soon enjoyed considerable independence since the central government in the Arab lands was unable to exercise effective control.[90] Caliphal authority had definitely dwindled in the wake of Caliph al-Mutawakkil's murder in 861 and no revenue or tribute was transferred from Makran and Sind to Baghdad ever since after al-Muʿtamid (died 892) conferred the government of Sind to one of his generals in 871.[91] But by the second wave of expansion into India under Mahmud of Ghazna (in 1025–6), the city of al-Mansura had nearly vanished which perhaps explains why the Moroccan traveller Ibn Batutta (1304–1377) does not even mention it.[92]

Shia-Sunni tussle in Sind

Like any other periphery of a centralised state, Sind had long become a refuge for marginalised and dissidents, free thinkers and atheists, such

[87] Al-Baladhuri: *Kitab Futuh al-Buldan*, p. 444.
[88] See Mehrdad Shokoohy: *Bhadresvar. The Oldest Islamic Monuments in India*, Leiden 1988, p. 4.
[89] Al-Baladhuri: *Kitab Futuh al-Buldan*, p. 444.
[90] Y. Friedmann: "al-Mansûra", in: EI(2), VI, pp. 439f.
[91] Wink: *al-Hind*, I, p. 131.
[92] Y. Friedmann: "al-Mansûra", in: EI(2), VI, pp. 439f.

as the Kharijites,[93] or supporters of the Qadariyya,[94] such as Mansur b. Jumhur (died in 751 in Sind), the dismissed governor of Iraq, who had been involved in a Shiʿite revolt in Iraq and subsequent conspiracy resulting in the murder of the caliph al-Walid in 715. Others followed Muhammad al-Baqir (died ca. 732), the fifth Shiʿite Imam, and claimed that Baqir had not died but would return as the guided one (*mahdi*). Yet, others wanted to hold his imamate. These Nizaris set up their centre in Uchh.[95] Lower Sind increasingly became politically and economically fragmented, to the extent that it was made up of some eighteen indigenised Arab tribes and competitive states. Ismaili proselytising (*daʿwa*) benefited from this fragmentation (see Excursus: Shiʿite).

When the governor of Abbasid Sind became sympathetic to the contesting Fatimid caliphate in al-Qahira (Cairo) showing his affiliation to the powerful Ismailiyya, major problems occurred. Soon the Fatimids were joined by those who considered themselves to be descendants of the Prophet via his daughter Fatima and who followed up to the sixth Imam, Jaʿfar al-Sadiq (died 765). Their caliphate had a long prehistory:

> It is the creation of a shiʿite secret society, which has conspiratively been working towards the fall of the Baghdad caliphate since the middle of the nineth century. The followers of the sect called themselves 'people of the truth' (ahl al-haqq), but were called by outsiders 'Qarmatians'[96] or 'Ismailis'. Having been developed in the region of the Persian-Arabic Gulf, the sect had established a net of secret cells through weavers and missionaries, a net that spread from Irak and Syria, Iran and Central Asia and the Indus valley (Sind); Yemen and Egypt..... The centre of the esoteric doctrine was the hope that God will soon send a saviour, the 'rightly guided' (*al-Mahdi*), who would replace the caliphal throne of the Baghdadian 'usurpers', who would unify the party and sect ridden umma and who would re-establish the true religion (*din al-haqq*) in its pristine,

[93] N.A. Baloch: "Kandâbîl", in: EI(2), IV, pp. 534ff.; Wink: *al-Hind*, I, p. 144; Mac Lean: *Religion and Society*, pp. 118, 120. The Kharijites emerged after the Battle of Siffin (658), which had ensued between ʿAli, the cousin and son-in-law of the Prophet, and Muʾawiya, governor of Damascus. This puritan group combined a radical egalitarianism with revolutionary zeal, and became popular among the al-Morawids and al-Mohads in North Africa.

[94] The adherents to this doctrine maintain that Allah had given man free will (*al-qadr*), implying that Allah could not know a man's actions in advance. Thus, responsibility and freedom were necessities of divine justice.

[95] Mac Lean: *Religion and Society*, pp. 142, 145.

[96] Called after Hamdan Qarmat (died after 899), who was an Ismaili propagandist in Kufa.

> paradisian urform—the cultless and lawless (sic!) devotion to God, like it had been in the times of Adam.[97]

The Ismailiyya developed chiliastic ideas; their leaders—the caliphs—were to hold extra-territorial powers. But by 899 they split into the loyal Fatimids and the dissident Qarmati factions, who did not acknowledge the Imamate of ʿAbd Allah al-Mahdi, the future founder of the Fatimid caliphate who ruled from 909–934. Instead they founded a powerful state of their own in Bahrayn.[98] When in the reign of al-Muʿizz (953–75) Ismaili *daʿwa* was supported, the Fatimids became particularly strong in India, and by 965 their Imam's name became part of the Friday sermon (*khutba*) in Multan,[99] thereby publicly acknowledging the community's allegiance to the current ruler.

The Ismailisation of Sind also witnessed the Hinduisation of *daʿwa* and support of Hindu temples allowing the retention of some of the elements of the converts' previous systems of belief and rituals. In this policy of accretion, that is the transfer of Islamic principles to the Indian religious universe and vice-versa, the *nabi* (prophet) becomes an *avatar* (incarnation of a god), ʿAli the incarnation of Vishnu, Fatima becomes Shakti.[100] Thus, conversion functionally provided for problem-solution by participating in a global horizon; at the same time conversion guaranteed coherence and continuity to a large extent.

The ideological tussle between the caliphates of Sunni Baghdad and of Shiʿi al-Qahira became a proper war, and with the knowledge of the economic significance of India, it translated into an economic rivalry between the Red Sea and the Persian Gulf. However, the full import of this conflict was to diminish later, due to the Turkish invasion and following that, the replacement with Central Asian power. Suffice it to say, that both the caliphates tried to dominate the Indian trade. The

[97] Heinz Halm: "Die Berberreiche des Westens", in: Noth and Paul (eds.): *Der islamische Orient*, pp. 195–216, here p. 199 (translation JM); on the rise of Fatimids see Heinz Halm: *The empire of the Mahdi: The Rise of the Fatimids*, Translated from the German by Michael Bonner, Leiden 1996.

[98] On the schism of 899 in the Ismailiyya see W. Madelung, "The Fatimids and the Qarmatis of Bahrayn", in: F. Daftary (ed.): *Mediaeval Ismaili History and Thought*, Cambridge 1996, pp. 21–73; F. Daftary: "Carmatians", in: *Encyclopaedia Iranica*, Vol. 4, pp. 823–832.

[99] On the Ismailis in Sind see S.M. Stern: "Ismâʿîlî propaganda and Fatimid rule in Sind", in: *Islamic Culture* 23 (1949), pp. 298–307; ʿAbbâs al-Hamdhânî: *The beginnings of the Ismaʿîlî daʿwa in Northern India*, Cairo 1956; also Farhad Daftary: *The Ismaʿilis: their history and their doctrines*, Cambridge 1990; Mac Lean: *Religion and Society*, pp. 126–153.

[100] Mac Lean: *Religion and Society*, pp. 137f., 151, 153.

demonstrative death penalty to the famous Sufi Mansur al-Hallaj in Baghdad in 922 had its roots in his alleged affiliations with the Ismailis. Visiting Sind in 905 he is said to have had some connections with the Qarmatians who, coming from Bahrayn, had settled in Multan and in parts of Sind. The fights between Ismailis and the Umayyads cost al-Hallaj his life.

Taking into account that the Muslim expansion into South Asia was primarily governed by economic rather than religious concerns it is understandable that Muslim Arabs did not fight in the name of Islam in the first place. Correspondingly, the Sanskrit epigraphic and literary sources hardly refer to Muslims in terms of religion, for many centuries to come. Instead they were referred to in terms of different ethnic and spatial origins: ethnic and regional terms were indigenised becoming Tajika (from the Arab tribe Taiyi), Parasika (Pre-Islamic Persia), Turuska (people from the North, also Turks before conversion), Yavana and Mleecha (the outsider, one who follows evil practices, according to Brahmanical understanding), often interchangeably used, sometimes overlapping each other. These "raiders and contestants for political power...were depicted...as among many claimants in a situation of...competition." These and other terms could also denote political authority in accordance with Hindu ideas, when for example in fourteenth century Vijayanagara the title of Sultan was transformed into Suratrana, i.e., Sultan among/of Hindu Kings, thereby leaving open the term of royalty in general rather than essentialise the term. This pragmatic approach harked back to the process of cultural encounter, and the adoption of Islamicate political culture by means of dress and title permitting Hindu culture to participate and change in this more universal and expanding political culture.[101] It is only much later and in different cultural and political contexts, that these terms acquired generic meanings that would highlight the difference of a social other with a different moral order.[102]

Up to the eleventh century Muslims managed to penetrate into many kingdoms of al-Hind basically as traders and soldiers and through

[101] See the enlightening article by Phillip B. Wagoner: "'Sultan among Hindu Kings': Dress, Titles, and the Islamicization of Hindu Culture at Vijayanagara", in: *JAS* 55 (1996), pp. 851–880, particularly pp. 862ff.

[102] See Brajadulal Chattopadhyaya: *Representing the Other? Sanskrit Sources and The Muslims (Eighth to Fourteenth Century)*, New Delhi: Manohar 1998, quotation, pp. 48, also pp. 54, 86–91; also Mac Lean: *Religion and Society*, p. 28.

forced migration, and began to participate in the local economy, so that by the time of the Abbasids Indian trade became the backbone of intercontinental Muslim economy.[103] While the internal Arabo-Persian Muslim tussle went on and weakened the expansionist power of Arab Muslim rule after three centuries, another local power, coming from the West, rose to prominence. These were the Turkic dynasties.

The question of Islamicity

Initially, scholars of hadith and Quran became important not only and primarily because there was a need for religious instruction but also to legitimise the complex process of expansion and settlement. Given the fact that there were different stages of development in the compilation of the Quranic text, of the tradition (*sunna* and *hadith*), the Islamic law (*fiqh*) and Sufism (*tasawwuf*), it was understandable that initially hadith-studies became prominent. The sunna of the Prophet, considered the second most important source for Islamic jurisprudence, was still in the making.[104] Indeed, with the vast and sudden expansion of Muslim lands, there arose a need to act according to Prophetic tradition and also to legitimise these conquests Islamically. The Prophetic ideal and that of the following two later sanctified generations, as recorded in the hadiths, could provide some orientation. In the face of this, the need to compile canonical hadith became even more important because fictitious, differing and even contradictory statements were increasingly being presented as hadiths. Moreover, the hadith-movement went hand in hand with a process of solidarity, affiliation and urbanisation; hence, hadith scholars sought and brought forth new ways of interaction and communication in new or conquered cities.

By the same token, one may find a number of scholars of Prophetic tradition (*muhaddithun*) in Sind. The majority of these scholars was counted among people of the hadith (*ashab al-hadith*) maintaining the primary importance of hadith texts. It is interesting to note that most of the Sindi Muslim religious elite were traditionists who focused on the study and transmission of Prophetic tradition. Apparently, the

---

[103] Wink: *al-Hind*, I, p. 7.

[104] For an interesting study on the development of sunna and hadith as sources of authority in early Islam see Daniel Brown: *Rethinking tradition in modern Islamic thought*, Cambridge: CUP 1999, Chap. 1.

textual piety of *ashab al-hadith* had some formal and structural similarities to the Sammitiyya textualism and literalism, such as the popular *Book of Discipline* (Vinaya Pitaka) consisting of Buddha's sayings. Thus *ashab al-hadith* being intelligible to textual Buddhists, and the Buddhist commercial and mercantile cooperation in Arab-Muslim mercantilism accounted for the disappearance of Buddhists in Sind during the Arab period. Hinduism however persisted.[105]

The historical conditions constituted the religious identity of the fledgling Muslim community. According to the medieval scholar Ibn Khaldun (1332–1406), a *science of the classification of the sciences* divided the sciences into transmitted (*naqliyya*) and rational (*ʿaqliyya*), sacred (*dini*) and profane (*dunyawiyya*) ones. The first (*manqulat*) comprises all branches of knowledge which owe their existence to Islam based on a divinely inspired law, such as the Qur'an, the sayings of Prophet Muhammad (*ahadith*), law and the principles of law, theology and auxiliary sciences such as grammar and syntax. The rational sciences (*maʿqulat*) are believed by some scholars to be fashioned on the Hellenistic, Judaic and Nestorian scientific traditions, consisting of logic, philosophy, astronomy, medicine, mathematics and metaphysics. The essential difference between the two branches is their ultimate source, from divine or respectively human inspired knowledge.

Thus according to S. ʿAbd al-Hayy (died 1923), the celebrated Indian historiographer and father of the late Abu al-Hasan ʿAli al-Nadwi (died 1999), and author of many books on Islamic scholarship, this first phase of Islamic scholarship between the seventh and tenth century can be distinguished with a stress laid on grammar, principles of jurisdiction, Quran, hadith, logic, and mysticism, that is mainly what has been called transmitted sciences (*manqulat*).[106] This evolution of Islamic scholarship—according to Peter Hardy—took place when Muslims, in particular Arab Muslims, were in their formative phase

> still sitting as pupils at the feet of the peoples they had subdued, learning the art of civilization. The study of Arabic grammar had begun; Islamic scholars were compiling the religiously authoritative reports of the sayings and doings of the prophet or his companions. Thinkers were raising theological issues of divine and human ordination and dissenting religious traditions like the Kharaji and the Shiʿa were contesting the government of the faithful. Even though Islam was still forging the intellectual weapons,

[105] Mac Lean: *Religion and Society*, pp. 53f., 95ff., 107–110, 155.
[106] See Sayyid ʿAbd al-Hayy: *Al-Thaqafa al-Islamiyya fi al-Hind*, Dimashq 1958.

> the sciences of tradition, theology, jurisprudence and history, that would enable it to meet argument with something more than conviction, it was still receptive to the impress of the civilization of Byzantium and Persia that the Arabs had conquered. Within wide limits Muslims were free to seek after and to do God's will in their own ways. There was as yet no established orthodoxy.[107]

Certainly there were attempts by Islamic scholars to establish singular processes of orthodoxy,[108] but this normatising trend increasingly produced heterodox movements. One early example of such traces can be found among the Ismailis. Movements such as those of the Sufis were looking for alternative worldviews to integrate the Islamic cosmos with that of the local environment, e.g. Hindu customs and systems. Many famous mystics can be encountered in this period, proclaiming religious pluralism, certainly not always altruistically and sometimes with political ambitions. Institutions for this endeavour were very much at hand, either existent in the new territories or brought in by newcomers. They all provided room for the development of a flexible Muslim culture capable of adapting to a new environment, as will be argued in the following chapter about Muslim space and Muslim divines.

[107] Peter Hardy in: Ainslie Embree (ed.): *Sources of Indian Tradition, Vol. I: From the Beginning to 1800*, New Delhi 1991 (2), p. 384.

[108] It should be noted, however, that Sunni Islam does not support the idea of orthodoxy. Unlike the Christian context there was no final process of singularisation and normatisation. Instead, in the history of the Muslim world the principle of pluralism prevailed, as can be gleaned from the evolution of Islamic law, based on long scholastic debates, bringing out a consensus broad and adaptable enough to guarantee a life in accordance to Islam in many different ways. This development made a central scholastic teaching institution superfluous. Thus the notion of orthopraxy as endeavours of "officially and established practices" of a religion seems to be more proper, as has been pointed out by W.C. Smith: *Modern Islam in India. A Social Analysis*, London: Victor Gollancz Ltd. 1946, p. 305. But out of convenience the term orthodoxy will be used.

EXCURSUS

HISTORIOGRAPHY AND SOURCES

Much has been written on historiography and sources, on memory permeating events selectively, and amnesia consciously deciding and unconsciously overlooking events. For example, religious pluralism was always inherent in it but, because of theological and historiographical constructions remained largely unrecognised. Yet, why have mutual interrelations and entanglements been bypassed in so many grand narratives? Why was it taken for granted that religions mutually excluded each other, that an individual could have one religion alone? The "other", constructed as counter foil, has not only an invisible history but also refers to a substantial influence on the comparative study of religion. Formation of a historical opinion has an inextricable connection between the presentation of past facts and the attitude towards the present. Facts can variously be described as researching, the narrative, the didactic and interpretative.

One finds *master narratives* of an Islamic history as against divergent 'sect histories'. Thus *narration of the history of Islam in xyz* is not an innocent process. It gets the scientist involved in a multi-layered process in which the narrative becomes inevitably rhetorical and the representation of the past is involved in a discourse of power, again dependent on non-academic discourses.

Polyvocality of history in the Muslim context is as difficult to document as in any other "church history". The idea has all along been to develop a master narrative of Islamic history[1] in annals, biographies and dynastic narratives. Issues most often discussed related to authenticity (from the beginning to ca. 1500 C.E.), and its relation to the sciences of the sayings of the Prophet and discrete anecdotes and reports (*akhbar*).[2] Historical sources of that time called "narrative accounts" (i.e. *ta'rikh*—chronicles) did try constructing a connected narrative of events,

[1] Standard work for early Muslim historiography is Franz Rosenthal: *A History of Muslim Historiography*, Leiden: Brill 1968 (2. revised ed.).

[2] R. Stephen Humphreys: *Islamic History. A Framework for Inquiry*, London: I.B. Tauris 1991 (revised ed.), pp. 69–91.

such as Tabari's (died 923) *History of Prophets and Kings*. This correlated with the collective tradition of *akhbar*: instead of interpreting the past, the author was to determine which of the reports about an event were acceptable on the basis of which he compiled them. Thus, we are left with little raw material but with constructed historical "facts" as Muslim historians were more concerned with political legitimacy, and the translation of the Prophet's redemptive mission into reality rather than with interdependence of social strata and norms. Normative Islamic historical thinking was informed by the idea that history would serve religion and law, a tendency with powerful after-effects. Single events and comprehensive narrations of Islamic history or universal chronicles were the major genres.

With the collapse of the Abbasid Empire, the expansions of Muslim rule and rise of the 'Gunpowder Empires' the historiographical hegemony of the Arabic language was increasingly challenged by the Persian language and tradition. Its impact was seen in linguistics and in themes and images carrying the Sassanian context. Historiographically, two trends emerged: the Arab tradition of hadith (*'ulum al-hadith*) concerned with the accuracy of data, going back to the great tradition of biography, useful for necessary posopographic studies to prove the authenticity of the chain of transmitters (*isnad*). The Persian context brought in the Sassanian tradition of epic writing with a "dramatic resolution" (i.e. Firdawsi (died 1020) and his epigones) which was—in contrast to Arabic history writing—not bound by religion. As a quasi-secularised language, Persian could create a literalised chronicle.[3] Both traditions, the "Arabic history of the age" and the "Persian history of the kings", however, focused on political prudence and moral admonition, which had an effect on historiography. New historiographical genres developed as well: the dynastic chronicles dealing with political wisdom and royal glorification, were mostly composed by men from scribal groups affiliated to the court. They provided little information on the non-elites. Thus, the literary production of political chronicles mainly reflected courtly life. Zia al-Din al-Barani (1285–1357) may be counted among such writers. Considered the most important political

[3] See Peter Hardy: *Historians of Medieval India: Studies in Indo-Muslim Historical Writing*, London 1960; C.H. Philips (ed.): *Historians of India, Pakistan and Ceylon*, London: OUP 1961; also Stephan Conermann (ed.): *Die muslimische Sicht (13.–18. Jahrhundert)*, = Jörn Rüsen/Sebastian Manhart (eds.): *Geschichtsdenken der Kulturen, Südasien*, Vol. 2, Frankfurt/M.: Humanitas Online 2002, 45–67.

theorist of the fourteenth century, he pondered about the ruler's role in an ideal Islamic state. Epistolography (*insha*) was another powerful expression of literary expertise, poetical literature, royal edict (*farman*) and collections of legal opinions (*fatawa*). Local histories, i.e., the histories of particular cities and regions, were usually produced in regions with a strong political autonomy.[4]

Biographical dictionary, another genre focusing on religious scholars (*ulama*), yielded detailed data not available in court histories.[5] Indeed, *ulamalogy* seems to be a viable way to writing Islamic history, since the sources here (*tabaqat* (classes)-works, *tadhkirat* (hagiographies), other kinds of biographical accounts), provide information on social and political contexts.[6] Mystical sources such as oral communication, letters and hagiographies of Sufi saints (*malfuzat, maktubat, tadhkira*) emerged as important genres of local history in the fourteenth century. Historians of the Aligarh school have drawn attention to the study of medieval Persian sufi discourses (*malfuzat*) as an important source of social history. K.A. Nizami: "There is no other type of literature through which we can feel the pulse of the medieval public".[7] But more important according to Carl Ernst, is that they "took on a canonical textual form that soon became the authoritative and normative genre both for members of the orders and for their lay followers. Transition from oral to written form was reflected in diverse literary styles adapted to different audiences" though many of these accounts are apocryphal and have to be read carefully.[8]

Sources for the reconstruction of medieval and Mughal rule are manifold: *malfuzat*, *faramin*, administrative handbooks (*dastur al-ʿamal*),

---

4 See A.K. Nizami: *On History and Historians of Medieval India*, New Delhi 1983.

5 Cf. Humphreys: *Islamic History*, pp. 129–136; cf. also: Stephan Conermann (ed.): *Die muslimische Sicht (13.–18. Jahrhundert)*, pp. 45–67; A.K. Nizami: *On History and Historians of Medieval India*, New Delhi 1983, pp. 6ff.

6 See Humphreys: *Islamic History*, pp. 187–208; cf. also: Roy Mottahedeh: "Review of R. Bulliet's *The Patricians of Nishapur*ʿ, in: *JAOS* 45 (1975), 491–495, here p. 495.

7 Khaliq Ahmad Nizami: *Some Aspects of Religion and Politics in India During the Thirteenth Century*, New Delhi: Idarah-i-Adabiyat-i-Delli 1961, p. 374

8 Quotation from Ernst: *Eternal Garden*, p. 62. For the historical significance of the rich hagiographies and *malfuzat* literature such as *Fawaʾid al-Fuʾad* by Amir Hasan Sijzi, *Khair al-Majalis* by Hamîd Qalandar, etc. see K.A. Nizami: *On History*, pp. 163–197, Ernst: *Eternal Garden*, pp. 62–84; Bruce Lawrence: *Nizam ad-Din Awliya; Morals for the Heart, translated and annotated*, intro. K.A. Nizami, preface S. Digby, New York 1992; Z.A. Desai: *Malfuz Literature: as source of Political, Social & Cultural History of Gujarat & Rajasthan*, Patna 1991; S.H. Askari: *Maktub & Malfuz Literature. As a Source of Socio-Political History*, Patna 1981; Jürgen Paul: "Hagiographische Texte als historische Quelle", in: *Saeculum* 41/1 (1990), pp. 17–43.

and *fatawa*, foreigner's account and travelogues, (made available to the public only recently), supplementing the history of Mughal empire, traditionally based on two outstanding though conflicting testimonies of the sixteenth century: Abu al-Fadl's *Akbarnama* which compiled data provided by a whole secretariat and ignored the vices of Emperor Akbar, and ʿAbd al-Qadir Badayuni's *Muntakhib al-Tawarikh* which fails to see the virtues but provides information on extra-courtly developments. The re-reading of old sources with new perspectives is only in embryonic phase, be it from the perspective of the subaltern, the margin or female historiography.

In the wake of the de-centralisation of Mughal rule, new forms and genres emerged such as institutionalised literary criticism, memoirs, biography and autobiography. The compilation of anthologies of poetry (*bayad*) and biographical collections of poets and scholars (*tadhkira*) extending beyond the classical hagiographies and of lexicons and encyclopaedia also became popular.

Following the tradition of *tabaqat-*, *sira-*, and *tadhkira*-literature, a number of Persian biographical dictionaries in the eighteenth and nineteenth centuries emerged, such as Shah Nawaz Khan's *Maʾathir al-Umaraʾ* (around 1750) and Ghulam Azad Bilgrami's (died 1786) *Maʾathir al-kiram* (written 1752, published in Agrah 1910). *Tadhkirah-ye ʿUlamaʾ-ye Hind* by Rahman ʿAli was followed among others by Sayyid ʿAbd al-Hayy al-Hasani's (died 1923) voluminous *Nuzhat al-khawatir* in Arabic. These sources have only recently caught the attention of historians.

With the colonial impact in the nineteenth century, new developments emerged.[9] Some authors have argued that biography evolved as an independent genre (out of hagiographical tradition), when texts turned from verse to prose. However the aim remained the same: *adab*![10] Biographies and even auto-biographies had been in place in the eighteenth century and became a major genre in the twentieth still linked with *adab*[11] as can be seen in the Middle East, especially in Egypt.[12]

---

[9] Basic readings on this see the contributions of Jamal Malik in: Michael Gottlob (ed.): *Historisches Denken im Modernen Südasien (1786–heute)*, = Jörn Rüsen/Sebastian Manhart (eds.): *Geschichtsdenken der Kulturen, Südasien, Vol. 3*, Frankfurt/M.: Humanitas Online 2002.

[10] Cf. Sisir Kumar Das: *A History of Indian Literature, Vol. 8: 1800–1910. Western Impact: Indian Response*, New Delhi: Sahitya Akademi, pp. 107f.

[11] Cf. Barbara Metcalf (ed.): *Moral Conduct and Authority: The Place of Adab*, Berkeley: UCP 1984, passim

[12] E.g. Fedwa Malti-Douglas: *Blindness and Autobiography: Al-Ayyam of Taha Husayn*, Princeton: PUP 1988; Ahmad Amin: *My Life: The Autobiography of an Egyptian Scholar,*

Against the backdrop of colonial expansion, the Muslim self-understanding needed historiography to highlight the glorious times juxtaposed to the modern with its new emerging societal formations. (Sir) Sayyid Ahmad Khan (1817–1898) was one of the early scholars who tried to demonstrate the compatibility of European education and rational thinking with Islam. He is considered one of the founders of historiography in modern Urdu, for his perception of the European enlightenment made him aware of the principle of change and movement in history. He had the greatest regard for the category ratio (*ʿaql*) and often referred to early Muslim philosophers such as Ibn Rushd (died 1198), who played an important role in the self-understanding and thought of the Islamic reform movement.[13] Khan's attempt to integrate science with Islam was opposed by traditionalist thought such as the school of Deoband.

Shibli Nuʿmani can be considered the founder of modern Muslim historiography in the Rankean tradition:[14] based on the historiographical works of Sayyid Ahmad Khan,[15] he combined the rational approach of modern source critique (as introduced by v. Ranke) with the didactical aim of Muslim historiography. The intent was to provide a solution to the prevailing social and political crisis as it was felt by the reformists. This was a quest for an ideal political rule. Thus historiography was crucial for a reformist Muslim education and had therefore, to become an independent subject for which Shibli struggled in the Nadwat al-ʿUlama and later in the Dar al-Musannifin in Azamgarh.[16]

Renewal of the cultural traditions gave way to the idea of a nation for Muslims, whence (Sir) Muhammad Iqbal (1877–1938) contrasted, much like the Hindu revivalists, the "materialistic" West with Eastern "spirituality." His was a Muslim nationalist historiography characterised

---

Writer, and Cultural Leader, translated by Issa J. Boullata. Leiden: Brill 1978; John Calvert: "The Individual and the Nation: Sayyid Qutb's *Tifl min al-Qarya* (*Child from the Village*)," in: *MW* 90, nos. 1–2 (2000), pp. 107–132.

[13] See Anke von Kügelgen: *Averroes und die arabische Moderne. Ansätze zu einer Neubegründung des Rationalismus im Islam*, Leiden: Brill 1994.

[14] cf. Das: *A History of Indian Literature*, pp. 262f.

[15] E.g. *Athar al-Sanadid*, vols. I–III, ed. by Khaliq Anjum, Dilli 1990; cf. M. Athar Ali: "Ta'rîkh. In Muslim India", in: EI(2), X, p. 297; C.W. Troll, *Sayyid Ahmad Khan. A Reinterpretation of Muslim Theology*, Karachi: OUP 1978, pp. 102f, 112–143.

[16] Cf. Neyaz Ahmad Azami: "Shibli on Muslim Education and Politics", in: *Islam and the Modern Age* 25:3 (1994), pp. 190–205; Christian W. Troll, "Muhammad Shibli Nu'mani (1857–1914) and the Reform of Muslim Religious Education", in: *Islam and the Modern Age* 24:1 (1993), pp. 1–19; also texts by Shibli Nuʿmani, introduced and translated by Malik, in: Michael Gottlob (ed.): *Historical Thinking in South Asia*, pp. 134–139.

by evolutionary ideas, by constant dynamics and movement. He believed that Islamic history had lost the dynamic element of its civilisation and was in need of a reconstruction of Islamic thought.

Another way of Muslim historiography was championed by A.A. Maududi (1903–1979) emphasising the incompatibility of traditional Islam with the modern nation state. His anti-Western tendencies influenced the Arab world, in particular the Muslim Brotherhood in Egypt and Syria. Thus, Maududi's view of history is linked to Shibli's envisaging a constant decline of Muslims.

Parallel to Shibli's 'rationalist historiography' and his epigones (e.g. Sayyid Sulayman Nadwi, to some extent), a traditionalist historiography evolved in the emerging *Tabligh* movement around the 1920s: literature was used in the legacy of the traditional historiography (*sira-*, *rijal-*, *manaqib*-literature) on the basis of *hadith* and *akhbar*—however, without applying the usual source critical tools from *'ulum al-hadith* and *usul al-fiqh*—and in the hagiographical tradition of prose writing. This is exclusively within the scope of *adab*, with predominantly edifying stories of the prophets, the companions of Prophet Muhammad, and stories of the Sufi saints. Protagonists of this tradition are Muhammad Yusuf Kandhlawi (1917–1965), and Muhammad Zakariyya Kandhlawi (died 1981).

This specific South Asian component of Islamic historiography was expressed by Sayyid Abu al-Hasan 'Ali Nadwi (died 1999), regarded one of the most famous Muslim historiographers of independent India. His work—comprising a multi-volume autobiography—shows the self-consciousness of Muslims who remained in independent India and symbolised the tension between national integration and Islamism in secular India.[17] His view of history, in contrast to Maududi's defeatist one, displays the Muslim achievements in South Asia, but he advocates an axiomatic supremacy of Muslims and takes up wide-spread essentialist arguments of the European historiography of the nineteenth century by citing Christian authors and Western philosophers. Supplementing

---

[17] For an excellent discussion of Nadwi's work and activities see Jan-Peter Hartung: *Viele Wege und ein Ziel. Leben und Wirken von Sayyid Abû l-Hasan 'Alî al-Hasanî Nadwî, 1914–1999*, Würzburg 2004.

the field of traditionalist historiography, many histories of religious institutions and movements can be found.[18]

In contradistinction to the conservative historiography, both liberal and Marxist historiographers have treated the idea of composite culture and composite secular nationalism as a powerful resource to combat communalism.

In Pakistan history and historiography developed a national identity and consciousness[19] although the new nation, after the Partition, had to work without many materials left remaining in Indian Archives.[20] As in India, the history of the freedom struggle acts as a folio for a master narrative for the nation state. Similar to Savarkar (died 1966), who claimed the 1857 revolt to be the first liberation fight, in Pakistan too the movement for autonomy was traced back to the likes of Tipu Sultan.[21] Nationalist historians such as Ishtiaq Hussain Qureshi (1903–1981) argued that India was divided by linguistic and racial differences—rather than by religious/sectarian ones—which then formed "political units".[22] He also endowed Pakistan's ideology with a secular identity by including the Indus culture and integrating Islamic tradition with modern achievements, criticising the shallow intelligence of technocrats and narrow-mindedness of what he called the orthodox scholars.[23]

---

[18] Such as Sayyid Mahbub Rizvi: *History of the Dar al-Ulum Deoband;* Muhammad Ishaq Jalis Nadwi and Shams Tabriz Khan: *Tarikh-e Nadwat al-ʿUlamaʿ, I–II*, Lucknow 1983; Muhammad Ibrahim Mir Siyalkoti: *Tarikh-e Ahl-e hadith*, Lahore 1952.

[19] Fundamental reflections on the role of history in Pakistan are to be found in K.M. Ishaque, "Role of history in the growth of national consciousness", *Journal of the Pakistan Historical Society* 17 (1969), pp. 25–39; D.R. Abdallah, "Tarikh ki ahmiyyat Iqbal ki nazr men", *Journal of the Pakistan Historical Society* 17 (1977), Part IV, Special Issue Allamah Centenary, pp. 1–21.

[20] For questions of the organisation of historical research in Pakistan see Khurshid Kamal Aziz: *Some Problems of Research in Modern History*, Rawalpindi 1969; Khurshid Kamal Aziz: *The Pakistani Historian*, Delhi 1994.

[21] M. Husain (ed.): *A History of the Freedom Movement*, Karachi 1957.

[22] Ishtiaq Husain Qureshi: *The Muslim Community of the Indo-Pakistan Subcontinent (610–1947) A brief analysis*, Gravenhage: Mouton 1962, p. 86.

[23] See texts by I.H. Qureshi introduced and translated by Malik, in: Gottlob (ed.): *Historical Thinking in South Asia*, pp. 246–249.

CHAPTER TWO

MUSLIM SPACE AND DIVINES (APPROX. 1000–1300S)

While the first wave of Muslim invasions in South Asia came from Arab homelands, their subsequent thrust into South Asia originated from Central Asians established in what is now Afghanistan. They came as raiders but stayed on as rulers establishing, in the process, a rich and versatile immigrant civilisation. While the Mongols destroyed much of West Asia, the left bank of the Indus remained more or less safe. The Sultanate of Delhi (1206–1555) was made possible only due to the permanence afforded to this region. Moreover, South Asia had already become a refuge for a variety of dissidents and fugitive scholars escaping the Mongol wrath. With the centre of Islam now in enemy hands, South Asia became Muslim world's cultural colony. At the same time, these immigrants to India also strengthened conservative trends at the beginning of the thirteenth century, juxtaposing Islam with the fortunes of their royal patrons. According to them, India became part of history only with the advent of Muslim rule.[1] Soon, Muslim court chroniclers and Sufis vividly recounted the Mongol destruction of their ancestral homelands. However, India's Islamic tradition was to become more versatile and inclusive, as the immigrant Muslim communities—different and contesting as they might have been—adapted to the Indian environment as the bearers of a different civilisation and faith. They increasingly expressed their concerns in shared cultural symbols and local languages rather than in the sophisticated cultural icons and language of the elite. The evolving vernacular literature gradually became self-conscious, and, embodying the local area identity, created specific regional codes. Thus documents and courtly communication

[1] Cf. Ainslie Embree (ed.): *Sources of Indian Tradition, Vol. I: From the Beginning to 1800*, New Delhi: Viking 1991 (2), p. 385; Richard M. Eaton: "Introduction", in: Richard M. Eaton (ed.): *India's Islamic Traditions, 711–1750*, Oxford 2003, p. 10; P. Hardy: "Some General Characteristics Analysed", reprinted in Eaton (ed.): *India's Islamic Traditions*, pp. 169–179.

were produced in local languages, creating new literary genres, such as the Sufi romance in Hindawi.[2]

Persianisation

With the eastern expansion of Muslims, Persian gradually became the Muslim language of the East, reducing Arabic to a merely scholarly language, and according to Bert Fragner gradually advanced to a basis for a universal religion, the first *Islamised* language as it were.[3] While Abu Rayhan al-Biruni (973–1050) wrote in Arabic, the Sufi ʿAli ibn ʿUthman al-Hujwiri (died around 1071) wrote in Persian, which was well received, not only due to the fact that Persian culture and language had a history in *al-Hind* in affiliating Persians with Indians.[4]

The Persianisation of Islam had started fairly early with the Abbasids who were supported by the Islamised Persian Khurasanians and the Shiʿite Dihqan aristocracy that was responsible for local administration and the collection of tributes. Baghdad was established to be the Persian counterpoint to the Arabic Damascus. To make sure that they were more than a regional power, the rulers in Baghdad adopted the pre-Muslim Persian title *Shahanshah* or 'king of kings', a title first used in the Indian subcontinent by the Mughal emperors.[5] Similarly in South Asia, Arab prudence was replaced by Persian pomp and paraphernalia with the Delhi court becoming the replica of the Sassanian court. By the same token, bureaucracy was expanded and hierarchised, and the link between state and religion was tightened through a policy of piety. Scholars (*ulama*), jurists (*fuqaha*) and Sufis were reduced to a quasi-priesthood. This contrasted with the more austere Arab Islam of the

---

[2] Cf. Aditya Behl: "The Magic Doe: Desire and narrative in a Hindavi Sufi Romance, circa 1503", in: Eaton (ed.): *India's Islamic Traditions*, pp. 180–208.

[3] For the lineage of Persian language, Persophonia or "the reign of the Persian language" in Central and South Asia see Bert G. Fragner: *Die "Persophonie". Regionalität, Identität und Sprachkontakt in der Geschichte Asiens*, Halle & Berlin: Das Arabische Buch 1999.

[4] Wink: *al-Hind*, I, p. 292; for a detailed discussion of Persianite India see Muzaffar Alam: "The Culture and Politics of Persian in Precolonial Hindustan", in: Sheldon Pollock (ed.): *Literary Cultures in History. Reconstructions from South Asia*, New Delhi: OUP 2004, pp. 131–198.

[5] Till the fifteenth century the ruler on the subcontinent acted as Sultan or representative of Caliph.

preceding centuries.[6] It should be noted, however, that orthodox scholars continued writing in Arabic in spite of the fact that Persian became the language of the court, administration and mystical lore.

Rulers often considered themselves to be warriors of God, *ghazis* or *mujahids*, or were made into such by Muslim chroniclers. For many of them, the Hindus were interesting primarily as converts and as capitation tax-payers.[7] However as in every cultural encounter, the subjects, in this case the Hindus had a major role to play. For despite the various discriminatory measures implemented by the future Delhi Sultans, the natives continued to be important members of society as ordinary labourers, architects, clerks, soldiers and officers. Moreover, the Sultans' cultural borrowing of Hindu sciences, symbols, mores and rituals as memory containers for the identity of religious communities, could endear them to their Hindu subjects.[8] The issue of *jizya* and to what extent the Hindus were subject to this tax in reality,[9] remains contested to this day. It is to be noted that this tax was collected in lieu of military service, but the problem gets compounded when we learn that so many Hindus fought in Muslim armies. It was only with expanding Muslim rule by the later half of the fourteenth century, that *jizya* was levied on non-Muslims as a discriminatory tax, but it was relaxed here and there. So it is quite plausible that Muslim-Hindu relations may have been acrimonious now and then. But on the whole it seems more plausible to argue that Muslim rulers were not always iconoclastic holy warriors.[10] They rather handled the problem with delicacy and pragmatism suited for such a multi-religious society. Most probably they distinguished between the peaceful and the rebellious rather than between Muslim and Hindu.[11] Clearly, the first dynasty pursued this policy, even though we find traces of discrimination and atrocities against their Hindu subjects. But then this seems to be an

---

[6] Wink: *al-Hind*, I, p. 22.

[7] Thus, Peter Hardy: *Historians of Medieval India, Studies in Muslim-Historical Writing*, London 1960, p. 114; see also K.A. Nizami: *Religion and Politics in India during the 13th century*, Delhi 2002, pp. 331–341.

[8] Cf. Peter Hardy: "The Growth of Authority over a Conquered Political Elite: The Early Delhi Sultanate as a Possible Case Study," in: J.F. Richards (ed.): *Kingship and Authority in South Asia*, Madison: University of Wisconsin 1978, p. 201.

[9] See Nizami: *Religion and Politics*, pp. 329–331.

[10] Whether "iconophobia" was inherently Islamic has been questioned by Oleg Grabar: *The Formation of Islamic Art*, New Haven 1987, p. 95.

[11] Cf. Peter Jackson: *The Delhi Sultanate. A Political and Military History*, Cambridge: CUP 1999, pp. 281–287, 295.

exception rather than the rule. Moreover, the underlying motivations for discriminatory acts were not always religious but had more to do with political legitimacy and loyalty.

The Delhi Sultanate was a strictly hierarchically organised Turkish military system with a Persian bureaucracy and culture. The strong Iranian underpinning of Turkic and Islamic cultures certainly goes back to the cultural interaction of dynasties with their conquered lands in Central Asia. Persian intellectual culture had a profound influence on scholarship, both esoteric and exoteric.

Constituents of the new system

Different constituents of the system such as sources of income, required management. There was *khalisa*, reserved lands or "crown" holdings from which revenue was directly collected; and there was *iqtaʿ*, the transferable revenue assignment in lieu of salary for service, through which the nobility was paid and in turn expected to render military and administrative services. This was a classical device for centralisation in Islamic states, which had been quite popular in South Asia and was adopted by Turkish invaders such as the Ghaznawids and their successors.[12] Thus the *iqtaʿ*-holder and assignee (*muqtaʿ*) were supposed to provide revenue collected from the *iqtaʿ* and to recruit warriors and scholars. In short, he was commissioned to take charge not only of a local territorial unit but of a local situation.[13] Given the transitory status of the *iqtaʿ*-holder, the *muqtaʿ* could convert the land into

---

[12] Cf. Andre Wink: *Al-Hind. The Making of the Indo-Islamic World. Vol. II: The Slave Kings and The Islamic Conquest. 11th–13th Centuries*, Leiden: Brill 1997, p. 212. For the *iqtaʿ*-system see I.H. Qureshi: *The Administration of the Sultanate of Dehli*, Karachi 1958(4), pp. 122–125; Nizami: *Some Aspects*, pp. 128ff.; Wink: *Al-Hind*, I, pp. 12f.; Irfan Habib in: Tapan Raychaudhuri and Irfan Habib (eds.): *The Cambridge Economic History of India, Vol. I: c. 1200–c. 1750*, Cambridge: CUP 1982, pp. 68–75; I. Habib: "Formation of the Sultanate Ruling Class of the Thirteenth Century", in: I. Habib (ed.): *Medieval India 1. Researches in the History of India 1200–1750*, Delhi: OUP 1992, pp. 1–21.

[13] Hardy: "Growth of Authority", 203. See also Iqtidar H. Siddiqui: *Perso-Arabic Sources of Information on the Life and Conditions in the Sultanate of Delhi*, Delhi 1992, pp. 167ff. Stephan Conermann: *Die Beschreibung Indiens in der "Rihla" des Ibn Battûta; Aspekte einer herrschaftssoziologischen Einordnung des Delhi-Sultanates unter Muhammad Ibn Tughluq*, Berlin 1993, elaborates on the prebendal system of the Delhi Sultanate. Similar grants were distributed in the form of booty during the Hindu expansion; see S. Bhattacharya: *Landschenkungen und staatliche Entwicklung im Frühmittelalterlichen Bengalen (5. bis 13. Jh.n.Chr.)*, Wiesbaden 1985.

hereditary units, especially those given to religious functionaries who received *iqta*ʿ in the form of *inʿamat*, i.e. income exempt from service, and to military and administrative office-bearers.[14] This system of *iqta*ʿ was not only important for the expansion of Muslim rule but, ironically enough, was also one of the important reasons for its downfall. In fact, Muslim expansion cannot be conceived without the *iqta*ʿ-system. Garrisoned space was needed to safeguard and expand the flow of traffic and trade, to keep "law and order" and to legitimise the ruling power. This was made possible through various supporting institutional infrastructures and personnel such as mosques, religious schools and their functionaries, exoteric and esoteric scholars and divines, as well as numerous *qasbah*s or market and garrison towns.

Mosques have been the prime manifestation of Muslim presence and at times the symbol of Islamic hegemony, though their architecture varied from region to region. They often adjusted to the area by adopting the architecture of the local environment thus showing cultural interaction and reciprocity rather than hostility and conflict.[15] Sometimes attached to the mosque was the *madrasa* which can be regarded not only as an important vehicle of the dissemination of knowledge but also of solidarity and identity in an expanding and often fluid Islamic universe. As a manifestation of social differentiation and diversification of scholarship, the institution of *madrasa*—often sponsored and patronised by the ruling classes and notables through religious endowment (*waqf*)—became prominent under the Sunni dynasty of Turkish Saljuqs, who ruled parts of Central Asia and the Middle East from the eleventh to fourteenth centuries. Under the patronage of the Saljuq wazir in the Abbasid caliphate, Nizam al-Mulk al-Tusi (died 1092),[16] the Madrasa Nizamiyya was inaugurated in Baghdad in 1067.[17] The wazir used *madrasa*s not only as a means to counter the rising Ismaili

[14] Cf. Jackson: *The Delhi Sultanate*, pp. 97–99, 101.

[15] On how architecture can be contextualised in its cultural meaning, see the excellent introduction by Monica Juneja (ed.): *Architecture in Medieval India. Forms, Contexts, Histories*, New Delhi: Permanent Black, pp. 1–105. See also the contributions by Mehrdad Shokoohy, George Michell, Catherine Asher, Brajadulal Chattopadhyaya and others (see Chap. 3).

[16] His mirror of princes, the *Siyasatnamah*, served to establish an autonomous policy without requiring religious legitimacy, yet conforming to shariʿa in the legalistic sense.

[17] On the evolution and early history of madrasas in different contexts see George Makdisi: *The Rise of Colleges. Institutions of Learning in Islam and the West*, Edinburgh: EUP 1981.

mission (*da'wa*), the spread of Shi'ite and Mu'tazila "heresies", but also as an important tool of mass education and a centre of communal social organisation, so that the counter-revolution of the Saljuqs was carried out through its reorganisation from private to a public institution. Based on the *waqf* and stipulated by the pious deed, the ideal was to receive a license to teach law and issue legal opinions.[18] This is how the foundation stone was laid for the establishment of state-loyal scholarship providing legitimacy to the state, whence secular law (*qanun*) became an alternative authoritative source to the *shari'a*. *Madrasa* institutions produced both theologians as well as service elites with a variety of specialists for different branches of knowledge, but the focus was on jurisprudence. In a way the *madrasa* became a model for quasi-universities in the Islamic world. The sciences of disputation (*'ilm al-khilaf*) became part of legal training, so that a doctrine of concession to the disputed doctrine (*mura'ah al-khilaf*) actually required the jurists to accommodate the opposing views. *Khilaf* was considered a blessing. Thus, rather than theology, law and jurisprudence claimed a central position in the tradition of teaching and learning to the extent that there were "no separate madaris exclusively for religious education... Theology became a regular subject in the madrasah curriculum in later periods..."[19] With the spread of school affiliation, urban societies could cluster under one or several of the schools of law.[20] This further encouraged pluralism and the acceptance of functional differentiation on the side of religious communities, as there were no exclusive *madrasas* for religious education. Thus, being a centre of dissemination of religious and secular Muslim thought the *madrasa* provided a prime vehicle and a proven infrastructure to consolidate the interior. It could serve state interests to push through also at the local level.

Another institution that needs to be mentioned here in some detail are the shrines of holy men. As we shall see below in some detail, proponents of mystical dimensions of Islam, the mystical orders, evolved in the eleventh century. With the passage of time, shrines developed around the graves and sarcophagi of their mystic leaders, and became

[18] See J. Pedersen and G. Makdisi: "Madrasa", in: EI(2), V, pp. 1123ff.

[19] Muhammad Khalid Masud: "Religious Identity and Mass Education", in: Johan Meuleman (ed.): *Islam in the Era of Globalization*, London 2000, pp. 233–246, here p. 235.

[20] Cf. Ira M. Lapidus: "Muslim Cities as Plural Societies: The Politics of Intermediary Bodies", in: Yukawa, Takeshi (ed.): *Proceedings of the International Conference on Urbanism in Islam*, I, Tokyo 1989, pp. 134–163, here p. 153.

centres of providing different levels of identity and social interaction. They monumentalised and actualised the memory of particular groups and appealed to a variety of social strata. It was through their cult and ritual that Islam became accessible to the educated elite as well as the uneducated masses. The shrine with its cult-networks offered them clear manifestations of the divine and integrated them into its ritualised performance, both as participants and as patrons.[21] This was so, because ritualised collective visits to the shrines and the holy men were—and still are—important social events which generated profitable earnings due to the interrelatedness of religious ritual and commercial activity: the anniversary (*'urs*) of a holy man's (*shaikh, pir*) death attracted peasants, artisans, merchants, and notables to exchange social and economic capital.[22] Moreover, the physical movement to these places is often linked to a spiritual one, namely the raising of a lower level of consciousness to a higher one. In more profane terms, it indicates the ascent of one social group into another or at least signifies a ritual overcoming of individual predicaments and social barriers. The visit is an act of affirmation, a sort of *hijra* to *dar al-Islam*, i.e. an emigration to a territory dominated by Islam. And the journey to the shrine assumes the status of a small pilgrimage. In sociological parlance, through this small pilgrimage the little tradition of Islam shares in the all-encompassing, centre-oriented great tradition of Islam radiating from Mecca.[23] The evolution of this complex sacral geography at once dissolves the centre-periphery hierarchised system wherein the shrine, as much as the *madrasa*, becomes embedded in a whole network of other similar institutions. Certainly, there were clashes between the representatives of mysticism and folk belief and those of orthodox practice right from the beginning, but the institution of the shrine underlines Islam's adaptability and its ability to shape a wide variety of identities and to provide them shelter in different locales.

[21] Compare Richard M. Eaton: "The Political and Religious Authority of the Shrine of Bâbâ Farîd", in: B.D. Metcalf (ed.): *Moral Conduct and Authority: The place of ADAB in South Asian Islam*, Berkeley 1984, pp. 333–356, here p. 334.

[22] The different issues of capital are with reference to Pierre Bourdieu: "The forms of capital", in: John G. Richardson (ed.) *Handbook of Theory and Research for the Sociology of Education*, Westport, CT: Greenwood Press (1986), pp. 242–258.

[23] See Dale Eickelman and James Piscatori (eds.): *Muslim Travellers: Pilgrimage, Migration, and the Religious Imagination*, London 1990.

Muslim space

This institutional Muslim network at the micro-level was integrated and supported through a whole network of *qasbahs* on a macro-level which was laid down by the Muslim newcomers.[24] Just like the Arab *masr* and *ribat*, the semantics of *qasbah* had a colonising—opening (*fath*) and controlling—connotation, as indicated by al-Baladhuri. *Qasbahs* seem to have become instrumental in Muslim expansion with the rise of the power of the ulama, when the sciences of hadith, exegesis, theology and jurisprudence increasingly became the principle of social organisation. As custodians of knowledge, they were powerful as interpreters of the divine and profane word. Initially, this knowledge was utilised to create personnel required for integrating the ruled land. Such a space was provided by the *qasbahs*, garrison towns and market places, which spread over the area, and built on existing infrastructural junctions. Subsequently, they became agents of Muslim culture and Islamicatisation, gradually appropriating non-Muslim space, introducing Islamic prayer and producing cadres of religious scholars and jurists, mostly sharing local customs.

Soon *qasbahs* became administrative units and centres of the Muslim military and service gentry which were to establish an intermediary economy, with particular products and services. They developed into Muslim sub-centres, legitimised by the presence of tombs and holy men and ulama, thereby becoming the prototype of a wealthy Muslim social environment in the fifteenth century. During the time of the Sultanate, different dignitaries, such as the official judge (*qadi*) and jurisconsultant (*mufti*), market supervisor (*muhtasib*),[25] scholars and mystics, revenue collectors and military were gradually added to the *qasbahs*. The increasing

[24] Qasbah literary means a newly dug well, overflowing water, as well as depth and interior. It also denotes cutting, and opening. The idea to open up new (agrarian) land for colonisation along the rivers (legally *ihya' al-mawat*, "the revival of the dead") also appears among other religious communities, such as in the savanna lands of western Sudan (see Rex S. O'Fahey: "Dâr Fûr in Kordofan. The Sultans and the Awlâd Najm", in: *Sudan Text Bulletin* VII (1985), pp. 43–63). Qasbah also denotes the city centre, a castle and the seat of the local ruler. In the Maghreb *qasbah* also means citadel; in Persian and Urdu *qasbah* is a market-town of a district with administrative and military tasks.

[25] There were parallels between *muhtasib* and the Greek *agoranomos* as well as *muhtasib* and the *dharma mahamatras* introduced by Ashoka. See Rafat M. Bilgrami: *Religious and Quasi-Religious Departments of the Mughal Period (1556–1707)*, New Delhi 1984, p. 171; B.R. B.R. Foster: "Agoranomos and Muhtasib", in: *JESHO* 13/2 (1970), pp. 128–144.

diversification of scholarly and administrative personnel was a reflection of the level of structural and functional differentiation of knowledge, and thus of societal complexity. Their function was to trickle down the official ideology to the local level, to legalise internal and external trade and, thus, to consolidate state power.[26] For their services the functionaries, including religious or quasi-religious dignitaries, received *iqta*ʿ or similar remuneration in the form of stipends (*muʿafi, inʿam, wazaʾif, amlak*)[27] and were conferred the supervision of religious foundations. These offices were not totally exempted from tax and were given for a limited time. Soon *iqta*ʿ were supervised by institutions particularly designed for that job, such as *sadrs* in the provinces and the *sadr al-sudur*, head of the department of religious affairs. As can be seen throughout history, *iqta*ʿ was not only given to Muslims who held some cultural and social capital such as those of Arab, Central Asian, Iranian and Afghan extraction (*ashraf*), but increasingly to members of other social and religious groups as well.[28]

In the course of time the space of the *qasbahs* and their inhabitants became even more important[29] as they were to play a decisive role in centuries to come, particularly in the later Mughal period. This was due to the fact that the *qasbahs* did not necessarily move towards reproducing the imperial "Islamic city".[30] The *qasbahs* displayed a normative autonomy as recruiting centres for the court and its apparatus. They

---

[26] See C.A. Bayly: *Rulers, Townsmen and Bazaars: North Indian Society in the Age of British Expansion, 1770–1870*, Cambridge: CUP 1983, pp. 349f.; Carl W. Ernst: *Eternal Garden: Mysticism, History and Politics at a South Asian Sufi Centre*, Albany: State University of New York Press 1992, pp. 47–51.

[27] *Muʿafi* and *inʿam* as well as *waqf* were most popular in the Sultanate of Delhi; see Bilgrami: *Quasi-Religious Departments*, pp. 59–98, 192. Also Iqtidar Husain Siddiqi: "Wajh-i-Maʿash Grants under the Afghan Kings (1451–1555)", in: *Medieval India: a Miscellany*, II (1972), pp. 19–44; Irfan Habib: *Agrarian System of Mughal India (1556–1707)*, Bombay 1963, p. 298.

[28] See Bayly: *Rulers*, p. 350. Also Ernst: *Eternal Garden*, pp. 48–50, 53–55; M. Athar Ali: *The Mughal Nobility under Aurangzeb*, Bombay 1970(2).

[29] See C.A. Bayly: "The Small Town and Islamic Gentry in North India: the Case of Kara", in: K. Ballhatchet and J. Harrison (eds.): *The city in South Asia*, London: Curzon Press 1980, pp. 20–48, here pp. 26f.; Muzaffar Alam: *The Crisis of Empire in Mughal North India*, Delhi: OUP 1986, pp. 224ff.

[30] It should be mentioned that this concept is primarily based on the notion of a deficient and parasitic city in the Orient, a notion developed by social scientists, such as Max Weber, and subsequently used by urban geographers and Orientalists. See Janet Abu-Lughod: "Islamic city—historic myth, Islamic essence, and contemporary relevance", in: *IJMES* 19 (1987), pp. 155–176; E. Ehlers and Th. Krafft (eds.): *Shâhjahânâbâd / Old Delhi. Islamic Tradition and Colonial Change*, Stuttgart 1993.

also provided for a moral community furnished with communal institutions, and their independent moral authority was often embodied by holy men. Even by the end of the nineteenth century an Englishman remarked, that these small towns

> owe their position and importance to their having been selected as capitals by Musalmán leaders of power varying with the size of the cities they founded and left behind them. The descendants of the leaders by whose aid they held their provinces still form the aristocracies of most of these towns. Their rapid growth was due to the fact that the surplus wealth of the provinces occupied was drawn into these permanent camps and attracted to them the handicraftsmen and traders who now form the bulk of their inhabitants...(of some places; J.M.) have had the added assistance in rising due to their importance of pilgrimage for low caste Hindus (too; J.M.).[31]

Thus it seems problematic to agree with the idea of rent-capitalism in Muslim environment with reference to *qasbah*s[32] although scholars such as tenth century al-Muqaddisi (died 988) who extensively travelled the Muslim world tended to establish a similar argument.[33] We contend that *qasbahs* became the sanctified nucleus of Muslim scholarship and imperial politics up to the nineteenth century, through Muslim institutions such as different offices held by the service elites as well as *madrasa*s and shrines.[34]

[31] D.C. Baillie: *Census of India, 1891, XVI: The North-Western Provinces and Oudh, Part I*, Allahabad 1894, pp. 94f.

[32] The concept has been championed by H. Bobek: "Zum Konzept des Rentenkapitalismus", in: *Tijdschrift voor Economische en Sociale Geografie* 65 (1974), pp. 73–78; see also Eugen Wirth: "Die Beziehungen der orientalisch-islamischen Stadt zum umgebenden Lande. Ein Beitrag zur Theorie des Rentenkapitalismus", in: E. Meynen (ed.): *Geographie heute, Einheit und Vielfalt. Ernst Plewe zu seinem 65. Geburtstag*, Wiesbaden 1973, pp. 323–333.

[33] However, one has to bear in mind that al-Muqaddisi adhered to the Balkhi-school of thought who interpreted geography in terms of Quranic revelation and considered Arabia to be centre of the universe, in contrast to the Iraqi-school that considered the world in universal terms dividing it into zones.

[34] Cf. Jamal Malik: *Islamische Gelehrtenkultur in Nordindien. Entwicklungsgeschichte und Tendenzen am Beispiel von Lucknow*, Leiden: Brill 1997, Chap. I: "Qasbah als Raum islamischer Tradition". See also Mushirul Hasan: *From Pluralism to Separatism. Qasbas in Colonial Awadh*, New Delhi: OUP 2004.

Mystical divines

As has been briefly mentioned, Sufism and shared religion are important, integral parts of South Asian Islam, so much so that J.S. Trimingham has called Indian Islam essentially an Islam of the holy men. While much of that is true, it would be too simple to reduce this major aspect of Islamicate culture to folklore, for major ideas and movements go back to mystics, which have had profound impact in the Islamic world: initially, orthodox individual mysticism (700–950) was motivated by discontent with the political and social situation around the ruling class and those who legitimised it, i.e. most of the orthodox scholars and jurists. It was also a movement complementing and contesting the establishment of legalism, which came to rule the lives of common Muslims. Outwardly *tasawwuf* was quietist and regressive, but inwardly it was powerful and activist: al-Hallaj's execution in 922 was a manifestation of a gradually increasing Sufi visibility; one that had become the symbol of anti-authoritarian and anti-orthodox public struggle.

The following accommodationist approach of Sufi apologists (950–1100) ran parallel to evolving eschatological ideas which influenced mysticism, especially in the wake of the believed disappearance (*ghaiba*) of the twelfth Shiʿite Imam in Samarra in 878. The work of al-Ghazzali (died 1111) paved the way to the much needed reintegration of exoteric and esoteric thought, and found its institutional form in mystical orders which became social mass organisations (1100–1300) and vehicles of Islamicatisation through lodges, monasteries and convents (*khanaqah*, *ribat*) and their specific discourses. The shaikh was bestowed with omniscience; the sacred genealogy (*silsila*) and mystical lore (*dhikr*) were sophisticated. These identity markers and rituals were most important for the rising communities, who gradually developed into prime mother orders along *khanaqah*s, shrines or tombs (*mazar*, *dargah*) of the powerful masters of mystical path (*tariqa*) and their followers and disciples (*murids*). Their deputies and successors (*khalifa*s) guaranteed the spiritual continuity that permitted the orders' presentation as an unbroken chain of succession of the Prophet.[35] Basically, the orders were named after their eponymous founders—such as Qadiriyya, Naqshbandiyya, and Kubrawiyya—but also connoted toponyms—such as Suhrawardiyya,

[35] Compare also Carl W. Ernst: "The Interpretation of the Classical Sufi Tradition in India", in: *SUFI* 22 (1994), pp. 5–10.

Chishtiyya, to mention the most important in South Asia. From West and Central Asia they spread out in different regions and carved their universe into spiritual territories or saintly realms (*walayat* or *wilayat*) which at times came to contest the sultans′ profane political domain (see below). All this happened at a time, when the Muslim world witnessed the fall of Baghdad; the realm of the mystic ʿAbd al-Qadir al-Jilani (died 1166) who had reconciled traditionalist Hanbalite legalism with ecstatic mystic individualism. Thus, it is the Sufi order that marks the highest political and social meaning of the mystic movement.

The first spell of institutionalisation of the orders was manifest in their integration with guilds and aspects of chivalry (*futuwwa/jawanmardi*) (approx. 1300–1700), when further Muslim expansion led to the establishment of major Muslim empires with Khurasan becoming a centre of mysticism. New aspects of an organised communal life were related to professionally associated *futuwwa*-organisations, which provided for morality and straightforwardness, but above all for masculine virtues in particular, such as pre-Islamic bravery and hospitality characterising socially free and unbound men (*fata*). The strategic inter-connections were exploited by caliph al-Nasir (died 1225) for integrating his empire. By the fourteenth century, the Sufi orders had become powerful enough to be constitutive elements for the establishment of empires, such as the Ottoman and Safawid Empires. Ruling aristocracies, such as the Mughals at times required their legitimating role to expand and consolidate their empires though, as will be argued below, the relation of the Sultans and subsequently the Mughal state to the Sufi orders was more complicated than simply one of dependence for the purpose of securing legitimacy.

In South Asia, Sufism attained such prominence and importance for a variety of reasons, particularly because of the vacuum created by the decay of Shiʿite-chiliastic powers between the eleventh and fourteenth centuries. By then several changes had occurred in its system: the interpersonal relationship between adept and shaikh and the introduction of the *silsila* now stressed narrow bonds and loyalties. The mystical stages (*maqamat*) were formulated; the authorisation (*ijaza*) and the affiliation (*baiʿa*) were introduced, so that the *khalifa* was now authorised to found a new social mass organisation. The evolution of the *tariqa* as a socially organised form of mystic relationships attracted urbane laymen,[36] the

[36] Lapidus: "Muslim Cities", 154.

nucleus of which were spiritually and territorially confined units, the *wilayat*, including urban centres and villages. Since vice-regents could be appointed and networks of spiritual centres all over the country could be established, the concept of *wilayat* can be understood in terms of its potential rivalry to the authority of the sultan.[37] Alternatively it can also be understood as a spiritual rivalry within the brotherhoods when it came to issues of agency and authenticity. The open kitchen (Persian: *langar*) became an important vehicle in spreading the egalitarian ideal of Islam, which contrasted with the strict rules of commensality in the Hindu system. The open kitchen was also a proven device to consolidate and expand power reminiscent as it was, of the Arab use of hospitality (*diyafa*) where meals were served free of charge (Arabic *mawa'id*) to people to programmatically weaken the power of traditional leaders and transfer their loyalty to the ruler.[38] Thus the spiritual leaders carefully cultivated traders, representatives of administration and military, thus becoming part of the religious, social and even political elite. They became a form of urban social organisation and gradually found their way into South Asia, shortly before Ibn al-ʿArabi (died 1248) tried to systemise the scattered Sufi ideas into a comprehensive albeit difficult whole, and when the celebrated Jalal al-Din Rumi (died 1273) became particularly famous for his didactic poems to make accessible the complex ideas to the non-initiated. Both of them and many others, directly or indirectly, were very important for the eventual Islamicatisation of South Asia, at a time, when the capital of the Abbasid Empire, Baghdad, was decimated by the Mongols in 1258.

Thus in Lahore Sufism had already begun to flourish before it became part of the Ghorid dynasty in 1186. Al-Hujwiri, coming from the Ghazna area, wrote his famous *Kashf al-mahjub*, the first comprehensive treatise on Islamic mysticism in Persian language. In it he wrote about Sufism:

> The true meaning of this name (*ahl al-tasawuf*; J.M.) has been much discussed and many books have been composed on the subject. Some assert that the Súfí is so called because he wears a woollen garment (*jámaʿ-i súf*); others that he is so called because he is in the first rank (*saff-i awwal*); others say it is because the Súfís claim to belong to the

[37] Cf. Simon Digby: "The Sufi shaykh and the sultan: a conflict of claims to authority in Medieval India", in: *Iran* 28 (1990), pp. 71–81.

[38] Khalil Athamina: "*Aʿrâb* and *Muhâjirûn* in the Environment of *Amsâr*", in: *SI* 66 (1987), pp. 5–26, here pp. 21f.

> *Asháb-i Suffa* (in Medina; J.M.) with whom may God be well-pleased! Others, again, declare that the name is derived from *safá* (purity). These explanations of the true meaning of Súfiism are far from satisfying the requirements of etymology, although each of them is supported by many subtle arguments.... I said that *safá* (purity) is the opposite of *kadar* (impurity), and *kadar* is one of the qualities of Man. The true Súfi is he that leaves impurity behind.... 'Súfí' is a name which is given, and has formerly been given, to the perfect saints and spiritual adepts.... "He that is purified by love is pure, and he that is absorbed in the Beloved and has abandoned all else is a 'Súfí'." The name has no derivation answering to etymological requirements, inasmuch as Súfiism is too exalted to have any genus from which it might be derived.... All that exists is the opposite of purity (*safá*) and things are not derived from their opposites. To Súfis the meaning of Súfiism is clearer than the sun and does not need any explanation or indication.[39]

Two major Sufi orders: Chishtiyya and Suhrawardiyya

Al-Hujwiri wrote before organised Sufism and mystical orders had evolved, two of them initially becoming most prominent in this part of the world: the Chishtiyya and the Suhrawardiyya.[40] The Chishtiyya was brought to South Asia by Hasan Muʿin al-Din (died 1236) from Chisht near Herat in Khurasan, who was later magnified in popular religion to the Prophet of Hind (*Nabi al-Hind*). He had come to Delhi in 1193—the year the Ghaznawid ruler of Ghazna, Muʿizz al-Din Ghori (assass. 1206), conquered the city (see below)—via Lahore where he had visited al-Hujwiri's tomb.

He ultimately settled in Ajmer in Rajasthan, near the Hindu holy lake of Pushkar, where he died in 1236. His shrine is most popular in Indian Islam and marks, like many other shrines, the site of local cults, which were practised there long before Islam.[41] Muʿin al-Din Chishti was one of the leading Muslim figures and a disciple of Najm al-Din al-Kubra (1145–1220) and Najib al-Din al-Suhrawardi (1097–1168), the author of *Adab al-muridin*, which became a handbook for Sufis in South Asia.

---

[39] ʿAli Ibn ʿUthman al-Jullabi al-Hujwiri: *Kashf al-Mahjub. The oldest Persian Treatise on Sufiism*, transl. by R.A. Nicholson, Lahore, 1953, pp. 30–34.

[40] Nizami: *Religion and Politics*, pp. 186–245.

[41] See P.M. Currie: *The Shrine and Cult of Muʿin al-din Chishti of Ajmer*, Delhi: OUP 1989.

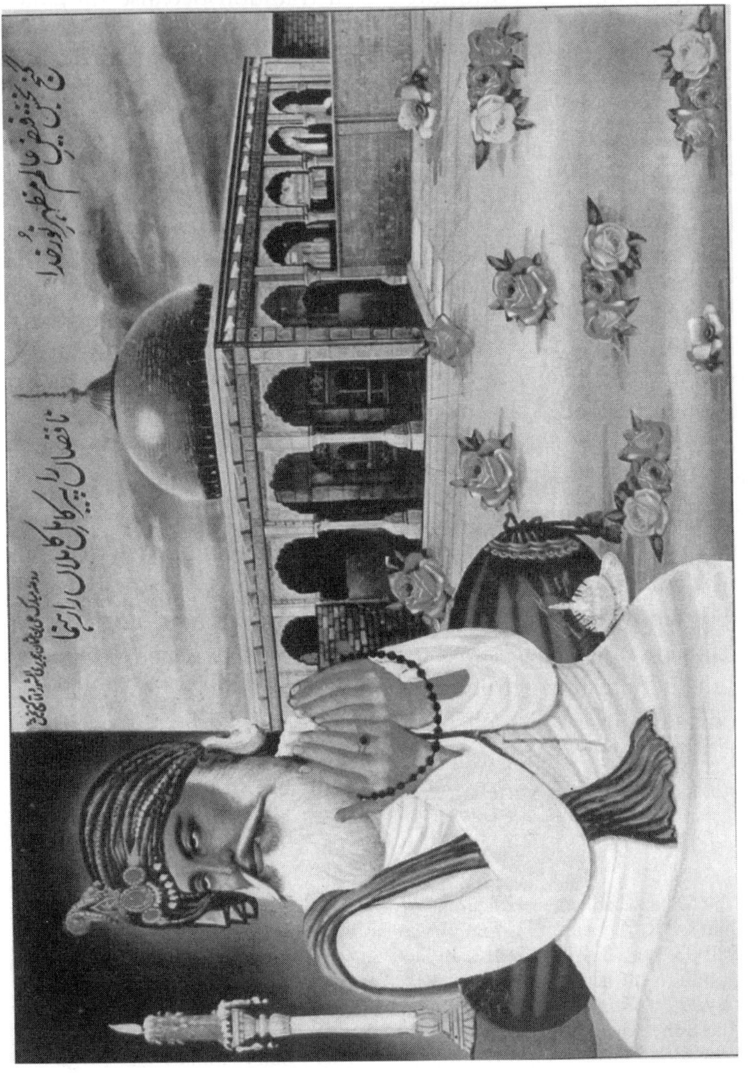

Mu'in al-Din Chishti praying in front of 'Ali ibn 'Uthman al-Hujwiri's tomb (also known as Data Darbar.
Source: Courtesy Museum of Ethnology, Munich.

Similarly, the Suhrawardiyya became important, the book *ʿAwarif al-Maʿarif* (Beneficial Effects of Gnosis) by Abu Hafs Shihab al-Din ʿUmar al-Suhrawardi (died 1234), the nephew of Najib al-Din al-Suhrawardi, providing orientation for their mystical ideas.[42] It is said that the Chishtis gravitated towards local tradition because they had reservations towards political participation and employment in government service, since it almost always involved actions disapproved of by the Islamic law, such as accepting salaries derived from non-shariʿa taxes. In sharp contrast the Suhrawardis, programmatically looked for political power and participation. For example, Iltutmish (reigned 1210–1235), the ascribed founder of the Delhi Sultanate, was a follower of Muʿin al-Din's successor, Qutb al-Din Bakhtiyar Kaki (died 1235) who was also offered the post of *shaikh al-Islam* (the post to govern religious affairs of the state) which the Sufi had in any case refused. At the same time Iltutmish was on good terms with the Suhrawardis through the missionary Shah Jalal al-Din Tabrizi (died 1244–45) who, due to competition with rival Sufis, migrated to Bengal to become active in the eastern part of *al-Hind*.[43] The post of *shaikh al-Islam* finally went to Suhrawardi shaikhs, considered to be predestined for that post due to their ideological proximity to the court.[44] Thus the rulers were flexible enough to use Sufi infrastructure to increase their influence, without ideological constraints. This led to quite a few contestations between the two orders who had had their own separate realm, i.e., *wilayat*, but which sometimes overlapped leading to conflicts which ultimately resulted in the Chishtis getting the upper hand. These two traditions produced many masters such as Bakhtiar Kaki's spiritual successor Farid al-Din Ganj-e Shakar (died 1265–6), who due to his devotional poetry also came to be venerated in the Sikh tradition. He settled in

---

[42] For the Suhrawardiyya see Nizami: *Religion and Politics*, pp. 255–263.

[43] For him see R.M. Eaton: *The Rise of Islam and the Bengal Frontier, 1204–1760*, Berkeley etc.: UCP 1993, pp. 73–77, 215–218. In fact, Sufi tradition appropriated Iltutmish by portraying him as an Islamic hero. See Muzaffar Alam: *The Languages of Political Islam in India. C. 1200–1800*, New Delhi: Permanent Black 2004, p. 86.

[44] For the Suhrawardi attitude towards the state see Nizami: *Religion and Politics*, pp. 263–272; for the discussion on this particular issue see Sunil Kumar: *The emergence of the Delhi Sultanate, 588–685/1192–1286*, unpublished Ph.D., Duke University 1992, pp. 191–194. I am thankful to Monica Juneja to have drawn my attention to this thesis. See also Sunil Kumar: "Assertions of Authority: A Study of the Discursive Statements of Two Sultans of Delhi", in: Muzaffar Alam, Françoise 'Nalini' Delvoye, and Marc Gaborieau (eds.): *The Making of Indo-Persian Culture: Indian and French Studies*, New Delhi 2000, pp. 37–65.

Pakpattan in Punjab at a major stop on the trade routes from Multan to Delhi.[45] His successor Nizam al-Din Awliya (died 1325) in Delhi gave an all-India status to the Chishtiyya. Many others exercised also great impact on the ruling parties, but at the same time there were regional localised orders such as the Firdausiyya in Bihar, the ʿAydarusiyya in Gujarat and Deccan.[46] In this sense the Sufi shaikh came to contest the power of the ulama and became a powerful source of authority in medieval India.[47]

It is of quite some interest to note why the Chishti tradition was most likely to attain its position of dominance and oust the Suhrawardi order, particularly during the Turkish Sultanate of Delhi. The Central Asian rulers may have preferred the Chishtiyya because it retained some features of nomadic culture.[48] It may also be because all three important men who received patronage at the courts of early Indian Islam happened to be followers of Nizam al-Din Awliya in Delhi: the poet and courtier Amir Khusraw (1253–1325), his fellow-poet Amir Hasan Sizji (1254–1328), and the celebrated historian Zia al-Din al-Barani (1285–1357). Khusraw's literary production had a major impact beyond the court. As Simon Digby puts it: "No other Indian Sufi Shaikh possessed a comparable panegyrist... and no rival Shaikh had a comparable publicist as disciple" as Khusraw and al-Barani. On the other hand, Amir Hasan's 15–year record of Nizam al-Din's famous conversations, the *malfuzat* called *Fawaʾid al-Fuʾad*[49] was widely read, an advantage denied to shaikhs of rival orders. These propagandists paved the way not only to the Chishti Sufi hegemony in South Asia during that time, but also provided for a Muslim sanctification of the newly appropriated land and for local Muslim identities which were required by immigrants and Muslim converts in the Delhi Sultanate. Even as the Sultanate of Delhi vanished, the Chishtis remained popular,

---

[45] For an illuminating portrayal of the shrine of Farid al-Din see R. Eaton: "The Profile of Popular Islam in Pakistani Punjab", in: *Journal of South Asian and Middle Eastern Studies* II (1978), pp. 74–92.

[46] Cf. Alexander D. Knysh: *Islamic Mysticism: A Short History*, Leiden: Brill 2000, pp. 281ff.

[47] Compare Simon Digby: "The Sufi Shaikh as a source of authority in Medieval India", in: *Purusartha, Islam et Societe en Asie du Sud* 9 (1986), pp. 57–77.

[48] Cf. Thierry Zarcone: "Central Asian Influences on the Early Development of the Chishtiyya Sufi Order in India", in: Alam et alii. (eds.): *The Making of Indo-Persian Culture*, pp. 99–116.

[49] Cf. Bruce B. Lawrence (trans. and ed.): *Nizam al-din Awliya: Morals for the Heart*, introduction by K.A. Nizami, preface by S. Digby, New York: Paulist Press 1992.

because the image and memory of the activities of the earlier Chishti shaikhs remained intact, and their disciples had established networks of influence and new centres, in Punjab, in Deccan and elsewhere. Moreover, Amir Khwurd (died 1368–9), the author of the *Siyar al-Awliya* (Biographies of the Saints; 1302), was instrumental in establishing the idea of the Muslim presence in India being a miracle (*karamat*) of the legendary Muʿin al-Din. The devotional legends around the Chishti saint certainly provided textual basis for the historical consciousness of South Asian Muslims.[50] Needless to say, Sufis preached social equality before God but they actually lived in spiritual and social hierarchies, as is obvious from their history, though there might have been exceptions such as Shaikh Hamid al-Din Nagauri (1192–1274), whose collection of conversations, *Surur al-Sudur*, is an important testament of a Sufi who modestly tilled the soil.[51]

Mechanisms of assimilation and refraction in the field of material culture were also discernable: the integration of local architectural forms by the new political leaders was to sustain the grandeur of the dynasties in popular memory (see Chap. 3). These were some of the constituent channels used by Muslims during their expansion in order to manage the new areas initially. They were used by the Turks, who were wise and at times also pragmatic enough to accommodate their policy and symbolic use of authority to the local environment. After all, the appropriation of South Asia was not possible without local acknowledgement and support. This appropriation occurred gradually, at times through bloodshed but as well through peaceful transfers of power. How then did the political control of South Asia take place?

---

[50] Cf. Digby: "The Sufi Shaikh", pp. 69–73. Alam: *Languages*, pp. 164–166, has argued that the Chishti myth was reproduced and reinvented again in the seventeenth century.

[51] For Hamid al-Din Nagori, see S.A.A. Rizvi: *A History of Sufism in India, Vols. I–II*, New Delhi: Munshiram Manoharlal 1978/1983, I, pp. 127–131; and Nizami: *On History and Historians of Medieval India*, pp. 163ff.

PART TWO

THE ESTABLISHMENT OF MUSLIM EMPIRE CULTURES: BETWEEN ISLAMIC AND ISLAMICATE

CHAPTER THREE

SLAVES, SULTANS AND DYNASTIES (APPROX. 1000–1400)

The Muslim political control of the sub-continent took place in several stages, starting with the Ghaznawids, Turkish nomadic tribes, and military slaves who were vassals of the Saljuqs. They represented an amalgamation of Islamic and Turkic cultures with a strong Iranian basis. These Turkish military slaves from Central Asia had been the most important export factor, having been separated from their tribal and other roots and capable of adjusting to the new environment quickly.[1] Because of their martial skills and alleged religious zeal they enjoyed a high reputation and therefore were provided with instruction in Islam and military drilling from their owners.[2] Becoming governors of the Samanids[3] in Eastern and Southern Afghanistan in the last quarter of the tenth century, the Ghaznawids gradually established themselves as independent amirs and sultans. By extending their power as far as Western Persia and the Ganges valley, they persianised the cultures of South Asia.[4] Under Toghril Beg (died 1063), the founder of the Saljuq dynasty, they entered Khurasan, a major cultural and political centre, and in 1055 conquered Baghdad and liberated the Abbasids from the Shiʿite Buyids. They, however, accepted the Abbasid caliph and appropriated the title of Sultan, which was the indicator of acquired authority in the Islamic universe. Distinguished in dynastical terms our narrative is thus:

[1] Cf. Jürgen Paul: "Von 950 bis 1200", in: Noth and Paul (eds.): *Der islamische Orient*, p. 219.

[2] See the classic work D. Ayalon: *The Mamluk military society*, London 1979.

[3] Samanids were the representatives of the Abbasids in Bukhara and the area around Khurasan, but were virtually independent. Known for their trade with Turkic slaves and the establishment of a slave army, they also introduced Sunnite Islam as state religion, and used sufi orders for converting local cultures.

[4] For the relation between Persian and Turkic cultures and institutions see P.B. Golden: *An Introduction to the History of the Turkic Peoples*, Wiesbaden: Harrasowitz 1992.

Ghaznawids and Ghorids

The active Muslim state of Ghazna initiated the first major conflict, when a ruler from the Punjab invaded the territory of the Ghaznawid leader Sebüktigin (died 997), a Samanid general of Turkish descent, who became an independent amir of a principality centred on Ghazna. Sebüktigin ruled from 977 to 997; his empire was consolidated and extended by his successor and staunch Hanafi, Mahmud of Ghazna (died 1030), who between 999 and 1027 entered India seventeen times on marauding raids.[5] Mahmud b. Sebüktigin, leader of the Ghaznawid dynasty, after having secured from the Abbasid caliph ʿAbd al-Qadir (reg. 991–1031) direct investiture of the governorship of Khurasan and Ghazna, began to conquer India (particularly Sind and Punjab)—not only to crush anti-Sunnite activities. Ismaili missionaries had been coming to Sind from Yemen, and Multan had become an Ismaili principality under the Fatimid caliph al-Muʿizz (953–975). In the *khutba*, his name was mentioned publicly acknowledging his authority.[6] Turning away the Fatimids, securing the routes for pilgrimage, and sacking Multan in 1006, Mahmud showed his loyalty to the Abbasids.[7] Consequently, the Ismailis had to emigrate or work secretly, for the Sunnite Ghaznawids did not hesitate to use the rhetoric of *jihad* or razzia (Arabic: *ghazwa*), which was a proven device to counter *fitna* internally and expand externally. Yet they continued to flourish as a secret organisation, and eventually merged into the Sufi school of Shaikh Zakariyya (died 1262), who was the founder of the Suhrawardi order in Multan.[8]

Somnath in historical memory

In Muslim elite discourse, the founder of the Ghaznawid empire and "helper of the Abbasids", i.e., a son of a non-Arab slave who rose to

---

[5] J. Burton-Page: "Hind", in: EI(2), III, p. 415.

[6] See S.M. Stern: "Ismaili propaganda and Fatimid rule in Sind", in: *Islamic Culture* 23 (1949), pp. 298–307.

[7] M. Nazim: *The life and times of Sultân Mahmûd of Ghazna*, Cambridge 1931, pp. 96–7; C.E. Bosworth: *The Ghaznavids*, Edinburgh 1964, p. 76; C.E. Bosworth: *The later Ghaznavids*, Edinburgh 1977, p. 31.

[8] Of how Ismailis adopted some Sufic pattern as late as in the fifteenth century, see Michel Bovin: "A Persian Treatise for the Ismâʿîlî Khojas of India: Presentation of the Pandiyât-i Jawânmardî", in: Alam et alii (eds.): *The Making*, pp. 117–128.

become a dynast, was considered to be the icon of Islam in *al-Hind*, bringing the Prophet Muhammad's iconoclastic endeavour to its completion.[9] Mahmud's state was portrayed as the stereotype of the Perso-Islamic "power-state", ethnically segregating the rulers—divinely-appointed as they were conceived to be—and the ruled, i.e., the mass of tax-paying subjects, the *ra'aya*. The destruction of the famous temple of Somnath, a well-known place of pilgrimage in Gujarat in 1026, played a major role in the making of this cultural memory; it became a crucial topic in Persian stories of Islamic iconoclasm, in 'epics of conquest' as well as in Hindu stories of recovery, in 'epics of resistance', at a time (fourteenth century) when the term "Hindu" had come to identify all indigenous religious traditions. Mahmud was considered a model ruler of an ideal Islamic state in the works of Zia al-Din al-Barani, the most important political theorist, who served several sultans of Delhi, and by other contemporaries such as Fakhr al-Din 'Isami (died after 1350) in his literary epic *Futuh al-Salatin* (1350–51). In doing so, Muslim chroniclers apocryphally projected their mental mapping onto the Somnath idol rendering it into the cultic centre of Hindu cosmology. Thus Mahmud's victory over it became a "synecdoche for the conquest of India" as Richard Davis has convincingly argued. Thus the stories of military programmes of conquest and resistance narrated by conservative elite courtiers made Mahmud the exemplary hero and Islamic warrior for the Muslims but for the Hindus an arch-enemy. This image of Mahmud was reproduced even later, by Muslim and Hindu chroniclers as well as British historians, transforming his victory over the temple into an archetypical encounter of Islamic monotheism with Hindu idolatry.[10]

In contrast to these powerful narratives that evolved over decades around Somnath, there is enough evidence that in everyday life many immigrant Muslims attracted by patronage like the leading poets such as 'Unsuri (died 1050), Farrukhi (died 1037) and also al-Biruni (died 1048) as well as Firdausi (died 1020),[11] were integrated into the local fabric and left traces of shared culture in the customs as well as architecture

---

[9] Friedmann: "Islamic thought in relation to the Indian context", p. 86.

[10] For a critical view of the narratives about Muslim raids and destruction of the temple see the illuminating study of Richard H. Davis: *Lives of Indian Images*, Princeton 1997, particularly Chap. 3, 4 and 6, quotation p. 94; also Thapar: *Somanatha*.

[11] Whose Islamist demand Mahmud could not fulfil, however; C.E. Bosworth: "Ghaznawids", in: EI(2), II, p. 1050.

and coinage.[12] The numismatic continuity did not correspond to the normative values of textual rhetoric implying reassurance to the indigenous population for their economic and administrative participation. Even Mahmud, the archetypical Islamic warrior of al-Barani and others, issued a Sanskrit version of the Islamic profession of faith, a bilingual Indian coin with a Sanskrit legend describing the Prophet as the *avatar* of God.[13] Indeed, "alliances and enmities were not based on identities of Muslim and Hindu, but on the identities and requirements of each of the smaller sects and communities."[14]

The dual administration of a divinely–appointed king on the one side, and subjects on the other was however, not applicable in reality, as can be gleaned from the writings of Abu al-Fadl Bayhaqi (995–1077), documented and analysed by C.E. Bosworth. Reflecting the spirit of the age, Bayhaqi in his political theory demands an authoritarian system: a society, metaphorically perceived as a human body, which he divides into three forces; the intellect/king; anger/the army; and desire/population. In this scenario the ruler had to be strong, with a strong army and a subject population trembling before the king. Yet rulers as well as secretaries were obliged to adhere to judicial and moral standards, in regard to the internal spy system, income, or hospitality.[15]

The state had to be run and income was important; sources of income were crown lands, confiscations, tributes to the rulers, normal taxation and war plunder. Since the treasures of Indian temples were used primarily to keep up a central bureaucracy and a well-equipped multi-ethnic professional army, the booty and revenue were immense: Mahmud could build a magnificent mosque in Ghazna to compete with the great mosque in Damascus. Tributes were usually collected by military force or through stipulations in the peace treaties between the Ghaznawid and local amirs. These were payable in cash, but also in elephants which had important symbolic meaning. A division of labour consisting of Turkish military commanders and Persian civil administration was introduced by the end of Mahmud's reign suggesting some degree of permanency but this could not prevail due to

[12] Cf. Mehrdad Shokoohy: *Bhadresvar. The Oldest Islamic Monuments in India*, Leiden 1988.

[13] Cf. Hirananda Shastri: "Devanagari and the Muhammadan Rulers of India," in: *Journal of the Bihar and Orissa Research Society* 23 (1937), p. 495. Ernst: *Eternal Garden*, pp. 52f.

[14] Thapar: *Somanatha*, pp. 120ff.

[15] Bosworth: *The Ghaznavids*, pp. 48–51, 63–65.

political instability.[16] Conversions did not occur nor was a permanent occupation even attempted Mahmud's main strategy being the *ghazwa*. Thus Islam did not really reach farther than the Punjab which became the Ghaznawids' frontier province.

Succeeding Mahmud

While there was entanglement of trade and social interaction at different levels, Masʿud succeeded Mahmud but was defeated by the Saljuqs in 1040 before he died in 1041 on a march to India. Masʿud's son Maudud tried to re-consolidate the empire that was heavily threatened by the Saljuqs, but died in 1048. In fact, the Persian part of the Ghaznawid Empire was already lost to the Saljuqs. His successors were unable to restore internal stability, but following a short but bloody intermezzo, the hereditary ruling family returned to power. One of its successors, Ibrahim, signed a treaty with the Saljuqs ceding to them several Western areas, which allowed him to raid the East and restore Ghaznawid power in the Punjab. When he died in 1099 after 40 years of rule, his son Masʿud embarked to conquer Kannauj, a loosely-knit territory under local lords and kings sacked by his father back in 1018,[17] but his death in 1115 caused fratricidal war. He was eventually succeeded by Bahram Shah (died 1157), who, like his predecessors was loyal to the Saljuqs. Thus the dynasty assimilated Persian influence, its language and cultures, and the form of government displayed customs of other Sunni empires within Persian territory, while they revered the Caliph.[18] Notwithstanding the centralising attempts made by the rulers, the empire gradually declined due to internal fractiousness and external threats such as the Ghorids, a local dynasty in East Khurasan with their capital in Firuzkoh.

With the invaders from Ghazna, Lahore had become the capital of the eastern part of the empire in 1031; it remained a frontier bastion for Muslim *ghazi* activity against Hindu-held territory for nearly two centuries.[19] The city developed into a centre of Islamic learning, particularly in the field of transmitted sciences (*manqulat*)—usually consisting

[16] Bosworth: *The Ghaznavids*, pp. 67–78.
[17] Wink: *al-Hind*, I, pp. 284f.
[18] C.E. Bosworth: "Ghaznawids", in: EI(2), II, p. 1050.
[19] C.E. Bosworth: "Mahmûd b. Muhammad", in: EI(2), VI, p. 64.

of Quranic exegesis (*tafsir*), the sciences of Prophetic tradition (hadith)—suggesting that Muslims were still in a transit-like state in South Asia. They were at the most beginning to look for consolidated power and hegemonic structure, which would give way to the study of logic, law and theology. The study of Sufism had already begun to flourish with al-Hujwiri (died around 1071). Amidst these contexts of permanency, settlement and caliphally accepted power, Islamic scholarship was further diversified. Along side the transmitted sciences, the *manqulat*, gradually *maʿqulat* evolved into a powerful part of Muslim education.

Sultanate of Delhi

Further incursions followed through the newly converted Hanafite nomads, the Ghorids, again through *ghazwa*-like raids, in Afghanistan. In 1175–76 they supplanted the Ismailis and Multan and Gujarat were attacked. Ten years later, Lahore was added to the Ghorid territories ending Ghaznawid rule in India. In 1191, the Ghorids advanced to Delhi, Ajmer and larger parts of Central India (Kannauj, Badayun, Gwalior) were subjected to the Turkic slave general Qutb al-Din Aybak (died 1210). Shortly after, Aybak, the first "slave king", was appointed the successor of Hindustan by Muʿizz al-Din Ghori who considered North India an extension of the appanage of Ghazna.[20] After his victory at Taraʾin against Rajputs in 1192,[21] Muʿizz extended Muslim political supremacy to Northern India by opening (*fataha*) up the route further south-east. He also tried to eradicate the Ismailis in Multan, before he was killed in 1206, leading to a fractionalisation of the Ghaznawid appanage.[22] The story of the Delhi sultanate begins shortly after this time.

The Sultanate of Delhi was ruled by several dynasties, starting from Aybak to Balaban, Iltutmish's slave, followed by the Khalajis and subsequently by the Tughluqs. This led to a regionalisation of Muslim

[20] Those involved in the incursions were composed of different social and ethnic groups, especially of Turkish background led by elite slaves, *bandagan-e khass*, who themselves gradually developed their own appanages, rose to power, and in this way laid the foundation for the Sultanate of Delhi. For an excellent discussion on the formation of Ghorid rule see Kumar: *The emergence of the Delhi Sultanate*, Chap. 1.

[21] This battle showed the superiority of modes of warfare which proved to be turning point for the Muslim conquest of South Asia, see Andre Wink: *al-Hind*, II, pp. 93, 109.

[22] C.E. Bosworth: "Mahmûd b. Muhammad", in: EI(2), VI, p. 64.

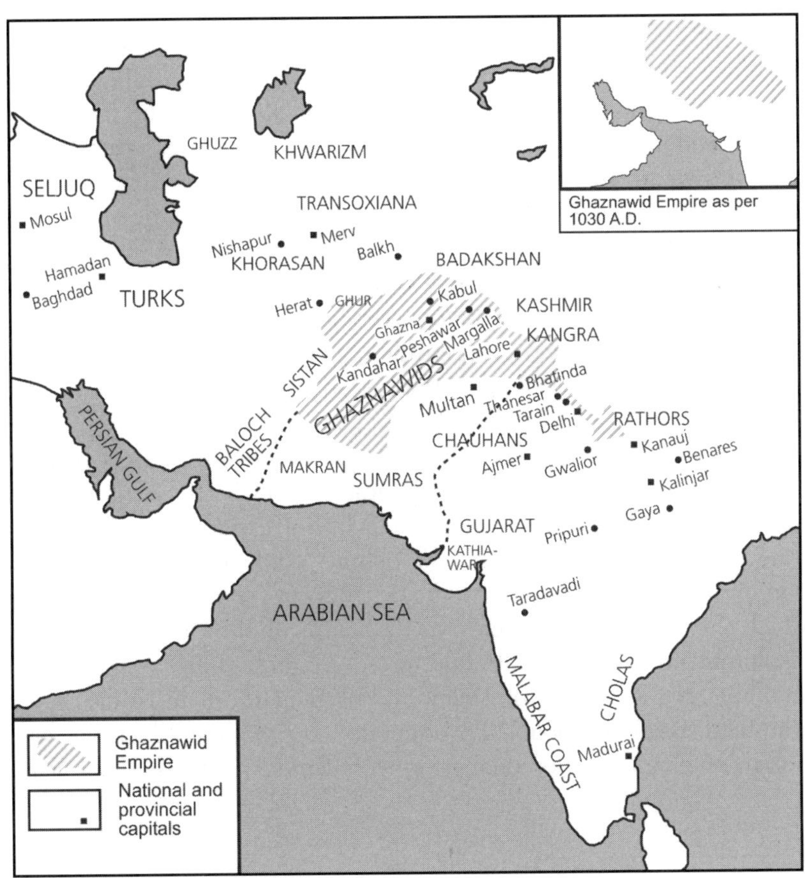

Map 4: Ghaznawids around 1100 C.E.

rule while Delhi as a regional Sultanate came under the tutelage of the Sayyids and Lodhis. The Muslim power was however reintegrated later by the Mughals through their policy of universal dominion.

The victories of the Ghorids, who moved into the Indian heartlands, became possible due to several factors. First, the Indian armies were relatively immobile. Their tactic was to move in packs, as solid columns, relying to a great extent on a bludgeoning force. Secondly, the Turkish slave nomads excelled in war techniques such as mounted archery and the use of cross-bows. Thirdly, the Turks had better access to well-bred war-horses, which made a method of shock and awe possible. Fourth, the swift horses drove the elephants, which had been the traditional war-vehicle in India,[23] although the Turks later used elephants in wars to their own advantage. Finally, the rhetoric of *jihad* which is evident in the declarations of immigrant *ghazi*s of Turk and Tajik descent was a mobilising force and attracted volunteers (*ghazi, mutatawwiʿa, mautauwiʿ, mujahid*), even under the Ghaznawids, which could swell the forces by several thousands.[24] They were not part of the regular troops and thus went out without salary or registration, adding an unpredictable force at a time of actual combat.[25] However, this is not to claim that *jihad* was perceived as a universal religious call for all Muslims, rather the notion was employed by the political agents as a means to their political ends. Yet, the Ghorids employed Hindus, especially the Rajputs, even though some of them had opposed Muslim expansion.[26] Economic transaction did not stop in spite of military conflict. So the dissemination of Islam was secondary to the desire for revenues and stability, for which the policy was "to leave in the hands of the rais and ranas no elephants, horses and wealth and to require these things every year".[27] In doing so, the Sultans of Delhi, and particularly their Turkish slaves who held social and political prominence, at times combined the symbolism of divinely ordered kingship with Turkish racialism:[28] the white

---

[23] Wink: *al-Hind*, II, 95.

[24] "those who perform supererogatory deeds of piety, those over and above the duties laid upon them by the Shariʿa, echoing the use of the verb tatawaʿa in Quran, 2:153/158, 180/184, 9:80/79, the term used in military contexts for volunteer fighters." C.E. Bosworth: "Mutatawwiʿa", in: EI(2), VII, p. 776; Bosworth: *The Ghaznavids*, p. 114.

[25] Jackson: *The Delhi Sultanate*, pp. 14–22; Wink: *al-Hind*, II, p. 91.

[26] Bosworth: *The Ghaznavids*, p. 110.

[27] Jackson: *The Delhi Sultanate,* 20, 123f; quotation p. 208.

[28] Ernst: *Eternal Garden*, p. 40; Kumar: *The emergence of the Delhi Sultanate*, pp. 171–181.

complexioned Turk set a contrast to the dark Indian; Turk became synonymous with Muslim.[29] This ethnic divide indicated the presence of boundaries and a powerful identity marker at court. Accordingly, this ethnic divide encountered much criticism from people such as the Chishti sufi Nizam al-Din Awliya.[30] Beyond the narrow world of the court and its peripheries, however, there was much shared or Islamicate culture,[31] as the material and textual culture tell us much about the fluidity and permeability of these boundaries (see below).

Resistance to Muslim invasion came from the privileged classes and the Rajput aristocracy rather than the Indian masses, for whom changes of government did not much matter. Some indigenous elites retreated into the countryside in reaction to the incursions. On the part of the immigrant community, the urban ulama primarily sought to understand the Indian universe through their elitist (*ashrafite*) perspective, which was often alienated if not arrogant. "No Indo-Muslim scholar of the 13th century sought to study the problems of Indian Musulmans and their relation with the Hindus in the light of the conditions operating in this country."[32] They considered Hindus as mere tax payers.[33]

Slave kings and the quest for legitimacy

After Muʿizz's assassination in 1206, fractionalisation set in. Aybak moved from Delhi to Lahore, where he founded his independent kingdom in 1208. In the following years, he settled post-Muʿizzian rival principalities and built the first minaret, Qutb Minar in Delhi, "indeed a symbol of the confidence of the Ghorid conquerors and their grip over the subcontinent".[34] Whether Aybak was a usurper remains an open question. His panegyrics such as Fakhr-e Mudabbir's *Shajarat al-Ansab* (The Genealogies; 1206), in which he also describes the rules of

[29] See Annemarie Schimmel: "Turk and Hindu", in: S. Vryonis (ed.): *Islam and Cultural Change in the Middle Ages*, Wiesbaden 1975.

[30] Cf. Kumar: *The emergence of the Delhi Sultanate*, pp. 177ff.

[31] Gilmartin and Lawrence (eds.): *Beyond Turk and Hindu*; also Dominique-Sila Khan: *Crossing the Threshold: Understanding Religious Identities in South Asia*, London: I.B. Tauris in association with The Institute of Ismaili Studies 2005.

[32] Nizami: *Religion and Politics*, pp. 80, 317f.

[33] See Annemarie Schimmel: *Islam in the Indian Subcontinent*, Leiden: Brill 1980, p. 9.

[34] See Mehrdad Shokoohy: *Muslim Architecture of South India, the Sultanate of Maʿbar and the Traditions of the Maritime Settlers on the Malabar and Coromandel Coasts (Tamil Nadu, Kerala and Goa)*, London: Routledge 2003, p. 133.

Islamic governance,[35] definitely do not share this view. However, Hasan Nizami in his *Taj al-Ma'athir*, the first chronicle written in the Delhi Sultanate,[36] gives a different view of Aybak.

When Aybak died in a polo accident in 1210, some of his army officers made his son-in-law and slave (*ghulam*), Iltutmish (1210–1235), the successor in opposition to Aybak's heirs and other potentates. Iltutmish, a slave of a slave and the commander (*muqta'*) of Badaun, is considered to be the founder of the Delhi Sultanate. With the palace revolt, the Delhi Sultan became the only Muslim sovereign in India to look after the Muslim ecumene until he died in April 1236. Iltutmish was able to consolidate his position through patronage and recruitment of a variety of immigrant experts, military adventurers, commanders and ulama who had fled the Mongol destruction as well as local experts in the fields of administration, military, governance and religious knowledge. In the face of this growing heterogeneity it became important to institute a collective loyal identity, at least among the most trusted slaves, the elite corps of Turkish slaves, the so-called Forty (*Turkan-e chihalgani*) given in return for faithful service.[37] Similarly, the Sultan's genealogy was related to legendary Persian rulers as was conveyed through collections of spiritual testaments (*wasaya*). The norms therein were considered acts of sagacity and wisdom. Subsequently, the Non-Arab, i.e. *'ajam*, was rehabilitated, both by endowing it with new self-confidence and creating a wider audience. At the same time liturgical Arabic was substituted by the more profane and indigenised Persian causing an accumulative character of the shari'a in a non-Arab culture of eastern Islam.[38]

The *madrasas* founded in Delhi and Badaun were called Mu'izziya, after Mu'izz al-Din Ghori, and focussed on rational sciences, due to the impact of immigrants from Khurasan and Transoxiana (today's Uzbekistan). It may be in the light of these activities that the Sultan obtained the investiture from the Abbasid caliph, who was influenced by the Mu'tazila, the official doctrine of the Abbasid government since al-Ma'mun's introduction of the inquisition (*mihna*) in 1229, the

[35] Muzaffar Alam: "Shari'a and Governance in the Indo-Islamic Context", in: Gilmartin and Lawrence (eds.): *Beyond Turk and Hindu*, pp. 216–245, here pp. 218–220.

[36] Jackson: *The Delhi Sultanate*, pp. 7f.

[37] For the ethnic and social composition of Iltutmish's slaves, their appointments and careers see Sunil Kumar: *The emergence of the Delhi Sultanate*, Chap. 2.

[38] For a brief discussion see Alam: "The Culture and Politics of Persian in Precolonial Hindustan", pp. 133–142; Alam: *Languages*, p. 141.

year when the independence of the Sultan of Delhi was recognised in Baghdad. Subsequently, he was bestowed with several titles. Sufis did not hesitate to appropriate the ruler as an Islamic hero, as can be read from both Suhrawardi as well as Chishti accounts, such as *Siyar al-ʿArafin*, a classical Indian hagiography written by the Suhrawardi court poet Hamid Jamali Kanboh, and the Chishti *Fawaʾid al-Fuʾad*.[39] So it was that Iltutmish received legitimacy from the highest Muslim authorities and thus transformed himself into a Muslim king now holding a title used by earlier Muslim kings to highlight their conquest of non-Arab lands.[40]

Up to this point the Sultans were pragmatic enough to imitate existing types of coinage with Hindu deities such as Lakshmi and Shiva, and Sanskrit letters, or popular indigenous motifs, such as Rajput horseman on the one side and Shiva's bull on the other. They regarded these as gestures towards Indianisation.[41] However, in the reign of Iltutmish, the issuing of a new coin in the name of "The helper of the leader of the faithful" (*Nasir Amir al-Muʾminin*), manifested loyalty to the Abbasids, thereby replacing the *Delhiwals* minted by Hindu rulers. A vast network of *qadi*s was laid throughout the country connected through the numerous *qasbah*s and the vast recruitment of ulama who would guarantee social and political stability. This is how the administrative duties were distributed.[42] The Madrasa Firoziyya at Uchh in Punjab became a centre where the much needed service elite were produced, with Siraj al-Juzjani, the celebrated pious historian (died during the reign of Balaban; 1265–1287), as its head in 1227.[43] In this expansionist process Hindus came to be *jizya*-payers, as can be derived from Fakhr-e Mudabbir's *Adab al-harb wa al-Shajaʿa*, dedicated to Iltutmish.[44] It needs to be reiterated however that Iltutmish's powers were greatly limited by other powerful courtiers and predominately military slaves due to what was the still fledgling nature of the Sultanate. Also, Sufis now increasingly intervened into politics, "who not only remained

[39] Alam: *Languages*, pp. 85, 87.

[40] Jackson: *The Delhi Sultanate*, p. 38.

[41] Ernst: *Eternal Garden*, pp. 52f.

[42] Schimmel: *Islam in the Indian Subcontinent*, p. 14; Nizami: *Religion and Politics*, pp. 169–185.

[43] For Juzjani see K.A. Nizami: *On History and Historians*, pp. 71–93; C.E. Bosworth: "Ucch", in: EI(2), X, p. 767.

[44] Hardy: "The Growth of Authority over a Conquered Political Elite", pp. 205–206.

quite unimpressed with Sultanate statements of piety and power but also produced their own contesting discursive texts", naming Delhi the "Sanctuary of Islam", *Qubbat al-Islam*, which was later transformed to *Quwwat al-Islam*, the "Might of Islam".[45]

Balaban's restructuring

Turkish slave (*mamluk*) states did not have a specific law of succession; the initial criterion for political power was the power of the monarch alone. Iltutmish introduced heredity as a principle of succession. His successors, among them his daughter Radiyya (ruled 1236–1240),[46] were not able to manage state affairs for long though. There were many rebellions in the *iqta*ʿ led by quasi-independent military slaves and by learned people as well. At the centre, political power wielded already in the hands of Ulugh Beg, the later Ghiyath al-Din Balaban, Iltutmish's former slave. Balaban (reigned 1266–1286), under whom the celebrated poet Amir Khusraw Dihlawi (1253–1325) rose to fame, had already planned to consolidate his position at Delhi court when he had begun to place young personnel loyal to him in strategic positions. As soon as he became sultan, he openly sought to destroy the Turkish nobility displacing the old lineage, although not completely.[47] His destruction of the corps of Turkish slaves, *the Forty*, was primarily for reasons of his own insecurity; they had started to compete with each other in their quest for pre-eminence. They were replaced with subordinates from different backgrounds. Many of the notables under Iltutmish and his heirs survived into the reign of Balaban if due to their merits and loyalty they had managed to gain the latter's protection. *Ghulam* status and ancestry still being qualifications for high rank, Balaban now also

---

[45] On this transformation see the enlightening piece by Sunil Kumar: *The Present in Delhi's Past*, New Delhi: Three Essays 2002, pp. 1–61.

[46] The fact, that a woman became sultana shows that royal women were a critical factor in the making of the Sultanate, though Raziyya had to discard her female attire to comply with the male attire of the day, but was soon removed by the old slave guard. Cf. Jamila Brijbhushan: *Sultana Raziya; her life and times*, Delhi: Manohar 1990.

[47] Cf. K.A. Nizami: *Some Aspects of Religion and Politics in India During the Thirteenth Century*, Bombay 1961, p. 143; SBP Nigam: *Nobility under the Sultans of Delhi A.D. 1206–1398*, New Delhi 1968, p. 42; Nizami: *Religion and Politics*, pp. 149ff.; for interesting details on the complex composition of Balaban's dispensation see Kumar: *The emergence of the Delhi Sultanate*, pp. 269–301.

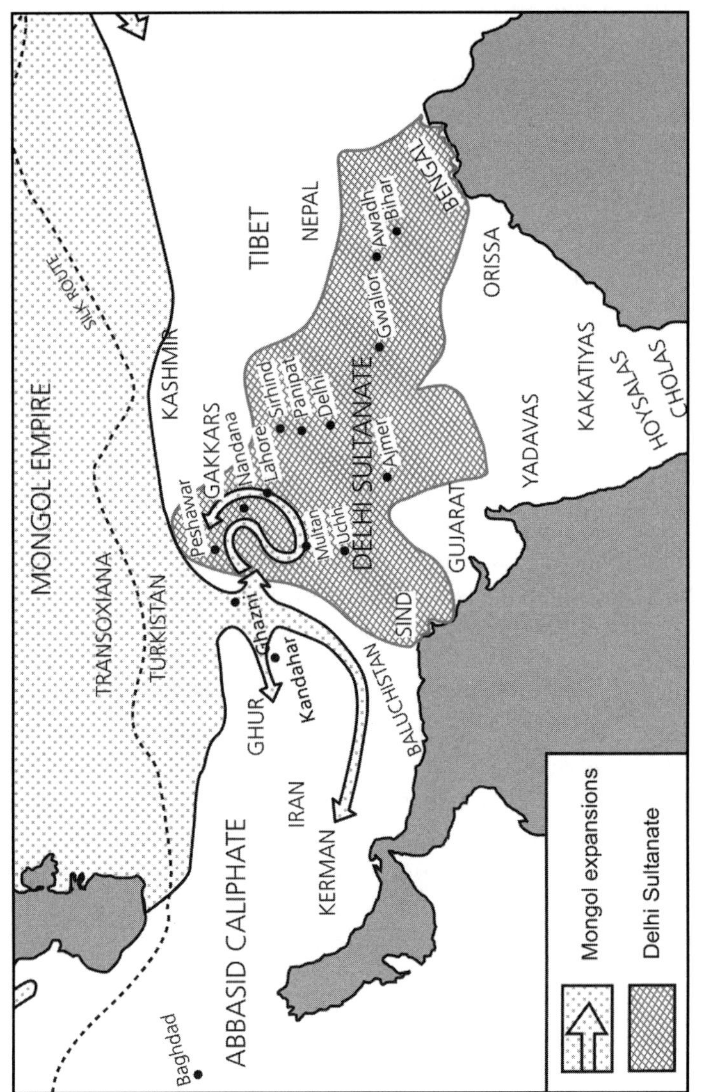

Map 5: Delhi Sultanate around 1235 C.E.

welcomed Islamised Mongol refugees, i.e., Afghans, from the Ilkhanat. Jalal al-Din, the later Khalaji ruler, happened to be one of them.

In his consolidating policy Balaban transformed small *iqta*ʿ into *khalisa*, since the old grantees had become too aged, had made their holdings hereditary, or had turned rebellious against the Sultan and held alliances with loyal rulers in the countryside. Therefore, he redistributed the land among his loyalists. The peripheries, the *mawas*, i.e., difficult and intractable terrain, had to be subdued in a systematic policy of deforestation. The driving away of pastoral and forest-dwelling people was followed by colonisation and sedentarisation, thus integrating the countryside with trade routes and adjoining qasbahs. This was accomplished by new systems of accountancy and information, carried out among others, by the newly introduced Afghans.[48] Large forts on the route to the North-West were constructed to block the Mongol advance into Sultanate territories.

At the same time Balaban claimed to be a descendant of the legendary Persian ruler Afrasiyab, thus attributing divinity to his lineage and himself. To maintain that he differed from other nobles, he initiated the customs of prostration (*sijda*) and kissing the Emperor's feet (*paibos*) in the courts—a reserved privilege. All important officers of the court had Iranian ancestry and their manner of functioning was essentially Persian. Thus, Balaban restored "the lustre of the Persian kings" (*darat-e salatin-e ʿajam*), a Persianised tendency informed by the *wasaya* collections of Iranian heroes and later pursued by the Mughals as well. Appropriating this genealogy for the Sassanian ruling house, had the function of lending a historical basis to the authority of the Sultans of Delhi, a trend also discernable in the literary production of scholars like ʿAwfi (died 1230). This also helped reproduce the caste-system, as Sassanian polity and social structure was based on the concept of class. In fact, during Balaban's reign the principle of racial superiority seemed to have reached ridiculous heights, as he went to the extreme of dismissing low-born persons from all government service and even ordered the inspection of genealogies of many families. His policy was partly legitimised by a collection of authoritative rulings, ascribed to Balaban, such as the Arabic *al-Fatawa al-Ghiyathiyya*.[49] Al-Barani, the champion of

---

[48] Jackson: *The Delhi Sultanate*, pp. 76–82, 95–96, 100; Kumar: *The emergence of the Delhi Sultanate*, pp. 287–293.

[49] In contrast, according to Zafarul Islam: "Origin and Development of *Fatâwâ*-Compilation in Medieval India", in: *Hamdard Islamicus* XX/1 (1997), pp. 7–18, here

Islamist writing, seemed to be quite happy with Balaban when he put this famous statement in the mouth of the Sultan, "whenever, I see a base born ignoble man, my hands reach for the sword." Yet, the mere power of the monarch and the recognition from tributaries that determined his political status and authority,[50] was increasingly challenged. Many potentates and rival groups, military slaves as well as "heretics" such as the Ismailis had to be subjugated. They were persecuted or went underground, providing much space for shared culture where language, customary law, dress and food of the regions were more important than religious identity.[51] At the same time the power of the ulama who were also involved in commerce and industry rose, the sciences of hadith and law gained in status. Moreover, the Sufi concept of *wilayat* challenged the Sultan's power; during Balaban's reign, no significant sufi hospice existed in Delhi. Thus the clique of Balaban remained stable only for some years (–1290) and was overthrown by Khalaji officers after some turbulence.[52] The hereditary *iqta*ʿ-system became a bone of contention for the Khalajis also. They built upon the perennial tensions between the centre and the peripheries, utilising the conflicts within the aristocracy, refuges, the *mawas*, being a prominent topic in the local histories of that time.[53]

Interventionism and integration

Jalal al-Din Firoz Shah (1290–1296) successfully challenged the rule of Balaban's successors and inaugurated the dynasty of the Khalajis, who were quite distinct from the Turks. It is true that the new Sultan promoted his tribesmen, but the fact that not too many of his loyalists hailed from the old aristocracy, shows, that the "ruling elite following Jalâl al-Dîn's accession bears the stamp of compromise... the real

pp. 8, 15f, it seems that this early *fatawa*-compilation gave due consideration to the prevailing situation, such as recitation of the Quran in Persian, Turkish and Indian languages, exemption of poor *dhimmis* from *jizya* and partnership of *dhimmis* and Muslims in matters of trade.

[50] Jackson: *The Delhi Sultanate*, p. 87.

[51] There was a variety of Muslim communities such as Bohras and Khojas in western India and the Mapillas in Malabar who intermingled with local people.

[52] J. Burton-Page: "Hind", in: EI(2), III, p. 416.

[53] Cf. Jackson: *The Delhi Sultanate*, 88–95, 124ff.; Ernst: *Eternal Garden*, pp. 55ff., 113; Kumar: *The emergence of the Delhi Sultanate*, pp. 271–275.

'Khalajî revolution' came with ʿAlâ al-Dîn",[54] who killed his uncle in July 1296, and had the older nobility eliminated.

ʿAla al-Din Khalaji (reigned 1296–1316) proclaimed himself sultan, seized Delhi, and made a number of conquests in Central and South India whose rulers became his vassals. He also stopped the Mongol raids. His regime was characterised by the introduction of administrative, agrarian and economic reforms. First of all, the internal espionage system was improved, among others, to subdue the Ismailis. The use of wine and matrimonial alliances amongst the families of the nobles was prohibited, Hanafi shariʿa laws implemented on the *dhimmis*, and the concentration of excessive wealth by individuals minimised. This was followed by new taxes levied and the confiscation of all rent-free lands, including religious endowments, many of which had become hereditary. The powerful *sadr al-sudur* (chief jurist) was to look after these issues, while the *malik al-tujjar* or *shahna-e mandi* (king of the market) supervised commercial activities. Thus ʿAla al-Din Khalaji's reign is known for the regulation of the market, a policy mainly based on a system of price control: the prices of commodities were reduced so that a horseman could be recruited for a comparatively small wage. The aim of this policy was to maintain a large standing army against Mongol threat. It was also to reduce the military power of landowners. This government interventionism went hand in hand with the replacement of the old Turkish nobility and influential economic groups such as brokers,[55] by Afghans and Indian slave soldiers. This was the start of a process of heterogenisation of the aristocracy, after the Khalajis discarded the theory of birth and heredity as well as the idea of racial superiority. Merit and loyalty replaced race as the basis for recruitment. While the establishment of the Delhi Sultanate had fostered urbanisation resulting in the development of a money economy, a new superior rural class had also emerged.[56] But ʿAla al-Din's pragmatic approach to royal authority did not replace the ethereal concept of the divine source of kingly power. On the contrary, the monumental architecture and its iconography initiated and completed by ʿAla al-Din (such as

---

[54] Jackson: *The Delhi Sultanate*, pp. 82–85, here 84f.

[55] For the discussion of these and similar groups see A.J. Qaisar: "The Role of Brokers in Medieval India", in: *IHR* I/2 (1974), pp. 220–246.

[56] Jackson: *The Delhi Sultanate*, pp. 156–161, 174f, 241–247, 249, 251f; S. Moinul Haq: "Khaldjis", in: EI(2), IV, pp. 920ff.; also Amir Khusraw in his *Khazâʾin al-futûh*, transl. Waheed Mirza, Lahore 1975, pp. 10ff.

Delhi's first congregational mosque) show his claims to moral authority, not only by maintaining the commands of shariʿa but actually reviving them. His claim to agency and authority was criticised by al-Barani and contested by al-Barani's spiritual leader, Nizam al-Din Awliya who had established his hospice in Delhi, and though his table-talks, the *Fawaʾid al-Fuʾad*, do not mention the earthly Sultan by name, the spiritual Sultan, i.e, the shaikh, criticised the mosques, pulpits and madrasas built by the Sultan at length.[57]

In contrast, many developments in the reign of ʿAla al-Din were well received by Nizam al-Din's successor, Shaikh Nasir al-Din Mahmud Chiragh-e Delhi ("the Lamp of Delhi") (died 1356), as can be gleaned from the pages of the celebrated *Khair al-majalis* (ca. 1354), a record of Chiragh-e Delhi's discourses, written down by Hamid Qalandar and considered to be the authentic voice of ordinary man.[58] Certainly, many scholars and service elite actively participated in these reforms and glorious campaigns, which also inspired literary panegyrics among Muslim courtiers such as Amir Khusraw. Meanwhile, the state-supported teaching institutions taught rational subjects most important for the service elite, reintroducing Arab language and judicial texts. *Maʿqulat* was also supported by ʿAla al-Din's successors[59] for this was the most pragmatic way to integrate a non-Muslim majority into the patronage system dominated by Muslims.

ʿAla al-Din Khalaji was succeeded by one of his sons, Qutb al-Din Mubarak Shah (1316–1320). So far the Sultans had reconciled themselves to the concept of a universal Muslim caliphate by calling themselves helper or right hand of the caliph, long after the cessation of the Abbasid caliphate whose imperial symbolism had played a significant legitimising role during the Delhi sultanate.[60] In contrast, Mubarak Shah initiated a process of emancipation that had long been in the making: he pronounced himself *khalifat Allah* in 1317–18, thereby contesting the

---

[57] Cf. Kumar: "Assertions of Authority", pp. 37–65.

[58] The Sufi opined that the Sultan was not motivated by militaristic considerations but by altruism and philanthropy; see Nizami: *On History and Historians*, pp. 177–179. For a critique on the authenticity of *Khair al-Majalis* see Ernst: *Eternal Garden*, pp. 68–71, 125; Paul Jackson: "Khair al-Majalis: An Examination", in: Chr. W. Troll (ed.): *Islam in India; Studies and Commentaries II, Religion and Religious Education*, New Delhi: OUP 1985, pp. 34–57.

[59] See Iqtidar H. Siddiqui: *Perso-Arabic Sources of Information on the Life and Conditions in the Sultanate of Delhi*, Delhi: Munshiram Manoharlal 1992, pp. 91f., 153ff.

[60] See Ernst: *Eternal Garden*, pp. 55–59.

authority of his predecessors, the Abbasid caliph, and the Prophet. The last caliph, al-Mustaʿsim, had been trampled to death by the Mongols in Baghdad in 1258. For the Sultans however, the caliphate had lost its meaning long before the Mongols brutally extinguished it. The rulers of Delhi had only been paying lip-service to the caliph in order to legitimise their rule and in all likelihoood to receive support to wage another *jihad* against infidels or heretics. Consequently, Mubarak Shah abrogated his father's repressive policy.[61]

Qutb al-Din Mubarak Shah was killed in 1320 by his favourite slave Khusraw Khan, a convert from a low-caste Hindu family, who had been able to muster a sizeable number of Hindu warriors. He virtually exterminated the power of the Khalaji dynasty, but his command did not last long (1316–1320). He soon was killed by a senior lieutenant of ʿAla al-Din, Ghazi Malik a son of a Turkish slave and a Hindu mother. Urged by the nobles of Delhi to accept the crown, under the title of Ghiyath al-Din Tughluq Shah I (1320–1324), he became the first Tughluqid, the head of a new Turkish dynasty,[62] who would pursue a policy of heterogeneity within Khalaji aristocracy.

The founder of this new Turkish dynasty based his power on soldiers and administrators from his own retinue in the north-west, though some old established families continued to hold offices. But he did not reign very long. He died in 1325, and was succeeded by his son Muhammad ibn Tughluq (reigned 1324–1351), under whom Ibn Battutta, the North African traveller in India between 1333 and 1342, became chief qadi of Delhi in 1333. The Sultan was ambitious to combine prophethood with kingship,[63] and as the first ruler regarded his empire as *dar al-Islam*, the abode of Islam. In pushing through his imperialistic approach, he succeeded in further crushing the power of the old nobility by undermining their *iqtaʿ* and co-opting foreigners and recent Hindu converts for administrative offices.[64] This Indianisation of the administration went hand in hand with his personal interest in philosophy, Islamic law and sufism. At the same time however, he denied the ulama any special privileges unlike his predecessor, and he

---

[61] Jackson: *The Delhi Sultanate*, pp. 158, 249f.

[62] S. Moinul Haq: "Khaldjis", in: EI(2), IV, 920ff., Jackson: *The Delhi Sultanate*, pp. 175–178.

[63] Schimmel: *Islam in the Indian Subcontinent*, p. 20.

[64] Jackson: *The Delhi Sultanate*, pp. 182–186, 250f.

was not on good terms with those Sufis who refrained from politics.[65] Whether this policy was inspired or not by the Syrian Hanbali scholar and jurist Ibn Taymiyya (died 1327), himself a Qadiri, seems to be questionable, as this Arab writer criticised some Sufi doctrines as much as he had Greek logic and philosophy.[66] Due to the Sultan's interest in philosophy, philosophers rose to new dominance in government councils. Similarly, his policy of encouraging scholars of different countries to migrate to India aimed to counterbalance the established scholars and mystics of his own empire. The rivalry usually focussed on the question of listening to music (*sama*ʿ).[67] Thus *sama*ʿ became an issue of Muslim identity which split society apart, as can be traced in the compendiums of mystics and scholars alike.

Expansion to the South

In 1337, only two years after his enthronement, Muhammad Tughluq abruptly decided to shift his throne with all his staff and army, and the Muslim elite to Devagiri / Daulatabad in the Deccan in order to expand his empire further southwards. Sufis resisted his call to accompany him, but once in the Deccan, the sultan tried to persuade the Deccani Indians to convert to Islam, with the help of Sufis, notably those of the Chishti network. This reciprocity between sacred and profane was crucial, for it revealed the political importance of the royal patronage of Sufism as a vehicle by which rulers sought legitimacy from religious institutions. He hoped to strengthen his position as "righteous" emperor and consequently to provoke less resistance. But neither did the Chishtis appreciate the Sultan's constant offer of employment in government service, nor did they like his travel directive which forcibly interfered in

[65] K.A. Nizami: "Early Indo-Muslim mystics", in: *Islamic Culture* 24 (1950), pp. 60–65.

[66] Cf. K.A. Nizami: "The impact of Ibn Taimiyya on South Asia", in: *Journal of Islamic Studies*, I (1990), pp. 125–134.

[67] *Sama*ʿ according to Shaikh Nizam al-Din, was "...a voice. Why should rhythm be forbidden? And that which is spoken is a word. Why should the comprehension of its meaning be forbidden? Samaʿ is also movement of the heart. If that movement is due to remembering God, it is beneficial, but if the heart is full of corruption, then samaʿ is forbidden." Nizam al-Din quoted in Lawrence: *Nizam ad-Din Awliya*, p. 356. Similarly, the discussion of the Suhrawardi Qadi Hamid al-Din, who legalised *sama*ʿ in Delhi. See Lawrence: *Nizam ad-Din Awliya*, pp. 348f.

the territorial organisation of the *wilayat*-system.[68] This caused conflict between Muhammad Tughluq and the leading *khalifa*s of Nizam ad-Din Awliya, adding to their already strained relations.

The shift to a new capital city seems to have been a failure eventually forcing the Sultan to return to Delhi. In the process, he had to leave many Muslims behind in the South, among them Sufis whom he had forced to accompany him and who now became the nucleus for autonomous Muslim cultures there. He thereby unwillingly enabled the development of new mystical branches, such as the order around Burhan al-Din Gharib (died in Daulatabad in 1340) and Muhammad Gesudaraz (died 1422), who, after a 64 years stay in Delhi became the leading Chishti Sufi in the Deccan during his last 22 years in Gulbarga. His tomb shrine (*dargah*, meaning also court or seat of power) and the cult associated with it, were rooted in the cultural symbols of the local population. In this way the social and cultural traditions of the North were consolidated in the Deccan (see also Chap. 4).

Tughluq's earning the investiture of the caliph in Cairo in 1343, however, could not save his long regime (1324–1351) from several famines, rebellions and insurrections. The nobility was given an even greater share in the *iqta*ʿ than before, so that the *muqta*ʿ acquired the right to inherit all privileges. In contrast, members of the military class who had been suffering under the revenue policy felt uneasy, so that many of his governors became independent potentates as was the case in Madura, the Deccan, Gujarat and Bengal. Some of these were permanently installed as in Maʿbar (1334–5), Gulbarga (1339), Warangal (1345–6), and Daulatabad. In the last case the result was the proclamation of an independent sultanate under ʿAla al-Din Bahman Shah in the Deccan. When Muhammad Tughluq died in 1351, the Sultanate was already on the brink of dissolution.[69]

Muhammad Tughluq was succeeded by his cousin Firoz Shah Tughluq (1351–1388), who was conferred titles by caliph al-Muʿtadid in 1353, and again, in 1355 received the investiture from the caliph in Cairo. The conferring of titles, however, did not render Firoz Shah an intermediary dealing in the caliph's name with the rest of South Asia, for he was not able to cover the losses Muhammad Tughluq had suffered during his reign. Nor were his campaigns successful, and at

---

[68] Ernst: *Eternal Garden*, pp. 216, 113.

[69] Schimmel: *Islam in the Indian Subcontinent*, p. 20, Jackson: *The Delhi Sultanate*, pp. 255–276.

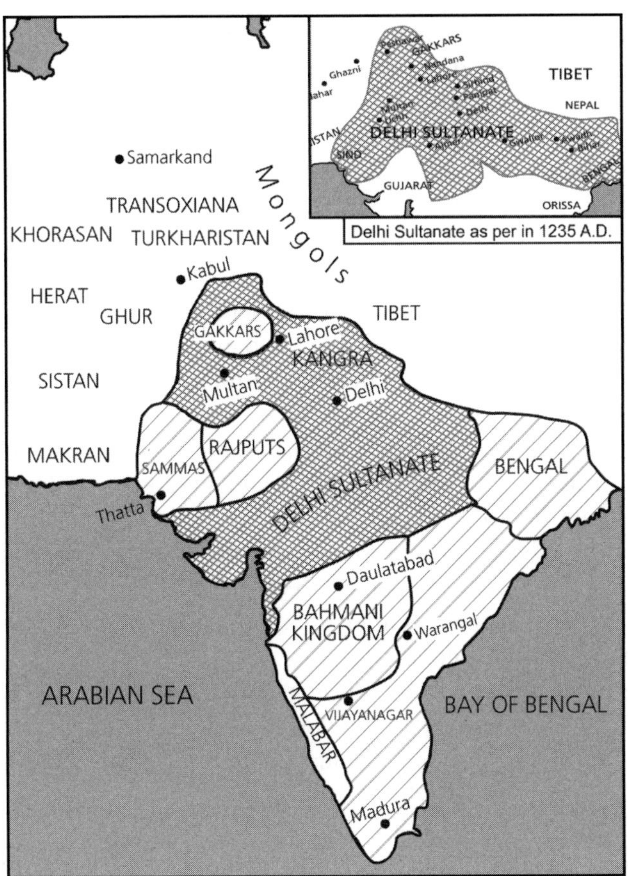

Map 6: Delhi Sultanate 1350 C.E.

court he gave too great an authority to his wazir Khan Jahan, who became the virtual ruler of Delhi.[70]

Collapse of Khalajis

Al-Barani considered this policy of alleged indifference towards Hindus and the lower strata as a lack of religiosity, basing his argument on ethnic grounds. He regarded the principle of heredity to be the only way to save Muslim rule from political upheaval and ethnic strife,[71] dismissing the infiltration of the ruling class by non-Turks, the root of which lay in Muhammad Tughluq's policy of rigorous cultural and religious integration. Instead, he not only advocated the reestablishment of the old order, but also a repressive policy against Hindus—inspite of being a disciple of Nizam al-Din Awliya. In his *Fatawa-ye Jahandari* (1358), a mirror of princes written in imprisonment under Firoz Shah, starting with Mahmud of Ghazna, al-Barani paints a portrait of the sound ruler posessing a rather Machiavellian amoralism, when putting kingship above Islamic law and ethics: the duties of a just and pious Islamic ruler stood in contrast to the sinful *padishah* of the Iranian tradition, the supreme ruler of the universe. In certain situations, al-Barani admits the sultanate had a potential for human weakness but also confused the head of religion (the prophet) with the head of government. He thereby tried to bridge the gap between *realpolitik* and prescribed shariʿa norms. Needless to say, his interpretation of the shariʿa focused on the interests of Muslims alone.[72]

Firoz Shah, who had his own huge corps of amirs, must have been in a critical situation when he followed al-Barani's advice. He was the first Sultan of Delhi to issue discriminatory sanctions against Muslim

---

[70] Jackson: *The Delhi Sultanate*, pp. 296–305; Schimmel: *Islam in the Indian Subcontinent*, pp. 21f.

[71] Nevertheless, it is al-Barani who has left us with an important precept (*wasaya*) of eminent rulers and statesmen, that of Balaban, in which we have several pieces of advice on the conduct of Muslim rulers. See Nizami: *Religion and Politics*, pp. 104–110, 150.

[72] See Nizami: *Religion and Politics*, pp. 114–117; Alam: "Shariʿa and Governance", pp. 222ff.; for al-Barani's perception of the Delhi Sultanate see Zia al-Din Barani: *Fatawa-ye Jahandari*, ed. A. Salim Khan, Lahore 1972. English *The Political Theory of the Delhi Sultanate (Including a translation of Ziauddin Barani's Fatawa-i Jahandari, Circa, 1358–9 A.D.)*, by M. Habib and Afsar Umar Salim Khan, Allahabad 1960, and by A. Begum in: *Medieval India Quarterly*, 3 (1957–58), pp. 1–87 and 151–197; see also Siddiqui: *Perso-Arabic Sources*, pp. 163ff.

heretics, and especially against non-Muslims, imposing *jizya* on Brahmans (*jizya-ye Hunud*) who had hitherto been exempt from it in the sultanate.[73] Yet, the *Fatawa-ye Firoz Shahi* also known as *Fiqh-e Firozshahi* compiled in Persian and Arabic gave guidance to *qadi*s and *mufti*s and tried to organise the relationship of Muslim rulers and non-Muslim (Hindu) subjects by providing them equal rights relating to the protection of life and property and to explain economic transactions in the Indian context, such as *hundi*, a traditional way of credit.[74] Similarly, the influential and monumental *Fatawa-ye Tatarkhani*—named after its initiator Tatar Khan (died 1337), a noble of Firoz Shah—seems to give ample evidence of the sultan's measures reflecting the social conditions of the day:[75] his policy restored land grants for the landed gentry and exempted them from paying certain taxes. The alleged prosperity and affluence during his time as suggested by the political chronicles is however, contested in the Sufi discourses such as *Khair al-Majalis*: where the common man is described as being in great difficulties.[76]

The restoration of land grants for the landed gentry proved to be decisive for the future of the Sultanate, for Firoz Shah's slaves and their offspring became a powerful force to form a new and independent aristocracy.[77] Therefore, his successors could not restore political power over these and other potentates and thus were not able to guarantee the important income from tax so vital for the empire. A weak centre and fragmented periphery made it easy for Timur (died 1405) to invade Northern India in December 1398, though it took another fifteen years for the Tughluq Sultanate to come to an end, with the death of Mahmud II in 1412. The armies of Timur destroyed and depopulated Delhi, the brain- and brawn-drain was so decisive that it took quite some time for restoration.

The Timurid invasion reduced the Delhi Sultanate to just one of many competing regional powers in South Asia. The centre was too weak to be the arbiter of various regional interests, the result of which was to be political and territorial fragmentation. Independent sultanates of Malwa, Jaunpur, Kashmir, Bengal, Deccan, Bijapur, Golconda,

---

[73] Schimmel: *Islam in the Indian Subcontinent*, pp. 21f.

[74] For this system of bills of exchange see L.C. Jain: *Indigenous Banking in India*, London 1929.

[75] Compare Islam: "Origin and Development of *Fatâwâ*-Compilation", here pp. 9, 13–15.

[76] K.A. Nizami: *On History and Historians*, pp. 2, 179f.

[77] Jackson: *The Delhi Sultanate*, pp. 187, 305–318.

Malabar, Sind and Gujarat came into being after having thrown off the Turkish yoke. This period also saw the growth of Shia Islam. However, amidst this fragmentation of political rule and cultural diversity, the major contribution of the Sultanate was the introduction of a monetary economy and a coercive administrative organisation, which through a hierarchical system of authorities was to control a vast area attempting to include even the villages. The organisation of Muslim scholarship hardly underwent any change, thus potentially being a ready ideological binding thread if such a need arose in the future. Perhaps to the Sultanate's great disappointment, the next dynasties to come were the utterly weak Sayyids (1414–1451) and Lodhis (1451–1526).

EXCURSUS

SHIʿITES AND SUNNITES

After Iran, the Indian subcontinent is home to the second largest Shiʿite population.[1] Post-Mughal centres of Muslim power—Bengal, Awadh and Haydarabad—were Shia. They produced one of the finest examples of composite culture, fusing and synthesising not only the cultural and religious traits of Shiʿism and Sunnism but also generally those between Hinduism and Islam. For its part, Sunni thought and institutions made a greater effort to compromise with Shiʿite Islam here than elsewhere, partly owing to the long history of Persian influences on the courtly culture even before the times of the Mughals. Similar to the Sunnis, Shiʿite groups are heterogeneous. There are several Shiʿite forms of cultural articulation that settled in South Asia, disseminated their ideas and established networks of social and political relations.[2]

After the death of the Prophet of Islam, Muslims split into groups of Kharijites, Shiʿites, and Sunnis over the issue of legitimate succession: whether it should be the outstanding merits in the cause of Islam (*sabiqa*) or close kinship ties with the Prophet's family (*nasab*). ʿAli's supporters insisted that only a member of the family can legitimately claim the mantle of the caliphate and thus established the institution of the Imamate. Imams are considered innocent and impeccable (*maʿsum*), endowed with spiritual and profane knowledge. Descendants from ʿAli's marriage with the Prophet's daughter Fatima came to be called the fiver, sevener or twelver Shia.

Different branches emerged out of complicated disputes over the succession of the leaders of Shiʿite communities, the Imams: first, there are the fivers who after the first four Imams accept Zaid ibn ʿAli

---

[1] Shiʿites represent approx. 10% of world's Muslims. Today almost 15% of Pakistani Muslims are Shiʿites; in Afghanistan they form about 15%, in India 3% and in Bangladesh close to 1% of the population.

[2] For an early overview see J.N. Hollister: *The Shiʿa of India*, London 1953. See also Yann Richard: *Shiʿite Islam, Polity, Ideology and Creed*, Oxford: Blackwell 1995, transl. by Antonia Nevill; Heinz Halm: *Shiʿism*, transl. by Janet Watson, new Material translated by Marian Hill, Columbia Univ. Press 2004 (2); Moojan Memon: *An Introduction to Shiʿi Islam; The History and Doctrines of Twelver Shiʿism*, New Haven: Yale University Press 1985.

(died 740) as their fifth Imam, rather than his brother Muhammad al-Baqir (died 743). Close to some ideas of Muʿtaziliyya these Zaidis do not believe in the Imam's infallibility and in the principle of *nasab*. Different contesting groups evolved within the fiver, some of them even succeeded in establishing an Imamate in Yemen.

A little more diverse were the followers of the sixth Imam, Jaʿfar al-Sadiq (702–765). According to these Ismailis, the eldest son—Ismail—was to inherit the right to rule. Thus Ismailis are often called Seveners, after Ismail, the seventh Imam. They established the Ismaili dynasty of Fatimids in Egypt, and subsequently branched out in different, mainly trading communities some of them extremely active under the spiritual guidance of the Agha Khan (see below).

In contrast, those who accept the first twelve Imams believe that Jaʿfar al-Sadiq preferred his younger son Musa al-Kazim (died 799), who continued the tradition until the twelfth Imam vanished in 872 (*ghaiba*) only to reappear at the 'end of times' as the Mahdi, a faith rejected by Sunnis. Since the doctrine of occultation, Twelver Shiʿites have been negotiating on the hidden Imam's representatives. It was only Ruh Allah Khumaini's idea of *Wilayat-e faqih*, guardianship of the Islamic jurist, that de-eschatologised Shiʿite discourse. He followed Muhammad Husain Naini's (died 1936) call for the ulama's political power: if ulama were ruling the state according to shariʿa, there was no need for Mahdi. Thus man was re-endowed with political power. Social revolution came to replace eschatological salvation.

In the cultural fabric and the Islamic sacralisation of South Asia, the Shia played an important role, particularly the Ismailis (7er Shia) who fled the Sunnite-dominated areas to find refuge along the river Indus. Their missionaries (*duʿat*) from Yemen and Egypt are said to have been responsible for converting parts of North Indian business communities and numerous low-caste Hindus to Islam, especially in Sind and western India in the ninth century.[3] When the Ismaili ruling elite established the Fatimide caliphate in Cairo (910 to 1171), the entanglement between commercial interests and religious activities grew stronger due to their benefitting from the Indian trade along the Red Sea route.[4] Multan became a major Ismaili centre; coins were

[3] See Dominique-Sila Khan: *Conversions and Shifting Identities. Ramdev Pir and the Ismailis in Rajasthan*, Manohar: Centre de Science Humaines 1997.

[4] André Wink: *AL-HIND*, I, p. 216; Farhad Daftary: *A Short History of the Ismaʿilis. Traditions of a Muslim Community*, Edinburgh: Edinburgh University Press 1998, p. 66.

minted on the Egyptian pattern. Much like the Sufis, Ismaili activists used local symbolism and wrote in Indian vernaculars rather than in Arabic or Persian. The emphasis on the veneration of the holy family (Muhammad, ʿAli, Fatima, etc.) and the shared symbolism around these figures was well received by the local population. Husain and his representation of redemption through sacrifice and martyrdom (in 680 in Kerbala) caught the imagination and devotion of Shiʿi masses and the respect of some non-Muslims.[5] Popular Shiʿism—much like Sufism—acted as an intermediary between the general population and the Muslim elite. In the shared cultural atmosphere of the subcontinent several Sunni Sufi orders or their branches drifted towards Shiʿism (e.g. several lines of the Kubrawiyya and the Niʿmatullahi). Whether some Sufis like Suhrawardis directly or indirectly, helped spread Shiʿism in India by using Ismaili terminology and ideas (such as esoteric exegesis) while practicing dissimulation and hiding their faith (*taqiyya*) in the guise of (Sunni) Sufism[6] may be questioned. In Sind, both Ismailism and Sufism flourished side by side. This mutual respect and personal union was based on the fact that Shiʿites and Sufis both suffered from marginalisation in Sunnite Abbasid-dominated territories. Both reciprocated in terms of structure and terminology, when eschatological ideas increasingly influenced the mystical fabric, especially from 872 on. By the thirteenth century, most of the eminent Sufi shaikhs claimed to be descendants of ʿAli: "Simultaneously the Sufi concept of the position of the shaikh came to parallel increasingly the Shi'i Imamate while ʾAli came to occupy almost as important a position in Sufism as he did in Shi'ism. These changes resulted in several Sufi orders gradually evolving from Sunnism to Shi'ism."[7]

In the eleventh and twelfth centuries, Hindus from the middle and upper castes such as *Vaishya*, made up of landowners, merchants and artisans embraced Ismailism in Gujarat, in order to benefit from the network of international maritime trade. These converts later became known as the Bohras, derived from the Gujarati "to trade". Indigenous converts became active in proselytising in areas today comprising Rajasthan, Madhya Pradesh and Maharashtra, while outside of South Asia there is a small Bohra community in Yemen. Since the twelfth century

[5] See David Pinault: *The Shiʿites. Ritual and Popular Piety in a Muslim Community*, New York: St. Martin's Press 1993.
[6] Farhad Daftary: *A Short History of the Ismaʿilis*, p. 198.
[7] Memon: *An Introduction to Shiʿi Islam*, p. 96.

the Bohras were partly reconverted to Hinduism, pressurised to convert to Sunni Islam, practiced *taqiyya* and thus experienced internal dissensions in various Bohra communities headed by different "absolute or unrestricted missionaries" (*daʿi mutlaq*), which further marginalised it. The most popular among them are the Dawoodi Bohras.

Similarly, the Ismaili community known as Khojas is comprised of merchants and landowners who converted from the Hindu Lohana caste in Sind in the fourteenth century. They are known for having developed a unique literary genre: devotional hymns (*ginans*) resembling *bhakti* and Sufi poetry, especially with devotional literature composed in the vernacular languages of western India/Pakistan.[8] The Khojas were flexible enough to adopt some Sufi terms and concepts such as *murshid* and *murid* to extend their realm, *wilayat*, as it were. Today Khojas are headed by the present Agha Khan, the fourtyninth direct descendant in a male line down from ʿAli, with followers in Pakistan, India, Iran, Yemen, and East Africa.

Some twenty thousand Khojas and Bohras migrated to East Africa in the early nineteenth century at the invitation of the Sultan of Zanzibar to boost economy and help build trading routes to Muslim countries. Over time they settled in the big cities of Tanzania, Kenya and Uganda. S.A.A. Rizvi[9] argues that the newly converted traders benefited from connections to Ismaili missionaries because these contacts helped build the trading routes to Muslim countries.

Apart from the Ismailis, the Ithna ʿAsharis or Imamis (Twelver Shia)—the biggest group among the Shiʿites—have been living in *al-Hind* in comparatively great numbers. Throughout the Delhi Sultanate Shiʿi traders, scholars and political refugees were patronised and entrusted with high posts in the Imperial service. Similarly, during the Mughal period Shiʿi influences remained strong,[10] yet, "tolerance of Shiʾism in Mughal India often fluctuated according to relations with Iran. The sixteenth-century Mughal-Safavid alliance gave way in the seventeenth to disputes over Qandahar, leading to restrictions on Shiʾis in India."[11] Even though Aurangzeb employed Shiʿites in the imperial

[8] Cf. Ali S. Asani: *Ecstasy and Enlightenment—The Ismaili Devotional Literature in South Asia*, London: Islamic publications 2002.

[9] Saiyid Athar Abbas Rizvi: *A Socio-Intellectual History of the Isna ʾAshari Shiʿis in India* Vols. 1–2, New Delhi: Munshiram Manoharlal 1986, Vol. 1, p. 149.

[10] Memon: *An Introduction to Shiʿi Islam*, p. 122.

[11] J.R. Cole: *Roots of North Indian Shiʾism in Iran and Iraq. Religion and State in Awadh, 1722–1859*, Berkeley/Los Angeles: UCP 1988, p. 25.

administration and gave them positions of the highest rank, he refused to tolerate public commemoration of Muharram. In contrast, his son Bahadur Shah participated in Shiʿi rituals.[12]

By the early eighteenth century regional centralisation gave way to the emergence of Shiʿite Awadh. According to Juan Cole, this promoted a liberal approach towards jurisprudence allowing the use of *ijtihad* as well as scholarly consensus (*ijmaʿ*). This *Usulism* stood in contrast to views which relied solely on Quran and hadith as sources of jurisprudence (*Akhbarism*) and Sufism. Usulis emphasised social closure and a Shiʿi communal identity which was important for the fledgling Nawwabi rule, yet ready to accommodate local cultures whenever necessary. A Shiʿi ruling group was established at the top of the social hierarchy, strengthened by Shiʿi military wing while the old Sunni clerical and mystical families were subordinated, with the exception of the Farangi Mahall. "Shiʾi Sufism might have acted as an ecumenical force, since pirs often had Sunni or even Hindu followers. The Shiʾism of the Usuli ulama emphasised strident communalism and such militancy ultimately would provoke a Sunni backlash."[13] In the early nineteenth century the government policy clearly followed Usuli exclusiveness and thereby enforced tensions among Sunnis and Shiʿis as well as between Muslims and non-Muslims. This trend was due to the transformation of a nebulous Shiʿi community in India into a formal religious establishment. This included emphasis on scripturalism and the exact observance of rituals.

Sufis were held in high esteem by the local population, because they felt much closer to them than to the Usuli ulama who scorned syncretic religious practices. This caused a fight between these groups which in turn led to the destruction of the mediating groups between Muslims and Hindus (Sufis and Hindu holy men) by the Usulis, which eventually contributed to the growth of communalism. Likewise Moojan Memon opines that the major coeval developments in Shiʿi community were the growing intolerance and hostility between Sunnis and Shiʿis on the subcontinent, which had not existed during the Mughal period, and the narrowing definitions of religion which rejected Sufism and philosophy.[14]

---

[12] Muhammad Umar: *Islam in Northern India During the Eighteenth Century*, New Delhi: Munshiram Manoharlal Publishers 1993, p. 169.

[13] Cole: *Roots of North Indian Shiʾism*, p. 151.

[14] Memon: *An Introduction to Shiʿi Islam*, p. 122.

In addition to these confessionalist trends, social changes enforced communalism. Economic, administrative and political developments seemed to have been more favourable to Hindu merchants than to the Muslim service gentry so that by the end of the nineteenth century, a Muslim "backwardness" was discernable. Frustration over their relatively deprived status made many Indian Muslims susceptible to increasing communalist propaganda. This was not exclusively or foremost a popular phenomenon; intellectuals did not shy from insulting and humiliating members of other sects and religions and in so doing creating an "indigenous other".

Growing influence and popularity of Shiʿism on the subcontinent in the eighteenth and nineteenth centuries and its increasing visibility provoked harsh reactions from the Sunni revivalist movements. In addition, the spread of Shiʿism in eighteenth century North India coincided with a relative decline of Sunni among the central Asian and Indian propertied classes. While many Shiʿis often allied with the British until the middle of the nineteenth century, Sunnis made them responsible for their loss in social status. Frequent urban disturbances of the late 1820s coincided with an economic downfall in North India.

Shiʿi-Sunni polemics were not only carried out in the contemporary intellectual literature (e.g. in Sunni Quranic exegesis). Ulama of both sects dwelt openly on the superiority of their faith. Sunni revivalism was directed against non-Muslims and the Shiʾi ruling class. Thus the beginning of the twentieth century saw frequent Sunni-Shiʿi clashes—especially in the United Provinces.[15]

Anti-British sentiments among Shiʿi clerics until the middle of the nineteenth century were rare. Shiʿi merchants and moneylenders lent and borrowed on interest and therefore benefited to a certain extent from the EIC. Starting in the 1840s, as government servants in the judiciary, Shiʿi ulama in Awadh came into conflict with British administrators who wished either to annex the state or to rule it by proxy. The annexation in 1855 and the abolition of the Shiʿi judiciary in Awadh

---

[15] See Imtiaz Ahmad: "The Shia-Sunni Dispute in Lucknow, 1905–1980", in: M. Israel / N.K. Wagle (eds.): *Islamic society and Culture: Essays in the Honor of Professor Aziz Ahmad*, Delhi: Manohar 1984, pp. 335–50; Mushirul Hasan: "Sectarianism in Indian Islam: The Shia-Sunni divide in the United Provinces", in: *IESHR* 27/2 (1990), pp. 209–228.

triggered the Shiʿis involvement in the upheaval of 1857, though they later attempted to obscure their participation.[16]

The *khilafat movement* did not attract many Shiʿi ulama in the beginning. But soon rumours of a British bombardment of Iraq's shrine cities led some to join in non-cooperation against the British. Many Shiʿis supported the Indian National Congress, partly because they were reluctant to entrust themselves to a Muslim state in which Shiʿites would constitute a minority. But their opposition to partition grew weaker over time. The founder of Pakistan was a Khoja, Muhammad ʿAli Jinnah.[17] He might have represented the majority of Shiʿi Muslims of the subcontinent when he aimed at creating a secular democratic society embodying the essential principles of Islam but he provoked protests from different sides. In the first decade of Pakistan's existence there was comparative peace between Sunnis and Shiʿis but the differences among them have intensified which is, to some extent, connected to developments in neighbouring countries, but also to the power struggle between different societal forces aggravated by re-migrants from Arab countries.[18]

---

[16] Cole: *Roots of North Indian Shiʿism*, p. 281.

[17] Cf. Ali S. Asani: 'The Khojahs of Indo-Pakistan: the Quest for an Islamic Identity', *Journal of the Institute of Muslim Minority Affairs* 1 (1987), pp. 31–41.

[18] This has been elaborated by S.V.R. Nasr: "The Rise of Sunni Militancy in Pakistan: The Changing Role of Islamism and the Ulama in Society and Politics", in: *MAS* 34 (2000), pp. 139–180; Saleem Qureshi: 'The Politics of the Shia Minority in Pakistan: Context and Development', in: Dhirendra Vajpeyi and Yogendra K. Malik (eds.): *Religious and Ethnic Minority Politics in South Asia*, Delhi: Manohar 1989, pp. 109–138; see also Mariam Abou-Zahab: "The Sunni-Shia conflict in Jhang (Pakistan)", in: Imtiaz Ahmad and Helmut Reifeld (eds.): *Lived Islam in South Asia*.

CHAPTER FOUR

MUSLIM HETEROGENEITY. MARGINS BECOMING CENTRES OF MUSLIM POWER (APPROX. 1300–1500)

In the years 1363–1415, Timur conquered Turkey, Syria and areas in North India. In 1366 he had succeeded in subduing his brothers and declaring himself ruler of the Mongol empire. Samarkand became the capital. By 1370 he was the master of Transoxiana, a largely Muslim and sedentary society. Using the slogan of orthodox Islamisation, he ransacked large parts of North India aiming to establish a vast Mongol-Turkish empire.[1] However, the dismantling of the Delhi Sultanate did not result from this Timurid devastation. Its downfall had much to do with a feeble political centre, which in itself was the acculturative result of successive administrative, economic, ethnic and cultural restructuring. As we have seen in the previous chapter, these acculturative tendencies produced a context in which different traditions interacted and contested over Muslim hegemony, thereby adding to the religious and societal complexity of South Asia. In this emerging and often fluid context, the dialectic between the social location of Muslim identities and its cultural articulation played a crucial role. On a higher plane, it was embedded within the greater dialectics between indigenous and Islamic cosmology. The complex, sacral geography resulting from such an interplay of cosmologies considerably weakened the centre-periphery relations if not altogether dissolving them, leading to different, sometimes also complementary regional entities such as in North Kashmir and Jaunpur, Malwa in the South of Delhi, Gujarat in the West, and Bengal in the East. Beyond Narmada River, the Deccan, Bijapur, and Golconda in Central India, were complemented by Maʿbar and Malabar in the Southern West and East coasts.

[1] For an account of Timur's invasion and conquest see Beatrice Forbes Manz: *The Rise and Rule of Tamerlane*, Cambridge: CUP 1999; *Malfuzat-e Timuri* or *Tuzak-e Timuri*, the memoirs of the Emperor, composed in the Chaghatay Mongol language, translated into Persian by Abu Talib Husaini, and translated into English by Major Charles Stewart: *The Mulfuzat Timury*, Holborn 1830, Lahore: Sang-e-Meel Publications 2000 (reprint), is commonly seen as a forgery of the Mughal period; see C.A. Storey: *Persian Literature: A Bio-bibliographical Survey, 2 vols.*, London 1927–1971, Vol. 1, p. 280.

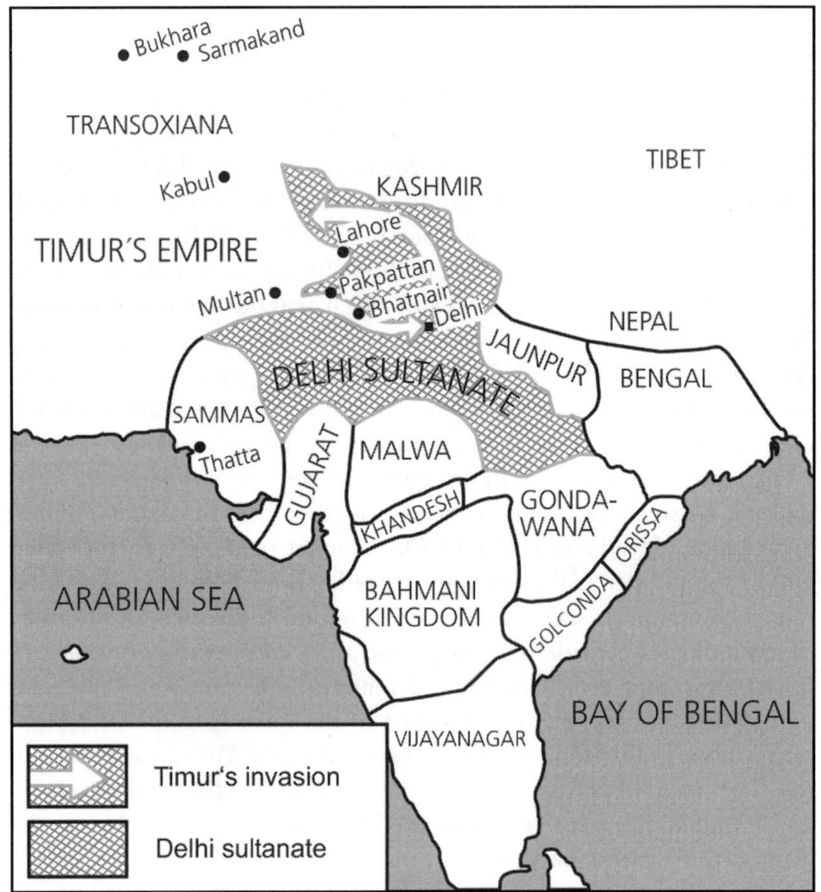

Map 7: South Asia around 1400 C.E.

Muslim power did not dissolve only because the Muslim rulers still needed legitimacy from the Islamic mainland. Thus coins continued to be minted in the name of the last Abbasid caliph even after 1258. Additionally, caliphal recognition was symbolically a challenge to the universal ruling claims of the Mongols. Meanwhile Muslim power had sought and also established some links and roots in South Asia resulting in most dynamic islamicated formations.

Inevitably, centrifugal forces asserted themselves anticipating the ultimate demise of the Delhi Sultanate. The Sultanate passed through the hands of two weak dynasties, the Sayyids (1414–1451) and the Lodhis (1451–1526), whose rule was brief but nevertheless had some political and administrative impact. The ensuing Muslim political heterogeneity and the evolution of several competing centres of Muslim power were shaped among other factors, by the activities of merchants and various Sufi orders. These orders, mainly originating in Central Asia in the twelfth century, swarmed out both westwards and eastwards. Their significant role in Islamic expansion in South Asia cannot be overlooked. The larger orders such as the Chishtis, Firdausis, Suhrawardis, Qadiris, Madaris and Naqshbandis, by utilising local institutions, symbols and languages, provided their members with the appropriate cultural tools with which they could productively engage with al-Hind. They informed the high culture of the elite with the local, regional symbols, thereby making it accessible to the masses within their own subaltern matrix, and at times becoming agents of high culture themselves. Needless to say, these processes of universalisation and parochialisation provided the basis for a variety of exclusive, inclusive and liminal religious identities. Thus acculturation took place as well.

The records left by the Sufi orders, though barely edited, provide detailed information on their early social history. In contrast to court chronicles, the conversation of Sufi masters with their followers and sympathisers inform us much more of the realities of contemporary life. People, cutting across class and religion, interacted with each other within the sacred space of hospices, convents (*khanaqah*) and shrines (*dargah*) and took home the advice of their holy masters. This first expansion of Sufi orders in the twelfth and thirteenth centuries was followed by a second one in the fifteenth century, so that the *A'in-e Akbari*, a major handbook on the Mughal Empire written by Abu al-Fadl (1551–1602), could boast a list of 14 major orders and many other individual Sufis who subsequently established sub-orders. The break up of the once centralised Delhi Sultanate into many independent power centres was accompanied by a shift in the power of the Sufi orders as well. As noted previously, the extinguishing of the Caliphate meant a crisis of legitimacy in the Muslim world. In South Asia some new means of legitimacy were provided with the coming of orders such as the Qadiriyya and the Central Asian Naqshbandiyya, both being quite urbane and elitist in their approach, and outwardly oriented. Thus, Sufi diversification was an important vehicle for disseminating Islamic thought and power throughout South Asia. However, this should not blind us to the fact that Muslim establishment, epitomised by the worldly king, could never succumb completely to the Islamising zeal of some Sufi orders and the ulama. Let us briefly look at the processes and levels of heterogeneity in which Muslim margins became centres of regional power after the Delhi Sultanate, from the North to the East to the South, on the eve of Mughal conquest.

Delhi after Sultanate

The fall of Baghdad in 1258 drove the Sultans to Cairo to receive legitimacy of their power. After the Timurid invasion and consequent regionalisation of Muslim power, the investiture from Cairo was sought after by various regional Muslim powers, thus creating a plethora of caliphally legitimised Muslim rulers in South Asia. This changed in 1414, when, Sayyid Khizr Khan (ruled 1414–1421) ordered the *khutba* to be read in the name of one of Timur's sons, Shahrukh (1377–1447), ruler of Herat. Khizr Khan's reign thus paved the way to the Afghans. Followed by Khizr Khan's son Mubarak Shah (1421–1434), this Sayyid dynasty came to an end after 37 years only, with ʿAla al-Din ʿAlam Shah having the dubious distinction of being the last of the Sayyids. In fact, the authority of this Sayyid did not even extend beyond Delhi and its surroundings, notwithstanding the support from Hindus as well as the Jains.[2] An important but perhaps unintended consequence of this loss of central authority was the growth of several independent centres of Islamic learning and culture under the patronage of local rulers. It was

[2] In fact, there are several Sanskrit inscriptions appreciating the rulers of the Delhi Sultanate, thus displaying not only the degree of patronage but also of a considerable "linkage and interaction between cultural elements, the diversity of which constituted the social and ideological situation of the period." See Chattopadhyaya: *Representing the Other?*, pp. 60, 65f., quotation p. 67.

in this context, that the Afghans, who had been migrating to northern India in search of employment for quite some time, became major contenders for political power since they had been major *iqta'dars* for some centuries wielding considerable power.

Lodhis, a clan of the Ghilzai tribe, who had become powerful in the days of Firoz Shah Tughluq (1351–1388) around the *iqta'* of Multan, became the first Afghan dynasty to rule Delhi. They legitimised their rule by tracing their lineage to Qais, alias 'Abd al-Rashid, a companion of Prophet Muhammad. It was the pious Bahlul (reigned 1451–1489), the first Lodhi Sultan, who set up an Afghan oligarchic rule in Delhi but could not really integrate the decentralised powers of the *iqta'dars*. Succeeded by his son, Sikandar Shah Lodhi (reigned 1489–1517), after the internecine struggles, Agra became the new capital in 1505. Still considering himself Sultan, he enlarged his territory by means of military action and a rigid implementation of Islamic policy targeted at the Shi'ites and eradicating Muslim folk-religious rites deemed as Hindu accretions. At the same time he was pragmatic enough to encourage Hindus to learn Persian in order to benefit from their administrative expertise. In a Hindu epigraphic account he is considered a just ruler.[3] Mysticism, particularly the Qadiriyya became so popular that Sikandar Lodhi became a disciple of Sayyid Muhammad Ghawth, a Qadiri sufi, who had settled in Uchh. While Sufi texts, such as Ibn 'Arabi's writings were read in many madrasas and khanaqahs, pilgrimage to the tombs of saints was prohibited.

Sikandar's son Ibrahim (ruled 1517–1526) tried to promote his own group at the expense of the old Afghan oligarchy. This policy met with severe resistance resulting in secession.[4] The governor of Punjab, Dawlat Khan Lodhi, peeved at being sidelined by Ibrahim Lodhi, invited Babur, the founder of the Mughal dynasty, to embark on his penultimate invasion of India in 1524.

We have previously seen that the Delhi Sultanate had become the refuge of numerous scholars, particularly from Khorasan, fleeing from the Mongol depredations (Chingis Khan, died 1227).[5] This *brain drain* was already severe during 'Ala al-Din Khalaji's rule (1296–1316) when Delhi boasted more than 50 leading scholars from Iran and Iraq. They

[3] See Chattopadhyaya: *Representing the Other?*, pp. 52f.

[4] For the Lodhis see J. Burton-Page: "Lôdîs", in: EI(2), V, pp. 782ff.

[5] For Chingiz Khan see J.A. Boyle: "Cingiz-Khân", in: EI(2), II, pp. 41ff.

transmitted the Persian culture of Baghdad which was reflected in the books they taught[6] as well as in the courtly rituals at Agra, the new capital of the Lodhis. Agra became a centre of Muslim learning at a time when the transmitted sciences (*manqulat*) were gradually being outnumbered by the rational sciences (*ma'qulat*).

Kashmir

Turning to the North, up until the eleventh century the picturesque valley of Kashmir was ruled by Hindu pandits, who had employed a large number of Turkish adventurers in their army. The Mongols destroyed this arrangement in 1320 and paved the way to an Islamic Sultanate to fill the vacuum. The first Sultan of Kashmir was a Hindu convert to Islam. Following a palace revolt, he was succeeded by Shah Mir from Swat. Shah Mir was an employee of the local Hindu ruler, but gradually became so powerful that in 1339, he ascended the throne as Sultan Shams al-Din, thus laying the foundation of his dynasty which was to rule Kashmir till 1561. His grandson Shihab al-Din (1354–1374) islamicated the administration with the help of the Kubrawiyya-Dhahabiyya which had been handed down by Sayyid 'Ali Hamadani (died 1385) arriving from Transoxiana in 1371. His *Zakhirat al-Muluk* (*The Treasuries of Kings*) elaborates the principles of the form and substance of power and governance, qualities, origins and obligations of rulers and the people, all discussed with reference to the shari'a.[7] Moreover, Kubrawis displayed their exclusivistic power by building Hamadani's shrine on the pillars of the biggest Hindu temple in Srinagar. In contrast to this, the indigenous Kashmiri Sufi order established by Nur al-Din (died 1438), is said to have actively pursued a policy of harmonious integration of different religious traditions. The Rishis, as they called themselves with reference to the Hindu term for ascetics, championed the cause of the poor and marginalised, in a form that was understandable and familiar to the poor and communicated in the language of the people. Yet, Nur al-Din converted quite a number of Brahmans. Thus the Rishis made Islam the focus of social identity among commoners,

---

[6] See I.H. Siddiqui: "Social Mobility in the Delhi Sultanate", in: I. Habib (ed.): *Medieval India 1*, Delhi: OUP 1992, pp. 22–48, here pp. 34f.

[7] Cf. Alam: *Languages*, pp. 43–46; I. Khan: *Kashmir's Transition to Islam—The Role of Muslim Rishis*, New Delhi 1994, pp. 4–35, 221–240.

and for centuries mystical poetry such as Nur al-Din's is said to have dominated the world views of Kashmiris, leading later generations to consider the *Kashmiriyyat* to be their self-understanding which integrated the local and the global.[8]

Religious centralisation was accomplished by Shihab al-Din's grandson Iskandar (1389–1413) who introduced the office of Shaikh al-Islam and enforced some shariʿa rules. However, his son Zain al-ʿAbidin (1420–1470) during his long reign consciously adopted a policy of religious tolerance, even abolishing *jizya*. He ameliorated the economic condition of his people by providing jobs, thereby not only benefiting from their expertise but also integrating them into the body-politic. The Shah Mir dynasty continued till 1561, but witnessed numerous ups and downs between different social groups led by Sufis. The Shiʿite Nurbakhshi order, founded by Shams al-Din Iraqi (1392–1464), had reached Kashmir in 1498, and was contesting the position of the well-entrenched Hanafi Sayyids. This tussle had a direct impact on the throne since the Nurbakhshiyya as well as the ulama had both become king-makers. When a cousin of Babur invaded Kashmir and seized power in 1540, Shiʿism and Sufi orders both were banned. However, in trying to enforce Hanafi law, Babur's commanders faced serious opposition from the nobles. Eventually a converted Shiʿite family seized power and ruled until 1589 when Akbar annexed Kashmir.[9] The incorporation of the Kashmir Valley into Mughal India did not, however, diminish Kashmiri independence and *Kashmiriyyat*. It seems "that it was precisely in the Mughal period that Kashmiri poets first began to self-consciously articulate a sense of regional belonging"[10] ushering in an era of cultural regeneration.

Jaunpur

Jaunpur, a famous centre of Muslim culture to the South-East of Kashmir, was founded in 1359 by Firoz Shah Tughluq to keep the Hindu

---

[8] See Khan: *Kashmir's Transition to Islam*. For a more critical and deconstructivist approach to *Kashmiriyyat* see Chitralekha Zutshi: *Languages of Belonging: Islam, Regional Identity, and the Making of Kashmir*, New York: OUP 2004.

[9] Schimmel: *Islam in the Indian Subcontinent*, pp. 44f; Mohibbul Hasan: "Kashmîr", in: EI(2), IV, pp. 706f.

[10] See Zutshi: *Languages of Belonging*, p. 29.

population under control. But the disaffected Hindus of the Eastern provinces always resisted his rule. Shortly before Timur's invasion (1398), Malik Sarwar, a former master of Firoz Shah's elephant stable and Grand Eunuch had successfully crushed the rebellion in 1394. Subsequently, Sultan Muhammad Shah entrusted him with the authority over eastern districts and also conferred on him the title of *Malik al-Sharqi* (Lord of the East). Thus Malik Sarwar became the founder of the Sharqi dynasty. The Sharqi kingdom led by Ibrahim Shah (Sharqi) (died 1440) developed into an important cultural and political area and Jaunpur became a centre of scholarship, soon to be called *Shiraz-e Hind*. In the wake of Timur's invasion many Muslim scholars found their way to the South, among them the great Shihab al-Din Daulatabadi (died 1445), the chief qadi, whose books became standard works of instruction in various madrasas. A grammarian and scholastic theologian, who wrote primarily in Arabic, he was also khalifa to Chiragh-e Dehli who, in turn, had been busy disseminating his ideas and extending his *wilayat* in the South. Whether it was under Daulatabadi's supervision that the voluminous Arabic work representing Hanafite school of law, the *Fatawa Ibrahimshahi* was compiled, is however, open to question.[11] Many more Sufis were to come to Jaunpur, among them the famous Chishti Ashraf Jahangir Simnani (died 1427), the spiritual leader of the political master Ibrahim Sharqi and a committed adherent of the Andalusian mystic Ibn Arabi's (1165–1240) idea of *Wahdat al-wujud*. Another important personality was the Sabiri-Chishti Ahmad ʿAbd al-Haqq from Rudauli (died 1434). A famous disciple of Rudaulwi's spiritual lineage was ʿAbd al-Quddus (born 1456), who left this area in 1491 for Gangoh in the Delhi kingdom, where he died in 1538.[12] ʿAbd al-Quddus Gangohi, a profound wujudi and Chishti-Sabiri, is known for his petitions seeking patronage of Muslim religious elite in the first place, as well as for his knowledge of how an Islamic government was to be run. Although he had studied local Hindu customs and was at times sympathetic to them, he nevertheless wanted *jizya* to be enforced on non-Muslims. In advising the Mughal emperor Babur to adhere to

[11] Compare Islam: "Origin and Development of *Fatâwâ*-Compilation", pp. 7–18, here p. 9.

[12] For Gangohi see Simon Digby: "Abd al-Haqq Gangohî (1456–1537 A.D.): The Personality and Attitudes of a Medieval Indian Sufi", in: *Medieval India—a Miscellany*, Vol. 3, 1975; Iqtidar Alam Khan: "Shaikh Abd-ul-Quddus Gangohi's Relations with Political Authorities: A Reappraisal", in: *Medieval India: A Miscellany*, IV, Delhi 1977, pp. 73–93; David W. Damrel: "The 'Naqshbandî Reaction' Reconsidered", in: Gilmartin and Lawrence (eds.): *Beyond Turk and Hindu*, pp. 176–198.

the shariʿa, the Chishti Sufi recognised the Mughals as the new political power. The Chishtiyya-Sabiriyya strongly favoured Ibn ʿArabi's monism and was thus more reconciliatory. It remained influential until the late nineteenth century and twentieth century, Warith Shah of Dewa Sharif (died 1903) being one of them. Many of the founding members of the famous seminar of Deoband, which was established in 1867 (see Chap. 10), were affiliated with this order. Whether ʿAbd al-Quddus contested the growing power of the Naqshbandiyya whose influence was profound on the early Mughals, is open to question.

In the fifteenth century, Jaunpur was to witness another dimension of Islam in the shape of a millenarian movement. Sayyid Muhammad Kazimi (born 1443), a Chishti Sufi from North India, on a pilgrimage to Mecca in 1495, declared himself Mahdi. This declaration offended the religious establishment and he was forced to leave the country. He died at Khurasan in 1505.[13] In the meantime, Jaunpur was absorbed into the Delhi Sultanate (1489).[14] Using *daʾira* as centres of dissemination, Kazimi's group was quite active in bringing his ideas to the hinterland. These ideas and infrastructure provided the basis for the Mahdawiyya, a sixteenth century millenarian movement, which spread as far as Sind and Gujarat. However, the movement polarised society between those having Mahdawi inclinations such as the Deccani nobles of Ahmadnagar and Golconda, and those persecuting them, such as the Afghan chieftains led by Sher Khan alias Sher Shah Suri (reg. 1538–1545).

Gujarat

The inhabitants of Gujarat (North of the Deccan, South of the Delhi Sultanate and West of Malwa), Hindus, Jains and Zoroastrians were well acquainted with Arab Muslim traders. The sea route between Basra and Gujarat had also been used by the mystic al-Hallaj when he embarked on his journey through India in 905. Such trade contacts may have led many Shafiʿite Arabs of the Red Sea area to settle in coastal Gujarat creating a predominantly Shafiʿite community. Soon, Ismaili missionaries from Yemen were dispatched to found a new

---

13 Schimmel: *Islam in the Indian Subcontinent*, p. 42.

14 After several battles with local potentates the city became the focus of governorship, but in 18th century its reputation faded away. J. Burton-Page: "Djawnpur", in: EI(2), II, pp. 498f.

Ismaili community in Gujarat. During the reign of Khalaji ʿAla al-Din Muhammad Shah (1296–1316) Gujarat was annexed, but it did maintain its independence. Later, Muhammad Tughluq conquered and installed Muzaffar Khan as governor of the province, who, however, declared himself to be the independent ruler of Gujarat in 1407. He also received an investiture from the caliph in Cairo in 1411. Muzaffar Khan's son Ahmad Shah did much to consolidate the fledgling state through his relentless iconoclastic policies and oppression of the Hindus (*jizya*), most probably enforced on the advice of Suhrawardi shaikhs such as the influential Burhan al-Din Qutb-e ʿAlam (died 1452).[15] This official 'Islamising' zeal contrasted with Islamicated Ahmadabad, the new residence of Ahmad Shah founded in 1411, which was to become a microcosm of what has been termed as "the 'Indian' interpretation of sacred space."[16] Its uninhibited architectural syncretism is most visible in Gujarati architecture and its trabeate style most obviously in the adoption of indigenous post-and-beam constructions also in religious buildings, such as mosques, tombs and shrines. The mechanisms of assimilation and refraction can be seen in the integration of Hindu and Jain forms in the richly carved pillars derived from local temple architecture which were made by local craftsmen.[17] Similarly, in the context of temple rituals, which are effective as receptacles of memory for the identity of religious communities, Hindu and Arabic terms were juxtaposed and mosques represented as dharmasthana displaying divinity as a locally comprehensible concept, although there were sectarian and theological conflicts as well.[18]

Notwithstanding this aesthetic, functional and ideological overlapping reflected in building activities involving a variety of socio-administrative actions, Ahmad Shah's successor Mahmud Shah (reigned 1458–1511) became known for his policy of internal security particularly in urban centres including ports. He actively encouraged the settlement of Sayyids and other members of the ashraf, while intermarriage was promoted which resulted in Hindu (Rajput) families losing their caste status. That Muslims of Gujarat share many Hindu rituals and also display a high rigidity in terms of caste practices seems to have its

---

[15] For him see Ziyaud-Din A. Desai: *Malfuz Literature: As a source of Political, Social, and Cultural History of Gujarat and Rajasthan*, Patna, 1991.

[16] Schimmel: *Islam in the Indian Subcontinent*, p. 67.

[17] Cf. G. Michell and S. Shah (eds.): *Ahmadabad*, Bombay 1988.

[18] See Chattopadhyaya: *Representing the Other?*, pp. 71–78.

roots in this policy of cultural assimilation. This particular autochthonous Islamisation continued to be sanctioned by Mahmud Shah's son Muzaffar (1511–1526) who was the last to receive an investiture from the caliph in Cairo.[19] His successor, Sultan Bahadur Shah (reigned 1526–1537) tried to strengthen his territory through centralisation. Nevertheless, the kingdom disintegrated in the following decades with the nobles partitioning it among themselves. The subsequent period of Gujarat's history is a dreary chronicle of civil war,[20] until 1575 and again in 1584 when Bairam Khan's son ʿAbd al-Rahim (1556–1627), tutor of Akbar's son Salim and a splendid military leader, made it a part of Mughal Empire.

Despite its political instability, Gujarat attracted a number of scholars, Sufis and poets, and Arab migrants who had become high ranking service families such as the *Nawaʾit*, elite Shafiʿi Muslims, reputed to be of Hashimite descent, who had been driven out of Iraq by al-Hajjaj. Among these Nawaʾit the famous ʿAla al-Din Mahaʾimi (died 1431) is credited with the first Arabic Quranic commentary in India called *Tabsir al-Rahman*, informed by the notion of Ibn ʿArabi's "Unity of being".[21] The Shafiʿite and Arab affiliated coastal region also attracted members of learned and trading families from Hadhramaut, among them the ʿAidarus family, who were important in disseminating Islamic knowledge and cementing the old ties of India and Arabia.[22] Another important personality was added when Sultan Bahadur Shah (died 1537) invited the Qadiri Shaikh Sayyid Jamal (died 1564) and set up a centre for him.[23] Later, the Qadiris connected Gujarat and Lucknow in the person of ʿAbd al-Samad Khudanuma (died 1697), the murshid of the Shaikh of the eighteenth century leading scholarly family of Lucknow, the Farangi Mahallis.[24] These scholarly traditions and networks were complemented by popular devotional literature as reflected in the poetry of Urdu's first great poet Khub Muhammad Chishti (died 1614),

---

[19] Schimmel: *Islam in the Indian Subcontinent*, 68f.

[20] J. Burton-Page: "Gudjarât", in: EI(2), II: pp. 1123ff.

[21] Schimmel: *Islam in the Indian Subcontinent*, p. 67; S. ʿAbd al-Hayy: *Nuzhat al-khawâtir wa bahjat al-masâmiʿ wa al-Nawâzir, I–VIII*, Haydarabad, 1956ff., vol. III, pp. 80f.

[22] See O. Lijfgren: "ʿAidarus", in: EI(2), I: p. 782. See now also the stimulating study by Engseng Ho: *The Graves of Tarim. Genealogy and Mobility across the Indian Ocean*, University of California Press 2006.

[23] Rizvi: *A History of Sufism in India*, II, p. 72.

[24] Cf. Rizvi: *A History of Sufism*, II, p. 73; for the Farangi Mahallis see below; also compare Malik: *Gelehrtenkultur*, pp. 140f.

or developed by immigrant Shattari Sufis, such as Shaikh Muhammad Ghawth Gwaliori (died 1563), both of whom described Sufi beliefs and practices, also supported by hadiths. Gwaliori's khalifa Muhammad ibn Fadl Allah Burhanpuri (died after 1620) in his *Gift addressed to the Prophet* (*al-Tuhfa al-mursala ila ruh al-nabi*) (1620) outlined main points of Ibn ʿArabi's "Unity of Being" and became instrumental in spreading mystical Islam to South East Asia.[25]

Malwa

Situated at the quadrangle of North India, the Deccan, the Western provinces and seaports of Gujarat, Malwa had great strategic and commercial importance. It attracted the attention of the Delhi Sultans who made it their province for nearly a century (1305–1402). Dilawar Khan, a descendant of the Ghorid Muʿizz al-Din, became governor in 1392. But it was his son Hushang (died 1435), who declared independence in 1406, after having poisoned his father and making Mandu his capital, embellishing it with magnificent buildings. He attempted to consolidate his empire by expanding trade related activities. For this purpose, he invited the powerful Jain businessmen to build up a home market. They subsequently, enjoyed royal patronage. In order to consolidate his military, he befriended the Rajputs. By all accounts, he sought to extend his territory whenever possible coupled with an internal policy of tolerance and cooperation towards the Hindu subjects, which however, did not prevent him from issuing coins in his own name.

Mahmud Khalaji I (1436–1469) tried to extend the borders of Malwa to areas such as Jaunpur, Gujarat and Deccan. His home politics were largely based on Jain economic and religious activities, which combined trade and pilgrimage patronised by the Sultan. At that time Jain merchants were closely associated with the administration and became instrumental in implementing a policy of perfect tolerance. To add to a peaceful situation, the interests of the peasantry were protected by improving agricultural concerns helping trade and industry to flourish, the opening up of a vast infrastructure of public institutions, such as hospitals, dispensaries, schools and colleges were to extend this policy

---

[25] Cf. Rizvi: *A History of Sufism*, II, pp. 284–286; Schimmel: *Islam in the Indian Subcontinent*, pp. 69f.

in the region.[26] Though Mahmud Khalaji I destroyed Hindu temples to finance his military campaigns, his religious policies sometimes gave his way to a *realpolitik*, such as in his alliance with a Hindu (*kafir*) against the Muslim Muhammad Shah of Gujarat. These alliances were sanctioned by the ulama. Sufis, notably of the Shattari order, led by ʿAbd Allah Shattari (died 1428),[27] also seemed to have played some role in this process of expansion.

While the reign of Mahmud's successor was peaceful, subsequent wars with neighbouring regions weakened the province. In the end, Malwa was reduced to a province of Gujarat. In 1535 the Mughal emperor Humayun attacked the area but it took many more years until Akbar could subdue the region in 1570. Under Mughal rule Malwa became one of the best revenue-yielding provinces of the empire. In the eighteenth century it came under the control of the Marathas.[28]

Bengal

Further to the East, since the beginning of the thirteenth century, Bengal had been invaded by the Persianised Turkish Muslims, first by Muhammad Bakhtiyar Khalaji (1201), shortly followed by Iltutmish (1230). Lakhnauti became the seat of government. Immigrant Sufis, such as Suhrawardi Jalal Tabriz (died 1244), were as important as Abu Tawʾama from Bukhara (died 1300) who had arrived in Delhi around 1260, drawing the attention of the people through his knowledge and spiritual power. In 1278 Abu Tawʾama acceeded Giyath al-Din Balaban's (1265–87), the Sultan of Delhi, request to leave the city for Sonargoan where he set up his khanaqah. He was interested not just in preaching Islam, but also in disseminating knowledge. For this reason he established a madrasa (the first of its kind in Bengal), which attracted students from home and abroad. Abu Tawʾama's disciple Sharaf al-Din Yahya Maneri (died 1381) who was born in Bengal and founded the Firdausi order of Bihar, became particularly famous for his "Hundred

[26] Cf. Upendra Nath Day: *Medieval Malwa. A Political and Cultural History, 1401–1562*, Delhi: Munshiram Manoharlal 1965.

[27] On ʿAbd Allah Shattari see J.S. Trimingham: *The Sufi Orders in Islam*, Oxford: OUP 1971, pp. 64, 97f. See Carl W. Ernst: "Persecution and Circumspection in Shattari Sufism", in: Fred De Jong and Berndt Radtke (eds.): *Islamic Mysticism Contested: Thirteen Centuries of Debate and Conflict*, Leiden: Brill 1999.

[28] T.W. Haig and Riazul Islam: "Mâlwâ", in: EI(2), VI: pp. 309f.

Letters" (*maktubat-e sadi*), one of the few works by an Indian Sufi that were included in the syllabus of Mughal madrasas. The letters were written in 1346/47 at the request of Qadi Shams al-Din, the governor of Chausa in western Bihar, to provide him with spiritual instruction. Therein Maneri's perception of Sufism is one of perpetual transformation of the self, a dynamic process of becoming, keeping the lover or searcher (*salik*) constantly searching for the beloved.[29] Similarly, the Chishti Nizam al-Din Awliya (1323) had encouraged settlements in Bengal. Thus, it was the shaikhs of the Chishti order who became the principal spokesmen for a Muslim perspective, such as Nur Qutb-e ʿAlam (died 1459), who had some influence on the Sultans even after his death. On the other hand, Suhrawardi Shaikhs, such as ʿAla al-Haqq and Shaikh Qutb-e ʿAlam (1388–1453) established a whole network of khanaqahs throughout Bengal.[30] Notwithstanding these accommodations, the mystical cosmos had its limits, be it in terms of defending the *wilayat* or contesting the court or seeking patronage.

Bengal became independent from the Delhi Sultanate under Shams al-Din Ilyas Shah (ruled 1342–1357) during Firoz Shah Tughluq's rule (1351–88). In 1352, he united the kingdoms of eastern and western Bengal for which he was called *Shah-e Bangala* by Shams-e Siraj ʿAfif in *Tarikh-e Firozshahi*.[31] The secession from Delhi saw an ideological alignment with West Asia, both Arab and Persian, but a political rooting in Bengal. This independence of a Bengal Sultanate found evidence among others in architectural grandeur, such as the largest mosque ever built on the Subcontinent, the Adina mosque in the capital of Pandua. The contradiction between ideology and politics however, resulted in tensions between the majority Hindu Bengali society composed of local peasantry, landholding elites and artisans, and the foreign Indo-Turkish (Muslim) ruling class, who stood for a purified, de-banglacised Islam. These tensions eventually resulted in a de facto Hindu political power

[29] See Paul Jackson (transl.): *Letters from Maneri; Sufi Saint of Medieval India*, New Delhi: Horizon India Books 1990. Riazul Islam: *Sufism in South Asia. Impact on Fourteenth Century Muslim Society*, New Delhi: OUP 2003, p. 450, writes that "Sharaf ud-din Maneri represented a reasonable blend of the two approaches. In practice the Maneri saint followed the example of the Chishtis in staying away from the courts, but he adopted a *via media* where the interests of the people or of deserving individuals were involved".

[30] Schimmel: *Islam in the Indian Subcontinent*, pp. 47f.; Richard M. Eaton: *The Rise of Islam and the Bengal Frontier, 1204–1760*, Berkeley: Univ. of California Press 1993, pp. 89f.

[31] A.H. Dani: "Bangâla", in: EI(2), I, p. 1014.

for some time, after Raja Ganesh rose to power. They were settled by Ganesh's son, who converted to Islam as Jalal al-Din, who ascended the throne in 1415 and ruled until 1431. By printing *khalifat Allah* on the coinage, he displayed his independence from Delhi and the Muslim mainland, but established ties with Mamluk Egypt. He also used Islamic rhetoric to unite the people against the threat of the Sharqi dynasty, though the religious elite were against this "infidel". Yet at the same time he supported local Bengali culture at the highest echelons of the administration, which found expression among others in Bengali-style mosques. Meanwhile, military slaves from Abyssinia were employed, whose influence steadily grew, leading to several palace revolts. Eventually, ʿAla al-Din Husain, an Arab from Mecca, who had risen to a high post, was able to become ruler in 1493. He and his son Nasir al-Din Nusrat Shah (1519–1532) are said to have brought peace and prosperity to the country, not the least by accommodating local society and culture.[32] The independent fate of Bengal was sealed when it was annexed by Sher Shah Suri and added to his Indian Empire. The region remained unstable until it became *suba Bangala* of the Mughal Empire in 1595.[33]

As an effort to legitimise Muslim rule in the eyes of the local population indigenous elements were combined with foreign Muslim symbols, such as the Bengal(i) coinage and the mosques from the fifteenth century onwards. Both, mosques and coins clearly displayed indigenous motifs which drew a connection to the Hindu heritage and elements of local culture. Later, the pragmatic Mughals were quick to follow, integrating the local symbols, both on the level of personnel as well as bringing cultural aspects into the administration. Thus the Mughals showed no interest in proselytising on behalf of Islamic faith. As elaborated by Richard Eaton, the consolidation of Mughal power coincided with an agricultural and manufacturing boom as well as the growth of overland and maritime trade. This boom was the result of the eastward movement of the rivers changing the area of cultivation, Bengal's politico-commercial integration with Mughal India and the increase in money supply due to the influx of silver meant to pay for locally manufactured textiles.[34] Indeed, Bengal was not alone; South Asia as a whole was

---

[32] Eaton: *The Rise of Islam and the Bengal Frontier*, pp. 40–69.
[33] Schimmel: *Islam in the Indian Subcontinent*, pp. 47–50.
[34] Eaton: *The Rise of Islam and the Bengal Frontier*, pp. 134, 202.

witnessing an economic boom at the time. The annexation of Bengal was basically informed by the search for new areas of cultivation and the revenue income attached to them. The political aim of the conquest was to create loyal clients at every level of administration, despite the conservative ulama's insistence that the emperors' "duty" was to convert the Hindu "infidels" to Islam.

Incorporation of Bengal into the Mughal Empire also led to an influx of a great number of Shiʿite traders who settled near the ports. Similarly, many soldiers and scholars of Persian descent settled in Bengal, though they could not threaten to dislodge the Arab Sayyids from their important positions. The region of Assam, which harboured rivals of the Bengal Sultans, had an active Sufi presence responsible for Islamicate practices amongst the local population. As a result, Assamese Islam became a mixture of local customs coexisting with Islamic faith. It was precisely this shared tradition, which would be challenged by revivalist movements of the eighteenth century such as the Faraidiyya (see Chap. 8).[35] It was due to this inclusive and flexible syncretism that the cultivating classes hardly regarded Islam as 'foreign', although this was not the opinion of some Muslim and Hindu literati.[36] This is certainly true for other regions as well and underlines the flexibility of Muslims in encountering other religious and cultural traditions. The developments in the Deccan were quite similar.

South to Narmada: The Deccan

Deccan was annexed to Delhi in 1318 after being subjugated by ʿAla al-Din Khalaji in 1294. Though considered a political disaster, the ill starred Muhammad Tughluq's change of the capital to Daulatabad in the South (1337) proved to be the most important vehicle by which North Indian Muslim ideas and institutions crossed the river Narmada. The status of being a tributary to the Sultanate was deeply resented by the local Muslims, culminating in the revolt by Deccani nobles led by ʿAla al-Din Hasan Bahman Shah (died 1358) in 1347, eventually establishing an independent kingdom called the Bahmani kingdom (1347). The Bahmanis, who were successful break-away officials of

[35] Cf. Schimmel: *Islam in the Indian Subcontinent*, pp. 49f.
[36] Eaton: *The Rise of Islam and the Bengal Frontier*, pp. 86–94, 310.

the Delhi Sultan, replicated the same Persian traditions. Their central government was divided into three main departments dealing with civil, military and judicial matters respectively.[37] This division of labour did not prove a hindrance in their constant endeavour to become the paramount power in Deccan, which involved them in costly protracted wars with the neighbouring kingdoms.

As in many cases, the master narrative tells us that Muslim leaders were blessed by holy men and sanctified in the name of Islam, in return for which Sufis and orthodox religious scholars were given material benefits, as exemplified by Persian poet ʿIsami who rose to fame after his *Futuh al-Salatin*. Scholars from Iran flocked to the new capital Gulbarga. The reign of Muhammad Shah I, despite the threat of neighbouring Vijayanagara,[38] witnessed a cultural blossoming, mainly through contacts with Iranians and Arabs. Arabic became quite popular in the Deccan, giving South Indian Muslim culture a specific blend, and was deliberately promoted by Sultan Firoz Shah (reigned 1397–1422), who had built for himself the palace city of Firozabad.[39] The shifting of capital to Bidar by Ahmad Shah Bahmani (1422–1436) not only underlined the need for massive fortifications against a Hindu environment. At the same time it monumentalised the Persian influence in its architecture. Again, Sufis were prominent in daily and court life, such as the Chishti Muhammad Gesudaraz (died 1422). Along with the Sunnis, the Shiʿites too had quite an impact. This as well can be gleaned from the reams of material left by the Niʿmat Allahi Sufis who settled there at the request of Sultan Ahmad Shah following the death of Gesudaraz.[40] A large influx of migrants from West Asia divided the Muslim population into contending groups such as the *dakhanis* and *afaqis* or *mulkis* and *ghair mulkis*.[41] The *dakhanis* were older settlers, mostly Sunni immigrants from North India but also mamluk Habashis of Abyssinia (later called

---

[37] H.K. Sherwani: "Bahmanîs", in: EI(2), I, pp. 923f.

[38] The emergence of Vijayanagar itself was the result of collusion with Muslim powers, often changing sides in the numerous battles which took place. Influences were expressed in terms of military and fiscal organisation, architecture and also in titulature. Thus the kingdom used Muslims in the army, at one instance having the commander-in-chief as a Muslim. See Burton Stein: *Vijayanagar*, Cambridge 1989; Wagoner: "Sultan among Hindu Kings", pp. 851–880.

[39] See George Michell and Richard Eaton: *Firuzabad: Palace City of the Deccan*, Oxford: OUP 1992.

[40] Schimmel: *Islam in the Indian Subcontinent*, pp. 51–54.

[41] Compare André Wink: "Islamic society and culture in the Deccan", in: Anna Libera Dallapiccola and Stephanie Zingel-Avé Lellemant (eds.): *Islam and Indian Regions*,

Sidis), who looked after the Deccani armies. These more or less Sunnite groups were sympathetic to Gesudaraz. In contrast, the *afaqis* or the new settlers or foreigners (*gharib al-diyar*), were mostly Shiʿites and Niʿmat Allahis from Iraq, Iran and Transoxiana. They gradually outnumbered the Deccani Muslims and Hindus, particularly Marathas for positions of major importance. They enjoyed greater patronage from the state because as recent immigrants, they had not developed roots and were thus considered more loyal than older Deccanis who could rebel by utilising their deep rooted and traditional networks.

The tussle between *afaqi* Shiʿites and *dakhani* Sunnis became quite massive, leading in 1450/51 to a massacre of immigrant Sayyids (Shiite) by indigenous nobles, harking back to the intermezzo of Muhammad Tughluq in Daulatabad. These tensions were the reflection of underlying socio-economic issues which were resolved by a former horse trader who rose to the wazirate, the Niʿmat Allahi Sufi Mahmud Gawan (died 1481). As supervisor of trade (*malik al-tujjar*) he centralised the administration, thereby streamlining the assessment of revenue and curbing the power of fiefdoms and local magnates.[42] In the following years, Yusuf ʿAdil Shah (ruled 1489–1510) established the Adilshahi dynasty of Bijapur in 1489 (1490–1686), which was to become the first Shiʿite state in al-Hind in 1503. To guard his independence from the Mughals and neighbouring states, Yusuf turned to Safawid Persia rather than to Ottoman Turkey. Despite attempted centralisation of administration and land revenue, governors of Bahmani provinces claimed autonomy consequently becoming independent which led to the fragmentation of Bahmani kingdom into several dynasties.[43] Ahmadnagar became a Shiʿite centre of the Nizam Shahis who ruled from 1490 to 1633, with a brief interlude of the Mahdawiyya occupying the throne between 1589 and 1591. The two largest kingdoms that emerged on the ruins of the Bahmani kingdom were Bijapur and Golconda. The provinces of Berar and Bidar were annexed by Ahmadnagar in 1574, which in turn was annexed in 1633 by the Mughal ruler Shah Jahan.

Wiesbaden 1993, pp. 217–227; Karen Leonard: "Hyderabad: The Mulki-Non-Mulki Conflict", in: V.K. Bawa: *The Last Nizam*, New Delhi 1992, pp. 54–62.

[42] H.K. Sherwani: "Bahmanîs", in: EI(2), I, pp. 923f.; H.K. Sherwani: "Mahmûd Gâwân", in: EI(2), VI, pp. 66ff.

[43] H.K. Sherwani: "Dakhan", in: EI(2), II, pp. 99f.

Bijapur

In Bijapur the Sunni—Shiʿite divide had devastating consequences for the kingdom. Various societal fissures which otherwise had profane reasons became camouflaged through this sectarian divide. It was only the external pressure of Vijayanagara which brought short term solidarity among Muslims in 1565. Again, Sufis, particularly the Chishtis had been active in the region since thirteenth century. Richard Eaton has argued that they became increasingly Deccanis, the so-called "rustic literati" thus enculturating themselves with the lower classes. Still others, such as the Chishti "literati Sufis" wrote mystic literature as well as popular lore. The language used for this purpose was suited to the clientele that it sought to address. Thus Persian, the language of the scholars and administrative class, was used as mystical literature while popular lore was usually composed in a vernacular so as to make it intelligible to the local population regardless of their class or educational level.[44] Even the female voice in Sufi ritual played an extremely important role in the dissemination of mystical ideas, when, in gendered opposition to *rekhta*, i.e., *rekhti*, there developed a subgenre of Urdu ghazal in which both the narrator and the narrative idiom is female.[45] Twelver Shia was the state religion for the better part of sixteenth century. However, the Safawid hostility towards Sufis and Sufi doctrines often resulted in Shia-Sufi enmity. With the return of Sunnite rule links to Safawid Persia weakened, the Iranian elite in the administration of Bijapur were replaced by the locals and Hindu ideas became part of Bijapur's cultural landscape. Towards the end of the sixteenth century, Bijapur reached the peak of its cultural and economic development under Ibrahim II (ruled 1580–1626). Portuguese traders as well as Hadhrami scholars and mystics made full use of this development and settled down in the centres along old trade routes. Among Sufis, the predominantly foreign "urban reformist" Shattaris and Qadiris[46] employed their influence to reform the court administration in order to create a system suited to their ideas and interests. As can

---

[44] Compare this argument in respect to grinding songs in R.M. Eaton: "Sufi Folk Literature and the Expansion of Indian Islam", in: *History of Religions* 14/2 (1974), pp. 117–127.

[45] See Shemeem Burney Abbas: *The Female Voice in Sufi Ritual: Devotional Practices of Pakistan and India*, Austin: University of Texas Press 2002, esp. pp. 118f. I am grateful to Carl Ernst drawing my attention to the female voice in Sufism.

[46] It seems that Qadiris settled down in Bijapur before they came to Uchh.

be well understood, they were particularly against Ibrahim II's process of Indianisation. It is unclear whether or not Muhammad ʿAdil Shah (reigned 1627–56), during whose rule Shivaji, the Maratha leader, rose to power (seizing many forts of importance between 1646 and 1648), pursued an orthodox Islamic policy and imposed *jizya* on Hindus. What is clear however, is that during the rule of Sultan ʿAli ʿAdil Shah II (1656–1672), the government became markedly anti-Hindu, thus fully igniting the fissiparous tendencies which during Muhammad's rule had only simmered beneath the surface.[47] The change in policy brought with it internal problems and Bijapur's inability to solve them. Its political decline (1646–1686) began soon after Bijapur's annexation by the Mughals. This was the price that Bijapur paid for maintaining a high degree of cultural autochthony, best exemplified by Deccani Urdu which took root here, making it immune to influences emanating from Delhi or West Asia.

Golconda

The other South Indian kingdom to emerge from the debris of Bahmani state was Golconda, founded as a Shiʿite state by Quli Qutb Shah (1512–43), who had been assigned parts of the area for his loyalty towards Muhammad Shah III. This Qutbshahi dynasty derived immense benefits from Golconda as it was the centre of trade and commerce, frequented by travellers, architects, calligraphers, scholars and traders. The city witnessed a vast increase in its population; the region prided itself on being the emporium and centre of the diamond trade of West Asia[48] and had good connections to major ports. It was quite natural that the region figured prominently in many an invader's list. In spite of many wars and internal rebellions, particularly against the *nayaks*, initially an elite body of Hindu royal servants with a military ethic, Golconda reached its peak under Sultan Ibrahim Qutb Shah (reigned 1550–1580). Ibrahim tried to heal a kingdom torn between immigrants, old settlers and natives by being fair in providing access to higher positions, extending this policy even to the Hindus. In contrast to his father's stressing the Islamic and Persian character of the monarchy,

---

[47] See in Eaton: *Sufis of Bijapur 1300–1700*, pp. 54, 198.
[48] H.K. Sherwani: "Golkondâ", in: EI(2), II, pp. 1118f.

Ibrahim presented himself in the idiom and style of an indigenous king eventually wining over the *nayaks*' loyalty.[49] His policy of official bilingualism—Persian and Telugu—and his patronage for Muslims as well as non-Muslims were maintained by the sultans that followed. His son and successor Muhammad Quli Qutb Shah (died 1611) laid the foundation for the new "City of Haydar"—Haydarabad. With growing wealth came increasing centralisation of the political system. Being a staunch Shiʿite ruling over Shafiʿite majority, Muhammad Quli developed close diplomatic relations with Safawid Persia, while trade with Persia and West Asia was made possible by the new diamond industry and a rigorous tax collection through tax-farmers, usually of the Telugu mercantile castes. Co-operation was sought between Brahmins in the fields of fiscal policy and revenue, and the *nayaks* for their capacities as troopers with their links to the regional aristocracy. Shiʿite influence on the Court trickled down, etching its memories on many buildings and cultural artefacts, not to mention the sublime genre of *marthiya*. This is not to deny the influence of Hinduism, which led to the creation of an indigenous syncretic episteme. Arabic continued to be the scholarly language making Golconda a heaven for quite a number of Arabic writers who came from Hijaz. Haydarabad, a major trade market on a main commercial route, could certainly avail of this patronage. The Qutbshahis resisted Mughal invasions by seeking help from Shiʿite Iran as well as from the Marathas, but finally, in 1687, they surrendered to Aurangzeb (died 1707),[50] who had by that time established Aurangabad as a contesting city attracting great parts of the surplus from Mughal administration.

Parts of the Deccan were then dominated by the Shiʿites. Partly by those immigrants who had steadily been absorbed by various Deccani courts and partly made up of old settlers. Therefore it took a long time for the Mughals to subdue the South. The Deccani kingdoms were always regarded as the vassals of the Mughals. It is no wonder then that Bhimsen (1649–1706), the court historiographer of Aurangzeb, refers to them as "zamindars". Shiʿite identity generated a common bond among the power holding dynasties and their vassals. The continuous influx of excellent Persian know-how and its application in administration

[49] For a detailed history of Muslims in Golconda see J.F. Richards: *Mughal Administration in Golconda*, Oxford: Clarendon Press 1975.

[50] Schimmel: *Islam in the Indian Subcontinent*, pp. 60–62.

and education further strengthened the cohesiveness of such bonds. It was but natural that Deccan would become the flashpoint in the ensuing battle of Mughal and Safawid interests. It is something of a historical truism that it is not distance but proximity, which persuades religious communities and dynasties to draw up boundaries, which are important for constructing the other. The history of South Asia perhaps best exemplifies this truism. To ignore those processes, which blurred the boundaries between various communities and gave expression to common human goals in the new language of shared tradition and syncretism, would be a one-sided reading of history.[51] The Deccani kingdoms' intimate relation with the Hindus is one such example, which, from the mid sixteenth century onwards, saw the meteoric rise of the Marathas, who having learned the fine arts of administration and warfare from the Deccani kingdoms, would eventually use them against the Mughals.

Maʿbar and Malabar

Muslims of this South-Western most coastal region trace back their lineage, as many others do, to Prophet Muhammad. Malabar's very location had made it part of Islam's maritime network, the Shafiʿite Arab Muslim tribe *Nawaʾit* being one of the major carriers of this infrastructure.[52] They played a vital role in the economy of Indian ports and thus benefited from the trust of the local Hindu rulers. It was only under the Khalajis (1308; ʿAla al-Din) that Muslims turned to military conquest of this region, when in 1310 Muslim armies despoiled the great Hindu temples of Maʿbar. When Ibn Battuta visited the Deccan in 1338 he found the Muslim sultanate with its capital at Madurai.[53] Muhammad ibn Tughluq (reigned 1324–1351) tried to conquer this region but Muslim armies were driven back by the forces of Vijayanagara.

---

[51] See the contribution by Hugh van Skyhawk: "Nasiruddin and Adinath, Nizamuddin and Kanipanath: Hindu-Muslim Religious Syncretism in the Folk Literature of the Deccan", in: Heidrun Bruckner, Lothar Lutze, and Aditya Malik (eds.): *Flags of Fame—Studies in South Asian Folk Culture*, Delhi 1993, pp. 445–468.

[52] J. Burton-Page: "Karnâtak", in: EI(2), IV, pp. 666f.

[53] A.D.W. Forbes: "Maʿbar", in: EI(2), V, pp. 937f.

Sufi networks were of great importance for Muslims as well as Hindus of this region too. There was a high level of acculturation making Malabar unique in terms of Arabic-Indian culture, where both, Arabic and Tamil languages, were in use. Qadiri affiliation seemed to be of particular significance. In spite of their alleged proclivities to Arabic culture, Qadiri Sufis were remarkably flexible in religious/ritual practices. They combined this with trade so that piety and commerce flourished side by side. The mutual use and adaptation of religious vocabulary and cultural elements in the southern Tamil-speaking regions may be exemplified in the seventeenth century epic *Cira puranam* or *The Life of the Prophet*, written by a major poet of the time, Umaru Pulavar, who had been taught by a Qadiri Sufi and was later patronised by merchants. The text is evidence of how Muslim figures are appropriated into Hindu popular piety and ritual, in which the Tamil landscape is transposed on Arabia, and Arab women are dressed like Tamilians and erotically described.[54] This approach was a result of cultural interaction still apparent among Tamil Muslims called *Marakkayar* from the Tamil word *marakkalam*, sailor.[55]

Similarly, though Muslim settlers were influenced by the architecture of the Yemen and the Persian Gulf, yet the very symbol of Islam, that is the mosques, were indigenised, missing minarets and the conventional *mihrab* or having a colonnaded portico in front of the prayer hall foreign to north Indian mosques or bursting with Jain and Hindu motifs such as lotus leaves.[56] By the same token, *dargahs* turned into centres where divine power was bestowed in ways acceptable to both Muslims and Hindus, not to mention their close links to the cult of indigenous Tamil deities. The *dargah* of Shahul Hamid (1491–1570), a Qadiri, who was patronised by Marakkayar shipping magnates in Nagore in the region of Tanjore in Tamil Nadu, on the East coast serves as a perfect example. His popularity was not limited to Tanjore. Tamil labourers

---

[54] See Vasudha Narayanan: "The Ramayana and its Muslim Interpreters", in: Paula Richman (ed.): *Questioning Ramayanas: A South Asian Tradition*, Berkeley: UCP 2001; and Vasudha Narayanan: "Religious Vocabulary and Regional Identity: A Study of the Tamil *Cîrâppurânam* ('Life of the Prophet')", in: Eaton (ed.): *India's Islamic Traditions*, pp. 393–410.

[55] See J.B.P. More: "The Marakkayar Muslims of Karikal, South India" in: *JIS* 2 (1991), pp. 25–44.

[56] Cf. Mehrdad Shokoohy: *Muslim Architecture of South India, the Sultanate of Ma'bar and the Traditions of the Maritime Settlers on the Malabar and Coromandel Coasts (Tamil Nadu, Kerala and Goa)*, London: Routledge 2003, pp. 61, 131, 132, 133. "In North India early minarets usually signified the Islamic conquest..." (p. 133).

in Malaysia have built a replica of his tomb in Penang/Malaysia. The shrine is still very frequently attended by Hindus, Christians, as well as Muslims.[57] Similarly, trade and the Sufi tradition also went together when, in the eighteenth century Muslims sought new markets along the coastline and expanded towards the interior to centralise regional dispensation, as did Nawwab Saʿadat Allah Khan (1651–1732), the founder of the *Nawaʾit* nizamat in Arcot.[58] And Sufi networks not only extended their own sacred realm but also that of the worldly rulers, the Walajah nawwabs of the eighteenth century being an example.[59] The Urdu-speaking Walajahs of the Arcot area had had their cultural roots in North India, as vassals of the distant Mughal overlord. They were made rulers by the British, integrating into an expanding trade with European companies on the Coromandel coast, though not without contesting the *Nawaʾit* nizamat, however. They created a formally defined community of Muslim believers out of various linguistic and status groups. Piety and benefaction were the pillars of legitimacy for Walajahi power. To construct networks of dependence throughout the region, links between pirs and power divinities were forged, their service elite was recruited from the North, exemplified in Nawwab Muhammad ʿAli's (died 1795) invitation to ʿAbd al-ʿAli Farangi Mahalli alias Bahr al-ʿulum (died 1810), the famous son of Nizam al-Din Sihalwi, the maker of *dars-e nizami* (see Chap. 7). The Walajah rulers also fulfilled the standard dharmic obligations, protected and endowed Hindu temples as well as supported Sufi foundations and shrines of cult pirs, particularly of Qadiri descent; they deepened relations with the Arab world by inviting scholars and sponsoring pilgrimages to Mecca and Medina.[60] Later, however, the situation became sour due to Sunni-Shiʿite

---

[57] Compare http://www.milligazette.com/Archives/15062001/04.htm, and http://www.aulia-e-hind.com/dargah/Nagoor.htm (accessed 29 Jan. 2008). I am grateful to Carl Ernst to share this information.

[58] See Muzaffar Alam and Sanjay Subrahmanyam: "Exploring the Hinterland: Trade and Politics in the Arcot Nizamat (1700–1732)", in: R. Mukherjee and L. Subramaniam (eds.): *Politics and Trade in the Indian Ocean World: Essays in Honour of Ashin Dasgupta*, Delhi: OUP 1998, pp. 113–164.

[59] The nexus between Sufis and ruler can be traced also in other regions during the eighteenth century as the Mughal Empire was breaking down. Paradigmatically see Nile Green: "Geography, empire and sainthood in the eighteenth-century Muslim Deccan", in: *BSOAS* 67/2 (2004), pp. 207–225.

[60] See Bayly: *Saints, Goddesses and Kings*; also Velcheru Narayan Rao, David Shulman and Sanjay Subrahmanyam: *Textures of Time. Writing History in South India 1600–1800*, New Delhi: Permanent Black 2001, for detailed studies of this region based on rich epic literary sources.

controversies (1792 and 1801) which was the excuse for the battles for social position and landed property between the Qadiris and Naqshbandis on the one hand and the Shiʿites on the other.

The matrilineal Mappila (Moplah) community is another product of the intense entanglement and reciprocity between Muslims and Hindus, though, like most of the Muslims in this region, they adhered to the Shafiʿi school of law.[61] Ibn Battuta paints a vivid picture of this part of India. In the fifteenth century, this region was firmly under Muslim rule, but following the visit of the Portuguese explorer Vasco da Gama in 1498, problems erupted between the Arab merchants and traders settled there and the emerging European traders and their companies. An account of Islam in Malabar and the Portuguese campaigns in India is given in the *Tuhfat al-Mujahidin* (Gift to the Holy Warriors) by Shaikh Ahmad Zain al-Din al-Maʿbari in ca. 1584. Written from a religio-political point of view, the author of this Arabic history of South India exhorts Malabari Muslims to wage *jihad* against the Portuguese for their atrocities.[62] However, despite the problems occurring with the Portuguese invasion, as portrayed in Zain al-Din's chronicle of local resistance movements, Muslim traders, who dealt in the rice trade along the Coromandel coast, could maintain their social and economic positions by collaborating with the Europeans in some instances, as can also be gleaned from a variety of sources analysed by Sanjay Subrahmanyam.[63] Their degree of integration and assimilation is also reflected in the Muslim architecture of Kerala: the *dargah*s and mosques of this area—as in most parts of South India—bear bilingual names and inscriptions: one Arabic and another in a local language representing a unique blend of the West Asian and South Indian architectural mix.[64] Moreover, the extensive use of timber in mosques

---

[61] On the Mappilas and European encounter see Roland E. Miller: *Mappila Muslims of Kerala: A Study in Islamic Trends*, Madras: Orient Longman 1992; Stephen Frederic Dale: *Islamic Society on the South Asian Frontier: The Mappilas of Malabar, 1498–1922*, Oxford: Clarendon 1980; Bindu Malieckal: "Muslims, Matriliny, and *A Midsummer Night's Dream*: European Encounters with the Mappilas of Malabar, India", in: *MW* 95/2 (2005), pp. 297–316.

[62] An English translation of this sixteenth century Arabic work is found as *Tohfut-ul-Mujahideen, an Historical Work in the Arabic Language*, tr. by M.J. Rowlandson, London 1833; see also N.R. Farooqi: "Early sufis of India: legend and reality", in Mansura Haidar (ed.): *Sufis, Sultans and Feudal Orders*, New Delhi: Manohar 2004; Shokoohy: *Muslim Architecture of South India*, pp. 241–246, 291–293, analysing Zain al-Din's shrine.

[63] Subrahmanyam: *Explorations in Connected History*, Chap. 2, pp. 17–44.

[64] See Mehrdad Shokoohy: "The town of Cochin and its Muslim heritage on the Malabar coast, South India", in: *JRAS* series 3/8 (1998), pp. 351–394; Mehrdad

represents a type of Indo-Islamic architecture peculiar to the region so that the mosques of Kerala differ immensely from Muslim structures of any other region in India.[65] Lying beyond the centres of power and patronage, such as Lahore, Delhi and Agra, the south Indian plateau maintained its independence from the Muslim North despite the short-lived conquest of Mughal emperor Aurangzeb in the late seventeenth century.[66] With increasing European involvement in South India in the eighteenth century the term Malabar came to be erroneously applied, as "Carnatic", to the coastal region alone.[67]

Linguistically, and religiously closely related to the Kerala and Tamil Muslims are those living in Sri Lanka, usually known dismissively by their Portuguese name "Moors". Partly descendent from Arab seafarers they settled in the important commercial junction of Ceylon during the eighth century. They kept links with their areas of origin and controlled foreign trade in Ceylon until they were devastated by the Portuguese in 1505. Thus many Muslim traders had to turn to agriculture. The Islamic revival came to them only in the nineteenth century via Kerala and Tamil Nadu, basically through Sufi orders and provided new vigour to the extent that Muslims were able to establish new educational institutions and their own media.[68]

Thus Islam and its actors definitely played a part in the expansion of Turkish imperialism, the ulama and the Sufis being cases in point. Particularly in South India, Islamic expansion had much to do with the decision of the Sufis to stay behind after Muhammad Tughluq's return to Delhi. At the same time it is not unproblematic to credit the Sufis as primarily responsible for the Muslim success, as has been argued in a powerful theory of Sufi warriors who are solely credited with the early expansion of Islam, particularly in the South.[69] While in some cases this might be true, the theory of Sufi warriors is itself

Shokoohy: "Architecture of the sultanate of Maʿbar in Madura and other Muslim monuments in South India", in: *JRAS* series n.s. 1/1 (1991), pp. 31–92.

[65] Shokoohy: *Muslim Architecture of South India*, p. 137.

[66] A.D.W. Forbes: "Maʿbar", in: EI(2), V, pp. 937f.

[67] J. Burton-Page: "Karnâtak", in: EI(2), IV, pp. 666f.

[68] See A.M.A. Azeez: "Ceylon", in: EI(2), II, pp. 26b; Christian Wagner: *Die Muslime Sri Lankas*, Freiburg 1990.

[69] See R. Eaton: *The Sufis of Bijapur*. Comparable phenomena are noticeable in other religious traditions, such as Christianity and Hinduism. See C. Walter: *The Warrior Saints in Byzantine Art and Tradition*, Oxford: OUP 2003; and D.N. Lorenzen: "Warrior ascetics in Indian history", in: *JAOS* 98/1 (1978), pp. 61–75.

UZBEK
Samarkand
Ferghana
Kashgar
MONGOLS
Balkh
BABUR
KASHMIR
SAFAWID
PERSIA
Ghazni
Kabul
Peshawar
Sialkot
Lahore
Kandahar
Quetta
Multan
DAULAT KHAN
LODI
LANGAHS
Panipat
Delhi
DELHI
SULTANATE
BIHAR
Kalat
Sukkur
Uchh
Agra
BALOCH
RAJPUT
CONFEDRACY
Kanauj
Gogra
ARGHUNS
Khanua
BENGAL
Thatta
GUJARAT
MALWA
GONDWANA
KHANDESH
BERAR
AHMAD
NAGAR
ORISSA
BIDAR
Warangal
GOLCONDA
ARABIAN SEA
BIJAPUR
Goa
VIJAYANAGAR
MALABAR COAST
BAY OF BENGAL
Calicut
Cochin
to
PORTUGAL
Columbo
Burbur´s invasion
Sailing routes to and
from South Asia

Map 8: South Asia around 1525 C.E.

based on much later historiography rather than primary sources. It might be erroneous to assert that the dislocation of Muslim religious groups implied missionary and battle-ready Sufis, as claimed by later historiographers. Similarly, the idea of Sufis as peaceful proselytisers shunning violence gained currency only in the nineteenth century to counteract the perception that Islam expanded by fire and sword alone. This perception had much to do with its adoption by the famous professor of philosophy, Thomas Arnold (died 1930), who taught at the Aligarh College (see Chap. 10), in his book "Preaching in Islam" (see also excursus: Conversion).

To summarise, the settlement of Muslims on the Western coast was highly informed by trade and commercial interaction and found its reflection in the social structure and material culture as it evolved in terms of pluralistic lived traditions. The eastward expansion of Muslim power ran parallel to political, agrarian and religious changes affecting the old Sanskrit civilisation. These changes primarily occurred due to economic reasons. Through sedentarisation and in some cases through rice cultivation and changes in riverbeds as well, agrarian people were integrated into religious institutions organised around charismatic figures. This process of integration resulted in various types of accommodations: the inclusion of other religions, whereby Islam existed parallel to other religious systems; identification with the local traditions, whereby Islam merged with local traditions, and finally the displacement of traditional religions by Islam—hence the reception, appropriation and obliteration of autochthonous ideas and institutions. Subsequently, Islamic reform added significantly to socio-political changes: on the one hand there was a 'routinisation of charisma' whereby holy men and their progenies became landowners. On the other hand, Muslim landowners often became holy men, thereby sanctifying bureaucratic authority. This multi-dimensional intermingling of the profane with the sacred served to deeply entrench Islam in the cultural memory of the people so that Islamisation outpaced the process of indigenisation. On an altogether different level, Islamic literary culture, handed down mainly by the Persianised and Arabised *ashraf*, was only marginally successful in the agrarian hinterland, where inclusion and identification were more important. Together, both tendencies had a profound impact on different cultures. Mutual encounters and interaction between Muslims migrating from the North, or having been settled there for many centuries, gave these regions their peculiar Indian Muslim traditions. As evident in local architecture, in the practice of religion and in Sanskrit epigraphical and literary sources, religiosity was not the prime marker of identity, distancing and exclusivism.[70] At the same time Muslim denominations contested with each other over the power to represent Islam, while depending on Hindu gentry at the same time. The coalescence of different interest groups opened numerous fissures such as those between the *ashraf* on the one hand and local converts and the lower classes (*ardhal*) on the other or between the *dakhanis* and *afaqis*, who found their theological rationalisation in different schools of thought, be they Sunnite or Shiʿite, Hanbali or Shafiʿi, mystic or orthodox. Considered in the light of our story, religious systems are cultural artefacts, which hold a mirror up to social realities. The expansion of Islamic cosmology is, therefore, grounded in the ability of its communicators—rulers, traders, scholars, Sufis, peasants, etc.—to absorb, reject or reinterpret, and in the flexibility of its institutions, such as *iqtaʿ* and *jagir*, the mosque, *khanaqah* and the *madrasa*, which function as centres of distribution, not only of piety but also of cultivated lands. Holy men combined piety with organisational skills in such mundane acts as clearing forests or reclaiming land, not to mention the pious acts of running a *khanaqah* and establishing a *wilayat*. These transmitters were remembered not only for establishing Muslim institutions such as religious endowments, mosques, shrines and *madrasas* but also for mobilising people to cultivate land.[71] The success of the Mughals depended to a great extent on how they utilised and built upon the existing structure bequeathed to them by their predecessors.

If the former director of the Nadwat al-ʿUlama, S. ʿAbd al-Hayy, is to be believed, this era marks the second epoch of Islamic learning. The service elite trained in the madrasas, studied selected works of various authors belonging to different schools. Thus, books, often included selections on *kalam* from the Muʿtazila, Ashʿariyya and Maturidiyya and selections on *fiqh* from the Hanafiyya. These books, therefore, displayed a broad inclusive perspective but were mostly brief and summarising. They were practically integrating while defining the boundaries of religious and cultural norms to the Muslim service elite within a Hindu majority environment. Yet, these books also reflected the hegemony of Muslim urban culture, as can be seen from the popularity of al-Hariri's *Maqamat* (eleventh century), which exemplified the zenith of

---

[70] See Chattopadhyaya: *Representing the Other?*; Davis: *Lives of Indian Images*, pp. 155ff.; Shokoohy: *Muslim Architecture of South India*.

[71] Eaton: *The Rise of Islam and the Bengal Frontier*, pp. 113ff., 268ff., 226.

Arab linguistic instruction.[72] On the whole, while the knowledge of law and logic served to legitimise the political rulers, the study of mystical treaties suggested a politics of cultural integration. In contrast to these, the study of transmitted sciences tended to stress Islamic orthodox rites. Perhaps for this reason such books were relatively few in number in India.[73] Yet, it was within the field of *manqulat* rather than *maʿqulat* that different methods of transmission and the evaluation of knowledge such as *ijaza, sanad, munazara, suhba*, etc.[74] developed. While the language of Islamic scholarship was exclusively Arabic, communications in administration, the courts and the interchange among Sufis were increasingly conducted in Persian. Persian connected South Asia with the wider Islamic world, though beyond the major trade and migrant routes such as Kashmir, Bengal and Tamil Nadu,[75] it hardly had an impact until the fourteenth century. It seems that the dissemination of an Islamic *Weltanschauung* followed the patterns of political power in terms of the shift from centre to periphery, providing adequate space for acculturation. Before describing the reintegration of this regionalisation of Muslim power, a brief look at the phenomenon of caste is in order.

---

[72] Compare Oleg Grabar: "The Illustrated Maqâmât of the thirteenth century: The Bourgeosie and the Arts", in: A. Hourani and S.M. Stern (eds.): *Papers on Islamic History, I. The Islamic City*, Oxford 1970, pp. 207–222. In the nineteenth century al-Hariri's *Maqamat* again became popular among urban reformist groups.

[73] See Robert L. Canfield (ed.): *Turco-Persia in Historical Perspective*, New York: CUP 1991; S.H. Nasr: "The Traditional Texts Used in the Persian Madrasahs", in: Nasr, S.H.: *Traditional Islam in the Modern World*, London 1987; Richard Bulliet: *The Patricians of Nishapur: A Study in Medieval Islamic Social History*, Cambridge, Mass. 1972; Cornell H. Fleischer: *Bureaucrat and Intellectual in the Ottoman Empire: The Historian Mustafa Ali (1541–1600)*, Princeton 1986; Halil Inalcik: *The Ottoman Empire; the classical age 1300–1600*, New York 1973, pp. 165ff.; R. Repp: "Some Observations on the Development of the Ottoman Learned Hierarchy", in: Nikki R. Keddie (ed.): *Scholars, Saints and Sufis*, Berkeley: UCP 1972; Katib Chelebi: *Balance of Truth*, English transl. from Turkish by G.L. Lewis, London 1957; G.M.D. Sufi: *Al-Minhaj; evolution of curricula in the Muslim educational institutions*, Lahore 1981 (first 1941); Naimur Rahman Farooqi: *Mughul-Ottoman Relations*, Delhi 1989.

[74] See Makdisi: *The Rise of Colleges*, pp. 99–152 et passim; Jonathan Berkey: *The Transmission of Knowledge in Medieval Cairo: A Social History of Islamic Education*, Princeton: PUP 1992; for some critical remarks see D.J. Stewart, in: *Islamic Law and Society* 1/3 (1994), pp. 367–376.

[75] See Mohammad Ishaq Khan: "The Impact of Islam on Kashmir in the Sultanate Period (1320–1586)", in: *IESHR* 23 (1986), pp. 187–205; reprint in: Eaton (ed.): *India's Islamic Traditions*, pp. 342–362; Tony K. Stewart: "In Search of Equivalence: Conceiving the Muslim-Hindu Encounter Through Translation Theory", reprint in: Eaton (ed.): *India's Islamic Traditions*, pp. 363–392; Narayanan: "Religious Vocabulary and Regional Identity".

EXCURSUS

CASTE

Describing India, al-Biruni (973–1050), who after living in India joined the Ghazna court in 1017 referred to Hindu-Muslim differences. He said the greatest obstacle that prevented any Hindu-Muslim rapprochement was the segregation that Hindus practised. Hindus considered "others" impure (*mleccha*). Intermarriage or even sitting with them supposedly was polluting. He marked Hindus as a religious group distinguished from Muslims and described them as being innately perverse.[1] Their reluctance to engage in social intercourse was the greatest obstacle to an egalitarian Islam.[2] Al-Barani was even more obsessed with Hindu low-born-ness. Notwithstanding a pristine Islam's egalitarianism, Islamic norms permit hierarchical structure, i.e., equality in Islam is only in relation to God, rather than between men. Early Muslims and Muslim conquerors in India reproduced social segregation among Muslims and the conquered religious groups. Similarly, Sufis who preached equality before God lived in spiritual and social hierarchies. The writings of Abu al-Fadl at Akbar's court mention caste, interestingly enough under the heading of 'Animal life'.[3] In the societal fragmentation of the eighteenth century, Muslim society further diversified the *ashraf* into Sayyids, Shaikhs, Afghans and Pakhtuns,[4] the common link being their foreign ancestry. However, these sub-classes of the *ashraf* showed both extreme professional and ethnic overlapping as well as distinction, to the degree that even the low professions could be considered Sayyids if they adhered to endogomy and their own social environment[5] and thus to their inherited cultural capital. Based on these perceptions another distinction was added: the *ashraf-ajlaf* dichotomy[6] (common folk; actually

[1] See al-Biruni: *Kitab al-Hind*, pp. 11, 91.

[2] Cf. A. Schimmel: *Islam in the Indian Subcontinent*, Leiden-Köln 1980, p. 7.

[3] Abul-Fazl Allami: *Ain-e Akbari*, Delhi 2001, Vol. III, pp. 126ff.

[4] Cf. Lalji: *Mir'at al-Auda'* (Pers. mss in A.M.U. Library; Tarikh No. 60), [pp. 88f.]

[5] Mirza Muhammad Hasan Qatil: *Haft tamasha*, translated from Persian into Urdu and edited by Muhammad Umar, Delhi: Maktaba Burhan, 1968.

[6] See Jafar Sharif with G.A. Herklots (1921 revised edition by William Crooke): *Islam in India or the Qânûn-i-Islâm. The Customs of the Musalmâns of India; comprising a full*

from Arabic: a body of any kind without a head upon it, hence, unsound in intellect), apparently reintroduced by contemporary social scientists as a powerful analytical tool.[7] Similar distinction is made in the table-talks of Sufis (*malfuzat*), but whether this implies that Sufis were free from "rigidity or principle of heredity in respect of birth and avocation",[8] has to be questioned. After all, the *ashraf* were followed by the low born classes, who were indigenous converts, and mostly comprised the artisan sections comparable to Shudras. The *ardhal* occupied the lowest category among Muslims who considered them polluting.

Certainly, the four levels of *ashraf* were reminiscent of *varna*, translated as colour, and corresponds with the four-fold division of Hindu society: Brahmans (priests), the Kshatriya (warriors), Vaishya (traders) and finally the Shudras (servants), followed by the so-called untouchables, or scheduled castes. While the untouchable remains a religious and social category, lower castes came to be known as Dalits, a political category, used in liberation movements[9] in nineteenth and twentieth centuries.

---

and exact account of their various rites and ceremonies from the moment of birth to the hour of death, Oxford: OUP 1921, reprint New Delhi: Oriental Books Reprint Corporation 1968, pp. 9, footnote 3.

7 See for example Imtiaz Ahmad: "The Ashraf-Ajlaf Dichotomy in Muslim Social Structure in Indian", in: *IESHR* III/3 (1966), pp. 268–278.

8 Compare S.H. Askari: *Maktub & Malfuz Literature. As a Source of Socio-Political History*, Patna 1981, p. 42.

9 Approximately one fifth of the population of independent India belongs to the group of *Dalits*, a conglomeration of several castes regarded to be "ritually polluted". *Dalit*-Muslims are mostly converts of low-caste Hindu descent; few claim Arab, Iranian or Central Asian ancestry. Not being integrated properly into the Indian Muslim community (*ashraf-ajlaf* divide) the *dalits* are at the bottom of the social hierarchy. Since caste-distinctions and caste-identity remains strong there, conversion of low-caste Hindus to Islam does not change their socio-economic status much. Since the early 1990s the so-called *Dalit*-movement tries to create a larger *Dalit*-identity which does not ignore caste-differences among the *dalits* themselves but at the same time enforces a collective identity in order to take concerted action against political discrimination. Within this development a specific *Dalit*-Muslim consciousness is enforced by low-caste Muslim organisations such as the "All-India Backward Muslim Morcha" (AIBMM)—established in 1994—to press Government to acknowledge the *Dalit*-Muslims the status of a "scheduled caste". So far this status and the benefits resulting from it have been denied Muslim and Christian *Dalits* while low-caste Hindus, Sikhs and Buddhists are regarded "scheduled castes". *Dalit*-Muslims (and Christians) are now more vocally protesting against discrimination and for their representation in official bodies and demand special social and economic development programmes for low-caste Indians. See Yoginder Sikand: *Islam, Dalit-Muslim Relations in India*, New Delhi: Global Media Publications 2004, pp. 47–65; also some contributions in M.K.A. Siddiqui (ed.): *Marginal Muslim Communities in India*, New Delhi: Institute of Objective Studies 2004. See also ʿAli Anwar: *Masawaat Ki Jung*, Vani Prakashan: Delhi 2001.

In the nineteenth century, colonial power considered the caste system to be a proven device for the organisation of manifold Indian identities in order to make sense of them[10] using the Portuguese term (*casto*), meaning pure or virgin. The caste system was of major interest to Europeans in the course of classical Orientalism. It was considered a necessary feature of Indian society to be understood by the colonial power.[11] In the wake of this Orientalism, a number of prominent caste theories were developed by Westerners and Indians alike. In the nineteenth century's history of ideas, some thought caste was created by ancient legislators, a system which was religiously determined, putting Brahmans in a privileged position. Photographs of natives served the purpose of displaying their peculiarities, as in *The Peoples of India*, published by the Governor of India in 1868 in eight volumes. In a more comparative approach, the scholars Max Müller and Max Weber considered caste an extreme form of Western hierarchical structures, with limited religious connotation. Weber's *Theory of Social Stratification* established that caste was merely an analogy to social rank or status group, with a division of labour, comparable to Europe's guilds system. Thus the historical models considered caste a pre-historic phenomenon, informed by concepts of purity and profession. In the twentieth century caste was considered in terms of hereditary groups separated by marriage patterns and physical contact, displaying a division of labour organised by hereditary occupations, that is *jati* (specie, root),[12] or by clusters of functional groups divided into sub-castes. In his *Homo hierarchicus*,[13] Louis Dumont distinguished the Indian value system on a purity-impurity basis determined by three social criteria: separation through marriage and physical contact, interdependence through profession and religious ritual, and finally hierarchy. The pure-impure dichotomy was based on reason rather than form.[14] Theoretical ideas provided the basis to debate caste in Islam, particularly in the Hindu environment.

---

[10] H.M. Elliot: *Encyclopaedia of castes, customs, rites and superstitions of the Races of North India, I–II*, 1st Indian reprint, Delhi: Sumit Publications 1985, first published 1870.

[11] Cf. Ronald Inden: *Imagining India*, Cambridge/MA: Basil Blackwell 1990, pp. 49–84.

[12] For example Celestine Bouglé: *Essais sur le régime des castes*, Paris: Alcan 1937.

[13] Louis Dumont: *Homo hierarchicus. The Caste System and its Implications*, Transl.: Mark Sainsbury, Chicago: UCP 1970.

[14] Declan Quigley: *The Interpretation of Caste*, Oxford: Clarendon 1995.

Caste among Muslims

The Muslim universe in South Asia provides ample opportunity to discover notions of segregation, though caste is sometimes considered as "qaum", a

> "patrilineal hereditary, [with] ranked occupation groups, conceptually endogamous. Each *qoum* [sic!] is named, and membership in a *qoum* is unalterably determined by birth. Sociologically, they might be classified as castes. They differ from castes as usually defined mainly in that they are without ritual or religious importance. But in view of their parallelism and continuity, through similar groups among Moslems in the Indus plain and United Provinces, with castes of the Hindu system" Barth refers to these as castes.[15]

Barth's universe being the Pakhtun tribes, he regards the notion of pure (*pak*) and impure (*paleed*) as equivalent to the notions of *ashraf* and *ajlaf*, the former being of lighter complexion and belonging to the dominant political elite, the latter being dark-skinned associated with ancestral professions as artisans and peasants.

Indigenous quasi-caste systems apart, the caste system is invariably Hindu. Muslims would willingly accept this "othering", which has found a basis in Muslim societies as shown even in pristine Islam.

This principle of social organisation is determined by hierarchy, ritual purity, endogamy and professional specialisation.[16] A hierarchy organised in terms of castes and based on ideology and religion prohibits social interaction among followers of different castes.[17] Muslims in India do mirror some of these criteria. This is partly true for the lower and middle classes who, for the most part are exogenous, while at higher levels endogamy can also be found. The reasons for endogamy have their roots in the desire to preserve one's own economic position rather than in the observance of Muslim culture and religion. Ritual purity is of secondary importance. As it is, professional specialisation creates interdependence and reciprocity between groups. Each caste or group was determined by specific profession in what is called the

---

[15] Fredrik Barth: *Political Leadership among Swat Pathans*, London: The Athlone Press 1959, pp. 16–22, here p. 16.

[16] See the critical remarks by Jürgen Osterhammel: *Die Entzauberung Asiens. Europa und die asiatischen Reiche*, München: Beck 1998, pp. 330ff.

[17] For the following see Imtiaz Ahmad (ed.): *Caste and Social Stratification among the Muslims*, New Delhi: Manohar 1978, pp. XX–XXXI.

jajmani-system, names often display these respective professions. It was based on extra-economic coercion. This system has now been replaced by a cash nexus based on the legal economic coercion which permeates Indian society.

Creation of social hierarchy among Muslims is particularly popular in India's south, though in a lesser form than among Hindus. This is founded primarily on non-ritual criteria such as considerations related to economic and cultural capital rather than to ritual alone, and therefore is more permeable. There is a distinction made between clean and unclean professional groups. Ideally speaking, among Muslims there is no ideological superstructure which would prohibit interaction between groups or castes. Ideally, Islamic notions of society forbid inequality, but similar delimitations are being rationalised through religion itself. The courtier and historian Zia al-Din al-Barani not only avowedly detested Hindus, in his *Fatawa-ye Jahandari*, he also vehemently stood for *ashraf* supremacy, referring to the Quranic text into which he read the division of *ashraf* and *ardhal*, as aristocratic birth and superior genealogy, being the most important traits of a human.

Caste exists, but is not justified in Islam. Imtiaz Ahmad speaks of a 'caste analogy', since the "Hindu ideological justification such as the pure-impure-dichotomy and determination by birth does not exist in the case of Muslims."[18] But there is a consciousness of status by birth though not as elaborate as among Hindus. Consequently, caste among Muslims does not restrict social intercourse as much as it does in the Hindu system.

The idea of endogamy, pride of birth and descent is popular among Muslims, but not based in an ideology of purity. Affluence and other secular factors seem to have more meaning for the determination of social status. Moreover, among Muslims there is no ritually pure caste with particular functions such as the Brahmans. On the other hand, the Sayyids, the direct descendants of Prophet Muhammad, are respected for their noble descent, but do not claim special ritual purity and do not have the charisma necessary for Brahmans. Some scholars also claim that the Muslim caste system is a result of cultural interaction with Hinduism acting as the retainer of the Middle Eastern heritage

[18] Ahmad (ed.): *Caste and Social Stratification among Muslims in India*, p. 11.

of social stratification or as the combination of Middle Eastern and South Asian models.[19]

As seen throughout Muslim history, the actors of Islam in South Asia adapted to local cultures while converted Hindus brought their social system to Islam. While the latter remained within a largely Hindu cultural universe, the Muslims retained many of its beliefs and practices. A high measure of shared culture was made possible, above all, through the creative interaction between indigenous and exogenous ideas and institutions. We focus on the transfer of Islamic principles to the Indian religious universe and vice-versa: the Prophet (*nabi*) becomes an incarnation of a god (*avatar*). But apart from these processes of acculturation, Islam harbours elements that allows for profound differences. Otherwise society would disintegrate into caste-like structures through the process of the Islamisation of society. Pre-Islamic principles of purity and unity of blood have survived the egalitarian postulates of Muslims, such as the descendants of Quraish, members of Prophet Muhammad's tribe who were categorised as being particularly noble. The so-called *nasab* principle stresses the descent, in contrast to precedence due to action (*sabiqa*).[20] Early Muslims distinguished between the so-called helpers in Medina—*ansar*—and the migrants from Mecca—*muhajirun*—particularly, when it came to distributing of booty.[21] This socio-religious segregation was further developed after incorporating non-Arab groups as subordinate 'clients' (*mawali*) of ruling Arab tribes. In the wake of Muslim expansion, Greek and Persian cultures with their already entrenched social hierarchies, had their impact.

Muslims scholars, mostly from 'high' castes, were generally sympathetic to a religious legitimacy of caste when referring to hereditary occupational and ethnic groups as an essential factor in deciding marriage.[22] Intermarriage is, therefore, difficult among certain sectors of Muslims. This stratification found its way into some Sunnite schools of law in the ninth and tenth centuries. They called for the hegemony of prophetic descent, as was the case in the Hanafi school of law,

[19] Marc Gaborieau: *Traditional Pattern of Dominance among South Asian Muslims*, Paris: Centre National de la Recherche Scientifique 1979.

[20] See Albrecht Noth: "Früher Islam", in: Ulrich Haarmann (ed.): *Geschichte der arabischen Welt*, München 1991, pp. 11–100.

[21] See Albrecht Noth: "Von der medinensischen 'Umma' zu einer muslimischen Ökumene", in: Noth and Paul (eds.): *Der islamische Orient*, pp. 81ff.

[22] ʿAbd al-Hamid Nuʿmani: *Maslah-ye kufw aur ishaʿat-e Islam*, New Delhi: Qazi Publications 2002.

most popular in South Asia. Accordingly, Arabs are considered socially higher than non-Arabs while among Arabs a Quraish is the noblest. Non-Arabs could be on par with Arabs, if their father and grandfather being wealthy Muslims could pay an adequate dowry. Moreover, an educated Non-Arab was equal to an uneducated Arab whence a Muslim scholar was considered of a higher position than a trader, while a trader was better than a businessman. Other schools of law such as the Shafiʿites and the Shiʿites considered the principle of descent to be even more binding.

This means that there is a quasi-caste system among Muslims in India, Pakistan and Bangladesh. Caste among Muslims is more of a form of social stratification that results from an adoption of Arabo-Islamic forms that were based on descent. Shared tradition and the mutual acculturative influences of Hinduism and Islam are important as they determine social interaction. This stratification is still very present, as can be seen in marriage advertisements in South Asian journals, but also among South Asian migrants to Britain and the USA. Structures are revived and cemented even in the diaspora when fair Sayyids of a certain status with a high education are seeking a marriage alliance.

CHAPTER FIVE

CULTURAL INTEGRATION TOWARDS A POLITICS OF UNIVERSAL DOMINION. THE MUGHALS (APPROX. 1450–1650)

Up to the mid-fourteenth century, Muslim influence in South Asia did not remain confined to the juridical level of rulers as witnessed by the Moroccan traveller Ibn Battuta who was affiliated with the courts. This influence was accelerated, albeit gradually, by the influx of Islamic mystics and scholars of various shades. Many Sufis settled along important caravan routes, where they sometimes also built fortifications. These establishments (*qasbahs*) grew into commercial-administrative-military bases at the regional level. Noted dignitaries and Islamic scholars established a network of clientele in these places. Over the years, a Muslim aristocracy (*ashraf* or *shurafa*) evolved which categorically differentiated itself from the rest of society perceived as "uncivilised" or "barbarian" (*radhil* or *ardhal*), both urban and rural, which included converted Muslims, though hierarchical concepts and class consciousness can be traced back to early Islamic times, that is, Islam had already become stratified before it was brought to India (see excursus: Caste). It was this discourse of stratification that lent concrete form to the idea of Islamic "superiority". Esoteric and exoteric ideas contributed to these developments resulting in the emergence and integration of regional powers contesting Muslim hegemony in South Asia. As mentioned earlier, they were glued together in a complex system of loosely allied groups informed mainly by ethnicity.[1] Internal differences allowed another invasion to conquer parts of Muslim ruled regions. The new dynasts brought changes; some radically new but more often they perfected the techniques of their predecessors in the Turko-Persian Sultanate of Delhi. The newcomers were the Mughals—a term acquiring its grandeur rather late[2]—who were Turks composed of segmental tribal groups. Thus unlike the Iranian Qizilbash or the Ottoman Sipahis,

[1] See D.D.A. Kolff: "A Warlord's Fresh Attempt at Empire", in: Muzaffar Alam and Sanjay Subrahmanyam (eds.): *The Mughal State*, New Delhi 1998, pp. 75–114.

[2] See Harbans Mukhia: *The Mughals of India*, Pondicherry: Blackwell 2004, pp. 2ff.

the Mughals had no coherent social or ethnic identity. Timur (died 1405), the great predecessor of the Mughals and "Lord of Conjunction" (*Sahib-e Qiran*),[3] had destroyed the policy of ethnic bonds when he established his power in Western Turkistan in fourteenth century, a process initiated by his predecessor Chingis Khan. So, the Mughals did not have to worry about internal tribal schisms and were free to concentrate their energies on expansion. Moreover, these Timurids did not have the rule of primogeniture, which made semi-open competition for high posts very common.[4] Central Asian cultural tradition thus latently but surely did play an important part in the development of the South Asian empire.

Setting the Mughal scene

The newcomers, moving eastwards, conquered South Asia without major difficulties. The founder of the Mughal dynasty, Zahir al-Din Babur (reigned 1494–1530), was the son of a Mirza of Fergana.[5] Succeeding his father, Babur conquered Samarkand but was unable to retain it. Moving further east he conquered Kabul in 1504, and, assuming the title of *Padishah* in 1508, became the leader of Timurids. In his eastward expansion Babur sought support from Safawid Shah Ismail, who in 1501 had promulgated the Twelver Shia as the state religion in the Persian Empire. Babur received this support in lieu of recognising the Safawid ruler as supreme leader, by reading the *khutba* in his name and by having his name printed on coinage together with the twelve Imams. However, the defeat of Shah Ismail by the Ottomans at Tabriz in 1514 left only the North of South Asia fit for expansion. Here the Lodhis still clung to power. The sultanate now was a loose confederation of semi-autonomous leaders under the leadership of various amirs or leaders of Afghan tribes. The amirs who based their power on family land grants or appanages were constantly fighting with other regional tribes and autonomous Muslim princely states. Babur

---

[3] Meaning that the conjunction of Jupiter and Venus was a fortunate birth date.

[4] This has been argued for the Rajputs; see Norman P. Ziegler: "Some Notes of Râjpût Loyalties During the Mughal Period", in: J.F. Richards (ed.): *Kingship and Authority*.

[5] For an excellent study of Babur contextualising his career in the light of the Emperor's autobiography see Stephen Dale: *The Garden of the Eight Paradises. Babur and the Culture of Empire in Central Asia, Afghanistan and India, 1483–1527*, Leiden: Brill 2004.

attacked India a few times between 1519 and 1526 without making major inroads. However, he consolidated his position by conquering Qandahar in Afghanistan. It was here that he received an invitation from Dawlat Khan Lodhi, the governor of Lahore seeking his help against Ibrahim Lodhi. In the ensuing battle of Panipat in 1526, Babur conquered Delhi. The *khutba* was recited in his name as King of Kabul and conqueror of Delhi. But before he could establish his dynasty, two major opponents, the Rajputs and the Afghans had to be subdued. A successful war for the faith (*ghazwa*) against the Rajputs in the South-West in 1527 brought him the best cavalry of India, while his eastern victory over the Afghans in 1529 exalted him to a *ghazi*, a new status that he had added to his seal and coinage. Agra rather than Kabul became the new capital.

A master narrative establishing a dominant normative history legitimised Babur's dynastic rule by tracing his lineage back to Timur. In fact, the role of memory and of the *narration of history* as a conscious and non-innocent process involved the representation of the past in a discourse of power and marginalised alternative narrative options. Indeed this was hardly something novel: the creation and use of establishment mythologies were pursued by the Ottomans and Safawids. Akin to the tradition of the renaissance, mythologies were important for generating a collective identity.

A major factor in the context of the establishment of Mughal rule was Babur's and his descendants' relationship with the Naqshbandis, who in the fourteenth century had become dominant in Turkistan and Transoxania, and soon followed the Mughals. Babur venerated ʿUbaid Allah Ahrar (died 1490), the great Central Asian Sufi and spiritual guide of the Timurids. Through royal patronage and nuptial agreements with Mughal service nobility, Naqshbandi Sufism soon became something like an aristocratic religious lineage. Around the same time, the Qadiri order gradually became important, having been introduced in this region via Uchh near Multan by Muhammad al-Husaini al-Gilani and expanded by his son Makhdum Shaikh ʿAbd al-Qadir (1429–1533).[6] As argued by Bruce Lawrence, this order displayed a poly-centric rather than a mono-centric view, meaning that they were not bound to a single lineage that could connect them with a foundational time and space, as was the case with the Chishtis, Suhrawardis and Naqshbandis. It might have

---

[6] It should be recalled from the previous chapter that the Qadiriyya had also entered the Bahmani sultanate in Deccan.

been this poly-presence that made the contesting of the hegemonies of two major pre-Mughal orders, Chishti and Suhrawardi, successful, eventually, leading to their replacement in the seventeenth century.

Babur conquered Lucknow and Ayodhya (1528), expanding eastwards as far as Bihar (1529), but could not really establish political control over the Ganga-Yamuna basin (*doab* or the land between two rivers) which had always symbolised the centre of various Indian Empires. His incessant military campaigns gave him little time to ponder about the development of political theory. But the exigencies of consolidation made Babur use proven devices such as providing "temporary or conditional territorial assignments given for the dual purposes of territorial consolidation and military stipends", the *wajh* or *tiyul*, to Timurid and Turkic language speaking, i.e., Chaghatay, loyalists in important forts. While trying to extend networks of loyalty through patronage Babur himself held only nominal authority over revenue collection and local administration which he had inherited from the Lodhis.[7]

A renaissance prince of Central Asia, Babur is famous for his autobiographical accounts. In his memoirs, *Babur Nama*, written in Chaghatay language he integrated his political views into literary, scientific, artistic and even geographical accounts. In his rather balanced picture of various aspects of Indian society, he stated, that Hindustan was a country of few charms however:

> The people of Hindustan have no beauty; they have no convivial society, no social intercourse, no character or genius, no urbanity, no nobility or chivalry. In the skilled arts and crafts there is no regularity, proportionality, straightness or rectangularity. There are no good horses, there are no good dogs, no grapes, no muskmelons or first-rate fruits, no ice or cold water, no good bread or cooked food in the bâzârs, no hammâms, no madrasahs, no candles, no torches or candlesticks... Except their large rivers and their standing-waters which flow in ravines or hollows, there are no running waters in their gardens or residences. Their residences have no charm, air, regularity or symmetry.[8]

This curiosity about and seemingly non-appreciation of South Asia coupled with the superiority complex of the Mughals influenced the

---

[7] See Dale: *The Garden*, pp. 406ff., quotation p. 407.

[8] Babur cited in Annette Susannah Beveridge: *Babur-Namah (Memoirs of Babur), I–II*, Delhi: D.K. Fine Arts 1989 (reprint), pp. 518–520, as quoted in S. Abdul Hai: *India during Muslim Rule*, Lucknow: Academy of Islamic Research & Publications 1977, p. 6, and Dale: *The Garden*, p. 369.

opinions of most Muslim rulers of Delhi. However, there are other examples of Muslim rulers not only appreciating Hindu influences but also being enchanted by them, as has been shown in the preceding chapters and will be documented in this and the following chapter.

Even Babur's son Humayun, who succeeded him in 1530, was unable to establish Mughal supremacy.[9] There were too many rival and competing parties, among them Humayun's three stepbrothers Mirza Hindal, who occupied Qandahar, Mirza ʿAskari and Mirza Kamran. The latter had conquered the northwestern border, strategically important for being a recruiting area of the powerful Mughal army. In this time of constant challenge to Humayun's rule the emperor sought the support of his aunt, Khanzadeh Begum, the sister of Babur. She managed to persuade Kamran to have the *khutba* recited in the name of the emperor, Humayun, a significant example of the impact noble women had on royal politics even in the sixteenth century.[10] Then there were the autonomous rival amirs, particularly in Bihar and Gujarat. Heading a fledgling empire Humayun encountered Afghan forces in 1540 at Kannauj and was forced to seek exile in Safawid Iran. South Asia was to witness a brief interlude of the Suris (1538–1555).

The Suri interlude

The Afghan chieftain Sher Khan alias Sher Shah Suri (reg. 1538–1545) created some major institutions on which the Mughals were later to build their empire. His imperial reorganisation included the introduction of a new administration as well as a two-chamber system. Administrative and fiscal reforms were paralleled by a vast network of roads with hundreds of *sarais* and bazars and postal stations, having

---

[9] Major sources for the reconstruction of Humayun's rule are *Humayunnama* composed in 1534 by Khwandamir, a courtly official; *Tarikh-e Humayun* or *Tadhkirat al-Waqiʿat* by Jawahar Aftabchi in 1587, and *Tadhkirah-ye Humayun wa Akbar* by Bayazid Bayat in 1591, and *Ahwal-e Humayun Badshah* composed Gulbadan Banu Begum, in 1587.

[10] This has been analysed by Ruby Lal: "Mughal India: 15th to Mid-18th Century", in: *Encyclopedia of Women in Islamic Cultures*, Leiden: Brill 2003, pp. 64–69, here pp. 68f., by referring to the *Ahwal-e Humayun Badshah* composed by Babur's daughter, Humayun's sister and Akbar's aunt, Gulbadan Banu Begum, in 1587. See also Gul-badan Banu Begum: *Humayun-Nama. The History of Humayun*, transl. with Introduction & Notes by Annette S. Beveridge, Lahore: Sang-e-Meel 1987, pp. 160f.; for the role of Mughal females see the interesting piece by Mukhia: *The Mughals*, Chap. III: "The World of the Mughal Family".

not only military significance but also linking the economy of Bengal to that of Northern India. Certainly, the network of *sarais* also served as 'listening posts' at a time when intelligence gathering had not evolved properly. These measures brought with them a much needed economic stability and were reportedly appreciated by the common people. The state assumed greater responsibility to encourage productivity.[11] The operation of this policy was possible only by using strategies of integration. Thus Sher Shah not only tolerated Hindus but also employed them in his inner circle. However, defeated by the Rajputs in 1545 at Kalinjar, the Afghans faced a war of succession. His son, Islam Shah (reigned 1545–1554) promoted a further separation of religion and politics but faced severe problems from rebellious notables, mainly the *ashraf*. Islam Shah's youngest son, Firoz Shah, was murdered by his own brother Mubariz Shah, who became the ʿAdil Shah (reigned 1554–56). However, the stigma of slaying one's own gave enough cause to ʿAdil Shah's detractors, mostly nobles and elements of the military, to foment trouble.

Towards universal dominion

Meanwhile, Humayun found shelter in Persia and converted to Shiʿism. For only as a Shiʿite, could he be supported militarily by the Safawids. A raid was planned on Qandahar, from where preparations were to be made to attack India (1545–54). Kabul was to be the point of embarkation, and supported by his loyal adviser Bairam Khan, Humayun successfully regained the throne just five years later. As noted earlier, the Sur dynasty was in disarray owing to numerous wars of succession. Humayun came to Delhi with many Iranians who were to change the Indian universe decisively. But only six months after having reclaimed the throne, he fell from the stairs of his library and expired.

In the previous chapter, we saw that Persian influence was already marked in several regional states as well as in the South. "The choice of Persian as a language of empire was, in very large measure, the outcome of specific Indian conditions inasmuch as the non-sectarian and

[11] See Iqtidar Husain Siddiqi: "The Agrarian System of the Afghans", in: *Studies in Islam*, Jan. 1965, pp. 229–253, quoted in John F. Richards: *The Mughal Empire*, Cambridge: CUP 1995 (reprint), p. 83.

liberal features of Persian idiom and expression made it an ideal vehicle through which the Mughals could effectively negotiate the diversities of Indian society."[12] The Persian influence became even more pronounced under Humayun's son, Abu al-Fath Jalal al-Din Muhammad "Akbar I" (1542–1605), who during his long reign managed to transform the nascent Timurid state into a multi-regional empire.[13] Employing intelligent political tactics of conquest, annexation and matrimonial alliance, Babur's grandson extended and consolidated his Empire. The very strength of the Empire made the Mughals autonomous from the Muslim courts of Istanbul, Cairo and Isfahan. Akbar succeeded his father Humayun at the tender age of thirteen, exercising power under the regency of the ever loyal Bairam Khan, until he ascended the throne in Agra in 1556. Imperial politics focused on his persona. Competition was either eliminated, as in the case of the alleged ambitions of Bairam Khan in 1561 or was co-opted through matrimonial alliances, particularly with the Rajputs. Akbar himself married a Rajput, who was to become the mother of his successor Jahangir (died 1627), the father of Shahjahan (died 1666).[14] A pragmatic policy on Sufi orders and religious endowments, such as the Chishti-shrine in Ajmer was envisaged. The Emperor paid regular visits to the most important Chishti figure of the time, Salim Chishti (died 1571), in whose honour Fatehpur Sikri was built and which was to separate the emperor's rule from what preceded. The city was conceived of as a microcosm of the Mughal Empire and served as its capital from 1570 to 1585.[15] The central task was to expand the empire through military interventions and eventually to culturally integrate the empire and attempt a harmonious interaction between Muslim, Hindu, Christian and other religious groups. An example of an experiment in integration is Fatehpur Sikri's famous discussion room, the *ʿibadat-khana*, in which Akbar joined in the deliberations of Jesuit, Hindu, Parsi, Jain and Muslim divines, before he moved to Lahore in

---

[12] Alam: *Languages*, p. 144. Compare also Fragner: *Die "Persophonie"*. See, however, the critical remarks by Mukhia: *The Mughals*, pp. 157f., pointing to the 'alien-ness' of Persian language even at court level.

[13] See Abu al Fazl Allami: *Akbarnâma*, trans. By H. Beveridge, I–III, Calcutta 1897–1921.

[14] In fact, royal women exercised quite some influence on the making of the Mughal world, as has been outlined by Lal: "Mughal India: 15th to Mid-18th Century", pp. 64–69; see also Mukhia: *The Mughals*, Chap. III: The World of the Mughal Family.

[15] Salim Chishti's exquisite white tomb is situated in the centre of the Jamiʿ masjid. For the architecture of Fatehpur-Sikri see Michael Brand & Glenn D. Lowry: *Akbar and Fatehpur Sikri*, Bombay: Marg Publications 1987.

1585 to focus on the Western edge of his empire. For the purpose of interaction, Mughal ruling classes also patronised Chishtis juxtaposing temporal authority (*jagir*) with spiritual/religious authority (*wilayat*). Thereby, Chishti piety was elevated into an almost imperial cult, serving Mughal cultural integration in the sixteenth century. This pragmatic approach of Mughal rulers found its manifestation inter alia in the Indian-Persian literary diction known as the Indian style, *sabk-e hindi*, or Safawid-Mughal style displaying the oscillating ideas and idioms of the Persian and Indian universes.[16]

Religious and matrimonial politics along with his unique techniques of war (technique of seizure) had made Akbar invincible. The power of the empire flowed from, and indeed was located in his very person, making the empire into what has been called a patrimonial bureaucracy.[17] Using this unique opportunity, Akbar attempted to neutralise the Muslim orthodoxy and sought to blur the boundaries of different religions, which could be acceptable to all. Much of his integrationist policy however, resulted from the very political aim of concentrating religious and political authority in his person. Akbar's support for Hindu religion and traditions and his call for tolerance can be read as an appreciable attempt towards a harmonious and equal cohabitation of different religions in the empire. In fact, he and his son Jahangir both were legitimised as authorised rulers by representatives of autochthonous religions as well, such as Jains.[18] However, these measures were never bereft of political motives, which were securing authority internally and extending power externally through expansion. To a very large extent, these successes of appropriating authority depended on those very Hindu landlords who had been variously subjugated. Akbar understood clearly that political situation of his times demanded a new ideological orientation.

Realising that stability of his expanding empire depended on securing the loyalty of all of his subjects, he issued a policy in 1564 which

---

[16] In "The Culture and Politics of Persian in Precolonial Hindustan" Muzaffar Alam convincingly argues that *sabk-e hindi* already had developed much before the Mughals. Paul E. Losensky: *Language & Literature Welcoming Fighani Imitation and Poetic Individuality in the Safavid-Mughal Ghazal*, Costa Mesa, Calif., 1998, critically assesses the term and its use, while Shamsur Rahman Faruqi: "A Stranger In The City: The Poetics of *Sabk-e Hindi*", in: *The Annual of Urdu Studies* 19 (2004), writes in its defence.

[17] As has been argued by Stephen P. Blake: "The Patrimonial-Bureaucratic Empire of the Mughals", in: *JAS* 39/1 (1979), pp. 77–94.

[18] See Chattopadhyaya: *Representing the Other?*, p. 85.

disapproved discrimination of Hindus on the grounds of religion. These subtle ways of propagating a coherent ideological concept to legitimise power were not devoid however, of several highly pragmatic elements. A "state history," focussing on the aura of Akbar, imbuing him with a prophetic halo and celebrated as *Akbarnamah* (completed in 1596), by his brilliant courtier Abu al-Fadl, was to become the dominant discourse for decades to come.

In establishing what has been called 'autocratic centralism' through a new form of epistemology, Akbar claimed a double authority in various forms, while flexibly interpreting the shariʿa.[19] Apart from the *farr-e izadi* or ray of God, which had come a long way from pre-Islamic Persian times via the Sultanate notion of the shadow of God transmitting divine effulgence from ruler to ruler, and *tauhid-e ilahi*, the royal cult which was meant to secure the nobles through a personal bond of allegiance to the ruler, a transcendental symbol was needed which could be acceptable to all existing religions of South Asia. This symbol was to take shape in the idea of the fire as the divine sun. A proven device, it was supplemented by elements of Islamic mysticism, in particular by the idea of illuminationist theory. Abu al-Fadl, Akbar's chief ideologue, murdered at Jahangir's behest in 1602 because of his influence over Akbar, was the chief architect of this theory. Abu al-Fadl himself, like his emperor, had a conciliatory attitude towards Hinduism, and the symbolic relationship between sun and king represented the conciliation between Hinduism and Islam, and in the long run became a solid pillar of the Mughal ideology of power. Akbar would exercise power over both the profane as well as the sacred worlds. Curtailing the authority of *sadr al-sudur* by nominating provincial *sadrs* served as an example of the reach of his power. This is not to suggest that the Mughals did not take recourse to orthodox ideas. Thus Humayun's son and Akbar's step-brother Mirza Muhammad Hakim (1554–85), the quasi-sovereign of Kabul region, was proclaimed king of Kabul

[19] Cf. J. Richards: "The Formulation of Imperial Authority under Akbar and Jahangir", in: Chr. W. Troll (ed.): *Islam in India. Studies and Commentaries*, Vol. II, New Delhi 1985; Peter Hardy: "Abu'l Fazl's Portrait of the Perfect Padshah: a political Philosophy for Mughal India—or a personal puff for a pale", in: Troll (ed.): *Islam in India. Studies and Commentaries*; S.A.A. Rizvi: *Religion and Intellectual History of the Muslims in Akbar's Reign, with special reference to Abu'l Fazl (1556–1605)*, New Delhi 1975; Alam: "Shariʿa and Governance in the Indo-Islamic Context"; and Muzaffar Alam: "Akhlaqui Norms in Mughal Governance" in: M. Alam et alii (eds.): *The Making of the Indo-Persian Culture: Indian and French Studies*, Delhi 1999.

by the old establishment and was legitimised by Islamic orthodoxy in 1580. Thus, on the whole, the Mughals were quite eclectic in their use of ideological formulations.[20] The discussions between Jesuits, Hindus and members of other religions created a shared court-culture, which was Akbar's personal way to reconciliation which was not forced upon the courtiers. Its demerit was that it would not outlive him. Apart from visual representations such as paintings and royal portraits that made up an iconography of the sacred,[21] as well as literary texts, an imperial coinage issued in 1577 also served the purpose of establishing Akbar's position as a lunar king who embodied justice, consolidation and discipline. Subsequently, in 1579, the "philosopher upon the throne" declared himself the highest religious authority through a *mahzar*, a public attestation or "infallible-decree", not only over Muslims but over all humans. A new calendar was introduced,[22] which made a programmatic break with tradition through the *tarikh-e alfi*, commissioned by Akbar from about 1581. This unfinished history of the Islamic millennium called for a new era starting from the death of Prophet Muhammad rather than from the *hijra*, thereby contesting the orthodox historiography. At the same time Akbar employed unique and quite unorthodox methods to instill a policy of piety, such as supporting women's *hajj*, initiated and organised by women, as documented in the *Akbarnamah*. These and similar activities of noble women in the making of the Mughal empire might have reinforced the Islamic face of the highly controversial Islamicity of the empire.[23]

Akbar's iconographical politics displayed the extent of his disassociation from Islamic orthodoxy and was paralleled by impressive reforms aimed at establishing cultural and economic integration. The administrative handbook *A'in-e Akbari* written by Abu al-Fadl sheds ample

---

[20] See Alam and Subrahmanyam (eds.): *The Mughal State*, pp. 22–23.

[21] The miniature painting depicts a variety of themes latently and openly displaying the role of noble and not so noble women in the context and making of Mughal glory. For a detailed analysis of the painting see Heike Franke: *Akbar und Ǧahângîr. Untersuchungen zur politischen und religiösen Legitimation in Text und Bild*, Schenefeld EB-Verlag 2005; see also the illuminating article by Monica Juneja: "On the Margins of Utopia—One more look at Mughal Painting", in: *The Medieval History Journal* 4/2 (2001), pp. 203–240.

[22] See also ʿAbdul Qadir Badauni: *Muntakhab al Tawarikh, I–III*, Calcutta: College Press 1865, transl. by G.S.A. Ranking/W.H. Lowe/S.W. Haig, Patna: Academia Asiatica 1973, Vol. 2, pp. 271–72; Rafat Bilgrami: "Akbar's Mahdar of 1579", in: *Islamic Culture* (1973), pp. 232–240.

[23] This has been outlined in Lal: "Mughal India: 15th to Mid-18th Century", p. 69.

light on this process of integration, partial as it might have been.[24] The centralisation and rationalisation of the revenue system demanded one third of the income to go to the crown. This income might have been the reason to put an end to the unpopular tax of *jizya* in 1564. But it should also be kept in mind that this changing source of revenue coincided with the recruitment of Rajput nobles into the imperial service. The Turanis who were the old, genealogically legitimised elites mainly from Central Asia, were replaced by new, indigenous Muslim and Hindu service elites directly responsible to the ruler. This reform led to rebellions of the old establishment in 1564 and 1574. It may be for this reason that *jizya* was re-imposed in 1575.[25]

A restructuring of the *iqta*ʿ system and of civil and military hierarchies called the *mansabdari*, imposed uniform royal standards demanding mounted (*sawar*) and armed (*dhat*) cavalrymen. Even the gentry submitted to this strict ranking system of the administrative and military apparatus, which eventually led to a militarised Mughal culture.[26] These wide-ranging fiscal, administrative, military and land reforms (*zabt*) in the 1580s were to proclaim Persian as the language of administration. They were primarily issued and supervised by the Khatri Hindu revenue minister, Todar Mal.[27] It was a system that had been experimented with earlier in one way or the other during the Sur Empire.

In the course of time the empire was able to incorporate large parts of South Asia including the kingdoms of Deccan, which derived their legitimacy from Safawid Iran.[28] The Shiʿite culture of this region fanned out over all of South Asia, especially over the regions of present day Pakistan, parts of North India and the Deccan. The pinnacle of this acculturation is best reflected in Mughal art, which is a blend of Persian and Indian elements. Soon the Dutch who had come to India

---

[24] See the critical remarks in: Muzaffar Alam and Sanjay Subrahmanyam: "L'État moghol et sa fiscalité", in: *Annales HSS* 1 (1994), pp. 189–217.

[25] Cf. Iqtidar Alam Khan: "The Nobility Under Akbar and the Development of His Religious Policy, 1560–1580", in: *JRAS* (1968), 29–36.

[26] For the important aspect of militarisation of Mughal culture in the context of empire-building see Kolff: "A Warlord's Fresh Attempt at Empire"; Seema Alavi: *The Sepoys and the Company. Tradition and Transition in Northern India 1770–1830*, New Delhi 1995.

[27] Similarly, the *waqf* under the Mughals; see Gregory C. Kozlowski: "Imperial Authority, Benefactions and Endowments (Awqâf) in Mughal India", in: *IJMES* 38 (1995), pp. 355–370.

[28] Cf. Nazir Ahmad: "Letters of the Rulers of the Deccan to Shah Abbas of Iran", in: *Medieval India: A Miscellany*, Vol. 1 Aligarh 1969, pp. 280–300.

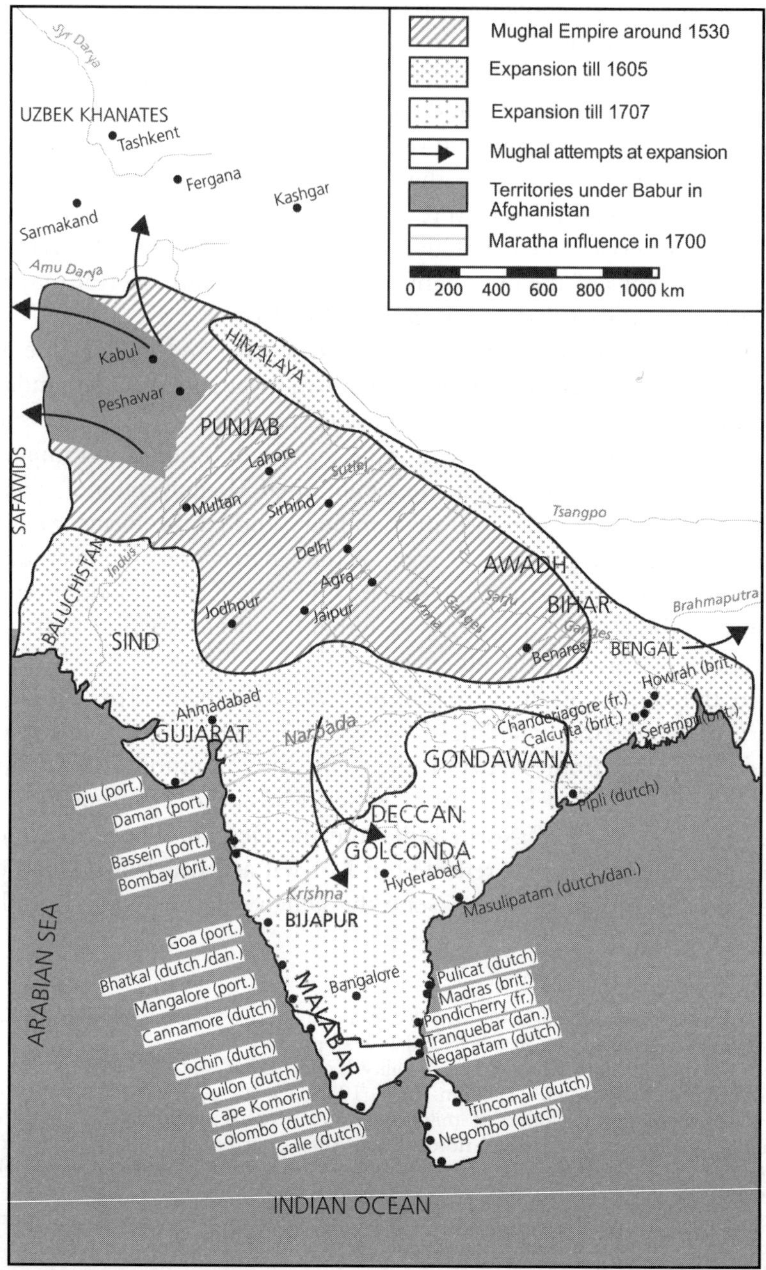

Map 9: Expansion of Mughal power

with their *Vereenigde Oostindische Compagnie* (VOC), established in 1599, replaced the Portuguese hegemony in the Indian Ocean. Their presence gave newer impulses to Indian art, particularly in the field of painting as Mughal painters began to use the representational techniques of the European Renaissance: the solar halo encountered by Mughal painters in European religious images was incorporated into their iconographic repertoire from Jahangir onwards.

Translations of Latin, Arabic and Sanskrit texts into Persian—the lingua franca of Mughal Empire—not only created more employment for the locals. They also reflected the fact that Persian had attained a status as the first language of the Mughals and their administration on all levels. And Persian became a vehicle for the process of cultural integration particularly on the higher level; knowledge of the language became a matter of prestige and wielded some cultural capital. It is however, not yet clear whether Akbar's well known translation bureau was an institutionalised expression of new ideas similar to those in Europe at that time. It was little understood as to why the Quran was not translated at all into Persian. It is also difficult to understand why Akbar did not use the printing techniques introduced by the Portuguese to India (Goa) in 1556 for his cultural politics. Whether printed books were considered useless because of a relatively high literary rate could be an argument still to be probed. Perhaps the reason may lie in the scholars' opposition to the printing technique on ethical grounds. Additionally, they might have feared losing their monopoly as agents of knowledge, this perhaps harking back to Brahmin tradition. There could also have been aesthetic reasons. Arabic script was considered sacred and demanded very high standards of beauty and symmetry which at that time could only be provided by calligraphers;[29] after all, there were many scribes who could copy books. In fact Akbar, when presented with a printed book, dismissed it as ugly, grotesque and gross. Nevertheless, he allowed the import of printed books.

Certainly printed books have the potential to democratise knowledge, resulting in changes in the power structures of society. In fact, the power and prestige of the learned not only depended on their monopoly on knowledge but through certain pedagogical practices, they also could

---

[29] See Francis Robinson: "Technology and Religious Change: Islam and the Impact of Print", in: *MAS* 27/1 (1993), pp. 229–251; Reinhard Schulze: "Die Islamische Welt in der Neuzeit", in: Noth and Paul (eds.): *Der islamische Orient*, pp. 366f.; A.J. Qaisar: *The Indian Response to European Technology*, Bombay 1982, p. 58.

shape a network of scholarly relationships, which could be a source of power in times of crisis or even otherwise. Traditional pedagogy not only created this intellectual field but also set the rules to operate within and master the codes of the field in order to be successful. After all, in what appeared to be a meritocracy based on piety, Islamic institutions were the most efficient channels of transforming cultural capital into economic capital.

At the same time the renaissance tradition supported further developments of a humanist worldview that would provide a predominant role for human beings endowed with reason. Mathematics, astronomy, historiography and philosophy gave primacy to the present time rather than to the past: the present became important because it could critically mediate the past—through an alternative teleology of universal history shifting from the framework of an Islamic community to that of humanity as a whole rather than territoriality.[30] These sciences came to be taught in many institutions throughout the empire. Consequently, sciences taught at the time of Akbar were predominantly rational (*ma'quli*) in the sense that they attempted to centralise the empire through a broadly liberal interpretation of the world. Many philosophical and legal texts, which had already gained importance during the Sultanate period, were re-read and taught. Persian became the dominant language, so much so that it became a major factor in religious studies contesting Arabic as the sole language of religious discourse. It seems that these rational sciences played an important role in the process of cultural integration and in consolidating the empire, as well as civilising nature as could be seen in the geometrical layout of urban topography.[31] These developments were also influenced by a tendency to popular piety, mystical orders and beliefs. That is why Ibn 'Arabi's idea of "unity of being" (*Wahdat al-Wujud*) became more popular here than in the rest of the Islamic world.[32] This ontological monism blurred the boundaries between religions which in a pragmatic sense was essential for the functioning of a Muslim minority. The rationale was that if "all is He" (*hama ust*), as propagated by Ashraf Simnani

[30] Compare Monica Juneja: "On the Margins of Utopia", pp. 211ff.; Mukhia: *The Mughals*, pp. 4ff., and Chap. I, on different ways of legitimacy of Mughals.

[31] See Attillio Petruccioli: "The Geometry of Power: The City's Planning", in: Michael Brand & Glenn D. Lowry: *Akbar and Fatehpur Sikri*, Bombay: Marg Publications 1987, pp. 49–64.

[32] For the influence of Ibn 'Arabi in South Asia, see William Chittick: "Notes on Ibn al-'Arabi's Influence in the Indian Sub-Continent", in: *MW* 82 (1992), pp. 218–241.

(died 1425) in the fifteenth century, then divinity must also be present among other non-Islamic, e.g., Hindu beliefs. Sufi orders like Chishtiyya and Suhrawardiyya, followed by the Qadiriyya enthusiastically preached similar pantheistic ideas, most notably Shaikh Muhibb Allah (died 1648) and Shaikh ʿAbd al-Rahman Chishti (died 1683) who tried to integrate the God Krishna into the context of *Wahdat al-Wujud*.[33] Consequently, this transference of divine benediction transmitted among others in songs and hymns also took place within the field of the Emperor's imperial construction.[34]

The Muslimness of "Pax Mughalica"

The stress on the discipline of philosophy and rational approach went back, among others, to major writers such as al-Farabi (died 950), Ibn Miskawayh (932–1030) and Nasir al-Din al-Tusi (1201–1274). Al-Tusi is considered one of the most important and influential Shiʿite scholars in the field of mathematics, geometry, astronomy, philosophy and theology. In 1259 he wrote his political treatise *Akhlaq-e Nasiri* which was essentially Aristotelian ethics read via Ibn Miskawayh (whose *Tahdhib al-Akhlaq*, Cultivation of Morals, he was commissioned to translate into Persian), with a practical orientation ideally providing for all persons, not only Muslims, the way to achieve perfection. His inclusivistic vision became quite popular, finding its way to India via immigrating Persian scholars and making profound impact even beyond the Mughal court. As Muzaffar Alam has stated, it was well read among the Mughal political elites and became an "undisputable source of Abul Fazl's non-sectarian ideology". It was consequently integrated into courses of ethics in the *madrasa* syllabus to become one of the "most favoured readings of the Mughal political élites." Many similar inclusivistic *akhlaq* texts followed,[35] elaborating upon imperial etiquette[36] and its discourse, perceiving political organisation in terms of cooperation achieved through justice. This justice was to be exercised by the ruler,

---

[33] See R. Vassie: "ʿAbd al-Rahman Chishtî and the Bhagavadgita 'unity of religion' theory in practice", in: Leonard Lewisohn (ed.): *The Heritage of Sufism, Vol. II: The Legacy of medieval Persian Sufism (1150–1500)*, pp. 368–377. Alam: *Languages*, pp. 96ff., 170.

[34] See Mukhia: *The Mughals*, Chap. IV: *Folklore and the Mughal Court Culture*.

[35] See Alam: *Languages*, pp. 46ff., quotation p. 61.

[36] On the detailed refinement of Mughal etiquette, including *paibos, zaminbos, sijda, kurnish, taslim*, dress, language etc., see Mukhia: *The Mughals*, Chap. II.

who was supposed to be affectionate and favourable, rather than using his power to command and seek obedience. Ideally, justice and mutual love were the cornerstones of government for emphasis on maintaining social balance and peace for all (*sulh-e kull*), rather than expressly concerned with religiosity.[37]

One may compare, in some way, the idea of *sulh-e kull* with the Vedic or Hindu idea of *dharma*, which means social order. The foremost duty of the king was to uphold *dharma*, maintaining the social order which meant accepting caste/*varna* as natural and given. Indeed, to prevent the mixing of castes (*varna-sankara*), for example, by inter-marriage was one of the most important duties of the king. Thus *sulh-e kull* could be read in terms that were not much of a departure from the status quo. In other words, the attempted blurring of boundaries was solely aimed at the upper castes. Within their respective boundaries, however, both the Hindus and Muslims were oppressive as far as the lower castes were concerned. Boundaries were already blurred as far as the lower castes of Hindus and Muslims were concerned. Indeed theirs was a more organic understanding of similarities united through their everyday life situations. In contrast, the upper castes, divorced as they were from the exigencies of everyday existence of lower castes, had to struggle hard to blur the boundaries.

Influenced by a strong political tradition of accommodation and relying on the liberal concept of social harmony, effected by *akhlaqi* norms and liberal Sufi texts, Akbar and Jahangir were able to adjust more flexibly to local Indian peculiarities in order to legitimise their wide-ranging reforms. Emphasis on the tradition of *sulh-e kull* meant support for both patrimonialism and equality between Muslims and non-Muslims, leading to increased confessional pluralism. In a sense the emperors' eclecticism was, in its historical sequence, a further development of the policies of some of his predecessors on the thrones of Delhi, Kashmir, and Deccan.[38]

The Mughal system attempted to integrate the empire through different policies, albeit not totally and homogenously. Socio-cultural diversity stretching from Central Asia to Bengal in the east and Deccan in the south required the creation and support of an alternative gentry. This

---

[37] On the impact of Nasir al-Din Tusi's political ideas on the Mughals see Alam: "Shariʿa and Governance in the Indo-Islamic Context", esp. pp. 229–231, 234.

[38] See Aziz Ahmad: *Studies in Islamic Culture in the Indian Environment*, Oxford 1964, p. 180.

support was sought to be created through the establishment of *madad-e ma'ash* grants and through the *zamindars* (vigilant revenue collecting intermediaries between the—mostly absent—*jagirdars* and local people). Even this was precarious and led to massive *zamindari* revolts. Thus the Mughal Empire resembled a mosaic of different regions, but a dynamic one: though changes were not sudden, yet they did have the capacity to incrementally alter forms over a long period of time. However, despite recurrent separatist movements, Akbar's reign supported cultural integration which went hand in hand with measures such as the upgrading of the state road network and system of mileposts (*kos minars*) to support trade and tie different parts of the empire together.

Akbar's son Salim, who was thought to be a gift from the shrine of Mu'in al-Din Chishti at Ajmer, was named after Salim Chishti. Only after a fierce revolt against his father Akbar in 1600, Salim became the successor known as Jahangir (Conqueror of the world), in 1605. First, Jahangir had to consolidate the internal frontiers, in particular to subdue the Rana of Mewar, head of Sisodia clan, and the Sikhs in Punjab, who had been contesting Mughal hegemony towards the end of the seventeenth century. Jahangir was somewhat more concerned with enriching his court with imperial culture through various objects and ideas, including his penchant for miniature paintings, which were renowned for their naturalism and further visualised political concepts.[39] He also tried to settle problems through what he considered a systematic public welfare, freedom and security. These changes were informed by social unrest and the existing contestations of power among local landlords due to the land and fiscal reforms introduced by Jahangir. Apart from this Jahangir also abolished taxes, centralised the market towns and prohibited wine production, which caused consternation amongst the landlords. He further Persianised court culture and made the Twelver Shia Imams revered even among Sunni Muslims. However, just like his father before him, he presented himself as the sun-king, while at the same time admiring the Qadiri saint Miyan Mir (1550–1636) of Lahore.

Jahangir's reign also saw an increase in European travellers to India and the advent of the European East India Companies. It was the beginning of latent influence, not only cultural and symbolic, but also commercial and economic. Networks of bankers and financiers increasingly

[39] Richards: *The Mughal Empire*, p. 101.

transferred revenue through bills of exchange (*hundi*), consequently meshing the fiscal system with commercial ones, enabling both the court as well as noblemen to participate in trade. Such "state mercantilism" was initiated by Jahangir but especially accelerated under his second son Khurram using the infrastructure provided by the network of *qasbahs*. Iranian influence might have played a role, but the important reason for resorting to "state mercantilism" was the Mughal court's desire to compete with the Ottomans and the Safawids.[40] While the Mughals claimed to have greater territory under their control, the Ottomans controlled Mecca, Medina and other holy sites. Wealth and territory were the prime reasons for Mughals to become the sole Sunni monarchs rivalling the Ottoman Sultans. Letters and other correspondences between the Mughal and Ottoman rulers show that the former claimed the title of caliph,[41] while Mughal painters portray Mughal Emperors as generous hosts to the Safawid ruler.[42]

Prince Khurram's succession to the throne was the result of the active role played by his mother, Nur Jahan[43] and some of her colleagues. Usually known as "Shahjahan" (King of the World) he was also the second "Lord of Conjunction". Subduing the initial rebellions he secured succession in 1628, making Agra his capital until 1648. After that he moved to the newly completed imperial city of Shahjahanabad, to rule the empire for another decade till 1658. During his period, the Afghans became powerful enough again to interfere with trade and commerce, making the Europeans the benefactors. It was natural therefore to shift the focus of administration gradually to the South.

The grandeur of Shahjahan's rule is expressed through the extraordinary monumental buildings, such as the Taj Mahal on the banks of the Yamuna.[44] Besides renovating the Lahore Fort and the Shalimar Gardens in Kashmir, the new capital of Shahjahanabad was built to

---

[40] See Alam and Subrahmanyam (eds.): *The Mughal State*, pp. 25–29.

[41] Thomas W. Arnold: *The Caliphate*, Oxford 1924, Ch. VIII: The Mughal Emperors in India, pp. 159–162.

[42] Juneja: "On the Margins of utopia", pp. 213 f; Franke: *Akbar und Ǧahângîr*, pp. 308–312.

[43] Again, the role of royal women in crucial matters of politics becomes evident. See the role of Nur Jahan as the "*Empress of Mughal India*" by Ellison Banks Findly: *Nur Jahan: Empress of Mughal India*, New Delhi: OUP 2001.

[44] Richards: *The Mughal Empire*, pp. 123–125; on the Taj see also Juneja: "Introduction", pp. 40–42, and the bibliographical notes therein, Catherine B. Asher: *Architecture of Mughal India (The New Cambridge History of India, I:4)*, Cambridge 1992, pp. 209ff. This monument can be considered a manifestation of guilt rather than of love, for his wife died giving birth to her fourteenth child!

display royal might reminiscent of Islamic glory and conquest.[45] Apart from this glorious imperial culture, Shahjahan patronised an intellectual movement, which tried to bridge the gap between Hinduism and Islam, and sought to evolve a common language for the representatives of both traditions. The reason for this movement was that the empire needed to be internally consolidated. An unsuccessful attempt was made to subdue the Uzbeks near the northwestern borders in order to expand the crown's land (*khalisa*). This reflected the power struggle between the monarch at the centre and the amirs and *jagirdars* on the peripheries. However, the clearing of forested land for colonisation eased some pressure as it added substantially to income accrued for the imperial revenue system, extracting vast sums from the production of Indian agriculturists, craftsmen and traders.[46]

Changes also occurred in the nobility with the relationship between the emperor and the elite becoming more formal. *Khanazadagi* replaced discipleship.[47] Similarly, the influence of Islamic orthodox ideas and movements, notably the Naqshbandiyya, grew stronger. Their ideas and institutions were transported by an influx of people from Central Asia. These developments gradually tightened the borders of religious identities, expressed in the fact that the shariʿa became the basis of official policy from 1633 onwards.[48] At the same time, connections to the Hijaz by supporting the pilgrimage to Mecca were to underline the policy of piety.

Negotiating religious boundaries

The policy of cultural integration provided space for pluralist texts such as descriptions of lived and shared religion in *Dabistan-e Madhahib* (The School of Religions) most probably written by Kaykhusraw Isfandyar (ca. b. 1618) in 1650s[49] or the adventures of Amir Hamza,

---

[45] See Stephen P. Blake: *Shahjahanabad; The Sovereign City in Mughal India 1639–1739*, Cambridge 1991; Ehlers and Krafft (eds.): *Shâhjahânâbâd*.

[46] Richards: *The Mughal Empire*, p. 140.

[47] See John F. Richards: "Norms of Comportment among Imperial Mughal Officers", in: B.D. Metcalf (ed.): *Moral conduct and authority*, Berkeley: UCP 1984, pp. 255–289.

[48] Newly built Hindu temples were to be demolished, while the birthday of the Prophet was celebrated in fervour. See Z.A. Desai and W.E. Begley (eds.): *The Shah Jahan Nama of 'Inayat Khan,'* New Delhi: OUP 1990, pp. 90, 118.

[49] For an English translation of this interesting text see *The Dabistan or School of Manners, Translated from the Original Persian with Notes and Illustrations*, trans. David Shea and

the *Hamzanamah*, commissioned under Akbar.[50] But it also encountered opposition and sharp criticism from orthodox quarters, as mentioned by the historian ʿAbd al-Qadir Badayuni, author of the celebrated unofficial history entitled *Muntakhab al-Tawarikh*. Thus in order to gain a comprehensive picture, Abu al-Fadl's liberalism should be read alongside the shariʿate perspective of al-Barani and Badayuni. Apart from scribal criticisms, there were revolts, outbreaks, and major religious groups which had more immediate impact. It is in this context that confessionalisation of Islamic culture in the sixteenth century should be understood wherein the identification of one's own local culture with the higher Islamic tradition became increasingly important. Basically, contesting eschatological movements at the end of the millennium redressed the grievances of those men who had lost their status in society due to Mughal imperialism. Differing religious interpretations and stricter enforcement of rules eventually resulted in the creation of distinctive communities of the faithful. These groups competed for the establishment of their respective faiths more firmly with the local population. They sharpened their religious profiles in order to draw strict borderlines, and developed numerous social techniques to instill doctrinal conformity and discipline. Sometimes cooperation with the Mughal court was necessary. Thus, their actions were crushed occasionally by military interventions, but usually neutralised by alliances or financial donations. One such example is that of the Mahdawiyya, led by Sayyid Muhammad Kazimi of Jaunpur (died 1505), which developed its own mobilisation institutions (*daʾira*), but was later accommodated socially and theologically by the Mughals. However, the Mughals were not so accommodating all the time. Anti-Mughal movements, if located within important trade routes such as those connecting the region with Central Asia and Iran, were subjected by sheer brute force. An example was the Rawshaniyya movement among the Pakhtun tribals in North West of the empire, which was led by Bayazid Ansari (1525–1576?), a former merchant transformed into "the perfect spiritual guide" (*pir-e kamil*) and "the axis of the age" (*qutb*). The "Enlightened Spiritual Master's"

Anthony Troye, vol. 3 (Paris, 1843); reprinted as *Oriental Literature or the Dabistan*, Lahore: Khalil & Co., 1973. On Dabistan see Fath Allah Mojtabaʾi: "Dabistan-i Madaheb," in: *Encyclopaedia Iranica*, vi, 1:532–534.

[50] See Musharraf Ali Farooqi: *The Adventures of Amir Hamza or the Dastan-e Amir Hamza* New York: Random House Modern Library, 2007.

(*Pir-e Raushan*) anti-Mughal sentiments were grounded in economic marginalisation resulting from the imposition of Mughal taxes. His social revolutionary messages were primarily articulated in Pushto. But since this Mahdi movement threatened the existing status-quo, it was crushed militarily and the sect declared heretic in Mughal sources.[51]

As has been outlined above, Akbar himself played the political millenarian card to consolidate his own position—a card that reflected synchronisms as well as connected or shared histories and faiths, e.g., the simultaneous appearance of Jewish, Christian and Islamic messianisms in different regions during the sixteenth century, as has been convincingly argued by Sanjay Subrahmanyam.[52]

In the sixteenth century, monistic *wujudi*-perceptions also demanded sharp and exclusivist identities that supported an idea of difference with a view to restore the influence of Sunni orthodoxy. The argument was that religious decadence and the political decay of the empire had reached new heights. It was in this context that the anti-Shia and anti-Hindu Shaikh Ahmad Sirhindi (1564–1624),[53] the "renewer of the Second Millennium" (*Mujaddid-e alf-e thani*), voiced a new articulation, albeit one based on old traditions. A native from East Punjab, Sirhindi had learnt at the feet of his father Shaikh ʿAbd al-Ahad (died 1599), who as a Chishti-Sabiri had strong *wujudi* inclinations and had been a disciple of ʿAbd al-Quddus (died 1537) in Gangoh. He settled down in Sirhind where he became a pious scholar. Thus Ahmad Sirhindi was firmly rooted in the Chishti tradition, until he very briefly met the itinerant Central Asian Naqshbandi Sufi Khawaja Baqi Billah (died 1603) in Delhi, becoming his khalifa in 1599. It must be noted that the early Naqshbandis coming from Central Asia hardly displayed exclusivism towards non-Muslims. In contrast, Ahmad Sirhindi seems to

---

[51] S.A.A. Rizvi: *Muslim Revivalist Movements in Northern India in the sixteenth and seventeenth centuries*, Lucknow: Balkrishna Book Co. 1965, Ch. II and III. Also Derryl MacLean: "The Sociology of Political Engagement: The Mahdawiyah and the State", in: Eaton (ed.): *India's Islamic Traditions*, pp. 150–166; Derryl N. MacLean: "Real Men and false Men at the Court of Akbar. The Majalis of Shaykh Mustafa Gujarati", in: Gilmartin and Lawrence (eds.): *Beyond Turk and Hindu*; Jamal Malik: "16th century Mahdism; The Rawshanîya movement among Pakhtun tribes," in: Dallapiccola & Zingel-Avé Lallemant (eds.): *Islam and Indian Regions*, Vol. I, pp. 31–59.

[52] See Subrahmanyam: *Explorations in Connected History*, Chap. 5: "Sixteenth-century Millenarianism from the Tagus to the Ganges", pp. 102–137.

[53] J.G.J. ter Haar: *Follower and heir of the Prophet. Shaykh Ahmad Sirhindi (1564–1624) as Mystic*, Leiden: Brill 1992; Yohanan Friedmann: *Shaykh Ahmad Sirhindî; An Outline of His Thought and a Study of His Image in the Eyes of Posterity*, Montreal 1971.

have been the first Naqshbandi who was profoundly anti-non-Muslim. He was a member of a group of Muslim functional elite and gentry, theologians, judges, and Sufis, who had relied on state patronage and had been uneasy with Akbar's inclusivistic policies allowing non-Muslims to participate in Mughal administration. Sirhindi responded to these concerns, particularly through his letters (*maktubat*), a method reminiscent of ʿAbd al-Quddus Gangohi, who was famous for his critical shariʿa-based epistles to the Lodhis and early Mughals nearly a century ago.[54] Sirhindi stressed strict observance of the shariʿa, the discrimination of non-Muslims, and criticised the monistic concept of Ibn ʿArabi (unity of being). This he reinterpreted by explaining the concept in terms of "unity of testation" (*wahdat al-shuhud*), which had already been formulated by the Iranian Kubrawi Sufi ʿAla al-Din Simnani (died 1336) two centuries ago.[55] In so doing, Sirhindi gave the ideas of Ibn ʿArabi a new social role, which aimed at changing society. After realising the experience of absolute unity (*wahdat al-wujud*), the Sufi (that is Sirhindi himself) returns to the world and sharing in the qualities of Prophet Muhammad, harmonises the degenerated moral order with the divine. In this perception the Prophet was endowed an even more prominent role. At the same time spiritual audition (*samaʿ*) was considered reprehensible, and silent *dhikr*, being a normative part of Naqshbandi ideas, was preferred. Thus, the basic boundary markers between different sufic and social groups were sobriety (*sahw*) and intoxication (*sukr*), rather than *wahdat al-wujud* and *wahdat al-shuhud*, but they added to the confessional trends.

Certainly, a number of important scholars opposed Sirhindi's views, even if many of them shared the idea of orthodox revival, such as the celebrated hadith scholar and Qadiri Shaikh, ʿAbd al-Haqq Dihlawi (died 1642). Being prominent among the Indo-Turani scholarly elite he authored a number of major books, such as *Akhbar al-Akhyar*, a biographical dictionary of Indo-Muslim Sufis. In *The Perfection of Faith*, ʿAbd al-Haqq paradigmatically made use of reason and tradition in order to prove God's omnipotence, which ran contrary to Akbar's prophet cult, which had endowed the emperor with divine power. His main

[54] David W. Damrel: "The 'Naqshbandî Reaction' Reconsidered", in: Gilmartin and Lawrence (eds.): *Beyond Turk and Hindu*, pp. 176–199, esp. 182–184.

[55] See H. Landolt: "Der Briefwechsel zwischen Kâshânî und Simnânî über Wahdat al-Wujûd", in: *Der Islam* L/1 (1973), pp. 29–81; and Pierre Lory: *Les Commentaires ésotériques du Coran d'après ʿAbd al-Razzâq al-Qâshânî*, Paris 1980, pp. 177–187.

contribution, however, seems to be the successful endeavour of giving a new impetus to the study of hadith,[56] which had been neglected for several centuries. And hadith studies did have strong institutional as well as discursive affiliation to the Arab peninsula: there the Naqshbandi from Delhi had met scholars such as the Muttaqi brothers Shaikh ʿAli and ʿAbd al-Wahhab from Central India, who had immigrated to the Hijaz in their quest for knowledge and piety.

So ʿAbd al-Haqq, whom Jahangir held in some esteem,[57] might have been looking for reconciliation between the extremes, when he severely criticised Sirhindi's self-proclaimed spiritual stage. Thus Sirhindi was imprisoned by Jahangir exactly because of his self-exalted position but was later pardoned.[58] However, Sirhindi's *silsila* known as the Naqshbandiyya-Mujaddidiyya became popular beyond the borders of South Asia due to its claim of authority elaborated in a theory of prophetology, with his descendants claiming to be the righteous leader in the quest for Prophetic sunna and the highest saint, the so-called *qayyum*. The new order took much from the Chishti-Sabiri attitudes and practices, which made it appealing to Indian Chishtis as well. But at the same time this branch was alienated from other Naqshbandis operating in South Asia.[59] Therefore, Sirhindi's response was a distinctively Indian purist answer to a widespread heterodox Sufism in the subcontinent.

Apparently, after an era of the development of a pluralistic religious milieu facilitated by *akhlaqi* norms and liberal Sufi texts, prophetic tradition and its relevance as an ethical ideal had returned to learned discourse and religious praxis, at a time when Mughal India was facing a major crisis on the eve of the fratricidal wars following Shahjahan's reign. When Shahjahan died, he left behind a yet unresolved political and ideational crisis, reflecting two major tendencies within South Asian Islam. The first was the liberal inclusivist string striving to safeguard balance between contesting interests, in the tradition of Amir Khusraw (died 1325), al-Biruni, Abu al-Fadl and Akbar. The second was orthodox exclusivism expounded by thinkers such as al-Barani, Badayuni and

[56] Hadith studies did not necessarily entail a traditionalisation of scholarship, as it also had the potential of newness—as the Arabic term *hadith*, e.g., news, itself suggests.

[57] Cf. Rizvi: *Muslim Revivalist Movements*, p. 173; Jahangir: *The Tuzuk-i-Jahangiri or the Memoirs of Jahangir*, Vols. 1–2, transl. and ed. by A. Rogers and H. Beveridge, Delhi: Atlantic Publishers 1989 (reprint), Vol. 2, p. 111.

[58] See Rizvi: *Muslim Revivalist Movements*, Ch. VI, pp. 287ff. Jahangir: *Tuzuk*, Vol. 2, pp. 91, 93, 161, 276.

[59] See Damrel: "The 'Naqshbandî Reaction' Reconsidered", esp. pp. 193f.

Sirhindi, who strove not only for shariʿa rule but also the humiliation and extermination of non-Muslim subjects. According to scholarly opinion, the former tradition was represented to some degree in the ideas of Shahjahan's eldest son Dara Shikoh, who is also known for having several texts translated from Sanskrit to Persian and vice-versa. A poor general and leader, he adhered to the ideas of the Qadiri order, which had started spreading across India from the Punjab, and which by then had reached Delhi and Agra via Sind and Deccan. Qadiris increasingly contested the Chishti hegemony during the seventeenth century,[60] as reflected in Dara's hagiographical testament of the Qadiri order (*Sakinat al-awliya*) in general, and of Miyan Mir and his successor Mullah Shah in particular. It is true that in his "The Meeting Place of the Two Oceans" (*Majmaʿ al-Bahrayn*) Dara elaborated on correlations between Sufi and the Upanisadic cosmologies, beliefs, and practices, and proposed that the Upanishads were necessary to be able to understand the Quran. Yet, as Carl Ernst has pointed out, Dara expressed contempt for the generality of both Hindus and Muslims; he had nothing to do with the common people of either community, but associated with the esoteric elites of both groups.[61] Similarly, one is reminded of the Shahjahan's third son Aurangzeb, who represented the tradition, that strictly obeyed the ritual commandments of the Quran, and called for religious orthodoxy, influenced by post-Sirhindi Naqshbandis. According to this scenario the ideological tussle took place at the court in Shahjahanabad, with Dara Shikoh being the designated heir, as well as in the Deccan, where Aurangzeb had successfully subjugated the Southern territories.[62]

Since the rules of succession did allow younger brothers to succeed to the throne, a bloody war of succession broke out while the aged Shahjahan was battling with death. Finally, the well-equipped army of Aurangzeb captured Shahjahan and defeated the three other brothers,

[60] In the sixteenth century, the Qadiriyya is mentioned as one of the highly respected orders but is not included among those recognised in India, according to *A'in-e Akbari*. However, Azad Bilgrami's *Ma'athir al-Kiram* dated 1752 mentions some important Qadiri Sufis. See also S. Moinul Haq: "Rise of the Naqshbandî and Qâdirî Silsilahs in the Subcontinent", in: *JPHS* XXV (1977), pp. 1–33.

[61] See the critical study by Carl W. Ernst: "Muslim Studies of Hinduism? A Reconsideration of Persian and Arabic Translations from Sanskrit", in: *Iranian Studies* 36 (2003), pp. 173–195.

[62] This scenario also gives way to the sweeping narratives that teleologically leads to partition in 1947.

Dara, Shujaʿ and Murad, who were subsequently executed between 1659 and 1661. This left Aurangzeb as the single great Timurid monarch ruling a unitary empire despite the fact that the civil war had devoured some of its income following an agrarian crisis.[63] The execution of Dara Shikoh in 1659 seemed to mark a decisive event in the cultural history of South Asian Islam, and probably gave way to some uncompromising Muslim attitudes towards Hinduism. However the coercive politics of "Pax Mughalica" make clear that Mughal Empire was hardly a close-knit system of power. It was rather more akin to a loose empire of "universal dominion" which accepted some autonomy within the social institutions over which it ruled.[64]

Yet, methods employed in this confessional trend corresponded closely with each other, eventually generating modernising processes in society and the state: it paved the way for the introduction of discipline and rationality, centralisation and bureaucratisation, and finally the enhancement of personal responsibility.

---

[63] See the brief but vivid narration in Richards: *The Mughal Empire*, Chap. VII.

[64] Refer to David Washbrook: "South Asia, The World System, and World Capitalism", in: *JAS* 49/3 (1990), pp. 479–508, here p. 491; also C.A. Bayly: *Indian Society and the Making of the British Empire*, Delhi 1990 (reprint), esp. Chap. I.

EXCURSUS

CONVERSION AND MISSION

The process of religious conversion attracts the attention and scholarship of psychologists, anthropologists, historians and theologians alike. It has been simply defined as the adoption of a new religion or a change in the orientation of one's faith; yet it is much more complex than this would suggest. Religious conversion is often experienced as a re-birth or awakening, leading to a sudden change in one's worldview, lifestyle and environment. Conversion does not occur at a specific moment. It is "not mere syncretism, neither can conversion involve a simple and absolute break with a previous social life"[1] but rather acts as a religious passage which is ongoing and partial.

The "convert as a social type"[2] has been constructed on the basis of how one uses language and procedure to prove herself/himself as a convert. In such a typology, we witness a change in the convert's "universe of discourse". She/he dissolves and reconstructs her/his past life. New meaning is given to old facts; everything is interpreted through a new worldview. The convert enters into a "master attribution scheme", through which she/he assumes a "master role", that is the generalisation of the convert role is seen as prestigious, daily routines carry added significance, a new identity is announced.

The convert does not simply replace her/his old belief system with another one. She/he will adopt new beliefs which are, at first, interpreted through an existing reference system.[3] The latter is enlarged through affiliation with a new group which performs and acts upon shared religious beliefs. In this sense, "...the worldview of the convert exists not only as abstract ideas but also as embodied reality, practising

[1] Diane Austin-Broos: "The Anthropology of Conversion: An Introduction", in Andrew Buckser and Stephen Glazier (eds.): *The Anthropology of Religious Conversion*, Lanham, MD: Rowman & Littlefield Publishers, Inc. 2003, p. 2.

[2] D.A. Snow and R. Machalek: "The convert as a social Type", in: *Sociological Theory* 1 (1983), pp. 259–289.

[3] Rebecca Sachs Norris: "Converting to what? Embodied Culture and the Adoption of New Beliefs", in: Buckser and Glazier (eds.): *The Anthropology of Religious Conversion*, pp. 171–181.

the adopted religion acquires not only the gradual assimilation of the meaning of terms and concepts based in the language and symbols of another culture, but also the performance of ritual postures and gestures requiring retraining of deep-seated somatic responses."[4]

The convert *is not converted* automatically. Usually, she/he will initially participate in rituals, freely and actively. Conversion to a new belief system comes later. Through these experiences, the convert relates to the adopted religion either with zealous adherence or selective performance. She/he may grow more "fanatical" or may remain syncretistic.

The process of religious conversion is often more emotional than it is intellectual; part of a quest to belong. The religious authority provides leadership, structure and order/organisation while the religious group provides acceptance and love. Faith offers a relationship to a transcendent being.[5]

Conversion to Islam in South Asia

There have been many theories on the main impulses triggering mass conversions to Islam in South Asia[6] are characterised as: "religion of the sword", "religion of social liberation", "Sufi missionary," "political patronage" and "ecological influences". To this list are added the "warrior Sufi", "immigration" and "forced conversion" theories.[7]

The forced conversion of non-Muslims to Islam characterises the "religion of the sword" theory. There is however, little evidence which supports the application of this process in practice. In fact, conversion of large masses to Islam was usually not forced though there were exceptions to it. Most Muslim kings showed tolerance or neutrality regarding the conversion of non-Muslims to Islam; only a few exercised political persecution. Eaton's research further shows that even though parts of India were exposed to the Muslim military force, there is "an inverse relationship between the degree of Muslim penetration and the

---

[4] Sachs Norris "Converting to what?", p. 171.

[5] Ulrike Popp-Baier: „Konversionsforschung als Thema gegenwärtiger Religionspsychologie", in: Christian Henning and Erich Nestler (eds.): *Konversion zur Aktualität eines Jahrhundertthemas*, Frankfurt am Main: Lang 2002, pp. 95–115.

[6] Ernst: *Eternal Garden*, p. 156.

[7] See also Peter Hardy: "Modern Muslim and European Explanations of Conversion to Islam in South Asia: A Preliminary Survey of the Literature", in: Nehemia Levtzion (ed.): *Conversion to Islam*, New York: Holmes & Meier Publishers 1979, pp. 68–99.

degree of Islamization."[8] Today, the largest share of Muslims in the subcontinent is found in eastern Bengal and the western Punjab.

The "religion of social liberation" theory puts forward the argument that conversion to Islam was motivated by the offer of equality to caste-weary Indians. It suggests that the conversion of "untouchables" and low caste Hindus was a means to escape the Brahmanic oppression and achieve social advancement. However, according to Eaton, conversion to Islam did not improve the plight of Indians, as demonstrated in the case of the *Dalits*.[9] On the contrary, conversion led to their exclusion from the Hindu community. Full integration of the convert into the Muslim community as a Muslim was not achieved. For the most part, Muslims of foreign descent generally avoided contact with converts and rather undertook efforts to display their exclusive *ashraf* status.[10] Although there are examples of *ardhal*-groups climbing up the social hierarchy, at no time in history did Hindus of low caste convert *en masse* to Islam or succeed in significantly improving their material standards or opportunities for social mobility (at least in the first generation). It is noteworthy that Chishtis and Suhrawardis only converted a few high caste Hindus and not the "suppressed Hindu masses" as the theory of the "religion of social liberation" would suggest. The influence of Sufism and of Islamic 'egalitarianism' did not motivate the Hindu lower classes to embrace Islam *per se*.[11] In addition, the suggestion that conversion was most likely in areas where Brahman culture was rooted is not defendable; evidence shows that "the less the prior exposure to Brahmanic civilization, the greater the incidence of subsequent Islamization."[12]

The "Sufi as missionary" theory suggests that Muslim mystics systematically brought Islam to Hindus through their preaching and by force of their character. While there may be a few examples to support this theory, the evidence suggests that Sufis did not set out to convert Hindus. It is suggested that the Chishti Sufis had initially refused to take part in their systematic conversion despite active propagations

---

[8] Eaton: *Rise of Islam and the Bengal Frontier*, p. 115.

[9] See Yoginder Sikand: *Islam, Dalit-Muslim Relations in India*, New Delhi: Global Media Publications, 2004, pp. 47–65. Also Excursus: Caste.

[10] For the *ashraf-ajlaf* divide see Imtiaz Ahmad (ed.): *Caste and Social Stratification among Muslims in India*. Delhi: Manohar 1978 (second edition, revised and enlarged).

[11] See Bruce B. Lawrence: "Early Indo-Muslim Saints and Conversion", in: Y. Friedman (ed.): *Islam in Asia, Vol. I, South Asia*, Boulder: Westview Press 1984, pp. 109–145.

[12] Eaton: *Rise of Islam and the Bengal Frontier*, p. 119.

by the Suhrawardiyya. The mystic of Sufi practices, legends of their miracles and their flexible interpretation of Islam were, however, often appealing to non-Muslims. Converts mixed their non-Muslim religious elements with their new beliefs and practices. Shattariyya members often mastered yoga and were ascetics who attracted Hindus, Buddhists and animists as well as Sufis of other orders. The Isma'ili sect is also said to have "freely adapted local Indian symbolism and integrated it with Islamic themes."[13] Some conversions to Islam took place in *khanaqahs* of famous saints.[14] Sufi shrines and tombs inspired non-Muslims and fostered a greater identification with, if not conversion to, Islam: "the graves of saints and martyrs remained more meaningful for the spiritual lives of village Muslims than the puritanical details of the Shari'a."[15] Today, the tombs of Sufi saints are frequented by Muslims and Hindus alike.

On the other hand, Eaton's "warrior Sufi" theory rejects the idea of the peaceful Sufi missionary. He argues that Sufis also served as warriors supporting Muslim armies: "if the Sufi's peaceful character can be supported by both written and oral traditions, so can his militancy."[16] Like other Muslims, Sufis believed that *jihad* was the only direct way to paradise. In a "holy war" against infidels of the subcontinent, the warrior Sufis religiously legitimised raids by Muslim generals. It is argued that Sufis abandoned their role as warriors only when and where the Muslim-Indian frontier disappeared. In this case, they would then devote their time to theology, writing and studying literature.

Those pursuing the "political patronage" theory posit that individuals and groups received financial rewards (tax relief and land grants) and political appointments for converting to Islam and for entering into mixed marriages. The reach of this type of influence diminished as one moved away from areas with a large Muslim population.

In his "ecological" theory, Eaton notes that conversion was most effective in areas least exposed to Brahmanical culture and shifted from

---

13 Ernst: *Eternal Garden*, p. 159.

14 The distribution of free food certainly attracted some poor Hindus too.

15 Saiyid Athar Abbas Rizvi: *A History of Sufism in India. Vols I–II*, New Delhi: Munshiram Manoharlal 1978, Vol. I, p. 432; see also Saiyid Athar Abbas Rizvi: "Islamic Proselytisation: Seventh to Sixteenth Centuries", in G.A. Oddie (ed.): *Religion in South Asia—Religious Conversion and Revival Movements in South Asia in Medieval and Modern Times*, Delhi: Manohar 1991, pp. 19–37.

16 Eaton: *Sufis of Bijapur*, p. 31.

tribal and nomadic lifestyles to agricultural existence under a political system run by Muslims, such as western Punjab and Bengal (see Chap. 4: Bengal and the South).

"Immigration theorists" believe that the majority of Indian Muslims are descendants of those which sailed across the Arabian Sea from the Iranian plateau. This is supported by evidence of Hindu converts dating back to the early arrival of Muslim merchants and Arab settlers on the subcontinent. The latter practiced *da'wa* and moved about freely; converting local rulers and the elite in the process. Arab traders and conquerors acquired Hindu wives and low-caste concubines which influenced not only the local 'non-Muslim' culture, but the growth of Indian Islam. New generations of Muslims multiplied. Converts gradually acculturated into the new tradition and syncretism or shared religion remained dominant; at times sheltering shifting identities.[17]

Evidence of forced conversion or Islamisation of tribes appeared between the tenth and fourteenth centuries. During this time, the Delhi Sultans converted tribal chiefs to Islam which meant the conversion of their entire tribe. While many chiefs eventually apostatised, converted tribal members had difficulties "reconverting" to their former religion and therefore remained followers of Islam. Forced conversion occurred on an even larger scale at the end of the eighteenth century in the context of increased communal conflicts as well as during the Mappila Rebellion (1921/1922).[18]

The evidence above demonstrates that religious conversion was a gradual process in which Hindu and other religious groups were (trans)forming Islam on the subcontinent. Often it reflected a mixing of Islamic beliefs and practices with other (un-Islamic) views and rituals which persisted. Therefore, conversion was not necessarily typified by a radical change of worldview or a situation of *tabula rasa*. It rather started with selective participation in rituals, with the eventual integration of new worldviews and beliefs into one's own system of reference. While some of the converts were attracted to pious Muslims, others

[17] Dominique Khan: *Conversions and Shifting Identities; Ramdev Pir and the Ismailis in Rajasthan*. Delhi: Manohar 1997; Bayly: *Saints, Goddesses & Kings*.

[18] J.T.F. Jordens: "Reconversion to Hinduism: The Shuddhi of the Arya Samaj", in: Oddie (ed.): *Religion in South Asia*, pp. 215–230.

sought social and economic improvement.[19] Thus, religious conversion aimed at solving problems, such as experiences of social and economic debasement, and helped maintain coherence and continuity.[20]

[19] Anthony Copley: *Religions in Conflict. Ideology, Cultural Contact and Conversion in late-colonial India*. Delhi: OUP 1997.

[20] See also the contributions by Monika Wohlrab-Sahr: "Symbolizing Distance: Conversion to Islam in Germany and the United States", in: K. van Nieuwkerk (ed.): *Gender and Conversion*, Austin 2006, pp. 71–92.

CHAPTER SIX

FROM UNIVERSAL DOMINION TO PRINCIPALITIES (APPROX. 1650–1800)

The politics of "Pax Mughalica" had already demanded further concession in favour of local landowners and middlemen. From the middle of the seventeenth century onwards, these persons were successful in appropriating rights over land and office into their own private jurisdiction, thereby escaping central control. Getting gradually stronger, they demanded participation in administration and also a stronger adherence to Islamic principles to stabilise their position. After all, these groups were the architects of those very principles themselves. So to counter these developments, which could guarantee imperial integration and universal dominion, a policy compatible with orthodox Islamic principles was to be pursued by *zamindars*, religious scholars and orthodox Sufis mostly of Turani stock. Such a policy also sought to expand borders or to annex certain regions in order to secure new and rich lands as happened in the North West, North East and South. Eventually this resulted in the largest expansion of Mughal Empire under the last emperor Aurangzeb (reg. 1658–1707), who added "Alamgir" or "Conqueror of the Universe" to his titles. Moreover, his reign required Islamic legitimacy since he had rebelled against his father and murdered his own brothers. Troubled by his own conscience, Aurangzeb sought to ameliorate his self-esteem by becoming a generous patron of the Holy Places, sending money to pious men living there and regularly invoking Islamic symbolism. This was followed by the enforcement policy of Islamisation of state culture in 1670 which, according to many historians, nearly suffocated the inclusivist court culture and further centralised the state.

From Islamicatisation to Islamisation

The court-cult of the Mughals known as *tauhid-e ilahi* or *sulh-e kull* (universal peace) was replaced in favour of an islamically legitimised normative order, which would go along with imperial culture. This demand had already been voiced by important Islamic thinkers, such as Khawaja Baqi Billah and Ahmad Sirhindi. The increasing influence of the Naqshbandi order, an immigrant group with immigrant clients and orthodox priests, might have influenced Aurangzeb to initiate this policy. In fact, the emperor had been on very good terms with Sirhindi's son Muhammad Maʿsum Naqshbandi (died 1668), the second *qayyum*, the highest saint, through whom the world would survive—according to local Naqshbandi version. Even in the Deccan there was an increasing influence of this order, as we shall encounter later in the chapter. Meanwhile, the Qadiriyya, which was relatively tolerant of non-Muslims by harking back to Arab tradition, and which was one of the formative influences on Dara Shikoh, fell on bad times under Aurangzeb.[1]

The coming of orthodoxy can be understood through various measures such as the introduction of special taxes levied on Hindu merchants in 1665 and the destruction of some Hindu temples in 1669 particularly in the important Hindu cities such as Varanasi and Mathura. Other discriminatory edicts followed. However, all this did not imply automatically that the emperor was completely hostile towards the Hindu tradition and people or that his policy was purely religious. His destruction of temples was mainly motivated by political considerations, to thwart political rebellions and to gain income, reasons very similar to Mahmud Ghaznawi's. After all, it took Aurangzeb 20 long years before he re-introduced the *jizya* for non-Muslims in 1679, shortly after the great Rajput rebellion (1678), when the Marathas forged an alliance with the Shiʿite Golconda,[2] and when the emperor started to expand into the Deccan, which eventually led to the annexation of Bijapur (1686) and Golconda (1687). On the other hand, he also provided land grants for the construction of Hindu temples, educational institutions and scholars. In fact, Khafi Khan (died approx. 1733), author of "The quintessential selection" (*Muntakhab al-lubab*) and historian whose family had been in Aurangzeb's service, tells us that *jizya* could not be levied and remained largely a tax on paper only. Similarly, the number of Hindu nobles and officials increased during 1679–1707, probably because the Mughals needed their services in their wars against Marathas. Finally, the destruction and desecration of religious structures such as Hindu temples as symbols of collec-

---

[1] Aziz Ahmad: *An Intellectual History of Islam in India*, Edinburgh 1969, p. 42.

[2] Satish Chandra: "Jizya and the State in India during the Seventeenth Century", in: Eaton (ed.): *India's Islamic Traditions*, pp. 132–149.

tive Hindu identities cannot always be explained in terms of Islamic zeal. It is true that temple destruction served legitimising purposes for Muslim rulers, but these temples were actually attacked as symbols of Hindu royal authority. The Muslim rulers made triumphal re-use of their building materials and their cultural memory by setting up other religious structures on the sites of the old. The basic issue was competition for greater historical recognition, for desecration represented a crucial symbolic act to delegitimise the rival sovereign and to incorporate his power and territory into one's own realm.[3] By the same token, reports of Aurangzeb's religious iconoclasm, particularly in the Deccan, are mainly legendary seeking the benefits of portraying an essentialised Islam. This was especially supported by later colonialist historiography.[4]

On the political level, things were getting increasingly difficult to manage with different forces challenging the Mughals. One of these challenges came from the Marathas of South, the encounter with which was often mistakenly understood, in terms of Islamisation.[5]

The Maratha War

Aurangzeb's strategy of Islamisation is primarily understood so because of his proclamation of *jihad* against the Marathas, who, under Shivaji Bhonsle (1627–1680) and his son Shambhaji (1680–1689), defended the Deccan region. As John F. Richards elaborates, as an open-status, peasant-warrior grouping, the Marathas held extensive prebendal rights under the ʿAdil Shahi rulers of Bijapur. They emerged as a regional power in Deccan, took charge of Pun and Bijapur, establishing a kingdom in Western Deccan organised and run by young Maratha warriors and Brahmin administrators. Their leader Shivaji, the symbolic figure of Maratha resistance struggle, benefited from the perpetually feuding Deccan Sultanates. Shivaji constructed an effective civil administration, decentralised the network of strongholds, controlled the important

[3] Gilmartin and Lawrence (eds.): *Beyond Turk and Hindu*, "Introduction", p. 15.

[4] For this argument see Asher: *Architecture of Mughal India*, p. 254; Carl Ernst: "Ellora Temples as Viewed by Indo-Muslim Authors", in: Gilmartin and Lawrence (eds.): *Beyond Turk and Hindu*, pp. 98–120, esp. pp. 109, 111f.

[5] Recent studies have rightly probed this simplistic equation of Maratha wars and Islamisation. See, for example, Stewart Gordon: *The Marathas 1600–1818*, Cambridge: CUP 1993.

overland caravan routes connecting Burhanpur[6] to Surat and he traded with the Persian Gulf and Red Sea. Income was also secured from raids into neighbouring territories. The Maratha success may have had to do with the fact that their power was based with some modifications on Mughal structures of governance such as *jagir*, and on the patronage of both Hindu and Muslim holy men to provide them with authority and power.[7]

When, in 1665, the Marathas tried to align with the Sultan of Bijapur, the latter faced the full force of Rajput Jai Singh, Aurangzeb's faithful supporter during the war of succession and viceroy of Deccan provinces. Shivaji had to surrender his independence by becoming a *zamindar* for some time. But when he realised that the Mughal army could be resisted,[8] Shivaji crowned himself as an independent Hindu monarch, thus challenging the Timurid emperor. In alliance with the Shiʿite ruler Qutb Shah of Golconda, Shivaji annexed much land in the South, before he died of fever in 1680. He was succeeded by his son Shambhaji.

The Marathas nearly restored their domination in the Deccan and this called for severe Mughal intervention. This became urgent because Prince Muhammad Akbar's rebellion against his father Aurangzeb had become the symbol of opposition during the 1680s, when he proclaimed himself emperor in 1681 for a short while. When Burhanpur was raided by Shambhaji's army and Muslim notables were deprived of their Islamic duties, Aurangzeb marched south, not destined to return to Northern India again. He used all his resources to control the southern borders of his empire, when he moved the capital from Shahjahanabad to Deccan, where he had been viceroy before, and where in 1644 a settlement named after him (Aurangabad) had been constructed. However, once in the Deccan in 1682, he seldom resided in this city which served him primarily as an administrative capital and imperial treasury. Instead, he lived in military camps, before he built Islampuri.

---

[6] Burhanpur was located at a central trade route between Surat and Agra, and in the seventeenth century it had acquired considerable economic importance.

[7] Stewart Gordon: "Maratha Patronage of Muslim Institutions in Burhanpur and Khandesh", in: Gilmartin and Lawrence (eds.): *Beyond Turk and Hindu*, pp. 327–338.

[8] Cf. M.N. Pearson: "Shivaji and the Decline of the Mughal Empire", in: *JAS* 35 (1976), pp. 221–235.

To keep Marathas in check was a very expensive undertaking. Bijapur and Golconda, renamed *Dar al-Jihad*, had to be annexed, before the Timurid emperor could conquer the Maratha state in 1688, thereby adding to the empire more than a quarter of its former size.[9] But instead of stability, perennial raids haunted the Mughal Empire, plundering expeditions and banditry from different quarters supported by a growing number of frustrated *zamindars* and nobility. The insurgencies were primarily initiated by Marathas, whom Aurangzeb could not really stop, even after he proclaimed *jihad* against them in 1698. The battles were costly and adversely affected trade and agriculture. Moreover, change in the composition of the imperial elite during the Deccan wars, resulting from accommodation of large numbers of high-ranking Deccani amirs and loyal Maratha nobles, met with hostility from the traditional amirs, the *khanazads*.[10] Due to instability in Deccan, many Mughal officers failed to get any *jagir*. In the opinion of some high nobles, it was high time to end the drain of imperial resources in Deccan. On the other hand, the Northern provinces suffered from the absence of the emperor, which was not conducive to the patrimonial structure, so Aurangzeb had to put in considerable effort to pacify them. On the face of it, he seemed to succeed in achieving his objective but in reality those given increasingly more power to suppress political disloyalty and independent movements, became the de facto rulers. Ill and exhausted, Aurangzeb died in his encampment at Ahmadnagar in 1707.

Hanafisation of judiciary

Parallel to the emergence of the Marathan warlord Shivaji and Aurangzeb's exterior *jihad* with the Marathas, the Mughal ruler was also practicing interior *jihad* using the Islamic repertoire for a variety of purposes, Islamic law being the case in point. So far, shariʿa had been subject to considerable individual interpretations by local *qadi*s dependent on local customary law and practices, *ʿurf* and *ʿadat*. Several *fatwa*-collections had been produced before the advent of the Mughals, others before Aurangzeb came to power, and two *fatwa*-collections were

---

[9] Richards: *The Mughal Empire*, p. 223.

[10] M. Athar Ali: *The Apparatus of Empire: Awards of Ranks, offices and Titles to the Mughal Nobility (1574–1658)*, Delhi: OUP 1985, passim.

already compiled during his reign, one by the distinguished Kashmiri scholar and Sufi, Muʿin al-Din Muhammad ibn Khawajah Mahmud al-Naqshband (died 1674) called *al-Fatawa al-Naqshbandiyya*. The other was compiled by Mufti Abu al-Barakat ibn Hussam al-Din Dihlawi in 1698 known as *Fatawa-ye Majmaʿ al-Barakat*.[11] These compilations were usually in the form of responses given by a single scholar to a variety of questions. In order to streamline different interpretations of shariʿa and to use them for state purposes, Aurangzeb supported the attempt to impose a clearly defined homogenised legal system. To codify Islamic law he commissioned an authoritative *fatwa*-collection called *Fatawa-ye ʿAlamgiri*, which was to present a consensus of Hanafi school of law.[12] Thus, he patronised Muslim scholars and institutions of Islamic learning to strengthen Muslim orthodoxy towards securing legitimacy for the royalty. Accordingly, supervised by Shaikh Nizam Burhanpuri (died 1679) the *Fatawa* was written in Arabic, the language associated with the patronised ulama, while Persian was more associated with poets, historians and bureaucrats. More than three dozen scholars were engaged in 1664, i.e., before Aurangzeb introduced most of his laws (*qanun*) on the basis of the shariʿa, during 1668–1678. The scholars were to compile, systematise and review Hanafi law to aid *qadis* and *muftis* in their work. During the next eight years, from 1672 onwards, all scholars involved in the work were provided with proper salaries and necessary facilities. Such a conceptionalised, juridical codification and collective endeavour was new, probably anticipating the first steps towards modern state legislation; the compilation became authoritative because it provided a review of *al-Hidaya*, the most popular Hanafi compendium written by ʿAli ibn Abi Bakr al-Marghinani (died 1197),[13] as well as of those

---

[11] Compare Islam: "Origin and Development of *Fatâwâ*-Compilation", pp. 7–18, here p. 10.

[12] See Must'ad Khan Sâqi: *Maâsir-i-ʿAlamgîrî; A history of the Emperor Aurangzib-ʿAlamgir (Reign 1658–1707 AD)*, transl. and annotated by Jadunath Sarkar, Delhi 1986 (first 1947), pp. 58, 315f.; A.S. Bazmee Ansari: "al-Fatâwâ al-ʿAlamgîriyya", in: EI(2), II, pp. 836f. *Fatawa-ye ʿAlamgiri* was translated into Urdu by S. Amir ʿAli in 1890 and was also republished in Arabic in 1895; see GoI: Selections from the Records of the Government of India, Home Department: CCXCV resp. CCCXXXVI: *Reports on the Publications issued and Registered in the Several Provinces of British India during the year(s) 1891* resp. *1895*, Calcutta 1891 resp. 1896, p. 67 resp. p. 68; D.N. Marshall: *Mughals in India; a bibliographical survey of manuscripts*, London 1985(2), pp. 21, 174, 223, 323, 324, 377f., 380, 481.

[13] *Al-Hidaya* is an extension of the law manual *Bidayat al-Mubtadi'* written by al-Marghinani. It was translated by Charles Hamilton (transl.): *Hedâya, or Guide; A Commentary on the Musalman Laws, 4 Vols.*, London 1791.

fatawa-compilations produced by Indian Muslims such as *Fatawa-ye Ghiyathi* (ascribed to Ghiyath al-Din Balaban), *Fatawa-ye Tatar Khani* (during the rule of Firoz Shah Tughluq, reigned 1351–1388) and others. It was also considered to be normative because it enjoyed the authority of the Hanafi consensus of—most—learned scholars (*ijma*ʿ).[14] Thus, Hanafi lineage seemed to become an important channel for collectivisation, internally in terms of homogenising Sunni normativity, externally in terms of distinction from Shiʿites.

The *Fatawa* introduced new judicial terminology and called for *ijtihad*: the creative application of Islamic law to meet the challenge of changing social conditions, however, within the boundaries of its own—Hanafi—school of law; it aimed to qualify the role and restrict the freedom of the Muslim judiciary, i.e., of *qadi*s and *muftis*, and empowered Muslims who had a good knowledge of *fiqh* and a good character to issue a *fatwa*. Thus, the issue was, who should exercise *ijtihad*, the scholars or also the ruler or the commoner. At the same time the *Fatawa* stiffened the social hierarchy of a highly stratified system, at the head of which stood the emperor. Certain punishments reified the established categories: the noblest including ulama and sayyids (*ʿulwiyya*) were exempted from physical punishments, while governors (*umara*) and landholders (*dahaqin*) could be humiliated but not physically punished or imprisoned. The middle class (*awsat*) could not be physically punished but humiliated and imprisoned, while the lower classes (*khasis* and *kamina*) were subjected to all three categories of sentences: humiliation, physical punishment and imprisonment. The fourfold stratification evokes the Hindu social stratification. In some instances the *Fatawa* even disagreed with the consensual Hanafi law when it stipulated that rebels could be sentenced to death. Thus the categories of *fitna* and *fasad* which automatically implied the reprehensible possibilities of schism and rebellion[15] as well as those of *ashraf* and those of the lowest class (*min al-salifa* or *al-akhissa*) gained prominent symbolic meanings, so that the *Fatawa* became a source of legitimacy for the royal policies. In many cases the *Fatawa* preferred the legal opinions of

[14] See Muhammad Khalid Masud: *Fatawa Alamgiri*: Mughal Patronage of Islamic law (Draft paper for discussion); Alan M. Guenther: "Hanafi Fiqh in Mughal India: The Fatâwá-i ʿAlamgîrî", in: Eaton (ed.): *India's Islamic Tradition*, pp. 209–230; Islam: "Origin and Development of *Fatâwâ*-Compilation", here pp. 10f.

[15] See A. Wink: "Sovereignty and Universal Dominion in South Asia", in: *IESHR* 21 (1984), pp. 265–92, here pp. 276ff.

older Iraqi Hanafis than relying on later Central Asian and Ottoman ones. Apparently, this bias is grounded in the fact that the older Iraqi juridical traditions accounted for the peasants' private landholdings, which in turn had a practical impact in terms of taxes and duties.[16] However, it must be reiterated that the *Fatawa-ye 'Alamgiri*—sometimes alien to the Indian reality—did not substitute *siyasa*, i.e. the political power, which was to remain with the Mughal Emperor, as is exemplified by his *farmans*, the royal decrees, which were often in contradiction to the *Fatawa*. The early Persian translation of the *Fatawa* may be an indication of a trickle-down effect, i.e., ordinary judges at the local level may have applied it.[17]

Along with this *qanun-isation* which penetrated different spheres of life, there was an increased systematisation of flow of information, which might have been necessitated by increasing internal factionalisation due to the growing economic crisis. The rationale behind the re-constitution of the powerful office of *muhtasib* or censor in 1679, which had already been a part of the official establishment until Sher Shah Suri, was to guarantee Islamic norms and fix the prices. This again showed the increasingly functional difference between the ulama and their patronisers. A *muhtasib*'s municipal and market duties also included the suppression of heresy and thus transcended those of a simple market inspector. His duties were limited to public spaces however, similar to those of the indigenous Indian city magistrate or head of the city police, the *kotwal* whose function seemed to be a replica of those performed by the *hisbah*—state authority—in early Islamic times.[18] The *muhtasib*'s power, therefore, ended at the borders of the city's *mahallas*.[19]

Other Islamisation measures aimed at centralising and neutralising mystical orders, which tended towards autonomy and heterodoxy. Orders such as the Qadiriyya became the target of Aurangzeb's iconoclastic policies and were gradually co-opted within orthodoxy. Others such as Chishtiyya tried to continue the tradition of an inter-religious

[16] See Moez Khalfaoui: *Le pluralisme et l'anti-pluralism en Asie du sud au XIIe siècle. Le Cas d'al-Fatâwa al-Hindiyya al-'Alamjīriyya*, Erfurt (Ph.D. Islamic Studies) 2007.

[17] Cf. M.L. Bhatia: *Administrative History of Medieval India (A Study of Muslim Jurisprudence under Aurangzeb)*, New Delhi 1992; Guenther: "Hanafi Fiqh in Mughal India", p. 223.

[18] See Zameeruddin Siddiqi: "The Muhtasib Under Aurangzeb", in: *Medieval India Quarterly* 5 (1963), pp. 113–119, and Bilgrami: *Quasi*, pp. 171ff.

[19] Compare H. Inalcik: "Istanbul: An Islamic City", in: *JIS* 1 (1990), pp. 1–23, esp. p. 17.

harmony exemplified by Shah Kalim Allah Jahanabadi (died 1729) and Fakhr al-Din (1715–1785), both active in Delhi. But the "most important concession for the ulema and larger Muslim gentry throughout the empire was in regard to tax-free land grants" by which the emperor revoked Akbar's policy when in 1672 he resumed grants held by Hindus. Eighteen years later, Aurangzeb went for another concession by which he made all such land grants hereditary to religious scholars.[20] It must have been in this connection that the emperor confiscated an estate of a Dutch trader known as Farangi Mahall, i.e., the European quarter, in Lucknow to give it to the sons of Qutb al-Din Sihalawi (1631–1692), a reputed scholar of Islamic learning.

Islamic scholarship

Islamic teaching, which closely connected South Asia with the rest of the Islamic world, had been reformed in terms of its content but the stress was on the so-called rational sciences.[21] The system experienced changes of its literature taught within a pragmatic set-up initiated by a group of Sunni scholars initiated into the Qadiri order. It was through these scholars, subsequently known as Farangi Mahallis, that this kind of Islamic learning received further impetus in South Asia.[22] It was instrumental in legitimising the evolving powers that soon came to regionalise the Mughal Empire, possibly also in Awadh.[23]

The above-mentioned Qutb al-Din was a member of Muslim gentry from *qasbah* Sihala, and aligned with the so-called rationalist tradition of men like Fath Allah Shirazi (died 1589) who was invited to Akbar's court from Bijapur, and ʿAbd al-Hakim Siyalkoti (died 1656). According to S. ʿAbd al-Hayy, they had further developed the *maʿqulat* tradition and consolidated the third epoch of Islamic learning in South Asia. Qutb al-Din is said to have been the initiator of the fourth phase of Islamic learning. He was killed due to rivalry over landed property, as can be gleaned from his only available writing, *Risalat dar al-harb*. This treatise

---

20 Richards: *The Mughal Empire*, p. 174.

21 The different phases of Islamic teaching with the respective books taught are given in Malik: *Gelehrtenkultur*, passim.

22 For the Farangi Mahall see Francis Robinson: *The ʿUlama of Farangi Mahall and Islamic Culture in South Asia*, New Delhi: permanent black 2001.

23 For the process of regionalisation see the seminal work of Muzaffar Alam: *The Crisis of Empire in Mughal North India*, Delhi: OUP 1986.

is about the rules of waging war, which he wrote at Aurangzeb's behest. A detailed list of foreigners, breakers of treaties and non-Muslims was compiled in order to help identify and localise rebels. Qutb al-Din's murder prompted Aurangzeb to commemorate the dead scholar through a *farman* dated 1694 which the confiscated estate in Lucknow known as Farangi Mahall was given to his eldest son. The transfer of knowledge from the *qasbah* of Sihala to the cultural metropolis of Lucknow was effected by his third son, Mulla Nizam al-Din (1678–1748), who was to become the founder of *dars-e nizami*, the name for the way of teaching and the books called after him.

The teachings introduced by Mulla Nizam al-Din after the death of the last Great Mughal Aurangzeb made up of brief sections of highly sophisticated treatises, primarily in logic, philosophy and law—for the first time, written by contemporary Indian Muslim scholars as well—which were studied in depth. The aim was to provide solutions to everyday problems, while tradition and relationships to authority remained important as before. The teaching was so effective that Shiʿites and Hindus availed themselves of this education becoming so successful as to be later placed in different principalities as office-bearers in administration and military. The affinity to a Qadiri sufi and a former warrior, ʿAbd al-Razzaq (died 1724) of Bansa, a *wujudi*, proved to be important for appealing to a variety of social and religious groups living in North India, at a time when internal feuds were hampering political and cultural integration.[24] As Muzaffar Alam has argued, this scholarship represented the local version of Islam as well as a model for the life pattern of local Muslim gentry. They set the scene for and were also in accord with the evolving social and political alignments, which sought to reduce confrontations in the countryside.[25] It seems that the *dars-e nizami* sought to legitimise the evolving regional powers in the face of the decaying central political power (see Chap. 7).

Credit must be given to this educational system for the cultural integration, which it fostered. But at the same time it strengthened the traditional compliance with state/law and dependence on authority—*taqlid*,

[24] Again, one may encounter the impact of military culture on society, religion and economy. The nexus between Sufis and ruler can be traced also in other regions in the eighteenth century fragmenting Mughal Empire. See Green: "Geography, empire and sainthood".

[25] Muzaffar Alam: "Religion and Politics in Awadh society: 17th and 18th centuries", in: Dallapiccola and Zingel-Avé Lallemant (eds.): *Islam and Indian Regions*, Vol. I, pp. 321–350, here p. 348. Alam: *The Languages*, pp. 98–112.

which was most crucial for new power-holders at the peripheries of Mughal Empire. While *taqlid* was based on jurisprudence, philosophical theology was based on logic. This logic again was the logic of the state and administration where philosophical theology and law flourished. As Peter Gran has pointed out, *kalam* was most congruent with state domination.[26] So these scholars pursued a scholarly culture that was designed for "scribal groups", able to develop new administrative techniques.[27] This process had started with the increase in the numbers of theologians and jurists, important for the fledgling autonomous princely states.[28] One may speak of a specific education, which these groups regarded as the crucial attribute of social honour and cultural capital as well as being the qualification criteria, important for service elites.

The *dars-e niẓami* marked the fourth epoch and completed, according to S. ʿAbd al-Hayy, the development of the preceding epochs. *Maʿqulat* were predominant, formalising and standardising knowledge. A development that had started under Sikandar Lodhi, gained new heights under the Mughal emperor Akbar and was institutionalised in the form of *dars-e niẓami* under and particularly after Aurangzeb. This happened while the Mughal Empire was tottering into several autonomous successor states seeking legitimacy (see Chap. 7). However, the *dars-e niẓami* was/is as little monolithic as is Islamic law or Islamic 'orthodoxy'. Instead it was informed by highly pluralistic and divergent tendencies in terms of personal differences among scholars regarding the ways to teach and to write, depending on their contexts, functions and patronage as stipulated in the *waqfiyyat*, the deed constituting a domain, i.e., *madrasa*, into a pious endowment.[29] In fact, the local differences are noticeable even in contemporary times, such as in those between Lucknow and Delhi, Allahabad and Khairabad, Bareilly and Deoband. In the face of these differences and varieties in the *dars-e niẓami*, it seems difficult to generalise about its foci and developments, but later generations of scholars have always made the attempt to classify the scattered testimonies of their ancestors, thereby rationalising their experiences.

---

[26] Peter Gran: *Islamic Roots of Capitalism: Egypt, 1760–1840*, Texas and London: University of Texas Press 1979, pp. xvi, f. 50, 96.

[27] See David Washbrook: "South Asia, The World System, and World Capitalism", in: *JAS* 49/3 (1990), pp. 479–508, p. 499.

[28] In Europe this increase was possible by way of princely revolutions during the reformation. It was to bring about the expansion of higher educational institutions with relevant service sectors for the state apparatus.

[29] Compare J. Pedersen and G. Makdisi: "madrasa", in: EI(2), V, pp. 1123ff.

Reforms contesting scribal groups

At the same time new societal groups emerged due to trans-regional economic affiliations that supported the development of new social formations. The so-called Delhi school, evolving from the Madrasah Rahimiyya outside Shahjahanabad, established by Shah ʿAbd al-Rahim Dihlawi (died 1718), the father of Shah Wali Allah (died 1762), who had also been consulted during the compilation of *Fatawa-ye ʿAlamgiri*, was a centre of such new ideas.

The discourse of these reformers was characterised by severe criticism of their own Muslim/Hindu society. Similar developments can be found in other regions of heterogeneous Islamic world—the Hijaz and Yemen being a kind of emporium for new ideas[30]—at a phase of historical transition from the disintegration of empires to new territorial states in the eighteenth century, i.e., when society was experiencing far-reaching socio-economic and cultural transformations. The reformers sought to purify religion by getting rid of folk-religious rites and tried to interpret God's message individually and independently through the revealed text. This meant the loosening of immediate and direct ties of authority on the one hand and the reconstruction of Islamic society by themselves on the other, thereby referring to early Muhammadan time. This was *ijtihad* in the broadest sense, expressing a desire for differentiation.[31] It is likely, that the past that was referred to, seemed not to be perceived as an era of heroism that would return, but as a political and social utopia, which required individual effort in order to be lived and translated into reality. Thus, memory was to be energised through a mood of powerful expectation. Needless to say, this approach stood in sharp contrast to traditional pedagogy, which emphasised a compliance with the law and authority or *taqlid*, as was the case with the better part of the imperial service elites. One of the well-known reformers was Shah Wali Allah, who considered his mission to integrate various fragmented and contradictory articulations of Muslim history

---

[30] For the following see Jamal Malik: "Muslim Culture and Reform in 18th Century South Asia", in: *JRAS* 13/2 (2003), pp. 227–243.

[31] That does not mean that the "door of ijtihad" had been closed with the advent of the four schools of Sunni law, as the powerful colonial image of a static Islamic law wants us to believe. Wael B. Hallaq: "Was the Gate of Ijtihad Closed?," in: *IJMES* 16 (1984), pp. 3–41, has shown that *ijtihad* always existed, albeit in different forms. Compare also Rudolph Peters: "Idjtihad and Taqlid in 18th and 19th Century Islam", in: *WI* 20 (1980), pp. 131–145.

of ideas.[32] He looked for a way to bring together the deliberations of philosophers, theologians, and mystics. He, therefore, arranged these ideas in theoretical treatises, in the style of the discipline of religious studies, calling it "The Conclusive Argument of God" (*Hujjat Allah al-Baligha*). In addition, he criticised the hereditary prebendal system and its representatives, the landed gentry (*ashraf*), and fought for a new educational system appropriate to the new social forces that were emerging in the wake of the decline of central Mughal rule. After his return from Hijaz in 1733 where he had studied at the feet of well-known hadith scholars, Shah Wali Allah replaced many books on logic and philosophical theology taught in the *dars-e nizami* with books on hadith and mystical treatises. According to him, rational human knowledge as represented by the studies of logic for the service elite was only a preliminary truth. Prophetic knowledge was more reliable than rational studies of logic and philosophy. *Ijtihad* was the means through which he sought to establish a major synthesis between transmitted and rational sciences, while discourse on the sunna was granted a central place. The idea was to strengthen faith through rational proofs and call for unity among all Muslims especially against the Marathas, who by the second half of the eighteenth century nearly conquered one third of the subcontinent. Rational sciences were merely a means by which to establish the authenticity and inimitability of the shariʿa, which was more complete and trustworthy due to its divine inspiration than the temporary human rational deductions. In this way, the reformer succeeded in drawing a distinction between revelation and reason as well as relating them to each other and harmonising them. By not placing rational sciences directly in the service of the profane authorities, but apparently using them as an auxiliary device for the sacred, he was able to legitimise his social critique islamically. He was supported by emerging dynamic urban traders whose profit-making activities and credit-worthiness called for moral behaviour and action. This required religious legitimacy. Shah Wali Allah's deliberations challenged the authority of received legal authority and sharply contrasted with aristocratic patrician hierarchical ideas, which privileged distinction based on ascription rather than achievement. However, it must be mentioned

---

[32] On Shah Wali Allah see the contributions by Marcia Hermansen such as *The Conclusive Argument from God. Shâh Walî Allâh of Delhi's Hujjat Allâh al-Bâligha*, Leiden: Brill 1996.

that he considered Hindustan an exile (*ghurba*) and Arabic genealogy and language the pride of Muslims.

In addition to these reformist views, Mirza Mazhar Jan-e Janan (died 1782) revived the idea of cultural integration by adopting not only a tolerant attitude towards Hindu ideas but also accepted the Vedas as a revealed book. He called for political participation but refrained from worldly powers. However, the theological concessions did not prevent both scholars and mystics to criticise Shiʿite ideas,[33] a confessionalist tendency that was to increase in decades to come, and which was part of a fledging formation of religious communities.[34]

Parallel to claims of reinforcing *ijtihad*, the theoretical elaboration upon the ethical concept called the Muhammadan Path (*Tariqah-ye Muhammadi*) transformed "mystical piety" into "prophetic" or "action piety". Quite in accordance with these developments there was a rise in the study of prophetic tradition, the hadith, and transmitted sciences. Moreover, through "structural amnesia" or the shortening of the traditionally accepted ascription of the chain of authorities (*isnad*), a quick and effective affiliation with Prophet Muhammad—the perfect man—became possible, hence *imitatio muhammadi*. His sunna was considered paradigmatic for social and political reform. This individual and collective perspective and action motivated and oriented by religion represented a "Sunnatisation" of lifeworlds, which went hand in hand with a process of a subtle humanisation of the Prophet; practically experienced religion was conceptionally reflected.

At the same time, a developing anthropocentric world view coupled with a new consciousness of the equality of all human beings and a belief in universal human dignity seemed to find expression mainly in vernacular literatures, which were able to adapt and relocate local concerns into their regional traditions. Such were Marathi, credited with being one of the first modern Indian literary languages, Sindhi and Punjabi which produced popular poets, such as Shah ʿAbd al-Latif

---

[33] For Mazhar Jan-e Janan who was eventually murdered by a Shiʿite and his views on Hinduism see Yohanan Friedmann: "Medieval Muslim Views of Indian religions", in: *JAOS* 95/2 (1975), pp. 214–221. For the history around his *khanaqah* see Warren Edward Fusfeld: *The Shaping of Sufi Leadership in Delhi: The Naqshbandiyya Mujaddidiyya, 1750–1920*, PhD dissertation, Pennsylvania 1981.

[34] C.A. Bayly: "The Pre-history of 'Communalism'? Religious Conflict in India, 1700–1860", in: *MAS* 19/2 (1985), pp. 177–203, argues that in the eighteenth century the formations of distinctive religious communities provided the basis for later communalism.

(1689–1752) and Bullhe Shah (1680–1758). Urdu, too, became important, in particular its poetry. In Urdu poetry, morality and sensitivity emerged as new concerns and the new level of interpersonal relations and disclosure implied societal equality.

The metamorphosis of names as manifested in the nom de plume (*takhallus*), and freeing oneself from traditional bondage (*takhallasa min*)[35] seemed to have played a crucial role in the processes of increasing reflexivity and individualisation.

A new public was seen to constitute itself, articulating their interests in particular institutional spaces and patterns such as literary salons, the *musha'ira*—within sensible circles of friendship as it were. Here different societal groups could find a rank-free communication zone, which could function as an alternative to the court, where critical and receptive competence could be acquired and where class and intellectual heterogeneity prevailed.[36] Sufis, like the Naqshbandi Mir Dard (died 1785), were at the forefront of these developments. Thus the growing popularity of vernacular languages such as Urdu, ideally, linguistically and socially expressed the cultural emancipation process from the pristine culture languages of Persian and in part Arabic as well.

These ideas seemed to find resonance especially among new urban trading groups who had benefited from contacts with European traders during the crisis of Mughal Empire and who were located mostly along the borders of the up and coming "national markets" of the successor states (see Chap. 7). While in this context the individual seemed to become the subject to create an imaginative new order, this process of becoming a social and political subject—in the sense of a sacralisation of the human being and secular sacrality—was rejected by the major part of the service elite that adhered to *taqlid*. This does not, however, imply drawing a strict line between different social groups, but it gives a clue as to how diverse cultural articulations were. Thus the enfranchising approach was grounded in sound economic, political and social interests, as will be seen in the next chapter. These traders wanted to get rid of traditional social hierarchy and status and pleaded

---

[35] *Takhallus* in this sense could also mean interrogating or even abandoning traditional order, and, thus reconstructing the ego.

[36] Religion and politics were hardly debated, confessional and political antagonisms could be transcended. Focus was laid on feelings and sensitiveness. And since the ego was at the centre of discourse, these *musha'iras* often became fora not only for polemics. An academic work on the complex issue of *musha'ira* as a cultural and social institution is still to be written.

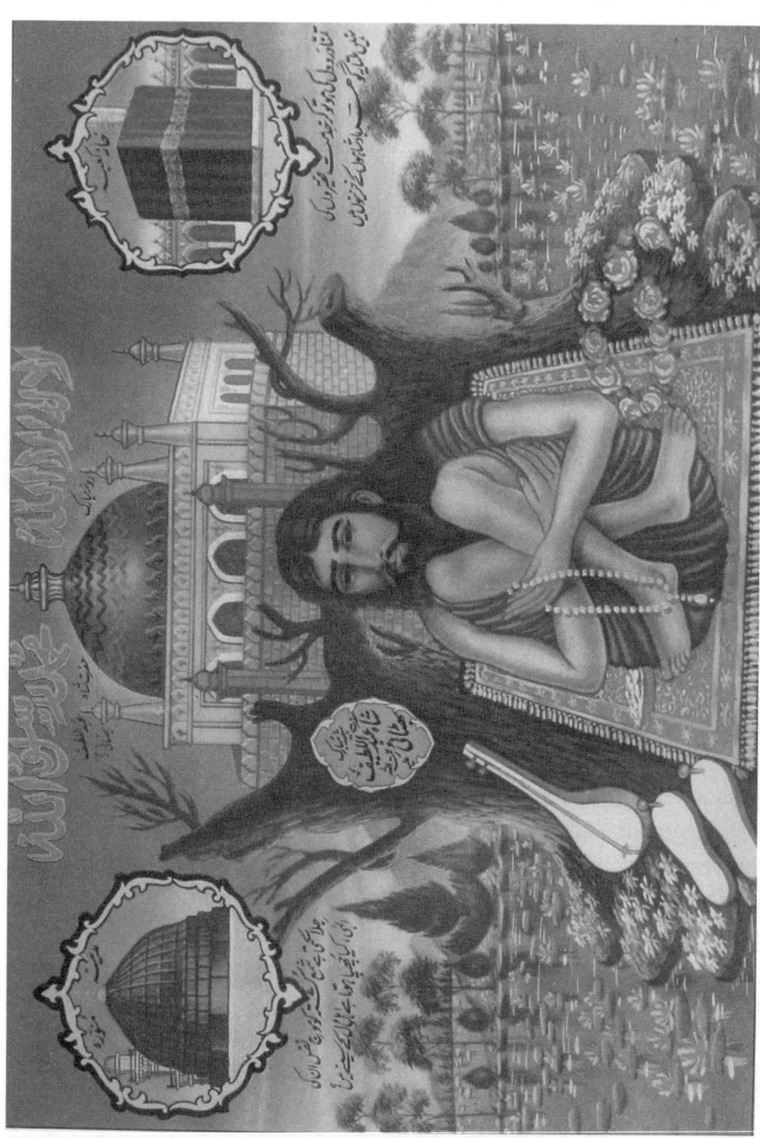

Shah ʿAbd al-Latif Bhitai
Source: Courtesy Museum of Ethnology, Munich

for more morality and virtue. Increasingly, the social esteem of person was more important than any ascribed status. In turn, this implied equality, which was most important for the rising trading communities crucial for the evolution of new regional states. These communities wanted to be credit-worthy and organised their income in a rational and calculating manner.[37] Common and untitled property was acquired through hard labour rather than inheritance. It did not consist of secure landed property but monetary and commodity assets, which, in order to be profitable, had to be risked again and again. Thus, these new trading classes were eager to create and maintain wealth; the aristocrat was fixated on its waste and consumption. It seems that new norms reflected the socio-economic changes. Thus one group subjected individual aspects of cultural practice to a dominating discipline of dogmatism and ideology as a principle of cultural heteronomy as was the case with the service elite, which fostered the study of *kalam* and law, both being based in logic (*mantiq*) that was most congruent with state law, as exemplified by the *dars-e nizami*. The other group stood for cultural autonomy and fostered particular discourses while calling for independent reasoning and stressing the role of vernaculars. In other words, while the first group referred to power hierarchy and was more localistic, the latter based itself empirically on evidence and consensus and was more puristic.[38] The contents of both these trends were critically debated. They represented the interests of old rural and new urban elites respectively. As important agents of change, these groups extended their realms of influence, eventually contributing actively to economic progress and political autonomy. Their debates over rationality, discipline and increased personal responsibility effected state and society. These were carried out passionately and seized the major part of the Islamic world with even the Shiʿites taking part in them.[39] It is in this context that the evolution of the new regional powers needs to be understood (see Chap. 7).

---

[37] Perhaps this can be read as a culturally specific 'protestant ethic of rationality'.

[38] Compare also Jan Assmann: *Das kulturelle Gedächtnis: Schrift, Erinnerung und politische Identität in frühen Hochkulturen*, München 1992, p. 117.

[39] Andrew J. Newman: "The nature of the Akhbârî/Usûlî dispute in late Safawid Iran. Part 1 and 2", in: *BSOAS* LV (1992), pp. 22ff. and pp. 250ff.

The Sufic impact

Before discussing issues like economy and politics, we need to deliberate on the impact of Sufi orders such as the Naqshbandis on the service gentry. As mentioned earlier, this branch of Sufism, similar to the Chishtis and other orders, was neither homogenous nor monolithic, as best described in the multifaceted biography of Ahmad Sirhindi. In Aurangabad in the Deccan, immigrant Turani Sufis were locked in contest with local Sirhindis settled there.[40] This ethnic division drove Aurangzeb to curb the latter's influence. In this, he was backed by the Turani Naqshbandis who had developed a vast network connecting Central Asian towns such as Bukhara and Balkh via Kabul, Peshawar and Lahore to Aurangabad.[41] Many of their followers and clients shared Central Asian descent and were recruited from the higher echelons of Mughal administration and military. Their attention to immigrant Turani soldiers served them to fix their hopes on Deccan as a new homeland in India. Men like Ghazi al-Din Khan, the founder of the famous Madrasa Ghazi al-Din outside Shahjahanabad's Ajmeri Gate, and his son, Nizam al-Mulk Asaf Jah (reigned 1724–1748) were both followers of the leading Naqshbandi Shah Saʿid Palangposh (died 1699) in the Deccan.[42] Palangposh's *khanaqah* and later the shrine, also enjoyed the patronage of Nizam al-Mulk, the future Nizam of Haydarabad, thus consolidating Naqshbandi influence in South.[43]

---

[40] Friedman: *Shaykh Ahmad Sirhindi*, pp. 7f. et passim; M.Z.A. Shakeb: "The role of the Sufis in the changing society of the Deccan, 1500–1750", in: L. Lewisohn and D. Morgan (eds.): *The Heritage of Sufis, Vol. 3, Late Classical Persianate Sufism (1501–1750)*, Oxford: Oneworld 1999.

[41] However, Aurangzeb did not refrain from paying homage to the Chishtis, in fact he often paid homage to their shrines. On Aurangzeb's relationship with the Naqshbandis see Y. Friedmann: "The Naqshbandîs and Awrangzêb: a reconsideration", in: Marc Gaborieau, Alexandre Popovic, Thierry Zarcone (eds.): *Naqshbandis; Historical Developments and Present Situation of a Muslim Mystical Order*, Istanbul: Institut Francais d'Études Anatoliennes 1990.

[42] Since multi-affiliation was common, the Nizam was also follower of the Chishti *silsila* of Kalim Allah and his first successor, and who was on good terms with the founder of the Madrasa Ghazi al-Din, outside the Ajmeri Gate of Shahjahanabad. For the *madrasa* see Margrit Pernau: "Introduction", in: C.F. Andrews: *Zaka Ullah of Delhi*, reprint with introductions by Mushirul Hasan and Margrit Pernau, Delhi: OUP 2003, pp. xlvii–lxxv; and Margrit Pernau: "Introduction", in: M. Pernau (ed.): *The Delhi College. Traditional Elites, the Colonial State, and Education before 1857*, Delhi: OUP 2006.

[43] Simon Digby: *Sufis and Soldiers in Awrangzeb's Deccan*, New Delhi 2001, pp. 5, 7ff., 13, 20f., 22, 29, 27; see also Green: "Geography, empire and sainthood".

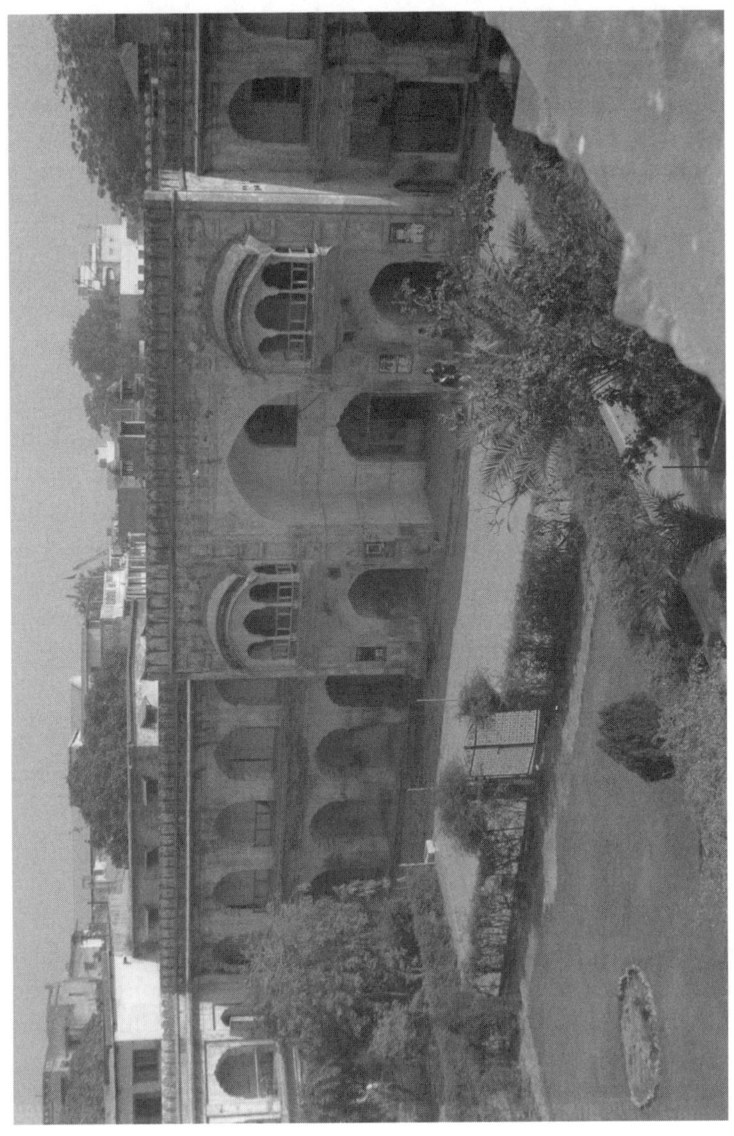

Madrasa Ghazi al-Din
Source: Jamal Malik (private archive)

In spite of this high level patronage enjoyed by the immigrants' Naqshbandi *khanaqah* of Palangposh under Aurangzeb, it failed to develop into a popular cult-centre among Muslim masses. Rather it was the Chishti tombs which were the repositories of sacred charisma, the Chishti establishment never letting the followers forget the selflessness of the order by reminding them of their non-alliance with state-power.[44] It is rather ironic but makes perfect sense that Aurangzeb opted to be buried in a tomb without a dome, with greenery open to the sky—like his sister Jahanara—near a Chishti shrine complex at Khuldabad rather than be interned in a Naqshbandi one, which can be explained as follows.

As has been argued by K.A. Nizami, the Chishtis assumed high sacredness only through their renunciation of worldly power, though Simon Digby convincingly showed the basis of the Chishti master-narrative (see Chap. 2). This renunciation was connected to the hallowed Indian philosophical tradition of '*tyaga*' or sacrifice. Since most of the Indians, whether Hindu or Muslim, shared the same appraisal for renunciation, the Chishtis could provide for some creative encounter between communities. Alternatively, the Naqshbandi association with power made this Central Asian order part of the state apparatus, which made identification with them difficult for the common people who were already reeling under high taxation. The Chishti popularity, therefore, can also be seen as a protest by the poor classes to carve out their own symbolic space of imagination. It is in this sense that Aurangzeb's burial in a Chishti space can be read as symbolically representing the acceptance of defeat on the part of his empire and all that it stood for. Indeed his death in 1707 heralded the demise of the Mughals though the empire could continue as titular head due to its sheer momentum and cultural capital earned in the past. On the other hand, for the poor and exploited it must have vindicated their belief in their *tariqa*, i.e., Chishtiyya, and unconsciously gratified them with a symbolic victory against the rich and noble, notwithstanding the fact, that Chishtis actually did not renounce all their associations with the state and power, as the close association between the Chishtis and the Sultanate of Delhi and the Mughals under Akbar shows.[45]

---

[44] Digby: *Sufis and Soldiers*, p. 28.

[45] In fact, Salim Chishti's tomb, and those of the members of his family, like Islam Khan who was even a Mughal *mansabdar*, are located at the highest spot of the Mughal capital city of Fatehpur-Sikri. But these were imperially built ritual centres with a view to providing sacred legitimacy to the rulers.

Apart from this suggested triumph, the Naqshbandiyya became unmistakably the leading order in South Asia and different from the older orders in several ways, by putting more stress on the elevation one's ego than the older orders, who tended towards a unity of the human being with God through meditation techniques. Further, all orders had one central book to base their ideology on. However, while the established orders such as the Chishtiyya taught their ideas by means of the authoritative oral statements (*malfuzat*), the Naqshbandiyya came to prefer epistles (*maktubat*). The Qadiriyya preferred poetry as the media vehicle to disseminate their ideas—all being means to grasp people's imagination and memory. Moreover, the Chishtis considered social activities as a means to achieve spiritual progress while the Naqshbandiyya believed rigorous discipline and asceticism to be their path. They also differed on the issue of *dhikr*. In contrast to many other orders, the Naqshbandis prescribed the silent *dhikr*. Similarly, most of them postulated Islamic exclusivism while others tried to accommodate and integrate other positions. However, these perceptions differing as they may have been were increasingly transcended by the increasing possibility of multiple memberships.[46]

It is precisely because of the diversity in South Asian Islam outlined above, that the "Pax Mughalica"—with its Turani bias and its process of singularisation and normatisation of cultural and religious dynamics—took place only partially, notwithstanding the policy of centralisation and bureaucratisation of different emperors, culminating in Aurangzeb's "Islamisation". Centralisation effected by the Mughals was reflected in the evolution of a common aesthetic taste inscribed in temples, mosques, palaces and fortifications, as has been shown by Catherine Asher. Centralisation can also be measured by the amount of revenue flowing into the royal treasury and the degree of autonomy granted to those formally conquered.[47] According to Khafi Khan, in line with the *Fatawa-ye 'Alamgiri*, no government official was severely punished but the peasantry remained exploited and harassed. Officers in charge neglected government orders. Moreover, the financial situation was fast deteriorating, as can be established in the fields of economy and trade.

---

[46] Cf. Knysh: *Islamic Mysticism*, pp. 284f.

[47] For this spatial diversity see Alam and Subrahmanyam (eds.): *The Mughal State*, pp. 33–46.

Financial aspect

The need to increase income made the empire finance itself primarily through internal resources, based on a revenue system, which taxed agricultural production and urban trade.[48] Even the Deccan was absorbed into the *zabt*-system. The search for new agricultural areas and the revenue attached to it, stood at the centre of Mughal imperial interests. As pointed out by Richard Eaton:

> Ruling over a vast empire built upon a bottom-heavy agrarian base, Mughal officials were primarily interested in enhancing agricultural productivity by extracting as much of the surplus wealth of the land as they could, and in using that wealth to the political end of creating loyal clients at every level of administration.[49]

The home market was to be stabilised and expanded. The support of domestic trade had given impulse to regional cities particularly in the Ganges valley. Demand for cash crops grew as market towns mushroomed to meet the needs of a booming overland trade.[50] Traders operating in the prosperous market towns benefited from this development. They were also affiliated with the local Sufi brotherhoods, which provided them with a much needed infrastructure stretching up to Central Asia. Even politically they were supported by the imperial conquest of the Deccan. The number of Hindu nobles increased tremendously at the Mughal court, reviving the system of a hierarchy of nobles established by Akbar (*mansabdar*-system) through which the power of Hindu officials started to increase.[51] The domestic trade, as well as the empire's preoccupation in the South supported the local nobility, who looked for further de-centralisation of the empire.

From the death of Aurangzeb till about 1720, the stability of the empire eroded severely. Internal security was ignored, giving way to internal violence. The *zabt* revenue system, which was not implemented throughout the entire empire due to regional variations, was prey to revenue farming. Tax collections diminished due to the missing links between centre and province. While the central authority weakened,

---

[48] Richards: *The Mughal Empire*, p. 185.

[49] Eaton: *The Rise of Islam and the Bengal Frontier*, p. 134.

[50] Richards: *The Mughal Empire*, p. 191.

[51] Under Aurangzeb, already leading generals and some mansab holders were Hindus. See M. Athar Ali: *The Mughal Nobility under Aurangzeb*, Bombay etc.: Asia Publishing House 1970.

regional potentates accumulated power and developed their own regional kingdoms. Thus in a way, political de-centralisation was paralleled by economic reorientation.

After Aurangzeb

Aurangzeb was succeeded in 1707 by his eldest son, Muʿazzam, the Bahadur Shah, a man more moderate than his father in religious matters. The Maratha wars had already had a harsh effect on the empire, affecting the regime's ability to enforce law and order. It became increasingly difficult to collect land revenue from the *zamindar*s. Rajputs, Sikhs and Jats as well as Marathas were the main problems, which Bahadur Shah could sort out only provisionally. His son Jahandar Shah succeeded him in 1712, only after fierce battle and intervention by the most powerful noble of the empire, Zulfikar Khan. The new emperor left Lahore, where his father had shifted the court, to Shahjahanabad. But things had changed irrevocably by then. Here ruled the powerful Zulfikar Khan, who gave the Rajputs extraordinary concessions. The Marathas were made feudatory in order to neutralise opposition. The emperor, preoccupied with these matters, could not check the growing fiscal crisis. Troops remained unpaid and landowners who were unable to live up to their *jagirs*, sold their lands. Tax bidders and their bankers were the main beneficiaries since they immediately collected on the discounted revenues. Having invited much resentment, Jahandar Shah was killed by Farrukh-Siyar who was supported by the ambitious Sayyid brothers of Barah, originating from Muzaffarnagar. His rule from 1713 till 1719 was exhausted by rivalling groups within the court nobility. They competed to influence him and sought to improve the circumstances of their extended families. Factionalism was increasingly becoming a matter of family rather than religious convictions. In order to secure a broader base, Farrukh-Siyar broke with Aurangzeb's policies, abolished *jizya* and made an amicable reconciliation with leading Rajputs and Marathas. Through a *farman* in 1717, he also permitted the European East India Company to carry out duty-free trade in major cities and areas such as Bengal, Surat and Madras. This was probably done also to curb the power of local potentates such as Murshid Quli Khan, who was appointed governor of Bengal in 1715. In the wake of these developments, it became increasingly difficult to defend the borders from Sikhs, Jats and Marathas, who as coherent groups, were themselves products of Mughal Empire. The Sayyid Brothers, the de-facto rulers were even willing to accept the Marathas as partners in the southern empire if they politically and militarily supported them at the centre.[52] Eventually, the Sayyid Brothers deposed and replaced Farrukh-Siyar with another puppet emperor called Muhammad Shah in 1719. The Sayyids played inclusive politics due to their own insecure position and for this reason they were criticised for following the anti-Timurid policies of Nizam al-Mulk Asaf Jah, who had become the master of Deccan after 1713. Eventually, Nizam al-Mulk defeated a Sayyid-Marathan coalition army in the Deccan in 1720.

The hereditary system weakened the centre. New social formations emerged and supported the evolving regionalism, which coincided with the establishment of regional and national markets. In what is remarkable but true, central control of provinces in the seventeenth century turned into provincial control of the centre in the eighteenth century, when a change from empire to territorial princely states took place. While the Mughal Empire had tried to integrate different cultures into an imperial unity and world economy, the evolving national markets in the princely states sought the regionalisation of imperial culture. Thus ironically enough the territorial disintegration of the Empire resulted in various levels of regional and local integration.

[52] Richards: *The Mughal Empire*, pp. 263, 270.

PART THREE

TERRITORIAL STATES AND COLONIAL RULE. ACCOMMODATION AND DIFFERENTIATION OF MUSLIM CULTURES

CHAPTER SEVEN

REGIONAL STATES, NATIONAL MARKETS AND EUROPEAN EXPANSION (APPROX. 1700–1800)

Between Aurangzeb's death in 1707 and British annexation of Bengal in 1757, the disintegration of the Mughal Empire into smaller principalities was, among others, the result of the increasing significance of market economy. This economy received support from different urban amirs as well as from the landed gentry united by their interest in keeping taxes and duties to their own liking. The penetration of money into the country-side destroyed parts of the traditional social structure and replaced it with interactions purely governed by cash nexus. At the same time, imperial expansion under Aurangzeb coupled with his long absence from the capital led to a weakening of control over gentry. This resulted in heavy loss of revenue, consequently making the centre as well as local landlords dependent on powerful financiers. The Emperor's increasing dependence on courtiers, both in the struggle for power and in the daily routine of the court, was a reflection of these problems. Though Muhammad Shah, the fourteenth Mughal Emperor, managed to seize power in 1719, the empire had already become truncated with the loss of Maharashtra, Awadh and Haydarabad. Large amounts of revenue stayed in the provinces, strengthening the local landlords as well as the new warrior states led by the Marathas, Jats, Sikhs or the invading Afghans in 1740s. Traditional cities declined while new market towns emerged to support economy and trade in new centres of commerce. Parallel to this, traditional harbour cities like Surat, Masulipatnam and Hugli were replaced by the new English and French harbours of Bombay, Madras, Pondicherry, Calcutta and Chandernagore. This enabled European trading companies to gradually get involved in the internal power struggles and to acquire numerous privileges by shifting sides most opportunistically. After the defeat of the Mughal army at Plassey in 1757, they went for direct annexation of provinces and by 1818 the East India Company (EIC), founded in 1600, had almost established an all-India rule.

Towards independent movements

Towards the end of sixteenth century the various "fiefdoms" and land grants became a central economic basis of Muslim communities in *qasbah*s. Apart from service gentry, there also developed rentier gentry, whose impact gradually increased, particularly since the Muslim gentry preferred to stay in their respective home-*qasbahs*. Besides fulfilling their imperial duties in administration and the military, they expanded the power and semantics of *qasbahs* by investing in water supply, mosques, religious schools, libraries, shrines, orchards and also big and high buildings, some of them up to five storeys. Far from being a philanthropic gesture, these investments served the *ashraf* as institutions through which later they could legitimately claim public property like land and buildings as their own. The economic and religious significance of these cities was reflected in the military might of the *qasbah*, manifested in citadels of the local potentates or *zamindars*, externally exhibiting their military importance and internally reflecting the prestige of their leaders. Thus, the military became one of the important cultural carriers. The development of marketplaces and literary culture transformed the *qasbah*s into an object of pride. Gradually, the concept of *watan* (home, residence, territory) gained considerable importance in the self-understanding of their inhabitants.[1] However, this newly attained pride for the home-*qasbah* was not without its problems. The struggle amongst the vassals replicated itself onto the religious elite. The relationship between the *madad-e ma'ash*-holding ulama and *a'immahdar*s on the one hand and land-hungry *zamindars* and military officers of the Mughals on the other became increasingly acrimonious as described in Qutb al-Din Sihalawi's treatise *Risalat dar al-harb* (see Chap. 5).

These conflicts were further aggravated by internal tensions at the court and the emperor's increasing dependence on politically influential gentry. Different new alliances at the court[2] and in the provinces saw the eventual triumph of *zamindars* who were able to acquire property rights also backed by religious scholars.[3] Towards the end of seven-

[1] See Bayly: *Rulers*, pp. 192, 352f.; Bayly: "Islamic Gentry", pp. 20–48.

[2] For the problems and tensions at court and the resulting movements for autonomy of the gentry see Satish Chandra: *Parties and Politics at the Mughal Court 1707–1740*, New Delhi 1972(2). Chandra's thesis is substantiated in Ali: *Nobility*.

[3] In the seminal work *The Agrarian System of Mughal India* (1963) Irfan Habib has argued that the dispersed landed gentry (*zamindars*) were able to oust the centralised

teenth century, orthodox pressure of *madad-e maʿash*-holders on the government became so acute that in 1690 Aurangzeb had to declare their properties to be hereditary, thus depriving the centre of extracting revenue from their subjects. This transfer of crown-land into private property also carried with it juridical and spiritual responsibilities, so that many vassals could now dispense secular as well as sacred justice. According to Muzaffar Alam, this led to secularisation and corruption of religious authorities and jurists.[4] The feebleness of the Mughal fiscal system led to more internal conflicts which ultimately led to autonomy movements by a wide variety of chiefs who had been high officials in Mughal administration. They began to regard their former fiefs as home provinces (*subah-e watan*). These new territorial lords, including nobles and important local officers, were closely affiliated with wealthy merchants and bankers,[5] who were more than willing to finance them due to their own interests in stabilising the evolving "national markets" (see below). In early eighteenth century, these landlords introduced various land and administrative measures resulting in what may be called "regional centralisation".

In particular, governors of some old provinces became virtually independent. A prominent example was Awadh, where under governors Nawwab Saʿadat Khan Burhan al-Mulk (nawwabship 1722–1739) and his successor Safdar Jang (1739–54), Shiʿite confession and rituals were introduced. The functional, state-legitimising *dars-e nizami*, developed by Sunnite scholars of Farangi Mahall in Lucknow, was more firmly established. Administration and revenue system were centralised. However, after the battle of Buxar in 1764, the weak Nawwab Shujaʿ al-Daula (1754–75) became a mere pensioner of the British (who had been working towards the establishment of colonial power, see below), and Awadh a buffer state against the Marathas.

Bengal, led by the Mughal Nawwab Murshid Quli Khan (died 1725), a Brahmin converted to Shiʿite Islam, became virtually independent in 1704 when he became head of the revenue department (*diwan*) of

---

nobility because the *zamindars* were able to benefit from the desperation of the oppressed peasantry.

[4] See Muzaffar Alam: "Some Aspects of the Changes in the Position of the Madad Maʾash Holders in Awadh, 1676–1722", in: Satish Chandra (ed.): *Essays in Medieval Indian Economic History*, Delhi 1987 pp. 72–80; see also Alam: *The Crisis of Empire*, passim.

[5] For the role of bankers in the South see Karen Leonard: "The 'Great Firm' Theory of the Decline of the Mughal Empire", in: *Comparative Studies in Society and History* 21/2 (1979), pp. 161–167.

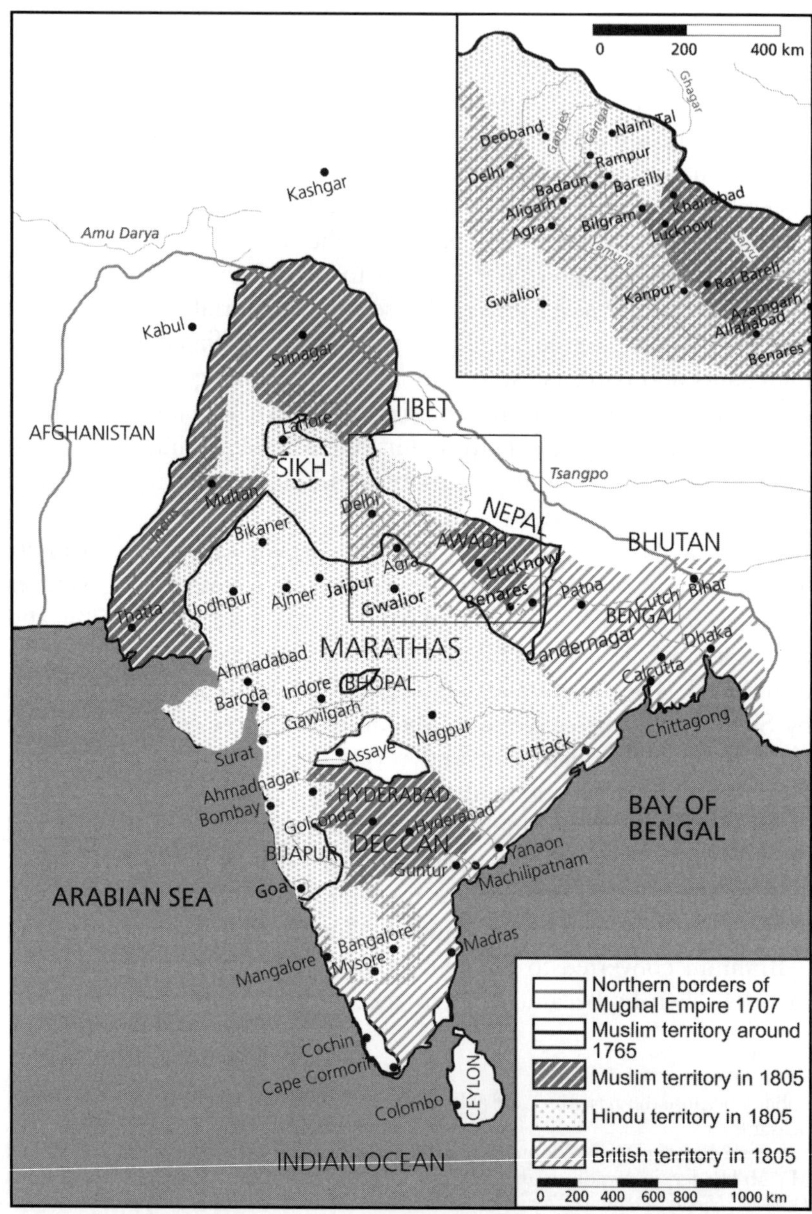

Map 10: Fall of Mughal rule in eighteenth century

the province with Murshidabad as the capital. An efficient centralised administration was set up, many of the Mughal land grants eliminated and collection of revenue in cash was implemented. Ironically enough, the British would use the existing power structure after defeating the powerful Alivardi Khan in 1756. In the war of Plassey in 1757, Colonel Robert Clive (1725–74), with the help of powerful merchant bankers led by Fatehchand Jagat Seth, the "banker of the world", defeated the governor of Bengal, Siraj al-Daula. He was replaced by the loyalist Mir Ja'far 'Ali. Attempts by Mir Qasim, who had been installed by the British in 1760 in place of Mir Ja'far 'Ali, to limit British exploitation resulted in the battle of Buxar in 1764, ending in humiliating defeat for the Nawwabs of Bengal and Awadh. In 1765 Clive took over the revenue collecting rights (*diwani*) of Bengal, Bihar and Orissa. By assuming the role of administrator in Bengal, the East India Company began to employ Europeans in the hinterland.

In the South, five Maratha states became nearly sovereign after 1720. Similarly, in 1724, in Deccan, Nizam al-Mulk Asaf Jah, the chief minister of the Mughal Empire, declared the wealthy state of Haydarabad to be his personal dominion. His successors were to become the most important allies of the British in India, continuing to rule until their integration into the Indian Union in 1948. Meanwhile, Nawwabs of Arcot and Carnataka enjoyed quasi-independent status in the western Deccan region.

Elsewhere, the Sikhs, under Ranjit Singh and after decades of struggle were finally able to establish their state with Lahore as capital in 1799. In Mysore, Haydar 'Ali established a formidable state in 1761, with centralised control and a flourishing export business. Succeeded by his son Tipu Sultan (Fateh 'Ali) in 1782, Mysore officially became an empire seeking confirmation from the Ottoman caliph. At the same time, the "Tiger of Mysore"[6] Tipu, interacted with the French and his self-understanding as "Citizen Tipu Sultan" and Tipu's membership in a Jacobin Club displayed some shifts from traditional politics when he applied new administrative and political techniques to his government. Giving high priority to morality and the improvement of living conditions

[6] Tipu had chosen the symbol of a tiger as a personal and royal insignia because it served different purposes: its use aligned Tipu with his Hindu dynastic predecessors and at the same time linked him within an Islamic context to the fourth caliph, 'Ali, the lion of the Prophet. By employing this shared symbol Tipu gained legitimacy; see Davis: *Lives of Indian Images*, pp. 149–152.

for his people, he devised a plan of some sort of state capitalism. But eventually, colonialism cut off his links with the lucrative Arab trade. To be sure, for the British, Tipu, who also initiated the compilation of juridicial opinions with special reference to *jihad* called *Fatawa-ye Muhammadi*,[7] became the "Oriental despot", as he attempted to face European mercantilist power with its own weapons of state monopoly and an aggressive ideology of expansion.[8]

National markets

The Socio-economic pattern of the national markets was primarily responsible for these developments.[9] These markets defined new economic relations within a specific limited region and required a centralised fiscal, administrative and military polity so that they could increase and speed up production. These markets were therefore characterised by the elimination of a number of internal duties which could hamper the burgeoning of trade. They were also characterised by standardisation of the tax-system within state boundaries and by protective customs at the borders. Their functionality was dependent on an already existing infrastructure, markets and functioning administrative centres as well as on the degree of socio-cultural integration of the local people. Areas that were not economically viable because of high administrative costs were exempted from the regulating agrarian system. These areas were mostly in the peripheries such as Afghanistan, Sind, Kashmir, and Orissa. Assessment according to the regulation governing land revenue system (*zabt*) by imperial officers was hardly possible in these mostly tribal areas.[10]

In sharp contrast, national markets provided space for new states whose borders increasingly defined the dominions of territorial power. In these states the idea of a "national culture" became more and more popular. Identity was established through a common communication structure, e.g., education and language, albeit vernacular, which

---

[7] Compare Islam: "Origin and Development of *Fatâwâ*-Compilation", here p. 11.

[8] See Bayly: *Indian Society*, p. 97; for an interesting account of European images of Tipu see Davis: *Lives of Indian Images*, Chap. 5.

[9] For the concept of a national market compare Fernand Braudel: *Civilization and Capitalism. 15th–18th Century*, Vol. III, New York 1986, pp. 277ff.

[10] Cf. Schulze: "Die islamische Welt in der Neuzeit", pp. 369ff.

became a central concern of the local courts. There was also a clear distinction between religious and secular authority in the sense that adherence to the same religion or caste did not prevent people from competing with one another economically. It was in these national markets that Muslim or more particularly the *ashraf* social structure acquired a four-fold hierarchy akin to the Hindu *varna* system. These four strata of the *ashraf* were the Sayyids, who derived their genealogy from Prophet Muhammad, followed by the Shaikhs who claimed to be descendants of his companions, the Afghans and the Pakhtuns[11] (see also Excursus: Caste). As Christopher Bayly notes, there was a tendency to emphasise community and sober ethics of work and worship. Under the great Mughals, especially Akbar, syncretism had dominated. But "religious syncretism was only one aspect of a wider amalgamation of different systems of knowledge which had considerable implications in the sphere of economic management", since existing Hindu classifications were adapted to Islamic nomenclature. The social stratification and diversification of *ashraf* coincided with the administrative needs of the seventeenth and eighteenth centuries which, among other things, necessitated a new science of book-keeping called *ʿilm al-siyaq*. The *Siyaqnamas* were to establish a connection between state agents and tradesmen, thereby binding them in close networks of communication and cooperation. The Europeans could later extend their hegemony building upon this rational calculative economic method already in use in South Asia.[12]

Similarly, the idea of *umma*—Muslim community—could be thought of not only in terms of unity of religion but also in terms of a cultural unity in a specific territory.[13] This shift in perception was important, because it gave expression to a variety of simultaneous developments: new emerging identities, through ethnic or sectarian grouping, informed by real as well as invented genealogies; local patriotism and

[11] Cf. Lalji: *Mirʾat al-Audaʾ* (Pers. mss in A.M.U. Library; Tarikh No. 60), [pp. 88f.].

[12] C.A. Bayly: "Pre-colonial Indian Merchants and Rationality", in: Mushirul Hasan and Narayani Gupta (eds.): *Indian's Colonial Encounter*, Delhi 1993, pp. 3–24, here pp. 6, 7, 13, 17f.

[13] In the course of time different meanings of *umma* evolved in legal and political thought to expand its semantics. It was only in the context of nineteenth-century colonialism that the term was reintroduced by Muslim avantgardists as a unifying anti-colonial political tool; see the brief but excellent article on "Ummah" by Ahmad S. Dallal in: John L. Esposito et al. (eds.): *Encyclopedia of the Modern Islamic World, 1–4*, New York and Oxford: OUP 1995, Vol. 4, pp. 267–270.

devotional religions,[14] centralised revenue systems, and the creation of standardised languages, which contested imperial Persian,[15] paralleled by the construction of libraries and shrines; promotion of architecture and literature and music; the extending of the teacher-student relationship; the writing of encyclopaedias and literary critical works. Every principality boasted its own religio-cultural "variety" cum "verity". Thus, the consciousness of a national identity was transported in cultural dimensions such as language, history, and art (see Chap. 6). It was important to make a name for oneself inwardly through integration and outwardly through distinction.

A novel characteristic of Bengal, Awadh, and Haydarabad was that the rulers' descendants inherited important offices. This was a clear break with Mughal tradition. Their regional centralisation and military fiscal policy also posed indirect regional threats to Mughal dominance. Externally they struggled with Delhi, and internally pursued centralisation on the regional level, not least in order to curb local *zamindari* power.[16] However, at the same time they reflected the vitality of Mughal tradition: in the decaying baroque era the successor states became prime political institutions. But since the idea of universal dominion of the Mughals competed with a gradually developing notion of a national state, the politics of nearly all dynasties hardly came to grips with the rationality of new order. The Mughal Empire was to become an *ancient regime*.[17] Notwithstanding the new social formations, they preserved Mughal forms and practices for their legitimacy. While the official language of diplomacy remained Persian, rulers encouraged the vernaculars. The perceived deficiency of the first stood against the power of productivity of the latter. Rulers of new territorial states also sought religious legitimacy acting as patrons for a variety of religious groups. In some instances, Sufis provided spiritual legitimacy for the new territories by connecting them with the older saintly geography of the Mughal centre and its distant origin, Central Asia. They thereby

---

[14] For the establishment of devotional monumental architecture see paradigmatically the Shiʿite ritual centre in Lucknow fusing political power and religious ritual, in Hussein Keshani: "Architecture and the Twelver Shiʿi Tradition: The Great Imambara Complex of Lucknow", in: *Muqarnas* 23 (2006), pp. 219ff.

[15] Compare also Muzaffar Alam: "The Pursuit of Persian: Language in Mughal Politics", in: *MAS* 32/2 (1989), pp. 317–349.

[16] Compare Alam and Subrahmanyam (eds.): *The Mughal State*, pp. 46–55.

[17] Cf. Schulze: "Die islamische Welt in der Neuzeit", here pp. 373f.

established a new, yet old sense of belonging, reflecting internal dynamics of social class rather than Islamicity.[18] The rulers also commercialised their administration, just in line with the demands of national markets, thereby empowering the groups involved, as noted above. At the same time they replicated the Mughal system in their new capitals of Lucknow, Haydarabad and Murshidabad, mirroring the Central Asian and Persian culture of Muslim aristocracy. Regional centralisation received impetus through a conscious policy of vernacularisation.

Certainly, not all the groups benefited from these developments. There were revolts by Hindu landowners, Sikhs, Rajputs and local raiders such as Jats and Afghans challenging internal peace.[19] It is certainly possible to understand this crisis of the Mughal Empire in eighteenth century as an overall decay. But more importantly it can be understood in terms of an actual struggle between entrepreneurs, military personnel and politicians for capturing economic and political hegemony.

There was hardly any direct attack on symbols of Mughal legitimacy by the successor states. Among others the Pakhtuns threatened it led first by the millenarian Rawshaniyya and then by the orthodox Khushhal Khan Khattak (died 1690) harking back to Sher Shah Suri. In the Northwest some Pakhtuns established autonomous territories and also threatened the Safawids. It took the Pakhtun leader Ahmad Shah Abdali, a Safawid subordinate, much effort to put down his Pakhtun rivals before he ransacked Delhi,[20] held by the Mughal emperor Muhammad Shah, who reigned from 1719 to 1748.

The conquest of Delhi in 1739 by Nadir Shah, who had seized power in Iran, accelerated the exodus from the former capital and strengthened the power of new princes. The contemporary literary genre called *shahr-e ashub* (shattered city) is witness to these developments. This process of

---

[18] "Sultans and Sufis colluded in these spiritual and cultural aspects of conquest through their promotion of a sacred Muslim geography and literature . . . that conformed to the predispositions of the Mughal ecumene . . . shrines . . . linking religious practice in their new homelands to ancestral traditions in their old ones." Green: "Geography, empire and sainthood", quotation p. 224.

[19] C.A. Bayly: *Rulers, Townsmen and Bazaars*; Alam: *The Crisis of Empire*; J.R. Cole: *Roots of North Indian Shī'ism in Iran and Iraq; Religion and State in Awadh, 1722–1859*, Berkeley: UCP 1988; Asim Roy: *The Syncretistic Tradition in Bengal*, Princeton: PUP 1983; Wink: *Land and Sovereignty*; Bayly: *Saints. Goddesses and Kings*; J.S. Grewal: *The Sikhs of the Punjab*, Cambridge 1990.

[20] Under Ahmad Shah Abdali Afghanistan extended from Central Asia to Delhi, and from Kashmir to the Arabian Sea. See M. Ewans: *Afghanistan: A new history*, London 2002.

regional centralisation was characterised by physical expansion, cultural integration, and administrative and military reforms, not without the help of European mercenaries. Islam and the re-emergence of patronage of Muslim scholars played a major role as well. A new sober and rational approach to the world had emerged, as can be observed in the popularity of the compact and rational teachings of the *dars-e nizami*. Mulla Nizam al-Din and his descendants and followers enjoyed patronage precisely because of this teaching, albeit with regional variations. Thus the Sunnite Farangi Mahall was able to produce many brilliant scholars and high officials, even in Shiʿite Awadh. Among them were the Mulla's son, the celebrated ʿAbd al-ʿAli (died 1810), the Mulla's nephew, Mulla Hasan (died 1794), and Maulana Haydar (died 1840). These and other scholars fanned into new (residence) cities, such as Lucknow, Murshidabad and Haydarabad, which manifested the might of new power holders who programmatically recruited scholars to provide teaching to the service elite and to legitimise the new territorial system, primarily through their scholarship of law. Making use of an elaborate teacher-student relation as well as spiritual affiliations, many scholars established new centres of knowledge, which fostered rational religious sciences, and whose protagonists taught at princely courts and disseminated this tradition of Islamic scholarship to regions such as Madras, Rampur, Arcot, Carnataka and even as far as Egypt, where they found willing supporters. Because of their functional approach they were soon to become leading servants in the colonial administration as well.[21] In fact, the Farangi Mahallis' patronage was well established even after the upheaval of 1857, so that the British census officer could state in 1869, that

> still they obtain thousands of favours from the Government of the Nawwáb Wazir...people come from far and near to be taught here, and obtain benefit from this family...the head of the family is looked on as the first Maulavi of the Sunni sect in Lucknow. Some of the family are still in receipt of pensions but they are badly off, and the number of their scholars has dwindled down almost to nothing. Yet they still possess considerable influence in the city.[22]

[21] Malik: *Gelehrtenkultur*, pp. 162–168.

[22] J. Williams (compl.): *The Report on the Census of Oudh, Vol. I; General Report*, Lucknow: Oudh Government Press 1869, App. E, V f.

Notwithstanding the teachings of Farangi Mahall and their role in the process of consolidation, both before and after British incursions, by 1780 Mughal power was reduced to the region of Delhi, until it also became part of British indirect rule in 1803, nominally reigned by Shah ʿAlam till 1806.

The Europeans

The national markets also provided space for yet another major actor: Europe. Various colonial powers, such as the French, Dutch and English, had been trying to extend their influence in Europe and competing materially and politically to control the new world economy. Their internecine war was basically to safeguard raw materials, markets, and even possibilities of emigration in what was considered to be unexploited and virgin regions. It is worthwhile to note that colonialism first took root within the boundaries of territorial (successor) states, i.e, within the borders of national markets. This means that colonialism did not expand into traditional and primitive societies but into closed political entities, which had replaced the Mughal Empire. In fact, the emergence of national markets coincided with areas of European trading companies, such as the Dutch East India Company, founded in 1602, and the English East India Company, established in 1600, whose major asset was its organisation as a joint-stock enterprise:

> Individuals could not hope to trade on their own so far away from Europe while the English Crown, unlike that of Portugal, did not care to commit its resources to so uncertain an undertaking. The joint-stock organization allowed merchants to share the risk of trade, and enabled them to raise further funds as needed. The access to resources provided by the company structure made the English a formidable competitor as they confronted India's indigenous merchant families. The Company gained further strength from its possession of centralized direction, through a 24-member Court of Directors, the stability of an archive, and a staff recruited for their specialized skills.[23]

International trade had stimulated the economic growth of the Mughal Empire, but this did not mean that wealth flowed automatically into

---

[23] B.D. Metcalf and Thomas R. Metcalf: *A Concise History of India*, Cambridge: CUP 2002, p. 43. For the history of the Company see Anthony Wild: *The East India Company: trade and conquest from 1600*, London 2000.

the Mughal treasury. European trading companies were quite consistent in obtaining imperial concessions from the 1610s onwards. The Dutch were exempted from payment of trans-toll in Bengal. Agrarian, industrial and processed goods exported to Europe were bringing in the necessary money. Articles for import included European goods or bullion, metal and coins. At the same time, the European presence in South Asia increased so that new trade began to be felt in Mughal India. Trading posts and industries, or "factories", were established in important coastal or delta areas again from the 1610s onwards, and by the end of seventeenth century, Indo-European trade was dominated by the Dutch and English companies.

In 1698, the British acquired *zamindari* rights over Calcutta which they eventually transformed into their commercial headquarters. Gradually, they acquired a strategic position from where they could create trouble for the Mughals. Their naval superiority made them the number one European pirate on the high seas. In 1702 Aurangzeb became furious enough to order his local officers to seize all European trading missions. But by that time the trade map had changed considerably. Bombay (Mumbai) had already replaced the old commercial Mughal centre of Surat. In the South, Europeans expanded by establishing enclaves at Pulicat, Madras and Pondicherry which provided refuge to thousands fleeing from political instability and war in the region. Bombay and Madras continued to flourish without major intervention by the Mughals, who were preoccupied with the Marathas.

Colonial impact

The trading companies integrated national markets into the colonial economy, depriving them of their economic independence. This was done mostly with the help and integration of local people, such as native informants, and alliances, whether in the South (Madras), where the British were able to defeat the French, or in Bengal. Native informants,[24] usually from higher social groups—the Muslim gentry or

[24] For the informants during the Mughal era, see Momin Mohiuddin: *The Chancellery and Persian Epistolography under the Mughals: From Babur to Shahjahan (1526–1658); a study in Inshâ', Dâr al-Inshâ', and Munshîs, based on original documents*, Calcutta 1971. For their relevance in colonial times see Michael H. Fisher: *Indirect Rule in India: Residents and the Residency System 1764–1857*, New Delhi 1991; Nicholas B. Dirks: "Colonial Histories

ashraf—enabled the foreigners to function in a world which otherwise was alien in several respects. Privileged through their assignments, the native elite also influenced colonial knowledge to a considerable degree, as we will see later. However, in serving the colonial power, the social status of the Indian service elite gradually decreased from that of *ashraf* of Indian society to that of *ardhal* or barbarians in the service of the British.

It is clear that the relatively swift colonial penetration of the Indian home market was possible only due to close connections between scholars, traders, taxes and politics. In Bengal big entrepreneurs were instrumental in establishing new economic relations. They became the financiers and at the same time consumers of British goods in India. The British, Dutch and French were important trade partners because they brought in silver and copper and bought Bengali clothes and silk. The Mughals benefited from this silver and copper which supported local artisans controlled particularly by Hindu businessmen. Having acquired political power by the mid eighteenth century, the British gave very low wages to the artisans so as to reap high profits. Moreover, company employees were privately given monopolies for trading in articles such as saltpetre and betel nut. Thus, part of the Bengali economy became increasingly dependent on the British.

But the first British success occurred in the South, in Madras and Arcot, which they could call their own after the Peace of Paris in 1763, which saw France ceding these parts to the British. With the bordering states they tried to set up a network of alliances, or otherwise dominated them militarily through their tightly-knit, elite military corps in order to secure their own defence.[25] The princely states were important buffer zones for the British against rebels and, later, against nationalism.

French and Indian interests had to be restricted by political interventions, in order to secure the British East India Company's commercial

---

and Native Informants: Biography of an Archive", in: Carol A. Breckenridge and Peter van der Veer (eds.): *Orientalism and the Postcolonial Predicament*, Philadelphia: Univ. of Philadelphia Press 1993, pp. 279–313; B. Cohn: "The Command of Language and the Language of Command", in: Ranajit Guha (ed.): *Subaltern Studies IV*, Delhi 1985, pp. 276ff.; Christopher A. Bayly: *Empire and Information. Intelligence gathering and social communication in India, 1780–1870*, Cambridge 1996.

[25] In fact, the company re-invented Mughal tradition in the attempt to establish its legitimacy by deliberately mythologising the performances of some historical figures. For this process of embodiment of military strength, compare Alavi: *The Sepoys and the Company*.

stakes. Thereby, trading privileges were transformed into absolute rights. Indians hired the Company's efficient troops, which had been evolving as a powerful establishment since the 1770s, at their own expense. This, however, could only be met by surrendering their revenue incomes to the Company. In order to maximise income, first, indirect rule was established in Bengal, often initiated by corporate bodies of merchants. This was considered a proven device, because it incorporated traditional indigenous political and economic structures. The reason for this was pragmatic as well as ethnocentric. The pragmatic reason was the cost-effectiveness through involvement of only a few Europeans; the ethnocentric reason being the belief that non-whites could only be controlled by their own leaders and systems. Utilising the vast network of Mughal infrastructure, the British set up a colonial information order. In this way vast colonies could be ruled remotely through the so-called "resident", the highest agent of indirect rule, while Indian officials acted as revenue collectors for the Company.[26] Thus, trade monopoly was gradually converted into a monopoly of territorial domination.

Penetrating the country

When Warren Hastings (died 1818) became the first Governor General of the Company's Indian territories in 1773, colonial expansion took on a new dimension. Close involvement with revenue further needed close involvement with the administration of justice. Civil courts were introduced, functioning under British responsibility in 1772, while the *Regulating Act* provided the Governor General with tremendous powers. The Company finally acquired a political mandate when the apparatus of Bengal's central government was established in the British city of Calcutta.

In order to further stabilise their power, the East India Company required a functioning land revenue system. Various experiments were devised so as to maximise revenue collection, eventually leading to the *Permanent Settlement* of land revenue in 1793 introduced by Charles Cornwallis (1738–1805), who held the posts of Governor-General of India and Commander-in-Chief of Bengal from 1785 to 1793, and

[26] See Michael H. Fisher: *Indirect Rule in India: Residents and the Residency System 1764–1857*, New Delhi 1991.

to be implemented by a new system of district collectors. This system guaranteed a constant flow of taxes, which was necessary to support traders, civil servants and tax collectors, all of which came to possess large land holdings over time. But at the same time the land revenue settlements led to the wholesale ruination of the peasantry as well as the old *zamindars*. These old ones were replaced by new speculative ones from the city having little empathy with the peasants. The new system thus created a new class of landowners, promoting the *zamindars* to landlords who now had contractual obligations to pay the government's revenue, i.e., 90% of the estimated revenue![27] Incidentally, they were predominantly Hindu in Bengal, but religious affiliation had hardly mattered so far and was only to become important later.[28] However, this new revenue system increased the influence of the established local Hindu elites of Bengal (*bhadralok*) who were socially comparable to Muslim *ashraf*. They were quick to occupy key positions in the emerging colonial administration and economy, and were at the forefront of the "Bengal renaissance".[29] The Muslims, in contrast, failed to utilise new opportunities, not so much because of religious reasons (they accepted interest from the money lending business), but primarily because their wealth was attached to hereditary landed property which was considered to be the only cultural and economic capital. Already by the end of eighteenth century this Hindu affluence was increasingly reflected through the construction of numerous temples. Also the change in balance of power between the Hindu and Muslim elite sometimes expressed itself through riots in urban areas which might have been based in the indigenous roots of later communalism. The Company tried to ensure "law and order"—since Indians were thought to be unruly—by introducing new legislation and regulations concerning taxes and land ownership rights. In doing so, the British connected India to the world market on a much greater scale. The intention, of course, was the thorough exploitation of India for their industrial needs back home.

---

[27] See Marshall: *The Eighteenth Century*, p. 32.

[28] In 1871 the colonial administrator W.W. Hunter observed that the Settlement was responsible for the downfall of Islam in Bengal. See his widely quoted book *The Indian Musulmans*.

[29] For the Bengal renaissance see David Kopf: *The British Orientalism and the Bengal Renaissance*, Calcutta 1969.

Changing the scene

But individual assessments in Bengal were cumbersome for the British and particularly harsh for the peasants. Later, they resorted to 'revenue farming' whereby the right to collect revenue was awarded to the highest bidders, who were mostly absentee landlords having profited through trading with the British. Despite their best methods, the revenue collection was much lower than what was assessed. Moreover, absentee landlordism coupled with the fragmentation of land made the yield under-productive. It was decided then to assess the revenue collectively. This was the ryotwari (*raiyatwari*)/*mahalwari* system in western and southern India, which guaranteed the continuation of big landholdings because revenue assessments were made collectively for the whole village/*mahal* rather than individually as in the case of permanent settlement areas. Therefore, this system introduced by Thomas Munro (1761–1827) seemed to shield the peasantry from much misery,[30] such as famines, which were a regular occurrence in Bengal. The overall misery of Indian peasantry was, however, compounded by famines and declining trade. Artisans, in particular weavers, were severely hit by increased imports. In the wake of these developments, *bhadralok* and traders from Calcutta found themselves hibernated between a decaying home market and European imported goods.

The economic and political expansion of the Company was not only limited to the borders of national markets of territorial states. It even went beyond these borders and had a tendency to place the Indian economy in the service of the Company. Europeans were looking at ways to make their fortune as entrepreneurs and were primarily interested in trade and business. In lieu of providing troops and cash to the Indians, they received different sorts of concessions for their private interests, with the East India Company's protections making their activities even more efficient and profitable. This indirect political intervention led to further political interference, which eventually allowed them to transfer the temporary and conditional land grants into private property supported by the British crown. The Company's armies were manned by Indian mercenary soldiers, known as sepoys (from the Persian *sipahi*), behind

[30] Yet, some influential literati mourned the old system's demise in their local texts; see Velcheru Narayan Rao, David Shulman and Sanjay Subrahmanyam: *Textures of Time. Writing History in South India 1600–1800*, New Delhi: Permanent Black 2001.

which, as P.J. Marshall argues, "were structures of command, linked ultimately to Britain, with a local hierarchy of officers, record-keeping and accounting...which built on the Mughal bureaucratic rules and a high standard of account-keeping...".[31] Nominally independent, the successor states were subdued, through different devices of fiscal and legal contracts, surrenders and privileges given to European traders. This was a clear step towards the establishment of British sovereignty in India. The devised way was the system of subsidiary alliances. Under the terms of this alliance, local rulers protected themselves from external aggression by using British troops, whom they had to maintain financially. For the British, it was a perfect arrangement since it was economical. If the protected regions were unable to pay, due to the increasing debts of local governors, they were liable to be annexed, which happened to parts of Awadh in 1801[32] while Delhi was annexed in 1803 to control the Marathas. South India was incorporated by the end of eighteenth century, when in 1792 Tipu was forced to cede half of his territory and Mysore was finally incorporated into the British realm at the battle of Seringapatam (1799). Hayderadad's Asaf Jah was integrated into the new system of "subsidiary alliances" introduced by Cornwallis' successor Lord Wellesley (Governor-General of India 1798–1805). While the Nizam signed off all his European (preferably French) contacts and any sort of foreign policy, the British supported him through military which he, however, had to pay himself.[33] Only the Northwest under the Sikhs remained unattended, and the British could not succeed there until the 1830s.

As will be recalled, Indian princes and governors sought to integrate their home markets before the arrival of the British. Attempts were made to create a uniformly standardised language. Knowledge was sought to be transmitted as uniformly as possible. Similarly, taxes and duties were made uniform within a territory, while they supplied manufactured goods that the British paid for with raw materials and

---

[31] See P.J. Marshall (ed.): *The Eighteenth Century in Indian History: Evolution or Revolution?* New Delhi: OUP 2003, pp. 27f. For a detailed study on the important role of military tradition in the Company's army see Alavi: *The Sepoys and the Company.*

[32] Compare Richard B. Barnett: *North India Between Empires: Awadh, the Mughals, and the British, 1720–1801*, Berkeley: UCP 1980, pp. 231ff.; Michael H. Fisher: *A Clash of Cultures: Awadh, The British, and the Mughals*, New Delhi: Manohar 1987, pp. 90ff.

[33] A more detailed discussion on this issue is found in Margrit Pernau: *Verfassung und politische Kultur im Wandel. Der indische Fürstenstaat Hyderabad 1911–48*, Stuttgart: Franz Steiner 1992, pp. 35–42.

precious metal. This regional centralisation, however, contrasted sharply with the nineteenth-century colonial attempt towards restoring the old system of landed property or universal dominion and integrating the colonies into the world market. This exploitation needed different layers of legitimacy. Consequently, the Company reproduced the nominalism of the Mughals through titles such as *Company Bahadur*, which was used even more by the natives! This 'invention of tradition'[34] furnished Mughal symbols for political legitimacy, which, however, was never received by the majority of Indians, mostly because of their economic exploitation. Parallel to these developments, de-industrialisation and de-urbanisation took place, which went back to the decrease in artisans' incomes leading to the desertion of traditional occupations. Some of them, such as metalworkers, were virtually wiped out; others, such as weavers, were flexible enough to survive. But the new developments made some artisan industries vulnerable at the hands of the commercial agents (*gumashta*) employed by *zamindars*, bankers and merchants. As a result, artisans depended more and more on the land, even in the lean seasons, rather than the loom as was the case earlier. Similarly, the old elite in the *qasbah*s was affected because demand for the goods produced there had faded due to lack of purchasing power. Consequently, the *qasbah*s gradually declined. The misery was compounded due to fragmentation of land holdings, which was the inevitable result of the above factors.

The global economic situation had made possible the establishment of territorial states through the evolution of national markets. They also determined the place which national economies were to occupy in the world system. The beginning of the industrial revolution in Western Europe (1795–1834) changed the terms of international trade. The demand for finished goods from India gradually gave way to raw material, which eventually was integrated into the industrial manufacturing. Economic liberalism, having been popular in England, supported capital owners who were able to buy whatever was not available in their own national market. In this division of labour, India was to become a supplier of raw materials for the new industrial cities mainly dominated by the British. Initially, the trade was lucrative for India, but international developments, such as the French continental blockade as well as fiscal

[34] Compare Terence Ranger and E.J. Hobsbawm (eds.): *The Invention of Tradition*, Cambridge 1983.

problems in 1810/11, had major negative impact on trade in agrarian products. Gradually, colonial interests had emerged from individual trading. The fact is that a mere handful of Europeans were able to rule India only due to a long-term unfolding of colonial politics which depended on contemporary situations and local indigenous forces and, therefore, was contradictory. In the meantime, they dissolved the territorial states through revenue collection, through their system of subsidiary alliances and by exploiting the Indian economy for their purposes. By 1818 the Company had nearly established its all-India rule.

EXCURSUS

ISLAMIC ENDOWMENTS

Religious Endowments (*waqf*: literary: confinement, prohibition)[35] in the Islamic context have been of prime importance for a variety of issues, such as colonisation, urbanisation, education, and institutions like shrines. The idea of endowment is rooted in a hadith, the Prophet's answer to ʿUmar b. ʿAbd al-Khattab's question on what best to do with his booty after the battle of Khaibar: "*If you like, you may hold the property as waqf and give its fruits as charity*."[36] It is also linked to the Quranic idea of charity, such as *sadaqa* and *zakat*, which is to do good deeds and to distribute proceeds as alms.

Basically, the idea of Islamic endowment is that the owner (mainly of real estate) gives up property rights by a formal act of endowment and assigns it to the legal ownership of God. Thus it becomes a property which cannot be transferred or sold. The purpose of *waqf* and the identity of the beneficiaries are stipulated in a deed (*waqfiyya*). One may understand two kinds of *waqf*: the private/family endowment (*waqf ahli*) that favours a particular person or family and the descendents, and the public endowment (*waqf khairi*) that favours the community as a whole. Since the transfer of such a property is a formal act, *waqf* deeds appoint an administrator. However, in most cases the *waqf* is administered by the donor him-/herself and his descendents. Although it started as a private initiative, *waqfs* were later controlled by the state jurisprudence, mainly by a *qadi*, to prevent nepotism and misuse.

---

[35] Gregory C. Kozlowski: *Muslim Endowments and Society in British India*, Cambridge: CUP 1985, pp. 10–21; Jamal Malik: "Waqf in Pakistan; Change in traditional institutions", in: *WI* 30 (1990), pp. 63–97; Franz Kogelmann: *Islamische fromme Stiftungen und Staat. Der Wandel in den Beziehungen einer religiösen Institution und dem marokkanischen Staat seit dem 19. Jahrhundert bis 1937*, Würzburg: Ergon 1999, pp. 25–37; J.-P. Hartung: "Die fromme Stiftung (*waqf*): Eine islamische Analogie zur Körperschaft?", in: H.-G. Kippenberg and G.F. Schuppert (eds.): *Die verrechtlichte Religion: Der Öffentlichkeitsstatus von Religionsgemeinschaften*, Tübingen: Mohr-Siebeck 2004, pp. 287–314.

[36] Ibn al-Hajjaj al-Qushairi Muslim: *Sahih Muslim*, Beirut 1955: *Kitab al-wasiya*, p. 15; Muhammad ibn Ismaʿil al-Bukhari: *al-Jamiʿa al-Sahih*, al-Riyad 1988: *Kitab al-Shurut*, p. 19, and *Kitab al-wasaya*, p. 28; Abu Daʾud: *Sahih Sunan Abi Daʾud*, al-Kuwait 2002: *Kitab al-wasaya*, p. 13.

Common endowments are mosques, hospices and convents (esp. hospitals and *khanaqahs*), religious schools (*madrasas*) and public wells (*sabils*)[37] thereby making up a major source for public welfare and social security. There are some very famous *awqaf*, such as the *Haramain*, al-Aqsa in Jerusalem, institutions of higher learning such as the Madrasa Nizamiyya in Baghdad, al-Azhar, the Jamiʿa Dimashq, the Jamiʿa Qurtuba (Cordoba), or tombs and graveyards belonging to a noble family (e.g. the Taj Mahal in Agra). They might also have a religious connotation, such as the graveyard Jannat al-baqiʾa in Medina.[38] Similarly, in South Asia *waqf* played a very important role. During the Sultanate and Mughal periods,[39] rulers followed the 'classical' way outlined above of dealing with endowments, and set up *awqaf* themselves (like West Asian rulers around the same period) by supporting their favourite shrines and *khanaqahs*, declaring them *waqf* under royal patronage. During the period of the centralised system, Mughal rulers took keen interest in the distribution of deeds, which were a means of controlling certain social and political groups, by making Sufis and ulama economically dependent on *awqaf*. The Mughal rulers gave deeds to Hindus and Muslims alike, especially during the reigns of Akbar and Jahangir. Some state-sponsored *awqaf* in that period, such as Jamaʿ Masjid Delhi, Badshahi Masjid Lahore, Taj Mahal, were important for the monumental architecture and Mughal power[40] while in later Mughal/Nawwabi time rulers used endowments to promote certain strands of religion, such as Shia Islam in Awadh, by endowing e.g. the *Imambargahs*.[41] Some non-state endowments were used to maintain economic independence from the political establishment, such as the Mujaddidi *khanaqah* in Old Delhi.

Under the East India Company (EIC), the *waqf* system was not changed and state policy continued, albeit in a different way to centralise the administration of the *awqaf* and the distribution of their deeds, in order to enhance control over these rather heterogeneous institutions. This was in line with a new jurisdiction for the status of land to impose taxes accordingly. Thus *awqaf* lands corresponded to EIC's religious policies. It was privileged, but nevertheless taxed.[42] Similarly, *awqaf*

---

[37] Cf. Gabriel Baer, "The *Waqf* as a Prop for the Social System (Sixteenth–Twentieth Centuries)", in: *Islamic Law and Society* 4:3 (1997), pp. 264–297.

[38] Cf. Ishfaq ʿAli: *Tarikh-e awqaf*, Lucknow 1984, pp. 148–187, 197f.

[39] Cf. Kozlowski: *Muslim Endowments*, pp. 21–32.

[40] Cf. ʿAli: *Tarikh-e awqaf*, pp. 198–215.

[41] Cf. Kozlowski: *Muslim Endowments*, pp. 27–32.

[42] Kozlowski: *Muslim Endowments*, pp. 37–40.

law played a crucial role in the course of standardising religious law under the EIC as 'Anglo-Muhammadan Law'. The regional as well as customary laws and the *waqf* administration were subordinated to the Anglo-Indian Courts.

Similarly, by reorganising the *awqaf*, the colonialists attempted to control the indigenous education system financed through religious endowments. For example, in 1884 the Department of Finance and Commerce, Gov. of India, suggested selling all *trusts*. Instead, "Government securities should be bought with the proceeds". This led to objections from *waqifs*, as in the case of the "management of the Saiyid Salar Endowment in Bahraich". These discussions lingered on until 1914.[43] Furthermore, emphasis was to be put on the public welfare-character of *awqaf*. This became a proven device for abandoning the family endowments—*awqaf ahli*.[44]

Endowments became central to British interests again during the discussion about their re-privatisation.[45] Some Muslims were against these measures, such as the doyens of reformism, S. Ahmad Khan, Shibli Nuʿmani and others. M.A. Jinnah, a young lawyer at the time, took up the issue and, during his opening address to the Indian National Congress in 1906, pleaded for the restoration of the rights of private ownership of Islamic endowments, which had come increasingly under British influence since 1887.[46] The *Privy Council* (the highest legal authority in the empire) had ordained in 1894 that Islamic foundations were to be considered as religious and charitable institutions, and that they

---

[43] See U.P. State Archives, Mahanagar, Lucknow, Gov. of U.P., *General Administration Dept.*, 1893, File No. 360C; File 77/1911; January 1913, A Proceedings Nos. 113–117 "Saiyid Salar Endowment, Bahraich". For the shrine see M. Garcin de Tassy: *Mémoire sur les particularités de la religion musulmane en Inde* (reprint), Paris: Labitte 1869, pp. 77–84; Kerrin v. Schwerin: "Saint Worship in Indian Islam: The Legend of the Martyr Salar Masud Ghazi", in: I. Ahmad (ed.): *Ritual and Religion among Muslims of the Sub-continent*, Lahore 1985, pp. 143–161; also Tahir Mahmood: "The Dargah of Sayyid Salar Masʿud in Bahraich: Legend, Tradition and Reality", and I.H. Siddiqui: "A Note on the Dargah of Salar Masʿud in Bahraich in the Light of the Standard Historical Sources", in: Troll (ed.): *Muslim Shrines in India*, pp. 24–43, 44–49.

[44] Kozlowski: *Muslim Endowments*, pp. 95–155.

[45] U.P. State Archives, Mahanagar, Lucknow, Gov. of U.P., *General Administration Dept.*, File No. 222/1911, June 1911, A Proceedings 1–5 and August 1911, A Proceedings 14–17: "Muhammadan Endowments in the United Provinces". Also U.P. State Archives, Mahanagar, Lucknow, Gov. of U.P., *General Administration Dept.*, File No. 23/1919: "Religious Endowments in the United Provinces", and "Proceedings of the Religious Endowments Conference held at Delhi on the 16th March 1914".

[46] Cf. Francis Robinson: *Separatism among Indian Muslims*, Cambridge: CUP 1975, p. 27 and p. 197; also S.Kh. Rashid: *Muslim Law*, Lucknow 1973^2, p. 150.

should be public and not remain in private hands. Thus, they were regarded as neither purely religious nor purely private, but rather as so-called "mixed endowments".[47] In this manner, the *waqfs* were removed from the private ownership of the Muslims[48] and Jinnah stated:

> If a man cannot make a *wakf alalawlaud* (a *waqf* in the name of his children; J.M.),[49] as it is laid down in our law, then it comes to this, that he cannot make any provision for his family and children at all and the consequences are that it has been breaking up Mussalman families.[50]

Jinnah, as a Member of Parliament not affiliated with the major party, presented a "private member's bill" to the Imperial Legislative Council in 1909 relating to reforms of the *waqf* system. By 1911 he had succeeded in pushing the bill through, so that in 1913 the *Mussalman Wakf Validating Act* was passed. Thus, the Act restored private ownership of *waqfs*.[51]

It is true that Jinnah won over an important section of the ulama for pushing through this *Validating Act*. However, the majority of the Islamic scholars had been against his plan. Strangely enough, the traditional upholders of Islamic culture did not have much to say in this matter,[52] except a verdict by the ulama of Farangi Mahall who called for a "separate department of Moslem Wakfs" in November 1917.[53] However, Jinnah's achievement won him the hearts of Muslims for his position.[54]

---

[47] Cf. Kozlowski: *Muslim Endowments*, p. 60; for the historical development of *waqf* cf. Rashid: *Muslim Law*, pp. 140–162.

[48] Cf. Kozlowski: *Muslim Endowments*, p. 5 and pp. 131–155; also S.Kh. Rashid and S.A. Husain: *Wakf Laws and Administration in India*, Lucknow 1973², p. 21.

[49] A Muslim was authorised to create a *waqf*, if it did not violate with Islamic injunctions, for, among other purposes, the maintenance and support wholly or partially for himself, his family, children or descendants. "A Wakf-alal-aulad can be created for the maintenance and support wholly or partially of the family, children or descendants of the Wakif....". Cf. Zia ul Islam Janjua: *The Manual of Auqaf Laws*, Lahore n.d., Part II, p. 60, Section 3 and p. 61 *Validity of Wakf-alal-aulad*.

[50] Jinnah cited in G.C. Kozlowski: *Muslim Endowments*, p. 187, see also pp. 181.

[51] Refer to text of the *Act* printed in Janjua: *The Manual*, p. 59 and in Raja Abdul Ghafoor: *Manual of Waqf Laws*, Lahore 1983, Part I, p. 142.

[52] "When it came to the consideration of questions on *awqaf*, the initiative belonged to those most committed to working within the institutional framework established by the British rule." Cf. Kozlowski: *Muslim Endowments*, p. 177.

[53] Gov. of U.P., General Administration Department, File No. 126/1917: "Religious Endowments in the United Provinces".

[54] Cf. Afzal Iqbal: *Islamization in Pakistan*, Lahore 1986, p. 30. The reasons for his commitment were diverse. On the one hand, he probably hoped to save the *waqfs* of the Bombay magnate Qasim 'Ali Jairaybhai Pirbhai, on the other hand he was

In Pakistan, as in various other Muslim countries, *awqaf* have been the target of state intervention for a fairly long time. In 1950 it was suggested to introduce a *Survey Act on Waqfs* in order to get to know the number and quality of the endowments in Pakistan and to nationalise them. This did not happen until Javed Iqbal, in his book, "*Ideology of Pakistan*" which appeared at the end of the fifties, called for abolition of shrines and crippling the power of *pirs* and their heirs, the *sajjadah-nashins*. He was exactly in line with his father, the poet-philosopher Muhammad Iqbal (1873–1938), who had criticised the shrine-cult and the lower ranks of the Islamic scholars. The *Awqaf Ordinance 1960* is said to have been formalised and pushed through Parliament due to this publication.

The "West Pakistan *Waqf* Properties Rules" of 1960 aimed at collecting the tremendous amounts of revenue from the endowments, particularly shrines of holy men, curbing their power and "regulating" the endowments, which were being "exploited" by *sajjadah-nashins* and the administrative successors. According to the *Rules*, the endowments were to pass into the hands of the State, apparently in contradiction to the *Mussalman Wakf Validating Act*, (1913). In order not to come under heavy criticism from the shrine managers, especially with reference to Jinnah's achievement in 1913, Section 3 of the *Mussalman Wakf Validating Act* was changed:

> '*Waqf* property' means property of any kind permanently dedicated by a person professing Islam for any purpose recognised by Islam as religious, pious or charitable, but does not include property of any *Waqf* such as is described under section 3 of the Mussalman *Waqf* for the time being claimable for himself by the person by whom the *Waqf* was created or by any member of his family or descendants.[55]

Thus endowments were no longer available for the economic well being of a Muslim and the State was able to intervene in foundations on a legal basis, without being in conflict with the *Validating Act*. But this nationalisation of *awqaf* was not in accordance with classical Islamic law, as also suggested by the *Council of Islamic Ideology (CII)* in 1981 and 1983: *Waqf* cannot be transferred or sold. This forbade the handing over of the *waqf* or its sale to a third party. Apparently, the position of

---

interested in building up his career. Cf. Kozlowski: *Muslim Endowments*, p. 152 and p. 179. Also the contribution of David Gilmartin: "Religious Leadership and the Pakistan Movement in the Punjab", in: *MAS* 13/3 (1979), pp. 485–517.

[55] Janjua: *The Manual*, p. 6.

the *CII* reflected strong public criticism at that stage. There were ulama and mystic divines in the *CII* whose well-being depended very much on endowments. Thus, some representatives of the Islamic tradition who were *CII* members could defend their material position and legitimise it according to their reading of Islam. Their argument, however, did not find any resonance in the Government policies. On the contrary, the *Federal Shariat Court* (*FSC*) set up in 1981, legitimised the nationalisation, as long as it was not in contradiction with Shariʿa, that is as long as "the main purpose of the *Waqf* is served and satisfied".[56] Thus the state was able through a politics of piety and accommodation to appropriate endowments.[57] Lately, this state policy has been challenging the traditional social fabric and cosmology, replacing it with agents of bureaucracy. Investment is done mostly in lucrative endowments, such as the Data Darbar in Lahore, the mausoleum of the great Sufi ʿAli al-Hujwiri.[58]

In independent India,[59] there are rich lands and lucrative real estate worth billions of rupees as *waqf*; the *waqf*-law of 1954 puts *awqaf* under the control of state administration, as represented by the Muslim *waqf*-Boards of respective Muslim denominations and respective federal states. As in Pakistan, the employees of the *waqf*-Boards receive state salaries. The amendment of that law in 1984 and the revision of the *waqf*-law in 1995 aimed at preventing misuse by administrators. This increasing state intervention was contested by leading personalities and bodies of the Muslim scholarship, such as the All India Muslim Personal Law Board.[60] Certainly, in India, as well as in other contexts such as Palestine, *waqf* can be used as a vehicle for religious/national authority to counter state interests and to (re-)establish an Islamic public sphere, because the institution of *waqf* establishes the normative and religious argument for such a sphere in Islam.[61] This is particularly the case since *waqf* has been playing a crucial role in the urbanisation process.

---

[56] Judgement of 21.6.1984.

[57] Cf. Malik: "Waqf in Pakistan", pp. 59–74.

[58] See the comprehensive overview by Ghafir Shahzad: *Data darbar kampleks. Taʿmir se takmil tak*, Lahore 2004.

[59] N.N.: "Qanun-e awqaf 1995. Ek sarsari jaʾiza", in: *Rahnumah-ye Dakkan*, January 06, 1996.

[60] Cf. Ahmed Mohiuddin Siddiqui: "Wakf Board wants Govt to pay Imams", in: *Deccan Chronicle*, January 07, 1996, pp. 1 + 9.

[61] Miriam Hoexter: "The *Waqf* and the Public Sphere", in: Miriam Hoexter, Shmuel N. Eisenstadt, N. Levtzion (eds.): *The Public Sphere in Muslim Societies*, Albany: Suny Press 2002, pp. 118–138.

It is argued that through *waqf* the particularity of Islamic public space in an urban environment can be delineated because *waqf* has a spatial, socio-economic and political impact. Urbanisation in major Muslim empires would not have been thinkable without *waqf* since it included many institutions such as schools, baths, shops, mosques, caravanserais etc. established by local people and still having a major impact upon urban living and trade quarters.[62] Similarly, different religious rituals and events, social services and education, cheap living and production are affiliated with it. *Waqf* is therefore an integral part of a moral economy. But because of its perpetuity *waqf* can also hinder modernisation and change. Thus, *waqf* is a major factor in the hands of Muslims to negotiate their position in independent India, and if used properly it can elevate not only the positions of Muslims in South Asia.

[62] E. Ehlers: "The City of the Islamic Middle East", in: *Colloquium Geographicum* 22 (1991), pp. 89–107.

CHAPTER EIGHT

CULTURAL ENCOUNTER, RECIPROCITIES, AND MUSLIM RESPONSES (APPROX. 1750–1870)

The socio-economic and political developments following the decline of the Mughal Empire and the beginning of European colonial power had a profound impact on both the colonialised culture and the colonialiser. The changes were reflected in normative aspects underlying the process of colonialisation, eventually finding their way into scholarship. In this context projection is considered a cultural technique for self-affirmation and demarcation, assigning a collective (negative) identity to the (colonialised) "other". This process of "othering" had different purposes: the other was denigrated, and the colonialists generated their identity in a specific colonial context, ultimately for the purpose of control[1] (see also Chap. 9). Indeed, some European enlightenment figures had even gone so far as to use the "Orient" as a didactic background to criticise their urban societies, thereby setting out the frame of reference for their identities. The literary technique of contextual alienation and distancing, such as can be found in Montesquieu's "Persian Letters" (1721) or Oliver Goldsmith's "The Citizen of the World; or Letters from a Chinese philosopher, residing in London, to his friends in the East" (1762), was born in this period. These and subsequent processes of projection were connected among, others things, with the fact that Europeans, as colonial masters, advanced to confront the world outside Europe. There they were faced with attitudes and norms that also forced them to question their perceptions. In doing so, they also tended to accept some of these strange ideas, and thus exposed themselves to some sort of cultural hybridisation which could then only be overcome by reconstructing their own culture as something "pure", in contrast to the "degenerate", "impure" culture of the colonialised. The construction of "purification"-discourse[2]—vis-à-vis the hybrid

---

[1] See the seminal work by Edward Said: *Orientalism, Western Conceptions of the Orient*, London: Routledge & Kegan Paul 1979.

[2] Compare the discussion in Robert J.C. Young: *Colonial Desire: Hybridity in Theory, Culture, and Race*, London: Routledge 1995.

other—was a proven device to establish a unilateral power-relationship that helped foster a global colonial identity and culture, the core of which lay in Europe. In this way, collective antagonisms developed, so that even the Oriental crusades which had been critically evaluated by European enlightenment scholars, were now for the first time perceived in terms of cultural clash. Analogously, Europe and Asia were constructed in the eighteenth century and very predominantly in the nineteenth century in terms of arenas of power politics. For instance, it was during this time that the eastern borders of Europe were conceptualised, with the Balkans and Transoxiana being considered as buffers or gaps between the two.[3]

Encountering the Orient. Imaginaries and reciprocities

Growing foreign interest in India provided the background for these developments. By the end of eighteen century, more and more Europeans, especially British, had come to India while some Indians had gone to Britain. It was during this period of flux that mutual perceptions changed, particularly so between 1790 and 1820. Gradually the newcomers from Europe came to dominate the economy and started demanding the use of the English language and imperial manners in spheres in which they operated. This type of cultural interaction was reflected in colonial efforts started under Charles Cornwallis (1738–1805), Governor-General from 1785–93. His efforts to reform the administration were informed by a policy of racist exclusion, nourished by cultural and religious ideas, whereby he replaced all senior Indian officeholders by Company servants. The reason given was that every Indian was assumed to be corrupt by nature.[4] Only British employees could guarantee morality and honesty of character. This orientalist (in Edward Said's sense of the term) discourse of alterity and identity was to have an important role to play later, as we shall see below and in the following chapters.

Based on various practical-philosophical ideas, nineteenth century colonial politics was perceived and consequently legitimised as evolu-

---

[3] Jürgen Osterhammel: *Die Entzauberung Asiens. Europa und die asiatischen Reiche*, München: Beck 1998, pp. 54f., 30–31, 68ff., 275–296 et passim.

[4] See Percival Spear: *The Nabobs: A Study of the Social Life of the English in Eighteenth Century India*, London 1963, pp. 80ff., 127ff., 137.

tionary and modern. In contrast, the "Orient" was constructed as a cultural space, diametrically opposed to the societal values and norms of the West, considered inherently universal. This mono-dimensional social evolutionism proclaimed Europe as embodying hegemonic power. In doing so, various discourses of othering about the Orient promulgated the societal decline, dogmatism, despotism, and irrationality of the region.[5] Historiography was a major means to this end: James Mill (1773–1836) in his *History of India*, 1806–1818, is held responsible for inventing the powerful periodisation of Indian history as Hindu, Muslim and British epochs. Interestingly, he conceded that Muslims only "substituted sovereigns of one race to sovereigns of another; and mixed with old inhabitants a small portion of new; but it altered not the texture of society; it altered not the language of the country; the original inhabitants remained the occupants of the soil; they continued to be governed by their own laws and institutions..."[6] Yet, Mill stresses the dichotomy of two civilisations: Hindu and Muslim. Mill's periodisation was subsequently replaced by contemporary historiography into categories such as antiquity, middle ages and modernity. This fostered the impression that communalism or ethnification was the main driving force in politics and consequently in Indian history and historiography. The celebrated translation project of H.M. Elliot and J. Dowson entitled *The History of India as Told by Its Own Historians* (London 1867–77)—a powerful collection of translations from mostly Persian sources, which also has been subject to criticism,[7] took up this trend.

It is at this historical juncture that we encounter the dialectical relationship between "Orientalism" and the claim to power. The backdrop of a postulated universal evolutionary history and the need for a consistent colonial hegemonic stand favoured the development of sciences specialising in the "Orient", such as Oriental Studies, Anthropology and Religious Studies whose underlying premise was derived from nineteenth century natural sciences. The orientalist sciences analyzed the object "Orient" in its historical development,[8] making use of

[5] This is convincingly illustrated by Osterhammel: *Die Entzauberung Asiens*, pp. 15–37.

[6] See Chattopadhyaya: *Representing the Other?*, pp. 14f.

[7] See for example S.H. Hodivala: *Studies in Indo-Muslim History: A Critical Commentary on Elliot and Dowson's History of India as Told by Its Own Historians*, 2 Vols. Bombay 1939–57.

[8] See the contributions by Sheldon Pollock: "Deep Orientalism? Notes on Sanskrit and Power Beyond the Raj", Vinay Dharwadker: "Orientalism and the Study of Indian

the Hegelian categories of alienation and reconciliation. In this way, colonial administrators were provided with a "scientifically proven" image of the development attained by the Orient, though alienated from its classical high culture. Cultural theories were to provide the colonialists with the orientalist image that ran counter to the historical one of classical high culture. On the basis of this construction, colonial measures to "reconcile" the Orient with its "alienated" tradition were to be implemented as an export of progress.[9] Thus terms like "modern" and "traditional" became scientific categories, evolving into an epistemological supremacy of Europe, firmly established politically. In this way authority was created on the object "Orient" not only for the Europeans but also gradually, through reciprocal perceptions, for the "Orientals" themselves. Subsequently, authority was derived from the instrumentalisation of the Weberian demand for "value-free" social sciences, that became "objective" in so far as they were considered to be not ideologically biased, but unquestionably "true."

Yet, the British—in a pragmatic culturalist twist—tried to link themselves to their Mughal predecessors by preserving the notion of "Indianess" and cultural unity. But in order to understand what "Indianess" meant, knowledge of languages was necessary. Therefore, in the second half of the eighteenth century, when the Indo-British encounter was still in the initial stage of "cultural encounter"[10] (see below) characterised by more or less fleeting and superficial contact, the British began to learn Indian languages and along with it initiated the process of classifying and categorising languages in hierarchical terms. The "classical" languages became Arabic, Persian and Sanskrit and affinity with European classical languages such as Latin and Greek was stressed. The so-called "vulgar languages" were affiliated with French and Italian dialects. In these processes of transfer and projection of ideas, the colonial masters did not hesitate in selectively appropriating the achievements of the

---

Literatures", and Rosane Rocher: "British Orientalism in the Eighteenth Century: The Dialectics of Knowledge and Government", in Breckenridge et al. (eds.): *Orientalism*, pp. 76–133, pp. 158–185, and pp. 215–249, respectively.

[9] See Ronald Inden: *Imagining India*, Oxford 1990, pp. 9 passim.

[10] According to Urs Bitterli there are several types of cultural encounter: *cultural touch, limited cultural contact, cultural collision, cultural assimilation.* See Urs Bitterli: *Die "Wilden" und die "Zivilisierten"; Grundzüge einer Geistes- und Kulturgeschichte der europäischen-überseeischen Begegnung*, München 1976; Urs Bitterli: *Cultures in Conflict: Encounters Between European and Non-European Cultures, 1492–1800*, Stanford: Stanford University Press 1989.

Orient and thereby obliterating traces of Oriental agency and creativity, as it were. For example, European studies in textual criticism and comparative religion relied heavily on the intellectual achievements of Mughal India.

Cases in point were Anquetil-Duperron (1731–1805) and Sir William Jones (1746–1794), who operated at a time when Orientalism was not yet a discourse of domination but of reciprocal relations: Siraj al-Din ʿAli Khan Arzu (1689–1756), the famous scholar and Persian and Urdu poet, had already ascertained the affinity of Persian and Sanskrit a few decades before Sir William Jones, while Anquetil-Duperron was highly influenced by Dara Shikoh's Persian translations. Both the Europeans, however, appropriated the works of their Indian informants without even mentioning their contributions. This was especially conspicuous, since it happened at a time when authorship was emerging as a prime principle of textual attribution and accreditation.[11] One could argue that in this way, agency was taken away from Indians and developments calling for emancipation gradually sank into oblivion. This blurring of history and scholarship culminated in the idea that the eighteenth century Orient was a place of chaos whose sources, it was proclaimed, were obscure. Subsequently, the Europeans excluded the Orient from history and made it clear how far they wanted to "Europeanise" the world.

The establishment of Royal Madrasa in Calcutta in 1781 was to reflect the British policy initiated by Hastings. It was at once the assertion of its sovereignty and at the same time the restoration and continuation of old Mughal imperial tradition. The necessary knowledge about people and country was to be supplied by the "Asiatic Society" in Calcutta, established by Sir William Jones in 1784 as a centre for Orientalists. The British rule of law and order in India had to be Indian, both Muslim as well as Hindu, as conceived by the British. Consequently, the Asiatic Society produced English translations of Hindu and Muslim law texts, such as the *Hindoo Law* and *Muhammadan Law*, in order to free the British from dependence upon Indian scholars, to dissolve judicial plurality and to help centralised jurisdiction. The English version of

[11] Compare Mohamad Tavakoli-Targhi: "Orientalism's Genesis Amnesia", in: *Comparative Studies of South Asia, Africa and the Middle East* 16 (1996), pp. 1–14.

the popular *al-Hidaya* was published in 1791, while the rather elitist *Fatawa-ye 'Alamgiri* (see Chap. 6) was not translated into English.

At the same time the intrinsic impact of reciprocity and mutuality of the colonial process may have found its political manifestation in indirect rule, though this system was not implemented in its totality. Too often the British administration got involved in internal affairs of colonialised societies very soon, at times resembling the French system of direct colonial administration. One manifestation of British indirect rule was the establishment of an honours system and the issuing of titles. Similarly, the system of "resident" relying on a network of indigenous people provided for the cultural success of imperialism. This success found its climax in the "invention of tradition" as it represented colonial authority in Victorian India through different ploys.

By the end of the century, the British were the sole European power in India. Their new imperial self-conscience was manifest in Lord Wellesley (Governor-General of India 1798–1805), Cornwallis' successor. He followed up the policy of subsidiary alliances to subdue the remnants of Indian independent power, i.e., the Nizam of Haydarabad, Asaf Jah, and Tipu Sultan in Mysore. Wellesley also saw the need for a new breed of civil servants to be trained at Fort William College established in 1802 at Calcutta. The college taught "modern" education considered crucial due to the supposedly "traditional" and "backward" character of India. Trained and instructed in Indian languages, these young servants were, so the idea was, to become more and more independent of their Indian informants. This transfer of knowledge was complemented by a college at Haileybury in England (1804), which was to become the cradle of the Indian Civil Service. At the same time, Fort William College hired and trained many Indian scholars who worked for the colonial administration. These Indians were important sources of information, for they furnished data in English or Indian languages. They collected, translated and discussed documents, and were able to write different comments, which could then be classified and analysed into knowledge *of* or *about* India by the colonial power.[12] Collection, classification and standardisation of written testimonies such as the personal laws were important. The traditional systems had recognised multiple laws even

[12] B. Cohn: "The Command of Language and the Language of Command", in: Ranajit Guha (ed.): *Subaltern Studies IV: Writings on South Asian History and Society*, pp. 276ff., here p. 322.

applicable to Muslims apart from their customary laws, which granted them much leeway to represent themselves in a plurality of ways. Now, this was considered unsystematic and arbitrary by the Europeans. So the colonial system had to simplify the texts through homogenisation to produce fixed and authoritative texts and make governance possible. The colonial making of *Hindoo Law* and *Muhammadan Law* is a case in point. The process of gathering information as a political strategy of control, which in turn had a profound impact on the development of vernacular languages, will be discussed in the next chapter.

Contesting Muslim publics

As it stands, British officials felt heavily inclined towards Indian/Muslim reformist scholars and Sufis. They paid them their respect, took advice in religious and family matters, as in the case of Shah ʿAbd al-ʿAziz (1746–1824), one of the sons of Shah Wali Allah.[13] It seems that the understanding, co-operation, and also the flow of information between officers of the East India Company and indigenous pietists developed due to mutual reform interests and common semantic allegiance. According to Wilhelm Halbfass, the interpretation and appropriation of traditional Indian concepts and terms were used at the beginning of the nineteenth century by experts and theoreticians of mission and colonialism to proclaim Christianity.[14] Similar ideas were formulated by the colonialised also:

> A venerable Maulavi from Kabul created a commotion in a Madras mosque in 1836 when he began preaching from the Bible against worshipping saints and prophets... Although this example is unique, it does underline the similarities in the reformist programs of Protestant Christians and Muslims.[15]

By implication it can be argued that the intellectual milieu was quite sober and even peaceful. In fact, some representatives of the East India

[13] On Shah ʿAbd al-ʿAziz see Muhammad Khalid Masud: "The World of Shah ʿAbd al-ʿAziz (1746–1824)", in: Jamal Malik (ed.): *Perspectives of mutual encounters in South Asian History 1760–1860*, Leiden: Brill 2000.

[14] Wilhelm Halbfass: *Indien und Europa: Perspektiven ihrer geistigen Begegnung*, Basel/Stuttgart: Schwabe & CoAG Verlag 1981, p. 66.

[15] Harlan Otto Pearson: *Islamic Reform and Revival in the Nineteenth Century India: The 'Tariqah-i Muhammadiyah'*, Ph.D., Duke University 1979 (unpublished), p. 190.

Company had been sceptical towards Christian missionary zealots in the eighteenth century, but with a parliamentary decree in 1813 (*East India Company's Charter*) they had to allow missionaries to work. It was in this backdrop of official permission to preach publicly that Muslims and Christians disputed and discussed matters of dogmatism and apologetics, sometimes in the presence of huge audiences, such as the well-known dispute between C.G. Pfander (died 1865) and Rahmat Allah al-Kairanawi (died 1891) in Agra in 1854.[16]

Apparently, there was a constant flow of information and co-operation: Lord Lake (1744–1808) occupied Delhi in 1803, defeated the Marathas under Daulat Rao Sindhia (died 1827), and took the old and blind Mughal emperor Shah ʿAlam II (1756–1806) under his protection only to reduce him to a pensioner. This was followed by some 50 years of peace at the cost of the British increasingly infiltrating the local culture, not only in terms of political intervention but also—and this was important for the colonial process—by emulating Mughal culture to the extent that they were called "White Mughals" and "Nabobs".[17] In the backdrop of these developments Shah ʿAbd al-ʿAziz issued interesting legal opinions (*fatawa*): he condemned folk religion, particularly the Shiʿite cult of saints, and called for catharsis. Furthermore, according to him, India was no longer a territory ruled by Islam, but *dar al-harb*—an abode of war, which he, however, carefully qualified.[18] The main issue of the *fatwa* pertaining to *dar al-harb* was certainly to legitimise economic transactions and social interactions between Muslims and non-Muslims, i.e., British conquerors rather than calling for the necessity of emigration (*hijra*) or the taking up of arms (*jihad*).[19] Shah ʿAbd al-ʿAziz even considered the Friday prayers permissible in that situation though it could only be performed in *dar al-Islam* because of the *khutba* being an essential part. This was so, because

[16] See A.A. Powell: *Muslims and Missionaries in Pre-Mutiny India*, London 1993. For the memorable dispute in Agra see Christine Schirrmacher: *Mit den Waffen des Gegners; zur Kontroverse zwischen Christen und Muslime im 19. und 20 Jahrhundert am Beispiel J.G. Pfanders mizân al-haqq und Rahmat Ullâh al-Kairânawîs izhâr al-haqq und der Diskussion über das Barnabasevangelium*, Berlin 1992.

[17] See William Dalrymple: *White Mughals. Love and Betrayal in 18th century India*, London: Harper Collins 2002; Spear: *The Nabobs*; Michael Edwards: *The Nabobs at Home*, London: Constable 1991

[18] See Shah ʿAbd al-ʿAziz: *Fatawa-ye ʿAzizi*, Karachi: Saʿid Kampani 1412 h. (reprint), pp. 454ff., 475, 581f., 582–586.

[19] *Hijra* was considered compulsory when performance of Islamic rituals was not allowed in *dar al-harb* any longer.

the regent of Delhi was still a Muslim, albeit blind[20] and installed by unbelievers (*kuffar*). His leading the prayer (*imamat*) was not considered necessary, his permission to pray was enough. In the same context, the Delhi scholar did not hesitate to propagate the learning of English in order to facilitate the entry into higher British service. The pro-British comments of Shah ʿAbd al-ʿAziz were however related to the restoration of confiscated landed property by the resident Archibald Seton. Other English officials such as William Fraser, secretary to General Ochterlony in Delhi in 1805, James Skinner (1802–1840), a Eurasian military officer, Alexander Seton, the first British Resident in Delhi, or Charles Metcalfe (1785–1846), all were also very much inclined towards reforms, such as the one postulated by Shah ʿAbd al-ʿAziz. He could, thus, be considered as an important mediator of that time, and also as one of those central figures who provided the colonialists with access to the contemporary Muslim discourse. His *fatawa* can be seen as attempts at integration for the Sunni Muslim community to gain a platform for their action—a platform which was lost at the advent of colonial power.

Such "integrationist" legal opinions soon fostered colonial thrust and appropriation. Colonial officials concluded from the aforesaid *fatwa* that the implementation of British law made perfect sense in territories not dominated by Islam. This was considered necessary since Muslims would accept the law of the present regent. Therefore, men like the Bengal civil servant W. William Hunter collected corresponding legal opinions, had them written down and published. In this way, the implementation of British law was greatly facilitated.

Other Muslim groups preferred to follow an "isolationist" position. They rejected any interaction with Europeans, such as Shah Ghulam ʿAli (1743–1824), who led the *khanaqah* of Mirza Jan-e Janan, the eighteenth-century Naqshbandi from the *silsila* of Shaikh Ahmad Sirhindi. Shah Ghulam ʿAli's *khanaqah* in the heart of Shahjahanabad attracted thousands of visitors from Asia and Africa and his Kurdish disciple Shaikh Khalid al-Baghdadi (died 1826) spread the teachings of this order in the Ottoman Empire and the Caucasus. The Shah was quite critical of the permissibility of seeking employment under the East

[20] The old Mughal emperor Shah ʿAlam II (reg. 1759–1806) had been blinded by the usurper Ghulam Qadir Rohilla (died 1789) in 1788. This was a proven device to disqualify the regents. According to the eleventh-century political theoretician al-Mawardi, a Muslim ruler had to be fit, physically as well as psychologically.

India Company. He was inspired by the Naqshbandi-Mujaddidi pietist ideals of guiding the fellow-believers to the right path by participating in politics and worldly affairs, but not at all costs. It was important to keep a distance from worldly power, particularly when it came to the British. In entertaining a particular notion of the British, these dignitaries created and perpetuated an exotic image of the *farangi* "other", paving the way to occidentalism. The following quotation is a case in point. It also shows the ambivalent character of the colonial process—of desire and disavowal. Ghulam 'Ali describes the interaction with Charles Metcalfe, the Resident at Delhi from 1811 to 1819:[21]

> Metcalfe, the European (Mitkâf Farangî) who was the ruler of Delhi also came there on the occasion. All of those present stood up out of respect for him, and I remained seated. When he sat down, I turned my back to him so that my eyes would not fall on his face. He asked from those present (who he was). They said he is such and such. He stood up and came near to me to kiss my feet. When he came close, the smell of alcohol came to me from his mouth. I became disgusted, and forcefully rebuking him, I drove him away from myself like a dog. He attacked a second time. Again I spoke to him sternly and didn't allow him to come near. When he returned to his own house he said to one of his servants, 'In all India I have seen this one true Muslim'.

Yet, besides this defensiveness Ghulam 'Ali considered it important to spiritually guide the Muslims in a situation of what they perceived to be increased depravity. The emulation of Prophetic tradition served as vehicle for ethical perfection which eventually would endow the community with the much-needed solidarity and identity. And men like him were concerned with urban artisans, particularly weavers, who suffered greatly under the colonial economy. They brought these groups together in guild-like organisations and thereby strengthened the Sufi orders, like the branch of the Naqshbandiyya in Delhi.[22] A transfer of knowledge through them to the colonial public was hardly possible. They used to

---

[21] See W.E. Fusfeld: *The Shaping of Sufi Leadership in Delhi: The Naqshbandiyya Mujaddidiyya, 1750 to 1920*, unpubl. PhD. thesis, Univ. of Pennsylvania 1981, p. 166.

[22] Compare Jamal Malik: "Islamic Institutions and Infrastructure in Shâhjahânâbâd", in: Ehlers and Krafft (eds.): *Shâhjahânâbâd*, pp. 56f. This points to a connection between handicraft, guilds and mystical orders, which is quite prevalent in West Asia. On the Naqshbandiyya-Mujaddidiyya in the Indian context see also Thomas Dahnhardt: *Change and continuity in Indian Sufism: a Naqshbandi-Mujaddidi branch in Indian environment*, New Delhi 2002.

have their own realm of discourse, which again could only be accessed by the Europeans through *integrationist* scholars and informants.

With increasing colonial impact, involvement and settlement, different cultural voices were articulated, such as the above-mentioned "integrationist" and "isolationist" ones, predominantly urban in nature. In contrast, in tribal and peasant areas, religiously legitimised revolts broke out. In many cases, *qasbahs* increasingly came to serve as retreats for cultural elites. They provided the points of departure for chiliastic insurrections which, in the first place, triggered off resistance against the immediate material exploitation by local landowners, traders, entrepreneurs and middle-men.[23]

The increasing colonial focus on ethnicity and religion (see below) might have fostered confessionalisation which produced several contesting movements. This can best be gauged from the polemical essay "*Tuhfah-ye Ithna-ye ʿAshariyya*" by Shah ʿAbd al-ʿAziz, who held the Shia responsible for political and moral decay, especially referring to the Shiʿite practice of *taqiyya*, which allowed any Shia to deny his/her religious identity in certain cases.[24] Many of these new movements maintained relations with the Arab peninsula—notably through the institution of *hajj* and *ʿumra*, their founders being inspired by the spiritual atmosphere prevailing there. But like the "Padri Movement" in Southeast Asia, these were indigenous movements, based on the Sufi reformist traditions of the eighteen century (see Chap. 6), and originally oriented against the restorative character initiated by colonial order. Such was the case in Gujarat under ʿAbd al-Rahman Mandwi, who organised weavers and peasants. Kenneth Jones has argued that these were new religious movements with three common components and aims.[25] First, they tried to reorder society in terms of social behaviour and custom, i.e., they provided normative guidelines; second, they stood for a

---

[23] For the following see M. Ahmad: *Sayyid Ahmad Shahid: His Life and Mission*, Lucknow 1975; Q. Ahmad: *The Wahhabi Movement in India*, Calcutta 1966; Rizvi: *Shâh ʿAbd al-ʿAzîz*; M.D. Khan: *Fara'idi Movement*, Karachi 1965; S.F. Dale: *The Mappillas of Malabar, 1498–1922: Islamic Society on the South Asian Frontier*, Oxford 1980; M.Z. Siddiqui: "The resurgence of the Chishti Silsilah in the Punjab during the eighteenth century", *Proceedings of the Indian Historical Congress, 1970*, Delhi 1971, pp. 408–420; D. Gilmartin: *Empire and Islam: Punjab and the Making of Pakistan*, Berkeley 1988, pp. 56ff.; Chr. Jaffrelot: *Les Nationalistes Hindous*, Paris 1993.

[24] See S.A.A. Rizvi: *Shâh ʿAbd al ʿAzîz: Puritanism, Sectarian Polemics, and Jihad*, New Delhi: Munshiram Manoharlal 1982.

[25] K.W. Jones: *Socio-Religious Reform Movements in British India (The New Cambridge History of India, III.1.)*, Cambridge 1989.

persistent demand for change even in the state sector; and third, their ideology was legitimised by religion. At the same time, their methods of operation changed. They gradually used professional missionaries, polemical treatises and new religious rituals of conversion. Later, this was paralleled by elected officials, regular meetings and annually published reports. Finally, after 1857 these religious movements came to have an organised philanthropy through hospitals, schools, orphanages and relief programmes. The ideology was based on a reinterpretation of doctrines and on new scriptural sources, emanating from the codification of their charismatic leaders' messages. The modification in social behaviour and its justification by religious authorities in light of the sunna as a symbol of the authority of Prophet Muhammad and as a source of continuity with the past[26] nourished the organisational structure of these new religious movements, originating in the pre-colonial and later in the colonial world. A revaluation of plurality, individuality, and contingency as well as an advancement of reflexivity generated a colourful diversity of individualised cults and movements.

The Muhammadan Path

Typologically, in the tribal context the *Mujahidin* or *Tariqah-ye Muhammadi*—not to be confused with the eighteen century ethical concept of the same name—needs to be mentioned, though its major activists came from agrarian backgrounds and the movement later also took its stride in major urban constituencies in Patna, Bareilly, Tonk, Delhi. It was established by the khalifa of Shah ʿAbd al-ʿAziz, Sayyid Ahmad of Rae Bareli (1786–1831) who came to Delhi from Shiʿite Awadh in 1804 and the powerful preacher Shah Ismaʿil Dihlawi (1779–1831). Similar movements emerged at around the same time in other parts of the Muslim world. They all stood for a type of Muhammadan catharsis, falling back upon their reformist traditions of the eighteen century, adhering to the wide network of the Naqshbandiyya and only gradually becoming active in the anti-colonial struggle. In India, members of the movement interpreted the *fatwa* pertaining to *dar al-harb* of 1803 by Shah ʿAbd al-ʿAziz in terms of a call for *jihad*. Their *jihad* was, however, not directed against the British but the Sikhs who had stabilised themselves in the Punjab and ostensibly prohibited Muslims

---

[26] See the interesting study on Prophetic authority by Brown: *Rethinking tradition*.

to practise their religion in regions under their control. Whether the protagonists of the "Muhammadan Path" and *Mujahidin* acted under the protection of the British, to weaken the stubborn Sikhs, is not yet clear. Fact is that the Punjab was soon annexed by the colonial power (1843). Sind followed suit in 1849.

Notwithstanding this encounter of an altogether new situation, different Muslim groups contested for Islamic hegemony. The statements of colonial as well as the nationalist historiography have to be questioned in this context. It remains an open question whether the prime reason for the emigration (*hijra*) of the members of *Tariqah-ye Muhammadi* from Delhi to the tribal area of Northwest Province around Balakot in 1827 was the *fatwa* of year 1803. In sharp contrast to nationalist historiography, the *hijra* of Sayyid Ahmad and Shah Isma'il seems grounded in debates with representatives of the traditional service elite, such as Fadl-e Haqq Khairabadi (died 1861), who hailed from a prominent ulama family of the Awadh region (on him see also Chap. 9). Just like the ulama of Firangi Mahall and Allahabad, the Khairabadis were *ma'qulis* and staunch supporters of *wahdat al-wujud* (unity of being), expounded by Ibn al-'Arabi. From the seventeenth century onwards, this scholarly tradition largely rejected the Islam of the Mujaddidiyya branch of the Naqshbandis, notably the notion of *wahdat al-shuhud* as propagated by Ahmad Sirhindi (see pp. 177f.). Fadl-e Haqq belonged to the Qadiri order; his father Fadl-e Imam (died 1826), a prominent writer, was supposedly the first Indian to accept the post of Mufti and *Sadr al-Sudur* under the Company. Fadl-e Haqq Khairabadi had been employed by the colonial administration since 1815, and ostensibly was to play a crucial role in the revolt of 1857 (see pp. 270ff.). It is said that at the instance of his employer he organised the expulsion of Shah Isma'il from Delhi, because the latter's polemic, *Taqwiyat al-Iman* (The Strengthening of Faith),[27] had caused great problems for the religious and social peace in the city.[28] This book is more like an Urdu edition of *Kitab al-Tawhid* written in Arabic by the eighteen century Arab reformer and Hanbalite, Muhammad b. 'Abd al-Wahhab (1703–1792) (see below). In *Taqwiyat al-Iman*, Shah Isma'il is very particular about traditional or transmitted sciences (*manqulat*) and radically rejects any sort

[27] The book was published first in 1824. See Shah Muhammad Ismail: *Support of Faith*, transl. by Mir Shahamat Ali, Lahore 1969.

[28] This narrative was championed by Mirza Muhammad Hairat Dihlawi in his *Hayat-e Tayyabah* (Dehli Matba' Faruqi, 1894), the biography of Shah Isma'il.

of veneration of holy men and adherence to schools of law. Moreover, he argues that God is capable of creating another Muhammad—the seal of prophets (*khatm al-anbiya'*)—but would not make him appear on earth. With this latter argument he attacked the traditional prophetology and in a way de-sacralised and humanised the Prophet. Fadl-e Haqq, in contrast, maintained that it was impossible that the Prophet should have a match.[29] The creation of a peer of the Seal of the Prophets was even beyond God's power. And in doing so he also instrumentalised his friend, the poet genius Mirza Ghalib (1797–1869), for whom he got some princely stipends.[30] Other important Delhi scholars were also involved in the issue, such as the famous loyalist, Mufti Sadr al-Din Azurdah (died 1868), who succeeded Fadl-e Imam Khairabadi to the post of *Sadr al-Sudur* and Mufti of Delhi in 1827. The debate is still relevant today and displays the heterogeneity of and contestation among Muslims in South Asia.[31]

In the worldview of *Tariqah-ye Muhammadi*, orthopraxy and the following of the sunna was most important. Yet, normative regulation which rejected innovation (*bid'a*) did not necessarily correspond to societal representation: the adherence to a *madhhab*, here Hanafiyya, was crucial. Only the reintroduction of the 'original/puritan', social system of Muhammad was capable of arresting the decadence of contemporary Muslim society as well as overcoming the increasing colonial impact. The reference to Shah 'Abd al-'Aziz's *fatwa*, who had called India *dar al-harb*, was exploited to mobilise the masses. Subsequently, the Jihad-movement set up a caliphate with new forms of political and societal centralisation, which actually contrasted sharply with those of the tribal society in today's North Pakistan. The ideas from the agricultural lands of the *qasbahs* in Awadh, such as Rae Bareli, could not readily be transplanted into tribal society. When its leaders were killed in a fight against the Sikhs, the movement survived with headquarters as far away as Swat and Patna under the leadership of Wilayat 'Ali (died 1853) and Sayyid Ahmad's brother Inayat 'Ali (died 1858). In Bengal the Jihad-movement was led by Sayyid Ahmad's disciple Titu

---

[29] In his reply *Tahqiq al-Fatwa fi Abtal al-Taghwa* (1825) he also declared Shah Isma'il a *kafir*.

[30] Cf. English translation of Ghalib's poem in R. Russell/K. Islam (tr. and ed.): *Ghalib; 1797–1869*, pp. 32–34. For the whole issue see Rizvi: *Shâh 'Abd al-'Azîz*, pp. 517–522.

[31] On this issue see Jamal Malik: "Letters, prison sketches and autobiographical literature: The case of Fadl-e-Haqq Khairabadi in the Andaman Penal Colony", in: *IESHR* 43 (2006).

Mir, or Mir Mithar ʿAli (died 1831). The Hanafi Karamat ʿAli Jaunpuri (died 1873) was important for indigenising the *mujahidin* ideas in a Bengali environment, but was against *jihad* as long as Muslims were allowed to practise their religious duties. After 1857 the movement was crushed by the British, particularly in the so-called "Wahhabi trials" of the 1860s.

These efforts provided solidarity and identity to the social fabric which had begun to suffer from colonial marginalisation. Their charismatic ideas appealed to Muslims also from the artisan groups in decaying weaving cities of the North, such as Allahabad, Mau and Patna. Their corporate identity fostered reform movements in the cities of Deccan and Central India such as Melapalaiyam in Tamil Nadu, even if the reform movements were regionally different.[32]

Reformers of the *Tariqah-ye Muhammadi* used the emerging printing press and disseminated their ideas of pure Islam in local languages such as Bengali and Urdu, as Marc Gaborieau has elaborated in detail.[33] It was during this period that the first Urdu translations of the Quran were produced, among others, by two younger sons of Shah Wali Allah, Shah ʿAbd al-Qadir (1754–1815) and Shah Rafiʿ al-Din (1750–1818). The vernacular media supported the development of diversified Muslim publics, which gradually became literate and emancipated to enter public spaces. As Francis Robinson puts it: "Increasingly from now on any Ahmad, Mahmud or Muhammad could claim to speak for Islam."[34] This, however, does not mean that the position of traditional scholars was totally undermined for they were mobile enough to accommodate these changes. Tradionalists such as Farangi Mahallis published some of the earliest Urdu newspapers, such as *Tilism-e Lakhnaʾu* and *Karnamah*. The *Delhi Urdu Akhbar* was issued in 1836.[35] Later, these publics were to become active participants in the discourse of nationalism.[36]

---

[32] Bayly: *Indian Society*, p. 166.

[33] See the contributions of Marc Gaborieau: "A Nineteenth-Century Indian 'Wahhabi' Tract Against the Cult of Muslim Saints: *Al-Balagh al-Mubin*", in: Chr.W. Troll (ed.): *Muslim Shrines in India*, New Delhi 1989, pp. 198ff.; Marc Gaborieau: "Late Persian, Early Urdu: The Case of 'Wahhabi' Literature (1818–1857)", in: Francoise Nalini Delvoye (ed.): *Confluence of Cultures: French Contributions to Indo-Persian Studies*, New Delhi: Manohar 1995, pp. 170–191.

[34] Francis Robinson: "Technology and Religious Change: Islam and the Impact of Print", in: *MAS* 27/1 (1993), pp. 229–251.

[35] See Margrit Pernau: "The Delhi Urdu Akhbar. Between Persian Akhbarat and English Newspaper", in: *The Annual of Urdu Studies* 18 (2003), pp. 105–131.

[36] For the identity-giving role of the media see Benedict Anderson: *Imagined Communities: Reflections on the Origin and Spread of Nationalism*, London 1983.

Itineraries of ideas

The colonisers wrongly identified this order with the Arabic puritan movement of the eighteenth century, the Wahhabiyya. In fact, the career of the term Wahhabiyya again sheds light on the creativity of encounter and translational deviations between Europeans and South Asians. The term Wahhabi was used pejoratively by the opponents of this eighteenth-century movement in Arabia in order to label a vague, exotic and plundering Bedouin community who, in their opinion, had deviated from Sunnite Islam. Additionally the aim was to reduce the movement to the personal convictions of one man, Muhammad ibn ʿAbd al-Wahhab, thus denying any divine legitimacy. First testimonies of these intra-Islamic debates were soon passed on by European travellers in Arabia. But the movement was given a religious colour much later and that too in India only. This happened when Europeans began documenting the doctrines of Arabic Wahhabiyya, considering both this and the Indian variety to be pan-Islamic and a political opposition, as can be derived from the *literature de surveillance.*[37] In doing so, the Western scholars introduced quotations from a reformist treatise written in Urdu in India in the first quarter of the nineteenth century—it was believed that "Indian Wahhabis" liberally used press and lithography.[38] Subsequently, "Wahhabi" mutated into a religious concept and was transplanted into the Arabian landscape. Thus Arabian "Wahhabis" came to be interpreted through the lense of Indian "Wahhabiyya". This was "othering" par excellence.

Actually this contextualisation dated back to early French Orientalism, as reflected in the work of Garcin de Tassy (1794–1878),[39] while living

[37] See R.S. O'Fahey and B. Radtke: "Neo-Sufism Reconsidered", in: *Der Islam* 70 (1993), pp. 52–87.

[38] See *Encyclopaedia of Islam*, Ed. by M.Th. Houtsma et al., Leiden 1934, IV, pp. 1175–1180, p. 1180. Especially important was the text by Shah Muhammad Ismaʿil *al-Sirat al-Mustaqim*. Soon after its publication the text was rendered into English. See Shah Muhammad Ismail: "Notice of the Peculiar Tenets held by the Followers of Syed Ahmad, Taken Chiefly from the *Sîrat al-Mústaqím*...", J.R.C. (transl.), in: *Journal of the Asiatic Society of Bengal* 1 (1832), pp. 479–498, and Shah Muhammad Ismaʿil: "Translation of the Takwiyat-ul-Imán, preceded by a Notice of the Author, Maulavi Isma'il Hajji", by Mir Shahamat Ali, in: *Journal of the Asiatic Society of Bengal* 13 (1852), pp. 310–372.

[39] For an interesting study of M. Garcin de Tassy, the author of many books such as *Mémoire sur les particularités de la religion musulmane en Inde*, Paris: Labitte 1869, see

and writing in Marseille, a centre of the eighteenth century Catholic movement. This Catholicism informed his object of study, so that he started off his Islamological work with a translation of the well-known Ottoman-Islamic catechism which expressed the views of a revivalist fundamentalist.[40] In the Indian context, de Tassy dealt with similar issues, namely the veneration of holy men and its critique by Indian Wahhabiyya. In his ethnographical study he came up with a trilateral distinction between esoteric (*sufi*), exoteric (*Wahhabiyya*) and popular Islam (*faqir*). He also compared Muslim holy men with Catholic saints. However, his sympathy for sufis and folk religion stood in contrast to most of his contemporaries who leaned towards Protestant ideals. And here lies the hermeneutic bone of contention. The French scholar seemed to perceive the Wahhabiyya-Saint-controversy in terms of the Protestant-Catholic-controversy. In imposing his perspective, he traditionalised Catholicism against the tradition of the Enlightenment, whose thinkers he, in fact, did not appreciate much. Thus, he communicated with Islamic culture from a Catholic background, and used Islamic symbolism as a projecting field for his Catholic perception. Moreover, through an Islamic framework, he reintroduced his Catholic view into the French discourse. His interaction appeared to be so close and ambivalent that Islamic culture became, more or less, part of his own identification process; thus the other, the peripheral and the excluded re-emerged in the midst of structures of meaningful. His reaction to the Enlightenment in Europe was a kind of re-invention of tradition when he made use of non-European traditions and reinterpreted European reforms through non-European repertoires.

This identification and interpretation was rooted in widespread colonial ignorance about other cultures and religions, which testifies to the lack of dialogical understanding and corresponded to the contemporary colonial hermeneutic monologue, which by now had become engraved in foreign images. The powerful book written by W.W. Hunter stiffened the image by suggestively asking "*Are they (the Indian Musalmans) bound in conscience to rebel against the queen*"? though he also criticised British negligence of Muslims in India. Later, many Muslim nationalists

---

Marc Gaborieau: "Muslim Saints, Faquirs and Pilgrims in 1831 according to Garcin de Tassy", in: Malik (ed.): *Perspectives of mutual encounters*.

[40] Compare Mehmed Birgili: *Exposition de la foi musulmane, traduite du turc de Mohammed ben Pir-Ali Elberkevi*, transl. by Garcin de Tassy, Paris 1822.

unconditionally regarded the "Muhammadan Path" as their forerunner and in that way constructed their lineages and master narratives. It was only in 1886 that the government dropped the term "Wahhabi" from official correspondence.

Turmoil in rural areas

Increasingly, repressive colonial revenue policy and the elimination of local industry by the Company fostered reactions. Thus there were other similar *jihad* movements active in Bengal, on the Malabar Coast and in the Punjab. In Bengal agrarian conflicts took on religious character. The Hanafi scholar Hajji Shariʿat Allah (1780–1840), after returning from a 20-year stay in Mecca, established the Faraidiyya movement in 1818, which fought against landholders, businessmen and money-lenders. In 1820, Shariʿat Allah travelled the length and breadth of Bengal challenging established Muslim nobles and landholders, by attracting their farm workers. Opposing popular worship at shrines of holy men and Shia heroes like ʿAli and Husain, the movement referred to Shah Wali Allah's innovative scriptural fundamentalism. It called the Muslims in a Shafiʿi environment to act Islamically, thereby sticking to Muhammadan ideals and duties, i.e., *faraʾid*. Only when the activities of the Christian missionaries gradually increased and the socio-economic situation of the Muslims became dismal—as was reported by the *General Committee for Public Instruction* in Calcutta set up in 1823[41]—the Faraidis turned against the factory owners, particularly the English indigo traders. The movement appealed to weavers in particular, and Shariʿat Allah became their spiritual leader. His son Dudhu Miyan (1819–1862) created an effective organisational structure in order to oppose the landlords, and he even postulated that no human being had the right to levy taxes on God's earth.[42] In 1841–42 several clashes between the peasants and the landlords occurred in Eastern Bengal, as a result of which Dudhu Miyan and a few of his campaigners were arrested by the British, but the movement's spirit survived and added to the restlessness of peasants of Bengal.

[41] ʿAbd al-Haqq: *Marhum Dihli College*, (reprint) Dehli: Anjuman-e Taraqqi-ye Urdu (Hind) 1989, pp. 13f.

[42] Bayly: *Indian Society*, 175; Ahmed: *The Wahhabi Movement*, p. 95.

In the South, on the central Malabar Coast, the Shafiʿi Mappila (see Chap. 4), whose foundations were laid within a few years of the *hijra* of the Prophet, i.e., even before Muhammad b. al-Qasim's conquest of Sind in 711–13, had evolved as a powerful inland cultivating group. Under Tipu Sultan they had enjoyed some privileges against their Hindu landlords. But under the impact of European colonialism, Christian foreigners and their Hindu allies, who had cut off the lucrative Arab trade, the Mappila gradually became a society of small traders, landless labourers and poor fishermen. Their resentment was displayed by a small portion of the populace in social protest articulated in religious terms, such as Mahdi movement and *jihad*, coupled with the emotion of oppressed people. They responded to a seemingly hopeless situation resulting in violent activities against their oppressors, whether British administrators or Hindu landlords (*jenmis*), and they willingly accepted what they thought was martyrdom. Later they joined the Khilafat movement (see Chap. 11).[43]

In rural Punjab, the Chishti order had been organised by the followers of Shah Kalim Allah (1650–1729), who in the eighteenth century had tried to infuse new life into the almost defunct Chishti organisation in Delhi. His idea of integration aimed at favouring and keeping good relations with non-Muslims in order to impress them with the teachings of Islam. But in the nineteenth century, the activity of the Sabiriyya, a branch of the Chishtis established back in the fifteenth century, no longer remained confined to missionary work; instead, it tried to re-convert Muslims, and to prepare them for *jihad* against Sikhs and other "infidels".[44]

Certainly, social protest movements with religious meanings emerged among other religious groups as well. One important scripturalist and pious movement, which was, however, confined to the educated middle classes supporting science and education and calling for democracy and Indian nationalism, was the *Brahmo Samaj*, founded by "the father of modern India", R.M. Roy (1772–1833). Christopher Jaffrelot calls Roy's movement strategic syncretism, because it recurred to Christian

[43] Cf. Miller: *Mappila Muslims*; Dale: *The Mappillas of Malabar*, K.N. Panikkar: *Against Lord and State: Religion and Peasant Uprisings in Malabar, 1836–1921*, Delhi: OUP 1989.

[44] Bayly: *Indian Society*, p. 185.

ideas and at the same time referred to the indigenous Golden Age, to protect Hindu identity from Europeans.[45]

The Muslim movements mentioned reflected the conflict between landholders and tenants, agrarian labourers or tribals, artisans and nobles. However, the initial enemy was mostly the immediate landlord rather than the infidel outsider. Yet, there was hardly any collective identity, because the solidarity of rural and tribal classes was disintegrated by religion, status and factional conflict.[46] At the same time, Islamic zeal replaced local cosmologies by Islamic ones. Strict monotheistic notions of Islam came to displace shared beliefs and practices embedded in indigenous societies. This led to what has been called "religious rationalisation",[47] though a clear distinction between pure and syncretistic was not always possible. In fact, both stayed popular, and shared the lived traditions, while the Prophetic example played a central role in the evaluation of contingency and individuality. The emulation of his ethics was at once inwardly and outwardly effected.

As we have seen, initially there were enough scholars who interacted with the colonialists by offering guidance to British while at the same time trying to pacify their religious communities by issuing relevant legal opinions. Only after 1830, when Christian missionaries interfered further and the government became a self-consciously 'reforming' agent, native fears began to assume wider proportions.[48] The emancipation which was part of these evolving new Muslim publics, however, did not correspond to authoritarian colonial interests. Thus, "traditionalisation" of India became necessary for the British in order to hinder a further self-conscious development, which could have seriously challenged foreign domination. It was partly based on insight into the South Asian discourse. The turn from cultural encounter to appropriation was thus completed. The East India Company still dominated India as if it was a colony run on private economy.

---

[45] See Chr. Jaffrelot: "Hindu Nationalism, Strategic Syncretism in Ideology Building", in: *The Indian Journal of Social Science* 5/4 (1992), pp. 373–392.

[46] Bayly: *Indian Society*, p. 176.

[47] See Eaton: *The Rise of Islam and the Bengal Frontier*, pp. 281–290, referring to Max Weber.

[48] See Bayly: *Indian Society*, p. 115.

CHAPTER NINE

FROM APPROPRIATION TO COLLISION AND COLONIAL STABILISATION (APPROX. 1820–1900)

At the beginning of the nineteenth century, Europeans decided not to wage war on one another and to establish what was called *Balance of Power*. Especially after the Congress of Vienna (1814–15), two issues became very clear. First, European wars were still and would continue to be waged outside Europe. Second, the principle of sovereignty,[1] demanded by the peace of Utrecht in 1713, was not valid for the non-European world. While the first issue had been a major feature of European colonialism—the contest for world influence among European powers—Britain, France and Portugal—the second was to be refined even more in the nineteenth century. By then, colonialism had made deep inroads into the Islamic world in general and India in particular. This process can be divided paradigmatically into three phases: from 1820, when colonial power was already firmly established, to the 1860s, when Muslim countries struggled for recognition in the changing geopolitical reality; and, from the 1860s to 1880, when nearly all Muslim countries lost their economic and financial independence and became dependent on the Europeans. From 1880 to 1910, most of these countries—apart from those controlled by the Ottoman caliphate—were subject to direct colonial, military and political control, where economic colonialism had become political colonialism. In political subservience, the traditional urban divines, particularly theologians, were responsible for the traditional legitimisation of the ruler. At the same time Islamic repertory was gradually used as an ideology and a mobilising force by the societal formations that had become partly integrated into the gradually evolving colonial sector.[2] In contrast to this, in the traditional agrarian

[1] The complicated issue of sovereignty is discussed with reference to international law and princely states, by Pernau: *Verfassung und politische Kultur*, pp. 33–59; similarly Jörg Fisch: *Die europäische Expansion und das Völkerrecht*, Stuttgart 1984, who challenges the unlimited nature of warfare by the colonial powers outside Europe.

[2] Cf. Jamal Malik: *Colonialization of Islam*, New Delhi: Manohar 1996, Chap. I; the sectoral approach has paradigmatic character and must deviate in individual cases.

sector Islam prevailed in the form of a quasi-egalitarian peasant culture based on the institution of *khanaqah* and *dargah*, attracting so many different representatives of the increasingly complex society, particularly the service gentry, independent traders and landlords such as *jagirdars, mansabdars, ta'alluqdars*. *Khanaqah*s and *dargah*s were still a major link between the central state, the middlemen and peasant society. This is not to share Charles Metcalfe's ideal of the Rousseauian dream of an eternal and egalitarian Indian peasant society.[3] Rather, as such, the success of Sufism primarily depended on its function to hide the contradiction between the metropolis and the countryside, between the state in its form of appropriator of surplus and its subjects and the peasants by "strategies of misrecognition".[4] At the same time the different and contesting cultural articulations of organised Sufism seem to have produced for the peasants alternative identities and solidarity systems in which they could imagine themselves as conscious agents of history, as can be traced from a number of Sufi and eschatological movements. How these movements transformed into various Muslim reactions to colonialism will be dealt with in the next chapter. Below we consider the process toward colonial stabilisation.

With the help of Indian wealth and especially Bengal revenues, the East India Company consolidated its authority over Bengal and acquired further territories in northern and western India. The introduction of an anti-tenant tax system, such as the *Permanent Settlement*, yielded higher income. In this way, the British army manned mainly by Indians could be financed through Indian taxes and the internal borders consolidated through colonialisation of virgin lands. Allies were restricted in their power, e.g., by being denied their rights to conclude treaties. This resulted in what was considered the pacified British realm, *Pax Britannica*. However, these new relations of dominance and property as well as the increasing economic pressure for artisans and peasants in particular fostered reaction that manifested itself in different ways and nourished the great upheaval of 1857.[5]

---

[3] See Devendra Nath Panigrahi: *Charles Metcalfe in India. Ideas and administration, 1806–1835*, Delhi: Munshiram Manoharlal 1968, pp. 6, and 88–102.

[4] Compare Pierre Bourdieu and Jean-Claude Passeron: *Reproduction in education, Society and Culture*, transl. Richard Nice, London 1990.

[5] Though in individual cases such as princely states, the situation might have been more complicated and ambivalent, particularly between 1800 and 1857.

"Traditionalising" India

As argued in preceding chapters, colonial power aimed at restoring parts of the Mughal system and its institutions by restructuring them in order to establish supremacy. In doing so, several methods were used to stabilise colonial rule, with the help and support of natives, adding to the colonial project of civilising mission, i.e. that colonies were backward, lacked civility and were at the opposite pole to enlightened Europe. The creation of 'traditional India' was becoming increasingly necessary for colonial legitimacy.

Traditionalisation of India harked back to the academic engagement with the colonialised region and the reception and selective appropriation of ideas of Indian pietists on the one hand and the obliteration of traces of Indian creativity on the other. Furthermore, we can argue that the well-known colonial criticism of the Orient was based on India's indigenous oriental criticism shaped according to Europeans' own convenience. Thus the colonial masters essentially were not the catalysts for "development" and "modernisation", because the catalytic moment was already there.[6]

The process of appropriation was complemented by demographic inquiries and the census first taken in 1871.[7] These were proven devices for social control. Back in England, the state supported its claim to legitimacy with technical and scientific achievements and social data.[8] India turned out to be an appropriate location to undertake similar legitimising projects, albeit in a different form. Unlike the collection of demographic data in the colonial motherland, which concentrated on territories and professions, in India the natives were primarily categorised according

---

[6] Christopher Bayly has been a pioneer who paved the way for this idea. See his monographs *Rulers, Townsmen and Bazaars; Empire and Information*; compare also H.L. Wesseling (ed.): *Expansion and Reaction. Essays on European Expansion and Reaction in Asia and Africa*, Leiden 1978; and Malik (ed.): *Perspectives of Mutual Encounters*.

[7] For the census see, for example, B.S. Cohn: "The Census, Social Structure and Objectification in South Asia", in: B.S. Cohn: *An Anthropologist among the Historians and Other Essays*, Delhi 1987; David Ludden: "Orientalist Empiricism: Transformations of Colonial Knowledge", and Arjun Appadurai: "Number in the Colonial Imagination", in: Breckenridge et al. (eds.): *Orientalism*, pp. 250–276, and pp. 314–340 respectively; Peter Robb (ed.): *Rural India: Land, Power and Society under British Rule*, London 1983. Also N. Gerald Barrier (ed.): *The Census in British India: New Perspectives*, New Delhi 1981.

[8] See Richard Lawton (ed.): *The Census and Social Structure: An Interpretative Guide to Nineteenth Century Censuses for England and Wales*, London and Totowa, NJ: F. Cass 1978; D.V. Glass: *Numbering the People. The Eighteenth-Century Population Controversy and the Development of Census and Vital Statistics in Britain*, London: D.C. Heath 1973.

to race, caste and religion in the 1870s.[9] This "orientalist empiricism"[10] had a controlling function and required "reform" and "modernisation" of traditional India—based on practical-philosophical ideas (see Chap. 8). Assigning and consequently creating new racial and religious identities to the colony helped translate the colonial situation in a manner that made the "other" comprehensible at home in England. This construction of an imagined Oriental identity does, however, say less about the peoples in the colonies than colonialists themselves, since the construction of the other can only be based on projections of elements of the self. By this complex process, India was to become the foil of an absent enlightenment, obscurantism, romanticism and ritualism, in contrast to enlightened Europe,[11] which could claim to operate, and ultimately control, the 'backward' and 'traditional' India in the name of progress and modernity. It is in this context that we can identify the other side of Orientalism: in addition to the essentialisation of the Orient, there is also a long-standing romantic idealisation of Eastern spirituality.[12]

Now that all information about India was available, the British could classify them in taxonomies to analyse them. Enumeration, essentialisation and appropriation of the social landscape exclusively served colonial domination and utilitarianism.[13] This "scientific" invention of traditional India helped establish an epistemological hierarchy, which determined the image of the Orient as an exotic region offering enough space for projections, yearnings, and traumata.[14] Thus the new and subjected region became, according to European notions of superiority, a vicious

---

[9] See Appadurai: "Number"; Henry Scholberg: *The District Gazetteers of British India: A Bibliography*, Zug, Switzerland: Inter-Documentation Company 1970. From 1871 onwards the British census in India defined group identities (communitas) in terms of caste, religious and ethnic affiliation. See H.M. Elliot: *Encyclopaedia of castes, customs, rites and superstitions of the Races of North India, I–II*, 1st Indian reprint, Delhi: Sumit Publications 1985, first published 1870. Also Nicholas B. Dirks: *Castes of Mind. Colonialism and the Making of Modern India*, Delhi: Permanent Black 2002, and Ronald Inden: *Imagining India*, London: Hurst 1990, who shows that caste and "Hinduism" were colonial inventions.

[10] Ludden: "Orientalist Empiricism".

[11] Wilhelm Halbfass: *India and Europe. An Essay in Philosophical Understanding*, Delhi 1990, p. 60.

[12] As has been discussed for instance by Richard King: *Orientalism and Religion: Postcolonial Theory, India, and 'The Mystic East'*, London 1999.

[13] See Eric Stokes: *The English Utilitarians and India*, Delhi: OUP 1992(3); Appadurai: "Number" in: Breckenridge et al. (eds.): *Orientalism*, pp. 314–340.

[14] Compare Halbfass: *Indien und Europa*, pp. 75ff.

country which could never improve by itself,[15] and which, therefore, needed guidance. The savages had to be civilised.[16]

"Modernising" India

The orientalist traditionalisation was programmatic and corresponded to the perceptions of the Victorian spirit, which had just begun to modernise a supposedly stagnant India now subdivided into castes, religions and races.[17] As the British began to define group identities in terms of race and caste and eventually very strongly in terms of religious affiliations and thereby justified their ethnic policy, "communalist" thinking was boosted, if not created[18] (see also Excursus: Communalism). In doing so, Europeans, such as Cornwallis (see Chap. 8), took individual cases concerning informants accused of mistranslating and manipulating information as proofs for their stereotypes. Indian knowledge was disparaged. And, by means of manipulating local narratives, Hindu-Muslim quarrels were generalised. European press, the forum of debate for these issues, was decisive in the proliferation of such images, and could be activated as a strategy of ascertaining oneself. Increasingly, any opposition was considered rebellious and seditious and was suppressed. Revolts against trade-stabilising measures of the colonialists, such as privatisation and transit taxes, were met with vigorous military action. However, the revolts increased, partly due to new laws prohibiting Indians to compete with the British. Labour had now to be remunerated according to specified rates (*Lascar Acts* 1820–24). Caste, religion and chaotic situations, as well as the idea of the despotic character of Indian rulers, served as a legitimising reference, as was exemplified through the monopolising activities of grain

---

[15] See Spear: *The Nabobs*, pp. 136ff.

[16] The invention of a backward Orient was most important for European enlightenment. See Bitterli: *Die "Wilden" und die "Zivilisierten"*.

[17] The historiography of the nineteenth century was well reflected in the colonial conception; see the bibliographical notes in O'Fahey/Radtke: "Neo Sufism Reconsidered", especially pp. 61ff.; also R. Inden: "Orientalist Constructions of India," in: *MAS* 20 (1986), pp. 401–46.

[18] The conceptualisation of society in terms of ethnicity and religion was reproduced in demographic data from 1871 onwards. Indian nationalists adopted this idea of ethnification and used it for their own communalist purposes. See S.B. Freitag: *Collective Action and Community*, Delhi 1990; G. Pandey: *The Construction of Communalism in Colonial India*, Delhi 1990.

traders and British interventionists between 1833–38 in Western India and Delhi, when continuous drought caused disastrous famine.[19] Thus the "preservation of empire", an idiom coined by William Bentinck (1774–1839), Governor General 1828–35, was important in the face of traditional Muslim space, the *qasbah*, which came to witness a renaissance in times of overall decay. The imagination of past pride of *watan* as a lived space, amounting to memorising the figures of collective memory, provided a spatial memorial frame which kept the memory of "homeland" alive even in its absence.[20]

For the British, who considered themselves messiahs of modernisation, it became increasingly urgent to reform the traditional and the orientalised region. This in fact ran parallel to safeguarding the East India Company's ability to act. Therefore, William Bentinck's reforms slashed budgets by employing cheap Indian workers at lower levels of administration and the cessation of military operations, but resulted in only limited improvement in trade.

Social reforms and changes in law were enacted. The elimination of traditional rites, so-called obnoxious customs was partly the result of pressure from the Christian missionaries. The British denounced ideas of honour and value system and the indigenous tradition manifested for example in widow burning (Sati; banned in 1829) as contingent. Against this presumably "dutiful act of religious volition" they set the principle of a universal ethos and their ethically motivated concern for the individual, what they called modernity in quest of the civilising mission of colonialism.[21] Similarly, robbery associated with travel rituals of certain tribes called "thugs" were also made unlawful. These and similar restrictions were the continuation of earlier British interventions into customary law. The introduction of the English education system

---

[19] The grain policy was not accepted unanimously but was a matter of controversy; though with the expansion of colonial rule Indian society became increasingly vulnerable to droughts and famines. For details see Sanjay Sharma: *Famine, Philanthropy and the Colonial State. North India in the Early Nineteenth Century*, Oxford: OUP 2001.

[20] For the identity-giving role of lived space see Assmann: *Das kulturelle Gedächtnis*, pp. 38f.

[21] Cf. Monika Horstmann: "The Debate on Sati in the Rajputana Agency", in: Malik (ed.): *Perspectives of mutual encounters*; Lata Mani: *Contentious Traditions. The Debate on Sati in Colonial India*, Berkeley and Los Angeles: UCP 1998. See also Jörg Fisch: *Tödliche Rituale*, Frankfurt: Campus 1998, who discusses the ambivalences of Sati-rituals from all over the world, in terms of socio-economic pressures felt by families to rid themselves of burdensome widows, and divine grace suggested in different male discourses; self-immolation as representing for the Hindus a path immorality has been discussed by Catherine Weinberger-Thomas: *Ashes of Immortality. Widow-Burning in India*, Chicago and London 1999.

offered Indians the possibility to join the lower ranks of the Indian Civil Service. Simultaneously, in 1835 Persian was replaced by English and Hindustani as languages of administration. Such measures weakened the supreme position of the service gentry, the *ashraf*, immensely, especially in the administration of justice.[22] Moreover, the *General Committee of Public Instruction* led by lawyer Thomas B. Macauley (1800–1859) proposed a radical Anglicisation[23] (Macaulay's *Codes of Criminal and Civil Procedure*, Draft 1841–42). Rejecting the Orientalists' veneration for India's past, he opined that a single shelf of a good European library was worth the entire native literature of India and Arabia. He wanted to create a "class of persons, Indian in blood and colour, but English in taste, opinions, morals and intellect" (Education Minute 1836) through *useful* education in natural sciences, mathematics, economy, philosophy, ethics and history. While the reforms manifested the Anglicists' victory over the Orientalists particularly on what was discussed of utility or efficacy of Oriental learning, the new educational system laid the seed for religious polarisation and marginalised the traditional education system, relegating it to the private realm[24]—thus "dini madrasa" (religious school). The nineteenth-century orientalist notion of "Islamic city", which was perceived as introspective (caused by confessional segregation), chaotic and disunited, divided into fragments and anti-nominal cells, can also be seen in this context.[25] This privatisation of Muslim space went hand in hand with the colonial discourse on the feminisation of Islam, which actually reflected the process of feminisation of Christianity back in Europe projected onto the colony:[26] Islam, and India, was perceived in terms of *feminality* that had to be tamed and subdued by the stark male British, and those affiliated with them. Soon

[22] Reform movements like Tariqah-ye Muhammadi and Faraidiyya took up this problem, radicalised it and thus sharpened the animosity between the religious communities.

[23] For the Anglicisation see also Anderson: *Die Erfindung der Nation*, pp. 95ff.

[24] For a brief but enlightening discussion of the criterion of "useful" instruction and "privatisation" of—religious—education, see Muhammad Qasim Zaman: *The Ulama in Contemporary Islam. Custodians of Change*, Karachi: OUP 2002, pp. 64–66.

[25] See Janet Abu-Lughod: "Islamic city—historic myth, Islamic essence, and contemporary relevance", in: *IJMES* 19 (1987), pp. 155–176; Ehlers and Krafft (eds.): *Shâhjahânâbâd*.

[26] See Michael B. Gross: "The Strange Case of the Nun in the Dungeon, or German Liberalism as a Convent Atrocity Story", in: *German Studies Review* 23 (2000), pp. 69–84; Irmtraud Götz von Olenhusen: "Feminisierung von Religion und Kirche im 19. und 20. Jahrhundert", in: Ingrid Lukatis et al. (eds.): *Religion und Geschlechterverhältnis*, Opladen 2000, pp. 37–47.

Muslim reformers adopted this orientalist critique to advocate Islamic education for women, as can be gleaned from religious advice literature, cornering women into narrowing, reformist-domestic chastity (see also Excursus: Gender).[27]

Thus, marginalisation and "privatisation" had a profound impact on Muslim reformers. The acceptance of functional differentiation on the side of religious communities can certainly be read in terms of a meaning of secularisation. Moreover, the reformers brought themselves to masculinise Islam through different discourses and practices, such as Islamic advice literature and puritan didactical literature for women, and they produced new visibility. Many Indian intellectuals followed the call for reform and founded socio-religious and later also political associations supported by rich assimilated Indians, such as the *British Indian Association* in Calcutta in 1851, or *Anjuman-e Islamiyya* and *Anjuman-e Himayat-e Islam* both in Lahore in 1869 and 1884 respectively. These associations and the emerging newspapers aimed at accelerating the Muslim public sphere not only to get informed by colonial concepts of normativity and civility, but also to de-legitimise the traditional set-up. The emerging culture of associations and societies thus enabled the discursive encounter with the British on the same cultural terrain, because they were accepted by the Europeans. Muslim intellectuals viewed these associations as a refuge that would show the right path between Hindus and British. The *Anjumans* provided for solidarity and identity and at the same time called for social responsibility which could be negotiated beyond the narrow borders of the associations, also in terms of a religious discourse. So it was in these forms of socialisation that the early reformist discourses took place.

At the same time, many traditional Muslim scholars were integrated into the colonial sector, probably to conciliate their gentry, but only at the lower levels in government offices and courts, and as interpreters of Islamic law. This was made possible through institutions such as the *Calcutta Madrasa* or *Madrasa Aliyya Kalkatta* founded by Warren Hastings in 1781, which partly adopted the teaching developed in Lucknow by the Farangi Mahallis and virtually taught throughout South Asia—albeit with local and personal differences. Another such institution was the *Delhi College*, established on the foundations of the Madrasa Ghazi al-Din, which disseminated colonial knowledge through Hindustani

---

[27] See the excellent discussion of this gendering process in Margrit Pernau: *Bürger im Turban. Muslime in Delhi im 19. Jahrhundert*, Göttingen 2008.

and Urdu translations.[28] The cooption of Farangi Mahallis, who by that time had already established an impressive scholarly network throughout South Asia, facilitated colonial penetration, but led to a political marginalisation of the conventional education system which was gradually replaced by the colonial one. This dichotomy lasted up to the contemporary period.

The new colonial culture demanded severe social readjustments. Thus new exclusive institutions with particular interests carrying similar new values emerged. Also new administrative centres were established to further unify and modernise the colony. This process of settlement along with new cultivation technologies, prohibition to migrate and coercive policies, was programmatically furthered by Dalhousie (1812–1860), Governor-General from 1848 to 1856. The whole process was facilitated by the fact that rural areas displayed capitalistic structures.[29] At the same time, traditional Muslim hegemony held by revenue farmers, local rulers, jagirdars and princes was dissolved through redistribution of land. These developments furthered uncertainty about the degree of colonial rule and met with several reactions couched in religious sentiments, eventually culminating in the revolt of 1857.

The revolt of 1857

Though by 1850 the East India Company had brought virtually the entire Indian subcontinent under its control to form a vast British Indian Empire, this was in no way a straightforward process of 'modernisation'. Many 'reforms' existed only on paper or were confined to tiny urban elites.[30] However, the colonial restructuring gave impetus to existing inner social antagonisms, which in conjunction with efforts of the British Government to annex further regions of the British Empire in India led to a number of upheavals eventually leading to the major outbreak of 1857. Three of the Company's native regiments (sepoy) in Meerut revolted against British officers because of the fear of ritual contamination stemming from a new kind of rifle cartridge. The revolt

[28] For an introduction to the history of the Madrasa and the College see Pernau: "Introduction", in: C.F. Andrews: *Zaka Ullah of Delhi*, and Pernau: "Introduction", in: *The Delhi College*.

[29] See Washbrook: "Problems and Progress"; Bayly: *Rulers*.

[30] Metcalf and Metcalf: *A Concise History of India*, pp. 89–90.

was received as a "freedom fight" or named a "mutiny", depending on different points of view. In it a large number of discontented groups joined forces, as had also been argued by Sayyid Ahmad Khan (1817–1899), the celebrated scholar of the nineteenth century (on him see Chap. 10). Muslim scholars, parts of the bureaucracy of the tottering Mughal Empire, notables, entrepreneurs, artisans and farmers, as well as *ta'alluqdari* landlords joined forces. The military was merely a catalytic agent, not the least because already in the 1850s problems had occurred when the Company tried to win over Indian soldiers for service in foreign countries (*General Service Enlistment Act of 1856*) and when the Company replaced the leaders of the army—Brahmans and Rajputs—by members of other castes. Moreover, their salaries had been reduced.[31]

It is meaningful for an understanding of the events to investigate in some detail how a leading Muslim scholar such as Fadl-e Haqq Khairabadi (died 1861, see also Chap. 8) perceived the colonial encounter and the developments that led to the upheaval of 1857. He already had grievances about colonial arrogance and dishonour, and in about 1827 he lamented the economic and social decline of Indians, which he related to the import of British manufactured goods. Interestingly, a similar statement was issued by the Mughal emperor in Delhi as a rallying call for the insurrection on 25th August 1857, seen as "the first manifesto in the European sense which has been published in India, the first list of grievances, the first step to stir up the people by promises unconnected with religion...The grievances of each class are specified, and a remedy promised if they will but fight boldly for the old regime."[32]

Fadl-e Haqq Khairabadi was charged by the British with instigating murder and high treason in a *fatwa*. The crucial *fatwa* was duly signed by more than 30 ulama, among others by the high Company employee Sadr al-Din Azurda (see above). It implied that if the British attacked Delhi, killed Muslims and appropriated their property, *jihad* would become an obligation (*fard-e 'ain*) for those able to resist militarily. And if the inhabitants of Delhi got weakened by *jihad*, those from the surrounding regions were to support them. Sayyid Ahmad Khan, who,

---

[31] For the role of military in the context of British rule in South Asia during upheavals before 1857 see Alavi: *The Sepoys and the Company*.

[32] Quoted in S.A.A. Rizvi and M.L. Bhargava (eds.): *Freedom Struggle in Uttar Pradesh; Source Material*, Vol. 1, Lucknow 1957, pp. 453–458, here p. 455.

as a loyal Muslim scholar and activist, had tried to pacify the British vis-à-vis the Muslims, later commented that this particular *fatwa* was baseless (*be-asl*), and was signed by many ulama only under pressure and threat. Most of them were loyalists anyway, and only a few would really have gone for *jihad*.

Although Fadl-e Haqq Khairabadi was not in Delhi when the *fatwa* was issued and thus did not sign it, he was sentenced to imprisonment for life and died in 1861 in exile on the Andaman Islands. There he composed some ciphered Arabic prose poems and *qasidas*: the *Risala thaurat al-hindiyya*, later reconstructed by his son, ʿAbd al-Haqq Khairabadi (died 1899), a scholar of the Delhi College. However, its authenticity may be questioned:[33] the colonial politics and the religious conversion of Indians connected with it were, according to him, based on these strategies: 1. The destruction of the traditional Islamic educational system and the standardisation of religious diversity. 2. The introduction of cash crops and monopolisation of the grain market, with the objective of making Indians materially dependent and thus to subject them absolutely. 3. The scholar from Khairabad also claimed that the British prohibited the Indians from observing their rites.

However, in the case of Khairabadi, one may suspect a judicial error of the colonial administration. This is more likely, since he had a namesake active in 1857; this error would give evidence to the profound ignorance or even to vindictiveness of the colonialists. It seems that the European conviction of its superior position hampered a deeper understanding of the independent character of Indian culture, and jeopardised the insight into the autonomy of other cultural forms. This might also be true in the case of an anti-British revolutionary council (*King Council* or *majlis-e mushawarat*), which is said to have been established during the revolt. Manned by 10 members from civil and military departments, the council worked towards a constitution, supposedly the first constitutional elaboration in Urdu for an independent India. The draft of these regulations used Arabic and Persian nomenclatures rather than British ones, and adopted many elements of European statesmanship. It is said that the council produced "a constitution based

---

[33] Translated and annotated by Muhammad ʿAbd al-Shahid Khan Sherwani, Mubarakpur 1985(4). S. Moinul Haq: "The Story of the War of Independence (being an English translation of Allamah Fadl-i-Haqq's Risalah on the War", in: *Journal of Pakistan Historical Society* V/1 (1957), pp. 23–57. For Khairabadi's biography and supposed involvement see Malik: "Letters, prison sketches".

on the principles of democracy" curtailing the power of the monarch. Nonetheless, the rebels proclaimed Bahadur Shah Zafar as the Shah of Hindustan, most probably to use the legitimacy of the Mughal crown as a symbol for unifying different groups. The fear of a potential renewal of Muslim rule supposedly drove many Hindus to the side of colonial masters. But by and large the loyalists differed from the rebels since the former had benefited from colonial administration and trade, whereas the latter had suffered persistently since 1801.[34]

Another centre of the 1857 upheaval was Awadh where the British monopoly of violence was shattered by the indigenous violence of the colonialised.[35] There the new tax policy implemented (*summary settlement*) had produced quite a number of insurrectional groups who joined the "mutineers". The battle of Lucknow took many months, but since Awadh was heavily colonialised, the British communication channels could not be cut. Also, there were quite a number of collaborators. The Muslim response itself was deeply fragmented. There were the *ghazis* and *jihad*-fighters in Delhi, mostly from Tonk and Bhopal, and particularly Bareilly and Patna, i.e., strongholds of the *Tariqah-ye Muhammadi*, but also from Gawalior and Najibabad, led by the above-mentioned Rahmat Allah al-Kairanawi, who apparently transformed himself from a fighter with a pen to one with a sword, as a result of marginalisation in the wake of colonial encroachment. Then there were men adhering to the Chishti-Sabiri order, who had developed a martial tradition against the Sikhs in Punjab. The battles in the districts of Saharanpur and Muzaffarnagar were, indeed, very Islamically tinged and waged by the powerful Muslim gentry previously affiliated to the Mughal court. Various *fatawa* from this region bear witness to an Islamic character of the struggle. Moreover, there were the *qasbah*s of Awadh where the Naqshbandis were active among weavers and people of the bazar. But, there was no commonality because Muslims were split religiously and socially and were not clear about the importance of *jihad*. The confiscation of revenue-free land had also had negative repercussions for religious schools and shrines. Furthermore, the trade and economic turmoil also created disgust. Big entrepreneurs did not call for *jihad*. Many were government servants and as such were

---

[34] See Bayly: *Indian Society*, pp. 187, 193.

[35] Compare R. Mukherjee: *Awadh in Revolt, 1857–1858. A study in popular resistance*, Delhi: OUP 1984.

apprehensive. Others, like Sayyid Ahmad Khan called for an internal reform of Islam. Moreover, cooperation with the Hindus made *jihad* difficult, so that after the colonial liberation of Delhi, cow slaughter and *jihad* were prohibited. Other leaders in Awadh tried to establish a common identity between Hindus and Muslims by creating a collective inimical image of the *Firangi*. Thus there was hardly any idea of a single community capable of being mobilised in times of collective need.[36] With lack of consistency, inadequate coordination, religious and social contradictions, collaboration on the side of the rebels and with modern colonial weaponry, the Europeans got the upper hand in 1858 after a long battle.

Civilising mission

After crushing the revolt of 1857, colonialists created a new official history, and vigorously introduced the reforms mentioned above and declared themselves as liberators of the Hindus from the tyranny of Muslim rule. Rebellious *ta'alluqdars* and Muslim scholars were persecuted. The revolt was interpreted in terms of a mutiny, considered a despicable crime against authority. The metaphor of "mutiny" was, after 1858, linked to the whole Islamic world, so that every Islamically tinged uprising was interpreted as mutiny. Consequently, rebels were hanged.[37] Interestingly, giving a vivid picture of the events in his "Dastambu", Mirza Ghalib complains among others that the "lowly ones, who have never known wealth or honour, now have prestige and unlimited riches" just to say that British should "see that justice is done".[38] For the nationalist movement, however, the rebels played the most important role as mythical heroes, being prominently portrayed in hagiographies. The reading of the ulama on this topic alone is, however, fraught with danger since there is exaggeration with regard to sacrifices they made and the numbers who became martyrs (*shuhada*) are increased. Thus one has to mention the *farman* issued by the Mughal emperor, Bahadur

[36] Bayly: *Indian Society*, pp. 180–190; see also Rajat Kanta Ray: *The Felt Community. Commonality and Mentality before the Emergence of Indian Nationalism*, Delhi: OUP 2003.

[37] See Schulze: "Die Islamische Welt in der Neuzeit", pp. 395f. This would go in line with Mukherjee's argument of a British monopoly of violence.

[38] See Ghalib: *Dastanbuy*, transl. and ed. by Khwaja Ahmad Faruqi, Delhi: University Press 1970, pp. 34, and 47. For an analysis of Ghalib's stand vis-à-vis 1857 see Pernau: *Bürger im Turban*.

Shah Zafar, in which he complains of *varna-sankara* (mixing of caste) by the British because of some of their liberal ideas such as equality of education. In contrast to the emancipative endeavours of the rebels suggested above, the imperial *farman* seems to be rather reactionary. If similar ideas existed in Indian ranks, to germinate and push through constitutional notions, then one may ask whether the revolt really aimed at restoring the old order, or whether the traditional historiography followed the "traditionalisation", which would, indeed, correspond to the politics of colonial restoration. Any other perception of the upheaval would have meant appreciating progressive forces.

We hardly know the view from the margin, such as the story of Umrao Jan Ada, a courtesan from Lucknow. Her portrayal by Mirza Hadi Ruswa (1858–1931) in the supposedly first Urdu novel tells a completely different story, seeing the so-called 'revolutionaries' as nothing more than trouble-mongers (*balwai*). Similar revealing information about the uneasy situation during the siege is provided by different other professions such as sweet- and wood-sellers, money-lenders, cobblers as well as some hungry sepoys, as can be read from the various Mutiny Papers,[39] which, however, have not been used by historians so far. Though the role of people such as Khairabadi remains alive in Urdu and Persian literature, we hardly find vernacular voices being heard in historical accounts that are important to ascertain the nature of the 1857 revolt.[40] A documentation piecing together such material lying in the dusty State and National Archives is of utmost importance, since these textually rich sources do provide an important and palpable insight into the variety of collective and individual decisions at a vital point of South Asian history. In fact, in the light of quite different views it becomes indeed a problem to definitely ascertain the nature of 1857 revolt.

The fact, however, is that India had been governed by British commercial entrepreneurs up to 1858, and became proper "British" only afterwards. As a result of the "mutiny", the Crown of England (i.e. Queen Victoria) took over the administration of India, now governed by a Viceroy, at the time Governor-General Canning. The British, on the one hand, reinvented Indian traditions when they adapted their own system of governance to the local set-up appropriating many of the

[39] I am thankful to William Dalrymple for sharing this insight with me.

[40] Therefore, it seems to be too early to state whether there were no upheavals in other areas as well, such as the Deccan and Bengal.

Persian norms, as a ritual expression of British power in India. Consequently, in 1876—the year of bad harvest and famines in India—Queen Victoria (1819–1901) accepted the title of Empress of India—*Kaiser-e Hind*—combining the imperial titles of Roman imperator, German Kaiser and Russian Czar—only 20 years after her ascending to the throne.[41] This semi-divine glorification of British rule was the apex and accomplishment of Mughal power, which, however, required guidance and management. Thus "modernisation" or "civilicisation", which initially took the shape of "Anglicisation" as demanded by Macaulay, became the political credo, ushering in constitutional reform that eventually gave some regular parliamentary security to Indian affairs. While some of these "modernising" developments took place in India first, before they found their way to England, the extension of the communication system, such as the telegraph line in 1861, and the opening of the Suez Canal as well as the Civil War in America which hampered the American cotton trade, further strengthened British control over India. An "official nationalism" was introduced which enabled the colonialists to retaliate legally, thereby establishing a definite power-relationship.[42] As outlined by Chris Bayly, "the more homogeneous society of peasants and petty moneylenders which emerged in the later nineteenth century was a more appropriate basis for a semi-European colonial state."[43]

After 1857

While the ethnification, or "communalisation" of local people—as is evident also in emerging colonial popular theories on martial races in the wake of the census—precipitated the decay of *qasbahs* when they became more and more the retreat and venue for "sectarian" and "communal" conflicts,[44] urban centres, where the colonial sector was

[41] This title was proposed by the Anglo-Hungarian Orientalist G.W. Leitner (died 1899), Principal Government College, Lahore from 1854–1886; the famous and functionally important Imperial Assembly in Delhi in 1877 has been analysed by B.S. Cohn: "Representing Authority in Victorian India", in: Ranger and Hobsbawm (eds.): *The Invention of Tradition*, pp. 165–209.

[42] See Anderson: *Die Erfindung der Nation*, pp. 89ff.

[43] Bayly: *Indian Society*, p. 144.

[44] See Pandey: *Communalism*; Hasan: *From Pluralism to Separatism*.

expanding rapidly, were soon caught by similar upheavals.[45] This goes back to colonial restructuring accompanied by profound changes in the socio-psychological sphere of colonialised societies. Culturally rooted systems of society, such as biological, spiritual and educational lineages and categories of social organisation (family, tribe, caste, profession, network of religious groups, clientele etc.), and their underlying values and relations were gradually replaced by abstract, anonymous state agents, whether by direct or indirect rule. As parts of traditional society were increasingly integrated into world market relations, a tremendous social upheaval took place. This complex process came about primarily in the wake of technical innovations, such as a perennial irrigation system for cotton growth, investment of capital, and privatisation of landed property: next to the traditional urban and traditional agrarian sectors, colonial urban and colonial agrarian sectors were established in order to implement colonial interests. Gradually, traditional sectors were colonialised and eventually integrated by using a colonial infrastructure, among others the newly invented railway. This complex process was paralleled by the recruitment and training of British civil servants, whose examinations were held only in England. Moreover, the age was deliberately reduced from 21 to 19 years in 1878, allowing only those Indians who attended school in England to qualify for admission.

Displaying British racist fears, this process also ushered in new societal formations. With increasing colonial penetration, traditional structures either stood on the verge of breakdown or looked for alternative structures or simply went underground. However, not all sectors were seized by the increasingly dominant colonial one, as their integration was not always profitable, such as in parts of the previously important nomadic sector and tribal areas. They were consequently marginalised, and are still socio-economically neglected areas. The cities were restructured in a way reminiscent of the ideas of Georges Eugène Haussmann (died 1891), who restructured Paris to save it from the urban mob.[46] Thus

[45] See W. Fusfeld: "Communal Conflict in Delhi, 1803–1930", in: *IESHR* 19 (1982), pp. 181–200; Freitag: *Collective Action*; Mushirul Hasan: *Nationalism and Communal Politics in India, 1885–1930*, Delhi 1991. According to Bayly communalism was existent even before British presence. See C.A. Bayly: "The Pre-history of 'Communalism'? Religious Conflict in India, 1700–1860", in: *MAS* 19/2 (1985), pp. 177–203.

[46] Compare E.J. Hobsbawm: *Sozialrebellen*, Gießen 1979, pp. 145ff. For the colonial city see A.D. King: *Colonial urban development: culture, social power and environment*, Boston, London 1976; David Arnold: *Police Power and Colonial Rule, Madras 1859–1947*, Delhi 1986; Narayani Gupta: *Delhi between two Empires, 1803–1931: Society, Government and Urban*

colonial urban planning became manifest in the establishment of military cantonments, civil lines and sadr bazars, segregated and sanitised, and developed into important economic centres to safeguard British interests especially in the colonial motherland. Hill stations, such as Shimla and Murree, were not only to serve as refuge for the hot summer, but also revived memories of "Englishness". Thus the number of urban colonial re-foundations increased, contesting with what came to be projected as the "Oriental" or "Islamic City". Some North Indian cities were even designed to become leading British trade centres. For example, Kanpur, a town several kilometres southwest of Lucknow, became a centre for the industrial economy in the interior of the subcontinent, the "Manchester of the East."[47] This was supported by the newly laid train line, which turned Kanpur into an infrastructural knot and a central emporium, where journalism flourished and many of the early presses were established.[48] After 1857, the increasing demand of the British Army as the most important investor and consumer, made possible the swift industrialisation of this colonial city.[49] At the same time, new handicraft and craftsmanship and new management were introduced. Parallel to the local economy that had been affiliated to the hinterland, the *qasbah*s, these colonial re-foundations developed new markets for the emerging small industries. The number of European companies and enterprises increased, constantly supporting new patterns of consumption and action. This produced new social needs, which were particularly popular among the parvenu groups. There were new goods for the new culture,[50] constituting groups that were located and oscillated

Growth, New Delhi 1981; V.T. Oldenburg: *The Making of Colonial Lucknow, 1857–1877*, Princeton, New Jersey 1984; A.D. King: *Urbanism, Colonialism, and the World-Economy; Cultural and Spatial Foundations of the World Urban System*, London/New York 1990; for interesting parallels in Egypt see Timothy Mitchell: *Colonising Egypt*, Cambridge: CUP 1988, pp. 63ff., 161ff.

[47] See Zoe Yalland: *Traders and Nabobs. The British in Cawnpore 1765–1857*, Wiltshire 1987; for Kanpur during the revolt see Pratul Chandra Gupta: *Nana Sahib and the rising at Cawnpore*, Oxford 1963.

[48] For the development of Indian journalism see Uma Das Gupta: "The Indian Press 1870–1880; a small world of journalism", in: *MAS* 11 (1977), pp. 213–235; for the development in Kanpur specifically see Nadir ʿAli Khan: *Hindustani Press, 1556–1900*, Lucknow 1990, here pp. 226–242; Nadir Ali Khan: *A History of Urdu Journalism*, Delhi 1991, pp. 121f.

[49] The military was the most important agent of imperialism—the iron fist in the satin glove of Victorian expansionism; see Washbrook: "South Asia", p. 481.

[50] See William Hoey: *A Monograph on Trade and Manufactures in Northern India*, Lucknow 1880, pp. 29ff., and Bayly: *Rulers*, pp. 441ff.

between colonial and traditional societies. The influential groups of Eurasians are the case in point. The means and methods of production and profit-making of different representatives of this primarily urban culture differed from one another. In this increasingly complex society the respective cultural articulations differed as well, mostly depending upon the social status acquired in the expanding colonial sector. These groups now increasingly opted for cultural and political participation. But in the cultural life under colonial rule this was hardly possible at that time. The cities, which had gathered massive potential of conflicts during the migrations even before 1857, were objects of thorough structural change by colonial power. Thus in the framework of colonial security policy, "nationalist" activities and big cultural or religious events could hardly take place, such as in Lucknow, where 20 years after the upheaval of 1857 the task of restructuring the government and politics was completed, initially followed by a dull and quiescent but stable period.[51] Analogous to this re-structuring, the colonial masters succeeded in creating many loyal aristocrats, in the countryside as well as in the cities,[52] thus "re-feudalising" the system by means of hereditary leaders. In the eyes of the gradually emerging reform movements with some kind of "middle class" habitus[53] such activities and events were mostly considered reprehensible while for the colonial masters they were illegal. After all, "official nationalism" required strict loyalty.

The new colonial education system and reforms

Parallel to these far-reaching economic, administrative and juridical reforms, a new education system suiting colonial interests was implemented. It was to be designed after the system in the colonial mother

[51] V.T. Oldenburg: *The making of colonial Lucknow, 1857–1877*, Princeton: PUP 1984, p. XXI.

[52] See Th. R. Metcalf: *The Aftermath of Revolt: India, 1857–70*, Princeton 1965, pp. 134ff.; C.A. Bayly: "Local Control in Indian Towns", in: *MAS* 5/4 (1971), pp. 289–311; F. Robinson: "Consultation and Control: The United Provinces' Government and its allies, 1860–1906", in: *MAS* 5/4 (1971), pp. 313–336.

[53] For the emerging social formations such as "middle class" in Lucknow between 1880 and 1930 see Sanjay Joshi: *Fractured Modernity. Making of a Middle Class in North India*, Delhi: OUP 2001. For literary and journalistic activities of these formations making Lucknow important again after 1857, see Ulrike Stark: *An Empire of Books: The Naval Kishore Press and the Diffusion of the Printed Word in Colonial India, 1858–1895*. New Delhi: Permanent Black 2008.

country whereby religion and its education was to be relegated to the private sphere. Again, this change did not occur without the support of the locals. The *Calcutta Madrasa*, for example, was to become the production centre for Muslim dignitaries in the sense of "intellectual compradors" who would help disseminate colonial systems and ideas. On July 20, 1860 Viscount Canning (1812–1862) was of the view that:

> The Mahomedans who had been educated there not only did not show any hostility to the Government during the period of the mutinies, but were better affected towards it than other members of the Mahomedan community...The aim of the Government when the College was founded was to enable the Mahomedans to acquire such an education as would qualify them for the various official posts to which they might reasonably aspire. A knowledge of Mahomedan Law, and a fair acquaintance with Arabic literature were considered in 1854 sufficient for this purpose; all dogmatical and abstruse disquisitions on science and religion, to which the older school of Muslim Teachers is prone, being set aside as unprofitable and beyond the scope of the Institution...most advantageous course will be to continue to act in the spirit of the reform of 1854.[54]

The institution was to become the ideal for further educational institutions and an important orientation point for religious scholars. The aim was to introduce a process of further secularisation, which was designed to serve British demands. Local groups were to participate herein and liaise between colonial power and local society. Since at this societal intersection there was an already-established elite able to make arrangements with the dynamic processes, the Europeans could hope for a fertile dissemination of English perceptions. After all, it had long been claimed that the educational standard was poor. In August 1871 a *Memorial* of the Muslim *National Muhammadan Association*, headed by the leading barrister at the *Bombay High Court* and leader of the Bohras, Badr al-Din Tayyibji (1844–1906), acknowledged the ostensibly poor state of local education by calling it decadent.[55] Providing legitimacy for change, he later added: "The backward condition of Muhammadan education in this country has, from the earliest days of British rule, attracted the attention of the Government of India. The question was examined at length by the Education Commission of 1882 and

[54] NAI, Home Dept. (educational) 2. July 1860, Nos. 1–8.
[55] See NAI, Private Papers Collection, *Badruddin Tayabji Papers*, No. 992.

the subject was again fully received in a big resolution issued by the Government of India in 1885."[56]

Following these statements, the British Crown showed keen interest in religious endowments (*waqf*) that had been the economic and ideological basis of local education.[57] Their stocktaking was followed by taking over some of them, which now were considered "permanent endowments", and which "should not be alienated by the trustees without the consent of Government".[58] Changes were to be implemented by the local governments. However, a uniform education reform in British India based among others on a policy vis-à-vis endowments was not possible, not the least because in several areas, like the Northwestern Provinces, Punjab and the Central Provinces, "Mussalman education...is by no means in a backward state."[59]

In the light of these plans, a considerable conflict potential developed, particularly as a result of the post-revolt policy. Muslim protestations demonstrated their increasing decline.[60] This Muslim protest met British interests of divide and rule, so that by means of the *Lord Mayo's Resolution* in 1871 Muslims were encouraged to organise themselves as Muslims and to seek concessions as a separate community. The space where the Muslim reform agenda was primarily developed and where the avant-garde of social and political movements of the Muslims were recruited was the *qasbah*. Hailing from these centres of traditional Islamic learning, the actors dramatically referred to new forms and methods of interaction and communication[61] by initially criticising their own traditionalism, paradigmatically reproduced in their system of teaching, i.e., the *dars-e nizami*. These groups constituted the broad Muslim public sphere, using forms of socialisation such as associations and media, in the context of an official nationalism.

The following process of political submission lasted from 1860 to 1935. The British Indian army was recruited from Punjab and segre-

---

[56] U.P. State Archives, Mahanagar, Lucknow, Gov. of U.P., Dept. of Education: *Muhammadan Education*: File No. 131/1913, p. 2.

[57] See G.C. Kozlowski: *Muslim endowments and society in British India*, Cambridge 1985.

[58] Regional Archives, U.P. Allahabad, Director of Education: File No. III-1 1886–87: "Control of Educational endowments" (Government Securities).

[59] Regional Archives, U.P. Allahabad, Director of Education: *Extract from the Proceedings of the Government of India in the Home Dept. (Education)*, Simla dated 15 July 1885, pp. 12f.

[60] Bayly: *Rulers*, pp. 357, 354–56, 455f., 190; also Cole: *Roots*, pp. 235, 285f.

[61] See Cole: *Roots*, pp. 287f.

gated according to castes and religions. Its major task was to secure the Northwest borders against Russia. Indian troops were also sent to Southeast Asia and East and South Africa and in 1914 even to Europe. All this was made possible through Indian taxpayers' money. These processes were introduced with the help of Muslim and Hindu groups, who, however, were deprived of climbing up the hierarchy of the colonial administration and who increasingly became alienated from the social environment that they themselves handed down. The introduction of local self-government did reduce state expenditures, for now local tax-payers had to pay for any improvements. But this at the same time supported political self-understanding, which became more and more conscious of its communal identity, following the motto: "no taxation without representation". How then, did differently situated Muslims articulate their interests in a system controlled by colonial power?

EXCURSUS

THE LANGUAGE ISSUE—URDU

Urdu today is among the most important languages in South Asia though academically it has lost ground. Its development seems contradictory: there are many—contesting—narratives surrounding its history, especially the term "urdu" and its literary origins.

Contemporary Urdu is comparatively young, an islamicated version of Hindustani, it boasts a rich literary tradition. It shares the grammatical structure and literary lineage with Hindi, and as such these are two languages with different scripts, as outlined by Christopher R. King.[1] Linguists agree that Urdu is rooted in a variety of languages like "Hindwi", "Hindi", or the toponyms "Dihlawi", "Gujri", "Dakani" or the way of talking like "Rekhta" (the mixed one with a few Persian words) and Khari Boli (the upright speech), sharing a linguistic and literary tradition with Hindi.[2] This led some scholars, the most prominent being Amrit Rai, to believe that Urdu is an offshoot of Hindi that received its cultural divide only through Wali of Aurangabad (Deccan) in 1702.[3]

Known as *zaban-e urdu-ye muʿalla-ye shahjahanabad* (the language of the exalted court of Shahjahanabad) it was confined to higher groups. Shortened to *zaban-e urdu-ye muʿalla*, then to *zaban-e urdu*, it finally came to *urdu* (literally: the court or campus). Though the word Urdu first appeared around 1780 in the first *diwan* of Mushafi (1750–1824), the language flourished when it became socially and linguistically very important, especially in its emancipation from the court language Persian from the eighteenth century onwards, though attempts at literary purification continued. It became a medium of communication among

[1] Chr. R. King: *One Language Two Scripts: The Hindi Movement in Nineteenth Century North India*, Oxford 1994.

[2] The linguistic context is elaborated by Shamsur Rahman Faruqi: "A Long History of Urdu Literary Culture, Part 1. Naming and Placing a Literary Culture", in: Sheldon Pollock (ed.): *Literary Cultures in History. Reconstructions from South Asia*, Delhi: OUP 2004, pp. 805–863.

[3] See Amrit Rai: *A House Divided: The Origin and Development of Hindi-Urdu*, Delhi: OUP 1990, who depicts Urdu as an artificial construct, a linguistic compromise and rather a conspiracy against a suggested and assumed linguistic unity. Quotation p. 101.

the royals and the wider population living in the Mughal encatchment areas, and the fledging princely states (compare Chap. 6 and 7).

Urdu's literary tradition is said to go back to Amir Khusraw (died 1325).[4] However, it is not easy to determine the beginnings of Urdu literature, as it came to be tied to "Muslim literature" and "Muslim literary tradition" thus making up an important pillar in Muslim cultural memory. Most "Muslim literature" in pre-modern times has been in Persian but literary tradition does not only comprise literature in Persian. Genres like *qasida, ghazal* and *mathnawi* were not confined to Muslims but also included Hindu poets "from the Persianising classes",[5] i.e. from elites. From the late pre-modern period, new types of popular lyric and poetry evolved. Both Muslim and non-Muslim authors composed *qissa*, the romance in indigenous languages.

The first of two theories about Urdu literature's beginnings claims that it started to flourish with Wali in Aurangabad (Deccan), bringing along a cultural change.[6] The second draws on the rise of Muslim dynasties in India,[7] recognising Urdu as a major element in the master narrative of the quest for Muslim self-understanding. Pre-modern Urdu is said to lack freshness as it borrowed too much from Persian[8] in terms of genres (*ghazal, qasida* and *marthiya*), grammatical structures, metaphors and words. Both theories seemed intertwined, however, but paradoxically the first notable tradition was founded in the South, Deccan and the Muslim courts of Bijapur and Golconda in the sixteenth and the seventeenth centuries. Dakkani-Urdu was confined to poetry, mostly panegyrics. After the conquest of the Mughals, poets of Deccan sought new patronage.[9] In Delhi the language of poetry was exclusively Persian. When Wali from Aurangabad came to Delhi's Mughal court, his Urdu poetry inspired even Persianised poets of the North like Hatim (1699–1781), who deliberately weeded out the composite Hindwi origin,[10] and Siraj al-Din ʿAli Khan-e Arzu (1689–1756), for his efforts to indigenise the language showed that poetry could also be composed in

[4] D.J. Matthews, C. Shackle, Sh. Husain (eds.): *Urdu Literature*, London: Urdu Markaz 1985, p. 20.

[5] David Gilmartin and Bruce B. Lawrence (eds.): *Beyond Turk and Hindu*, p. 56.

[6] Rai: *A House Divided*, pp. 226ff.

[7] Matthews et alii: *Urdu Literature*, p. 20.

[8] Muhammad Sadiq: *A History of Urdu Literature*, Delhi: OUP 1995, p. 15.

[9] Matthews et alii: *Urdu Literature*, p. 54.

[10] Vasudha Dalmia: *The Nationalization of Hindu Traditions. Bharatendu Harishchandra and Nineteeth-Century Banaras*, New Delhi: OUP 1996, p. 157.

Rekhta and *Dakkani*; moreover, he showed that the new mixed language can even surpass Persian in its ability of expressing metaphors and images.[11] This ambiguity can best be gauged from *Rekhti*, the feminine form of *Rekhta*, with its own—at times shameless—vocabulary of female convention due to sexual segregation.[12] In gendered opposition to *Rekhta* it is still used in Sufi songs.[13] As literary language it was used, however, exclusively by men, displaying the masculine imagination of female emotions, such as Nawwab Saʿadat Yar Khan Rangin (1756–1835), the classic of *Rekhti*.

Then emerged the phenomenon of the *ustad* (teacher)—*shagird* (pupil) relationship; the new literary codes of conduct and expression had to be specifically learnt. Emphasis was on the accuracy of language and issues of conduct were developed in literary gatherings, the *mushaʿiras*.[14] A more refined variation of Urdu is said to have been evolved by Hatim, who stressed the simplicity and purity of language.[15] He had a great impact on the next generation of Urdu poets in the eighteenth century, such as Mirza Jan-e-Janan Mazhar (1699–1781), Mir Taqi Mir (1722–1808), Mirza Muhammad Rafi Sauda (1713–1781), Khwaja Mir Dard (1721–1785) and Mir Hasan (1727–1786). Sauda, the leading satirist and panegyrist of Urdu literature during the eighteenth century and a student of Hatim, focused mainly on writing *qasidas*,[16] not only in praising, but also satirising nobility.[17] Mir Taqi Mir's topics, in contrast to the energetic poetry of Sauda, were rather introverted and poignant, but well-received by commoners. His *ghazals'* main characteristic was the poet depicting himself as the one suffering from love, caused by the beauty of a woman, who is in most cases indifferent or has fallen for someone else. Notwithstanding these classical genres, Mir

---

[11] Faruqi: "A Long History of Urdu", p. 848.

[12] Compare Gail Minault: "Other Voices, Other Rooms. The View from the Zenana', in: Nita Kumar (ed.): *Women as Subjects. South Asian Histories*, Calcutta, Stree, 1994, pp. 108–125; Carla Petievich: "*Rekhti.* Impersonating the Feminine in Urdu Poetry", in: *South Asia. The Journal of South Asian Studies*, Special Issue, Vol. XXIV (2001), pp. 75–90; short but excellent, Pernau: *Bürger mit Turban.*

[13] See Shemeem Burney Abbas: *The Female Voice in Sufi Ritual: Devotional Practices of Pakistan and India*, Austin: University of Texas Press 2002, esp. pp. 118f.

[14] C.M. Naim: "Poet-audience interaction at Urdu mushaʿiras", in: C. Shackle (ed.): *Urdu and Muslim South Asia; Studies in the honour of Ralph Russell*, London: SOAS 1989, pp. 167–173.

[15] He revised his first diwan and offered a simpler version. In some of his *ghazals* it becomes clear which parts or words he removed to simplify the written language.

[16] The *qasida* is not necessarily tied to certain topics. Its speciality is the overstated adulation of different topics, such as the beloved, nature or even religious figures.

[17] Matthews et alii: *Urdu Literature*, p. 67.

also criticised religious establishment and wrote an autobiography. In contrast, Khwaja Mir Dard's Sufi poetry reveals his pain about the political situation in Delhi while Mir Hasan excels in *mathnawi*. Yet, there was Nazir Akbarabadi (1740–1830), whose heroes were common men. These poets depicted Delhi's political, social and economic situation when the power centre gave way to decentralisation and new territorial states.

Lucknow became a competitor for patronising Urdu literature, and masters of Urdu poetry received support from Nawwab Asaf al-Daulah's court. This two-school theory offered a framework for Urdu critical tradition and many cultural, political and historical comforts.[18] Lucknow became a new Urdu centre because of Delhi's decline due to recurring invasions by the Marathas, Persians and Afghans and increasing impoverishment[19] which also was to become a major genre, the *shahr-e ashub* (shattering of the city). The nobility of Delhi migrated to Lucknow, among them Sauda and Mir.[20] The Nawwabs of Awadh, Shiʿis and patrons of Urdu literature and poetry, provided support for the *marthiya* genre in North India. Its purpose was to establish loyalty through rituals and devotionalism by commemorating the battle of Kerbala in 680.

During this time literary criticism flourished, namely in the form of memoirs, biographies and autobiographies. The compilation of anthologies of poetry (*bayad*) and biographical collections of poets and scholars (*tadhkirah*)—extending beyond the classical hagiographies—and of lexicons and encyclopaedia became popular. The three earliest (Persian) biographies of Urdu poets were written between 1752 and 1754.[21] But it was the colonial scholars who produced the first grammar of "Hindoostanee Language" in 1796: it was John Gilchrist, who later worked at Calcutta's Fort William College, to introduce works from various poets, in the mixed dialect called *Oordoo* (military camp). The British misconception of Urdu having evolved from Muslim army camp-markets was reproduced by Mir Amman Dihlawi, a British employee, in a prose romance, *Bagh o bahar* (Garden and spring), a translation of

---

[18] Frances W. Pritchett: "A Long History of Urdu Literary Culture, Part 2. Histories, Performances and Masters", in: Pollock (ed.): *Literary Cultures in History*, pp. 864–911, p. 878.

[19] Carla Petriovich: *Assembly of Rivals. Delhi, Lucknow and the Urdu Ghazal*, New Delhi 1992, pp. 26f.

[20] Matthews et alii: *Urdu Literature*, p. 81f.

[21] For some initial discussion on these issues see Jamal Malik: "Muslim Culture and Reform in 18th Century South Asia", in: *JRAS* 13:2 (2003), pp. 227–243.

Amir Khusraw's classic epic "Qissa Chahar Darwish", in 1803 at the Fort William College.[22]

In the nineteenth century the British directors of Fort William College approved Hindustani as the lingua franca suitable for literature, speech and prose and which could easily be learnt. In doing so the colonialists codified and standardised the languages and made script crucial as the indigenous knowledge could only be written in some script.[23] Subsequently the College published books but the main genre of interest was *ghazal*. Prose written at the college remained confined to the British and their native informants. One of the first Urdu *dastan*, the *Fasanah-ye 'Aja'ib* by Rajab 'Ali Beg Surur (1781–1867) was published in 1824 and became very famous. Thus Urdu poetry and Persian prose were popular among the literate people.[24] Besides, Muslim scholars and mystics—notably the activists around *Tariqah-ye Muhammadi*—played an influential role in developing Urdu prose. Translations of the Quran, the Bible (in Hindustani in 1741) and the New Testament (1814) were followed by mystical treatises. Urdu came to be identified with high Islam. Similar developments can be traced in Hindi standardised by religio-cultural actors to serve their notions of purification.[25]

Among Urdu writers of the nineteenth century the most prominent is Mirza Asad Allah Khan Ghalib (1797–1869), whose writings were highly influenced by the political circumstances, among others the upheaval of 1857. His letters in Persian and Urdu offer a rare insight into life in Delhi.[26] However, to establish the first Urdu novel with the coming of *Umrao Jan Ada*, a story about the career of a Lucknowi courtesan during the fall of that city, written by Mirza Muhammad Hadi Ruswa (1856–1931) in 1905, seems to be as questionable as ignoring Mir Taqi Mir's autobiographical account.

When in 1832 the vernacular—Urdu—was made the language of the court, the need for judicial translators arose, and when English replaced Persian as the official language in 1835, Urdu textbooks were needed. This in turn fostered many encyclopaedic and grammatical works. Urdu was thus supported by some European scholars of the Orient, such as

---

22 Faruqi: "A Long History of Urdu", p. 811.

23 For an excellent discussion of this process see Salil Misra: "Transition from the Syncretic to the Plural. The World of Hindi and Urdu", in: Malik and Reifeld (eds.): *Religious Pluralism*, pp. 268–298.

24 Pritchett: "A Long History of Urdu", p. 880f.

25 Dalmia: *Nationalization of Hindu Traditions*, p. 151.

26 Matthews et alii: *Urdu Literature*, p. 116f.

Felix Boutros (died 1863) a French Orientalist, who established Delhi College Vernacular Translation Society, Aloys Sprenger (1813–1893) and W.G. Leitner (died 1899), both leading scholars in their fields. Similarly, Urdu periodicals supported prose. Agha Hasan Musawi Amanat (1816–1859) could counter this development through his *Indra Sabha* (1843), but this drama became more popular in Europe because it satisfied the other side of orientalism, the romantic other.

After 1857 some Muslims turned towards Muslim discourses to bolster their presumably shattered Muslim identity. It is in this context that Sayyid Ahmad Khan (1817–1898) established the Urdu Defence Association. His most famous disciple was Altaf Husain Hali (1837–1914), who composed the *musaddas*, entitled "The Tide and Ebb of Islam", which was to become one of the most important literary works of the Aligarh movement. Similar developments can be traced in the Hindi/Nagari context when protagonists of both languages polemicised against each other to gain access to the cultural and economic capital guarded now by the British,[27] and to refine their respective Muslim and Hindu cultures. Therefore, official recognition was important.

Muslim-Hindu cooperation during the Khilafat movement could have reunited Urdu and Hindi, but the confessionalisation had already gone a long way. Muslim League and Hindu Mahasabha used the language issue for mobilising purposes, thus making language a component of national identity. With the Hindi-Urdu controversy, Urdu ultimately became communalised by urban, educational, skilled and hegemonic forces in the quest for jobs and access to the market.

Notwithstanding these identity issues, in the twentieth century Urdu literary culture developed a progressive attitude and focused particularly on socio-political issues. Poetry, novels, short stories and essays were the boulevards of the free-thinking idioms. The most popular modern poet was Muhammad Iqbal (1877–1938) who considered Islam as the guiding force. In his *Shikwa* (Complaint to God) he measured, like Hali, the past splendour of Islam, but he also went beyond dwelling on the past, while dealing with action, movement and development, and finally with the idea of an independent state for Muslims.[28]

---

[27] See King: *One Language, Two scripts*, p. 184, who elaborates on different allegations hurled against the two languages by Hindi and Urdu protagonists respectively.

[28] Matthews et alii: *Urdu Literature*, p. 145.

The rise of the Urdu short story spearheaded the establishment of the *Progressive Writers' Association* (*PWA*), which launched its first all-India meeting in 1936 under the chairmanship of Premchand (1880–1936), the doyen of social-realist fiction. Their initial anthology called *Angare* (Burning coals) (1932) dealt with issues of gender and religion, making use of new literary devices like interior monologue and stream of consciousness. This caused widespread protest from traditionalist quarters and British masters. Consequently, the anthology was banned. Internal ideological tensions soon split the movement.[29] Having a strong impact on Urdu, the movement of *adab islami*[30] and its predecessor, the *halqah-ye arbab-e dhauq* (Circle of Possessors of Good Taste) (1939), emerged in reaction to this new literature.

Among the *PWA* was the celebrated Saadat Hasan Manto (1912–1955), the Indian Kafka, whose descriptions of the partition in 1947 are well known. Another important figure was Faiz Ahmad Faiz (1910–1984), who is acknowledged as the utmost modern-day Urdu poet.[31] Even though Urdu became more and more tied to Muslim identity, popular Hindu writers also wrote in Urdu, like Krishan Chandar (1914–1977) and Rajindar Singh Bedi (1920–1987).

After partition Hindi became one of many official languages of India, Urdu the official lingua franca of Pakistan to help integrate the multi-ethnic and multi-lingual state, thus cementing the confessionalisation of the language issue. There have since been a number of initiatives to promote and standardise Urdu such as the Urdu Language Authority in Islamabad. Being the mother tongue of some 4%—basically *muhajirs* from Punjab and Bihar—Urdu had to compete with Bengali, Punjabi, Sindhi and Pashtu.

However, Urdu literature kept an important place in Indian society and culture. Through media, Urdu literature spread among people, even those who did not know its script. Today Urdu still is cultivated in centres such as Delhi, Lucknow and Haydarabad. And since the different states of India are governed according to the three-language

[29] Carlo Coppola (ed.): *Marxist Influences in South Asian Literature*, Vols. 1–2, Michigan: East Lansing 1974. Interestingly, the anthology was reprinted in Hindi only recently, but the controversial passages, e.g., those hinting at sex and religious abuses were omitted. Moreover, several important Persian and Arabic words were replaced by Sanskrit idioms.

[30] In *adab islami* man and his interaction with God are made of prime importance, criticising agnosticism and obscenity considered to be propagated by the *PWA*.

[31] Matthews et alii: *Urdu Literature*, pp. 169f.

formula, i.e. Hindi, English and a regional language, Urdu potentially can manage to survive in certain areas, though it has been made into a major issue in the context of Muslim identity. However, while Urdu publications are decreasing in number—because more and more Urdu-speakers turn to Hindi or English in India—the cultivation of Urdu continues also in the Gulf States, Europe and North America, due to migration.

In retrospect, this minoritisation of Urdu might serve the purpose to ghettoise Indian Muslims—who are often considered by Hindu nationalists to be un-loyal to India—and exclude them from participation in democratic processes. This in turn provokes Muslim activists to call for minority rights in which the language issue becomes a major vehicle in the communal mobilisation. Thus with the constitutionalisation of Hindi/Urdu, Urdu was reduced to a communal—marginal—language.

CHAPTER TEN

INSTITUTIONALISATION OF MUSLIM COMMUNITIES AND THE QUEST FOR A NEW ISLAMICITY (APPROX. 1860–1900)

The self-understanding of new social formations were to some extent influenced by European interaction, both in urban centres and in the *qasbahs*, as well as in other semi-urban regions, where their base had been built on a long cultural and intellectual tradition. Most of these formations were informed by the idea of the privileged position of Muslims. In an act of self-reflection, of an inward perspective so to speak, these new Muslim communities based their discourses on recent knowledge and experiences, particularly in the wake of the great upheaval of 1857, which had shattered Muslim rule and established firm colonial power, producing a serious crisis. They negotiated the new situation through a variety of forms and institutional patterns, which gradually became important vehicles of communication, be it for traditional Islamic learning and discourse, for treatises, pamphlets, newspapers, novels or even paintings. Their movements varied from "traditionalist" to "modernist", thereby expanding the semantics of *sharif*: the notion of *noble* as part of a (Mughal/Nawwabi) social group was enriched by the idea of *noble* as a moral quality, thus establishing distinction and distance from Mughal/Nawwabi concepts.[1] Appealing to changing *ashraf* clientele associations (*anjumans*) and assemblies (of believers) (*jama'a*), press and publishing houses in Calcutta, Bombay, Kanpur, Madras, or the famous Naval Kishore Press in Lucknow[2] became instrumental in establishing Muslim visibility in the public sphere. Eventually, in the formation of these socially and religiously competing communities, an evolving "middle class" used these media to adapt and adopt the new values, to reshape them and render local, i.e., transform into middle-class values, that which might have been perceived as foreign, and not only

[1] See Gail Minault: *Secluded Scholars. Women's Education and Muslim Social Reform in Colonial India*, Delhi 1998, pp. 4f. For a precise description of *sharif* culture, see David Lelyveld: *Aligarh's first Generation*, Princeton: PUP 1978, pp. 35–56.

[2] For Naval Kishore Press see Stark: *An Empire of Books*.

to respond to local educational and social needs, to champion reforms, found schools, and to foster public activity in the Muslim community. The foremost task was to juxtapose these institutions with "civility" in their quest for a new Islamicity, which went public, as it were, at times with Prophet Muhammad as the normative example, being the focal point of Muslim religious discourse. Some of these new identities still dominate Muslim public opinion in South Asia and beyond.

Incremental Muslim public: The "traditionalist" context

An early variation of this self-understanding of Muslims was the radical 'reformist' position taken by the movement called Ahl-e Hadith, which is said to have found its way to South Asia from Yemen from 1830s onwards, though the term Ahl-e Hadith seems first to have been used in 1864.[3] The movement found some of its activists in the Jihad-movement, most of whom quietened after 1857, while its reformism drew inspiration from Ibn Taymiyya (died 1328), Shah Wali Allah and the Yemenite scholar Muhammad al-Shaukani (1760–1834) in particular, who focused on the study of hadith to reform the judicial and social system. The Arabised Ahl-e Hadith refused to acknowledge any authority of legal schools (*madhahib*) and also the emerging modernism which had started rallying behind Sayyid Ahmad Khan (1817–1899) (see below). Instead, these hadith-based reformists claimed a purified religious Muhammadan life, the sunna, represented by authentic hadith, and rejected shared religious practices as well as pilgrimages connected to shrine cult and visits to the grave of the Prophet Muhammad which they consider as—heretical—innovation (*bid'a*). Yet, Sufism remained a form of ethical self-determination. In so doing Ahl-e Hadith showed clear ideological overlapping with Shah Wali Allah and Sayyid Ahmad Isma'il's iconoclasm, as they claimed to be their real heirs. At the same time *ijtihad* is allowed for members of the educated elite as well, rather than concentrating Islamic agency purely in the hands of ulama. Known as *ghair muqallid* (those who reject, even oppose, *taqlid*, which they consider a deviation from the sunna) these quietists found their

---

[3] It is very difficult to attach a certain founding date to this movement, because of its having different centres throughout South Asia.

social basis, primarily among trading communities and upper class Muslims from different regions, including Muslim notables, landholders and ulama, from whom they also obtained patronage by means of different intellectual and social networks. One of their leading personalities was the administrator and financier Siddiq Hasan Khan al-Qanauji (1832–1890), who married the powerful Begum of Bhopal, and who is said to have written many important books. The intellectual leadership was, however, provided by various emigrant scholars from Yemen, and Nadhir Husain (died 1902) from Delhi. ʿAbd al-Rahman Mubarikpuri (died 1935), who polemicised against the Hanafi school of law,[4] and Muhammad Ibrahim Arawi (died 1901), an early activist of the Nadwat al-ʿUlama (see below), tried to institutionalise the movement, among others, by establishing a number of religious schools. Later, Thana Allah Amritsari (died 1948), a prominent member of the Jamʿiyyat al-ʿUlama-ye Hind (see below) provided the movement with some structural elements by initiating All-India Conferences.[5]

Next to this rather urban, mercantile movement, the Hanafi movement at Deoband, a *qasbah* near Delhi, evolved in 1867. Like in the case of the Ahl-e Hadith, Deoband's protagonists were recruited to a great extent from the *ashraf*, such as Muhammad Qasim Nanautawi (1833–77) and Rashid Ahmad Gangohi (1829–1905).[6] They kept a certain degree of distance to the colonial regime, although a few found jobs in the civil service. The movement which eventually led to the establishment of the famous seminary in Deoband was intended to reform Muslim education and society from within, rather than adopting English education and the Western "infidel" culture, thereby contributing to the development of a new Urdu religious literature. The proven way to put this into practice was by means of rigorous training in transmitted sciences (*manqulat*), particularly the study of hadith, to acquire a common platform to safeguard the interests of Sunni Hanafi scholarship and to

[4] Muhammad Qasim Zaman: "Commentaries, Print and Patronage: "Hadith" and the Madrasas in Modern South Asia", in: *BSOAS* 62 (1999), pp. 60–81, p. 64.

[5] The movement has been analysed in quite some detail by Claudia Preckel: *Islamische Bildungsnetzwerke und Gelehrtenkultur im Indien des 19. Jahrhunderts: Muhammad Siddîq Hasan Khân (st. 1890) und die Entstehung der Ahl-e hadît Bewegung*, Bochum/Erfurt (Ph.D. Islamic Studies) 2005; and Martin Rixinger: *Sanāʾullāh Amritsarî (1868–1948) und die Ahl-i-Hadîs im Punjab unter britischer Herrschaft*, Würzburg: Ergon 2004; see also Brown: *Rethinking tradition*, pp. 27ff.

[6] For the Deobandi tradition, see Barbara D. Metcalf: *Islamic Revival in British India: Deoband 1860–1900*, Princeton 1982.

create scholars who would embody Islam. In doing so, they emphasised their affinity with the Delhi tradition and the "Muhammadan Path". On the other hand, they reformed the system of education along the lines of the *Delhi College*, introducing a fixed curriculum, system of examinations and certificate.[7] Soon the Deobandis spread a net of affiliated *madrasas*, the financial base of which was to be constituted by individual donors, rather than traditional *waqf* institutions. Qasim Nanautawi opined in one of his eight principles:

> So long as the Madrasah does not have any regular and definite source of income, it will continue to exist—Inshâʾ Allâh, provided there is an honest reliance on and faith in His mercy and compassion; and when it comes to possess a definite source of income, e.g., some substantial property in the form of land or factory or a promise of permanent donations from some rich person of honest intentions, then it appears the Madrasah will be divested of the feelings of fear and hope—a perennial source of submission to the will of Allâh—and, with this, will be deprived of the 'hidden' source of unfailing assistance; and its workers will start quarrelling amongst themselves. Therefore, in matters of income and constructions there should always remain a certain lack of certainty of means.[8]

Graduates of the *madrasa* disseminated Deobandi thoughts as far as Punjab, Northwestern Frontier Province, Afghanistan and Bengal. Beside its educational function, many *fatwas* on questions of proper religious practise were issued and in fact published by a proper *fatwa* department. Soon the movement entered Indian politics (see below). Both movements, the Ahl-e Hadith and the Deobandis, attempted to legitimise the new social realities within the framework of Islamic world-views more or less by addressing the "traditional" sector rather than the

[7] It is debateable whether these institutional and organisational features alone marked the secularisation in Muslim learning, as some scholars have pointed out. As we have noted already for the eighteenth century, at least initial forms of secularisation by means of diversification in the field of religious and quasi-religious establishment and some sort of division of labour had been introduced in the wake of the political decline of the Mughal Empire and regionalisation of imperial culture. A proper degree of secularisation in the field of Muslim educational and political thought presupposes elaborated in-depth studies of the texts taught in the *madrasas*. These studies are, however, still to be done. See also the interesting discussion by Muhammad Qasim Zaman: "Modernity and Religious Change in South Asian Islam", in: *JRAS* Third Series 14/3 (2004), pp. 253–263.

[8] As quoted in Ziya-ul-Hassan Faruqi: *The Deoband School and the Demand for Pakistan*, Lahore 1963, p. 26.

colonial, though there was societal overlapping. Their vehicles of articulation were theology and the sciences of hadith in particular.

The Islamic discourse was complemented by a third important group: the Hanafi *Ahl al-Sunna wa al-Jamaʿa* (The people of the tradition of the Prophet and the Community), also called *Barelwis*, after Bareilly, the birthplace of their central figure Ahmad Rida Khan (1855–1922).[9] He was not only an acclaimed master of religious poetry in praise of Prophet Muhammad (*naʿt*) but was also famous for his many *fatwas* issued in response to questions posed by Muslims from all parts of the country. The Barelwis thus claimed to have received questions from outside India such as the Haramain in Arabia, but many queries seemed to have been fabricated to provide legitimacy for Ahmad Rida Khan by well-known Hijazian scholars who sympathised with his views. In this way the judicial ground was provided to the Barelwi polemics against other schools of thought such as the Deobandis and the Nadwis in particular (see below). The movement was primarily active in the agrarian society of Northern India. While the scripturalists (Deobandis and Ahl-e Hadith) were and still are inclined to the Naqshbandi order and appreciated the idea of the "unity of testimony" as propagated by Ahmad Sirhindi (1564–1624), the Barelwis tend towards the Qadiriyya and towards popular Indian interpretations of Ibn Arabi's complex philosophical idea of "unity of being". They attach great importance to the idea of a living Prophet Muhammad, who possesses knowledge of the unseen (*ʿilm al-ghaib*) and is omnipresent, being invested with God's pre-eminent light. Barelwis organise and take part in popular festivals, and consider themselves true Sunnis (Ahl al-Sunna wa al-Jamaʿa), their ritual practice being centred on Sufi shrines, particularly the periodic observance of the death anniversaries (*ʿurs*) of the founder of the Qadiri order, Shaikh ʿAbd al-Qadir Jilani Baghdadi (died 1166). They claim that individual believers need the Prophet's intercession with God if they hope for His forgiveness. Yet, both Deobandis and Barelwis seem to be safeguarding their Hanafite tradition and, thus, are an explicit rejection of Ahl-e Hadith.

According to S. ʿAbd al-Hayy (died 1961), who had developed some ideas about the reform periods of the syllabus, this era marked the fifth

---

[9] The Barelwi movement has been portrayed by Usha Sanyal: *Devotional Islam and Politics in British India: Ahmad Reza Khan Barelwi and his Movement 1870–1920*, Delhi 1996.

phase of Islamic learning. Apparently, this period was characterised by an increase in the number of commentaries, glosses and meta-glosses evolving in a culture of interpretation which—as has been argued by both colonialists and urban Muslim reformers—had ossified and traditionalised Islamic education and thus brought the stream of tradition to a halt.[10] Orientations towards law, the tradition of the prophet, and towards Sufism and folk-religious practices define the various groups, the proponents of which exercise influence over different regional, social and sometimes even linguistic bases. They differ on issues of doctrine such as *taqlid*, *tasawwuf* and the definition of innovation (*bid'a*). Common to all these *ashraf* groups was that they did not in the first place aspire for political leadership. But all of them postulated reforms of religious education while the emulation of sunna and hadith—which had become a decisively useful means of safeguarding Muslim identities—was paramount by way of pious action in order to re-establish the cultural and political hegemony of Muslim power. Thus, the contest over Islamic agency in the form of dogmatic debates takes place particularly between Deobandis, Barelwis, and Ahl-e Hadith. Presently, however, the inner-Islamic conflicts fuelled by them are taking on violent forms, due to lack of national integration, particularly in contemporary Pakistan.

Meanwhile, the expanding and complex colonial society had increasingly fostered intellectual exchange with local cultures. The bilingual intelligentsia, which emerged out of this oscillating process between different, at times also overlapping societal sectors, i.e., the colonial and the traditional, consisted of government bureaucrats, lawyers, and especially intellectuals who acquired knowledge and social status through traditional and non-traditional channels, such as English education. And there were also *ta'alluqdars*—more or less representatives of the re-established and loyal aristocracy—who considered themselves to be "an enlightened aristocracy".[11] They all constituted the urbane elite

[10] On the evolution of interpretative culture and the stream of tradition in the context of cultural memory compare the illuminating ideas by Assmann: *Das kulturelle Gedächtnis*, pp. 93ff. On the other hand, these additions provided the tradition, i.e., the major texts, with perennial re-reading and in this way reflected the discourses in changing circumstances. It seems therefore most important that these commentaries, glosses and super-glosses on the major texts be studied carefully with a fair amount of hermeneutical expertise. For a preliminary assessment see Zaman: "Commentaries, Print and Patronage".

[11] Metcalf: *Land*, pp. 318–326.

that was but seldom regarded as belonging to the scholarly group in the narrow sense but who represented throughout the *ashraf* culture of the *qasbahs*, where they still possessed landed property. Due to their being socially embedded in the colonial context this elite derived its identity from here, however. Soon they began to increasingly claim importance to define *modernity* (*jadidiyyat*) and *tradition* (*riwayat*), just in line with their colonial masters; thus, they equated colonial society with advancement, dynamism and development, while autochthonous society was considered stagnant, conservative and barbaric. Stereotypical colonial dichotomies were adopted to play a decisive role in the future. Having acquired eminence through interaction with colonial rule, this Muslim avant-garde saw itself as the only legitimate group to replace the conventional scholarship and to establish civility—*sharif* hood as it were.

"Modernist" fora

One possibility to overcome the tension between what was perceived as modernity and tradition was to establish an inwardly directed discourse, just as the reformist Deobandis or the Barelwis did. Reciprocating to this "traditionalist" and inward-looking discourse, an explicitly "modernist", outwardly directed discourse emerged, though there were interactions and reciprocities at various points, when interaction took place through a variety of channels of understanding and reciprocal obligation, built on informal personal networks. This adjustment with the colonial system was attempted by different new philanthropical organisations such as the Muslim *National Muhammadan Association*, under the leadership of Badr al-Din Tayyibji (1844–1906); the Bengali magistrate ʿAbd al-Latif (1828–1893) called for the *Mahommedan Literary and Scientific Society* in Calcutta, and Amir ʿAli (1849–1928), the brilliant lawyer and religious thinker of Calcutta, who was ambivalent toward Western Christian civilisation, headed the *Central National Mahommedan Association* in 1877.[12] However, the most influential cultural articulation of Muslim elites and intellectuals rather than ulama and Sufis was the one centred on

[12] For an excellent discussion on philanthropic organisations in the context of identity formations see Pernau: *Bürger im Turban*.

Sayyid Ahmad Khan (1817–1899),[13] who, in 1863 founded the *Aligarh Scientific Society* with a reform agenda. But on his return from England in 1869/70 Sayyid Ahmad was completely convinced of European superiority. In 1870 he founded the *Committee for the Better Diffusion and Advancement of Learning amongst the Muhammadans of India* in Varanasi, and postulated unconditional "civil servant-like" behaviour, through which alone the self-perceived Muslim malaise was to be overcome. By this time, colonial encroachment of state administration and civil society was paralleled by the attempt to integrate Indians into Municipal Councils, nominated and co-opted, and later elected. This politics of *self-government* was, however, not designed to provide political participation or strengthen the institutions of self-government but to nominate their loyalists. At the same time groups of Hindus, primarily those having a literate tradition, were quick to acquire new educational opportunities offered by the British. Bengal was first to do so, also because Ram Mohan Roy started a movement against Sati and emphasised "modern" English education as far back as the early nineteenth century. With their increase in numbers in the field of education and representation in the expanding colonial sector, Muslims felt threatened and left out. Sayyid Ahmad articulated their fears when he opined that their own minority ("we") had to be protected against the dominant majority of the Hindu "other", a concept also used in Mughal times.[14] This discourse did not necessarily imply sowing the seeds for the "Two Nations Theory" later espoused by the *All India Muslim League* which was founded in 1906 (for the League see Chap. 11). Rather, his line was tactical and can be looked at in the context of the loss of 1857.[15] Altaf Husain Hali (1837–1914), one of the close associates of Sayyid Ahmad Khan at Aligarh, biographer of Mirza Ghalib, literary critic and a member of the Muslim elite aptly put down this Muslim fear in his elegy "*The Flow and Ebb of Islam*" (1879).[16] Khan's loyalty earned him colonial respect so that with the help of the British he set up the

[13] See Lelyveld: *Aligarh's first Generation*; S.M. Tonki: *Aligarh and Jamia; Fight for National Education System*, New Delhi 1983; Chr.W. Troll: *Sayyid Ahmad Khan: A Reinterpretation of Muslim Theology*, Oxford 1979; A. Ahmad/G.E. v. Grunebaum (ed.): *Muslim Self-Statement in India and Pakistan 1857–1968*, Wiesbaden 1970, pp. 25ff.

[14] The myth of Muslim backwardness was ontologised by W.W. Hunter (*The Indian Musalmans*, 1871), whose information in major part was meant to be applicable to Bengal; but Muslim intellectuals and nationalists generalised this information.

[15] Scholars from Aligarh usually focus on the secular nature of Sayyid Ahmad Khan; see for example K.A. Nizami: *Secular Tradition at AMU*, Aligarh 1992.

[16] See Altaf Husain Hali: *Musaddas. The Flow and Ebb of Islam*, translated and with a critical introduction by Christopher Shackle and Javed Majeed, Delhi: OUP 1997.

Mohammedan Anglo-Oriental College at Aligarh in 1876 (which received its charter as a university in 1920 only), at a time when widespread agitations were demanding the Indianisation of the Civil Service the higher ranks of which were still inaccessible to Indians.

Embedded in mystical tradition, notably the Naqshbandiyya-Mujaddidiyya and *Tariqah-ye Muhammadi* and dedicated to the writings of Shah Wali Allah, the reformer of Aligarh launched his well-known Urdu-journal, *Tahdhib al-Akhlaq* (The Refinement of Morals) in 1870, reminiscent of Ibn Miskawayh's (died 1030) *Tahdhib al-Akhlaq*. Indeed, Ibn Miskawayh, like Sayyid Ahmad Khan, had given prime importance to the intellect as a means to attaining morality and knowledge of the sublime. *The Muhammadan Social Reformer*, as the English rendering of the journal was called, became the promoter of Urdu as a scientific language. But *Tahdhib al-Akhlaq* not only stood for sufic endeavour, *via purgativa*, and a rational approach to the moral content of prophetic tradition. In the first place, this polishing of manners was to provide for an accommodation and to demonstrate the compatibility of European education and rationalist thinking with the tradition of Islam. The equation of the "word of God" with the "work of God" was his credo in the quest for both civility and Islamicity. Thus he reinterpreted Islamic theology in terms of dynamic evolutionism and scientism, thereby arguing against traditionarians such as Deobandis, his ardent enemies who called him pejoratively a naturalist (*nechari*), and he was severely refuted by Jamal al-Din al-Afghani (1838–1887), the doyen of what has been called pan-Islam, who considered Khan a tool of British imperialism.[17]

S. Ahmad Khan was one of the first to question the content and authenticity of hadith. In response to western orientalists' challenging the authenticity of hadith—such as William Muir (1819–1905)—he called for new scientific approaches. In doing so he assigned the method of biblical criticism to hadith, thereby demythologising Muhammad's life. The Quran only was the ultimate source; the Prophet was functionally reassessed as a normative model for human behaviour.[18] This stand was taken up by Chiragh ʿAli (1844–1895) and later radicalised by

---

[17] For al-Afghani, who disguised his Shiʿite heritage in order to appeal to the larger—Sunnite—universe, and his criticism of Ahmad Khan see Nikki R. Keddie: *An Islamic Response to Imperialism: Political and Religious Writing of Sayyid Jamal al-Din "al-Afghani"*, Berkeley: UCP 1968; Nikki R. Keddie: *Sayyid Jamâl ad-Dîn 'al Afghânî'; a political biography*, Berkeley: UCP 1972.

[18] Compare Brown: *Rethinking tradition*, pp. 32–37, 65, passim.

Ahl-e Qur'an (see Chap. 12). Certainly, the endeavour to sacrifice sunna at the altar of rationalism was part of Khan's historiography and new historical consciousness vis-à-vis colonial criticism, which he passionately pursued. Thus, he can be regarded one of the founders of historiography in modern Urdu, which was further developed by the Shi'ite judge Amir 'Ali and Shibli Nu'mani (1857–1915). In his attempt to reform he was joined by many other scholars such as Chiragh 'Ali who wrote *A Critical exposition of the popular Jihad* (Calcutta 1885) to underline Islam's pacifism, and also introduced new approaches to Islamic law.[19] The movement initiated by the loyal Sayyid Ahmad Khan transmuted into the vanguard of politicised Muslims after his death and is believed to have become "the source of modernist and rational thinking among the Muslim elite and at the same time provided the catalyst for latter day Muslim political 'separatism' and 'communalism'."[20] And it also raised the question of religious authority.

In 1870s this blend of piety, mysticism, rationalism, and new habitus did appeal to articulated groups having access to colonial media, for the Muslim avant-garde perceived the emerging Hindu nationalism as a threat to their status. Nationalism took different forms, such as that of Hindus increasingly demanding the implementation of Hindi and the abolition of cow slaughter. The appeals of Muslim minorities were, therefore, appreciated by the British who offered some concessions, for in this way the evolving nationalism dominated by Hindus could be balanced. While in the middle of the nineteenth century the British had been critical about Muslims, now they could hope that Muslims would seek their support against the Hindu majority and thus be loyal. Sayyid Ahmad Khan was the one who had called for loyalty and it is in this context that the British supported the Aligarh movement, which much later became the Aligarh Muslim University.

However, restrictive colonial measures such as the introduction of the *Vernacular Press Act* 1878[21] by the conservative Viceroy Lord Lytton (Viceroy of India 1876–1880) did not prevent loyal Indians from arguing for some liberalisation of colonial policy. When the idea of giving more rights to "Indian subjects" emerged, the liberal Viceroy Lord

---

[19] For Chiragh 'Ali see Ahmad and v. Grunebaum (eds.): *Muslim Self-Statement*, pp. 5, 49ff.; Hardy: *The Muslims of British India*, pp. 112–114.

[20] Ayesha Jalal in Sugata Bose and Ayesha Jalal (eds.): *Nationalism, Democracy and Development. State and Politics in India*, Delhi: OUP 1997, p. 82.

[21] Sadhan Bose Nemai: "The Vernacular Press Act (1878) and Indian Nationalism", in: *Bengal, Past and Present* XCVII/2 (1978), pp. 115–127.

Ripon announced the *Ilbert Bill* in 1883, enabling Indian judges to issue verdicts about Europeans suggesting the equality of Indian ability.[22] This caused a storm of protest among Europeans living in India, and eventually had to be annulled. At the same time, a new generation of liberal nationalists from the educated elite became increasingly vocal. They found a forum in the journal *Voice of India*, established in 1883.

Striking a balance

As the Aligarh movement was not able to integrate the intellectuals, leaving out mystics and ulama, other Muslim forces began to form an alternative loyal interest group. In doing so they referred to the reconstruction of the early Islamic era, similar to contemporary reformers in the Arab world such as Syria and particularly Egypt. For their ideas they utilised print media in the vernaculars and in this way they continued publishing religious pamphlets and tracts, increasingly undermining the authority of traditional dignitaries because, according to them, proper Islamic behaviour was possible now without them and was in any case accessible to everyone. They began to determine the Islamic discourse, but found themselves in a normative dilemma between their tradition and the colonial. This tension was aptly expressed by the satirist Sayyid Akbar Husain Illahabadi (1846–1921):

> Our belly keeps us working with the clerks—Our heart is with the Persians and the Turks

His critique of the Anglicisation of Indian and Muslim education and Western civilisation in general, however, did not deter him from sending his son to London for higher education! It is also entirely clear that such a tension could hardly trouble a low-caste Muslim for whom the glory of Turks and Persians meant little.

The background of the Muslim reform was, among other things, the ongoing discussion on *dars-e nizami* which was by now—approx. 150 years later—burdened with books on logic and *usul al-fiqh*, showing the

[22] For the *Ilbert Bill* see Chandrika Kaul: "England and India: The Ilbert Bill, 1883: A case study of the metropolitan press", in: *IESHR* 30 (1993), pp. 413–436; Mrinalini Sinha: "'Chathams, Pitts and Gladstones in Petticoats': The Politics of Gender and Race in the Ilbert Bill Controversy, 1883–1884", in: Nupur Chaudhuri and Margaret Strobel (eds.): *Western Women and Imperialism: Complicity and Resistance*, Bloomington and Indianapolis: Indiana Univ. Press 1992.

interdependence of the study of law and centralised state power. But in doing so, the reformers considered loyalty to be a very great virtue, similar to many Salafis in Egypt, in order to safeguard the influence of their own group in a colonial urban culture. It is therefore characteristic that in 1892 an Indian *Deputy Collector* in the "Manchester of the East", i.e. Kanpur, demanded the establishment of the "Council of (Islamic) scholars" (Nadwat al-ʿUlama). This happened at a time when the *Council Act of 1892* secured colonial import and export interests,[23] thereby denying the indigenous chamber members the right to vote—because election was considered to be incompatible with oriental spirit. The Nadwa was aimed at embodying this desire for reform, and intended to find new ways of expressing knowledge, organisation and literature in a new environment and at the same time to serve as a stabilising and integrating force, ensuring political loyalty. By means of a legal institution and a college, social service and missionary activities, voluntary organisations and publication of a journal, the Nadwis tried to administer their appeal to "solidarity traditionalism", i.e., the deliberate use of solidarity-giving elements at the cost of discriminating elements. In this attempt, Urdu served as the common language even in the academic discourse for a little while. Some Nadwa members, like Shibli Nuʿmani showed some profound parallels to Egyptian Salafis, such as the *al-Manar* group around Rashid Rida (1865–1935). The Indian-Arab affinity was further developed by Shibli's most famous student, Sayyid Sulaiman Nadwi (1884–1953).[24]

The Nadwat al-ʿUlama was a product of the colonial system. Their aim—the stabilisation of imperial unity—was reflected in the new image of Islam the council members created themselves. Being purely religious was not enough; what was required was "useful" education. By way of a profound reform of "backward" *qasbahs*, British power was to reach areas hitherto untouched. For this purpose, however, the Nadwa had to rely on the help of further traditionalist scholars, who also had access to sufi orders, especially the popular Naqshbandiyya. Thus after a short phase of inner reform under Shibli Nuʿmani and after the Khilafat movement of 1919–24 (see Chap. 11), these traditionalists came back to the helm.

All these fora accelerated Muslim consciousness thereby increasing dissemination of political issues on a local level through the vernacular

---

[23] For the *Council Act* see Madhvi Yasin: "The Indian Councils Act of 1892: An Analytical Study", in: *JIH* 55 (1977), pp. 255–264.

[24] On the Nadwa see Malik: *Gelehrtenkultur*.

press, by public oratory and religious sermons in local mosques. In this way they not only tried to bring the *religious* that had been rendered *private* since colonial intervention back to the public but also provoked tensions among traditional Muslim and Hindu groups pleading for yet more political participation.

A revised role of historiography was important in creating a new Muslim consciousness. The case of Sayyid Ahmad Khan has been mentioned. Shibli was another major force in re-establishing Muslimhood. He can be regarded as the founder and the pioneering practitioner of the critical Islamic historiography in Urdu. Having been active in the Aligarh movement, Shibli was also influenced by Thomas Arnold (died 1930) who had been teaching there and wrote *The Preaching of Islam* (Aligarh 1896) arguing that Islam spread by means of missionary efforts rather than by military conquest. At the core of the efforts of Shibli stood the working out of a new philosophical theology (*ʿilm al-kalam*) following Ibn Rushd (1126–1198) who, during his time, had rejected any contradiction between the revealed truth and the truth of rationality and who played an important role in promoting the case of *salafi* reformers.[25] Moreover, the knowledge of English was considered to be the only way to acquire recent knowledge which was necessary to reform Muslim historical writing. Various places and mainly the recently established Nadwat al-ʿUlama offered patronage for Shibli's efforts for a while. Shortly before his death he founded the *Dar al-Musannifin* in Azamgarh. One of his big projects was a critical history of Persian poetry in five volumes (*Shiʿr al-ʿajam*), which is considered to be a standard work even today. In his planned encyclopaedia of Islamic history he wanted to link secular and Islamic approaches. Similar to the Salafiyya movement, the reconstruction of the Golden Age of the Prophet Muhammad and the four caliphs was of central importance to him, as only by creatively adopting these role models could contemporary Muslims, who had moved away from the right path, attain a new and better life. History for him therefore served as moral lesson and as a means to social progress. Inspired by the series "Heroes of the Nations" in contemporary England, he started the series "Heroes in Islam" writing several biographies.[26] The historical method, according

---

[25] Troll: *Sayyid Ahmad Khan*, pp. 169f., 199.

[26] Texts by Sayyid Ahmad Khan and Shibli Nu'mani, introduced and translated by Jamal Malik, in: Michael Gottlob (ed.): *Historical Thinking in South Asia. A Handbook of Sources from Colonial Times to the Present*, New Delhi 2003, pp. 124–127, 134–139.

to Shibli, consisted of a synthesis of traditional Islamic sciences like chronicles and hagiographies on the one hand and Western objective analysis on the other, an approach elaborated in the introduction of his *al-Faruq*, published in 1898.

Politicisation of Islam

All these institutional and intellectual developments took place in a colonialised environment. They eventually had an impact on the national movement, as they evolved in the Khilafat struggle influenced among others by al-Afghani, the famous Muslim activist who visited India in the 1850s and 1860s. However, nationalism as prescribed by the British definitely could not allow a democratic progress, for India's large agrarian society was governed by remote control from above, as it were. This was incompatible with a democratic process.[27] The Anglicisation and growing desire for participation, especially in the Indian Civil Service, led to further frustration. Indian voices had to articulate their interests from a solid platform. But none of the known centres, neither Deoband and Farangi Mahall,[28] nor Aligarh and Nadwat al-ʿUlama, or any of the diverse Hindu organisations, were in a position to serve as a common platform. Moreover, the *Ilbert Bill Controversy* 1883–1884 showed that a nationally organised mobilisation had some positive effects.

Therefore, the *Indian National Congress* founded in 1885 was designed to take up the task. The Congress was supported financially and intellectually by A.O. Hume (1829–1912), a retired British Indian Civil Service officer, and founded by English-educated Indians including a few economic magnates in Bombay—where industrial development had taken place. The Congress was mostly manned by middle-class Hindus, who "moderately" argued for greater participation and representation in British-Indian politics. This in turn supported the development of journalism and of a strong middle class that gradually became

---

[27] Rothermund in Kulke/Rothermund: *A History of India*, p. 270.

[28] They still yielded considerable influence over a well-functioning press and extensive book markets. The "Jewels of Paradise" (Bihishti Zewar) written by the famous Deobandi scholar, Ashraf ʿAli Thanawi, became an authoritative guide to behaviour, politeness, and etiquette for middle-class women and is the most popular reading material in South Asia even today. Cp. B.D. Metcalf: *Perfecting Women*, Berkeley 1991.

"extremist" and increasingly called for more rights. Scholars of the powerful Deobandi tradition welcomed the founding of Congress and the spirit of co-operation between Muslims and Hindus in secular matters (*muʿamalat-e dunyawi*). In this regard the leading Deobandi Rashid Ahmad Gangohi gave a statement in 1888, in which, however, the idea of Islamic superiority was maintained:

> If Hindus and Muslims go mutually into an economic transaction which neither harms religion nor contradicts Shariʿa, and the problem of interest or invalid sale does not appear, then the transaction is permissible and legal. But no contact should be held with Sayyid Ahmad Khan[29]...and one should establish contacts with Hindus. However, the contact is prohibited if Shariʿa is ignored, or Muslims are weakened, and Hindus are strengthened.[30]

This statement points towards economic issues that were quite important for the Muslims, due to the decline in their position after 1857, especially in trade, commerce, and banking; many leading Muslim scholars had migrated to Arabia, whereas Hindus adapted more quickly to the new order and, therefore, seized profitable positions. However, Sayyid Ahmad Khan, to the contrary, rejected the Congress as a mere Hindu institution. Instead, he demanded representation exclusively for Muslims and in this context he and several colleagues founded the *Muhammadan Anglo Oriental Defence Association* in 1893. In doing so, he seemed to contribute to confessional tensions.

In contrast, during the initial phase of the Aligarh College, Sayyid Ahmad Khan had spoken of Hindus and Muslims being the two eyes of mother India, partly because the College was financed by Hindu landlords. He turned away from the Hindus, because he and his colleagues, such as the novelist Deputy Nazir Ahmad (1836–1912), preferred moral and educational reforms in the Muslim quest for civility rather than constitutional and elite politics of reform of the Congress, which eventually would come to be dominated by Hindus.[31] In doing

---

[29] Deoband attacked Sayyid Ahmad Khan's exclusive standpoint since he had questioned the superiority of the Islamic scholars, and had rationalised religious options in his *Principles of Exegesis*. For the debate between the Deoband and Aligarh schools, cp. Ahmed et al. (eds.): *Muslim Self-Statement*, pp. 66ff.

[30] Sayyid Muhammad Miyan: *ʿUlama-ye haqq awr un ke mujahidanah karname*, Delhi 1975, p. 101.

[31] See Nazir Ahmad: *The Son of the Moment*, translated by Mohammed Zakir, Haydarabad: Orient Longman 2002.

so, these Muslim scholars discursively maintained collective categories of solidarity which required group compulsion and loyalty as well as friend-foe identification. Apart from this identity-political reform-cum-demographic argument, one could argue that Sayyid Ahmad Khan himself could not de-class or de-ashrafite himself, remaining the factional leader of the fledgling Muslim service class whose chances were intrinsically connected with the colonial British Raj. The incipient Hindu middle class had done the same in their outright denunciation of the revolt of 1857. As a rule, middle classes have looked for strong state support throughout their history; this includes middle class in Europe. Thus it was in the interest of this class to remain aloof from the rising tide of nationalism championed by the Congress. Sayyid Ahmad, therefore, should not be made responsible for 'creating' the feeling of insecurity among Muslims. He was merely articulating their life chance positions. Certainly he was trapped within his own class position and on this he cannot be faulted. But he seemed also fully convinced of the Ashrafite position—in terms of *sharif* as a moral quality and as part of a social group—that God had entrusted matter of knowledge and guidance to the higher castes only and thus they were the natural leaders of the community, as is exemplified by his comments on Muslim weavers (*julahas*) who had the temerity to participate in the 1857 revolt. Thus, it was not only the feeling of insecurity but also the fact that the Congress was increasingly highlighting the plight of the low-born (*ridhalah*) rather than the high-born (*ruasa*) which made him uncomfortable with the emerging national movement.

Thus the emerging Hindu nationalism came to stand diametrically opposed to the different loyal fora of Muslim elites, who as representatives of Muslim interests became identity-politicians in their formulation of common concerns. At the insistance of the Indians, the British were forced to make the first concession in the form of the *Council Act* of 1892. This Act provided a very limited right to Indian representation in provincial legislatures and the Imperial Legislative Council, thereby enhancing the legitimacy of British rule. But the Act alarmed the Muslim elites, since under no circumstances would they go for democratic representation, insisting rather on parity. This intensified animosity between the representatives of both religious communities, especially between urban Muslims and Hindu landowners and traders. Other religious communities such as Christians, Jains, Sikhs and also the Untouchables added to the communalising tensions. The *Hindi-Urdu controversy* rendering both languages icons of religious identity (around 1900) and the prohibition of cow-slaughter by the colonial masters saw the Muslim avant-gardes calling for the rights of Muslims by founding their own organisations: the *Urdu Defence Association* in 1900 (which became the *Anjuman-e tarraqi-ye Urdu* in 1903),[32] the *Muhammadan Political Association* in 1903 and *All-India Muslim League* in 1906 (see Chap. 11), while all the time referring seriously to the axiomatic superior position of Islam in India, so plausible for them.[33] The colonial masters could therefore legitimately assume that some Muslim groups continued to seek their support against the Hindu majority, such as the Nadwis, Aligarhis and the *Muslim League.* On the other hand, Ahmad Rida Khan (Barelwi) opposed these movements as well as any anti-British movement—though he was not particularly pro-British. His argument was that the British did not interfere in the internal religious affairs of Muslims, though his social base of peasants also suffered due to British economic policies. Whether this indifference had to do with the control of shrines and its relationship with the state is open to question. In contrast, the majority of traditional Islamic scholars, such as Deoband, and members of the Ahl-e Hadith demanded a peaceful coexistence with Hindus and cooperation with Congress, while the Muslim League could reap the harvest for its own politics at a time when demand for 'Pakistan' became inevitable and Sir Sayyid was no more. The formation of religious communities with formal institutionalised patterns clearly hinted at internal modernisation processes of religious institutions. Thus, colonial reforms and a state of

[32] The language Hindi, as it emerged at the close of the nineteenth century, is based on the grammar of Urdu. It differs from Urdu in the form of script and degree of-sanskritisation; Urdu being rich in Arabic and Persian loanwords. The controversy particularly reflected the already existent economic competition between the two religious communities. Thus the controversy became religiously laden. Christopher King: *One Language Two Scripts: The Hindi Movement in Nineteenth Century North India*, Bombay: OUP 1994; Salil Misra: "Transition from the Syncretic to the Plural. The World of Hindi and Urdu", in: Malik and Reifeld (eds.): *Religious Pluralism*, pp. 268–298; Shamsur Rahman Faruqi: *Early Urdu. Literary Culture and History*, Delhi: OUP 2001; Amrit Rai: *A House Divided. The Origin and Development of Hindi/Hindavi*, Delhi: OUP 1984. For a regional study see K. Dittmer: *Die indischen Muslims und die Hindi-Urdu-Kontroverse in den United Provinces*, Wiesbaden 1972.

[33] For a summary cp. F. Shaikh: *Community and Consensus in India: Muslim Representation in Colonial India 1860–1947*, Cambridge 1989. The idea of dynamic Islam and stagnant Hinduism is still quite widespread among Indian Muslim dignitaries.

communal aporia demanded the development of a unified national Indian front which came to constitute a mix of pan-Islamic, pan-Indian and local interests, eventually reinforcing—at least in the imaginations of the actors involved—the notion of ontologically monolithic religious blocs: Hindus and Muslims.

EXCURSUS

GENDER

The image of Muslim women and of India has been shaped by colonial reforms and modern identity-formations. Not that women enjoyed a better image in pre-colonial times, but there was a marked shift in how colonial rule and reform used feminality.

In early Islam, women enjoyed some mobility, given the Quranic injunctions elevating their position in traditional Arab society of Mecca and Medina. However, championing the cause of women did not prevent Prophet Muhammad and the second caliph ʿUmar from demanding that sons (auladakum or abnaʾakum; your sons) learn swimming and archery while for daughters spinning would suffice.[1] For them a smattering of morality, religion and household management was considered enough.[2] Too much knowledge of writing and reading in them was considered potentially disruptive of men's lives, as can also be read from Persian prose and *adab*-literature of the eleventh and following centuries.[3]

In the Indian context, both Muslim and Hindu elite women remained invisible behind veils, yet many enjoyed influential positions in scholarship or at court. They had a profound impact on court politics, when they negotiated the prescriptive, thereby translating, recasting

[1] Hadith quoted in Ibn Hajr al-Asqalani: *Lisan al-mizan*, 6 vols., Haydarabad: Matbaʿa Majlis Daʾirat al-Maʿarif, 1329–31, Vol. 3, p. 112, No. 368.

[2] On the role of women in early Islam see Harald Motzki: "Dann machte er daraus die beiden Geschlechter, das männliche und das weibliche ... (Koran 75:39)—Die historischen Wurzeln der islamischen Geschlechterrollen", in: *Veröffentlichungen des "Instituts für Historische Anthropologie e.V."* (eds. J. Martin and T. Nipperdey), Vol. 5/2, Freiburg/München 1987, pp. 607–642, and A. Degand: "'Wie im Prozeß um einen Esel'—Geschlechterrollen in der islamischen Literatur des 7./13. bis 9./15. Jahrhunderts", ibid., pp. 643–676.

[3] Such as Kai Kaus ibn Iskandar's *Qabus Nama* (*A Mirror for Princes*), transl. Reuben Levy, New York 1951) and Nasir al-Din Tusi's *Akhlaq-e Nasiri* (*The Nasirean Ethics*), trans. G.M. Wickens, London: George Allen & Unwin 1964; compare the excellent study by Gail Minault: *Secluded Scholars. Women's Education and Muslim Social reform in Colonial India*, Delhi: OUP 1998, pp. 23f. On different male discourses on women from judicial, social and political perspectives see the contributions in Afaf Lutfi al-Sayyid Marsot (ed.): *Society and the Sexes in Medieval Islam*, Malibu, C.A.: Undena 1979.

and appropriating the imperial vision.[4] Some even became leaders in politics and reformers in their own right, like the Central Indian State of Bhopal's Begums, who in the nineteenth century were also ardent supporters of female education. Still others developed the high culture of courtesans, such as in Lucknow,[5] with all its cultural and political impact on society. However, women battled male chauvinism, be it Muslim or Hindu, rationalised by theological discourses discriminating space into controlled public (male) and unregulated private (female).[6] This was even more the case in colonial rule. "These impressions (of male chauvinism; J.M.) formed part of an overall pattern of cultural criticism of India, designed both to justify British assumption of imperial control, and to convert Indians to their 'civilising mission'."[7] Ironically, colonialism supported this chauvinism. In early colonialism the *Nabobs*[8]—an epithet for Europeans returning with fortunes from India under Robert Clive (died 1774)—cared little about morality and openly kept mistresses. However, with the arrival of nineteenth-century European moralism in India, a large number of *memsahibs*, respectful designation of married English women, came to the subcontinent.[9] Eventually, Muslim women were confined to the private sphere, symbolising the inner, spiritual life, equating gender with the domestic, so dear to Victorian patriarchs. This private, yet uncolonialised space of the home was to be colonialised and made public, first by colonial rule

---

[4] So far little academic work is available on the role of women other than on household customs and rituals. Their impact on politics and other public fields has been focused on only very recently. See for example Ruby Lal: "Mughal India: 15th to Mid-18th Century", in: *Encyclopedia of Women in Islamic Cultures*, Leiden: Brill 2003, pp. 64–69; and Ruby Lal: "Historicizing the Harem: The Challenge of a Princess's Memoir", in: *Feminist Studies* 30, No. 3 (2004), pp. 590–616.

[5] For the politics of the Begums of Bhopal see Claudia Preckel: *Begums of Bhopal*, New Delhi: Roli Books Pvt. 2000; Shaharyar M. Khan: *The Begums of Bhopal. A Dynasty of Women Rulers in Raj India*, London: I.B. Tauris 2000; for the courtesans see V.T. Oldenburg: "Lifestyle as Resistance: The Case of the Courtesans of Lucknow", in: Douglas Haynes and Gyan Prakash (eds.): *Contesting Power: Resistance and Everyday Social Relations in South Asia*, Delhi: OUP 1991, pp. 23–61.

[6] See Faisal Fatehali Devji: "Gender and the Politics of Space: the movement for women's reform, 1857–1900", in: Zoya Hasan (ed.): *Forging Identities. Gender, Communities and the State*, Delhi 1994, pp. 22–38.

[7] Minault: *Secluded Scholars*, p. 2.

[8] For the Nabobs see Percival Spear: *The Nabobs: A Study of the Social Life of the English in Eighteenth Century India*, London 1963; for their process of reintegration in England see Michael Edwards: *The Nabobs at Home*, London: Constable 1991.

[9] For this process see J.K. Stanford (ed.): *Ladies in the sun. The Memsahibs' India, 1790–1860*, London: The Galley Press 1962; Indira Ghose (ed.): *Memsahibs Abroad; Writings by Women Travellers in Nineteenth Century India*, Delhi: OUP 1998.

but eventually by the Muslim reformers defending religious traditions. Embedded into colonial structures, the latter tried to respond to the changed conditions of British rule. To harmonise private and public life, they defined Muslim society and culture in the new context and delineated norms and roles for women. Subsequently, articulate religious scholars and reformers produced a number of discourses—legal, mystical, orthodox—as well literature offering religious advice to women.[10]

Women had been active in cultural and politically important areas before colonial expansion, but now rigid compartments and norms were generalised when women witnessed marginalisation informed by puritanical evangelicalism. Colonial impact and reform intertwined. The emerging male Muslim public could not tolerate influential women, as can be seen in the changes in the lifestyles of courtesans or even in poetry, which provided for ambiguity. The result was a feminisation of the colony: India was perceived in terms of feminality that had to be tamed and subdued by the strong British masculinity. This perception inspired Muslim reformers when they advocated Islamic education for women. This can be seen in literature carrying religious advice indicative of evangelical didacticism. Eventually this boiled down to the Islamisation of everyday life, predisposed women to their gender and thus restricted their decision-making and responsibility. The male-dominated gender-specific discourse on education (*ta'lim o tarbiyat*) relegated women to the narrow confines of reformist-domestic chastity, as can be read in many a novel of that time—thus, the advancement of male control in religious reform movement. However, it also paved the way for women to take up various professions. Paradoxically, the new image of women produced male identity through regulations, considered binding for women. The aim—civility—was to be reproduced through the conscious labour of women. Thus the perceived civilising mission which Muslim men received from the European was passed on to women: women were important for character building and for endowing men with civility, by which they would be recognised in the colonial pantheon. Of prime importance for the acceptance of new standards were education and the liberation from *purdah*, though many

[10] See Margrit Pernau: "Motherhood and Female Identity. Religious Advice literature for women in German Catholicism and Indian Islam", in: Margrit Pernau, Imtiaz Ahmad, Helmut Reifeld (eds.): *Family and Gender. Changing Values in Germany and India*, New Delhi: Sage 2003, pp. 149–158.

women had been active under the veil.[11] Many Urdu novels had this pedagogical aim as exemplified by Nazir Ahmad Dihlawi's (1833–1912) *Mirat al-'Arus* (The Bride's Mirror) and Altaf Husain Hali's (1837–1914) *Majalis al-Nisa* (Assemblies of Women). Scholars like these seemed to dismiss the old princely order set up by the British in the wake of 1857 in favour of an anglicised—albeit chaste, Victorian—culture which they communicated through the medium of fiction, but also through non-fictional texts and journals, printing technology being of prime importance for their dissemination.[12]

With the Women's India Association, led among others by Dr. Annie Besant (1847–1933), women re-entered the public realm only after World War I. During the colonial era, such movements failed to achieve much politically. Change came with massive participation of women in non-cooperation that emerged in the wake of the Khilafat movement. Finally, when women constituted more than half of the people imprisoned, male politicians became aware of women's potential. This led to some legislative improvement in the status of women, such as the "Child Marriage Restraint Act (1929)". Moreover, in an Indian National Congress session in 1932, Nehru introduced the "Fundamental rights resolution", recognising the judicial equality of men and women, followed by the "Shariat Application Act (1937)" and the "Dissolution of Muslim Marriage Act (1939)". The acts served as surety for maintaining community identity as well as religious and political interests. The Muslim League appreciated women's participation as "a product of political calculations, and not a sign of a sea-change in its attitude towards women."[13]

Political strife and mass arrests in 1942 saw renewed participation of women in the independence movement.[14] The first public calls by women for the abolition of *purdah* came to be heard. Similarly, Muslim women, especially the women's subcommittee of the Muslim League,

[11] For these arguments see the excellent works by Minault: *Secluded Scholars*, Chap. I: Role Models, and pp. 55ff., and Margrit Pernau: *Bürger im Turban*.

[12] Cf. Nazir Ahmad: *Mirat al-'Urus*, transl. *A Tale of Life in Delhi a Hundred Years Ago. The Bride's Mirror*, Delhi: Permanent Black 2001. In fact, Urdu emerged as a language of public discourse at that time. See David Lelyveld: "The fate of Hindustani: Colonial Knowledge and the Project of a National Language", in: Breckenridge/van der Veer (eds.): *Orientalism*, pp. 189–214.

[13] Ayesha Jalal: "*The Convenience of Subservience: Women and the State of Pakistan*", in: Deniz Kandiyoti (ed.): *Women, Islam and the State*, London 1991, pp. 77–114.

[14] See Azra Asghar Ali: *The Emergence of Feminism among Indian Muslim Women*, Oxford 2000.

actively struggled for Pakistan, thus linking the political awakening of Muslim women to the struggle for a separate Muslim state and potentially offering a new discursive field to re-negotiate the sexual territory in Muslim society.[15] Apparently, women's appearance in public was no longer considered a threat to male honour. It was rather a sign of cooperation, but this was to be primarily seen as such among the elite. The Indian constitution of 1950 acknowledged this role of women in national movements by guaranteeing the right to vote to women above the age of 21. On a political level, this was an attempt to solve the women's issues that had existed within the traditional social system. A decade later, some amendments to the "Family Law Ordinance of 1961" addressed various aspects of personal status, such as divorce, child custody and alimony in Pakistan linking female literacy with the workforce.[16] However, to a large extent the female half of the South Asian population continued to be ignored politically, socially and economically. In fact, in South Asia social reality is gendered, not only among Muslims but also the Hindus.[17]

In a gendered context, Muslim patriarchs used shariʿa as an effective tool to curtail women's rights, as well as to socialise and create Muslim identity as interplay between the religious community and the state. One example is the "All India Muslim Personal Law Board" (heart of the masculine Muslim identity), created in the 1970s and pretending to reform the regressive and misogynous Muslim Personal Laws. The Law Board does not accept women members to maintain patriarchal hold over female identity and the conservation of the family unit, which was in a process of redefinition, especially in urban centres.

Since the 1980s, communal and religious fundamentalist groups have attracted a large number of women. This explains the calls for a uniform civil code for the identity of Muslims in India. In 1985, the Supreme Court ruled that a divorced woman (Shah Bano) was entitled to alimony from her husband (see also Excursus: Communalism, and

---

[15] David Willmer: "Women as Participants in the Pakistan Movement: Modernization and the Promise of a Moral State", in: *MAS* 30, 3 (1996), pp. 574, 578.

[16] Cf. Anita Weiss: "Benazir Bhutto and the Future of Women in Pakistan", in: *Asian Survey*, 30, 5 (1990), p. 440; also Lucy Caroll: "Muslim Family Law in South Asia", in: *Encyclopaedic Survey of Islamic Culture*, Vol. 18 *Perspectives in Islamic Law*, New Delhi 1998, pp. 173–187.

[17] See Shahnaz Rouse: "The Outsider(s) within", in: Patricia Jeffery and Amrita Basu (eds.): *Appropriation Gender: Women's Activism and Politicized Religion in South Asia*, London 1998, p. 58.

Chap. 15). As a consequence, Muslims feared that Islamic practice might be modified by non-Muslim institutions. Many Muslims regarded this ruling as a confrontation between shariʿa and the Civil Law, and as a decision against Islam.[18] The claim was that alimony by a husband had no basis in Islam, and the ruling was therefore against Islam. Pressure from a Muslim lobby finally led to R. Gandhi's neutralising the Supreme Court's verdict and getting the "Muslim Women (Protection of Rights on Divorce) Act" of 1986 pushed through: the husband was let off while Shah Bano did not receive any alimony. Instead, under the bill, the woman's relatives were responsible for her maintenance, and if they failed to do so the *waqf* board would pay it. As a result, every divorced Muslim woman in India finds herself without means to support herself, *waqf* boards being the only source.

The response of Muslims was, however, not the only significant reaction to the ruling. It was primarily a reaction of right-wing Hindu organisations that welcomed the ruling. The Muslim traditionalists saw their own integrity threatened by an outside anti-Muslim organisation and reacted in force. Arun Shourie's opinion that "fundamentalists have frozen Muslim Personal Law to what it was 40 years ago" thus hits the mark, considering the current influence of traditionalist Muslim scholars on society. Progressive and reformist opinions hardly seem to have any support among Muslims that view traditional scholars as the only legitimate promoters of Islam. This monopolistic position prompted the secular state to accept traditional views alone as influential, because of the predominant perception of Muslims being a monolithic society in which law and identity are one and the same thing. Thus dissent becomes marginalised and silenced. The state's position, on the other hand, becomes accepted among the Muslim society because many see this extra-legal position as a privilege and try to defend it, while at the same time this position also presents a target for the opponents of a pluralist discourse. The traditional views and customs are thus supported by half-hearted reform attempts, where the state appears as a protector

[18] Since the available sources of and on Islamic law were not sufficient to sort out this problem—because they consider alimony legal only for the three-month period of *ʿidda* after divorce—the Supreme Court referring to Quran 2:240ff., found that a husband is obliged to pay alimony to his divorced wife in case she is unable to provide alimentation for herself. This drew severe reactions with the argument that the Court was not authorised to refer to the Quran and other sacred texts, since this gave too much power to the secular court.

of Islam, and Muslim women especially, while using the politics of "othering" to attack Muslims as a stagnating community.

Changes in the political landscape after 1986 support this view. Hindu-nationalist parties were enabled to assail the Muslim minorities, by attacking cultural pluralism and secularism as something undermining the integrity of the Indian state. The issue of women became a battleground, as it gave nationalists a chance to claim that a state should be based on Hindu laws and traditions, and not on some notions of a secular state. This debate brought Muslim women right into the centre of the communal political imagination. The question of their rights was the focus of debates on the issues of conservatism versus modernisation; pluralism versus national integrity; secularism versus equality of women; a uniform civil code versus distinct religious laws.[19]

Similar tendencies can be delineated in Muslim majority countries, where women served as symbol of progress and, what is more important, as custodians of cultural identity, because of their seemingly being less assimilated into society as a whole. Here one has to mention the Muslim fundamentalist critique of the West and its modernity which centres on moral decline, particularly that of sexual morality. The "social pathologies" of European societies resulting from the modernisation process are often used as reference points of a Machiavellian strategy that is out to capture power. Indeed, a key dimension of Muslim politics is the controversy over the meanings attached to "woman" as a generic symbol, invested with diverse ideological meanings, particularly by established religious authorities and Islamists who claim to be the defenders of family integrity and of the roles and rights of women.[20] As such, women are pivotal to contemporary Muslim politics, because they are seen as the guardians of tradition. In this context, "woman" is often a mere symbol while real women have no agency, "their exalted, symbolic status does not translate into any form of agency."[21]

Similarly, women can also become icons of ethnic and national identity as well as national success, as in South Asia. A similar reactionary position is advocated by Indian Muslim parties, as, for example, in the case of the "Women's Quota Bill", which requested at least one-third of the Lok Sabha seats for women. It seems cynical that most Muslim

[19] Cf. Hasan (ed.): *Forging Identities*, p. xix.

[20] See Eickelmann/Piscatori: *Muslim Politics*, pp. 96–99.

[21] Susan Starr Sered: "Woman as Symbol and Women as Agents. Gendered religious Discourses and Practices" in: Myra Max Feree, Judith Lorber, Beth B. Hess (eds.): *Revisioning Gender*, New Delhi: Sage Publications 1998, pp. 193–221, here p. 199.

women defend patriarchal structures, especially those belonging to traditional Islam-parties. In other words, women are promoters as well as the victims of these policies of patriarchal ideologies.

This tendency is deep-rooted. While the Islamic identity of women in India, and their minority status, limits their social range by reducing access to multiple identities and loyalties, it binds women to local traditions by using a complex socialisation process. Particularly, women at the local level in South Asia are hardly controlled by the state and religion, but rather by the family, which is the main and the only source of support, and changes are only possible if the family agrees.[22] The difference between Muslim women in India and females in other predominantly Muslim societies lies in the struggle to define their legal and social role, which in India is caught between state and Islam.

In addition, the socialisation process is a source of support for traditional gender roles. One example concerns the *Bihishti Zewar* (Heavenly Ornaments), written by the renowned Muslim scholar, Sufi and divine, Ashraf ʿAli Thanawi (died 1943). This popular book defines, much in the tradition of religious advice literature, conventional middle-class manners for Muslim women while seeking to eliminate as non-Muslim innovations any "Hindu" or cultural practices. It offers advice to women to lead a good life. It serves as a guide for respectable women, and sets out the core of a reformist version of Islam that has become increasingly prominent across Muslim societies in the past hundred years and can be found in nearly every household.[23] Even though these approaches towards women were not revolutionary, like the teachings based on religion and lessons on hygiene or household, they still changed the perception of local Muslim values.

Despite general perceptions of Islamic and Islamist discourse as limiting—such as the case with the *Hudood-Ordinances* which as a reaction called for the *Women's Action Forum*—the discourse paradoxically enables women to liberate themselves from traditions which advocate their submission to male dominance. Accepting and reinterpreting the reformers' and Islamists' strictures and using Quran and sunna as a

---

[22] See Farida Shaheed, "The Other Side of the Discourse, Women's Experience of Identity, Religion and Activism in Pakistan", in: Jeffery and Basu (eds.): *Appropriation Gender*, pp. 143–164.

[23] For a partial English translation and analysis of this famous book see Barbara Daly Metcalf, *Perfecting Women: Maulana Ashraf ʿAli Thanawi's Bihishti Zewar*, Berkeley: PUP 1990; Minault: *Secluded Scholars*, Chap. II: A Suitable Literature.

basis, some women started postulating emancipation based on Islamic discourse itself. As argued elsewhere, Islamist discourse has become a powerful emancipative tool for the youth—against the traditional cultural baggage of their parents. Young Muslim women increasingly use the veil to symbolise Muslim identity, and transform feminist critique into an Islamic one, creating a gender-segregated public sphere.[24]

[24] Compare Nilufer Gole: *The Forbidden Modern. Civilization and Veiling*, The University of Michigan Press 1997; Nilofer Göle: "The Gendered Nature of Public Sphere", in: *Public Culture* 10(1) (1997), pp. 61–81; also Minault: *Secluded Scholars*, Chap. VI: Daughters of Reform. For new educational developments in Pakistan and beyond see Katharina Fleckenstein: *Al-Huda International: Institute of Islamic Education for Women*, (Ph.D. Islamic Studies) Erfurt (in progress).

CHAPTER ELEVEN

COLONIAL REFORMS, THE KHILAFAT MOVEMENT AND MUSLIM NATIONALISM (CA. 1900–1947)

Growing discontent

In Bengal, the largest province in British India with approximately 80 million people, one third of them being Muslims, homogenising imperatives of nationalism had meanwhile become more radical, especially in Calcutta, nurtured by, among other groups, respectable Bengali upper castes, the *bhadralok*, who arose during colonial times. To rid Calcutta of the troublesome Bengalis of the eastern regions, the colonial rulers partitioned Bengal in 1905,[1] thereby creating a Muslim majority province consisting of East Bengal—with its influential Hindu educated middle class—and Assam, and designed to transform the Bengali-speaking population of West Bengal, Bihar and Orissa into a minority. In fact, in partitioned West Bengal, Oriya- and Hindi-speaking Biharis far outnumbered the Bengalis. Thus the national movement was made to look like a ridiculous Bengali idea which was not equally shared by other linguistic groups.[2] Also the loss of Dacca to East Bengal was supposed to take the winds out of the sail of increasing Bengali radicalism. This gave a snub to radical Hindu nationalists and widened the gap between Hindus and Muslims. Meanwhile, the partition of Bengal created severe problems for the British, for the boycott of British goods, initiated in Bengal, was starting to acquire the character of a mass movement, the *swadeshi* movement, which called for promoting the culture of their 'own country'—anticipating Gandhi's political tactics.[3] In political terms this meant *swaraj*, independence, and its call spread around the country. Apparently the British had underestimated Bengali nationalism

---

[1] This resulted in communalist movements because many Muslims led by the initiator of the scheme called "Muslim All-India Confederacy", Nawab Salimullah (1884–1915) from Dacca, were in favour of this plan, while the Hindus rejected it.

[2] See Sumit Sarkar: *Modern India, 1885–1947*, Basingstoke: Macmillan 1989 for relevant data.

[3] See Sumit Sarkar: *The Swadeshi Movement in Bengal, 1903–1908*, New Delhi 1977.

at a time when Bengalis had already 'imagined' themselves as a nation and as a 'people with history'.[4] In the Bengali jurist and landlord Fazl al-Haqq (1873–1962; President of the All-India Muslim League from 1916–1921) and subsequently in the Assamese ʿAbd al-Hamid Khan Bhashani (1885–1976; member of Congress and later of the All-India Muslim League), they later found proven leaders for their interests.

Similar discontent grew in Madras among its Telegu-speaking people, who supported *swadeshi* developments in Bengal, and in commercialised Bombay, particularly in the fields of steel and textile. In Punjab discontent with colonial rule heightened as well, partly due to high water rates and control in canal-irrigated colonies. This was juxtaposed with increasing tensions between Sikhs, Hindus and Muslims, which had led to the emergence of movements such as Arya Samaj (1875) in Punjab. The Malabar Coast was another troublesome area of rural violence. Though these developments were followed by colonial repression, the *swadeshi* Bengali anthem *Bande Mataram* ("Hail the Mother (India)" written by the Bengali novelist Bankim Chandra Chatterjee, died 1894, in 1875) became the voice of nationalistic endeavour to be heard in the country. All this discontent had reasons based in political and economic monopolisation, exploitation and the increasing friction among different social and religious groups in a market dominated by colonial power.

Colonial repression was followed by compromise, when in 1906 the Liberal Party won election in Great Britain, though the colonial government meanwhile pursued its communal politics with added vigour. Instead of providing space for territorial and parliamentarian representation, the idea evolved of seeking communal representation. Already early in 1906 a delegation of Muslim leaders from the Muhammadan-Anglo-Oriental College in Aligarh headed by the powerful Ismaili, the Agha Khan III (1877–1957), had the initiative for separate electorates presented to Viceroy Lord Minto at Simla. Shortly thereafter, the *All India Muslim League* was founded in Dacca (see below), initially manned by feudal lords and some lawyers and traders, most of whom were not anti-British. More or less integrated into the colonial system from

---

[4] For the construction of this imagination see Partha Chatterjee: *Nation and its Fragments. Colonial and Postcolonial Histories*, Princeton: PUP 1993, as well as his chapter on the writings on Bankimchandra Chattopadhyay (1838–1894) in *Nationalist Thought and the Colonial World: A Nationalism as a Derivative Discourse?* London: Zed Books for the United Nations University, 1986.

which they derived their legitimacy, they started to lobby Muslim interests and functioned as an alternative to the *swadeshi* leaders. Thus the partition of Bengal sparked off not only Hindu nationalism but also an organisation of Muslim political orientation.

When in 1907 Congress witnessed a schism between the extremists led by B.G. Tilak (1844–1920), and the moderates under the leadership of G.K. Gokhale (1866–1915), over the question of tactics, the increasing radicalisation of Congress and the Muslim demand for separate electorates were met with the constitutional reform of 1909, the so-called *Morley-Minto Reforms*. The reforms provided for some rights for Indians, such as to move resolutions for the first time, but they also safeguarded Muslim interests—particularly of the League's United Provinces leadership from Aligarh and Lucknow—through political representation called separate electorates, denounced by the Congress.[5] This move not only was to provide more legitimacy for the British, but also that only Muslims were to decide over Muslim candidates; thus religion became central for matters pertaining to identity and politics. However, there were also alternative voices calling for some cooperation with Congress, albeit under British protection, such as Hakim Ajmal Khan (1863–1928) who represented the Muslim League, and the Congressite M.A. Ansari (1880–1936).[6] Radical nationalism could thus be neutralised, and the *Indian Councils Act 1909* proved to be the right decision to weaken the nationalist tendencies of the Indian National Congress—at least for the time being.

In 1911, the year when it was decided to shift the capital of British India from Calcutta to an area south of Old Delhi (Shahjahanabad), establishing a new administrative metropolis in New Delhi, his Majesty at the Delhi Durbar in a show of 'magnanimity' announced the annulment of Partition. With this shift British rule tried to gain legitimacy through continuity,[7] and it also suggested that the move recalled the glorious Mughal past and extended recognition to their religious community, "a suggestion that failed to consider that what Muslims

[5] See Mushirul Hasan: *Nationalism and Communal Politics in India, 1885–1930*, Delhi: Manohar 1991, pp. 84f.

[6] On Ajmal Khan see B.D. Metcalf: "Nationalist Muslims in British India: The case of Hakim Ajmal Khan", in: *MAS* 19 (1985), pp. 1–28. On Ansari see Mushirul Hasan: *A Nationalist Conscience: M.A. Ansari, the Congress and the Raj*, Delhi: Manohar 1987.

[7] See Robert E. Frykenberg: "The Coronation Durbar of 1911. Some Implications", in: Robert Frykenberg (ed.): *Delhi through the Ages. Essays in Urban History, Culture and Society*, Delhi: OUP 1986, pp. 369–90.

remembered more recently about Delhi was the humiliation of the dismissal of the last Mughal, old and blind, after the Mutiny."[8] With this annulment, however, Muslim elites found themselves in a difficult position, as they had to give up their privileges and, therefore, started rethinking their loyalty. Even if the different fora represented various interests, the reforms showed that colonial masters could be forced to comply with Indian interests.

Such was the case in 1913 when M.A. Jinnah established his reputation when speaking for the re-privatisation of Islamic endowments (*waqf*). The League's longstanding leader, initially a member of Congress, was an affluent barrister of Victorian manners from Bombay, belonging to the prosperous business community of Gujarati Ismaili Khojas[9] and was married into a Parsi family. Many Muslim scholars, therefore, observed him with suspicion. As a supporter of the demand for the right of self-determination for all Indians (*Lucknow Pact*, 1916), he joined the League in the same year while retaining his Congress membership. The *Pact* was built on the notion of religious separatism, which the Congress had opposed for so long: Muslims were to be over-represented in Muslim minority provinces and under-represented in majority provinces such as Bengal and Punjab. The *Muslim League* was granted a veto right on minority issues.[10] To be sure, not all Muslims were in tune with the League. There were many ways to react, as in the case of Bengali Muslims who preferred representation on the basis of population rather than separate electorates and weightage in councils and local bodies. In other cases contests were obvious, such as between Barelwis and Deobandis. But the Pact ushered in an era of Congress-League co-operation. And in the light of sacrifices made by Indians in a war forced upon unknown and unknowing people but referred to as World War I, the voices for autonomy had become louder. Home rule loomed on the horizon. The *Montagu Declaration* of August 1917 was to meet some Indian demands, thereby shattering Indian nationalist unity. Its aim was to bring about a responsible government in India as an integral part of the British Empire by increasing the

---

[8] Stein: *A History of India*, p. 296.

[9] Khoja is a mutated form of Khwaja, usually designating a follower of the Agha Khan but also referring to Nizari Ismailis, who had split off from the Ismaili community (see also excursus: Shiʿites).

[10] C.H. Philips (ed.): *Select Documents on the History of India and Pakistan, 1858–1947*, London 1972, vol. 4, pp. 1–22; for a detailed analysis of the Pact see Hasan: *Nationalism and Communal Politics in India*, pp. 81ff.

number of Indians in administration, and gradually developing self-governing institutions.

The Khilafat Movement

The idea of autonomy reinforced the latent ethnification and was continued in the *Montagu-Chelmsford Reforms* (1919) which provided for Indian participation but kept intact the separate electorates of 1909 which had initiated the process of distributing power according to the numerical strength of a community; in so far Muslim majority provinces came to play a major role in the political bargaining. The *Reforms* introduced "diarchy": major portfolios, such as home, revenue and finance were reserved for the central authority, i.e. the British, education, health and local government for provincial legislature, i.e. Indians. Diarchy did not suit Indian demands, however, and was rejected by both League and Congress. Against the backdrop of post-war economic depression and food riots in major colonial harbour cities and in Bengal, unrest intensified. In order to stop the rise of pan-Indian nationalism, the colonial state now armed themselves even more rigidly and reacted with drastic repressive measures, continuing martial law even after World War I.[11] Following the *Rowlatt Commission* 1918, the *Anarchical and Revolutionary Crimes Act* (*Rowlatt Act*) of 1919 was meant to suppress political mobilisation. The act was passed by the Imperial Legislative Council against the will of Indian representatives, and eventually resulted in the massacre of Jallianwala Bagh (1919) in Amritsar, when British troops led by General Dyer mercilessly fired, without any warning, at a peaceful meeting. Later, Dyer was rewarded for his 'patriotic duties'.

It is in this context that India saw the emergence of a new leader, Mohanchand Karamdas Gandhi (1869–1948), who had returned from South Africa in 1915, where he had been a barrister. In India he soon became most powerful in the Congress leadership.[12] Having proven his abilities as a leader in the civil disobedience campaign, he managed

[11] The feeling of insecurity among the colonial rulers and their segregation has been the subject of literary works such as the novel *A Passage to India* (London 1924) by E.M. Forster.

[12] See Dietmar Rothermund: *Mahatma Gandhi. An Essay in Political Biography*, Delhi 1991; for a stimulating analysis of Gandhi's career between 1915 and 1924 see Stein: *A History of India*, pp. 299–310.

to win over sections of the Muslim public by way of cooperation with the ulama and to spearhead the Khilafat movement by supporting their demand for British recognition of the Ottoman sultan as Caliph. In return, the ulama supported the Indian nationalist struggle against British rule. Gandhi's non-violent protest (*ahinsa*), the campaign for non-violent force (*satyagraha*) and non-cooperation stood for the renunciation of titles, resignation from government service, in particular from police and military, and non-payment of taxes, as well as the boycott of imported British goods, and eventually political independence.

Since the middle of the nineteenth century a pan-Islamic sentiment had developed in favour of the Ottoman Sultan Abdulmajid I (reigned 1839–61), the root being the common colonial experience, forced by a common ideography and common dress (e.g. fez and beard). These symbolic items were influenced by al-Afghani's pan-Islamic messages and inspired leaders of Muslim communities to consider themselves as one community. In the process of elevating religious identity, the Ottoman Caliphate became the symbol of sovereignty that brought about a feeling of solidarity and commonality.

The British threat to the Ottoman caliph and the parcelling of the Ottoman Empire under the allied powers as a result of World War I (Treaty of Sevres 1920) was considered unacceptable to Muslim intellectual elites in India. Relations between Ottomans and British worsened when in World War I the Ottomans sided with the Germans against the allied forces. The Ottomans were defeated and lost much of their territory, while the Arabs were seeking independence from their Ottoman overlords. Although the Mughal emperors in their heydays had often ignored the sovereignty of Ottoman caliphs, the later Mughals presiding over a tottering kingdom had begun appealing to Istanbul to rescue them from the European threat. In fact, the Friday *khutba*s in some Indian mosques publicly acknowledging the community's allegiance to the contemporary Ottoman sultan, Indian Muslims began to look to the Ottomans as the last remaining Muslim empire able to compete with Western power. Support of the caliphate was combined with anti-British sentiments to bring about a Hindu-Muslim *entente.* Elite Muslim grievances had already been aggravated by the annulment of the partition of Bengal in 1911. The Kanpur mosque-affair in 1913, which had led to the desecration of a mosque by the British, had the effect of uniting Muslims from different quarters. Finally, the campaign for the *Muslim University* in Aligarh started in 1912. They all served the establishment of new mass mobilising institutions and strategies.[13] The issue of the caliphate also led to a politicisation of traditional scholars, which in connection with mystical orders such as Naqshbandiyya, Qadiriyya and Chishtiyya became prominent. Notwithstanding the religious rhetoric giving life to the Khilafat movement, the unease with which many ulama entered into an alliance with the Indian National Congress cannot be explained in terms of Pan-Islam alone, because it had a strong political (nationalist) pan-Indian component, including a variety of individual motivations of its actors, as Gail Minault has elaborated.[14]

In fact, a number of societies and organisations were founded in the wake of local initiatives having political, religious, social, and philanthropical agendas, some of which eventually became trans-local, national and global. In these societies traditional and reformist scholars, Sufis and intellectuals gathered under the slogan of Pan-Islam to transcend their particular interests in the struggle for the well-being of their country against the foreigners, the British: Deobandis and the Ahl-e Hadith, particularly the group around the Begum of Bhopal, already had established contacts with the Ottoman rulers at the beginning of the twentieth century, the "Association of Helpers" (*Jam'iyyat al-Ansar*) being founded in 1909 for this purpose by Mahmud al-Hasan (1850–1920), one of the earliest students of the seminar in Deoband. Mahmud al-Hasan sent the activist 'Ubaid Allah Sindhi (1872–1941)[15] to the Amir of Afghanistan with a decree of *jihad* against the British in silk handkerchiefs, but soon was caught by the colonial administration and detained in Malta for three years until 1920.[16] In the following years the communication network of the Deobandis and Sufis was extended to Sind and Afghanistan by 'Ubaid Allah Sindhi. Sufi shrines had been

---

[13] Freitag: *Collective Action and Community*; G. Minault & D. Lelyveld: "The campaign for a Muslim University, 1898–1920", in: *MAS* 8/2 (1974), pp. 145–188; Hasan (ed.): *Communal and Pan-Islamic Trends*; Mushirul Hasan and Margrit Pernau (eds.): *Regionalizing Pan-Islamism. Documents on the Khilafat Movement*, Delhi: Manohar 2005.

[14] The excellent study by G. Minault: *The Khilafat-Movement: Religious Symbolism and Political Mobilization in India*, New York 1982; see also the detailed study by Naeem M. Qureshi: *Pan-Islam in British Indian Politics. A Study of the Khilafat Movement 1918–1924*, Leiden: Brill 1999.

[15] Sindhi was a student of Mahmud al-Hasan and is largely responsible for the development of a nationalist historiography, particularly over-emphazising the Delhi tradition around Shah Wali Allah and his descendants.

[16] See Syed Mohammad Mian: *The Prisoners of Malta*, transl. from Urdu into English by Mohammad Anwer Hussain and Imam Manak, Delhi 2004.

centres of *mujahidin* activity in nineteenth century, and from time to time they had become centres of protest against the government. The Khilafat movement would not have won such a large following if the ulama and the sufis had not been actively supporting the cause. In Afghanistan a shadow government was established under the leadership of socialist forces, among others ʿUbaid Allah Sindhi, to counter colonial power.[17] The Farangi Mahallis entered into a phase of institutionalisation from 1905 onwards, when in 1913 the "Association of Servants of the Kaaba" (*Anjuman-e Khuddam-e Kaʿba*) was founded by ʿAbd al-Bari Farangi Mahalli and the Muslim intellectuals such as Mushir Husain Kidwaʾi (died 1937) at Lucknow to support the caliph.[18] All these efforts finally found their institutional manifestation in the "Association of the Scholars of India" (*Jamʿiyyat al-ʿUlama-ye Hind*; JUH) in 1919, initiated primarily by Deobandis and Farangi Mahallis, and joined by members of the Ahl-e Hadith.[19] The association demanded adherance to Islamic tenets, a strengthening of the relationship with the Islamic world, i.e., the Ottoman Empire in particular, and fostering Muslim-Hindu amity. The holy places of Islam were to be defended, separate shariʿa courts and a zakat system was to be established. The Indian National Congress under the leadership of Gandhi accepted these demands. This "solidarity traditionalism" found its climax in a *fatwa*—the so-called *muttafiqa fatwa*—on non-cooperation and civil disobedience issued by ʿAbd al-Bari Farangi Mahalli in 1920.[20] By the same token, the *Jamʿiyyat* stood for a composite nationalism (*muttahida qaumiyat*) delineated only in 1938 (see Chap. 12). Since the members of the *Jamʿiyyat* considered themselves religious guides, rather than politicians, they continued to emphasise the

---

[17] S.F.D. Ansari, *Sufi Saints and State Power. The Pirs of Sind, 1843–1947*, Cambridge 1992; K.H. Ansari, "Pan Islam and the making of the early Muslim Socialists," in: *MAS* 20 (1986), pp. 509–37.

[18] "The Anjuman was... a significant step toward cooperation between the ulama and the Western-educated Muslims, and it provided a pattern for future operations." Minault: *The Khilafat-Movement*, p. 37.

[19] Francis Robinson: *Separatism among Indian Muslims; the politics of the United Provinces' Muslims 1860–1923*, Cambridge: CUP 1974; P. Hardy: *The Muslims of British India*, Cambridge 1972; Parvaiz Rozinah (ed.): *Jamʿiyyat al-ʿUlamaʾ-ye Hind. Dastawizat markazi ijlasha-ye ʿam, 1919–1945*, vols. 1–2, Islamabad 1980; Yohanan Friedmann: "The attitude of the Jamʿiyyat al-ʿUlamaʾ-i Hind to the Indian national movement and the establishment of Pakistan," in: *Asian and African Studies* 7 (1971), pp. 157–180; Yohanan Friedmann: "The Jamʿiyyat al-ʿUlamaʾ-i Hind in the Wake of Partition", in: *Asian and African Studies* 11 (1976), pp. 181–211.

[20] See the *muttafiqa fatwa* on non-co-operation reproduced in Qureshi: *Pan-Islam*, pp. 443f.

correct observance of shariʿa and concentrated on religious and legal dimensions of community life rather than immediate political aspects. As long as Muslims integrated in the colonial set-up recognised their guidance in matters of religion, the two groups—traditional ulama and Western-educated Muslims—could work together. Some groups, such as Barelwis and some scholars of Farangi Mahall did not follow the *fatwa*. Similarly, the Pirs of Sind were divided on the issue.[21]

In the same year, 1919, Bombay witnessed the founding of an *All-India Khilafat Committee*, which started as a purely urban institution initiated by intellectuals and major entrepreneurs. Using both existent Sufi and Congress Party infrastructure as well as symbolism, the committee successfully approached traditional groups of the society. Rites, *khutbas*, journals and Urdu poetry mediating political as well as emotional messages were of particular importance in fostering a common identity.[22] The role of media and vernacular periodicals in particular was important, such as the Lahore-based newspaper *Zamindar*, edited by Zafar ʿAli Khan, which became a passionate organ of young Muslim political assertiveness. Leading figures in the movement, such as the ʿAli Brothers, Muhammad ʿAli (1878–1931) and Shaukat ʿAli (1873–1937), realised that religion and a communal (religious) identity among Indian Muslims was the only way in which a mass mobilisation for their political interests could be acquired.[23] In 1911 Muhammad ʿAli launched the powerful English-language weekly *Comrade* in Calcutta, and in 1913 the Urdu weekly *Hamdard*, both of which were banned by the government later. Finally, the Salafite Abu al-Kalam Azad (1888–1958), who had become famous through his widely circulated journal *al-Hilal* published from Calcutta after 1912,[24] announced the founding of a "Party of God" (*hizb Allah*). He even agitated for armed resistance (*jihad*) if non-cooperation failed. The obligation for emigration (*hijra*)—to Afghanistan—was considered as one possibility of the anti-colonial struggle in the 1920s. Some scholars, such as Kalam Azad, issued relevant *fatawa* calling India *dar al-harb*, which

[21] See Mushirul Hasan: *Nationalism and Communal Politics in India*, pp. 160f.
[22] Compare G. Minault, "Urdu Political poetry during the Khilafat Movement," in: *MAS* 8 (1974), pp. 459–71.
[23] See M. Hasan: *Mohamed Ali: Ideology and Politics*, New Delhi 1981; M. Shan: *Freedom Movement in India—The Role of Ali Brothers*, New Delhi 1979.
[24] *Al-Balagh* was the successor of *al-Hilal*. Azad was also editor of *Vakil*, one of the best known and stylistically excellent Urdu newspapers, which dealt with national and community problems.

meant that Muslims were obliged to wage *jihad* or had to emigrate.[25] This *Hijrat* movement proved a disaster.[26] After mostly Muslim peasants had sold their belongings at throwaway prices, thousands set out for the Afghan border in July/August 1920. But since all *muhajirs* were not allowed to enter Afghanistan, several thousands returned disillusioned and penniless to the plains of India; many died during the journey. Many of those entering Afghanistan were soon exposed to privation and starvation because the country was not prepared to provide food, water and lodging to them. Indian Muslims were disappointed.

For some time, the cooperation between nationalist Hindus and Muslims, between Congress and League in the Khilafat movement counterbalanced British imperial policy, but with increasing radicalism many Muslims left the movement, especially those well-established in the colonial system, such as members of the *Muslim League*. Communists affiliated with the Congress called for independence and nationalisation of means of production and media, as was formulated by the leader of the "Khilafat workers conference" Hasrat Mohani (1877–1951). Other Muslim groups, such as the Barelwis associated with Ahmad Rida Khan, stayed away from the non-cooperation, the Khilafat movement, and the *Hijrat* movement, because these movements were dominated by Rida Khan's Deobandi rivals, whom he accused of sympathising with the unbelieving and "unclean" Hindus, though there was some opposition against him within the Barelwi movement on these issues, particularly with regard to Non-Cooperation and Khilafat. The Shiʿite minority, on the other hand, did not recognise the caliph for dogmatic reasons because they actually considered the Sunnite authority to be a usurper, but, sharing the anxiety over the decline of Muslim power, some of them eventually realised the need for Muslim sovereignty and joined the Sunnis in supporting the Ottomans and the non-cooperation movement.

In the South East, in Malabar, shortly before the collapse of the Khilafat movement in 1921, agrarian discontent among Muslim peasants was led by descendants of Arab merchants who had settled there from the eighteenth century onwards. In the nineteenth century the Mappila

[25] See I.H. Douglas: *Abul Kalam Azad; An Intellectual and Religious Biography*, eds. G. Minault and Chr.W. Troll, Delhi 1988; for the *fatwa* issued by Azad see Quershi: *Pan-Islam*, pp. 188ff.

[26] See the analysis of the *Hijrat* movement by Dietrich Reetz: *Hijrat: The Flight of the Faithful: A British File on the Exodus of Muslim Peasants from North India to Afghanistan in 1920*, Berlin: Das Arabische Buch 1995, based on one single British source, however. More detailed is Qureshi: *Pan-Islam*, pp. 174–232.

Maulana Azad during the Khilafat Days
Source: P.N. Chopra, *Maulana Abul Kalam Azad—unfulfilled dreams*, New Delhi: Interprint 1990, p. 20.

(see Chap. 4) witnessed a reform movement led by scholars, who were connected to the Salafis, among others. During the Khilafat struggle, Muslim peasants established a Khilafat kingdom and revolted against their Hindu landlords, some of whom they also converted forcibly, and whom they considered agents of the colonial state. Thus one of the first acts of these peasants was to burn the record-books of the landlords so as to save themselves from payment of debts. So this Mappila rebellion was not necessarily linked to the Khilafat movement but the British government considered the Khilafat movement responsible for this outbreak. It "marked the beginning of a cycle of inter-communal riots, especially in North India, which culminated in the reinforcing of a sense of inferiority among the majority community."[27] Eventually a special force named "The Malabar Special Police" was organised to provide a permanent solution to the "Mappila problem".[28]

End of Hindu-Muslim entente

Thus the caliphate had the symbolic power to integrate a variety of—contesting—social and regional Muslim and also Hindu forms of cultural articulation for a broader cause, and the Khilafat movement had different meanings in different regional contexts. As Burton Stein has argued, "the khilafat cause became transformed from the protection of a remote and archaic Turkish monarch into a mobilisation against the proximate and dangerous British enemy."[29] The abolition of the Ottoman Caliphate in 1924 by Muslims themselves led by Mustafa Kemal (1881–1938), curtailed the vigour of the Khilafat movement. In India the Khilafat Committee faced financial problems, the Congress split into ideological factions, and the latent rivalry between colonial-educated Muslims and ulama for Muslim hegemony became much more explicit. Thus the Khilafat movement did not succeed in preserving the caliphate, or uniting Indian Muslims politically or forging a permanent Hindu-Muslim nationalist alliance. But it did

---

[27] Christophe Jaffrelot: *The Hindu Nationalist Movement in India*, New York: Columbia University Press 1996, p. 20. The *madrasa* played a vitally mobilising role when, in the early twentieth century, leaders such as ʿAbd al-Qadir Moulavi (1873–1932) realised the need for reform including both secular and religious subjects. Also, Malayalam was now taught in *madrasas*, underlying the nationalist zeal of the people.

[28] For the Mappila Rebellion of 1921–1922 and for further reading in reference to Khilafat movement see Qureshi: *Pan-Islam*, pp. 445–457.

[29] Stein: *A History of India*, p. 307.

provide a basis for political mass mobilisation so far unknown in India. It intensified the spread of political and religious ideas via the media and forms of propaganda, and made Hindus and Muslims and even Christians more aware of their religious identity. In fact, Hindu-Muslim contradictions blazed up again, showing that there were problems simmering beneath the surface: maintenance of old privileges among different elites as well as access to an increasingly feeble market took religious colour and led to many "communal" outbreaks, in urban centres as well as in the hinterland, where landlords and tenants were of different religions, such as in Bengal. Moreover, many Muslims in the League felt increasingly uncomfortable with the different political and especially economic agendas of the Congress and the League, and with Gandhi's populist political propaganda[30] and the growing influence of the Hindu Mahasabha[31] upon Congress. Communal clashes led the leaders of the Mahasabha themselves to suggest the division of India into Hindu and Muslim territories. In this context both Hindus and Muslims based their narratives on some notion of a Golden Age. Hindu revivalism glorified the Gupta period of the fifth and sixth centuries C.E., i.e. the period of Brahmanical ascendancy following the threat of Buddhist heterodoxy, rather than the Aryans of the Vedic era. Muslims referred to the Quran, sunna and the pristine glory of early Islamic times. Others, such as those associated with the anti-loyalist forces in the Aligarh movement who came to be known as the Jamia Millia Islamia, were led by people such as Zakir Husain (died 1969) to start working for an alternative education system in Delhi.[32]

[30] Jinnah himself was against the prominence of any form of religion and politics, but he made Gandhi responsible for the communal drama when he "told him that he (Gandhi) had ruined politics in India by dragging up a lot of unwholesome elements in Indian life and giving them political prominence, *that it was a crime to mix up politics and religion the way he had done*." Richard Casey, Governor of Bengal, in his dairy on 6.12.1945, in *Transfer of Power*, VI, p. 617, quoted in H.M. Seervai: *Partition of India; Legend and Reality*, Bombay 1989, p. 13.

[31] Thus there was considerable communalist activity in the Congress. An extreme position of *Mahasaba* was formulated later by M.S. Golwalkar (1906–1973), who suggested the expulsion or discrimination of Muslims in his *We, or our nationhood defined*, Nagpur 1939 (see excursus: Communalism). It should be noted, however, that the severest critics of Golwalkar's ideas came from within the Congress. Gandhi was eventually killed by them.

[32] For the Jamia Millia Islamia as a nationalist alternative to the Aligarh College see Muhammad Talib: "Jamia Millia Islamia. Career of Azad Talim", in: Mushirul Hasan (ed.): *Knowledge, Power & Politics. Educational Institutions in India*, New Delhi: Roli Books 1998, pp. 156–189.

Jinnah preferred to withdraw from Congress and dedicated himself fully to the League.

The Muslim League and the demand for a Muslim state

The fora of Muslim political elites represented neither the interest of the wider population nor that of Muslim scholarship. They remained an exclusive circle of entrepreneurs and influential landowners as before, mostly from the United Provinces, reinvented as centres of Muslim separatism only later.[33] Therefore, the *Muslim League* suffered a severe loss of popularity during the Khilafat agitation (1915–1924),[34] while it became possible for a few Muslim scholars and intellectuals to find an audience for their ideas among the majority population.

In the backdrop of an increasing population and diminishing access to resources, the colonial power again reacted with repression followed by political concession. At the same time the so-called *Delhi Proposals* of spring 1927—Jinnah's brainchild—attempted to calm down increasing communal tensions by foreseeing joint electorates under certain conditions, given under mounting pressure from important Muslim groups.[35] But the *Proposals* encountered opposition from Congress, causing more friction in the Indian leadership. It was the Simon Commission in Nov. 1927 which again united Congress and League. With not a single Indian on its panel, the Commission was to look into the possibility of reform, but it was rejected by various groups such as merchants, students and politicians. Congress and League both pressed for "dominion status" for India as had been conceded to the white dominions of the British Empire under the Statute of Westminster of 1926. Others around Jawaharlal Nehru stood for independence. The Hindu Mahasabha opposed the compromise between the League renouncing separate electorates and the Congress agreeing to accept a fixed Muslim minority

[33] In these minority provinces Muslims were better represented among the intelligentsia—13% of the population were Muslim in that area, but they occupied 45% of the administrative positions.

[34] In 1915 the *Defence of India Act* was promulgated to reduce Indian participation.

[35] Such as proportionate representation of Muslims in Bengal and Punjab in legislative councils, one-third seats in central legislature be reserved for Muslims, Sind made into a Muslim-majority province, and reforms be extended to the Frontier Province; see Mushirul Hasan: "The Communal Divide: A Study of the Delhi Proposals", in: Hasan (ed.): *Communal and Pan-Islamic Trends in Colonial India*, pp. 281ff.

representation in legislative bodies. Instead, the Mahasaba demanded that Congress support "re-conversion" of non-Hindus. In this situation, the League turned to the Simon Commission to protect the separate electorates. Thus Hindu-Muslim unity collapsed and gave way to yet a new wave of communalism.

Communalism reached the pinnacle in late 1920s when the All Parties National Convention considered, among others, the *Nehru Report* (published in Aug. 1928) which had proposed to abolish separate electorates and discard weightage. The most contentious issue was the rejection of 33% representation for Muslims in the central legislature. This was a reflection of the urban "petty bourgeois" Hindus in the United Provinces (formerly Awadh and Northwestern Provinces and Agra) and the Punjab who, like Nehru and Gandhi, were uncomfortable with the concessions they had to make to Muslims. Muslim groups of higher social strata in United Provinces feared that as minorities they would never be able to win a fair proportion of seats in joint electorates.[36] The *Nehru Report*, granting Muslims only 25% of the legislative representation, was adopted by Congress. The League split into two factions, one around Jinnah, the other around Miyan Muhammad Shafiʿ (died 1932), general secretary of the Punjab Muslim League.

According to Ayesha Jalal, Jinnah demanded parity in the central government. His vision was that of a secular polity "where there was real political choice and safeguards."[37] But after the *Nehru Report* he came up with his "14 Points", published later in 1928, and which elaborated the future state of India, but evoked hopes for a separate Muslim territory as well. The "14 Points" put forward, among other things, the demand for separate electorates, provincial autonomy, a federal system of government and a constitution. However, a separate Muslim state was not yet mentioned. Therefore, the "14 Points" also became the basis for the Muslim elites' unity and their homogenising slogans, enabling them to negotiate with both the Hindus and the British as a stronger entity.

---

[36] For an analysis of the Nehru Report see Hasan: *Nationalism and Communal Politics in India*, pp. 248–281.

[37] Ayesha Jalal: *The Sole Spokesman; Jinnah, the Muslim League and the Demand for Pakistan*, Cambridge 1985, Reprint Lahore: Sang-e Meel 1992, p. 122.

Muhammad Iqbal

Meanwhile another Muslim figure rose to political fame, Muhammad Iqbal (1877–1938).[38] Born in Sialkot in Punjab, he studied English and Arabic in Lahore and completed his studies successfully in 1899 in philosophy. When he arrived in Europe in 1905 for advanced study, he was still a nationalist and at the same time a pantheist. Very early in his life he learned about Oriental studies and the Western critique of civilisation and concluded that both the materialism of Europe and the esotericism of the Orient were problematic. After he had been awarded the doctorate on the basis of his dissertation "Development of Metaphysics in Persia" in Munich in 1907, he became a member of the British Committee of the All-India Muslim League, only to return to India in 1908 to get involved in politics. In the wake of the *swadeshi* movement, which swept the country, his numerous poems first lamented the loss of Muslim power by the British colonialists in his Urdu poems "Complaint" (*Shikwa*, 1911) and "Answer to the Complaint" (*Jawab-e Shikwa*, 1912).[39] Soon he would argue for Muslim independence and emancipation in his Persian "Secrets of the Self" (*Asrar-e Khudi*, 1915). He pointed out the development of the national spirit against colonial rule, only to give the fledgling *self* a voice. Many other poems followed such as "Mysteries of Selflessness" (*Rumuz-e bekhudi*, 1918), "The Message of the East" (*Payam-e Mashriq*, 1922) and "The Sound of the Caravan Bell" (*Bang-e Dara*, 1923),[40] reflecting his commitment to the Khilafat and non-cooperation movements.

In view of the worsening Muslim decline and the growing tension between Muslims and Hindus, particularly after the collapse of the Khilafat movement in 1923–24, Iqbal began to politicise the principle of his ontological dynamics, by pointing to the necessity of a Muslim autonomy in South Asia: history to him was evolutionary, and had to

[38] Much has been written on Muhammad Iqbal; see Annemarie Schimmel: *Gabriel's Wing, A Study into the Religious Ideas of Muhammad Iqbal*, Leiden 1963; Iqbal Singh: *The Ardent Pilgrim. An Introduction to the Life and Works of Mohammad Iqbal*, New Delhi 1997; P. Hardy: *Partners in Freedom and true Muslims. Political Thought of some Muslim Scholars in British India 1912–1947*, Lund 1971. See also next chapter.

[39] Compare Muhammad Iqbal: *Shikwa & Jawab-i-Shikwa; Complaint and Answer; Iqbal's Dialogue with Allah*, transl. with intro. by Khushwant Singh, Delhi: OUP 1992(2).

[40] For an interpretation of these two collections in particular see the excellent study of Stephan Popp: *Muhammad Iqbal's Romanticism of Power. A Post-Structural Approach to His Persian Lyrical Poetry*, Wiesbaden: Reichert Verlag 2004.

be interpreted ethically.[41] The universe and life were locked together in a transcendental dance of creation, as it were. Decline was due to lack of dynamics and stagnation. Human action, he argued, led to movement, also implying the appropriation of nature. The movement in history is therefore necessarily a move ahead. Only the verve of life, the *élan vital*, as the ontological reality of change and movement, as well as *ijtihad*, the independent reasoning, would lead to the—de-territorialised—perfect human being or the Muhammadan reality—which did not need independent territory, but strove for *umma*. Besides his numerous poetry collections his prose text *Reconstruction of Religious Thought in Islam* (Lahore 1930) gives further theoretical explanations for *ijtihad* and the application of analytical deduction, showing his debt he owed to Shah Wali Allah, Sayyid Ahmad Khan, and European philosophers such as Goethe, Nietzsche and Bergson.

In the 1920s Iqbal entered local Punjabi politics, and by 1927 he, as one of the leaders of the Punjab Muslim League, denounced any cooperation with Congress when he rejected the *Delhi Proposals* that foresaw joint electorates under the condition that Muslim seats in the central legislature would at least be one-third of the total. The idea of a Muslim homeland matured to reach the first peak in Iqbal's famous Presidential Address to the Annual Meeting of the All-India Muslim League on December 29, 1930 in Allahabad, when the poet-philosopher expounded the idea of two nations in India, i.e., a "Consolidated Northwestern Muslim State" on the subcontinent:[42]

> It cannot be denied that Islam [...] has been the chief formative factor in the life-history of the Muslims in India [...] (and has) transform(ed) them into a well-defined people. [...] Muslim society, with its remarkable homogeneity and inner unity, has grown to be what it is under the pressure of the laws and institutions associated with the culture of Islam. [...] Is it possible to retain Islam as an ethical ideal and to reject it as a polity in favour of national politics, in which a religious attitude is not permitted to play any part? This question becomes of special importance in India where the Muslims happen to be in a minority. [...] I would like to see the Punjab, North-West Frontier Province, Sind and Baluchistan

---

[41] Compare the brief introduction to Iqbal's historical view with paradigmatic texts by Malik, in: Gottlob (ed.): *Historical Thinking in South Asia*, pp. 163–167.

[42] Cp. Ahmad et al. (eds.): *Self-Statement*, pp. 148ff.

> amalgamated into a single State. [...] the formation of a consolidated North-West Indian Muslim State appears to me to be the final destiny of the Muslims, at least of North-West India. [...] I therefore demand the formation of a consolidated Muslim State in the best interests of India and Islam. For India it means security and peace resulting from an internal balance of power; for Islam an opportunity to rid itself of the stamp that Arabian imperialism was forced to give it, to mobilize its law, its education, its culture, and to bring them into closer contact with its own original spirit and with the spirit of modern times. Thus it is clear that in view of India's infinite variety in climates, races, languages, creeds, and social systems, the creation of autonomous States based on the unity of language, race, history, religion, and identity of economic interests, is the only possible way to secure a stable constitutional structure in India. [...].[43]

The speech became the landmark in the struggle for an independent state, though one may question the meaning it acquired for Muslim nationalists. After all, the text of the "Resolution" seemed more like an expression of frustrations of the Punjabi urban professional groups than a well-thought-out scheme to which the Muslim League did not pay much attention initially; his views—poetical and political—seemed to be confined to Punjabi urban middle-class Muslims as major channels for emancipation and dynamism.[44]

Jinnah, meanwhile, went to Cambridge, where he came into contact with the Pakistan National Movement and its leader Rahmat ʿAli[45] (died 1951), who studied in Europe and was inspired by Iqbal's idea of a separate Muslim territory. Extending it further in 1933, Rahmat ʿAli gave a name to the imagined territory: "Pakstan" or "Land of the Pure", which at the same time is said to be an acronym of "Punjab, Afghania (North-West Frontier Province), Kashmir, Sind and Baluchistan." However, Rahmat ʿAli's idea of a sovereign Muslim state neglected Muslims in the minority provinces and also in Bengal.[46] After his return to India, Jinnah worked to enforce the League's claim of being the sole representative of Indian Muslims although the party was initially manned

---

[43] Muhammad Iqbal, 'Presidential Address', in: *Speeches and Statements of Iqbal*, Lahore: Al-Manar Academy 1948(2), pp. 3–6, 8, 13, 15, 34–36.

[44] See Popp: *Muhammad Iqbal's Romanticism of Power*.

[45] Compare K.K. Aziz: *Rahmat Ali, a Biography*, Lahore 1987; Rahmat Ali: *Now or Never: Are we to Live or Perish For Ever?* Cambridge 1933.

[46] Rahmat ʿAli therefore coined another Muslim state *Bangistan* (for Bengal) in 1942. See Rahmat Ali: *Bangistan: The Fatherland of the Bang Nation*, The Bangistan National Movement, Cambridge, Sept. 1946.

by influential landlords, later also by entrepreneurs and economic magnates. Since the end of the 1930s, the League's slogan was that Muslims would be suppressed in an independent, democratically ruled India—an idea that had been nurtured in Aligarh. These sentiments were aggravated by the government's discussion about greater devolution of power in India in 1935 (*Government of India Act*) in its capacity as a federation of autonomous provinces under the condition that at least half of the Princely States would cooperate, which, however, they did not. Thus the implementation of further autonomy did not take place; rather, the 1937 elections, resulting from the Act of 1935, led to diarchy in the provinces.

Political manoeuvring

Initially the idea of a separate land was alien to the overwhelming majority of Indian Muslims, as can also be seen in the concept of composite nationalism. So in the 1937 elections, the League could not even win in the Muslim majority provinces.[47] In Punjab the feudal Unionist Party won, while in Bengal, despite entering into an alliance with other parties and being also supported by well-to-do groups, the League was not successful. It received approximately one quarter of the seats reserved for the Muslims. Apparently, the League had only a small following among the Muslim masses: the dominant party of NWFP, *Khuda-ye Khidmatgar* (see Chap. 12) was a Pakhtun nationalist movement, allied with Congress; the JUH never accepted the two-nation theory; the Ahrar party in Punjab refused to join the League, accepting instead the political and economic objectives of the Congress. In Bihar, the Momin Ansar Conference (Party of Muslim Weavers) remained opposed to the League. Baluchistani nationalists were also opposed to the division of the country. Furthermore, many organisations with Muslim members, such as the Shia Conference, the State People's Conference, Trade Unions, and Kisan Sabhas had adopted the same political platform as the Congress. Thus Congress won the majority in

[47] The League's limited representation and franchise was due to the diversity of Indian Muslims. See Mushirul Hasan: *Legacy of a Divided Nation; India's Muslims Since Independence*. Delhi: OUP 1997.

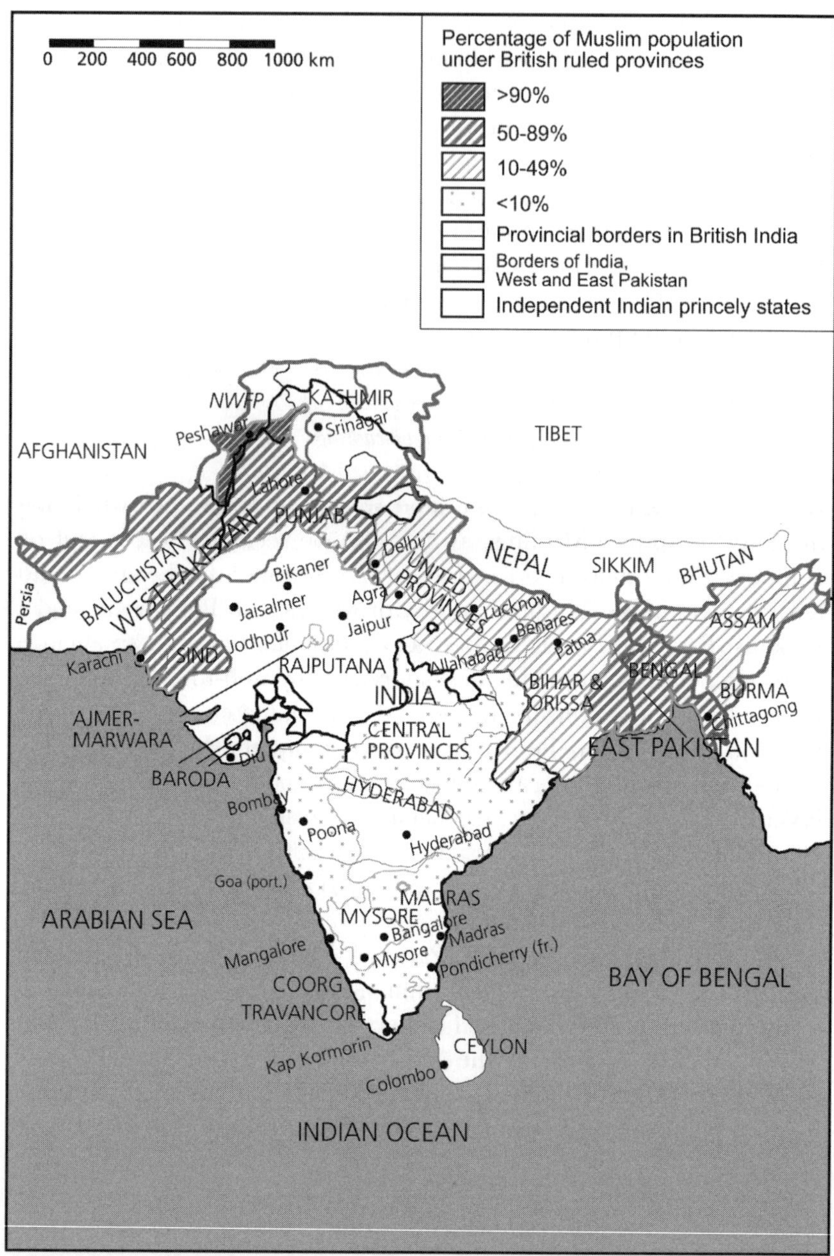

Map 11: South Asia between colonialism and independence (1937–1948)

those provinces where it formed the government; the Muslim League received an insignificant number of the Muslim vote.

After this debacle, Jinnah started to work vigorously towards the creation of a common Muslim identity with political aspirations opposed to those of Congress which gave boost to a lingering Muslim separatism. He insisted that "Honorable settlements can only be achieved between equals, and unless the two parties learn to respect and fear each other, there is no solid ground for any settlement." In developing the "Two-Nation-Theory", Jinnah now—as usual in the English language—publically spoke of a common Muslim identity and of national aims of the Muslims. He was celebrated as the "great leader" (*Qa'id-e A'zam*), and, in March 1940, finally, demanded a separate territorial entity which would integrate all Muslim *qaums*. His identity-politics made use of the affective semiotics of the word *qaum* which could refer to collective identity such as caste, profession, region and religion but also to people with a distinctive culture and civilisation, language and literature. In his presidential address at the Lahore session of the Muslim League he said: "The history of the last 12 hundred years has failed to achieve unity and has witnessed, during the ages, India always divided into Hindu India and Muslim India." This address became known as the "Lahore Resolution".[48] As its declarations deliberately were kept vague and ambiguous (e.g., the problem of Muslim minorities and foreign policy remained open), the "resolution" should be regarded as a working paper for negotiations with leaders of Muslim majority provinces, with the British and also with the Congress rather than a blueprint for the establishment of a Muslim nation. Rahmat 'Ali was by then conveniently forgotten.

The League played a populist tune by means of journals, religious scholars, symbolism, and terminology, thereby creating a preference for an imagined community of brethren. Islam is endangered, all Indian Muslims constitute one single community and deserve a nation of their own, was the message conveyed. This emphasised the affiliation to the Arabic-Persian cultural area and petrified the division between Muslims and non-Muslims, no matter whether Hindus or other. By way of an exclusive Muslim territory, the Muslim League promised religious, social, and political equality, as well as economic benefits to Islamic scholars, young intellectuals, entrepreneurs, the unemployed, and

[48] Philips: *Evolution of India and Pakistan*, pp. 345–5.

even farmers. A protected market and state support, no more Hindu majority, the unlimited prospect for feudal lords to appropriate land, these were all reasons to hope for Muslims running industries, banks and Muslim trade. The slogan *Pakistan ka matlab kya, la ilaha illa Allah* (What does Pakistan mean? No other Deity than Allah!) seemed to be the consensual common denominator of the various and also contesting groups, i.e. *qaums*, involved. Of all the social groups, the Muslim middle class in the Indian metropolis and especially in the cities and *qasbahs* of the United Provinces, Calcutta and Bombay seemed to have responded most to this Muslim separatism[49] though other areas were also involved, such as Punjab and Sind where particularly *pirs* and their institutions were mobilised by the Muslim League which also witnessed some opposition there.[50] Only gradually did the balance of power within the League swing from moderate, constitutional lawyers toward the advocates of religious self-assertion and broad-based political mobilisation. The rise of a new type of young educated Muslim brought a new approach to Muslim politics and rejected the loyalist approach of earlier Muslim modernists—they were willing to agitate. In this context, the rise of the Muslim League has been interpreted in its success in manipulating the discontent and fear among various classes that resulted from the policies of the Congress ministry. The policies seemed to threaten Muslim landlords, the urban elite as well as working populations.[51]

Although World War II imposed certain constraints upon the nationalist demands, the "Atlantic Charter" of August 1941 inaugurated a new perspective on the people's self-determination. While the League could further prove its strength in the 1945–46 elections, the colonial rulers had no clear concept of how to proceed. The *Cabinet Mission Plan* of March 1946 fell back on an offer made during the War (*Cripps' Offer*, 1942), allowing a Muslim state within an Indian federation. But,

[49] Francis Robinson has elaborated on this at quite some length in his *Separatism among Indian Muslims*. Paul Brass: *Language, Religion and Politics*, Cambridge: CUP 1974, has argued that the elites alone manipulated the masses for their own purposes.

[50] For detailed studies of these separatist processes in different areas see David Gilmartin: *Empire and Islam: Punjab and the Making of Pakistan*, Berkeley: UCP 1988; Ian Talbot: *Provincial Politics and the Pakistan Movement; The Growth of the Muslim League in North-West and North-East India 1937–47*, Karachi: OUP 1988, and Ansari: *Sufi Saints and State Power*.

[51] Thus Seyed Nesar Ahmad: *Origins of Muslim Consciousness in India. A World-System Perspective*, New York 1991, p. 178.

as Congress under the leadership of J.L. Nehru (1889–1964) did not agree to abide by the recommendation of the Cabinet Plan after the transfer of power, the League withdrew itself from the plan. In this respect it has been assumed that "it was the Congress that insisted on partition. It was Jinnah who was against Partition."[52] Apparently, Jinnah initially was in favour of Indian unity, similar to other Muslim leaders. But in 1943 he expressed his opinion against a federation,[53] just in contrast to Husain Ahmad Madani (1879–1957), Principal of Dar al-ʿUlum Deoband, and chief spokesman of JUH, who in April 1946 was in favour of one Centre and one Constituent Assembly, with Hindus and Muslims sharing parity both in the government and in the Central Legislature.[54] Elections should be based in joint electorates coupled with reserved seats.[55] Gandhi, however, was against this parity: "The Muslim majority Provinces represent over 9 crore of the population as against 19 crore of the Hindu majority Provinces. This is really worse than Pakistan. What is suggested in its place is that the Central Legislature should be formed on the population basis. And so too the Executive."[56]

Independence and Partition

As the Viceroy wanted to go ahead with the plan, Jinnah resisted and, on August 16, 1946, called for a *Direct Action Day*, which unleashed the communal bloodbath of Muslims and Hindus in Calcutta. To avoid further worsening of the situation, a plan of partition was worked out hurriedly under the new Viceroy Mountbatten (1900–1979) (*Plan Balkan*).[57] The plan did not maintain the unity of India, but proposed

[52] Jalal: *The Sole Spokesman*, p. 262.

[53] See Ahmad et al. (eds.): *Self-Statement*, p. 155.

[54] This idea of a composite nationalism was outlined in Madani's book *Muttahida Qaumiyyat aur Islam* in 1938 (see Chaps. 12 and 15). In the course of Madani's political activities he was also detained in Malta for his involvement in the so-called *silk-letter conspiracy*, but after his release in 1920 again became active in the freedom struggle against the British. See Syed Mohammad Mian: *The Prisoners of Malta*, transl. from Urdu into English by Mohammad Anwer Hussain and Imam Manak, Delhi 2004.

[55] Compare Seervai: *Partition of India*, p. 43.

[56] Gandhi quoted in *Transfer of Power, VII*, p. 466, in Seervai: *Partition of India*, p. 44.

[57] The role of Mountbatten has been questioned by A. Roy: "The high politics of India's partition", in: *MAS* 24 (1990), pp. 385–415.

Muslim majority provinces at the cost of the partition of Punjab, Bengal and Bihar.[58] *Divide and rule* changed into *divide and quit.*

The problem was one of interpretation over the 'residual powers', the Congress insisting that it remain with the centre, the League arguing for a loose federation. The Congress plan was within the concept of a multi-lingual, multi-religious nation state, the like of which had not been experimented before. To let go of it meant the death of many ideas which the Congress had cherished for decades. Thus it would be wrong to blame the Congress for Partition or for that matter the Muslim League. The subsequent creation of Bangladesh (see Chap. 13) did prove the Congress right that religion could not be the basis of a nation state on the Indian subcontinent.

In August 1947 West and East Pakistan were separated from India rather hastily. The following migration of about 15 million people was accompanied by unbridled massacres, the wounds of which have not healed yet. It is only recently, in the wake of the fiftieth anniversary of independence, that contemporary literature and historians have started dealing with the traumatic experiences of partition intensively to focus on the fate of ordinary people. This marked change in partition historiography also draws attention away from usually male-dominated party politics and channels of mobilisation to a more de-centred popular experience. The studies also show that the experience of partition was not singular. Often it meant very different things to different sets of Muslims—and Hindus. Although politically aligned with the Muslim League, large numbers refused to leave their villages and towns when it dawned upon them that partition would mean only a change of locality.[59]

---

[58] The experiences of Punjab and Bengal have been two dominant nodes of research on Partition in India, but the experience of Bihar is a third case that researchers have been marginally concerned about. Though communal riots occurred in Bihar during 1947–8, Bihar's case seems to be peculiar in that no separatist movement emerged from Bihar, unlike Punjab and Bengal. Thus it would be important to study this 'third case' to enrich our understanding of the history of Partition in India and Pakistan.

[59] See Leslie A. Flemming: *Another Lonely Voice: The Life and Works of Saadat Hasan Manto*, Lahore 1985; Alok Bhalla: *Stories about the Partition of India*, 3 Vols. Delhi 1994; Saros Cowasjee and K.S. Duggal (eds.): *Orphans of the Storm: Stories on the Partition of India.* Delhi: UBSPD 1995; among the historians who have been working towards giving voice to the victims of partition are Mushirul Hasan (ed.): *India Partitioned: The Other Face of Freedom*, 2 vols., Delhi: Roli Books 1995; on those who explore the trauma and loss suffered by women see Ritu Menon and Kamla Bhasin (eds.): *Borders and Boundaries*, New Delhi: Kali for Women 1998; see also Mushirul Hasan (ed.): *Inventing Boundaries:*

With the tragic legacy of an uncertain future, a young refugee sits on the walls of Purana Qila, transformed into a vast refugee camp in Delhi. Picture taken by the American photojournalist Margaret Bourke-White in 1947 Courtesy Visage images representing Getty images.

The princely State of Haydarabad with its Hindu majority decided to remain independent, though there was the People's Movement in Haydarabad State[60] which did want a merger with India. Soon, Haydarabad was merged forcefully with the Indian Union in 1948 through a *Police Action*.[61] Pakistan in turn supported the "war of independence" by the Muslim majority in Kashmir, where India sent her troops in response to a request for help made by the then ruler, Maharaja Hari Singh, and the leader of the National Conference, Shaikh Muhammad ʿAbd Allah. The Muslim-Hindu divide in Kashmir has a long history:[62] unlike in Mughal India with its Muslim ruler being on top of a layered authority and maintaining an equidistant approach to all religions, in the Dogra-ruled Kashmir, the Hindu ruler not only centralised all power but also created a Hindu sovereignty facilitated by a colonial withdrawal after 1846 when the treaty of Amritsar was signed. Soon the already developing conterminous religious and class divisions were further strengthened when the small Hindu minority acquired disproportionate influence in administration and landed gentry. Socio-economic difference ran conterminous with religious identity-politics. While this did not seriously challenge Dogra rule for almost a hundred years, one might ask whether the concept of *Kashmiriyyat* glossed over the major fault lines between Hindu-Muslims relations, to produce an argument for Kashmir to be the natural part of secular India.[63] Chitralekha Zutshi is probably right in saying that "The 'happiness' of the Kashmir Valley, particularly for India's colonial masters, perhaps had more to do with its geographical attributes, which rendered it a cool haven for

---

Gender, Politics and the Partition of India, Delhi 2000; S. Kaul (ed.): *The Partitions of Memory: The Afterlife of the Division of India*, Delhi 2001. Compare the interesting overview on partition historiography by Yasmin Khan: "Asking New Questions about Partition of the Indian Subcontinent", in: *History Compass*, Blackwell Publishing Ltd. 2004, http://www.history-compass.com/popups/print.asp?items=7554, accessed 25.04.2005.

[60] There were quite a number of people's movements in the princely states. See Y. Vaikuntham (ed.): *People's Movements in the Princely States*, New Delhi: Manohar 2004.

[61] Compare Margrit Pernau: *The Passing of Partimonialism: Politics and Political Culture in Hyderabad 1911–1948*, New Delhi: Manohar 2000.

[62] For an interesting discussion of religions in Kashmir see T.N. Madan: "Religious Ideology in a Plural Society: The Muslim and Hindus of Kashmir", in: *Contribution to Indian Sociology* 6 (1972), pp. 106–41.

[63] These and other topics are dealt with by Mridu Rai: *Hindu Rulers, Muslim Subjects: Islam, Rights, and the History of Kashmir*, Princeton: PUP 2004, and Chitralekha Zutshi: *Languages of Belonging: Islam, Regional Identity, and the Making of Kashmir*, New York: OUP 2004.

the heat-weary British, than with any peculiarities of the people in the region."[64] In fact, the Kashmir conflict has led to a number of armed flare-ups between Pakistan and India, and remains one of the most crisis-prone areas in South Asia even now. Pakistan witnessed severe problems of national integration, which were to tear apart the multi-ethnic and multi-lingual country divided into two realms.[65]

In the nineteenth century, India played a vital role for the British economy, as a market as well as producer of raw materials, as a job market as well as military resource. The costs of these goods were all borne by the Indian tax payer. It was, therefore, important for the British to keep India in a de-centralised form of government as inexpensively as possible, and also by integrating important social groups. But these groups increasingly raised their voices, particularly after 1880, to gain autonomy. After all, they had access to the dominant, colonial language as well as to the new channels of communication by which they could reach a larger audience. The administrative reforms and political decentralisation occurring in 1920 and 1935 were born from the necessity to stabilise British authority and also to give more rights to the Indians. They could not, however, work together. Gradually, in the late 1930s, India was able to improve its terms of trade, so that British investments in India decreased. The number of local traders and businessmen increased. India no longer looked attractive as a job market for the British, and the Indian army could not be modernised for lack of funds. Decentralisation was thought to be one possible way to finding new possibilities to hold on to India. When this did not work out, the colonial power had to quit, however, leaving behind the heavy burden of a colonial legacy.

Meanwhile, the vacuous solidarity between Indian intellectuals and traditional higher social groups was being tested by new groups demanding an independent Muslim territory. These new diverse groups, lacking any unity whatsoever, in no way represented the whole of Indian Muslims. As the following chapter shows, they were too divergent in terms of their backgrounds, affiliations, loyalties, channels of communication and, most importantly, interests.

---

[64] Zutshi: *Languages of Belonging*, p. 4.

[65] From the point of view of international law see also Patrick Hönig: *Der Kaschmirkonflikt und das Recht der Völker auf Selbstbestimmung*, Berlin: Duncker & Humblot 2000.

EXCURSUS

COMMUNALISM

"Simply put, communalism is the belief that because a group of people follow a particular religion they have, as a result, common social, political and economic interests."[1] Thus, politicised religious identity claims primary loyalty.

There are many arguments on communalism, some seeking its indigenous roots in conflicting eighteenth century activities of Muslim and Hindu groups, which later turned into nationalism.[2] It is also seen in protest traditions of each religious community—going as far back as considering Buddhism a Hindu protest movement! The majority of scholars thinks it has been used as a political tool in the colonial context; that is the politicisation of primordial—religious—identities. The colonial codification of (religious) law for different communities, helped reify and essentialise communities as tolerant, martial or otherwise. This transformed the Indian population into a universe defined primarily in terms of religion and caste.[3] Consequently, a new—colonial—historiography evolved suggesting that Muslims and Hindus had been contesting each other ever since. Such an understanding of Indian history figured prominently in James Mill's effort when he divided it into Hindu, Muslim and British periods. Mill's notion was perpetuated by Elliot und Dowson in 1849, who postulated that only the British would

---

[1] Bipan Chandra: *Communalism in Modern India*, Delhi: Vikas Publishing House 1984, p. 1.

[2] Cf. Christopher A. Bayly: *Origins of Nationality in South Asia. Patriotism and Ethical Government in the Making of Modern India*, New Delhi: OUP 1998, pp. 210–237; C.A. Bayly: "The Pre-history of 'Communalism'? Religious Conflict in India, 1700–1860", in: *MAS* 19 (1985), pp. 177–203. There is a long tradition of constructing the Hindu Self and Muslim Other, and vice versa, but the discourse was not primarily religious; the Muslim was hardly referred to in religious terms. See Ian Talbot: "Inscribing the Other, Inscribing the Self: Hind-Muslim Relations in Pre-Colonial India", in: *Comparative Studies in Society and History* 37 (1995), pp. 692–722; also Muzaffar Alam and Seema Alavi: "Negotiating Identities: People, Culture and Politics in an Eighteen Century Indo-Persian Text", in: Malik (ed.): *Perspectives of Mutual Encounters*, pp. 228–259.

[3] Cf. Gyanendra Pandey: *The Construction of Communalism in Colonial North India*, New Delhi: OUP 1990.

make "our native subjects more sensible of the immense advantages accruing to them under the mildness and equity of our rule".[4]

In constructing this communalist master narrative, local myth and oral tradition were often uncritically reproduced as historiography in the gazetteers, which again became the basis for further history writing. This process went hand in hand with the production of powerful stereotypes such as the "bigoted Julaha", the fierce Pathan, the intriguing Brahman, the criminal Pasis, etc. Since these characters became transpersonal and trans-individual, timeless and spaceless, they suggested a primordial essence attached to specific castes and/or religions feeding into communalism. Thus, communalism was seen as an expression of caste, as the all-defining culture of India.[5]

Thus, the split into two major religious groups can be traced back to colonial times, when religion came to be considered as the only binding identity. Religion would outweigh other variables of composite identity such as society, gender, culture, economy and politics. As such communities had their specific history and culture, excluding and contesting each other. Seen from this angle, communalism is a strategic taxonomy to make sense of the Indian others' difference. This correlated with the notion of *commune* popularised by the Parisian commune since 1871, symbolising autonomy, so that the Viceroy of India, the Marquis of Dufferin, could state in 1888, that "The most patent characteristic of our Indian cosmos is its division into two mighty political communities as distant from each other as the poles asunder...".[6]

When this colonial historiography began to be contested by local historiography, Hindus and Muslims had already been constructed into two different monolithic groups. Divisions developed further in the 1920s and 1930s in the *Minority Report 1924* and culminated in the *Nehru Report* of 1928 which stated, "The communal problem of India is primarily the Hindu-Muslim problem".[7]

Some nationalists tried to restore religious pluralism by secularising historiography or integrating Hindus and Muslims in the Khilafat

---

[4] Elliott in Chandra: *Communalism*, p. 213.
[5] Pandey: *The Construction*, p. 108.
[6] Dufferin quoted in Chandra: *Communalism*, p. 26.
[7] Pandey: *The Construction*, pp. 8f.

movement. But after the collapse of this movement, communal outbreaks increased. They were rationalised by protagonists of communalism. Among Hindu groups there were the Arya Samaj founded in 1875,[8] which became radicalised in the course of the reconversion-movement (*shuddhi*) under Swami Shraddhanand (1856–1926) and the Gurukul-movement.[9] This attempt to shape Hindu community found its counterpart in Muslim movements such as Tablighi Jama'at. People like V.D. Savarkar (1883–1966) postulated that religions not originating in India were non-Indian and thus strange to this soil. The "cultural nationalism" formulated in his *Hindutva* (Hinduness) of 1923 culminated thus: "The Hindus are the nation in India—in Hindusthan, and the Moslem a minority community."[10] Similarly, M.S. Golwalkar (1906–1973) was specific in his *We: Our Nationhood Defined* (Nagpur 1939).[11] A major argument was that Hindus had always been ruled and persecuted by the brutal Muslims. Both Savarkar and Golwalkar were highly appreciative of Nazi Germany and the treatment of minorities there. So their concept of nationalism was not indigenous, as the Hindu Right argues. Muslims used similar arguments like Shaukat ʿAli in 1929: "Hindus have been habituated to slavery and they would remain slaves."[12]

---

[8] Cf. Kenneth W. Jones: *Arya Dharm. Hindu Consciousness in 19th-Century Panjab*, New Delhi: Manohar 1989.

[9] Cf. Harald Fischer-Tiné: "'The only hope for fallen India'. The Gurukul Kangri as an Experiment in National Education (1902–1922)", in: Georg Berkemer et alii (eds.): *Explorations in the History of South Asia. Essays in Honour of Dietmar Rothermund*, New Delhi: Manohar 2001, pp. 277–99; also Chr. Jaffrelot: "Hindu Nationalism, Strategic Syncretism in Ideology Building", in: *The Indian Journal of Social Science* 5/4 (1992), pp. 373–392.

[10] Savarkar postulated the concept of *Pitrabhoomi* (Fatherland) and *Punyabhoomi* (Holy Land). His argument was that for the Hindus both *Pitrabhoomi* and *Punyabhoomi* were in India, while for the Muslims and Christians they were elsewhere. For the Muslims, their *Punyabhoomi* was in Mecca while for the Christians in Jerusalem. These minorities therefore can never be trusted fully and their loyalty to India would always remain suspect.

[11] "The non-Hindu peoples in Hindusthan must either adopt the Hindu culture and language, must learn to respect and hold in reverence Hindu religion, must entertain no ideas but those of glorification of the Hindu race and culture, i.e., they must not only give up their attitude of intolerance and ungratefulness towards this land and its agelong traditions but must also cultivate the positive attitude of love and devotion instead—in one word, they must cease to be foreigners, or may stay in the country, wholly subordinated to the Hindu nation, claiming nothing, deserving no privileges, far less any preferential treatment—not even citizen's rights." Golwalkar quoted in Chandra: *Communalism*, pp. 217f. For these men and ideas see Bruce Graham: *Hindu Nationalism and Indian Politics. The Origins and Development of the Bharatiya Jana Sangh*, Cambridge: CUP 1990.

[12] Cited in Chandra: *Communalism*, p. 220.

Hindu and Muslim leaders are themselves objects of communalism, and try to mobilise traditional concepts of self-identification which are broad enough to provide the basis for new identities. Thus communalism returns to tradition but does not restore it, in a situation where the state and its agents are not able—due to failing national integration—to push through their institutions and thus provide alternative structures to the historically developed lineages and patterns of social organisations. The state's failure to de-institutionalise these historical patterns of social organisation ultimately reactivates them. Put into a religious discourse, they become prominent channels for mass mobilisation: it seems as if communalism is a logical result of failing national integration or a "back-door nationalism",[13] when religion becomes an instrument in the hands of a few who, due to their level of education and wealth, can afford to think along these lines and capitalise on religious sentiments, especially among the economically weak. Slaughtering, music in front of mosques, disputes over land, molesting of women and elections etc. are occasions when conflicts erupt on an ad-hoc basis.

The twentieth century witnessed the emergence of umbrella organisations that promoted communalism, like the All-India Muslim League, the Shiromani Gurduvara Prabandhak Committee of the Sikhs,[14] and the Hindu-dominated Akhil-Bharatiyya Hindu Mahasabha.[15] In the wake of partition a number of radical movements evolved under the aegis of the Hindu Mahasabha, such as the 'National Volunteer Corps' (Rashtriyya Swayamsevak Sangh, RSS) (1925) and the World Hindu Council (Vishwa Hindu Parishad, VHP).[16] Later, under Indira Gandhi (1917–1984), the communalisation of Indian politics led to the emergence of other communalist parties, such as the Bharatiyya

[13] Romila Thapar et al.: *Communalism and the Writing of Indian History*, New Delhi 1977 (2), pp. 39–61.

[14] Cf. Mark Juergensmeyer: *Religious Nationalism Confronts the National State*, Delhi [et al.]: OUP, 1996, 93; Marla Stukenberg: *Der Sikh-Konflikt. Eine Fallstudie zur Politisierung ethnischer Identität*, Stuttgart: Steiner 1995, pp. 49–51.

[15] Cf. Thomas Blom Hansen: *The Saffron Wave. Democracy and Hindu Nationalism in Modern India*, New Delhi: OUP 1999, pp. 74–6 et passim; Partha S. Gosh: *BJP and the Evolution of Hindu Nationalism. From Periphery to Centre*, New Delhi: Manohar, 2000, pp. 63–71.

[16] Cf. A.T. Embree: "The Function of the Rashtriya Swayamsevak Sangh: To Define the Hindu Nation", in: Martin E. Marty/R. Scott Appleby (eds.): *Accounting for Fundamentalisms. The Dynamic Character of Movements*, Chicago: UCP 1994, pp. 617–52; P. van der Veer: *Hindu Nationalism and the Discourse of Modernity: The Vishva Hindu Parishad*, in: ibid., pp. 653–668.

Jana Sangh that later turned into the *Indian People's Party* (Bharatiyya Janata Party; BJP).[17]

In the confessionalisation of communal identity, history is an important tool. The construction and establishment of master narratives of a dominant history against divergent 'sect histories' or in relation to historical constructs of other religions is as important as the role of memory in the representation of the past. History is being reinterpreted to conceptualise the world anew. To re-invent this—religious—tradition, elements of past and local institutions are used to appeal to broader masses. Panegyrics and iconography and the cult of manliness[18]—such as that provided by the re-imagination of Shivaji and Aurangzeb as the apex of religious zeal—and the deliberate use of a variety of religious paraphernalia as well as rituals and symbolic behaviour are proven devices to mobilise people.[19] "A sadhu is the best political worker you can ask for... He travels long miles, meets scores of people, and can subsist on almost no food or clothing. Above all, he will not emerge as a rival politician."[20] The reciprocal demonisation is as important as the mythologisation of one's origin and history. The "saffronisation of history" in India and the re-writing of history under Zia al-Haqq in Pakistan are cases in point.[21]

Major issues in the communal encounter are sacred body (Shah Bano), sacred space in Ayodhya (Babri Masjid-Ramjanmabhumi-controversy),

---

[17] Cf. Gosh: *BJP*; Hansen: *Saffron Wave*; Chr. Jaffrelot: "The BJP in Madhya Pradesh: Networks, Strategies and Power", in: Gyanendra Pandey (ed.): *Hindus and Others; The question of identity in India today*, New Delhi: Viking 1993, pp. 110–137, is an insightful overview of the early development of the BJP.

[18] For the analysis of the masculinity of these myths, see Anuradha Kapur: "Deity to Crusader: The Changing Iconography of Ram", in: Pandey (ed.): *Hindus and Others*, pp. 74–107. The masculisation has a long history of colonial effeminacy of Hindu males later prominently adapted in the Hindu nationalist discourse to counter the Muslim Other. "This dominant view of the Muslim proclivity for producing children as a calculated strategy for outnumbering the Hindus demographically is an argument that continues to resurface in contemporary *Hindutva* discourse." Thus race is fused with nation. See Zaheer Baber: "'Race', Religion and Riots: The 'Racialization' of Communal Identity and Conflict in India", in: *Sociology* 38(4) (2004), pp. 701–718, quotation pp. 706f.

[19] For the different channels of mobilisation see Freitag: *Collective Action and Community*. Tapan Basu et. alii: *Khaki Shorts, Saffron Flags*, New Delhi: Orient Longman 1993 give a detailed view into the different Hindu strategies in early 1990s. Also Neeladri Bhattacharya: "Myth, History and the Politics of Ramjanmabhoomi", in: Sarvepalli Gopal (ed.): *Anatomy of a Confrontation*, New Delhi: Viking 1991, pp. 122–140.

[20] Malkani, BJP Vice-President, quoted in *India Today*, 30 April 1991, p. 52.

[21] See Basu et alii: *Khaki Shorts, Saffron Flag*; K.K. Aziz: *The Murder of History*, Lahore: Vanguard 1993.

sacred law (Muslim Personal Law-Uniform Civil Code-controversy),[22] and language (see excursus: Urdu and Gender, and Chap. 15).

The Ayodhya issue went back to the eighteenth century when a Hindu sect—the Ramanandis—started re-inventing the cult of Rama (Vaishnavites), and was backed by the Shiʿite Nawwab Safdar Jang against the Shaivites. Until 1855 the place was frequented by both Muslims and Hindus for prayers and worship. During the so-called Hanumangarhi affair some Sunnis started arguing that the temple of Lord Hanuman in Ayodhya had been built on a former mosque. This Sunnite argument was actually to pressurise the Shiʿite Nawwabi ruler, who now was in difficulties, to protect either the Sunni Muslims or the agitated Hindus. When the Ramanandis encountered Sunni Muslims militarily the latter fled into the Babri Masjid where they were killed by the former, who eventually occupied the place to call it the historical birthplace of Rama. The issue lingered for a century, the British being hesitant to take sides. It was only shortly after independence, in March 1949, that idols of Rama and his wife Sita were found in the dome of the Babri Mosque, thus underlining the Hindu claim on this sacred space. This laid the basis for renewed communal upheavals. The government closed down the mosque, declaring it disputed area. The VHP, which was leading the agitation to claim Babri Mosque as the birthplace of Rama for Hindus, was supported by the then Prime Minister Indira Gandhi when the Babri Mosque started to become politicised from 1983 onwards. In 1986 Rajiv Gandhi used the symbol of the Babri Mosque to reignite communal passions and handed over the keys to the VHP, which called the space Ramjanambhomi, birthplace of Lord Ram.[23]

---

[22] Much has been written on these issues; see for example Gopal (ed.): *Anatomy of a Confrontation*; Asghar Ali Engineer: *Lifting the Veil: Communal Violence and Communal Harmony in Contemporary India*, Bombay 1995; J.-P. Hartung: "The Land, the Mosque, the Temple", in: Bonney (ed.): *Ayodhya 1992–2003*, pp. 31–44; H.A. Gani: *Reform of Muslim Personal Law. The Shah Bano Controversy and the Muslim Women (Protection of Rights on Divorce) Act, 1986*, New Delhi: Deep & Deep Publ. 1988; Ali Asghar Engineer (ed.): *The Shah Bano Controversy*, Haydarabad: Orient Longman 1987.

[23] It is Rama rather than Shiva who becomes the rallying ground for Hindu nationalists: Rama is the upholder of the traditional system of Hindu caste hierarchy (*varna*). It was to maintain this traditional balance that Rama killed Shambukh, a low caste claiming to be as learned as the Brahman. Rama also represents a patriarchal God when he doubts Sita and asks her to go through the test of fire, *agni-parikhsa*. It is not a coincidence that the initial camp followers of the RSS were Maharashtrian Brahmins and later in north India, the BJP became and still is an upper caste Hindu phenomenon. Shiva, on the other hand, seems to be problematic to appropriate in this way because he is most heterodox and liminal. He cavorts even with the lowest of the lowly, the

The reopening of the mosque has been seen as the tribute to the victory of the All India Muslim Personal Law Board in the Shah Bano case.[24] Communal riots[25] followed and eventually led to the demolition of the mosque by Hindu fanatics in Dec. 1992.[26] The tensions generated what Peter van der Veer called "Religious Nationalism".[27] Thus communalism is "a modern ideology that incorporated some aspects and elements of the past ideologies and institutions and historical background to form a new ideological and political discourse or mix", it is not a revival of traditional ideology, and it is not a primordial feeling.[28] Insofar communalism can be considered near some sort of nationalism.

Naturally, economic dynamics lead to a new level of competition and conflict, mostly in industrial cities where the Muslim share is relatively high (15–60%):[29] by the end of the 1950s, for example, the tensions were results of economic misery and increasing social disintegration in urban centres. In the recent past the Hindu-Muslim communal outbreaks have increased from 240 in 1972 to 525 in 1985[30] culminating in the riots following the destruction of the Babri Mosque and later in Gujarat in 2002. Lately, this communalism is gradually being carried into rural areas where in 1985 some 46% and in 1995 more than 50% of the conflicts took place. As noted above, the patterns to explain communalism are often derived from the "divide and rule" policy of the colonial masters, from the "Two Nation Theory" and the

---

Chandals, who even lost their caste identity, and in one of his many popular forms is half man half woman—*ardhnarishwar*—which makes it difficult for any patriarchy to appropriate him. It should also be noted that Rama remains a north Indian god since the Ramanandis are a north Indian phenomenon. In the south—stronghold of the Shaivites—the BJP and their Ram have never been popular. I am thankful to Arshad Alam to have drawn my attention to this interesting context.

[24] See Hasan: *Legacy of a Divided Nation*, pp. 253–357.

[25] See S.K. Gosh: *Communal Riots in India*, New Delhi: Ashish Publishing House, 1987, p. 36.

[26] The way the violence evolved and was used by politicians remind of Paul Brass' thesis (*The Production of Hindu-Muslim Violence in Contemporary India*, Seattle, WA: University of Washington Press, 2003) who opines that the communal battles are "pogroms" rather than "riots," carefully initiated by political leaders.

[27] Peter van der Veer: *Religious Nationalism: Hindus and Muslims in India*, New Delhi: OUP 1996.

[28] Chandra: *Communalism*, pp. 6, 9.

[29] Gosh: *Communal Riots*, p. 36.

[30] Raghuraj Gupta: "Changing Role and Status of the Muslim Minority in India: A Point of View", in: *Journal; Institute of Muslim Minority Affairs* 5/1 (1984), p. 193.

educational backwardness of Muslims.[31] Rarely ever is any reference made to the Muslim nationalist movement, which itself was not able to accept secularism in modern India. It still makes—albeit latent—use of a sedimentary religious vocabulary and symbolism and in this way perpetuates communal identity. Post-1947 Muslim communalism, however, does not dispose of the structural framework to operate as such.

Different explanations of increasing communalism were furnished in the last couple of years: the failure to institute genuine structures of participative democracy plus the uneven and contested economic liberalisation favoured restricted sectors and groups—such as the growing middle classes—at the expense of poorer sections. Failing investments in rural production, mainly resisted by the new agrarian rich, has led to uneven distribution and an increasing rift between rich and deprived. The result was increasing social tension articulated in popular political movements, whether traditional or religious.[32] Others opine that there is an intrinsic connection between global capital, economic growth and Hindutva which is conducive to economic growth, its ethics reflecting the spirit of Indian capitalism.[33] Yet others outline how ethnically divided societies like India deal with globalisation. The deliberately slow introduction of market reforms harks back to the interaction between domestic politics defined by ethnicity and international economy. But the reforms based on global capital have brought Hindu nationalism from margin to the centre. In playing the communal card, the BJP has made Hindutva a legitimate phenomenon in politics. However, in the era of economic globalisation the BJP has relinquished its explicit ideological commitment to *swadesh* (homeland) and has come to accept economic liberalisation.[34] Another set of arguments, such as those of T.N. Madan and Ashis Nandy, reconsiders the value and plausibility of imported (Western) secularism for the Indian political fabric. The former considers secularism a Christian legacy not suitable for India, for it marginalises religion in public life while Hinduism mandates

---

[31] For the following see N.C. Saxena: "Historiography of Communalism in India", in: Hasan (ed.): *Communal and Pan-Islamic Trends*, pp. 302–313.

[32] See Stuart Corbridge and John Harriss: *Reinventing India: Liberalization, Hindu Nationalism and Popular Democracy*. Cambridge: Polity Press 2000.

[33] Cf. Thomas Blom Hansen: "The ethics of Hindutva and the spirit of capitalism", in: Thomas Blom Hansen and Christophe Jaffrelot (eds.): *The BJP and the Compulsions of Politics in India*, New Delhi 1998, pp. 291–314.

[34] Cf. Baldev Raj Nayar: *Globalization and Nationalism: The Changing Balance in India's Economic Policy, 1950–2000*, New Delhi/Thousand Oaks/London: Sage 2001.

that religion be part of the state. The latter stresses the non-sense of secularism making a distinction between private and public and seeks a recovery of religious tolerance inherent in traditional Hinduism[35] which is different from modern Hindu naationalism. Achin Vanaik[36] counters that these scholars would ontologise—as it were—religion, rendering it something essentially Indian.

Measured by standards derived from economic and political modernisation theories, communalism necessarily becomes a social pathology and an expression of political underdevelopment and failing national integration. Communal identity is rejected as it would add to economic stagnation, and contradict the apparently positive results of modernisation. Yet others argue that communalism emerges in a required differentiated and political group-consciousness and therefore ascertains identity. It produces political leaders chosen from the midst of their indigenous constituencies, and as such can be a healthy sign of democracy, when competing group solidarities in the same political system based in ethnic, linguistic or religious identities can thus flourish.[37] Another string of discourse is put forward by Zaheer Baber who looks at the *racialisation* of communal conflict, not only in terms of being biologically constructed as has been the case with totalitarian ideologies but predominantly in cultural terms, i.e., cultural racism.[38] Yet, any meaningful understanding of contemporary communalism has to take into account the shift from ad-hoc violent outbreaks to a more organised system of engineering riots with the complicity—active or passive—of the state, as the Sikh pogrom in Delhi in 1984 and Gujarat in 2002 showed.

Militant and politicised forms of re-invented traditions have filled up the public sphere, and the mass mobilisations in the name of tradition are all around. It has pushed the lived, shared experiences of the people into the corners of their private lives—they have been domesticated and silenced. Whether it is worthwhile to recognise and revive

---

[35] See T.N. Madan: 'Secularism in its Place', in: *JAS* 46(4) 1987, pp. 746–758; Ashis Nandy: "The Politics of Secularism and the Recovery of Religious Tolerance," in: Veena Das (ed.): *Mirrors of Violence: Communities, Riots and Survivors in South Asia*, Delhi: OUP 1990, pp. 69–93.

[36] See Achin Vanaik: *The Furies of Indian Communalism. Religion, Modernity and Secularization*, London: Verso 1997.

[37] See for example Amrita Basu: "The dialectics of Hindu nationalism," in: Atul Kohli (ed.): *The Success of India's Democracy*, Cambridge 2001, pp. 163–189.

[38] Compare the thought-provoking article of Zaheer Baber: "'Race'".

the—sedimentary—tradition of religious pluralism has to be probed, for pluralism means more than mere plurality and diversity; it implies active engagement with plurality which has to be created and which requires participation. Thus religious pluralism is more than mere tolerance; it is the active attempt to understand each other. In fact, pluralism does not displace or eliminate deep religious commitments but is the encounter of commitments—against communalism.[39]

[39] See the contributions in Malik and Reifeld (eds.): *Religious Pluralism*.

PART FOUR

NEGOTIATING MUSLIM PLURALISM AND SINGULARITY

CHAPTER TWELVE

THE MUSLIM PUBLIC DIVIDED (APPROX. 1930–1960S)

Apart from the Deobandis, Barelwis, Ahl-e Hadith, Aligarhis, Nadwis and Shiʿites, many other regional and trans-regional groupings with specific ideas and organisational structures emerged, at times sharing different religious traditions; a number of new thinkers, movements, organisations and parties also evolved—messianic, missionary, quasi-fascist, Islamist, modernist, secular, most of them contesting for the agency to represent Prophetic authority as the embodiment of Islamic morality and space. We will discuss the most important ones before pursuing the historical narrative of South Asian Muslims in the context of the Muslim League.[1]

Messianism

Long before Muhammad Iqbal (1877–1938) formulated his idea of a "Consolidated North Western Muslim State" in 1930 (see Chap. 11), the millenarian *Ahmadiyya* had already established their power in Punjab under the charismatic leader Mirza Ghulam Ahmad (1835–1908) of Qadiyan in 1889.[2] In 1882, he claimed to have received a divine message, on the basis of which he proclaimed himself a *mujaddid* (renewer of faith who averts the process of deterioration). Initially Ghulam Ahmad strove to defend Islam from Christian and Hindu missionaries, but soon he also demanded its reformation. He claimed to be the *masih-e mauʿdud* (promised messiah) and the mahdi, subsequently claiming to be the saviour of both Islam and Christianity. Violence was

[1] Still valid and useful are Ahmad et al. (eds.): *Self-Statement*; W.C. Smith: *Modern Islam in India. A Social Analysis*, Lahore: Muh.Ashraf 1969 (reprint); A. Syed: *Pakistan, Islam, Politics and National Security*, Lahore 1984.

[2] The most important source on this movement is still Y. Friedman: *Prophecy Continuous: Aspects of Ahmadi Religious Thought and Its Medieval Background*, Berkeley 1988; see also Charles H. Kennedy: "Towards the Definition of a Muslim in an Islamic State: The Case of Ahmadiyya in Pakistan", in: Dhirendra Vajpeyi and Yogendra Malik (eds.): *Religious and Ethnic Minority Politics in South Asia*, Maryland: Riverdale, and London: Jaya Publishers 1989, pp. 71–108.

to be replaced by peaceful preaching. Even though Ahmadiyya ideas contradicted the very finality of Prophet Muhammad and thus called massively into question the prophetic authority—discussed in different Muslim publics and annoying those who claimed to represent and were competing to be authoritative interpreters of the Prophetic legacy, i.e., ulama and intellectuals, they were quite popular even beyond the realm of Punjab. According to Ghulam Ahmad the prophethood continued, he himself being a Sufic inspired prophet within Islam. He offered some liberal interpretations of Islam but at the same time remained conservative. After his death one of his veteran associates, Nur al-Din (died 1914), became successor. Under this Khalifa al-Masih I, the movement expanded its missionary activities, particularly in England. Internal schism led to a division of the Ahmadiyya into two groups: the Qadiyani Ahmadiyya and the Ahmadis of Lahore. The first published an article in which all Muslims outside their movement were considered *kafirs*, while the second, considered Ghulam Ahmad just a *mujaddid* rather than a prophet and stressed the unity of all Muslims. In 1914 the Qadiyani Ahmadiyya founded the Anjuman-e Taraqqi-ye Islam (Association for the Advancement of Islam), introduced an elaborate administration and soon was able to propagate its cause far beyond Indian borders under the leadership of Mahmud Ahmad (died 1964). Though the movement adopted a formal election procedure in the 1950s, the *khilafat* was kept within the family with the succeeding *khulafa* being Mahmud Ahmad's sons.

Loyalty to the government in power was a major principle of the movement, due to which the Qadiyanis joined neither the *Khilafat* and non-cooperation nor the *Hijrat* movement. Ambivalent towards the struggle for independence, they were reluctant to support the Congress, which in case of independence did not guarantee missionary activities and conversion. They also could anticipate what to expect in a country run by non-Ahmadi Muslims, after facing the first severe attack from the militant Sunnite Majlis-e Ahrar organisation in 1934. Nevertheless, the majority soon shifted from Qadiyan to Punjab in Pakistan to build a new city called Rabwa (calling to mind the hill where Jesus and his mother were given refuge by God; Quran 23:51). There they faced the first major problems in the 1950s, in the context of constitution-making, reintroduced by the Ahrar and supported by a number of ulama. They failed. Due to orthodox pressure, the Pakistani constitution of 1973 took up the issue of the finality of Muhammad's prophethood, and introduced discriminatory propositions to declare the movement un-Islamic in 1974 (thus contradicting article 20 of the constitution of 1973).[3] This was followed by further anti-Ahmadis laws in 1984 which led to an exodus of many of its members—including its then leader Mirza Tahir Ahmad—giving this missionary movement great popularity outside South Asia.

The Ahmadiyya can be considered one of the first local movements that soon evolved into a trans-national one operating outside India—and Pakistan—with hundreds of mosques built all over the world especially in South Africa, South East Asia and Europe. Aiming at conversion of the non-Muslims, this became internationally one of the most renowned movements of the twentieth century, with major publication programmes in different languages.

Quranic scripturalism

The Ahl-e Hadith had changed the study of prophetic tradition into a major normative discourse, differing from those adhering to a school of law, such as the Hanafis. Yet, the propagation and study of hadith as a perfect means to establish moral Islamic behaviour with a radical reference to the Prophet was also supported in the context of Hanafite lineage itself, such as the case of Deobandis and Barelwis. The bone of contention revolved around rituals, ritual prayers in particular, and the status of the Prophet and his tradition. But not all submitted to this hadith fundamentalism. S. Ahmad Khan accommodated Muʿtazalites' idea of dubious origins of hadith literature which did not correspond to their construed version of a rational-philosophical Islam. ʿAbd Allah Chakralawi (died 1930) from Punjab radicalised these ideas, questioning the significance of established norms and practices derived from sunna. He therefore looked directly towards the Quran for guidance in matters of belief and practice and demanded intra-textual quranic interpretation (*Tarjumat al-Qurʾan bi ayat al-furqan*; 1906). Using the term Ahl-e Quran he considered the holy text to be the exclusive source for Muslim normativity—the only revelation (*wahy*) of the Prophet—at the expense of hadith. This revaluation of the function of Muhammad's

[3] Which proclaims every citizen's right to profess his own religion, subject only to such limitations as are prescribed by law or are necessary to protect public order and morality.

prophecy stood in contrast to the traditionally accepted reference system relating to the Prophet. This sort of quranic scripturalism was propagated in different organisations and through different journals, such as *Isha'at al-Qur'an*. His exegetical extravagances caused, however, divisions, such as the one involving Ahmad Din Amritsari (1861–1936), who humanised the Prophet and called prophetic authority into question. The Prophet merely delivered the message, his sunna was limited time and space. Distinction was made between god and *muhaddithun* rather than between god and the prophet. Thus, historicisation of *hadith* and rehabilitation of the Quran demanded re-interpretation of the sacred text with much openness and flexibility. However, Ghulam Ahmad Parwez (1903–1986), in tune with his mentor Aslam Jairajpuri (1881–1955), did not discard those practices and rituals, which were in continuous use among the Muslims, such as prayer and pilgrimage. He therefore adhered to the usual Hanafi tradition. The message was that the Prophet Muhammad, being a paradigm rather than an exemplar, could be emulated by human beings, among others by the leader of a true Islamic state. Parwez's "Resurgence of Islam" (*Tulu'-e Islam*) movement was a major channel to propagate these rather secular ideas among urban educated youth such as college educated students and elites. In so doing he provided them with yet another tool of *ijtihad* and agency against traditional Muslim scholars who considered him infidel (*kafir*) and thus was to become influential in certain political circles. As Daniel Brown puts it, the "denial of the authority of prophetic sunna *required* an attenuation of Prophetic infallibility."[4] However, these different strands of hadith scepticism did not translate into an agreed upon set of dogmas and consequently the ideologues never considered themselves as a new or distinct sect. Yet, these subjectively constructed and non-institutionalised systems of ultimate meaning questioned and replaced the indispensability of traditional religious forms and leadership resulting in religious individualisation. The more profane side to the story is that this was done to counter Ahl-e Hadith's claim to hegemony in the Punjab.

---

[4] For the Ahl-e Qur'an see Brown: *Rethinking tradition*, pp. 38ff., 44–49, 70ff., passim, quotation p. 66. Also Ali Usman Qasmi: *Revisioning Islam: The Ahl al-Quran Movements in Punjab*, Ph.D. forthcoming University of Heidelberg, who rightly distinguishes different strands. For Ghulam Ahmad Parwez see Ahmad and v. Grunebaum (eds.): *Muslim Self-Statement*, pp. 21f., 167–181.

The famous journalist, diplomat and scholar, Muhammad Asad, alias Leopold Weiss (died 1992)[5] who had converted from Judaism to Islam in 1926, was one of many players in the debate on the preferences of prophetic sayings and their use as second source—after the Quran—of Islamic law. Thus, he ardently wrote in favour of hadith as the prime source for Muslim normativity in his *Islam at the Crossroad* (1934), saying that the Prophet's "wonderful life was a living illustration and explanation of the Qur'an, and we can do no greater justice to the Holy Book than by following him who was the means of revelation." Needless to say that he demonstratively argued from a rationalist position which sought to encounter both orientalist propositions such as Ignaz Goldziher's, as well as Muslim modernists' staunch critique of the authenticity of hadith, such as that of Chiragh ʿAli's. Thus, adherence to sunna did not vanish; rather it re-emerged with new vigour.

Mission

The *Tablighi Jamaʿat* ("Missionary Community"), by "living hadith" and using a variety of missionary methods, was to become one of the most visible religious movements world-wide.[6] It, therefore, needs some detailed analysis. Its proselytising campaign was, initially, to confront Hindu movements such as the *shuddhi*[7] which attempted at re-conversion of ex-'Hindus', particularly of the lowest castes. The Tablighi Jamaʿat was founded around 1934 by Muhammad Ilyas Kandhalawi (1885–1944) in Mewat near Delhi, which had become a crucial area for Hindu-Muslim antagonism. Initially, the movement targeted tribal groups such as the Meos of Mewat.[8] Soon the Jamaʿat's intellectual centre was established in Madrasa Mazahir al-ʿUlum in Saharanpur,

[5] See Günther Windhager: *Leopold Weiss alias Muhammad Asad—Von Galizien nach Arabien, 1900–1927*, Wien 2002.

[6] See Muhammad Khalid Masud (ed.): *Travellers in Faith. Studies of the Tablîghî Jamâʿat as a Transnational Islamic Movement for Faith Renewal*, Leiden: Brill 2000; Yogi Sikand: *The Origins and Development of the Tablighi Jamaʿat*, New Delhi: Orient Longman 2002; Barbara D. Metcalf: "Living Hadith in Tablighi Jamaʿat", in: *JAS* 52 (1993), pp. 584–608.

[7] This was a later incarnation of the Hindu revivalist movement Arya Samaj established by Dayanand Saraswati (died 1883) in Bombay in 1875.

[8] For Mewat and mission among Mewatis as a primarily non-religious process producing homogenous group identity see Shail Mayaram: "Rethinking Meo Identity: Cultural Faultlines, Syncretism, Hybridity or Liminality?" in: Mushirul Hasan (ed.): *Islam, Communities and the Nation. Muslim Identities in South Asia and Beyond*, Delhi: Manohar

while Basti Nizamuddin in Delhi became the administrative centre with a fledgling publication activity. The Islamising mission of this Deobandi puritan, yet pietist and sufi endeavour[9] invited Muslims to enter the realm of "true" Islam, as outlined in its most famous books such as *Hayat al-Sahaba*, written by the second amir and Ilyas' only son, Muhammad Yusuf Kandhalawi (1917–1965), and *Tablighi Nisab* (The Curriculum for Proselytising), later named *Fada'il-e A'mal* (The Virtues/Rewards of Action), based on stories on hadith written between 1928 and 1940 by Muhammad Zakariyya Kandhalawi (died 1982), the nephew of the movement's founder. The movement's stress on 'correct moral behaviour' by strictly following the prophetic example was soon transformed into a trans-national struggle by the second amir, who took office in 1943. Soon the Nadwat al-ʿUlama joined in, carrying its modest but effective ideas far beyond the South Asian region, not least because of the activism of the late principal of the Nadwat al-ʿUlama, Abu al-Hasan ʿAli Nadwi (died 1999), in the Arab world. By 1965, when the third amir Inʿam al-Hasan (1918–1995) took charge, the movement had spread to more than 90 countries. By 1995 it had become so big that the concept of *imamat* was given up in favour of a council (*shura*) of three scholars from the founder's family, based on one of the institutional structures, the *mashwara*, consultation.

The internationalisation of the movement was made possible through a flexible, yet hierarchical organisational structure based on personal relations between the amirs and councils (*shura*) at all levels, from local to trans-national. The Tablighi Jamaʿat was and still is a grass roots movement, self-financing, and without fee or salaries for the members, though with limited female participation. This rather loose approach towards official structures is also reflected in a deliberate absence of any welfare or educational programme. Similarly, there is no official document or prolific literature as in the case of the Ahmadiyya. However, of prime importance for the movement is the six-point plan of action, known as *Chhe batein* (six points), which regulates the life and action of the Tablighis: 1) the article of faith (*kalima*), 2) the prayer (*salat*), which stresses the significance of mosque and *daʿwa* to enhance commonality. 3) Knowledge and remembrance (*ʿilm awr dhikr*) serve to integrate

1998, pp. 283–307; Shail Mayaram: *Resisting Regimes. Myth, Memory and the Shaping of a Muslim Identity*, Delhi: OUP 1997.

[9] While pristine mysticism as propagated by early Sufi masters is accepted, the veneration of holy men, however, is repudiated as an unlawful innovation, e.g., *bidʿa*.

different Islamic perceptions such as Sufic and orthodox. 4) Respect for a Muslim (*ikram-e Muslim*) serves to cultivate Muslim brotherhood. 5) Sincerity of purpose (*ikhlas-e niyyat*) serves to earn Allah's pleasure. 6) Devoting time (*tafrigh-e waqt*) is considered conducive for practical tabligh activities, through which the Tablighi absolves himself or herself from profane distractions and futile talk.

These six points are put into practice by Tablighi Jamaʿat's methods, which represent Sufi elements such as a 40-day Sufi practice of reclusion (*chilla*) and *dhikr*, as well as public gatherings (*ijtimaʿat*), groups (*jamaʿats*) making rounds (*gasht*) in the vicinity to call people to observe prayers, and invitation to prayer (*daʿwa*), including teaching (*tadris*) and disputation (*munazara*). *Daʿwa* is considered a spiritual struggle while missionary travel (*chilla*) gives the concept of *hijra* a central meaning. The *gasht* provides with a liminal state, making proper Islamic behaviour possible. Thus physical movement and trans-national travel are means for the renewal of faith (*tajdid*), and serve to enlarge the movement's legitimacy.

Due to the Tablighi method the movement could appeal to a variety of social strata and professions across ethnic lines, prevalent in the petty bourgeoisie: tradesmen, junior civil servants, as well as wealthier social circles. Their annual meetings, at its headquarters in Raiwind in Pakistan, not far from Rabwa, evolved into the second-largest gatherings in the Muslim world after Hajj. Moreover, the movement has been able to attract leading government officials, politicians, intelligence service and also armed forces and sportsmen, particularly after independence. Khalid Masud opines that "(I)its focus on individual reform and faith renewal, without social concerns, has produced a strong sense of separation between personal and social morality. This does not seem to have been the vision of Mawlânâ Ilyâs."[10] In fact, Ilyas opined that "the aims of modern political authority and the aims of Islam do not conform. If Islam as a religious system is to make any progress, it must be separated from politics." The movement's programmatic eradication of shrines and the cult attached to them,[11] its criticism of secularism,

[10] Masud: *Travellers in faith*, p. 31.

[11] Like other Muslims they want to emulate the life of Prophet Muhammad, to '*sunnatise*' their life-worlds, and perform *imitatio Muhammadi*. This more or less literal negotiation with religious truth, salvation or asceticism brings Tablighis near to reformist positions, which consider folk-religious practices to be un-Islamic because they were inserted into Islam by charlatans and spiritual delinquents who were then uncritically followed by the ignorant masses.

modernism, Hindus, Jews and Christians, as well as its restrictive stand on women, is as notable as its constant attempts to "invite" even non-Muslims to Islam. Regardless of Tablighis' ostensible indifference to political issues such as independence and a separate Muslim state, the seemingly quietist stand of this ethically orientated movement has to be questioned. Dale Eickelman and James Piscatori have shown aptly that "the competition is over the right to manipulate the symbolic capital of Islam and, ultimately, territory: who speaks for Islam *here*?" Thus, in the long run the proposed internalised Islamisation—by imitation of sunna and reference to hadith—involves the expansion of the sphere of interest that is identification with—territorial—space.[12] This gradual externalisation of internalised Islam seems to be in line with Abu al-Hasan ʿAli Nadwi's ideas of an all-encompassing Islamisation, which stands in contrast to the Islamisation supported by men such as the doyen of political Islam, A.A. Maududi (see below).

Non-violence

In the 1930s a non-violent, non-missionary association again emerged among the Pakhtun tribes of North-Western India under the leadership of Khan ʿAbd al-Ghaffar Khan (1890–1988), popularly called as Badshah Khan. His "Servants of God" (*Khuda-ye Khidmatgar*)—also known as "red shirts", called so by the police to vilify them as communists—established in 1929, entered nationalist politics when they adopted methods and teachings of Pakhtun culture and combined it with Gandhi's credo of non-violence. Ghaffar Khan referred to Islam only as a source of ethical precepts, of which the oath each "servant" had to take bore witness: "I am a *Khuda-ye Khidmatgar*, and as God needs no service I shall serve Him by serving his creatures selflessly...and shall treat every Pakhtun as my brother and sister." The majority of his followers were poor peasants from the Peshawar Valley. Tribal chiefs as well as many landless labourers did not share the ideas of the "Frontier

[12] See Eickelman/Piscatori: *Muslim Politics*, p. 153. It has also been argued that Tablighi Jamaʿat turned from apolitical to explicitly anti-political. See Mumtaz Ahmad: "Islamic Fundamentalism in South Asia: The Jamaat-i-Islami and the Tablighi Jamaat of South Asia", in: Marty, Martin E. and Scott R. Appleby (eds.): *Fundamentalism Observed*, Vol. 1, Chicago, London 1991, pp. 457–530.

Gandhi", who was able to integrate different elements such as local tradition of non-violence, the idea of Pakhtun nation, and Islamic-trans-communal movement, in order to transcend tribal feuds and intra-family rivalry that kept Pakhtun society divided. So he distanced himself from political power due to its innate moral corruptness, rejected Muhammad Iqbal's plan of a "Consolidated North Western Muslim State" (see Chap. 11), and in 1931 allied with the Congress Party, which did not interfere with Pakhtun ethnicity—including Sikhs and Hindus. Consequently, pro-Congress Muslims who wanted to create an autonomous Pakhtunistan boycotted the referendum for the creation of Pakistan in 1947, desiring a plural undivided India. In 1948, the movement was banned by the Pakistani government and as an organisation that opposed the Muslim League and Pakistan, the *Khuda-ye Khidmatgars* were branded as traitors or enemies of the new Muslim state. Ghaffar Khan, who stood for Pakhtun autonomy in Pakistan, was imprisoned on charges of sedition.[13]

Militancy

In 1931, shortly after Muhammad Iqbal made his plan public, the physicist ʿInayat Allah Khan al-Mashriqi (1888–1963) founded the paramilitary movement called *Khaksar* (the Humble) in the Punjab. Al-Mashriqi—called as such by Arabs attending the Khilafat conference in Cairo in 1926—did not want to cooperate with the Muslim League, scholars and Sufis. In his magnum opus "al-Tadhkirah", published in Amritsar in 1924, and in other books, he like the Ahl-e Qurʾan, stood for the doctrine of sufficiency of the Quran; on the other hand he advocated a totalitarian Islamic government on the Indian Subcontinent, equally distant from democracy and communism. Ideologically and institutionally he leaned towards German National Socialism.[14] Yet, it would probably go too far to interpret the movement in terms of some

[13] Sayed Wiqar Ali Shah: *Ethnicity, Islam and Nationalism. Muslim Politics in the North-West Frontier Province 1937–1947*; Karachi: OUP 1999, p. 247.

[14] In fact, al-Mashriqi claimed to have met Adolf Hitler on a tour to Europe. This quasi-fascist approach calls to mind contemporary Hindutva ideology and movements such as the RSS (1925), which also proclaimed a uniform and compulsory drill and a strict hierarchy, thereby fostering racial superiority.

sort of clerical fascism.[15] His famous ten principles comprised inter alia the belief in the unity of God, the unity of the *umma*, in *jihad* and *hijra*, and in the world hereafter. Although he rejected mystical approaches outright, his millenarian movement nevertheless used the principles and symbolism of Sufi orders to win popular support, a tendency found among political religious movements of the day.[16] However, it can be seen as a modified form of 'agrarian traditionalism' among disintegrated middle classes, who had moved from feudal village economy and notorious canal colonies to the lower rungs of a new industrial economy. Traditional Islam no longer suited them:

> "The alim will get the opportunity to snatch away (the citizens) from the grip of unjust capitalists and political swindlers, to rule the world under the laws of the Book of Nature...to look upon mankind as a whole instead of dividing it into various small nations, to permanently stop war...and to establish a new political Paradise, corresponding to the Paradise of his own scientific findings, through which eventually mankind will build up one community with the aid of knowledge from the Book of Nature."[17]

Needless to say, the *ʿalim* was al-Mashriqi himself.

During the "Great Depression", al-Mashriqi in a very short period won the support of a large number of urban traders as well as peasant migrants for his association. He, being the amir of a strictly hierarchical movement with an elaborate organisation, called for 'actionism', the spade being the symbol of action used by the Prophet Muhammad at the occasion of the Battle of the Ditch, "when the condition of the Muslims was that of extreme weakness and the power of the enemies of Islam was at its extreme height." The movement was, however, contested by a variety of organisations. ʿAbd al-Ghaffar Khan called them creations of the British to curb the power of the *Khuda-ye Khidmatgars* in the North West. After independence, Khaksars continued to oppose partition. Due to their involvement in violent incidents they were controlled by Pakistani government but have since been politically active as Khaksar Party.

---

[15] For a broad definition of clerical fascism see Roger Griffin: "The 'Holy Storm': 'Clerical fascism' through the Lens of Modernism", in: *Totalitarian Movements and Political Religions*, Vol. 8, No. 2. (2007).

[16] See Jamal Malik: *Die Khaksar Bewegung*, M.A., University of Bonn 1982 (unpublished).

[17] Quoted from J.M.S. Baljon: *Modern Muslim Koran Interpretation 1880–1960*, Leiden 1961, p. 76.

Political Islam

The effort for renewal of Muslim cultural traditions in the first two quarters of the twentieth century had given rise to the idea of an Islamic territory, advanced by a specific nationalist historiography, as elaborated by Muhammad Iqbal who was the vantage point for many a movement and organisation in the 1930s (see Chap. 11). Taking into account that Iqbal was voicing Muslim interests of the Punjabi urban middle-class in the first place, his political views proved to be most important for the movement that led to partition of India and the creation of Pakistan, a state for Muslims as heralded by the Muslim League,[18] to which we have referred to earlier. It is against this backdrop that yet another prominent movement arose in the 1930s, when Abu al-Aʿla al-Maududi (1903–1979) from Aurangabad/Deccan formulated his political ideas about state and government which still have great impact on the Arab world as well.[19] Initially he sympathised with the Tablighi Jamaʿat, through the influence of the anti-Shiʿites Abu al-Hasan ʿAli Nadwi and Muhammad Manzur Nuʿmani (died 1997), a prominent Deobandi scholar, author of the popular Urdu book *What Is Islam?* (*Islam kya hai?*), and editor of the well-known Urdu journal *al-Furqan*. Maududi, however, soon rejected the movement bitterly due to its ostensibly a-political stand but used its trans-national network as a vehicle for the dissemination of his ideas formulated in his Urdu writings. These ideas were transmitted and also absorbed by leading members of the Egyptian Muslim Brotherhood, such as Sayyid Qutb (1906–1966), by means of translations into Arabic arranged under the supervision of a staunch Ahl-e Hadith, Masʿud ʿAlam Nadwi (died 1954). Like many Islamists of his time, Maududi was an autodidact who was widely read in European non-fictional literature. He started his career as a journalist working for the Deobandi-based association *Jamʿiyyat al-ʿUlama-ye Hind* (JUH), but distanced himself from the Jamʿiyyat and in 1932 founded his own Urdu-language journal *Tarjuman al-Qurʾan* in Haydarabad/Deccan, which he soon published from Punjab

[18] See also Gilmartin: *Empire and Islam*; and Markus Daechsel: *The Politics of Self-Expression: the Middle Class Milieu of Early 20th Century India and Pakistan*, London/New York: Routledge 2006.

[19] For an authoritative documentation and analysis of the Jamaʿat and Maududi see Seyyed Vali Reza Nasr: *The Vanguard of Islamic Revolution: The Jamaʿat-i Islami of Pakistan*, London 1994; Seyyed Vali Reza Nasr: *Mawdudi and the Making of Islamic Revivalism*, New York 1996; also K. Bahadur: *The Jamaʿat-i-Islam of Pakistan*, Lahore 1983.

whereto he was invited at the behest of Muhammad Iqbal in 1938. On an endowment of eighty acres in Pathankot, a non-Muslim majority area in the extreme north of Gurdaspur in Punjab, they planned to establish the *Dar al-Islam Trust* to work towards a future Islamic leadership. Though Maududi left for Lahore only two years later, the foundation was laid for his movement in Pathankot.

Maududi's ideas stood in contrast to JUH, which postulated composite nationalism (*muttahida qaumiyyat*), standing for an independent, multi-religious India in which Muslims and Hindus would have their separate institutional structures. This concept of composite nationalism was unique in Islamic thought. The Deobandi scholar Husain Ahmad Madani in his book called *Muttahida Qaumiyyat aur Islam* (Composite Nationalism and Islam) in 1938, refuted both M.A. Jinnah's arguments for Islam being the basis of nationalism, as well as Muhammad Iqbal's notion of territorial nationalism.[20] Abu al-Kalam Azad (died 1958), who had been a staunch nationalist siding with Gandhi, was one of the main architects of this multi-religious approach, deducing an all-Indian perspective from the experience of a shared history, just in contrast to his initial Salafite position. The drift towards Indianness culminated in his idea that no religious tradition was allowed to claim final and absolute truth. Azad's pluralistic concept of society read the Quran merely in terms of a postulate to submit to God and to live a righteous life in accordance with the individual's respective religious conviction. Azad thus represents one of the conflicting views concerning Muslim identity in South Asia. The other rested with Iqbal and certainly with Maududi.

Maududi, consequently, also spoke out against Muhammad Iqbal's idea of a Muslim state (territorial nationalism), which the philosopher had formulated shortly before his death in the debate with Husain Ahmad Madani in 1938. Maududi postulated a third alternative when he began to Islamise the political discourse of the nationalists: an Islamic state must correspond to the divine order, which has to be realised on earth. A Muslim should believe in the sovereignty of God rather than

[20] As Peter Hardy has pointed out, Madani envisaged a temporary coalition between Hindus and Muslims rather than an immersion of the Muslim community into a nation dominated by a Hindu majority. See P. Hardy, *Partners in Freedom and true Muslims*; Zaman: *The Ulama in Contemporary Islam*, pp. 32–37. It should be mentioned that Madani made frequent reference to the covenant of Medina, yet his concept of composite nationalism, was narrow as it drew clear borders around a Muslim-Sunnite identity (see below Chap. 15).

A.A. Maududi
Source: *Haftrauza Zindagi*, Lahore Oct. 1979, p. 21

in the idea of a government *of* the people, *by* the people, and *for* the people.[21] Thus the Muslims did not represent a nation, but the party of God, which acts as God's agent on earth (*khalifa*). For this aim, he considered self-purification as a prerequisite, which he much later based on his peculiar interpretation of the "four basic Quranic terms" (the one who is worshipped (*ilah*), the lord (*rabb*), religion (*din*), worship (*ʿibadat*).[22] Towards the end of the 1930s he was convinced that the creation of a Muslim state—the outline of which was formulated by Iqbal—was not becoming of a good Muslim, and, therefore, the idea of an Islamic state was incapable of being realised. To put his ideas into practice, in 1941 Maududi was instrumental in the foundation of the "Islamic Community" (*Jamaʿat-e islami*), strictly hierarchically organised, under the leadership of its amirs. From 1942 onwards Maududi postulated the sovereignty of God (*hakimiyyat-e ilahi*). The human beings would only be representatives of God (*khulafa*), in a universal, ideologically Islamic nation. The notion of such a *khilafat* was derived from the Quran 24:55[23] which in practice not only poses the question of agency but also rejects the search for individual autonomy rather than modernity and therefore potentially opens the doors for coercive Islamisation.

After 1947, Maududi tried to materialise this idea of an imagined nation in the constitution of Pakistan (see Chap. 13) to where he, along with the majority of his community eventually emigrated. Thus he accepted the idea of a nation-state which he had rejected earlier. His argument to establish an Islamic state was substantiated by the idea that the wrong interpretation of the Quran's basic principles had led people astray. This had resulted in the loss of religious and cultural identity, due to, among others, misguided mystics (Sufis). Pakistan, he elaborated, should not become a classical nation state but an ideological nation, and should be a manifestation of divine sovereignty, which the Muslims had to organise according to their ideological guidelines:

---

[21] Compare Syed: *Pakistan*, p. 35.

[22] See Syed Abul-Ala Maududi: *Four Basic Quranic Terms*, Engl. transl. by Abu Asad, Lahore 1996 (4).

[23] The verse 24:55 reads: "Allah has promised to those amongst you who believe and do righteous actions that He will certainly grant them khilafah (succession) on the earth, as He granted it to those before them; and that He will grant them authority to practice their religion, the one that He has chosen for them; and He will change their state from one of fear in which they lived to one of peace and security. They will worship Me alone, not associating any partner with Me. But whosoever disbelieves after this, then they are the rebellious ones."

> The Qur'an not only lays down principles of morality and ethics, but also gives guidance in the political, social and economic fields. It prescribes punishments for certain crimes and enunciates principles of monetary and fiscal policy. These cannot be translated into practice unless there is a State to enforce them. And herein lay the necessity of an Islamic state.[24]

The concept of history fused by the notion of constant decay, which he had already developed in his *Muslims and the Present Political Crisis* (1937–1939), was the basic motivation for Maududi's activism.[25] Education was the means to achieve proper Islamic identity, which had much to do with the Prophetic ideal and whose true representative he considered himself. Consequently, Maududi vehemently opposed the doctrine of the sufficiency of the Quran. He did realise that the hadith was not as reliable as the Quran, yet he emphasised its importance for Islamic tradition. Following Shibli he regarded the message (*matn*) more important than its authoritative chain (*isnad*). A true *faqih* could instinctively "judge what the Prophet would have said or done in [any] circumstance." Thus the revitalisation of sunna was an inevitable step in the modernisation of Islamic faith. By internalising the temperament (*mizaj*) of the Prophet, Maududi was, like many of his contemporaries, interested in re-evaluating the contents of Islam while keeping his privileged position within the religious establishment.[26]

The organisational pattern of the Jamaʿat is complex. The party is led by amirs, who are selected by a council called *shura* for five years. There are three cadres of movement members: the regular members (*rukn*) selected after scrutiny; the other two, i.e., workers (*karkun*), and sympathisers (*muttafiq*), have no voting privileges. Office holders receive salaries. At the same time this bureaucratic organisation provides the power to reproduce the structure from the national to the town level. This ensures efficiency and operation supported by a vast publication wing and study circles, which are major tools to disseminate their ideas far beyond Pakistan. Thus after having being disillusioned in the elections, the Jamaʿat has not only been reorganising its student wing, the Islami Jamʿiyyat al-Tulaba as a militia, but has also been successfully

---

[24] A.A. Maududi: *The Islamic Law and Constitution*, Lahore 1969 [1955], 158f.

[25] A brief introduction of Maududi's historical view with paradigmatic texts is given by Jamal Malik in: Michael Gottlob (ed.): *Historisches Denken im modernen Südasien (1786 bis heute)*, Vol. III, Frankfurt a.M.: Humanities Online 2002, pp. 304–308.

[26] See Brown: *Rethinking tradition*, pp. 49, 75ff., 78ff., 127, 131.

entering various organisations, such as trade unions, the army and educational institutions.

Eventually, the party's founder, Maududi, gained great fame throughout the Islamic world and became a member of several societies, such the consultative board of the International Islamic University in Medina in 1961, and of the Rabita al-ʿAlam al-Islami in 1961. His "Community" won much influence, especially among young intellectuals and the middle class in the following years. (See also Excursus: Islamic Fundamentalism)

These and other groups such as mystical orders and their spaces of retreat, that is the shrines as the loci of shared lived religion, interacted and vied with each other for political and moral authority in the new territories of South Asia: West- and East-Pakistan and India. Muslim mystical culture and shared religion did play some role in the making of such movements, in terms of organisational structure, symbolism and semantics, even though their leaders formulated their resentment over these traditional patterns of social and religions organisation and were particularly distinguishable about them. Nevertheless, they took recourse to them in a notable form. Increasingly this complementing side of the complex Islamic and Islamicated fabric had been contested by emerging urban Islamic reform movements, pan-Islamic and Salafi endeavours and eventually by the ideologised Islamic movements. The latter used the language of urban colonial and colonialised culture and had acquired access to the media which turned out to redound to their advantage. In deliberately silencing and obliterating Sufism they tried to render themselves into the sole agents of Islam, regardless of their contesting opinions. In doing so they were quite successful, though on a limited scale; the notion of mystical ideas and folk-religious practices as being un-Islamic and charlatanism inserted by spiritual delinquents is very popular even in academic circles, institutionalised Sufism, in the shape of orders for example, is hardly visible in the public arena. Apparently, echoing the colonial process of feminisation of Islam, now the visibility of shared religion was relegated by these reformist trends to the female and the private, the *khanaqah* and the shrine. Despite all these male-dominated reforms, these spaces of lived and shared religion provide important alternative sources for identity and solidarity for women and generate new patterns of social interaction not available in Muslim spaces controlled by men: the mosques. The annual festivals in and around so many shrines dotted and dispersed around large parts of South Asia are cases in point. Thus shared religion is very prevalent on the level of lived Islam, exposing the failure of reformist and politicised movements to dispose of this rather gay and complex side of Islamicated traditions present in every nook and corner of the societies.

Due to versatile diachronical and synchronical contexts the formation of religious communities mentioned above provided for yet another level of complexity of civil-societal forms of Islam. The communities have, however, developed differently, at times contesting with each other, at times interacting, overlapping and excluding, yet never losing sight of the normative centrality of Prophetic tradition. We shall, however, turn to the story of Pakistan and subsequently Bangladesh first, before dealing with India and its Muslims.

CHAPTER THIRTEEN

THE INTEGRATION OF NATION-STATE AND SECESSION (APPROX. 1947–1990S)

The creation of Pakistan, originally the fifth largest Muslim state in the world and one of the most populous, was the highlight of a policy of colonial ethnification. According to the sympathisers of the new Muslim state, its creation seems to have been born out of the Muslim bourgeoisie's fear of being discriminated against by a Hindu-dominated Indian bourgeoisie. In this context, Jinnah is even said to have talked about the emasculation of the entire Muslim nation and the establishment of the Hindu majority Raj on the subcontinent in 1943. Correspondingly, the creation of Pakistan was also connected to the hope of finding an exclusive and protected market. To this end, different social sectors had been mobilised promising heaven on earth in a Muslim state. The Muslim feudal elite tended to accept the new state because they feared, among other things, the socialist programme of the Congress that had been devised right after the 1937 elections and their loss of majority in the new state.[1] Many other Muslims had opted for Islam intending to bring about economic emancipation and gain the right to social self-determination. However, the apparatus of the new state, the military, the civil administration and economy, continued to run along colonial lines so that social, cultural, national, and even religious integration proved difficult if not impossible to achieve.[2] The majority of Muslims had remained in India, bound to the land as landlords or tenants. The indifference of these Muslims to partition

---

[1] Due to personal unions and ties of loyalty, feudal forces were also to be found in the Congress; in fact, in Bihar feudal elements were in the forefront of Congress leadership. Part of the reason for this was that candidates had to finance their own elections. Under such circumstances, the very upper caste landlords whom Congress rhetorically fought against were in a position to subvert the party's own agenda. This very much applies to the latter-day Communist Parties also. In Bihar for example, the Communist Party of India is known as the party of Bhumihars, an upper caste of Brahmins who also till the land. Most of the land is concentrated in this population till now.

[2] See R. Jahan: *Pakistan: Failure in National Integration*, New York 1972; H. Frey: *Der Indisch-Pakistanische Konflikt in den Jahren 1957–1968*, Wiesbaden 1978; K.B. Sayeed: *Politics in Pakistan*, New York 1980.

and the call for a secular, multi-religious India by those Muslim scholars who retained their traditional rights to land in *qasbahs*, was significant. The lived Muslim tradition of shared religious practice can be seen as another reason for their reluctance to migrate to Pakistan. And, there was a discrepancy between political loyalty to the Muslim League and partition, and the idea of changing locality. Thus the *Pakistan Movement* and the partition even today represent "an uncertain place in historical narrative even for historians of Pakistan."[3]

Problems of national integration

West Pakistan attracted the bulk of the Muslim intelligentsia and capital. The vast majority of the migrants (*muhajirs*) from independent India made up one fifth of the West Pakistani population. They had a profound impact on political, economic, and religious life of the new state. The remaining minority, who migrated to East Pakistan, amounted only to 2% of that population. Approximately one third left for urban areas, comprising up to half of the population in urban centres of the western wing of the new Muslim country. In Karachi, Muslim trade communities from Punjab, Bombay, Gujarat and the United Provinces started to dominate and monopolise the new and protected market for their own economic purposes. Similar developments occurred in East Bengal which, before partition, had been an agricultural hinterland for the metropolis Calcutta: the vacuum created by the emigration of non-Muslim landlords, traders, bankers and civil servants to India was programmatically replaced by Urdu-speaking *muhajirs* from the United Provinces, Bihar and also Punjab.[4] Due to their traditions, and particularly their language, they identified more with West Pakistan's ruling elite—who were conversant in Urdu even if some of them were not native speakers—than with the Bengali-speaking population. This sort of communal tradition was reflected in discriminatory policy: while in 1955 the majority of the population of Pakistan was living in the Eastern wing, they were highly under-represented in the higher

[3] Gilmartin David: "Partition, Pakistan, and South Asian History: In Search of a Narrative", in: *JAS* 57, 4 (1998), pp. 1068–1095.

[4] It should be noted that quite a number of Hindus from India migrated to Karachi and other urban centres in Pakistan in search of jobs. They were given Pakistani citizenship. Research on the fate of this minority is still pending.

echelons of the military and civil services (4% and 7% respectively). Until 1960, East Pakistan generated more than half of foreign currency, but received barely one third of the imports.

In this way, *muhajirs* soon enjoyed a hegemony which enabled them to control and manipulate the economy 1,500 kilometres away in East Pakistan, which differed from West Pakistan ethnically and linguistically as well as in terms of culture. The introduction of Urdu and various taxes and tariffs were means to this end. Even though only a minor percentage of Pakistanis spoke Urdu as their native tongue (2%), Jinnah, himself barely able to speak Urdu, requested, in March 1948, the introduction of Urdu as the official national language, even in East Pakistan. This cultural chauvinism vis-à-vis Bengalis was rooted in a long tradition, which considered them as incomplete and degenerate converts in the eyes of many North Indian Muslims.[5] These linguistic and cultural problems were symptomatic of the tensions between a colonialising West and a colonialised East. They laid down the foundation for the Bengali quest for self-determination, a quest already articulated in 1949 by the moderately socialist *Awami League*. This party was established in Dacca to call for provincial autonomy in reaction to Muslim League claims to be the exclusive legitimate Muslim political party. In 1952, the first ethnically motivated crisis erupted, fuelled by the Bengali versus Urdu language controversy. Not only had *muhajirs* in East Pakistan refused to adapt to the local Bengali conditions, but the Bengalis had also been denied their identity, to the extent that "(T)they found it difficult to fill out their money order forms or understand the value of the money written on stamps, etc. because Bengali was nowhere to be found on any of these documents."[6] This behaviour of the *muhajirs* mirrored the traditional resentment of North-Indian *ashraf* against "lower classes", i.e., the *ajlaf*.[7] Thus the *Awami League* became the vehicle for the Bengali attempts at secession, whereas Islam continued

[5] Already in 1917 similar tendencies had arisen when Bengali was considered not to be a proper language. In opposition, the journal *Al-Islam* had called for Bengali linguistic self-determination; see M.G. Kabir: "Religion, Language and Politics in Bangladesh", in: Rafiuddin Ahmed (ed.): *Religion, Nationalism and Politics in Bangladesh*, New Delhi: South Asian Publishers 1990, pp. 35–49, here p. 38; Asim Roy: "The interface of Islamization, regionalization and syncretization: the Bengal paradigm", in: Dallapiccola and Zingel-Ave Lallemant (eds.): *Islam and Indian Regions*, pp. 95ff.

[6] Sayeed: *Politics in Pakistan*, p. 275, quoted in Frey, p. 47.

[7] A point articulated even in North India during the 1930s and 1940s by ʿAbd al-Qayyum Ansari (1905–1973) and the nationalist All India Momin Conference.

to play an important if not uncontroversial role. The party won the 1954 elections and was able, for a short period, to head a provincial government. It was the most powerful political organisation in the country, as one spokesman opined, and with a strong culturalist idea it eventually symbolised tendencies for secession from West Pakistan with its dominant Islamic tradition.[8]

Similar to East Bengal, the integration of the NWFP was not an easy task. With the Frontier Gandhi ʿAbd al-Ghaffar, who supported the Congress, the NWFP had developed a tradition of anti-colonial struggle. But the Province's annexation to independent India was impossible at this stage. However, in spite of sympathy with the movement of *Khuda-ye Khidmatgar*, most Muslims of the NWFP gave their votes to the Muslim League. Incidentally, during the regional parliament votes, the party of Ghaffar Khan abstained, making the process easier for the League. In Sind, the local traders had been forced to retreat after the arrival of colonial and Indian merchants, but now they started to regroup under G.M. Syed (died 1992), a staunch Sindi nationalist, Sufi and spokesman for the landless peasants (*haris*) of Sind.

The contrast between national ideology (urban elites) and the social basis (predominately agricultural society), between the Muslim League and cultural nationalisms, between secularists and urban Islamists, became vigorously evident during the constitutional debates of the 1950s, though there were also in-between positions such as that of Muhammad Asad, who had been invited by Muhammad Iqbal to contribute to the establishment of the new state. Asad's proposal, which was published as "Islamic Constitution-Making" in 1948 was, however, not implemented. M.A. Jinnah, who legitimised the Pakistan movement by using Islamic symbols for mass-mobilisation, had clearly appealed for a strict separation of religion and politics. This ambivalence threw the fathers of the constitution into a dilemma. The rift between those who opted for a continuation of colonial heritage, and those who called for the expansion of the influence of Islam widened. The tensions between neo-colonial and traditional forces as well as representatives oscillating between neo-colonial alliances and traditional patterns of organisations, including politico-Islamic parties in the social fabric of the state, could not be expressed more clearly.

---

[8] See Lawrence Ziring: *Bangladesh. From Mujib to Ershad. An interpretative study*, Karachi: OUP 1992.

The Islamic factor

Maududi was one of the first to call for an Islamic constitution.[9] His political vision and idea were articulated in his writings and put into practice by the Jamaʿat-e Islami (see Chap. 12), when his group was forced to face the issue of the role of religion in politics. Maududi consistently confronted the Pakistani government on this pertinent issue, questioning the state's legitimacy. Other factions supporting this project were the pro-Pakistani faction of the Deobandi *Jamʿiyyat al-ʿUlama-ye Hind* (JUH), which, in 1945, had founded a subsidiary, the "Association of Muslim scholars" (*Jamʿiyyat-e ʿUlama-ye Islam*; JUI; see below) under the leadership of Shabbir Ahmad ʿUthmani (died 1949) and Mufti Muhammad Shafiʿ (died 1976). The JUI, which supported the idea of a separate homeland for Muslims, however, had to struggle for a long period to be accepted by the Pakistani elites because it stood in the shadow of the Indian nationalist JUH. The JUI remained a religious organisation virtually until the late 1960s, when general elections were announced. It was only after the collapse of the Ayub Khan regime that this organisation entered the political mainstream (for the post-secession career of the JUI see Chap. 14).

Another party which was to play some role in the political scenario was the "Association of Pakistani scholars" (*Jamʿiyyat-e ʿUlama-ye Pakistan*; JUP). The JUP was formed in 1947 by Barelwi scholars who had migrated to Pakistan. Under the leadership of Abu al-Hasanat (1896–1961) and ʿAbd al-Hamid Badayuni (1898–1970) the JUP tried to give legitimacy to the cause of Pakistan and the Muslim League, unlike the JUH and in some ways unlike the JUI. In doing so, the JUP postulated Ahmad Riza Khan, the consolidator of the Barelwi movement, to be the first Muslim to have proclaimed the two-nation theory. Being primarily engaged in social activities—mainly in the settlements of refugees in Sind[10] and rural Punjab—the JUP remained politically insignificant for more than two decades. Only in 1970 did it enter the political realm, though it had already established a Sufi organisation in 1948, a student wing in 1968, and later, in 1980 founded a writers'

---

[9] For the constitutional activities of Maududi see also Zaman: *The Ulama in Contemporary Islam*, pp. 102–106.

[10] How the experiences of *muhajirs* in Sind link with the evolution of the identity of Pakistan, has been elaborated by Sarah Ansari: "Partition, migration and refugees: responses to the arrival of Muhajirs in Sind", in: *South Asia* 18 (1995), pp. 95–108.

association. In 1970 its leader Shah Ahmad Nurani (1926–2003) started propagating a campaign for the Islamisation of Pakistan (see below). Later, JUP changed sides several times—allying itself even with its main adversaries, the Jamaʿat-e Islami and JUI. Unable to withstand the pressure it underwent, it split in two major factions, the Nurani faction and the faction of ʿAbd al-Sattar Khan. Its success—even as a religio-political party—lies in its reliance on oral tradition, drawing its constituency from the followers of *pirs*—preferably from the Qadiri lineage—, observance of ritual traditions associated with saint worship, and usage of millenarian postulates and symbols.[11]

These Islamic parties and some other dignitaries campaigned for the creation of Pakistan and requested an Islamic state without delay, a state which was supposed to represent a wide array of conflicting Muslim identities and ethnic and linguistic groups.[12] Prime Minister Liyaqat ʿAli Khan (died 1951) complied with these demands. According to the *Objectives Resolution* (1949) elaborated by the fathers of the constitution-making process, Pakistan was to become an Islamic state. State orders and laws would not be allowed to contradict the Quran and sunna. The question as to who would create this legal framework, and how, remained unanswered. The propositions of the "Ulama Board" which were published in the same year were deemed unacceptable. Instead, a constitutional committee, primarily manned by West Pakistanis, declared Islam of only auxiliary importance. Moreover, the committee discriminated against the Bengali majority, which led to further problems. The 1956 constitution would treat the issue of parity between West and East Pakistan thus: Bengalis were offered more participation in administration and military, as well as more development support, if they abandoned their request for "one man one vote" as demanded by the Awami League.

Thus, a group of scholars duped by the constitutional committee, including Maududi, met in 1951 in order to discuss these matters. The members of the forum were divided on interpretations of Islam. In this situation, none of the scholars had the capability to oppose

[11] This has been elaborated in Jamal Malik: "The Luminous Nurani; Charisma and Political Mobilisation among the Barelwis in Pakistan", in: Pnina Werbner (ed.): *Person, Myth and Society in South Asian Islam*, Social Analysis 28 (1990), Adelaide, pp. 38–50.

[12] See Overview by D. Khalid: *Pakistan and Bangladesh*, in: W. Ende/U. Steinbach (eds.): *Der Islam in der Gegenwart*, München 1984, pp. 274–307. For the constitutional debates see L. Binder: *Religion and Politics in Pakistan*, Berkeley 1961.

Maududi's elaborate political ideas, as few of them had anything meaningful to add to the debate. The resulting manifesto contained 22 basic points which called for the creation of an Islamic national identity for Pakistan. The forum itself laid claim to an influential position within this identity. The politically dominant sector, the administration and the army, were of course opposed to this manifesto, as it called for an ostensibly egalitarian Islamic system. Dominated by Punjabis and *muhajirs*, this sector sought to hinder the development of this movement led by Islamists like Maududi. As a reaction, in 1952–53, a campaign against the Ahmadiyya was launched by Islamic groups spearheaded by the Jamaʿat-e Islami and the Majlis-e Ahrar-e Islam, which had been founded in Lahore in 1931 to "liberate" Islam from a Hindu-dominated Congress. In the background of an increasingly unstable domestic political scenario,[13] this pressurised the government.

The anti-Ahmadiyya movement was the Jamaʿat-e Islami's ticket into the mainstream of Pakistani politics, because by questioning the Islamic credentials of (Ahmadi) state functionaries the party vented the pent-up feelings of other schools of thought as well as ethnic and social groups disappointed with the official policy. Some of these disappointed groups found themselves organised under the pan-Sunnite movement called *Majlis-e Khatm-e Nubuwwat* (Organisation for the Finality of Prophethood) which transcended sectarian and social boundaries in the struggle against Ahmadi 'heresy' and became quite active also trans-nationally—very much like the Ahmadiyya itself.

A centralised government was installed in 1955 under "One Unit", rather than a confederation of various regions. This policy relied primarily on urban elite, mainly Punjabis and *muhajirs*, and was reinforced by a policy of linguistic discrimination, which strengthened the role of the favoured classes in the urban markets. While a large part of the rural population drifted into poverty, the state distanced itself increasingly from the bulk of the population. A prominent example is the change of capital from Karachi to the planned city of Islamabad

---

[13] Muhammad Zafarullah Khan was an Ahmadi and Minister of Foreign Affairs of Pakistan in the cabinet of Khawajah Nizam al-Din, who was a Bengali. Non-Ahmadi Punjabis and the *muhajirs* were against constitutional parity between the two wings of Pakistan and started using the simmering reservation against the Ahmadis. When the conflicts threatened to widen, the military was called out by Governor-General Ghulam Muhammad in the Punjab.

in the 1960s, which consequently begins at *Zero-Point*, symbolising the political divide between rulers and the people.

It took nine years for the first constitution to be introduced in 1956.[14] Again, one of the dominant factors was the economic and social interests of the influential colonial sector, incarnate in the form of bureaucracy and military, which resorted to an authoritarian system of rule to preserve their status. Feudal problems in the predominantly agrarian society led to upheavals and thus to the decay of political culture. Parliamentarian movements and social unrest as well as the emergence of socialist and communist formations in the neighbourhood resulted in the power-holders' curtailing parliamentary democracy. This attitude had its foundations in the deep-rooted, albeit fabricated fear of Indian "aggression", as well as severe internal political problems. The rise of socialist and communist forces in the Middle East, South Asia and in Southeast Asia created the necessity for a military alliance between Pakistan and the USA, which came into being in 1954. In 1956, when Egypt's Gamal ʿAbd al-Nasser nationalised the Suez Canal, Pakistan joined the Baghdad Pact signed by Iraq, Iran and Turkey in 1955, which in 1959 developed into the mutual defence and security organisation called CENTO (Central Treaty Organisation) in which Pakistan, Turkey, Iran, Britain and USA joined together.[15]

Military intervention

In 1958 the situation worsened when the conflicts caused by various promises, on the occasion of the first free elections, were utilised by the military for a coup d'état led by the military commander Ayub Khan (1907–1974). The official reason given was that the military intended to free the country from power-hungry and corrupt politicians. But, in reality, it was rather an attempt by the old elite to secure their resources, since subsequent events proved that the dominant classes continued to amass riches, instead of creating a new, Islamic state in any form whatsoever. In doing so, they did not hesitate to use unscrupulous means, such as corruption and suppression. Thus, the status-quo of

[14] See Ahmad et al. (ed.): *Self-Statement*, p. 206.

[15] The US American-inspired Baghdad Pact emerged as new system of security against communist activities in the region, including material and technological support by the USA. Similarly, CENTO was to curb communist activities.

the colonial administration and hierarchy were maintained, while the majority of the population was still kept away from participation in the political system.

One could argue, on the other hand, that India may have been weakened by the post-partition events, losing rich agricultural lands in West Punjab and East Bengal, the cotton and jute for her industries in Calcutta[16] and Bombay, as well as the markets necessary for the sale of the finished goods. Whether this really mattered to the country at that time is open to question however India was busy solving its own problems i.e. accommodating refugees from Pakistan, laying out Five Year Plans, maintaining secular credentials as the Partition was a recent experience, championing democratic values through the idea of 'diversity and composite nationalism', and entering the arena of world politics while building new institutions. Moreover, despite losing Pakistan, India had enough agricultural lands (including part of Punjab and part of Bengal, which are still the largest wheat and rice growing states), commercial hubs and resources to market it in order to strengthen its economy. Yet, India had problems in recognising the legitimacy of the new state which has to be understood in the context of *realpolitik*: the geopolitical situation of Pakistan and China seem to be the only threats to India's security. It might be for this reason that a country like India must see to it that Pakistan and China are not overpowered. Thus in the background of West Pakistan's military suppression of the increasingly secessionist tendencies in East Pakistan championed by the Awami League, the ambiguous role of Indian military intervention in the Eastern part of the Islamic republic in 1971 would make sense.

In Pakistan Islam was primarily used to legitimise Pakistani leadership. It was, however, secondary to the presence of Western military forces, economic ambitions, and development and modernisation programmes. A policy of *laissez-faire* was used, instead of pursuing an "Islamically" sanctioned social equality, whatever its structure might have been.

Consequently, Ayub Khan tried to subordinate the religious establishment, both ulama and Sufis, and their institutions—religious schools and Islamic religious endowments in particular—to a centralised political

---

[16] East Bengal had figured as the agricultural hinterland of Calcutta before partition. After the Hindu merchants had emigrated, the resulting vacuum was filled by Urdu-speaking Muslims from Bihar, Calcutta and West Pakistan, not by local East Bengalis.

system in order to link potentially independent forces to the state.[17] This sort of nationalisation policy was to utilise the religious scholars' deep-rooted and traditional autonomy for the crucial nation-building process and to attach them to the state-run infrastructure. Connecting notions of traditional as well as political Islam to a modern political system seemed to be an adequate measure to motivate ulama and Sufis for national ideology. The institutional affiliation of religious schools to the state machinery was to be paralleled by curricular reforms which, however, aroused a feeling of deficiency and insecurity among the representatives of religion.[18] They, therefore, established umbrella organisations for religious schools—just prior to the proclamation of the *West Pakistan Waqf Property Ordinance 1961*. The Ordinance actually aimed at looking into the possibilities to appropriate religious endownments, which together with the stipulations by pious deeds had traditionally been the basis for *madrasa* education.

The main tasks of these umbrella organisations (*tanzims* and *wafaqs*) were to reform and to standardise their educational system, which followed what was left of the *dars-e nizami* with different interpretations specific to their schools of thought, and of course, to counter state authority collectively, trying to keep their endowments. But as the ulama are no monolithic block, they organised themselves, their adherents and their centers according to different schools of thought, that is Deobandis, Barelwis, Ahl-e Hadith, the Shiʿites. The Jamaʿat-e Islami, which in 1974 founded its national headquarters at Mansura in Lahore, set up their Rabita al-madaris al-Islamiyya only in 1982.

Major problems started to arise when Ayub Khan, who had the skill to split Muslim public opinion through different alliances with important Muslim dignitaries, promulgated the *Muslim Family Law Ordinance* in 1961. This ordinance managed to harden the fronts between him and the Muslim public because it stood for a modernist interpretation of personal law, thus demanding the abolition of the monopoly of Muslim scholars over legal matters. Furthermore, it implied a revision of the policy towards the influence of the Quran and sunna, which had figured as sole sources of interpretation for the legal structure of Pakistan, but was reduced to "the teachings and requirements of Islam"

[17] For the following compare Malik: *Colonialization of Islam*; also Zaman: *The Ulama in Contemporary Islam*, Chap. 3.

[18] Cf. *Report of the Committee set up by the Governor of West Pakistan for Recommending improved Syllabus for the various Darul Ulooms and Arabic Madrasas in West Pakistan*, Lahore 1962.

in the 1962 constitution.[19] Loyalist Islamic scholars were co-opted in two important constitutional bodies: the *Council for Islamic Ideology* and the *Islamic Research Institute*. However, while suggestions by the first neither became public nor were they ever implemented, the modernist writings of the latter's chairman, Fazlur Rahman (died 1988), aroused much controversy. The bone of contention was—again—Prophetic sunna, at a time when Ghulam Parwez articulated his hadith criticism with patient visibility. In slight contrast, Rahman interpreted sunna in terms of societal dynamism: based on the spirit of Muhammadan mission, the Muslim community was itself responsible for creating sunna. Thus, he spoke out against *muhaddithun* who would promote rigidity of sunna instead of contextualising hadith. Hadith should be understood as a quarry for an ongoing process of negotiating the normative, the sunna.[20] No wonder Rahman had to leave the country due to pressure from ulama.

All these changes in policy and ideas intensified the activities of Islamic parties, mainly in Punjab. There the politics of modernisation and centralisation had provoked a social change which had left behind the lower classes, especially in the small urban centres. It was in these areas where most of the Jamaʿat-e Islami members were recruited, hailing from the educated lower-middle class, including *muhajirs*. Thus, the Islamic parties, i.e. the JUI and JUP as well as the Jamaʾat-e Islami, were able to gain a considerable amount of support for their activities. Under these circumstances, a national integration would have no means of success.

The government was unable to continue its policy of an official nationalism, being incapable of creating a mutually beneficial relationship between national ideology and social basis, and to generate a movement to integrate the ethnically, religiously and socially heterogeneous groups in the country. A number of problems became virulent in the interior, as for example the situation of farmers and workers, who were more and more threatened by the rulers' policy of modernisation, particularly through the Green Revolution. The semi-feudal rulers appropriated the land as soon as it was evacuated, at the expense of the tenants. Tenant-friendly laws were blocked in Parliament. The number

[19] The dropping of sunna and thus hadith caused a reaction from Islamic groups, so that amendments were introduced one year later: Pakistan was renamed "Islamic Republic" and "Qurʾan and Sunna" were reintroduced. See Ahmad et al. (ed.): *Self-Statement*, pp. 214–219.

[20] Compare the discussion in Brown: *Rethinking tradition*, pp. 102–107.

of unemployed agricultural workers soared, while in urban centres migrant Muslim merchant communities such as the Memons, Bohras, Khojas and Ismailis monopolised the economy. According to the 1951 census, migrants composed almost half of the population of larger cities in Pakistan. Many of the immigrants from India brought vast amounts of capital with them to generate as much profit as possible, especially in foreign trade. Soon they built their own consumer goods industry, without facing any competition due to the ban on imports. The prices of agricultural products were kept low by simultaneously controlling imports and keeping the excessive rupee exchange rate, even after the Korea-Boom. In this way, it was possible to keep cheap imports for industry, cheap agricultural raw materials and stable food prices. This development prevented the rise of salaries. Consequently, agricultural production stagnated, the situation of foreign trade led to a rise in prices. This, in turn, hit the lower classes first, who then began to react. Already in 1959, a quarter of the private industrial capital and a fifth of the Pakistani industry was under control of seven individuals, families or foreign companies, nearly all of them non-Bengali.[21]

In 1959 Ayub Khan introduced the system of Basic Democracy, based on 80,000 "basic democrats", who were to prevent the emergence of particularistic tendencies of political parties just in line with One Unit. But already in 1956, ʿAbd al-Ghaffar Khan from NWFP, G.M. Syed from Sind, Miyan Iftikhar al-Din from the Punjab and ʿAbd al-Samad Achakzai from Baluchistan founded the *Pakistan National Party* (PNP) to formulate resistance against One Unit, so that by 1964 basic democracy was unable to impede the rise to power of opposition, which had been campaigning against Ayub Khan's subsequent policy of integration: the "Combined Opposition Party" (COP), led by the sister of M.A. Jinnah, the mother of the nation (*madar-e millat*)[22] Fatima Jinnah (1893–1967), against Ayub Khan. The COP received its main support from influential merchants in Karachi who had suffered under Ayub Khan's politics, due also to the shifting of the capital from Karachi to the north. His relationship with Islamic scholars was equally strained (see above): they opposed the new constitution, though he was able to co-opt some important scholars and Sufis.[23] Eventually, internal tensions split the

[21] Frey: *Der Indisch-Pakistanische Konflikt*, pp. 66, 126.

[22] The concept of *millat* is grounded in ties of faith while *qaum* (nation) is not faith-based.

[23] See, for example, the illuminating article by Katherine Ewing: "The Politics of Sufism: Redefining the Saints of Pakistan", in: *JAS* 42/2 (1983), pp. 251–269. The

COP when the *Awami League* requested autonomy for each ethnically defined province, professing a weak centre and the decentralisation of bureaucracy and of the military. The PNP, which came to stand as the symbol of provincial demands, tried to extend its influence into the eastern wing. It was well received by ʿAbd al-Hamid Khan Bhashani (1885–1976), one of the champions of Bengali cultural nationalism. To satisfy Bhashani, PNP was renamed *National Awami Party*. In 1966, a similar request towards autonomy was reinforced in the *Awami League* by the Bengali state-socialist Shaikh Mujib al-Rahman (1922–1975): "The history of East Pakistan is the history of exploitation", he had already proclaimed in 1957.[24] The state was in danger of breaking apart; secession loomed large on the horizon.

Secession or independence

The national situation worsened due to Mujib al-Rahman's demands, the war against India in the Kashmir region and the sacking of the Minister of Foreign Affairs, Z.A. Bhutto (1928–1979). These internal and external problems generated a huge potential for unrest, which Bhutto articulated through his *Pakistan People's Party*, established in Lahore in December 1967. This party called for an Islamic socialism, in order to calm down the people since Islamic scholars had declared Bhutto and his system to be atheist. Its main support groups were the impoverished rural population, small entrepreneurs and industrial workers, as well as students. Its programme advertised the abolition of One Unit and called for a crusade against inequality and exploitation of the working force as well as against the 22 families who supposedly had divided Pakistan's wealth among themselves, and which was a powerful slogan introduced by PPP's chief economist, Mahbub al-Haqq (1934–1998). Bhutto's programme increasingly brought him into conflict with the bureaucratic and military leadership. He tried to contain the PPP's impact by making electoral promises and hints at a possibility of self-determination. Bhutto's campaign in West Pakistan called the *Awami League* back to action in 1968.[25] In this situation, a sick Ayub

---

politicisation of Sufism does not, however, mean that meditative practice and the rituals of music have ceased to exist in Sufi circles in Pakistan today.

[24] See L. Ziring: *Bangladesh*, pp. 35f.

[25] In 1966 the Awami League had put forward their six points, which hardly reflected the interests of the masses but only those of the (upper) middle class. Only through

Khan resigned in March 1969, followed by General Yahya Khan as president. Under Yahya Khan's leadership, the One-Unit was abolished in 1970, and the Bengali demand for proportional representation was granted. Consequently, 138 seats of the four West Pakistan provinces were confronted with 162 East Pakistani seats in the national assembly. In the first general elections in December 1970, Bhutto only gained 60% of the West Pakistani vote (the Jamaʿat-e Islami and others were routed), while the *Awami League* could boast 98% of the East Pakistani vote,[26] thus gaining the absolute majority in the National Assembly.

This landslide victory threatened the centre in West Pakistan, which saw the East Bengali resources in danger. A policy of mediation was thus out of question. East Pakistan sank into anarchy, as atrocities and rebellions tore apart the country. The Bengalis were rebelling against some elements of the Biharis and Punjabis in particular, because they were still clinging to their leading positions. The atmosphere of civil strife worsened when, during the flood catastrophe of November 1970, help from Islamabad arrived too late. The ensuing full-scale rebellion was drenched in blood by West Pakistani elite troops in the Operation Searchlight with the help of al-Shams and al-Badr, which were militant wings of Jamaʿat-e Islami and operated openly as assassination squads. The following guerrilla war of the Bangladesh liberation force, the *Mukti Bahini*, and the support of India brought about a defeat of the government troops, who surrendered in November 1971. In the aftermath, over a million dead had to be mourned, while over 10 million people migrated to India where they were considered refugees. In the midst of blood and tears, the sovereign socialist Bangladesh ("Land of Bengali-speakers") was declared by Mujib al-Rahman in December 1971.[27]

their 11 points issued in 1968 did the Awami League become popular, when it called for the nationalisation of banks, insurance companies and industries, demanded lower taxes for peasants, and higher wages for industrial workers. The common enemy was the exploiting Punjabi.

[26] In the preparations of the 1970 elections, the Awami League had of course made some allowances for Islam; no law was allowed that conflicted with the Quran or sunna.

[27] For a complete history of Bangladesh see Ahmed (ed.): *Religion, Nationalism and Politics in Bangladesh*; L. Ziring: *Bangladesh*. The secession was also to become a topic in literature, see: M.U. Memon: "Pakistani Urdu Creative Writing on National Disintegration: The Case of Bangladesh", in: *JAS* 43 (1983/84), pp. 105–127. M.U. Memon: "Partition Literature: A Study of Intizār Husain", in: *MAS* 14 (1980), pp. 377–410.

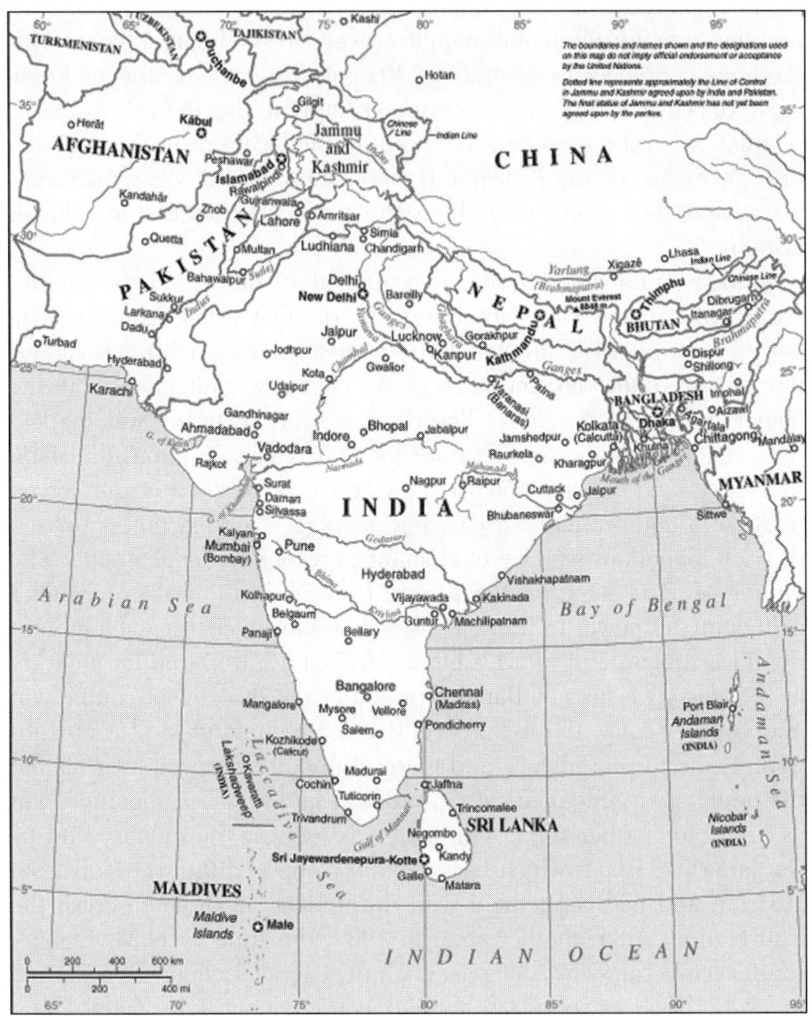

Map 12: Contemporary South Asia
Source: Courtesy UN Cartographic Section, South Asia no. 4140, Rev. 3, January 2004

Land of Bengali-speakers

The creation of the new state had been an expression of linguistic and cultural identity which, in combination with poor living conditions, had had a politically mobilising effect, carried by the bourgeoisie. But the imagined collective identity of Bengali Muslims was fragile. Once again the elites had promised a brighter future to the (Bengali-speaking) population, and once again they were to be deceived. In the tradition of exploitation by the British and following them the West Pakistanis, it was now their own ruling elites who started exploitation in colonial fashion.

In the new Bangladesh, politics remained the domain of the bureaucratic and military elite. Mujib became the first Prime Minister. The constitution of 1972 proclaimed secularism and socialism. Religious parties were outlawed, and parts of the economy nationalised, but the owners remained the same. The emphasis on secularism was marked by aversion to Islam, more so since the West Pakistani Jamaʿat-e Islami had legitimised military violence. However, even Mujib was soon forced to strike a compromise with Islamic factions,[28] among others to woo the rich oil nations who were reluctant to recognise the new state. The famine of 1974 intensified civil unrest, which in the wake of Mujib's arrogating all power to himself instead of introducing new blood into the government, cost him his life in 1975 and introduced the military as the true governors of Bangladesh. After the subsequent coup d'état and counter-coup, the military, under the command of Zia al-Rahman, came to prominence and enjoyed popular support, as it offered the population some political aspiration. Islam now became important as a tool for mobilisation. This tool was used by the military and by the Jamaʿat-e Islami which had originally opposed the secession from Pakistan and had cooperated with the military in order to crush the insurrection. After another coup in 1982, this time by H.M. Ershad, Islam even became the state religion, and general elections were allowed in 1986. These elections saw Ershad as the winner. Like Zia al-Haqq in Pakistan (see Chap. 14), he was attempting to legitimise his claim

[28] Mujib not only retained the madrasa education but also increased their grants; see Enayetur Rahim: "Bengali Muslims and Islamic Fundamentalism: The Jamaʿat-i-Islami in Bangladesh", in: Rafiuddin Ahmed (ed.): *Understanding the Bengal Muslims*, Dhaka: Univ. Press Ltd. 2001, p. 248.

to power by using state-controlled Islamisation, when he among others established nearly 2,000 new *madrasas*,[29] though he knew that an Islamist option had no chance in Bangladesh: "Our people have never believed in the fundamental variety of Islam. But, at the same time, they are religious-minded and want to see Islam's ideology and ideals reflected in society. That is why we made it the state religion."[30] He was supported by the bourgeoisie and the military, under the leadership of Mujib's daughter and leader of the secularly oriented Awami League, Shaikh Hasina, while the Jamaʿat-e Islami, active since shortly after the secession and able to gain increasing support ever since, was content to take a role in the opposition. The state-forced Islamisation progressed further during the following years, in contrast to the historical roots, Islam enmeshed with the cultural dynamism of this region. In August 1994, the imprisoned writer and women's rights activist Taslima Nasrin was freed on bail and went into exile to Sweden. She had been writing about the discrimination against Hindus and women in Islamic Bangladesh in her book "Lajja" (Shame), and subsequent charges of blasphemy had been brought against her.[31] After the resignation of the wife of Zia al-Rahman, the Prime Minister Khaleda Zia (the leader of the right wing Bangladesh National Party (BNP)), Shaikh Hasina was elected in the 1996 polls, when she sought support of Jamaʿat-e Islami. She stayed in office until 2001 but was again ousted by Khaleda Zia, in a scenario in which the Jamaʿat-e Islami (JI) played the increasingly prominent—Islamising—role of king-maker. In fact,

> The growth of the JI is (also) facilitated by the absence of any ideological divide between the Awami League and the BNP; both of these parties embrace extremely personalized ideologies centred completely on the two leading ladies themselves. JI on the contrary, does not suffer from any of

[29] Enayetur Rahim: "Bengali Muslims and Islamic Fundamentalism", p. 260.
[30] Ershad quoted in *Far Eastern Economic Review*, Vol. 23, March 1989, p. 23, in Ahmed: *Religion, Nationalism and Politics in Bangladesh*, p. 28.
[31] In the wake of the demolition of the Babri Masjid in Dec. 1992, Hindu minorities in Bangladesh had been harassed and persecuted. The author held responsible some Muslim groups in and around Sylhet, an industrial town. This brought the "Soldiers of Islam" from Sylhet to the platform who issued a *fatwa* in Sept. 1993. It was only after Nasrin was quoted in the Indian newspaper *The Statesman* on 9 May 1994 to have claimed to rewrite the Quran, that the people were mobilised against her.

> these negative associations and instead enjoys the reputation of being a clean, ideologically firm and corruption-free party.[32]

The Islamic parties have since been in the forefront, though there is a marked divide between them and the cultural-modernist Bengali-Muslim middle class. How the scenario developed in Pakistan and India will be discussed in the following two chapters, following the excursus on Islamic Fundamentalism.

---

[32] Cf. Sreeradha Datta: "Ascendance of the Jamaʿat-e-Islami in Bangladesh", in: *ISIM Review* 13 (2003), pp. 44f. For the career of Jamaʿat-e Islami in Bangladesh see also Enayetur Rahim: "Bengali Muslims and Islamic Fundamentalism"; and B.M. Monoar Kabir: "The Politics of Religion: The Jamaat-i-Islami in Bangladesh", in: Ahmed (ed.): *Religion, Nationalism and Politics in Bangladesh*, pp. 118–136.

EXCURSUS

ISLAMIC FUNDAMENTALISM

It was argued in the last decade of the twentieth century that political Islam was a new Muslim concept and self-understanding, which emanated from an ideology[1] evolving in the 1930s from the need to distance itself both from the politically-dominant colonial sector and the adherents of Muslim traditions that passed on from generation to generation. And like colonialism and popular religion, political Islam cannot be a monolithic system of cultural expression, but rather should exhibit versatility.

Abu al-Aʿla Maududi (died 1979) was one of the first to ideologise Islam or islamise the political discourse of the nationalists, developing a system equated with Islam (*nizam* = Islam) compatible with Western ideologies. Central to Maududi's ideology was a revolutionary movement to be realised through his party, the Jamaʿat-e Islami (established 1941), with members drawn from an urban milieu.

This new Muslim identity expresses a bipolar field of tension between colonial and indigenous realms.[2] Ideally speaking, each has been accommodating within itself, insofar as conflicts could be settled in an internal arrangement. This provides for social coherence assigning a specific place in the world. In contrast, the new liminal identity resulting from bipolarity is part of the composite social relationships within modern Muslim society: people caught between the boundaries of different sectors, on the borders of indigenous and colonial societies. These groups comprise far less definite, closed, social sectors than segments of different overlapping strata. They are chiefly to be found in the lowest to middle levels of the colonial hierarchy as well as in the intelligentsia. Working for and within the colonial—and later

[1] For the following see D.F. Eickelman and J. Piscatori: *Muslim Politics*. Princeton, New Jersey: PUP 1996; S.V.R. Nasr: *The Vanguard of Islamic Revolution: The Jamaʿat-i Islami of Pakistan*. London: I.B. Tauris 1994; M. Riesebrodt: *Fundamentalismus als patriarchalische Bewegung: Amerikanische Protestanten (1910–28) und iranische Schiiten (1961–79) im Vergleich*. Tübingen: J.C.B. Mohr 1990; R. Schulze: *Geschichte der Islamischen Welt im 20. Jahrhundert*, München: Beck 1994.

[2] See Malik: *Colonialization of Islam*, Chap. I.

(post)-colonial—economy, they continue to find themselves in an inevitable normative dilemma.

These groups thus oscillate between the indigenous and the colonial. Ideally speaking, with ambivalence and flexibility in their constitution, they ignore structural differences in traditional and modern economic and social sectors. They thus constitute hermetic layers of identity not normally construed as socially cohesive. Obviously, rapid social change has called into question what had hitherto been obvious, social disintegration leading to intense problems of identification and to reorientation, and enhances the necessity of shifting loyalties and religious opportunism.

Having partly broken away from historically evolving lineages and categories of social organisation, such as a learned network, kin group and family, these identities are increasingly dependent upon a network of social relations which are not required when firmly bound by other sets of relationships and social capital. A high degree of social incoherence seems to correspond to an increasing desire for approval and for impact and so for the construction of relations and networks.[3]

This is aggravated by the fact that the usually distant and unaccountable agents and institutions of the state are themselves incompletely diffused into society. This situation can precipitate an identity crisis, confronted with the question: 'Do I want to be like I am?' or 'Am I a good Muslim?' As a result of this reflective inquiry and an inner consciousness, a new construction of identity is possible, towards one that asserts: 'I want to be different!' This desire for difference leads to a transformation of identity, through catharsis and rebirth. The conflict arising between the multiple identities and different realms of operation such as a modern world of work and a traditional world of living can be resolved in at least three ways:

1. Integration, i.e., adapting or modernising one's tradition which continues to be articulated in Islamic symbols and terms;
2. Isolation, i.e., enriching or even replacing the world of modern production with tradition;

Or, the most interesting field which, however, is difficult to qualify and quantify

[3] Cf. B. Streck: "Netzwerk: Der transaktionale Einspruch gegen das Paradigma der Struktural-funktionalen Ethnologie", in: *Anthropos* 80 (1985), pp. 569–586.

3. Substitution, i.e., the creation of a substitute culture—which provides a temporary refuge from the sharp contrast between modern and indigenous, such as urban crime, consumption of narcotics, or the world of cinema. The veneration of saints may also be considered here.

Each of these possible resolutions depends on the respective social position of the individual and the social prestige s/he assigns to it. In short, the higher a person stands in the colonial and (post)-colonial hierarchy, the greater is the tendency towards modernisation, in which Islam serves as a reservoir of social and cultural experiences and as a collective point of reference (for example integrationism). Also, the higher the degree of social disintegration and the fewer the chances of upward social mobility, the greater is the inclination towards traditionalisation and, in the medium-term, even willingness for radicalism, hence isolationism.

The integrationist pattern was pursued by leading Islamists like Abu A'la al-Maududi and other functionaries of Islamist organisations. They largely originate from this field of tension between indigenous and colonial sectors. One might call them border-liners such as representatives of the middle ranges of administration, skilled labour, students, lawyers, physicians, engineers, and new professionals bound up in the (post)-colonial system, and relatively highly placed in society. Only in the rarest cases have they had a traditional religious education, yet they partly still live in a context of historical lineages and categories of social organisation. Due to their integration into the (post)-colonial system, they adopt terms and ideas central to this distant and unaccountable (state-)system and recognise them as part of their own biography. Islamic terms such as "*dastur*" (Persian for constitution) and "*shura*" (council) are extricated from their religious context and given new ideological values such as "constitution" and "parliament", without, however, renouncing their Islamic identity. Party system and nation-state, for instance, are interpreted as having always been Islamic. With this authoritative replacement, traditional boundaries are transcended and modern developments within the Islamic semiotics legitimised. In this process of 're-invention of tradition', network behaviour and code—or identity-switching are most important, because they provide reciprocal translation of symbols and terms enabling action on different societal levels. To the outsider—for example, to the (post)colonial sector—the Islamist argues ideologically, limiting the use of Islamic symbols to the indispensable. To the insider—that is the indigenous society—s/he deliberately pursues the theological argument. The Islamic cult is reinforced, the theological discussion, however, is of debatable theological value. It is this network behaviour that is responsible for the particular dynamics of political Islam, which usually promises a righteous society here and now through catharsis: a transformation from corruption to purity, from *Jahiliyya* (pre-Muhammadan times; here: conditions of ignorance) to Islam.

This *Jahiliyya* was, according to Islamists, a result of the modernisation policies of the state and its incomplete diffusion into society. Thus Islamists call for a return to the righteous society and for the reconstruction of an idealised, pure, yet de-culturalised Islamic context which would guarantee the integration of Muslim community (*umma*). This required Muslims to live according to the sunna of the Prophet, based on a trans-national view of the golden age of the Prophet and the generations that followed immediately. This radical re-invention of tradition seems to be grounded in a heritage under which the generationally transmitted canon became blurred and lost, as happened in the process of obliteration and appropriation by colonial power in the eighteenth and nineteenth centuries (see Chap. 9). The only way to legitimate revival is thus to go back beyond this obliterated tradition. The floating gap between the Muhammadan past and the current Islamic individuals can be bridged only through an immediate genealogical link, for example the Muhammadan era itself, hence the reference to the central tradition of Sunni Islam in its period of development, and the reference to *al-Salaf al-Salih*, the pious forefathers. As avantgardists and exponents of the imagined Islamic society, or *jamaʿat*, they can thus distinguish themselves from the ordinary Muslims and secular politicians, from *creatio ex nihilo* as well as from the continuity of the real tradition. They consequently consider themselves authorised to establish renewal—*tajdid*—thought necessary to respond to the changes of modernity. *Ijtihad*, for example, the maximum effort to ascertain, in a given problem or issue, the injunction of Islam and its real intent, was the proper channel for that renewal. With such arguments people like Maududi created a new authoritative and formative past while the absence of historical records allows thinkers like him to see themselves as exponents of the imagined Islamic society.

Aspects of their critique are systematised in a history of salvation and formulated as an integrist programme which, however, has a clear integrationist character. In contrast to their slogan "islamise modernity", their Islamic tradition is modernised, since the imagined Islamic society is to compete and correspond with Western achievements. This would only be possible in a centralised Islamic state over which the Islamists would wield control as the agents of God's sovereignty on earth, as with the Jamaʿat-e Islami. The Quran and sunna would be the ideal basis for a universal, legally ethical monism. In such an imagined Islamic territory, ideas such as nationalism, pluralism, democracy and human rights have little value; democracy and political secularism are considered to be outcomes of Christian clericalism, as they are perceived to be purely European in their essence. These and other terms are genealogically assigned to European history only. Thus Islamists regard the dogmatic self-definition of early Islam as the Islamic nature, the essence. Any historical processes after this time are simply ignored, actually denied. The main concern is to establish a unique and synchronic Islamic identity. These kinds of Islamist ideas are always postulated within the boundaries of a nation-state through such ideas have some transnational potential. This nation remains untouched as the prime frame of reference: it is not only an important feature for cultural autonomy, but also offers space for an encompassing cultural identity which can integrate particular and regional identities. Here lie the limits of Muslim unity and Islamic identity. Political Islam then provides the imagination of the realisation and reconstruction of a society within a nation-state.[4] Political Islam and religious fundamentalism preach a solidarity traditionalism,[5] which is primarily oriented to a life in this world and has certain ideas of what reform should be about. On closer inspection, however, its postulates reveal mere prophecies, pieces of advice, threats and general desiderata with little consistent programme. It fails to solve factual problems, offering mostly regressive attempts at solutions, precisely because its orientation is mythical, hence restorative, and hardly utopian, that is social-revolutionary. Yet, fundamentalists do not reject modernity such as increasing bureaucratisation and rationalisation but modernism, that is, the search for individual autonomy, and therefore can be seen as some sort of alternative modernity.[6]

---

[4] Initially Maududi had denied the necessity of a nation state for the realisation of a true Islamic society. This was the prime reason for his party to oppose the creation of Pakistan initially.

[5] That is to say a traditionalism that consciously and selectively interprets tradition for the sake of solidarity and therefore rejects discriminatory elements or apologetically reinterprets them; see Rothermund: "Der Traditionalismus als Forschungsgegenstand".

[6] See Bruce Lawrence: *Defenders of God. The Fundamentalist Revolt against the Modern Age*, University of South Carolina Press 1995.

Since the 1980s, when political Islam was said to have failed, we have witnessed a change in the Islamist discourse. According to O. Roy and G. Kepel,[7] Islamist movements had their peak in the 1980s. It has been argued that this phase of "post-Islamism"[8] ushered in terrorist attacks as a last attempt to regain political power—not least because Islamist theories have the potential to accommodate religious radicalism. At the same time, however, alternatives have emerged characterised by a process of self-re-invention as democratic movements to mark out the Islamists' social and political territories and to enlarge them, albeit within the boundaries of the nation-state.[9] Their positions are constantly re-negotiated vis-à-vis government, external patrons, other Islamist groups, and their respective target audiences. This involves competition and control of a variety of institutions as well as disagreement over the interpretation of symbols, because symbols are integral to any political system, be it religious, modern or even post-modern—and—Muslim politics,[10] and are not only used by political elites but also by the recipients of their discourse as it lends meaning to their action. They express the values and norms of a political community. There is a constant struggle concerning people's imagination and memory, and following that, over the chances and resources in a free market. The interaction takes place through a variety of channels of understanding and reciprocal obligation, often built on the resilient framework of informal networks of trust and responsibility. Therefore, Islamic—even fundamentalist—principles must constantly be reinterpreted. The result is a flexibility of ideas and divergence over time and space when faced with social reality. Indeed, it is in the gap between divine plan—*shariʿa*—and human understanding—*siyasat*—that the

---

[7] See Olivier Roy: *The Failure of Political Islam*, tr. by Carol Folk. Cambridge: Harvard University Press 1994; Gilles Kepel: *Jihad. Expansion et decline de l'Islamisme*, Paris 2000.

[8] The Islamist decline theory has been critically discussed by Guido Steinberg: "Der Islamismus im Niedergang? Anmerkungen zu den Thesen Gilles Kepels, Olivier Roys and zur europäischen Islamismusforschung", in: Bundesministerium des Inneren (ed.): *Texte zur Inneren Sicherheit. Islamismus*, Berlin 2004(3), pp. 19–42, particularly pp. 28ff.

[9] Y.Y. Haddad: "Islamicist Depictions of Christianity in the Twentieth Century: the pluralism debate and the depiction of the other", in: *Islam and Christian-Muslim Relations* 7/1 (1996), pp. 75–89; A. Kian: "Women and Politics in Post-Islamist Iran: the Gender Conscious Drive to Change", in: *British Journal of Middle East Studies* 24/1 (1997), pp. 75–96.

[10] On how Muslims use specific Muslim symbols and discourses, see the enlightening book by Eickelman and Piscatori: *Muslim Politics*.

perennially fertile space of critique can be found.[11] This can intensify competition and conflicts. *The Satanic Verses* controversy is a case in point, when the banning and burning of the book was an Islamic demonstration to punish what was considered un-Islamic. The alternative is that multiple centres of power and contenders for authority come to certain accommodations. This can indeed be an indication of negotiation to the relative satisfaction of all. It is these different discourses that reflect the complicity of Muslimhood. This is particularly true in the field of the latent and open tensions between, say, ulama, Sufis and *mufakkirun*. There seems to be enough societal and economic overlappings, and cross-connections, as well as personal unions between, for example, Islamists and traditional Muslim scholars (ulama) so that both can come to terms with one another. In the process, given boundaries and norms are shifted, displaced, and extended. This has been the case since the 1980s, when Islamists have increasingly realised the potential of the ulama as custodians of change along with their various institutions and networks and have sought their alliances.

Thus, making sense of religious fundamentalism can be possible only if the complex and dynamic perspectives are contextualised. One can contend that studies on Islam should be read in the light of articulations of particular social and cultural realities negotiating over boundaries between spheres of social activity and institutions. Approaching 'Islamic' culture normatively does not contribute much towards understanding of the phenomenon. Islamicity is the linguistic and symbolic expression of this negotiation, a process of appropriating a meta-physical world, a system and repertory through which human beings represent the world. Fundamentalism is one such expression.

---

[11] Brinkley Messick as quoted in Eickelman and Piscatori: *Muslim Politics*, p. 16.

CHAPTER FOURTEEN

FROM THE PULPIT TO THE PARADE GROUND (APPROX. 1970–2002)

In what was left of Pakistan, Zulfiqar Ali Bhutto attempted to introduce his brand of "Islamic Socialism", with little success in solving the pressing economic and social problems.[1] The constitution of 1973 defined Islam as the state religion and determined the distribution of power between the central and provincial governments. The state was to be Islamised in nine years. However, Bhutto's policy of nationalisation led to an impoverishment of significant parts of the lower middle classes which had supported the Pakistan People's Party in 1970; the ensuing social tensions found expression in political unrest and opposition, which in turn were subdued by force.

Towards Islamisation

Islamic parties appeared to offer alternatives in this tense situation. Calling for the establishment of the so-called "Muhammadan System" (*nizam-e Mustafa*),[2] the political party of the Barelwis, the *Jam'iyyat-e 'Ulama-ye Pakistan* (JUP) spearheaded the movement against Z.A. Bhutto. Its leader, Shah Ahmad Nurani (died 2003), was nominated candidate for the position of Prime Minister by the member parties of the "United Democratic Front" against the PPP. 'Islamisation'—in contrast to "Islamic socialism" which provided for some Islamic provisions—was their slogan: the goal was not a radical isolation from the socialist, 'un-Islamic' realm of state economics—which included interest-bearing transactions and accounts—but rather the co-ordination with and integration of traditional Islamic customs into the modern economy. Discontent against the PPP had risen particularly in economically

---

[1] For the following see S.J. Burki: *Pakistan under Bhutto*, New York 1979; L. Ziring: *Pakistan: The Enigma of Political Development*, Boulder 1980; S.J. Malik: *Islamisierung in Pakistan 1977–1984*, Stuttgart 1989.

[2] Al-Mustafa, the chosen, selected one, is an epithet of Prophet Muhammad.

developed areas, where the gap between traditional socio-economic systems and modern ones was most apparent. The Islamic parties became a rallying point for people in these areas, pulling in elements of the middle class, petty tradesmen, industrial workers and intellectuals. They strove for an alternative to the besieged Bhutto system, which was coerced into making considerable concessions in 1977: the Ahmadiyya was declared a non-Muslim minority in 1974, the power of the *Council for Islamic Ideology* was elevated, Muslim Friday was declared the weekly holiday instead of the Christian Sunday; and certificates from some religious schools were nationally recognised for the first time. Beyond that, Bhutto's foreign policy was of some concern to the USA, since he seemed to stand up for the interests of the Third World, colluded with communist countries and threatened to develop and produce nuclear weapons.

Despite the wide-ranging opposition from the "Pakistan National Alliance"—a conglomerate of nine parties from the far left to the far right—Bhutto's party surprisingly emerged as the largest in the 1977 elections. Alleging fraud, the opposition demanded new elections, which further intensified the conflict. The slogan of the day introduced in 1970 by JUP once again generated solidarity and mobilised people: "We'll take the bullets in our chest, we'll bring *nizam-e Mustafa*" (*sine par goli kha'enge, nizam-e Mustafa la'enge*). A slogan that stood in stark contrast to the secular one used by the PPP: "Victory or death, we will bring about socialism" (*marenge, mar ja'enge, soshalism la'enge*).

The Zia era

When the already unstable nation appeared to fall apart, the military—having been sent back to their barracks after 1971—intervened in 1977, while readily responding to the calls for a "Muhammadan System" which was led jointly by Islamic parties. The commander in chief, Zia al-Haqq, promised elections within 90 days of seizing power (subsequently delayed by several years), ordering Bhutto's arrest and his eventual execution in 1979. He then consolidated his power by various changes in the constitution under the pretext of constructing an Islamic social system. In a questionable referendum in 1984, he arranged for himself to be acknowledged as the only legitimate ruler, the Ahmadiyya was practically declared illegal. Similarly, the non-party elections of 1985 affected only a few individual parliamentary seats, making the emergence of any serious opposition impossible. Against the backdrop of a brutal war in Afghanistan led by *mujahidin*, "freedom fighters" trained and supported in Pakistani *madrasas* with the help of foreign, in particular US money, arms and US-sponsored textbooks,[3] to counter Soviet invasion (see below), Zia's top-down Islamisation endeavours were supported by a motley alliance: the military and civilian bureaucracy, leaders of differing Islamic parties such as the Jamaʿat-e Islami and the traditionalist Deobandi Jamʿiyyat-e ʿUlama-ye Islam (JUI) and also the increasing circle of the Tablighi Jamaʿat. The majority of the Sunni scholarly establishment, however, and also the Shiʿite minority (less than a fifth of the population) opposed these policies—not because they disagreed with the intensity of Zia's Islamisation, but because it did not match their own diverse Islamic ideas. For one, the speed of implementation and the intent of Islamisation were obscure,[4] secondly, the Federal Shariat Court set up in 1980 issued verdicts—in the case of stoning to death (*rajm*)—to the extent that the hadiths cannot abrogate the Quran because they suffer from infirmities. Under pressure of ulama this verdict was reversed. This showed that the centrality and function of sunna as a legitimising force was very much alive.[5] After all, the ulama considered themselves to be the prime agents of prophetic tradition as well as movers of reform and change in accordance with the Islamic concept of *islah* (reform)—mandating change to eradicate unlawful innovations (*bidʿa*) for establishing the common good, the *maslaha*. This made challenging the state even more legitimate. However, the military regime put considerable pressure on religious scholars by 1982 through a series of ploys: generating economic dependency through the wide-spread and sophisticated Islamic charity system, the *zakat*[6] that had been nationalised since

[3] Rashid Ahmed opines in Chap. 1 of his celebrated *Taliban: Militant Islam, Oil and Fundamentalism in Central Asia*, Yale Univ. Press 2000, that "US funds were matched by Saudi Arabia and together with support from other European and Islamic countries, the Mujaheddin received a total of over US$10 billion. Most of this aid was in the form of lethal modern weaponry given to a simple agricultural people who used it with devastating results."

[4] GoP, Ministry of Justice and Parliamentary Affairs (Justice Division): *The Comparative Statement of the Constitution as it stood before the 20th March, 1985 and as it stands after that Date*, p. 54, states: "'Law' includes any custom or usage having the force of law but does not include the Constitution, Muslim personal law, any law relating to the procedure of any court or tribunal or, until the expiration of ten years from the commencement of this Chapter, any fiscal law or any law relating to the levy and collection of taxes and fees or banking or insurance practice and procedure."

[5] Brown: *Rethinking tradition*, pp. 135–138.

[6] The root of the term *zakat* (from the Arabic *zakâ*) means "to purify" and "to grow", i.e., to purify the annual wealth (cf. Sura 2:219). The required duty amounts

1980—and also by the recognition of religious school-certificates issued by umbrella organisations of affiliated religious schools. This led to an increase of newly founded *madrasas*, and consequently to a spectacular glut of graduates causing tremendous problems, adding to alarming escalation of the existing conflict potential, giving rise to a variety of radical groups. This activated hitherto latent sectarian violence which can be considered as resulting conflict in terms of state power arrayed against marginalised citizens (see below).

The policy of Islamisation

The Jamaʿat-Islami gradually became political ammunition in the hands of authoritarian regimes precisely because of its reformist ambitions which it only felt to be realised in a strong—Islamic—state as the embodiment of alternative modernity. This Islamist state-apologetics was supported by the state, as was evident in the results of the Islamisation policy when Zia al-Haqq backed up the programmes of the Jamaʿat-e Islami wholeheartedly. In the following we will consider the Islamic institutions, such as *waqf, zakat* and *madrasas* in particular.

In fact, the Islamisation policy in Pakistan since Zia al-Haqq generated a new phase of institutionalisation in religious schools through, among others, their conditional recognition by the University Grants Commission.[7] To be so recognised, the students were supposed to be taught a modernised syllabus lasting sixteen years, which meant that the teachers would have to follow the suggestions of the National Committee on Religious Schools established in 1979. The report of the Committee suggested taking

> ...concrete and feasible measures for improving and developing Deeni-Madrassahs along sound lines, in terms of physical facilities, curricula

---

to 2.5% of the annual savings. While those liable to pay *zakat* are not specified in the Quran (cf. Sura 21:73, 19:31, 19:55, 7:156, 2:3, 2:43, 2:177, 2:83, 5:12, 5:55, 9:11, 9:18 et passim), those entitled to receive *zakat* are specified in Sura 9:60. For the Shia an additional rule says that a non-*Sayyid* (i.e. a non-descendant of the Prophet) may not give any *zakat* to a *Sayyid* as a *Sayyid* does not need any alms. Instead, the *Sayyid* may receive *Khums*, i.e., one fifth of the annual deposits of a non-*Sayyid* (cf. Sura 8:41). Half of this *Khums* again belongs to the *Imam* or his representative. The descendants of the Prophet may give *zakat* among themselves as well as to needy non-*Sayyids*.

[7] For the following see Malik: *Colonialization of Islam*; Jamal Malik: "Traditional Islamic Learning and Reform in Pakistan", *ISIM Newsletter* (Leiden) 10 (2002), pp. 20–21. Also Zaman: *The Ulama in Contemporary Islam*.

> and syllabi, staff and equipment...so as to bring education and training at such Madrashahs *in consonance with the requirements of the modern age and the basic tenets of Islam*...to expand higher education and employment opportunities for the students of the Madrassahs...integrating them with the overall educational system in the country. (emphasis mine)

However, the idea of this reformed Islam provoked considerable reaction because it stood in stark contrast to the concepts of most of the ulama, but with the insistent pressure of the government and its support—e.g., through *zakat* money, as we shall see—and with the equating of their degrees with those of national universities in 1981/82, they became more and more convinced of the potentially positive consequences this policy might have for them. They did adopt the curriculum by merely adding subjects from the formal primary education system to their own syllabus, and Arabic instead of English was used on the certificates. Thus the ulama showed their ability to gain official recognition by effecting minor changes, and they were gradually able to exercise more influence on the government. Theoretically, these degrees, once recognised, were to open up economic mobility and possibilities of promotion for the graduates. However, there was no concrete plan of how and where the now officially examined masses of religious scholars would be integrated into the job market. This myopic planning done mainly by government officials and some co-opted ulama soon led to new challenges.

Parallel to these administrative and curricular reform measures, the economic situation of *madrasas* changed and, indeed, improved by means of money disbursed through the central and provincial *zakat* funds set up by the government in 1980: ten per cent of the alms collected from current accounts through *zakat*-deducting agencies go to religious education if curricular reform and political loyalty are observed.[8] These additional financial resources enhanced the budgets of religious schools considerably, constituting up to one third of their annual income, and were exclusively at the disposal of the rectors of

[8] It should be pointed out that the Shia community has been exempted from *zakat* and *'ushr* (dues on agricultural output, i.e., *the tithe*) for theological reasons and political pressure. Shia landowners were, however, faced with a higher land tax above the corresponding value of *'ushr*. It is interesting to note that under these circumstances *zakat* evasion occurred increasingly. Sunnis produced affidavits to prove their Shianess. It is clear that the *zakat* system became a bone of contention in the tussle between those who wanted a Sunnite Islamisation and the Shi'ites; see Malik: *Colonialization of Islam*, pp. 102–107.

these schools, i.e., the ulama. This certainly created new expectations and new patterns of consumption.

Changes in religious establishment

As a result of these changes, a new dimension of mobility of these scholars and their centres of learning can be discerned, with far-reaching consequences as early as the 1990s. First, the prospect of *zakat* grants resulted in a mushrooming of *madrasas*, mostly in rural areas. In response, the government introduced various measures to try to stem the tide, but this only raised new problems. Second, the number of the graduates of religious schools at various academic levels is constantly on the rise, as these institutions now also offer formal primary education with officially recognised degrees. Third, Islamisation policy brought in a new phase of institutionalisation among umbrella organisations, so that the number of affiliated schools increased tremendously. Fourth, each school of thought has its own reserved area, be it tribal, rural, urban, trade-oriented or even strategic: Deobandis in the Northwestern Frontier Province and Baluchistan where tribal society prevails, as well as in parts of Punjab and Sind; Barelwis in rural areas of Sind and Punjab, where an elaborate cult of holy men is most popular; Shiʿites in the Northern Areas and in some districts of the Punjab dominated by religious practices not necessarily appreciated by dominant Sunni scholarship; the Ahl-e Hadith in commercial centres and important internal markets; and the Jamaʿat-e Islami primarily in urban and politically sensitive areas such as the NWFP and "Azad Kashmir" that seemed to have attracted a number of radical groups from various regions outside Pakistan.

In the wake of the formalisation and reform of religious schools, an increasing trans-provincial north-south migration from rural to urban areas can be observed, a sign of the degree of spatial mobility of the young religious scholars, which reflects networks of scholarship: students from specific regions look for schools and teachers who comply with their cultural perceptions and ethnic affiliations. They search for corresponding institutions and affiliations that create identity-giving sub-structures in an urban environment which may otherwise be perceived as alien and even hostile. Eventually, the migrant scholars-to-be found in the metropolis contributed to conflicts, often religiously sanctioned but motivated by economic and social contestations. The number of religious schools and their students has grown in a spectacular way in urban, and even more in rural areas. Thus, not only cities have become locations of increasing conflict; the hinterland also has been increasingly drawn into the sphere of religiously legitimised battles. Islamisation policy has thus promoted institutionalisation of different groups, but since contemporary regimes are not able or willing to integrate religious scholars into the national fabric, their increasing marginalisation, politicisation and even radicalisation are the results, though they have been regarded by state officials as the heirs to and preservers of Muslim identity in colonial as well as in post-colonial times.

The increasing numbers of young theologians, with degrees equivalent to an M.A. in Arabic/Islamic Studies, are increasingly confronted with government reform measures that lack plans for dealing with the labour market. The promised Islamisation and plans to improve the literacy rate have not translated into jobs for them; on the contrary, the lack of proper measures comprises a potential source of internal conflict. It is only as teachers of Arabic, having been promoted since 1979, that some young scholars have found jobs. These courses are, however, targeted at Pakistanis seeking work in the Middle East.[9] On a different front, the military, against the background of the cold war, has been encouraging the recruitment of religious scholars since 1983—with foreign aid. In the medium term, this has led to new values and structures in the army, especially at middle and lower levels of command.

With the official support of religious scholars in the 1980s and even in the 1990s, the political strength of representatives of this section

[9] These students are part of the considerable number of labour migrants who find jobs in Arab countries from where they remit huge amounts of money that make up to a large part of the country's foreign income. The remittances are often used to subsidise the families, to build representative houses and to provide for different consumer goods. This has caused initial brain drain, as well as changes in living standards and patterns of behaviour. But with the remigration in the 1980s and the dislocations going had in hand, the repercussion of these migrants can be marked also in terms of religious practices. They have been increasingly looking for Islamic groups that would provide them with a proven legitimacy for their new status. The sectarian groups that emerged in the 1990s provide them with such contexts (see below). The literature on migration is huge. See Jonathan Addleton: *Undermining the Centre: The Gulf Migration and Pakistan*, Karachi: OUP 1992. A general overview is provided by Robert E.B. Lucas: "International Migration to the High Income Countries. Some Consequences for Economic Development in the Sending Countries", in: *Bulletin for Comparative Labour Relations* 55, April 2004.

of Islamic traditions has increased profoundly. Thus, the Islamisation policy—or better the politics of de-traditionalisation—has ultimately forced the politically dominant sector to rethink its own position. In such a situation of tension the centre may be pushed onto the political defensive, a position from which it could extricate itself only by violence, and with increasing alienation from the rest of the society. This danger exists especially where state institutions can offer no adequate alternatives to indigenous social and educational structures and historical patterns of social organisations, such as extant and functional endowments (*waqf*), charities (*zakat*) and religious schools (*madrasas*), and when thousands of unemployed religious scholars with access to large segments of society are not successfully integrated.

At the same time, the existing historically developed structures and categories of social organisation, providing alternative space to the state-centred social formations and ideas, are increasingly weakened through Islamically sanctioned measures designed to introduce legislation into remoter regions and to consolidate the market according to an Islamic nomenclature. The elaborate state-run *zakat*-system, the nationalised *waqfs* and also methods of Islamic economy such as profit-and-loss-sharing accounts are cases in point to legitimise and extend state interests. An ideologised historiography and re-writing of history, the strengthening and standardisation of Urdu as a national language with a religious impetus, but also the establishment of an extensive administration have been thought to be primary means of reaching this target. But actually state diffusion into society has been incomplete due to failing national integration and corresponding institutionalisation. In the meantime, however, foreign interest groups in alliance with the colonial sector recognise new possibilities for market transactions and expansion. This rather short-sighted policy of Islamisation has caused major, unforeseen, though not unforeseeable sectarian problems in a partly functioning traditional society.

Taming the religious

Given that after the mysterious death of Zia al-Haqq in 1988,[10] the democratically elected government of the Pakistan People's Party (PPP)

[10] Together with a number of high military functionaries he was killed in a plane crash in August 1988. The circumstances of the crash were not clarified.

under the leadership of the daughter of former prime minister Z.A. Bhutto (executed 1979), Benazir Bhutto (assassinated 2007), mistrusted the active participation of regional forces and especially the participation of the advancing religious dignitaries. Her poor domestic and economic policies were perpetuated by Nawaz Sharif, who successfully challenged her in the national elections on the ticket of the Islamic Democratic Alliance. But these unbalanced policies led in the 1990s to uncontrolled Islamisation from below through various means such as favouring the ulama through constitutional amendments, and ultimately dramatising the issue of Islamic agency between ulama and state.[11] In October 1999, the tense situation led to another coup under General Musharraf.[12]

Between 1977 and the end of the millennium, the policy of Islamisation boomeranged unstoppably. Instead of the avowed formation of a harmonising Islamisation, new increasingly radicalised rival Islamic groups entered the scene in all sects. Specific ethnic and language-related identities are now increasingly legitimised on religious grounds. From the cities, these groups infiltrate the countryside where they provoke regionalism and thereby endanger the stability of the remaining parts of the colonial state. Thus, the raised expectations have pushed many graduates of religious schools into the hands of different players; the rhetoric of Islamic symbolism and *jihad* has shown that it can be effectively used as a means of self-defence against foreign encroachments, and there has been a constantly increasing pressure on the state by religious elements. In fact, the representatives of Islam can be seen as a source of limitation on state power, as has been the case also historically:[13] The Council of Islamic Ideology, set up in the 1960s, and the Pakistani Federal Ministry of Religious Affairs, have been issuing objectionable Islamic proposals. Similarly, the failure to reform either the Blasphemy Law in 1994 and 2001,[14] or the *madrasas* in 1995 is

---

[11] Compare Zaman: *The Ulama in Contemporary Islam*, Chap. 4.

[12] For Musharraf's coup and his political vision of Kemalism see Jan-Peter Hartung: "Gottesstaat versus Kemalismus", in: *Religion, Staat, Gesellschaft* 1/1 (2000).

[13] Historically speaking, the activities of the ulama can also be seen as a means to limit caliphal despotism. See Richard W. Bulliet: "Twenty Years of Islamic Politics", in: *Middle East Journal* 53 (1999), pp. 189–200, and John Kelsey: "Civil Society and Government in Islam", in: Sohail Hashmi (ed.): *Islamic Political Ethics. Civil Society, Pluralism, and Conflict*, Princeton 2002, as quoted in Mohamed A. Bamyeh: "Civil Society and the Islamic experience", in: *ISIM Review* 15 (2005), pp. 40f. Also Barber Johansen: *Contingency in a Sacred Law: Legal and Ethical Norms in the Muslim Fiqh*, Leiden: Brill 1999, pp. 189–218.

[14] The idea was that, instead of filing a blasphemy case with the police, a senior administration official should oversee the procedure. Blasphemy has become a major

simply a reflection of the aggressive mood of both Islamic traditionalists and Islamists, based on what has been called 'paranoid Islam'.[15] In May 2000, Islamic parties were powerful enough to demand several Islamic provisions,[16] some of which were instantly met by the government. But in order to increase control over the religious establishment, the current regime came up with yet another *madrasa* reform proposal in August 2001, designed to establish a Pakistan Madrasah Education Board and a Pakistan Madrasah Education Fund as well as model *dini madaris*. This policy clearly aims at controlling some 20,000 *madrasas* with approximately three million students[17] and more than 50,000 mosques—a solid power-structure indeed.

The control of the ulama and their followers seems to be even more important since there has traditionally been a movement across the porous borders of Pakistan and Afghanistan, India, and the Kashmir valley. This is especially true of Pashtuns in Pakistan, who outnumber their fellow Pashtuns in Afghanistan. They are linked by family networks, student-teacher loyalties, legal and illegal commercial connections, and religio-political solidarity. Thus despite the Pakistani government's recent strict policies against foreign students, Afghan students of religious schools have vowed to continue their Islamic education in Pakistan.

Radicalisation of the religious?

The reforms thus envisaged by the state have produced an imbalance that has resulted in a variety of problems, some of which were tem-

---

issue in Pakistan and is used as a weapon to arbitrarily criminalise opponents. See for example Asif Shazad: "Holy Terror", in: *Herald* (Karachi), 34/7 July 2003. See also Christian Stahmann: *Islamische Menschenrechtskonzepte und das Problem sogenannter 'islamischer' Menschenrechtsverletzungen in Pakistan seit 1977*, Heidelberg: Ergon 2005.

[15] Thus called by Salman Rushdie in his article "Yes, This Is About Islam" published in *The New York Times* on 2 Nov. 2001: "This paranoid Islam which blames outsiders, 'infidels', for all the ills of Muslim societies, and whose proposed remedy is the closing of those societies to the rival project of modernity, is presently the fastest growing version of Islam in the world."

[16] That is 1) integration of special Islamic provisions of the constitution of 1973 into the Provincial Constitution Order of Oct. 1999. 2) Keeping separate electorates for Muslims and non-Muslims at district and local level. 3) Implementation of Friday as the holy day. 4) Banning of anti-Islamic activities of NGOs. 5) Guarantee of Gov. not to touch *madrasas* and *jihadi* groups.

[17] A recent World Bank report from 2005 counts less than half a million students, which seems highly underestimated.

porarily alleviated through what was called *jihad* in Afghanistan. In the wake of these developments, newer identities and several branches of *madrasas* have emerged, enhancing the state of sectarian fights. To be sure, these branches do interact in a variety of channels of understanding and reciprocal obligation which are often built on the resilient framework of informal networks of trust and responsibility. One, may, however distinguish several groups: the students of religious schools in general have been subject to several reforms from within and without, and have played a quietist role.[18] However, because of their traditional ties with Afghanistan and other neighbouring countries and as a result of the use of *jihad* rhetoric, some of them were used as foot-soldiers in the Afghanistan civil-war. A subset of this first category, therefore, became the second group—the *mujahidun*[19] who sought to "reassert their independence by overthrowing the leftist Afghan regime propped up by Moscow."[20] In order to keep these rather diverse and contesting and ethnically organised groups under control and to maintain a grip on the region for economic and political purposes, yet another version was established by those interested: the Taliban.[21] Their declared aim was the restoration of peace, disarmament of the population, enforcement of *shari'a* law and the defence of Afghanistan's integrity and Islamic character. Many *mujahidun* too followed the call of Mulla Muhammad Omar, the shy and mysterious leader of the Taliban. Thus both the *mujahidun* and the Taliban have much in common; apart from same ethnic lineages and educational background they are also known for their forced recruitment and molesting of young children in *madrasas* and refugee camps in Pakistan. As far as the fourth category of *jihadis* is concerned, many of them can be traced back to the Taliban and

---

[18] It is banal to point out that an ordinary *madrasa*-student can join the mujahidin, who themselves, like the Taliban could have joined *jihadi* groups.

[19] The mujahidin became warlords who in the course of the war in Afghanistan had divided the country into fiefdoms. They fought in a bewildering array of alliances, betrayals and bloodshed, switching sides again and again.

[20] This was a major theme in the textbooks designed for the *madrasas* between 1986 and 1994 in a programme sponsored by a $50 million USAID grant; see Mahmood Mamdani: *Good Muslim, Bad Muslim. Islam, the USA, and the Global War Against Terror*, New Delhi: Permanent Black 2004, pp. 136f.

[21] The word *taliban* is actually the Persian plural of the Arabic word *talib*, student. Thus 'students of (religious) schools'; most of them had been students in Pakistani *madrasas* preferably in NWFP and Baluchistan where they found a network of schools and ethnical affinities before they emerged at the end of 1994. The name Taliban was to make clear that they categorically rejected the party politics of *mujahidin*.

mujahidun themselves, others to groups returning from battlefields such as Kashmir, Afghanistan, and Chechnya. Their leaders usually hail from the middle-class and are often secularly educated men, rather than *madrasa* students, though *madrasa* students also join the militant and radical groups in the global upsurge of religious violence. There is little doubt that some of their organisations run private armies, collect compulsory donations, and indulge in militant activities. Some of them, such as *Jaish Muhammadi* (Muhammadan Army), *Harakat al-Ansar* (Movement of (Medinian) Helpers), *Lashkar-e Tayyiba* (Soldiers of Medina), are the armed wing of the Centre for mission and guidance (*Markaz-e da'wat wa irshad*) established in the Punjab in 1986 by Ahl-e Hadith, have made a regional conflict, the Kashmir cause, their raison d'être, under the shibboleth of Prophetic tradition—probably under patronage of Pakistan's Inter Services Intelligence. Thus it is true that the struggle for victory over a super-power—the Soviet finally withdrew in 1989—and an alleged affiliation to some global network enhance the radicals' feeling of Islamism—no matter how blurred and intangible it may be. It must be stressed, however, that it is the objective material conditions coupled with the symbolic power of regional conflicts, such as those in Palestine and Kashmir, that make up for the explosive mixture because these conflicts represent the suppression of whole nations. However international and global these organisations may be, they have risen primarily as a result of internal problems caused by political mismanagement, and they have subsequently been exploited by external powers. The dramatic flaunting and celebration of military power on national occasions such as Pakistan Day[22] and the propagation of *jihad* in textbooks even in formal schools and on television for the cause of Kashmir are cases in point.

This state-promoted violence and hatred from childhood onwards might be part of the painful nation-building process and the invention of an ideology broad enough to accommodate the various groups involved, but it certainly fails to instil tolerance and acceptance of plurality among students.

This rather grave scenario is certainly different from the Indian scene where the government has started to launch similar reform programmes which were met by severe reactions from the ulama, fearing

[22] This is the celebration of the passage of the Lahore Resolution passed at a meeting of All India Muslim League at Minto Park Lahore on March 23, 1940.

a profound change in their—sometimes flourishing—*madrasas* and so the loss of Islamic identity. In Bangladesh, the situation is quite similar where the *madrasas* are witnessing a boom.[23] It must be reiterated that religious schools in these areas provide at least some kind of education and survival. What is more important, perhaps, is their use of a variety of religious symbols to articulate the predicaments which people face in highly fragmented societies that have become increasingly subject to globalisation through its prime agent, the post-colonial state. The growing presence and visibility of religious power in the public sphere represents this struggle between state and religious scholars and their institutions that have been exploited by different groups but at the same time been denied their share. In the context of these developments the making of an epitomising prophet was easy: the 'Ladinist' saviour, who would lead the campaign against suppression. But the basis of this Islamic radicalism still has very profane reasons:[24] social conflict, poverty, and political suppression. The basis is not the Quran, but social reality, which is formulated by means of Islamic symbolism. Formerly, violence was legitimised nationally; today use is made of the Islamic repertory, not because this violence is, or has become Islamic or religious, but because the political discourse has shifted. Thus, it is merely formulated Islamically rather than conditioned by Islam.

Some religio-political parties have been capitalising on this new situation, such as the Deobandi JUI which had been politically successful in NWFP in the 1980s, for it postulated the implementation of shari'a laws, Islamic economic and social reforms. Back in the 1970s, the party had been benefitting from the use of historically developed patterns of social organisation, such as ethnic bonds, mosques and their umbrella organisation of religious schools. Eventually it entered into a coalition with the National Awami Party (NAP) and thus managed to form provincial governments in two provinces, NWFP and Baluchistan, Mufti Mahmud being chief minister of NWFP from 1971 to 1973. The Islamisation of the region under him influenced the subsequent political scenario in so far as the JUI cooperated with the "Pakistan National

---

23 An overview on *madrasas* in Bangladesh is given by Amr Abdalla, A.N.M. Raisuddin, Suleiman Hussein: *Pre-primary and Primary Madrasah Education in Bangladesh*, prepared for the Basic Education and Policy Support (BEPS) Activity, United States Agency for International Development, July 2004 (http://www.beps.net/publications/BangladeshMadrasahStudyFINAL.pdf, accessed 18 Aug. 2005).

24 Though one might argue from a specific Muslim point of view that there is no distinction between sacred and profane at all.

Alliance" against Z.A. Bhutto in 1977 and later at times also supported the policy of Zia al-Haqq as well as the Islamic Democratic Alliance government of Nawaz Sharif (1990–1992). However, the JUI was against state interference into *madrasas*, it boycotted several schemes initiated by the Zia regime, such as the reform of religious schools and the state-run *zakat* system of 1980, particularly in Sind. In doing so, the JUI thereby also became a vehicle of provincial nationalism for some time.

Under the leadership of Fadl al-Rahman (born 1953),[25] the son of the late Mufti Mahmud, the JUI became increasingly anti-Shiʿite, as can be witnessed in the activities of the Punjab-based communal *Anjuman-e Sipahan-e Sahaba*,[26] a militant splinter group of the JUI established in Jhang/Punjab in 1985 which strives to excommunicate Shiʿism; even other contesting Sunnite groups such as the Barelwis are persecuted, while trying to make Sunni celebrations constitutive of state ceremonials. In 1985 senators Samiʿ al-Haqq[27] and Qadi ʿAbd al-Latif, both JUI, introduced the Shariat Bill to the National Assembly. The intellectual centre of the JUI has lately shifted—in the wake of intra-provincial migration—from the North to the South: the *Dar al-Ifta wa al-Irshad* in Karachi.

Although the JUI has not been very successful in gaining political influence at national level, it is one of the most powerful political and social forces, particularly in the NWFP and Baluchistan. Having its base among the Pashtuns, it holds control over a large number of religious schools all over the country that have been recruitment centres not only for thousands of young male religious scholars, but also for Afghan *mujahidin* who fought Soviet power. Later the *madrasas*, in particular the one led by JUI, have also been very actively supporting and training Taliban by helping to establish the "Islamic Emirate Afghanistan" that lasted from 1995 to 2002. It also facilitated the government's relations with the Taliban. This also enhanced the profile of the Deobandi

[25] It is said that Fadl al-Rahman is on good terms with Mulla Omar due to spiritual and family ties.

[26] The *Sipahan-e Sahaba* stand, as the name suggests, for the devotion to the Prophet's companions. Thus "the sahaba must be rescued from Shiʿi vilification, their honor guarded, their memory revived and revered". They publish a monthly journal called *Khilafat-e Rashida*, and are supported by the middle classes and the commercial bourgeoisie. See Zaman: *The Ulama in Contemporary Islam*, pp. 118ff.

[27] Samiʿ al-Haqq heads one the largest religious schools and centres of *mujahidin* and later Taliban, the Dar al-ʿUlum Haqqaniyya, Akora Khattak, near Peshawar. For this school see Malik: *Colonialization of Islam*, pp. 202–209, 227ff., 240f.

ulama in Pakistan.[28] The success of the Taliban, therefore, cannot be understood without referring to the Pakistani scene. They were successful because of their ethnic homogeneity and their radical elimination of the quasi-anarchical situation in Afghanistan led by warlords. But their alliance with Usama bin Laden (born 1957) who had been living in Afghanistan under their protection since 1996 resulted in the expulsion of the Taliban regime by foreign powers—at least for the time being.

This development has repercussions for Pakistan; some speak of "Talibanisation of Pakistan" because after the Taliban takeover of Kabul, the JUI openly declared revoking the electoral politics of Pakistan. Many analysts believe that quite a few religio-political parties such as the JUI have a wide international *jihadi* network, such as in Tajikistan, Chechnya and, of course, Kashmir.

One may also consider different alliances between Islamists and groups adhering to traditional scholars, such as the Deobandis in Pakistan. The alliances go back to the dynamism that developed in the wake of the Islamisation policy and the subsequent strengthening of parts of the religious establishment, connected to *madrasas*. The dynamism became evident when the traditional Islamic educational institutions came to be known as breeding grounds for terrorism and training camps for *jihad*, as had already been suggested by the Pakistani Anti-Terrorism Ordinance 2001, one month before the attacks on the World Trade Centre and the Pentagon. Yet, a number of them had been nourished and financed by foreign donors for political purposes. Also in secular India, *madrasas* have become subject to scrutiny and suspicion. This suspicion goes back to the late 1970s when Zia al-Haqq initiated his Islamisation policy, which is becoming graver each day, if one considers the intolerable sectarian situation in Pakistan particularly between Sunnite groups and Shiʿites.

The Shiʿites had been demanding more rights in terms of rituals, endowments and schooling for a long time, but it was the Sunnite Islamisation policy which brought many of them together politically under the umbrella of the newly founded Movement for the Implementation of the Jaʿfari Law (*Tahrik-e Nifaz-e Fiqh-e Jaʿfariyya*) in 1980,

[28] Again, it is hard to speak of a monolithic bloc of Deobandi ulama in Pakistan. Men such as Samiʿ al-Haqq and Fadl al-Rahman head different branches of the JUI, while scholars such as Taqi ʿUthmani from Dar al-ʿUlum in Karachi excel in Islamic scholarship and are well known for their intellectual contributions. See Zaman: *The Ulama in Contemporary Islam*, pp. 135ff. et passim.

coinciding with the Iranian Revolution. The movement was led by Mufti Jaʿfar Husain (1916–1983), who pushed through the *zakat*-exemption for Shiʿites. He was succeeded by ʿArif Husain al-Husaini (1946–1988). Having been under Ruh Allah Khumaini's influence in the *madrasas* in Iran, al-Husaini deliberately played an offensive if not aggressive card by trying to push through Shiʿite interests in a self-conscious and collective way which in fact might have threatened the rather loose and dispersed Sunnite establishment. After his assassination, the movement became more moderate and even docile and was renamed *Tahrik-e Jaʿfariyya Pakistan*, dropping "implementation" for there was no issue of overthrowing Sunnism in Pakistan. Others became radicalised and founded the extremist group known as *Sipah-ye Muhammad* in 1991, which acts to combat Sunni onslaughts.

The alternative religious

In any case, sectarian identities are imagined to be constructed by reference to reform and change in what are considered ignorant and backward areas, and to enlighten them with "true" Islam. As has been the case with many nineteenth century reform movements aiming at *qasbahs*, the current policies are attempts to impose urban Islam on rural areas, to replace heteropraxy by orthopraxy, feudal oppression and corruption by empowerment. This postulated rationality against backwardness is the official face of state power arrayed against increasing numbers of marginalised people: the alarming increase of kidnappings for ransom in the cities as well as in rural areas, the killing of whole families by senior family members because of lack of material resources are causes of major concern. The Islamic repertory is, however, driven by a highly sectarian—Deobandi as well as Shiʿite—imagination, which can indeed be conducive to creating solidarity. The centres of the dissemination and proliferation of such ideas and forms of congregation can be the *madrasa* and sectarian organisations. They are led by laymen but are provided with ideological justification by well established ulama. Support comes mostly from the middle classes and local commercial bourgeoisie and urban professionals, often themselves from a rural background, but also and increasingly from the returnees from the Arab countries. The latter seems to be quite prone to these sectarian Sunni radical movements because they can help the remigrants in their quest for socially and economically vertical mobility against a feudal establishment which happens to be held by Shiʿites. This attack on entrenched social and economic privileges extends the influence of the ulama, and thus at the traditionalists, to dominate the Islamist, hence modernist, discourses,[29] and eventually becoming an agent of Islamisation from below rather than being inexplicably irrational actor.

Madrasas and Islamic learning traditions can thus be embodiments of a variety of resistance patterns. On the one hand, they appear to be the local resistance forces arrayed against the universalising and homogenising notions of secular modernity as stipulated by the state from above. On the other hand, they are exposed to the challenges of homogenising and globalising notions of Islam emerging within the religious discourses, that is to say, from below. These forms of resistance do have the potential to evolve into some radicalism, as the resistance adopts itself to the political economy of *madrasas*. On the positive side, however, these forms also provide for creative alternatives allowing accommodation and appeasement from within, as one can witness tremendous internal dynamics in these institutions. Interestingly enough, the language they speak is becoming increasingly similar to the one imposed by the state: homogenising and globalising, yet pluralistic and localising. Their homogenising notions of Islam target and contest the Muslim other rather than the non-Muslims. This sort of skirmish between local factions competing for scarce resources "from below" provides authoritative agency which seems to be necessary for survival in the same religious domain. Outwardly, these Islamic scholars might appear to be striving solely towards a universal Muslim identity. In their struggle for financial betterment, *madrasas* can try to resist the centripetal and centrifugal forces of secular modernity when they stress their particular identity as Muslims, Sunnis and Shiʿis. Again, it is in the contestation with other Muslim groups rather than with non-Muslims that they engage in their own "homogenising" forms of religious resistance. There is a clear universalising contestation to the homogenisation attempts of the state as well as those of traditionalist *madrasas*. Thus, alternatives to these "homogenising" forms of religious

[29] This has been elaborated by S.V.R. Nasr: "The Rise of Sunni Militancy in Pakistan: The Changing Role of Islamism and the Ulama in Society and Politics", in: *MAS* 34 (2000), pp. 139–180; Saleem Qureshi: 'The Politics of the Shia Minority in Pakistan: Context and Development', in: Dhirendra Vajpeyi and Yogendra K. Malik (eds.): *Religious and Ethnic Minority Politics in South Asia*, Delhi: Manohar 1989, pp. 109–138. See also Mariam Abou-Zahab: "The Sunni-Shia conflict in Jhang (Pakistan)", in: Ahmad and Reifeld (eds.): *Lived Islam in South Asia*.

resistance do exist and remain open to shifting connections and diverse forms of religious understanding to the extent that Islam and Islamic learning is vernacularised to fit local needs in the widest sense. It is this rare pluralistic approach that finds precedents in Muslim history, where the principle of pluralism was that which prevailed and was commonly accepted, such as Islamic law. In fact, it was this law that evolved from long scholastic debates, bringing about a consensus that is adaptable enough to guarantee a life in accordance with Islam in many different ways, harking back to the science of disputation mentioned earlier. This development rendered the singular and normative religious dynamics and a central scholastic teaching institution superfluous. It implied active engagement with plurality which required participation, beyond mere tolerance, and it did not displace or eliminate deep religious commitments but was rather the encounter of commitments.[30] In the current situation this pluralism is hardly detectable, however. Thus the International Crisis Group in its report on "The State of Sectarianism in Pakistan" states:

> Sectarian conflict in Pakistan is the direct consequence of state policies of Islamisation and marginalisation of secular democratic forces. Co-option and patronage of religious parties by successive military governments have brought Pakistan to a point where religious extremism threatens to erode the foundations of the state and society. As President Pervez Musharraf is praised by the international community for his role in the war against terrorism, the frequency and viciousness of sectarian terrorism continues to increase in his country.[31]

This is even more problematic since the "real damage the CIA did was not the providing of arms and money but the privatisation of information about how to produce and spread violence—the formation of private militias—capable of creating terror."[32] In the light of these developments, Musharraf's announcement of a crack-down on violent organisations in 2002 can hardly diminish the significance and power of these groups, because they reflect systemic problems. Unless these problems, e.g. material conditions of the people and regional conflicts,

[30] More on these issues see Jamal Malik (ed.): *Madrasas in South Asia. Teaching Terror?* London: Routledge 2008.

[31] See International Crisis Group, Asia Report N° 95, 18 April 2005: http://www.crisisgroup.org/library/documents/asia/south_asia/095_the_state_of_sectarianism_in_pakistan.pdf, accessed 19 April 2005.

[32] Mamdani: *Good Muslim, Bad Muslim*, p. 138.

are tackled, these groups will start operating under different names, change their modus operandi or move their operations elsewhere, making use of trans-Islamic networks. As a popular diviner has opined, a reaction was brewing: 'This government is paving the way to Islamic revolution by creating hurdles for the Islamic parties.' He hastened to add that '[t]here may not be instant reaction but they will respond once the dust is settled.... We are just watching the situation but the silence will not last for long.... The timing of this announcement by the president [e.g. crack-down, J.M.] has raised suspicion in the minds of religious people. It is being done under U.S. pressure.' And he asked: 'If they were terrorist groups, then why were they allowed to operate for such a long time?'.[33]

The criminalisation of the ulama therefore seems not to be an option. In a country that is heavily under their socio-cultural and religious influence, a dialogue of bullets is a dead end. Instead, it is more important to integrate these sections of society properly in order to prevent another cold war that no one can handle, especially against the backdrop of the evolution of what has been called "globalised Islam".[34] Whether the enigmatic policy of enlightened moderation enunciated by Pervez Musharraf can integrate the country can much be doubted, because the initial tussle between the secular bureaucracy, civil society and military does not show any interest in getting the ulama to the discussion. So religious leaders with their various and flexible repertoires will serve as channels of the have-nots, whose number is—one may add—constantly on the rise. The sunna as a legitimising principle in a time of socio-economic uncertainty and cultural and political flux seems to be of prime importance. Moreover, it benefits women to challenge the old patriarchal understandings of faith when looking for an opportunity to increase their knowledge about their own religion. But apparently, neither government education nor the traditional *madrasa*-system were able to fulfil those wishes. Cases in point are instruction groups in hadith even for women, such as the al-Huda International.[35]

---

[33] *The News*, January 15, 2002, p. 11.

[34] See Olivier Roy: *Globalised Islam: The Search for a New Ummah*, London: Hurst 2004.

[35] See Katharina Fleckenstein: *Kontinuität und Wandel islamischer Bildung für Frauen in Pakistan: Die Al-Huda International* (Ph.D. Islamic Studies Erfurt) (in progress).

Yet there are other, indigenised forms of religious socialicisation and cults embedded in local cultures and facilitated by mystical ideas. Among these one must count the ubiquitous Sufi shrines located all over the country, making up a complex sacred geography that is recreated again and again not only by regular feasts but also through a wealth of Islamic tradition, also in the shape of precious manuscripts of Islamic scholarship located in these shrines[36] and endowing them with eternal sanctity. These spaces of liminality provide important alternative sources of identity and societal niches for women and much needed alternative spaces for marginalised groups. They are equally important to politicians and other VIPs in their daily routine of addressing their constituencies.[37] These lived traditions very much determine the circle of everyday life without, however, necessarily adhering to the mystical superstructure[38] guaranteeing both continuity and change. This scene of shared religion is complemented by organised Sufism to be found in religious formations such as local-cum-global Naqshbandiyya-Gamkoliyya originating from the NWFP, and the reformed Sufi organisation Minhaj al-Qur'an founded by Tahir al-Qadiri, who dispose of an international network[39] that is linked to the Prophet-authenticating Sufi practices.

These endeavours are complemented by learned and ingenious contributions from old established and new formations of religious communities, however epistemologically different, heuristically distinct and societally diverse. They are politically conformist and religiously revivalist, limited to national universe or are operative globally that oscillate between Islamic and Islamicate. Next to those articulations and communications of religious experience already mentioned, Israr Ahmad's *Tanzim-e Islam* deserve reference. Scholars such as Javed Ghamidi and Muhammad Khalid Masud have influenced strongly the academic discourses on modernist Islam and have induced new

---

[36] See for example Ahmad Munzawi: *Fihrist-e mushtarak-e nuskhah-ha-ye khatti-ye farsi-ye Pakistan*, vol. III, Islamabad: Markaz-e Tahqiqat-e Farsi-ye Iran wa Pakistan 1984.

[37] See Carl W. Ernst and Bruce B. Lawrence: *Sufi Martyrs of Love: The Chishti Order in South Asia and Beyond*, Palgrave: Macmillan 2002.

[38] Compare K.P. Ewing: "*The Modern Businessman and the Pakistani Saint: The Interpenetration of Worlds*", in: Grace Martin Smith and Carl W. Ernst (eds.): *Manifestations of Sainthood in Islam*, Istanbul: The Isis Press 1993, pp. 69–84.

[39] See Pnina Werbner: "Seekers on the path"; Ron Geaves: "Learning the lessons from the neo-revivalist and Wahhabi movements", in Jamal Malik and John Hinnells (eds.): *Sufism in the West*, London: Routledge 2006, pp. 127ff., and 152ff. respectively.

arguments in the intricately designed plot of humanisation, thereby drawing from Islamic scholarly tradition.

All these variations, routinisations and institutionalisations of the religious charisma amount to internal modernisation processes of cultural articulations and can be considered to have evolved by ongoing competition from below, the Prophet being present in one way or the other. They show continuous religious vitality, and shatter the postulated hegemony of securalisation paradigms. Whether secular political parties or military oligarchy and their supporters are able to bridge the appalling gaps between different actors to integrate all these versatile contesting trends that make up for a plural, yet fragmented society—with or without the prophetic ideal—is yet to be seen.

EXCURSUS

THE SOCIAL STRUCTURE OF MUSLIMS IN INDIA

Given the fact that Partition has caused considerable socio-economic dislocations and socio-psychological problems at the individual as well as collective level—not to speak of the extreme political effects of migration—, one might have thought of a variety of forthcoming academic enquiries into the social structure of Muslims in India, be it just for the sake of academic curiosity or for nagging political purposes. Yet this topic—despite of its being a crucial point, especially after its chequered history—did not find much interest in academia or in political discussions for many years. This is even more striking in that deep-rooted reciprocities had evolved between the carriers of the diverse Muslim and Hindu cultures after more than one thousand years of social, cultural, religious and political cohabitation. As has seen shown in preceding chapters, the interaction between minorities and majorities indeed left profound traces of mutuality as far as religiously interpreted group-building processes are concerned. They can be retraced in a variety of forms of cultural articulation when religion becomes a linguistic and symbolic expression of minority-majority conflicts. By contrast, independent India is commonly perceived as a land of Hinduism alone, though overlapping semantics are obvious when it comes to central identity markers: the foundation stone of Qutub Minar, the highest brick minaret in the world, was laid by the first Sultan of Delhi, Qutb al-Din Aybak (died 1210) in 1193, and was completed during Firoz Shah Tughlaq's rule in 1368. The Taj Mahal, awe-inspiring through its timelessness and built by the fifth Mughal emperor Shahjahan (1592–1666), is probably more popular as an Indian landmark than any Hindu Mandala amongst foreigners. However, a few scholarly works on Muslims in independent India have come done to us so far, most of them by cultural and social anthropologists; a smaller number was commissioned by the government. Therefore, a detailed ethnographic study of the variety of Muslim cultural articulations in independent India is not available, so that in the following it is attempted to give a broad overview of the social and religious complexities of Muslims, their composition and distribution, an overview that will necessarily be sweeping and neglects the actual polyvocality of different actors in the dialectic of the global and the local, the universal and the particular, assimilation and resistance to it.[1] Thus some general observations will be attempted after a short quantitative survey. Briefly, religious differences and religious similarities, also with reference to family structure, are touched upon in order to provide an impression of the state of affairs of this highly contingent and contested field.

The composition of Indian Muslim Society—the quantitative aspect

The major part of the world's Muslim population today lives in the large countries of South Asia, e.g., Pakistan, India, Bangladesh. This population amounts to three times that of the Arab Middle East, and accounts for more than one third of the total Muslim world population. To be precise, in 1991 the number of Indian Muslims amounted to more than 120 million, and 140 million by the end of the millennium. This makes up about 12% of the contemporary Indian population. In contrast, the share of Indian Christians and other religious communities is negligible.

According to demographical estimates in late 1980s,[2] Muslims in India are spread nearly all over the federal territory; they range from a high concentration of approx. 75% in Jammu and Kashmir, and approx. 27% in West Bihar and Assam, up to the lowest marker of 1% in Orissa.

In regions showing a proportionately high Muslim population (more than 10% of the respective population) Muslims can be identified as predominately living in rural areas, whereas they tend to be mostly urban in regions where they proportionately make up only 10%. Since

---

[1] For some interesting studies see the contributions in the edited volumes by Imtiaz Ahmad: *Caste and Social Stratification among the Muslims*, New Delhi: Manohar 1973; *Family, Kinship and Marriage among Muslims in India*, New Delhi: Manohar 1976; *Modernization and Social Change among Muslims in India*, New Delhi: Manohar 1983; *Ritual and Religion among Muslims of the Sub-continent*, Lahore: Vanguard Books Ltd. 1985, and by T.N. Madan (ed.): *Muslim Communities of South Asia*, New Delhi: Manohar 2001(3); by M.K.A. Siddiqui (ed.): *Marginal Muslim Communities in India*, New Delhi: Institute of Objective Studies 2004; see also Aijauddin Ahmad (ed.): *Muslims in India; Vols. I–III*, New Delhi: Inter-India Publications 1993–1995; the *Rajinder Sachar Report on Muslims* (2007) came up with interesting findings about Muslim under-representation in government employment and security agencies.

[2] S. Muthiah (ed.): *An Atlas of India*, Delhi: OUP 1990, p. 10.

1947 they have been recorded with a higher fertility rate compared to Hindus and they are more urban in relation to the national average: 27% as compared to 18%. This is especially true in those areas that have witnessed economic boom and fast urbanisation such as in the Northwest (Haryana, Punjab), West (Gujarat, Maharashtra) and South (Karnataka, Andhra Pradesh). In the East (Orissa) and Northeast (Bihar, Bengal), the majority of Muslims is predominantly of rural character, traditional urban centres still providing some contingency and permeability for socio-economic chances. There seems to be also some indication that Muslims from the South tend to be urban and politically active due to their relative prosperity, while North Indians still benefit from the traditional pre-partition fiefs which are, however, noticeably dwindling.[3]

During Partition millions of Muslims, many of them of urban background, migrated from India to West-Pakistan, mainly into urban Punjab and Sind.[4] Their urban preference subsisted in the new territory, so that according to estimations about 50% of these emigrants found a new home in urban West-Pakistan. This migration of Muslims and Hindus was followed by massacres; their painful histories have been dealt with in different ways, among others in fictional literature.[5] About one third of these emigrants is said to have come from urban areas, including intellectuals, government employees, doctors and jurists as well as businessmen, a number of whom had been politically active, such as during the Khilafat movement and the following period of political manoeuvring. In Muslim as well as Hindu narratives this brain-drain inevitably changed the social fabric of urban as well as rural Muslims who were left or stayed behind, ushering in severe repercussions for

---

[3] Zafar Imam: "Some Aspects of the Social structure of the Muslim Community in India", in: Zafar Imam (ed.): *The Musalmaans of the Subcontinent*, Lahore: Vanguard 1980, pp. 71ff. also Moonis Raza et al.: "Muslims of India-Some Aspects of Regional Demography", in: Imam (ed.): *The Musalmaans*, p. 129.

[4] For the following see Zafar Imam: "Some Aspects", pp. 74ff., also Chapter 11: *Independence and Partition.*

[5] It is only recently that social scientists, anthropologists and historians have started to give voice to the popular experience of Partition and its sometimes inconceivable sufferings. See the thought-provoking article by Yasmin Khan: "Asking New Questions about Partition of the Indian Subcontinent", in: *History Compass*, Blackwell Publishing Ltd. 2004 (http://www.history-compass.com/popups/print.asp?items=7554, accessed 25.04.2005). For some disturbing images see Khushwant Singh: *Train to Pakistan*, with Partition photographs by Margaret Bourke-White, New Delhi: Roli 2006, which makes a great visual impression of affliction and distress.

them in terms of their politico-economic decline and leading to a vacuum devoid of chances to actively participate in civil society. Due to the exodus and the following restructuring of administration and landownership, Indian Muslims, so the powerful narrative, came to lack economic resources to compete with other communities.[6] This again gave vent to Muslim complaints in independent India, for without proper political leadership they would retreat into a defensive, quietist culture, grasping at straws of the secular-oriented Congress party. As a—socially constructed—religious minority, they henceforth were perceived to be a monolithic unity, irrespective of their ethnic, linguistic, economic, social and religious differences. The grand narratives discursively endowed this imagined collective Indian Muslim identity with some lasting agency and normative significance, culminating in the ulcerating perception that Indian Muslims were discriminated against (see Excursus: Communalism). On the other hand, they played some role in elections.

Against the background of the political programme of a promising Nehruvian era that stood for composite culture, secular nationalism and communal harmony,[7] the economic situation of Muslims was improved. Reforms between 1948 and 1956 sought to enhance Muslim social mobility in administration and economy by reforming educational institutions. These measures, however, basically promoted urban groups at the cost of rural population. The resulting rural exodus and increasing unemployment ratio gave vent to societal tensions, particularly in urban centres. Thus rural migration to urban areas exacerbated communalism and vice versa. Urban Muslims whose societal performance depended on Congress politics generated leaders for rural Muslim masses who had signed in for the Congress party *en bloc*. This voting behaviour further advanced the idea of a homogenous Indian Muslim community, reminiscent of the "joint electorates" which had been introduced by colonial power in 1909, when the border-line became religious identity, and when communities were to vote for their coreligionists only. This vision of "joint electorates" had cast a dark cloud over secular India for it determines the imagination of some religious politicians from

[6] As will be discussed in Chapter 15, there has been a powerful discourse on Muslim backwardness without, however, ample empirical proof. This discourse serves both sides, Muslim as well as Hindu power elites.

[7] One of the stalwart supporters of this approach was Mohammad Mujeeb (1902–1985); see his *The Indian Muslims*, Delhi 1967.

both sides, Muslims as well as Hindus. However, beyond these powerful assumptions of primordialism discursively inaugurated and endowed with communal meaning, there is much commonality and overlapping in terms of lived religion. Indeed, the idea of a unified Muslim community high-jacks the social structure and cultural articulation—not to speak of different forms of religious community building and institutionalisation. Therefore, it seems reasonable to refer to a conglomerate of different societies among Muslims.[8] How then can the social structure of Indian Muslims be summed up?

The social structure of Indian Muslims

Though there are no definite statistics on the social structure of Muslims available, some general statements about their complex formation and their stratification can be made primarily on the basis of anthropological research (see also Excursus: Caste).[9] A broad distinction can be made. First, there were the dominant political elites, i.e., traditionally the landed aristocracy (*ashraf*) who played a crucial role particularly in the Mughal and colonial periods. Peasants, artisans, military and administration were dependent on this aristocracy to some degree,[10] an aristocracy who had received estates for their military and administrative services and for tax collection. A number of them had been able to convert these transferable revenue assignments in lieu of salary for service into private ownership during the end of eighteenth century. Many of them depended on functional intermediaries which contributed to the evolution of absentee landlordism. With the colonial implementation of *Permanent Settlement 1793* these (absentee) landholders acquired these fiefs as personal property, while middlemen wielded considerable power. Post-independence land reforms (*Zamindari Abolition and Land*

[8] Raghuraj Gupta: "Changing Role", p. 184.

[9] For the following see Imtiaz Ahmed: "Economic and Social Change", in: Zafar Imam (ed.): *The Musalmaans*, pp. 234–253; Ahmad: *Caste and Social Stratification among the Muslims*.

[10] This system has been called prebendal patrimonialism, which, on the basis of new research, can be interrogated, particularly in the face of the autonomy and autocephaly enjoined in *qasbahs*. See however, Stephen P. Blake: "The Patrimonial–Bureaucratic Empire of the Mughals", in: *JAS* 39/1 (1979), pp. 77–94; Peter Hardy: "Islamischer Patrimonialimus: Die Moghulherrschaft", in: Wolfgang Schluchter (ed.): *Max Webers Sicht des Islam*, Frankfurt a.M. 1987, pp. 190–216.

Reforms Act, 1950 and Rules, 1952) sought to abolish this absentee landlordism, ushering in repercussions in the social and economic fabric of the—Muslim—landed gentry and those sectors affiliated to it.

Secondly, the majority of Muslims in contemporary India belong to the peasantry; they can be divided into several categories. When during the 1960s the Green Revolution promoted powerful peasants, the neglected and poor groups of agricultural labourers and landless peasants were forced to look for job opportunities in different professions such as craft and industry. For that purpose they rushed into towns and cities.

Thirdly, there were the artisans, who were closely connected to the landed gentry; their trade was usually limited to local markets. The traditional patronage system (*jajmani*) linked them through hereditary bonds to a household of patrons, to whom they provided services according to traditional occupational specialisations. In turn, they were provided food and shelter. Reforms abolished this sort of moral economy in the 1950s. The following rural migration constricted the market for traditional artisans, while at the same time the establishment of new urban markets encouraged the demand for new craftsmanship. These reforms had a severe impact on employees and servant classes in rural areas, while the urban service sector could benefit from the expansion of urban markets. Many artisans managed to establish themselves as traders and entrepreneurs, and with economic improvement they diversified the Muslim social fabric.

The educated middle classes—many of whom migrated to Pakistan—traditionally had considered education as an investment. But as the job market for Muslims at higher ranks of administration and military seems to be quite limited in secular India, most of these classes would start to renounce education. Instead they increasingly tried to establish themselves in the job market, as a result of which they forfeited much cultural capital. Therefore many of them are to be found in trading sectors and lack higher education.[11]

Another group comprises the traditional trading community, which has held a quite strong position in terms of both economic and cultural capital since the Mughal period and has been able to consolidate itself, though members of other religious groups flock to this sector too. This

[11] For recent data on the distribution of Muslims in public service see Raghuraj Gupta: "Changing Role", p. 191, Table IV.

social and economic heterogeneity among Muslim cultures is maintained even when it comes to their religious affiliations, the different contesting Muslim organisations being evidence of a living plurality.

Religious differences among Muslim cultures

It is a truism that various Muslim cultural articulations reflect different social backgrounds. But given the fact that different players are informed and determined by the same attitudes and interests in the discourse of agency and normativity including the daily struggle to maintain a livelihood, the contest becomes dramatic. Different branches of Deobandis, Ahl-e Hadith and Barelwis, as well as various Shiʿite groups, not to speak of adherents of various Sufi congregations, are cases in point. This is especially true in the case of the social construction of these elements of the population when they all share a common frame of reference. Islamicity in this context is merely the symbolic expression of this negotiation. Since the normative level of their discourses is constantly changing, one has to focus on their versatile lived traditions rather than on their written testimonies alone. Again, for analytical purposes two broad areas can be distinguished, without denying the actual societal complexity of lived religion.

Broadly speaking, the rural population is functionally organised into traditional networks of lineages and forms of institutional patterns like tribes, families and patronage. Generally they tend to adhere to esoteric Islam which is permeated by custom-centred and shared traditions. The predominance of this seemingly integrative and inclusive lived religion in rural areas is the result of a personal union between local landlord and religious and spiritual master who holds power over his constituency.[12] Therefore, one may speak of an indigenisation of Islam: the Muslim community is interwoven with non-Islamic elements, though, within an Islamic symbolism.[13]

In contrast, the urban population at large tends toward what has been called religious scripturalism, as is propagated for example by religious politicians, even though shared religious patterns among poorer as well

[12] See Imtiaz Ahmad and Helmut Reifeld (eds.): *Lived Islam in South Asia. Adaptation, Accommodation and Conflict*, New Delhi 2004.

[13] Also see Gopal Krishna: "Piety and Politics in Indian Islam", in: Madan (ed.): *Muslim communities*, pp. 148 and 160.

as well-to-do urban sections can be observed to quite some extent in urban sectors as well. Scripturalists do find their social base primarily among middle and lower strata, and generally speaking, they represent a de-culturalised, de-territorialised Islamic purism or Islamisation (versus Islamicatisation and indigenisation).[14] This essentialised discourse of difference, mingled with and supported by the feeling of being an oppressed minority, necessarily leads to exclusion and isolation from what they consider a dissenting and errant religious and cultural Hindu environment. This discourse advances religiously motivated conflicts. Besides these general differences between urban and rural sectors, there is a variety of disputes between different Muslim groups as there are different Sunnite schools of thought or between the Sunnites, the Shi'ites and so on. These groups run different organisations that help create and perpetuate societal cohesion, identity and solidarity in an environment that is perceived as crisis-ridden in the background of a failing welfare state which still is in its infancy or even completely absent.

The interaction of Islamic cosmology with the indigenous also has considerable impact on the social structure and organisation, if kinship, modes of exchange among Muslims, "brotherhoods", tribes, lineages and caste system or "caste analogy" are considered. Indeed, in a Muslim context caste-linked principles of social organisation are legitimised by Arabo-Islamic principles of kinship and descent; they serve as a determining factor for social relations among Muslims in South Asia (see Excursus: Caste).

Religious similarities

In India there is an extremely rich variety of religious traditions. Most of them evolved and/or existed in the same territory, shared the same social habits and cultural mores. Yet it was this proximity rather than distance which persuaded religious communities to draw up boundaries. However, the blurring of these boundaries was and still is a constant process that marked interaction and encounter all along. Therefore semantic and normative affinities between religious traditions can be

[14] See Gopal Krishna: "Piety and Politics"; see also S.C. Misra: "Indigenisation and Islamisation in Muslim Society in India", in: S.T. Lokhandwalla (ed.): *India and Contemporary Islam*, Simla 1971, p. 369.

found to a remarkable extent. One example is accretion, that is, when the original cosmology structurally remains unchanged, and new ideas are merely added on or identified with existing entities of the religious pantheon. Again, one may generally look at rural and urban cultures. In urban society a bias in Islamisation prevails due to tendencies of delimitation between minority and majority, often instigated and exploited by religious politicians. Islamic orthopraxy indeed can provide for the much-needed identity, solidarity and social coherence, particularly for migrated peasants and newcomers in the new urban environment. In contrast, in a rural context shared religious traditions are most popular, local and Islamic are intermingled or exist side by side. This results in a complementarity or reciprocity as well as ritual and religious pluralism. In this context, the life-structuring religious rites exhibit special significance, because they provide for some change in the monotonous rural life, and they create and strengthen solidarity among the local population through collective rituals. The very loci of these most popular traditions are Sufi shrines with their veneration cult that contrasts notions of scripturalist Islam. Shrine cults can be discerned among both Hindus and Muslims alike, to the extent that Hindu Sufis or Hindu offshoots of Sufi orders and vice-versa can be found to quite some extent. Hindu musicians would perform in Muslim holy shrines, the number of Hindu visitors exceeds that of Muslims.[15]

However, shrines attract both Muslim and Hindu worshippers for different reasons: Hindus construct the saint as a deity; for Muslims s/he is an extraordinary person endowed with *baraka*. Thus, Muslims can displace local superhuman agencies and situate Islam within the local context; they Islamise the indigenous. According to Sudhir Kakar this can result in Muslims being regarded as impure representing the alien and the demonic, apprehended as a reification of the unconsciously despicable.[16] In contrast, the symbolic repertoires of regional saint cults reinforce beliefs in the universalism of Islam and Hinduism. Thus heterodoxy and orthodoxy do not necessarily contradict but overlap at the level of life-worlds. Therefore, Islam in India is both formal and trans-local, because of its orientation towards normative Islamic

[15] See for example Thomas Dahnhardt: *Change and continuity in Indian Sufism: a Naqshbandi-Mujaddidi branch in Indian environment, New Delhi 2002*; Dominique-Sila Khan: *Conversions and Shifting Identities. Ramdev Pir and the Ismailis in Rajasthan*, Manohar: Centre de Science Humaines 1997.

[16] See Kakar, Sudhir: *The Colours of Violence*, New Delhi: Viking 1995.

texts and centres in the Arab and Persian lands, as well as ritual and local, because of its tendency to adjust to the life-structuring cultural environment or to reciprocate to local cosmologies.[17] The net result is Islamicatisation: the social and cultural complex, which evolved historically in the encounters among actors of different religious traditions.

Family system

Similar processes of mutuality can be indicated when it comes to the family–system. Again, a number of similarities between actors of Muslim and Hindu communities can be indicated:[18] Muslims live, as do Hindus, mostly in joint family systems. In the absence of a state welfare system, a joint family system is considered to be by and large the ideal and most meaningful way of life.[19] The son would live at his paternal house. Joint family system, patrilinearity and patrilocality are even more popular among and practiced more rigidly by Muslims than by Hindus, most probably to secure the economic and cultural capital. Also, patterns of social interaction between different family members and internal familial power structure are similar between Muslims and Hindus: matrimonial and mother-son relations are endowed with crucial meaning; the family system is highly sophisticated and functionally laid out with each one family member having a specific social role and function in relation to others: the maternal uncle traditionally has different functions as compared to the father-brother, the mother-mother has particular assignments in comparison to the father-mother. Thus, all family members reserve their specific titles.

Extra-familial groups and organisations are responsible for arrangements related to marriage, ownership and estate as well as issues pertaining to inheritance. Arrangements and practices of marriage and inheritance are carried out on the pattern of local customs; mostly these traditional rites are quite expensive and cause heavy loss and debt for the family, especially when it comes to a dowry. Thus, providing

---

[17] Compare Imtiaz Ahmad: *Ritual and Religion*, pp. 4–15; Imtiaz Ahmad (ed.): *Lived Islam*.

[18] The following is based on Imtiaz Ahmad (ed.): *Family, Kinship and Marriage among Muslims in India*, New Delhi: Manohar 1976, pp. XXII–XXXII.

[19] See for example Akos Östör/Lina Fruzzetti/Steve Barnett (eds.): *Concepts of Person: Kinship, Caste, and Marriage in India*, Delhi: OUP 1992; Patricia Uberoi (ed.): *Family—Kinship and Marriage in India*, Delhi 1998.

information about the unborn child's gender is prohibited by law, while the death rate of new-born girls among Hindus is as high as among Indian Muslims. Polygamy and the rather easy possibility for male family members to get divorced point to the discrimination of women also existent in Hindu traditions.

For sure, industrialisation has increasingly blurred the internal structure of authority and interaction among Hindus as well as Muslims who have developed strategies of inclusion and exclusion, exhibiting many cultural complexities. And since the lower ranks of the social hierarchy are now beginning to witness increasing economic mobility due to rapid industrialisation, manpower-export to Arab countries and the quota-system, the number of caste and communalist conflicts has grown larger. However, one may conclude that there are striking similarities between different religious communities in every aspect of structuring of their lives. Islam in India thus has a twofold meaning: it has allowed different Muslim communities in India to legitimate their local customs or to integrate them with the *shari'a* which is flexible and adjustable. At the same time Muslims are able to construct an authentic Islamic picture for themselves and to maintain it by means of the Islamic repertory. Yet, Muslims are an integral part of the cultural complex in which they interact with non-Muslims. Indeed, the negotiations of minority and majority depend on their reciprocity; they share the same frame of reference, and constitute a cultural ensemble.

As can be seen, Islam in independent India is a reflection of a variety of religious norms, societal interests and in particular contextually embedded cultural actors. Thus there is nothing like a homogenous monolithic Indian Muslim community; religious identities can transcend religious and religiously legitimated boundaries, because the actors can activate different identities in different contexts. In fact, identity matters in context, when linguistic affinities and secular and profane interests such as economic transactions cut across religious particularisms in the quest to create secular relationships of mutual support. Needless to say, the dialectic of religion and politics plays a determining role in people's trajectories.[20]

---

[20] See T.N. Madan (ed.): *Muslim Communities of South Asia*, New Delhi: Manohar 2001(3).

CHAPTER FIFTEEN

INDIAN MUSLIMS OR MUSLIM INDIANS? (APPROX. 1947–2002)

In independent India, the situation of the majority of the Muslims (about 14% of the population)[1] and their religious and political leaders ushered in a state ostensibly desolate as in Pakistan; political independence in 1947 neither solved economic problems nor eradicated communalism. Due to a lack of economic resources following the exodus in 1947 of many businessmen, traders and intellectuals to Pakistan, majority of Muslims staying in India increasingly suffered introversion. The restructuring of the Indian administrative body, the supposed lack of political guidance, and increased industrialisation eventually forced the impoverished self-dependent Muslim artisans, weavers and lower middle class Indian Muslims to engage in occupations that did not pose a challenge to the Hindu majority.[2]

However, one should look at how Indian Muslims have been successfully able to build a discourse of economic and educational backwardness of the community in post-Partition India, while at the same time they considering themselves superior to other communities in the country as they often trace back their history with extreme eulogy and nostalgia. Though they have clung to this debate of 'backwardness', there is an absence of any solid empirical findings on all India scale. Most studies reveal the backwardness of the community, including government reports, but they have their weakness in the motives and the way in which survey or research was carried out. This attracts the attention to severe methodological problems that support this argument. Interestingly, one hardly comes across a study (even by right wing parties) that punctures this discourse at any level. So the discourse of backwardness has not been challenged so far, perhaps, because there

[1] The Muslims in independent India are predominantly urban as compared to the national average: 27% as compared to 18%.

[2] For some data on the Muslims in the public sector see Raghuraj Gupta: "Changing Role and Status of the Muslim Minority in India: A Point of View", in: *Journal; Institute of Muslim Minority Affairs* 5/1 (1984), p. 191, Table IV.

is no need to unearth this reality as it has become a commonplace by now, and it also serves the purposes of the power elites in the country—both Hindu and Muslim. It is on this basis that the demand for reservation can be a legitimate one.[3]

To start with, the religious representatives of the Muslim elites who remained in India sought to imagine a corporate Muslim identity—as did those in Pakistan—irrespective of the fact that Muslim communities themselves are highly differentiated in terms of education, social, cultural and economic capital (see Excursus: Caste). The representatives of this mostly urban religious elite, who also hailed from *qasbahs*, holding on to the fabulous narratives of a glorious past, usually supported some kind of an Arabised or Persianised version of Islam, and proclaimed their own normative definitions as the only valuable ones. So they considered "their" community as a religious minority—in contrast to a national minority. The elite put forward mainly religious demands; economic and political considerations hardly figured in their agenda.[4] The isolation of the Muslims from the Hindu majority, which both sides fostered, in an ontological twist, translated into a master narrative of the under-representation of Muslims in the public sector, military, trade and the economy. Thus, the communities increasingly became concerned with issues like the maintenance of "their" language, "their" space and "their" personal law.

Individuals, groups, institutions

It is argued that the major problem for Indian Muslims was the lack of intellectual leadership, and of a powerful organic integration figure. Abu al-Kalam Azad was made Education Minister of India but was absorbed and neutralised by the administrative pressure. The late head of Nadwat al-ʿUlama, Sayyid Abu al-Hasan ʿAli Nadwi (died 1999), could have

[3] For the latest refer to the *Rajinder Sachar Report on Muslims* (2007) that finds among others a dramatic Muslim under-representation in government employment and security agencies but a significant over-representation in prison.

[4] S.J.R. Bilgrami: "Nationalism and Indian Muslims: Problems and Perspectives", in: Zafar Imam (ed.): *The Musalmaans of the Subcontinent*, Lahore: Vanguard 1980, pp. 155ff., Raghuraj Gupta: "Changing Role", p. 192, and Moin Shakir: "The Muslim Political Elite", in: Imam (ed.): *The Musalmaans*, p. 171.

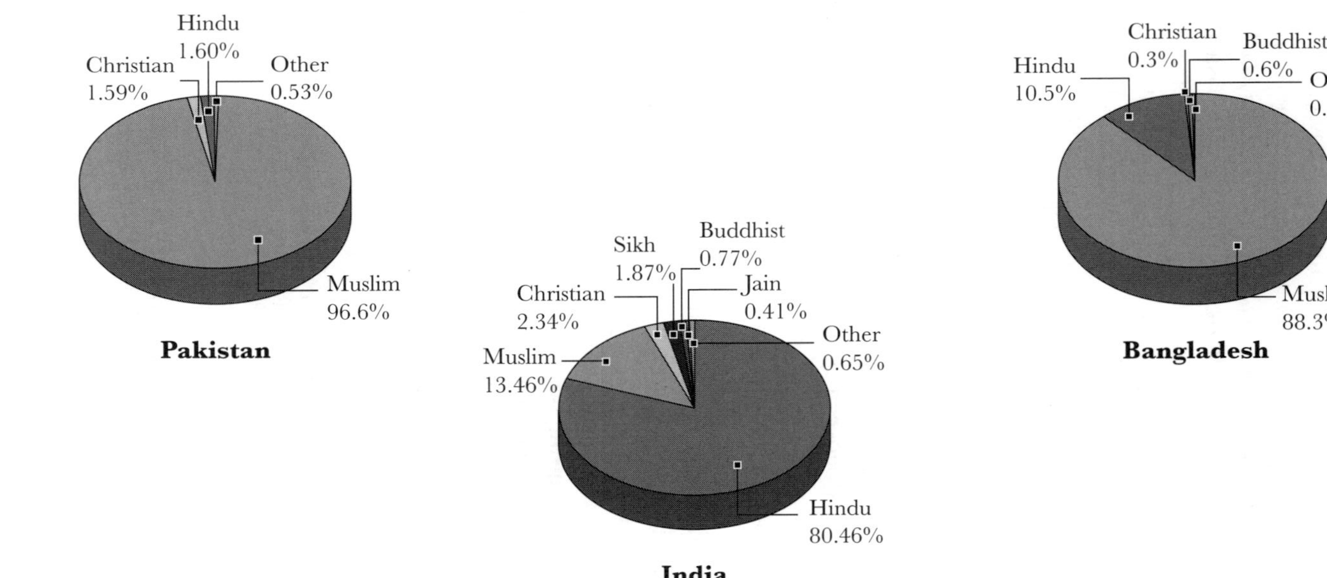

Abridged form of pie charts published in the story "After partition: India, Pakistan, Bangladesh" in BBC <http://news.bbc.co.uk/go/pr/fr/-/2/hi/in_depth/629/629/6922293.stm> on 2007/08/08

claimed a charismatic position for himself.[5] He became popular among sections of the Indian Muslims with his biography of Sayyid Ahmad Shahid, published in Urdu in 1939. His entrée to the Arab World was his famous *What Has the World Lost with the Decline of the Muslims?* written between 1944 and 1947; the book was originally published in Arabic and subsequently translated into several languages. Before a backdrop of emerging pan-Arabism and the Arab socialism of Nasser, Nadwi pleaded for a revival of an Islamic consciousness with the Arabs and urged them to reintroduce all-encompassing Islamic principles. At the same time he called to refrain from the evils of nationalism because this would divide Muslims. He and his Nadwat al-ʿUlama as well as the Ahl-e Hadith—also in Pakistan—might have been supported by Saudi Arabia financially, notably through the network of International Islamic Universities with its centre in Medina established in 1961, and the Muslim World League in Mecca.[6] It seems likely that in this context the affiliations between Arabia and India became a major topic in his and Nadwa's imagination. However, Nadwi, who entertained relations to both, mystical institutions and Tablighi Jamaʿat, but also to a number of Muslim organisations in Arab countries, publicly criticised the Islamist ideas of Maududi: social change in accordance with Islamic ideals, he said, would have to be preceded by an alteration at the individual level—Islam was an internalised message of God to men rather than an externalised political one.[7] Yet, while Nadwi was generally open to harmonising postulates and recognised the importance of national integration, his endeavours remained branded by the consistent and traditionally overloaded idea of Islamic superiority: Muslims, he claimed, had awakened every country and also India from a deep slumber and had led it to the heights of civilisation:

[5] On Sayyid Abu al-Hasan ʿAli Nadwi see Jan-Peter Hartung: *Viele Wege und ein Ziel. Leben und Wirken von Sayyid Abû l-Hasan ʿAlî al-Hasanî Nadwî (1914–1999)*, Würzburg: Ergon 2004; Zaman: *The Ulama in Contemporary Islam*, pp. 161–177. There are others, who consider Sayyid Shahabuddin to be the integrating force. Cf. Thomas Blom Hansen: *The Saffron Wave. Democracy and Hindu Nationalism in Modern India*, New Delhi: OUP 1999.

[6] For a comprehensive study of the League see Reinhard Schulze: *Islamischer Internationalismus im 20. Jahrhundert*, Leiden: Brill 1990. For Saudi patronage see Zaman: *The Ulama in Contemporary Islam*, pp. 175f.

[7] The critique was published only in 1979 but actually was the culmination of a process that had been under way since 1943, when Nadwi parted with Maududi. See Jamal Malik: "Between National Integration and Islamism: Lucknow's Nadwat al-Ulama", in: Mushirul Hasan (ed.): *Knowledge, Power & Politics. Educational Institutions in India*, New Delhi: Roli Books 1998, pp. 221–238.

> Taking a leap from the obscurity of dark ages, each one of these countries took its rightful place in the comity of nations and made valuable contributions towards human knowledge and culture...(and) the lands they (i.e. Muslims) conquered were actually reborn, with a renewed zest and vigour, in a new and brighter world.[8]

Moreover, Nadwi regarded Zia al-Haqq's policy of Islamisation in Pakistan, which had been supported vigorously by the Jamaʿat-e Islami, to be a promising 'Islamic revolution'. So Nadwi's concept of communal harmony is determined by distinction and essentialised—albeit disguised—notions of Islamic identities, reminiscent of Husain Ahmad Madani's Islamist trap (see below).

In contrast to these semi-inclusivist stands, there were/are also more inclusivist ones in contemporary India, such as those of Syed Zainul Abedin (1928–1993) and Wahiduddin Khan (born 1925) as portrayed by Christian W. Troll.[9] While Abedin, the founder of the "Journal of the Institute of Muslim Minority Affairs", argued, that "a qurʾanically-informed *umma* consciousness is demanded of the believers, together with the full recognition of the existing nation state" identifying this idea with the words of Sura 103:3 "to exhort one another to truth and to exhort one another to endurance", Wahiduddin, on the other hand, advocates absolute *ijtihad*—the creative application of Islamic law to meet the challenge of changing social conditions beyond the boundaries of one's own school of law—in contrast to a limited *ijtihad*, a primary demand for openness to opportunities that offer themselves to Islam in the modern world.[10] Consequently, he argues against a coercive *shariʿa* and for a separation of religion and politics. Both men are developing ideas and strategies as to how Muslims could thrive as a minority within a democracy ruled by a non-Muslim

---

[8] Abu al-Hasan ʿAli Nadwi in S. Abdul Hai: *India during Muslim Rule*, pp. 2f.

[9] See the brief remarks in Christian W. Troll: "Plurality of Religion and Plurality in Religion", in: Malik and Reifeld (eds.): *Religious Pluralism*, here pp. 89–96.

[10] Absolute *ijtihad* is the prime demand of practical necessity. The need of abrogation and the re-interpretation of the Quranic text, Wahiduddin argues, is determined by changing social context, and as such is a kind of adjustment between ideal and practical conditions, in the backdrop of issues related to pluralism, inter-faith dialogue and peace. Presupposition is, however, the reintroduction of tolerance of criticism. See Yoginder Sikand: "Peace, Dialogue and Daʿwa: An Analysis of the Writings of Maulana Wahiduddin Khan", in: *Islam and Christian-Muslim Relations* 14/1 (2003), pp. 33–49; on his view on the ulama see Zaman: *The Ulama in Contemporary Islam*, pp. 181–185, 189.

majority in a state governed under a modern constitution. So both scholars do advocate peaceful proselytism but at the same time create and recreate the notion of Muslims being a—minority and yet united—religious entity.

As far as groups and institutions are concerned, mystical orders had been over centuries the transmitters of Muslim culture and have represented the indigenous social and educational structures and historical patterns of social organisations. After World War II and in the light of the foundation of new nation-states, these forms of socialisation were marginalised by the ideological and political centre. One of the key mechanisms, among others, was the appropriation of their economic base through the nationalisation of religious endowments. This decline was mainly initiated by state agents, representatives of political Islam as well as Islamic reformism.[11] Yet, this marginalisation does not affect the general popularity of saint cults or devotionalism, as is evident from the visits to shrines.[12] Tablighi Jama'at function at a trans-national level actually tries to counteract these phenomena by calling for a restructuring of Islamic mores.

Other historically developed patterns of social organisation, such as *madrasas* did increase in number after independence, probably to provide the Muslims with a broad institutional framework on the micro-level.[13] Several attempts have been made to reorganise the numerous

[11] A comprehensive overview on these developments is provided by E. Sirriyeh: *Sufis and Anti-Sufis. The Defence, Rethinking and Rejection of Sufism in the Modern World*, Richmond 1999, esp. Chap. 6. In the context of literary works see Jamal Malik: "The Literary Critique of Islamic Popular Religion in the Guise of Traditional Mysticism, or the Abused Woman", in: Helene Basu & Pnina Werbner (eds.): *Embodying Charisma: Modernity, Locality and the Performance of Emotion in Sufi Cults*, London: Routledge 1998, pp. 187–208.

[12] There is a vast literature on shrines. See Troll (ed.): *Muslim Shrines in India*; C.W. Ernst & G.M. Smith (eds.): *Manifestations of Sainthood in Islam*, Istanbul 1993; Curie: *The Shrine and Cult of Mu'īn al-Dīn Chishtī*; Imtiaz Ahmad (ed.): *Ritual and Religion among Muslims of the Subcontinent*, Lahore: Vanguard 1985; also Helene Basu: *Habshi Sklaven, Sidi-Fakire: Muslimische Heiligenverehrung im westlichen Indien*, Berlin 1994; contributions to Dale F. Eickelman/James Piscatori (eds.): *Muslim Travellers: Pilgrimage, Migration, and the Religious Imagination*, London 1990.

[13] See Kuldip Kaur: *Madrasa Education in India; a study of its past and present*, Chandigarh: Centre for Rural and Industrial Development 1990, p. 225; for *madrasa* education in India in general see S. Maqbul Ahmad: "*Madrasa* System of Education and Indian Muslim Society", in: S.T. Lokhandwalla (ed.): *India and Contemporary Islam*, Simla 1971, pp. 25–36; Mohammad Akhlaq Ahmad: *Traditional Education among Muslims; A Study of some Aspects in Modern India*, Delhi: B.R. Publishing Corporation 1985.

religious schools, not only, because "the scope for the intellectual development of Muslim community through these institutions is tremendous", but also because "75 per cent of the Muslims, especially in Uttar Pradesh, Bihar and Bengal are literate because of these *maktabs* and *madrasas*."[14] The estimation that there are "more than 20,000 maktabs and madrasas in India", housing several thousand students,[15] seems, however, too low.

The Madrasa Education Board Calcutta established shortly before independence, the Central Wakf Council founded in 1965, and the Deeni Talimi Councils in U.P., in West Bengal, Assam and Bihar in 1978 and 1981 tried to integrate formal education (mathematics, geography, history, etc.) and set up a network of religious schools, providing some financial aid. Their degrees are recognised not only by several Indian universities, but also by al-Azhar in Cairo, and Medina University of Saudi Arabia. The potential of *madrasa* education for Muslim reform, development and mobilisation is recognised even by Muslim intellectuals who postulate that "a special effort...must be made to get the information to these institutions."[16] However, "a special effort" might imply state intervention, which again is not fully compatible with the constitutional autonomy granted to private religious, cultural and educational institutions in India. But since *madrasas* claim that they increase literacy, they adhere to the objectives of the Constitution which envisage common development for all citizens. Insofar their argument is not religious but very modern and in line with the literacy demands of the state.

Thus the pressure on the government to support Muslim educational institutions has increased. This has led to programmatic attempts to modernise the *madrasa* system, notably under the eighth Five-Year Plan, 1992–1997. The objective of the scheme of "Modernisation of Madrasa Education", launched in 1993–94 and administered by the Ministry of Human Resource Development, was to encourage these institutions by giving them financial assistance to introduce science, mathematics, social studies, Hindi and English to their syllabi. Registered volunteer

---

[14] Kaur: *Madrasa Education*, p. 254.

[15] See Kaur: *Madrasa Education*, p. 210; see also Anjuman-e Nida-ye Islam (ed.): *Fihrist Madaris-e ʿarabiyya diniyya*, Kalkutta: Anjuman-e Nida-ye Islam 1404/1983.

[16] Cited in *Muslim India* 127 (July 1993), p. 323.

organisations existent for at least three years were considered for assistance. For the ninth Five-Year Plan (1997–2002) a meagre grant of 916,5 million Indian Rupees was allocated but the amount actually released did not exceed 160 million Indian Rupees earning the comment that "to make the Scheme viable an allocation of at least Rs. 500 crore should be made for the Scheme in the Tenth Five Year Plan."[17] So far, the plan has been refused by major *madrasas* because they argue that the scheme has primarily been linked to the issue of "national security" rather than educational reform. But perhaps the more important reason for the lackadaisical response of the *madrasas* is to do with their notion of knowledge (*ʿilm*) and their guarding of what has been called the "private sphere". In their understanding, *ʿilm* pertains only to religious education which—according to this argument—was dichotomised from the public by the colonial intrusion. Thus by pointing out that their activities relate to the religious sphere only, they might justify their exclusion of modern subjects by arguing that there are many schools for that—secular—purpose, a tendency also clearly discernable in Pakistan.[18] In this scenario the introduction of modern subjects might defeat the very purpose for which they exist.[19] Changes in the social base of *madrasa* education may however force these institutions to reform: increasingly *madrasas* build "modern" institutions on their premises. It seems that the developments and changes in Indian religious schools therefore will remain more or less private initiatives.

An interesting but little known development took place in Kerala where the Islahi (reformist) movement founded the Kerala Jamiyyattul Ulama in 1924. This "Association" soon split into progressives (Kerala Nadvathul Mujahideen) and conservatives who founded the All Kerala Ulama Organisation (Samastha Kerala Jamiyyattul Ulama). This society at present runs nearly 8,500 *madrasas* in various places in Kerala with more than one million students, co-ordinated and supervised by the Samastha Kerala Muslim Education Board (started in 1951). The

[17] See Hamdard Education Society: *Evaluation Report on Modernization of Madrasa Education (UP)*, New Delhi 2003; an interesting overview is provided by Amir Ullah Khan, Mohammad Saqib and Zafar H. Anjum, *To Kill the Mockingbird. Madarsah* (sic!) *System in India: Past, Present, and Future*, http://www.indiachinacentre.org/bazaarchintan/pdfs/madarsas.pdf (consulted 20 Feb. 2004).

[18] See K.K. Aziz: *The Murder of History*, Lahore: Vanguard 1993.

[19] Cf. Arshad Alam: "Understanding Madrasas", in: *Economic and Political Weekly*, May 31, 2003.

Arabic language plays a major role.[20] The Jamaʿat-e Islami (Kerala branch) joined the fray at a later stage in 1944, by attempting to integrate both religious and secular education. These organisations started Arabic Colleges also, particularly after Independence as an alternative to the traditional system while those affiliated to the Samastha Kerala Jamiyyattul Ulama follow the Deoband model with some modification in their syllabus. The Arabic colleges run by the Mujahideen and the regional Jamaʿat-e Islami follow a comparatively modern method. Students join these colleges only after completing high school to learn modern methods of Arabic learning: an emphasis is on the study of Malayalam including instruction in social studies.[21]

But all these formations of religious communities and social organisations did not provide for common political leadership. In fact in secular India, Muslims tended to be more or less a-political when it came to not using Islamic rhetoric for obvious political reasons. Similarly, the followers of Maududi, the Jamaʿat-e Islami, were forced to compromise. While Maududi had led about one third of his followers to Pakistan, the remaining 200 members founded the "Islamic Community of India" (Jamaʿat-e Islami Hind). Although this hierarchically structured community would also prefer a sovereignty of God in India, they nevertheless adopted the quietist way: well-being and success are accounted for in the hereafter, a change in the present situation is seemingly secondary.[22]

Initially, the vacuum left in the wake of the prohibition of the Muslim League in India was filled by the Jamʿiyyat al-ʿUlama-ye Hind (JUH), the apex religious body comprising primarily the followers of Deoband school. Being the only nation-wide body to represent Muslim interests in the first place, the JUH worked at first towards social and religious reforms, but was not able to integrate the broad Muslim pantheon, mostly due to its Deobandi and the Ahl-e Hadith dominance that collided with Shiʿites, Barelwis and other denominations. Usually it is stated that the isolation of Muslims from sensitive administrative and military positions as a consequence of the Indian-Pakistani wars over Kashmir

[20] http://www.samastha.net/madrasas.html (visited 4 June 2007).

[21] See Shareena Banu: *Education and Religious Identity among Muslims of Kerala: A Study of Selected Schools in Malappuram District*, Ph.D. Jawaharlal Nehru University, New Delhi (in preparation).

[22] See Irfan Ahmad: "Power, Purity and the Vanguard: Educational Ideology of Jamaʿat-i Islami of India", in: Malik (ed.): *Madrasas in South Asia.*

in 1947–48, 1965 and 1971, as well as the land-reforms of late 1950s aggravated the economic problems of the Muslims—though the land reforms targeted the landlords but gave a semblance of assertion to the lower strata of all religious communities be they Hindus or Muslims. Against the background of this narrative context the Jamaʿat-e Islami Hind and the JUH, actively working for Muslim betterment, began to enjoy enhanced acceptance. Today, both groups are represented in India on a wider national level, as opposed to regional organisations. Particularly on the level of small industry and commerce and of higher educational institutions the Jamaʿat-e Islami Hind enjoys—just as it does in Pakistan and Bangladesh—quite a degree of popularity. Similar to the JUH, it engages in mission, social services, publication, preaching in mosques, etc. Lately, the JUH has sought public recognition for its activities in India, their office in New Delhi has consequently become the nerve centre through which they disseminate their ideas through various publications, holding meetings on topical issues facing the community and the country, issuing audio tapes of prominent ulama associated with the organisation, etc.[23] The JUH also commissioned a propaganda film made on their organisation by the well known Indian film maker Mahesh Bhatt. Such activities make the JUH much more visible to the public and, in a sense, can be read as a desire on the part of the organisation to be 'seen' within the public space. Among its many activities, for example, the JUH pamphlets and booklets mention the work the party did after the Godhra train incident in Gujarat in early 2002, which was followed by massive communal riots leaving many hundred Muslims dead. For an association which considers itself *the* religious organisation of Muslims in the country, a response to a disaster like the one in Gujarat would be expected. The very fact that the JUH advertises its effort probably indicates that it seeks more public recognition than it actually gets, though the JUH has the moral capital to find such recognition. Its role during the freedom movement of the country has been consistent, always siding with the nationalist Congress Party at that time. It is perhaps with such an intention to rejuvenate its moral capital that the JUH has recently published 'Composite Nationalism and Islam', a book printed by a renowned publishing

[23] Among their most recent activities, mention must be made of organising a meeting in the India Habitat Center in New Delhi, a venue which seemed of late to seek to replace the India International Center as the 'sacred space' of Indian intellectuals.

house with an extensive introduction by Barbara Metcalf. The book is a translated version of *Muttahida Qaumiyyat aur Islam* written by Husain Ahmad Madani in 1938 (see Chap. 11 and 12). The original tract was a response to many of those Muslims (like Muhammad Iqbal) who were critical of the JUH aligning with the seemingly Hindu Congress Party. The text seeks an alliance with the 'Hindus' and wants to justify it along Islamic lines. However, a closer reading of the text belies such 'composite' hopes, since Ahmad Madani seems to fall into the Islamist trap, as his composite nationalism does not really transcend boundaries of religious differences. Outwardly—towards the non-Muslim other—he seemed to accept their religious traditions for the sake of a concerted struggle against colonial rule. The text itself questions the validity of composite nationalism as it "is needed only till such time as different *aqwam* (nations, J.M.) and different religions exist in a country. When the entire nation becomes Muslim (*jo keh awwalin asli maqsad hai: "which is the prime real aim"*), where is the need for it? I have termed it 'temporal and special' for this reason."[24] So Ahmad Madani not only disqualifies other religions on the ground of their being false ("While being aware of the truth of their (other religions; J.M.) falsehood, it (Islam; J.M.) is ready to mingle with them; co-exist with them and even establish reciprocal ties with them."[25] He also holds the view that ultimately Hindustan be Islamised: "*jab tak tammam Hindustan ke bashinde musalman nah ho jain*", which is tactfully omitted in the English version.[26]

Madani's argument seems to be informed by the idea of an imagined Arabised pan-Islamic community combined with an innate Muslim superiority-complex which is very much grounded in Islamic thought itself, a complex that has far-reaching consequences, particularly for Muslim minorities world-wide. Inwardly—towards the Muslim other—we find a similar bias when it comes to Ahmadis, Shi'ites and Barelwis, not to speak of women who are not accepted as equal partners and, therefore, fail to qualify for the re-invented covenant of Medina. Thus,

---

[24] Maulana Hussain Ahmad Madani: *Composite Nationalism and Islam*, transl. from Urdu into English by Mohammad Anwer Hussain and Hasan Imam, Delhi 2005, p. 150; *Mutahidda Qaumiyat aur Islam* (Urdu original, republished by JUH), p. 55. Also, pp. 139f. of the translation: "This problem will continue to bedevil India till the light of the true religion dispels its darkness."

[25] Madani: *Composite Nationalism and Islam*, p. 117.

[26] Quoted from *Mutahidda Qaumiyat aur Islam* (Urdu original, republished by JUH), p. 55; see however, p. 151 of translation.

Madani's concept of composite nationalism is built around a narrow Muslim-Sunnite identity.

Turning to politics, the self-inflicted failure of the political leadership combined with rising communal problems in Bihar and Orissa in 1964 and the weak socio-economic position as well as the increasing political tensions between Pakistan and India led many Muslims to look for some kind of parliamentary representation: representative democracy was the most important instrument of empowerment for them and was an inherent expression of their socio-material condition of daily existence.

The political system was marked by a highly complex, sometimes romanticised and colourful social mosaic of the ideology of composite culture and secular nationalism. While some religious and political leaders became 'reformed Muslims' and sought to separate lived religions along confessional lines, composite culture has been a living presence in the life of Muslims and Hindus, an outgrowth of working together and a part of the social habitus, for many centuries, as can be gleaned particularly from literary texts.[27]

Following the general elections in 1964–65 the overall Nehruvian mood eventually created a desire to integrate religion into the official 'rationalisation and disciplinarian project'.[28] The result was among others, the establishment of the All India Muslim Majlis-e Mushawarat (AIMMM) (Muslim Consultative Committee) in Lucknow in 1964, under the leadership of Dr. Syed Mahmood (died 1972), the former deputy foreign minister, who once opined that "only Muslims can save this nation from doom". The AIMMM, a loose coalition of different Muslim groups mainly from North India was however too broad in terms of its ideological positions to become a serious political party. After a split initiated by Dr. ʿAbd al-Jalil Faridi (died 1974), who had organised the U.P. Muslim Majlis in 1968, the AIMMM came to focus purely on the conservation of Muslim cultural life as was subscribed

---

[27] Such as Saadat Hasan Manto, Rajindar Singh Bedi, Amrita Pritam, Qurratul Ain Haydar and Ilyas Ahmad Gaddi, just to mention a few. See for example the short stories of S.H. Manto ("The Writings of Saadat Hasan Manto", *in: Journal of South Asian Literature* 20/2 (1985) and *Kingdom's End and other Short Stories*, transl. by Khalid Hasan, London 1989), and the novels by Qurratul Ain Haydar such as *River of Fire*, New York 1999, and Ilyas Ahmad Gaddi's *Fire Area*, New Delhi 2002.

[28] A fine example for this powerful trend is Mohammad Mujeeb: *The Indian Muslims*, Delhi 1965.

by some Deobandi scholars.[29] In Haydarabad, the All India Majlis-e Ittihad al-Muslimin was reorganised and stood for Muslim supremacy in Deccan, despite being in a minority position.[30] Again in 1972—after the creation of Bangladesh—another attempt was made to integrate Muslims under one platform with the All-India Personal Law Board (AIMPLB), established by Muslim scholars against the backdrop of Indira Gandhi's attempt to introduce a Uniform Civil Code.[31] The intervention of the Board was to guarantee the continuation of 'personal laws' of Muslims.[32]

The linguistic restructuring of the Indian states had further fragmented a manufactured but trans-regional Muslim collective identity.[33] This further proves that different social groups, lifestyles and life-chances are not conducive to a unified Muslim definition of what is called a homogenous Muslim minority. Other interests, loyalties and affiliations such as economic, social, caste, etc. do indeed transcend religious barriers between Hindus and Muslims, and their plurality of social identities often is more important than their religious affinities. This was mirrored in the electoral behaviour, when Muslims did not necessarily vote for Muslims; this corresponded to the Muslims voting *en bloc* for the Indian National Congress before the Emergency (1975–77). It is banal but important to note that Muslim-ness is a factor only in the context of opposition, that is, a propagated Hindu-ness, which has had major repercussions for the social fabric in India, as has been the case lately.[34]

Yet, despite all the cultural overlapping and compositeness,[35] there are limits to mutual assimilation between Hindus and Muslims. Militant

---

[29] *The Statesman*, 22.1.1988; see Theodore P. Wright, Jr.: "Muslim Education in India at the Crossroads: The Case of Aligarh", in: *Pacific Affairs*, 39 (1966), pp. 50–63.

[30] See Omar Khalidi: "Mawlâna Mawdûdî and the Future Political Order in British India", in: *MW* 93 (July 2003), pp. 415–427; Margrit Pernau-Reifeld: *Verfassung und politische Kultur im Wandel. Der indische Fürstenstaat Hyderabad, 1911–48*, Stuttgart 1992, pp. 271–3, 288–98, 349–368.

[31] Indira Gandhi was assassinated by her own bodyguard in 1984, when the Sikh community was angry over 'Operation Blue Star' ordered by her to combat Sikh insurgency in Punjab.

[32] For an analysis of the "The Changing Position of the Muslims and the Political Future of Secularism in India, c. 1947–1986", see Mushirul Hasan: *Islam in the Subcontinent. Muslims in a Plural Society*, New Delhi 2002, pp. 361ff.

[33] Moin Shakir: "The Muslim Political Elite", p. 170.

[34] Rajani Kanth: "A Muslim Political Culture?", in: Imam (ed.): *The Musalmaans*, pp. 140f.

[35] See I. Ahmad (ed.): *Caste and Social Stratification among the Muslims*, New Delhi 1973; (ed.): *Family, Kinship and Marriage among Muslims in India*, New Delhi 1976; (ed.): *Ritual*

Hinduism, which seemingly re-invents Hindu tradition by reviving and idealising the role of the legendary Maratha leader Shivaji (died 1680), provides the contemporary—modern—social fabric for the much needed legitimacy of historicity. The Hinduised role of Shivaji and "cultural nationalism" was first championed by V.D. Savarkar (1883–1966) in his *Essentials of Hindutva* (1924) (see Excursus: Communalism). The Shiv Sena, the Army of Shiva or Shivaji, founded in Bombay in 1966 by Bal Thackeray, which was originally formed to stand up for the privileges of Maratha workers in Bombay against the immigrant South Indians, became one of the major communal parties in Maharashtra: by 1980s Shiv Sena declared that Muslims had lost their right to live in India because of the creation of Pakistan to which they should emigrate.[36] Correspondingly, after the Bharatiyya Janata Party (BJP) came to power as the single largest party in 1999, a Hinduised revision of school books and a linguistic purism were called for. Romila Thapar had commented that BJP was trying to semiticise Hinduism: the earlier earthly pluralism of Hinduism was sought to be replaced by one Book (Ramayana) and one God (Ram).[37] Thus they were trying to make Hinduism look more and more like Islam while opposing it at the same time!

This passionate and collective enthusiasm for essentialism can be found on both sides, Hindu and Muslim: both invent themselves as communities in the process of reinventing their own past. The identity politicians campaigning for election votes, constrict the heterogeneous Indian Muslim community in such a way, that one might too easily tend to speak of a monolithic Indian Islam. In fact, the recent separation of different personal law boards for Shiʿites, Barelwis and women from the All India Muslim Personal Law Board dominated by Deobandis, Ahl-e Hadith and Nadwis in 2005 shows this Muslim plurality and contest very aptly.

---

and Religion among Muslims of the Sub-continent, (reprint) Lahore 1985; (ed.): *Modernization and Social Change among Muslims in India*, New Delhi 1983. In the South the degree of assimilation seems to be much higher than in the North. See Susan Bayly: *Saints, Goddesses & Kings*.

[36] See Bruce Graham: *Hindu Nationalism and Indian Politics; The Origins and Development of the Bharatiya Jana Sangh*, Cambridge: CUP 1990.

[37] For a critical analysis of the Ram-tradition see Romila Thapar: "A historical perspective on the story of Rama", in: S. Gopal (ed.): *Anatomy of a Confrontation*, pp. 141–163.

The issues

Whether the increasing Muslim assertion since 1977 had any relationship to the coup d'état of Zia ul-Haqq in Pakistan and the Iranian Revolution in 1979 is open to question; what can be safely argued is that since the 1970s religion increasingly has become the major discursive vehicle to articulate the interests of Muslim minorities, not only in South Asia but also world-wide. This importance attached to religion became manifested at the Delhi Milli Convention in 1977 as well as in other regional and national fora. The major issues around which Muslim politics in India has been negotiated are the maintenance of the status quo on personal law, the preservation of places of worship and the promotion of the Urdu language. These symbols help to generate a unified group feeling and solidarity because they are necessary signs of identification; their usage creates social and religious norms, which are only comprehensible to an informed, sacral-liturgical community. They therefore become constitutive elements exclusive to a particular group which must belong to the same semantic family. Such symbols are expressed also in narratives of genealogical and social origin; Arabisation and Ashrafisation can manifest the collective group consciousness. The politics of religious symbolism has an important function in evoking social and religious norms because it lies beyond grammatical speech and addresses the sub-consciousness underlying these norms. As a pre-language, such symbols can be used by a moral authority: the religious politicians. Religion thus has a major impact on the collective Muslim mind such as can be seen in the wake of the mobilisation in the case of the Shah Bano affair (see Excursus: Gender), the issue of Salman Rushdie and Babri-Masjid (see Excursus: Communalism).

Shah Bano

The AIMPLB was most active during the famous Shah Bano case in 1985, when the Indian Supreme Court overruled a Muslim personal law—which was the domain of Muslim traditionalists—by granting a 62 year old Muslim woman alimony and thereby threatening the limited legal autonomy provided to the Muslim minority in India. As this was interpreted as an attempt to change the Muslim Personal Law (which had acquired a quasi sacred status despite the fact that it had been created by the British), the JUH and other Muslim traditionalist forces, such as Nadwi who had been chairing the AIMPLB since 1983, intervened successfully. These representatives of Muslim-patriarchal interests claimed to protect Islam from the arbitrariness of the secular state. They argued that Hindu judges of a Hindu-dominated state had interpreted the Quran to that extent. They did not mention, however, that the Supreme Court also underlined the need for a Uniform Civil Code, which is not written in the Shashtra but is part of the directive principles of the Indian Constitution. While most Muslim modernists appreciated the Supreme Court's verdict, the Congress-led government under Rajiv Gandhi gave in to Muslim orthodox pressure and reversed the ruling of the Court. Eventually, this affair caused a major split among secular Muslims who called for a Uniform Civil Code, and religiously minded Muslims who considered religious identity to be their dominating national identity. In fact, the pertinent call for minority rights has been a powerful instrument in the hands of quite a number of Muslims, religiously minded as well as secular.

Rushdie

This sense of insecurity was further aggravated during the Rushdie Affair in 1989. The affair had little impact in Pakistan, though the Jamaʿat-e Islami in Pakistan was responsible for mobilising the first protests against "The Satanic Verses" for its "blasphemous" dream sequences of Prophet Muhammad. Iranian leader Ruh Allah Khumaini's edict, imposing the death sentence on Rushdie, grabbed the headlines in 1989, but the Islamic world's fury was ignited by the Indian Jamaʿat-e Islami. Soon, the book was banned in India. In a secular state which stood for both the guarantee of the rights and freedoms of different religious communities and the freedom of thought, this ban—like any ban—was highly problematic. The reason for the ban, however, had a political rather than a religious motivation and lay most probably in the value potential Muslim voters had for the Congress that had been dominating politics since independence: more than 50 million Indian Muslims up until then, barring the elections of 1977 (Emergency) had, more or less voted *en bloc* for the Congress which was considered the secular guarantor of their rights and interests. The Muslim sensitivity to the issue is based in the fact that over the course of Muslim history Prophet Muhammad had become the sublimation of the sublime, a perfect individual, a moral and aesthetic ideal which is to be followed.[38] Any criticism of him would have severe repercussions. It is precisely in this context that the Barelwis for whom the Prophet enjoys the special status for his omnipresence, were "collectively more prepared to register the insult contained in the book"[39] than any other groups. So the Rushdie affair as well as the result of the election demonstrated that Muslims in India could not be neglected even in political terms.[40]

Babri Mosque and its aftermath

Muslims had traditionally tended to vote for the Congress in Indian elections—particularly because of their lack of parliamentary representation. However, the Emergency under Indira Gandhi (1975–77) changed their voting behaviour decisively when Indian Muslims lost confidence in the Congress.[41] This loss of confidence was further aggravated during the issue of the Babri Mosque, in which Rajiv Gandhi's government

---

[38] See, for example, the *dala'il* and *shama'il* literature: Muhammad, the beautiful and spiritual model. Thus said Rudi Paret, a German Orientalist: "In case of emergency, the Muslim might deny his faith, but he would never be willing to utter a word of slander against Muhammad or to renounce him, even though he were facing death in case of refusal to do so." And the Canadian W.C. Smith explained: "Muslims will allow attacks on Allah; there are atheists and atheistic publications, and rationalistic societies; but to disparage Muhammad will provoke from even the most 'liberal' sections of the community a fanaticism of blazing vehemence." (quoted in A. Schimmel: *And Muhammad is His Messenger*, Chapel Hill, NC, 1985, p. 5). This tradition is based in the reverence for the *sahaba*, so that the biographies (*tabaqa* and *sira*) of the *ashab al-nabi* were indemnified from scrutiny. This correction (*ta'dil*) of the *sahaba* is still untouchable, it supersedes collectively all the following generations.

[39] J. Nielsen: *Muslims in Western Europe*, Edinburgh: Edinburgh University Press 1992, p. 159. See also Pnina Werbner: "Allegories of Sacred Imperfection: Magic, Hermeneutics, and Passion in 'The Satanic Verses'", in: *Current Anthropology* (Chicago) 37 (1996), Supplement.

[40] In Britain the Rushdie Affair has turned Islam into a new strength, into a new agenda for multiculturalism, for a fundamental revision of the national self-image of Britain as it moves to becoming a more self-consciously plural society. The mobilisation against the book and its author brought together rival Muslim sectarian groups and factions from all over England. As a united force they could demand the ban of the book and reciprocally promised to end the unrests in ghettos and restore social peace; see W. Schiffauer: *Fremde in der Stadt. Zehn Essays über Kultur und Differenz*, Frankfurt am Main: Suhrkamp 1997, pp. 39–42.

[41] See V. Graff: "Le désarroi des musulmans indiens. Chronique d'une crise annoncée", in: *Hérodote* 71 (1993), pp. 116–139.

had a rather ambivalent position (see Excursus: Communalism). Rajiv Gandhi's electoral calculations had seen Muslims founding the "Babri Masjid Movement Coordination Committee" in 1986 initiated by the then parliamentarian Sayyid Shihabuddin (b. 1935) and the "Babri Masjid Action Committee" under the advocate Zafar Yab Jilani from Lucknow. This was the year that the Babri Mosque was opened only for Hindus.[42] The Muslims' vote was a reaction to the increasing communal tensions which had worked their way into rural areas and regions dominated by the Congress such as Bhagalpur in Bihar. In contrast, areas led by the opposition were rather peaceful. The communal tensions culminated shortly before the election in 1989. Reason was a little mosque which was said to have been built at the behest of the Mughal emperor Babur, on the ruins of a temple, the Babri masjid in Ayodhya. The mosque had not been used by the Muslims since 1948 when a local court had ordered its closure after the mysterious appearance of the idol of Lord Rama. However it was only after the establishment of the Ramjanambhumi Temple Trust by some nationalist Hindus on 1 Feb. 1986, that the matter caught the national attention which subsequently led to a number of communal riots in and around Ayodhya. Two weeks before the elections, on the 9th of November 1989, Rajiv Gandhi allowed the Vishwa Hindu Parishad (VHP) to lay the foundation stone (*silanyas*) of the temple. The reason for Gandhi's benevolence vis-à-vis Hindus was to win them over as voters. The position taken by BJP was even clearer and much appreciated by many Hindu voters. Rajiv Gandhi was on the point of losing his Muslim constituency; a group of Islamic scholars had proclaimed in a *fatwa* that Muslims should give their vote to the opposition because the Congress would allow the demolition of the mosque and the reconstruction of the temple. Subsequently, Rajiv Gandhi lost his Muslim as well as his Hindu constituencies. To compensate the Muslims he promised to make the Prophet's birthday a public holiday and stressed the secular stand of the Congress as the patron of the Muslims. He also promised to compensate for each family that lost a member in the communal riots in Bhagalpur in 1989. But all these concessions came too late. The elections were won by the

[42] This reopening of the mosque has been seen as a tribute to the victory of the Muslim Personal Law Board in the Shah Bano case. See Mushirul Hasan: *Legacy of a Divided Nation*, New Delhi: OUP 1997, pp. 253–357.

moderate Janata Dal under V.P. Singh in an alliance with the Hindu fundamentalists just after Rajiv Gandhi's assassination in 1990 by an activist of the *Liberation Tigers of Tamil Eelam* (LTTE).[43]

In order to counter the perceived 'Hindu division' through the implementation of the Mandal Commission Report which had recommended 27% reservations for backward castes, the leader of the Hindu Right BJP, L.K. Advani, started the open use of panegyrics and iconography to mobilise Hindu masses, most importantly through his *rath yatra* (lit. car festival) from Somnath[44] to Ayodhya in 1990, whipping up religious sentiments and demanding the construction of a Ram temple in Ayodhya. His *yatra* left a blazing trail of destruction as the country was engulfed by serious communal riots.[45] The BJP's politics of Hinduism (Hindutva) ultimately led to the demolition of the Babri Mosque in 1992 by the Hindu Right.[46] Muslims at their end started to globalise this local conflict by seeking international support, among others through the Mecca-based Muslim World League, of which Abu al-Hasan ʿAli Nadwi was a leading member.[47] The Muslims, highly fragmented and barely united, could not form a united position, thus enabling the VHP to announce the temple reconstruction works in spring 2002. But the

---

[43] The LTTE was formed in 1976 and began its armed campaign in Sri Lanka for a separate Tamil homeland known as the Tamil Eelam (state) in the Northern and Eastern provinces of Sri Lanka in 1983. It is known for its intensive guerrilla tactics, including suicide attacks.

[44] Somnath has become a major symbol for an imagined Hinduness vis-à-vis the image of Muslim hostility. This strategic essentialism suggests an innate antagonism between Muslims and Hindus. For a critical review of the narratives about Muslim raids and destruction of the temple see Thapar: *Somanatha*; Davis: *Lives of Indian Images*.

[45] However Laloo Prasad Yadav, then Chief Minister of Bihar, from Janta Dal Party, had him arrested by the police when he was crossing Madhubabi district in Bihar that led, along with Laloo's popularity, Muslims to shift their favour from the Congress to this charismatic figure. Though Laloo did not do much for the Muslims, during his time however he ensured that no communal strife took place in the state, which was a relief for many Muslims as it was always the minority that had to suffer in such situations.

[46] The way the violence evolved and was used by politicians is discussed in Paul Brass' thesis (*The Production of Hindu-Muslim Violence in Contemporary India*, Seattle, WA: University of Washington Press, 2003). Brass opines that these communal battles are "pogroms" rather than "riots" carefully initiated by political leaders.

[47] The internationalisation of the Babri Masjid-Ramjanmabhumi issue has been dealt with by Jan-Peter Hartung: "The Land, the Mosque, the Temple. More than 145 Years of Dispute over Ayodhya", in: Richard Bonney (ed.): *Ayodhya 1992–2003: The Assertion of Cultural and Religious Hegemony*, Leicester and New Delhi 2003, pp. 22–28.

incident of train burning in Godhra which killed many Hindu pilgrims (*kar sevaks*) and which was followed by a state sponsored pogrom of Muslims in Gujarat, perhaps led to the postponement of this plan by the VHP. The BJP being the ruling party had come under criticism from its allies on the handling of the Gujarat issue where the BJP was ruling as well. Their allies threatened to bring down the government if the situation was not brought under control. It was under this threat that the VHP, considered very close to the BJP since they share the same ideological moorings, decided to postpone their plans for the temple construction at the demolished site of Babri Mosque. However, the issue remains alive till today and the struggle over sacred spaces is an active manifestation of political contest between different religious groups. From the point of view of Muslim religious leaders, the demolition of the Babri mosque, which had become even more sacred after its demolition, is an attempt to desecrate Muslim space and thus to wipe out their religious identity by non-Muslims. It must be added here that in countries like Pakistan the demolition of mosques by the "Islamic" state is hardly an issue since the 'perceived looming threat' of a non-Muslim majority is absent.

The Kashmir issue

The Kashmir issue has been another area of contestation between some of the heirs of Islam and those of the state, though it has remained peripheral to the politics of North Indian Muslims. In fact, the resolutions passed by different Muslim organisations hardly mention Kashmir at all. However, some Muslim radical groups supposedly infiltrating from Pakistan to Jammu and Kashmir are encountered by the *All Parties Hurriyat Conference* established in 1994. The *Conference* pursues a peaceful solution of the Kashmir problem with the Indian Government and aims at integrating groups such as the Jamaʿat-e Islami (Jammu wa Kashmir) and the *Jammu and Kashmir Liberation Front* (JKLF). The JKLF had begun to call for militant resistance against the Indian troops in "occupied" Kashmir in 1989, the year that the Soviets withdrew from Afghanistan. Since then the JKLF had been nourished by groups recruited outside Kashmir.

Hindu Communalist parties have pushed Muslims to be on the defensive, particularly when these parties propagate that Muslims are primarily Muslim and not Indian, and therefore, have exterritorial loyalties.[48] A 'Hindu past' is glorified—such as the cult attached to the temple of Ayodhya (see Excursus: Communalism).[49] Urdu is seen as a Muslim language and is neglected by the State, leading—according to Muslim politicians—to a shrinking Urdu market.[50] All this culminates in the so-called "Muslim problem", which suggests a homogenised Muslim identity. This in turn is taken up and used by communal Muslim groups, such as the Jamaʿat-e Islami Hind, Tablighi Jamaʿat, All India Majlis-e Mushawarat, All India Taʿmir-e Millat, Jamaʿat-e Ahl-e Hadith and their respective student organisations, for their own purposes, though there are also violent quarrels among Muslims themselves. One can think of the recurring riots between Sunnis and Shiʿites in Lucknow and elsewhere on the occasion of Muharram,[51] or the fights between the followers of the Barelwis and the Deobandis, fights that are also re-enacted among South Asian Muslim migrants and their offspring in the U.K.[52] Religion has become an instrument in the hand of a few and a catalyser for political unrest: "...whereas religion may ideally define political conduct, in effect, religion is only another vested interest in the struggle for domination and supremacy subject to the machinations of the master-minds of the power game."[53] In doing so, formations of religious communities come to the fore, not only contesting space and interrogating religious and religiously legitimated boundaries, but as actors of civil societal in the public sphere in which they compete. Thus, cultural praxis embedded in culturally conditioned systems of symbols has the capability of challenging master narratives and to compromise callous ideals which otherwise might be impermeable. The sufi song, the *qawwali*, brought to western audiences by the late Chishti Nusrat Fateh ʿAli Khan (died 1997), is one of such many

[48] See Anwar Moazzam: "The Indian Muslims", in: Lokhandwalla (ed.): *India and Contemporary Islam*, p. 199.

[49] For the BJP strategy see also Chr. Jaffrelot: "Hindu Nationalism, Strategic Syncretism in Ideology Building", in: *The Indian Journal of Social Science* 5/4 (1992), pp. 373–392. See also Chr. Jaffrelot: "Les pièges de l'instrumentalime... et de la répression", in: *Cultures et conflicts* 8 (1992–93), pp. 91–109.

[50] Thus many articles in the journal "Muslim India", New Delhi, edited by Sayyid Shahabuddin.

[51] See for example Mushirul Hasan: "Sectarianism in Indian Islam: The Shia-Sunni divide in the United Provinces", in: *IESHR* 27/2 (1990), pp. 209–228.

[52] Cf. Pnina Werbner: "Factionalism and Violence in British Pakistani Politics", in: Donnan Hastings and Pnina Werbner (eds.): *Economy and Culture in Pakistan; Migrants and Cities in a Muslim Society*, London: MacMillan 1991, pp. 188–215.

[53] Rajani Kanth: "A Muslim Political Culture?", p. 149.

examples of shared religion, and how music can convey the message of religious pluralism.

Prospects

Although currently, the public debate in South Asia is dominated by secular-political parties and by the military, the increasing esteem of religious-political parties cannot go unnoticed, in a region, where a large number of people live below the poverty line. One can detect instances of ethno-political conflicts, in which the own group is idealised and the image of the enemy constructed, the own origin and history elevated and the other's right to exist negated. Mythical explanations generate solidarity but also provoke upheavals; the revolution of rising expectations can then only be suppressed by radical means. Cases like those of Salman Rushdie and Taslima Nasrin, but also the increasing number of confessional conflicts, the destruction of the Babri Mosque in Ayodhya all indicate that the multiplying conflicts within society take religious (Islamic) forms of expression. These are cases in which emotionalised processes of identity-building are actualised and the performance and power of religious symbolism becomes evident. Whether the re-elected Congress government—after an intermezzo of the coalition led by BJP—will be able to re-store the 'unity in diversity' is still to be seen. The recent conflicts between Sunni and Shiʿite groups in Pakistan as well as India and Bangladesh only show that the generated violence does not stop at national borders, but that it rests under the influence of hegemonic interests—also of foreign regimes. Moreover, the dramatic impact of the former Taliban regime on the entire region nourishes doubts as to whether a process of democracy really can take place or if some embedded alternative is to be found which would be commensurate with local norms, institutions and discourses.

This is more important in light of the fact that there are nearly half a billion Muslims living in the three major countries on the subcontinent, with a tremendous increase in population—from 1.7%, to 2.7%. Simultaneously, their standard of living and education and access to basic facilities is declining each day. These millions of people can fall prey to the many trans-national religious organisations operating throughout the subcontinent and beyond.

In order to understand these complex processes one has to contextualise the situations and the different religious sentiments attached to them. This calls for the translation of social and cultural codes and repertoires. This is especially important since there is constant interaction between minorities and majorities; both constitute a cultural ensemble sharing the same frame of reference and much mutuality. A frame of reference, one must add, which is becoming more brittle with each passing day.

AFTERWORD

Thus the teleologically oriented perspective closes and comes to an end. Even if we dislike the grim scenario, it is a reality occupying not only our minds but also the public sphere and holding much visibility. One can well argue that beneath these influential and effective images that tend to reduce major cultural achievements to the realm of religious fanaticism, other more lenient and Islamicated forces are at work. The whole universe of lived tradition and shared religion is the case in point which facilitates cultural interaction and provides healthy spaces for reciprocity. We may consider the profound impact of institutions and the lore of mysticism and lived Islam that inform everyday life, whether in urban or in rural areas, enabling people from different walks of life to come together in an atmosphere of sharing and participation.

Preconditions for this entangling scenario were provided well in advance, that is, with the early Muslim settlers, when Arabs encountered Hindus and Buddhists in their quest to expand their influence over a market extending far beyond al-Hind. The area around the Indus delta and the coasts of South India proved to be reasonable starting points. Rather than expanding Islam by fire and sword the Muslims turned out to be indifferent to conversion. The observance of Prophetic traditions so important to these fledgling Muslim communities was kept in tune with political pragmatism. The accommodation of non-Arab polytheists into the Muslim taxonomy corresponded to conversion of non-Muslims in order to participate in a global Muslim horizon. Furthermore, the correspondence between the textual piety of hadith scholars and Buddhist textualism and literalism provided for even more interaction on the level of Arab-Muslim mercantilism, in a time when the study of transmitted sciences was most important. Yet, a singular process of orthodoxy could not emerge, for there were too many different groups contesting over Islamic agency, contestations that eventually resulted in proxy wars between early Muslim Arab dynasties on Indian soil. As a result of these interactions a basis was laid for a colourful plurality of religious practices and communities. Indigenous culture became Islamicated and Islamic religion indigenised, but what happened in most cases was probably a mixture of both. Thus, the impact of Muslim did not vanish with the Arab retreat; rather it accelerated, coming this time as it did from the North.

The major structural change occurring during this shift was the introduction of Persianised culture, involving ethical texts, Persian literary cultural pathos, sufi liberal texts and the flexible Islamic law of the Hanafi tradition. These sources were to provide non-sectarian and humane alternatives for Muslims in South Asia. The channels used to spread and disperse these ideas were versatile and were based on meeting traditional religious and non-religious institutions and infrastructures to provide for pluralistic religious milieus. These rather accommodationist positions were encountered by different orthodox scholars and practitioners. The creation of Pakistan as the embodiment of a Muslim majority state distinct from a Hindu majority state seems to anticipate that the latter (orthodoxy) won the day and that an homogenous Muslim identity emerged—on either side of the border. But this was not the case; far from it, thanks to the existence and persistence of several virtually contesting Muslim ideas in plural and pluralist contexts. The extreme poles of the disputes were represented by those who sought affiliation and also patronage in the Arab context, focusing perhaps unnecessarily strongly on the Arab Prophet as a crucial ethical ideal for solidarity and identity purposes on the one hand. On the other hand, there were the more indigenised, Islamicated, forms of articulation embedded in shared religion of the *ʿajam*. In between *ʿarab* and *ʿajam* there was a plethora of voices arguing for balanced encounter that sought creative paths between both poles, complementing precisely these different and at times contestant Muslim positions.

The tussle between *ʿarab* and *ʿajam*, however, was decided in favour of the latter, when non-Arabs could boast the only functioning Muslim Sultanate East of Baghdad. Arabic was substituted by the more profane Persian which eventually caused an accumulative character of the *shariʿa* in a non-Arab culture of eastern Islam. Precisely to counter this process of blurring the *shariʿa*, some sultans at the behest of scholars and Sufis alike re-introduced the Arab language and law books, while others tried to limit the assimilative Sufi discourses to keep the sultanate working. The institution of *ijtihad* proved to be of utmost significance for both sides since it had always been the perennial duty of Islamic scholars to take care of this most precious device of Islamic law. Even in later centuries this device was reactivated, the issue being as to who should exercise *ijtihad*: the scholars or rather the ruler or the common man. Thus issues of both agency and normativity both were at stake. These antagonisms were not only crucial in terms of culture clash between *ʿarab* and *ʿajam*, they were also extremely important for the operationalisation of different Muslim political systems in a pluralistic context. The breaking apart of several political entities to become independent Muslim principalities was possible precisely because of these different, conflicting and overlapping tendencies formulated in religious terms. Muslim heterogeneity facilitated the ability of the margins to become centres of Muslim power, especially through Shiʿites flocking from neighbouring Western regions.

Islamic mysticism encouraged belief in the unity of pluralism, particularly in the fifteenth and sixteenth centuries, transported by poems and songs in particular. Personal unions between Hindus and Muslims were common; Prophet Muhammad came to be seen as an *avatar* of Hindu gods. Yet, people like al-Barani and Sirhindi wanted not only *shariʿa* rule over the country but also the humiliation and extermination of their Non-Muslim subjects. In contrast, the Mughals built on these different tendencies and strove to safeguard balance between rivalling interests. In their project to implement universal dominion, which came to be reflected paradigmatically in the notion of "peace with everybody" (*sulh-e kull*), different players can be discerned: some Sufis such as Sirhindi and ʿAbd al-Haqq strove for restoration of Sunni orthodoxy, particularly in the face of growing Shiʿite influences. It is in this context that the study of Prophetic tradition gained renewed impetus after several centuries of neglect. Apart from individual figures that provided the necessary theological and juridical expertise, the encompassing Moghul policy of universal dominion witnessed a growing plurality of competing religious groups. In their encounter with the monarch as well as with each other they were forced to acuminate their religious profiles, to define the strict and distinctive confessional identity-boundaries between them. Moreover, to produce doctrinal conformity and disciplined behaviour among their own members, a wide range of social techniques were developed. This competition from below was to a great deal responsible for processes of institutionalisation and routinisation of the religious. In effect, the methods employed by these different groups were similar. In some cases cooperation with the holders of political power was thought to be essential, in others millenarian movements challenged the holders of power. In any case, the moral and ethical role of the Prophet Muhammad in the making of such religious communities was an important point of reference. Considering these developments in terms of a "confessionalisation paradigm"[1] might help in understanding similar developments in the context of Muslim empires and beyond in contemporary perspective.

It may be a coincidence that these religious communities produced certain modernising effects in state and society: rationality and discipline, bureaucratisation and centralisation, and, going along with these developments, a heightened personal responsibility for life, in a conscious attempt to ideologically instrumentalise one's own confessional affiliation in the skirmishes with the confessional other. For in the course of events it was precisely these effects that changed the character of religion. Henceforth, regionalisation of imperial culture ushered in various levels of regional and local integration, whereby devotional religion went hand in hand with patriotism and centralised revenue systems. Patronage was a major means to realise these steps towards territorial independence. Thus, on the occasion of colonial penetration, national markets had developed which were later used by Europeans as springboards for economic and political conquest. Two major trends can be delineated among urban Muslims: on the one hand, established elites holding to law and a quasi-standard set of education designed for scribal groups to run the virtually independent states; and reformers who challenged precisely this system and called for processes of religious individualisation, on the other. The reinforcement of *ijtihad* increased reflexivity and individualisation of religion, while Prophetic sunna was considered paradigmatic for social and political reform. Practically experienced religion was conceptually reflected, the sacred was humanised, and the humane was sacralised, as can be traced in the writings of the age, such as pious texts and poetry mass-circulated in the bazar. Just as in the pietist tradition, there was a critical consciousness of existing institutions and of religious "superstition". The visibility of publicly accessable spaces such as poetry meetings was a common feature in other institutions such as libraries, coffee-houses, and baths, the number of which increased rapidly during this period.[2] It is no wonder therefore, that contemporary Indian travellers to Europe could perceive similar institutions in Europe within their own cultural

[1] Following Wolfgang Reinhard and Heinz Schilling (eds.): *Die katholische Konfessionalisierung*, Gütersloh: Gütersloher Verlagshaus 1995.

[2] It would be worthwhile to enquire about this aspect of material culture with the tools of urban anthropology and urban geography.

categories.[3] Thus this indigenous process of emancipation was also receptive for colonialists who at times even indulged in cultural mimicry, a mimicry that could be selfless but which was also important in embracing the colonial process. At the same time, this process threatened colonial deployment. Therefore, the semantic of traditionalisation and—following that—of modernisation of the Orient was to endow the colony with "civility" and to safeguard economic exploitation. This was the major colonial project.

In the face of the following wide-raging changes, it took Muslims many decades to restore Islam as a normative force in the public mind; emphasis on hadith and the centrality of the Prophet were the major vehicles in that endeavour—though the positions varied from conflict to complement. Thus the initial process of emancipation in eighteenth century was radicalised in nineteenth century. One may consider this phase in terms of neo-confessionalism, characterised by a high degree of diffusion of Islamic learning and piety, facilitated through media, increasing mobility in Muslim world and pan-Islam sentiments. Islamic puritanism played an importantly expanding role because it appeared in different—sometimes contradictory—forms, such as scripturalist, yet sufic. The latter was integral to society and prominent even as urban reformist movements were trying to get rid of it. The revival of ritual activities and scriptural norms was important to establish distinct contesting confessional groups, functionally attributed to scholarly culture (beyond traditional scholarship) in the public sphere. These groups were later complemented by yet others during the anti-colonial struggle.

Even if the macro-political scenario of Muslim South Asia looks rather grave—considering issues of communalism and sectarianism for example, and the low standard in terms of education, income and political participation; on the micro-level the fate of South Asian Muslims is not so bad. After all, they have at their disposal a vibrant religious context which has the capability to act in the form of societally self-organising networks, networks that have been helping people right

---

[3] Such as was the case with Abu Talib al-Isfahani or Munshi Ismail, Dean Mahomet, Lutfullah or al-Tantawi; see C. Stewart (transl.): *Travels of Mirza Abu Taleb Khan in Asia, Africa and Europe During the Years 1797 to 1803, 2 Vols.* London 1811, reprint 1972; Michael Fisher (ed.): *Dean Mahomet, Travels of Dean Mahomet: An Eighteenth-Century Journey through India*, Berkeley 1997; S. Digby: "An eighteenth century narrative of a journey from Bengal to England: Munshî Ismâ'îl's *New History*", in: Shackle (ed.): *Urdu and Muslims*, pp. 49–66; Shaikh Lutfullah: *Autobiography of Lutfullah: An Indian's Perceptions of the West*, ed. Edward B. Eastwick, reprint, ed. with an Introduction S.A.I. Tirmizi, New Delhi 1985.

from the beginning in 1947, when the state had little infrastructure of its own to offer. The potential for the formation of religious communities is immense, competitive and versatile. In attending to their constituencies as competitors these religious communities can negotiate as actors of civil society in the public sphere. And what is more important: because they are much more rooted in society than the agents of the anonymous state, they can challenge the limited authority of state. Religion, as it appears de-privatised, becomes a representative player in civil society helping to shape or at least affect that society. To this extent, it is not only the nation-state that defines religion, but also that religious actors themselves exert a major impact on the state. This is indeed a truism, but considering the fact that different players are informed and determined simultaneously by very different models and attitudes at the same time in same localities, this contest becomes dramatic. Yet, it is not only the condition of "the contemporaneity of the non-contemporaneous" (Ernst Bloch), which has been asserted all around, particularly in the context of globalisation. Indeed, religion is a special mediator to communicate this non-contemporaneousness—via memory, visualisation and repetition. What is both bewildering and fascinating is its sheer dimension and magnitude in South Asia. Consider: one community of the faithful considers belief in universal human dignity and human rights motivated by religion while the other rejects this claim for secular sacrality with similar arguments, precisely at the same time and from the same space; one religious community demolishes the remains of ancient history in the name of the Prophet, the other cherishes them in the name of precisely the same prophet; one concedes hadith to have prime importance for the understanding of the divine message and Prophet Muhammad its paragon, while the other questions the infallibility of the sunna to assign man the faculty of interpreting Quran, whether *ashraf*, *ajlaf* or *ardhal*. In other words, when subjectively construed, shared religious, institutionalised and non-institutionalised systems of ultimate meaning and truths are increasingly and expeditiously replacing traditional Muslim religious forms, be it in Muslim minority or majority regions, when some sort of religious individualisation takes place, affirming the idea of the dignity of the human being, while at the same time atrocities are committed in the name of God, reconciliation of the contemporaneity of the non-contemporaneous is hardly possible.

Whether these tensions—deep as they may be—can be smoothed over through the homogenising vigour of modern nation-states and globalisation is open to doubt. To be specific: state policies that function to extend the process of globalisation and homogenisation and seek to impose transcultural values look for recognition and acceptance of this process as a 'de-cultured' one. However, this globalisation meets with a variety of reactions and encounters resistance, in a process of external global pressures interrelated with distinct local struggles. Thus, the recent expressions of religious "resistance" in the context of formations of religious communities in a space of autochthonous cultural articulation, or the non-contemporaneous as it were, can be seen as a response to the political economy of globalisation and state penetration proceeding "from above." At the same time, religious communities have developed their own dynamics vis-à-vis the ever encroaching state and respond to local skirmishes between local factions competing for scarce resources "from below". Their engagement in homogenisation and contestation in the pursuit of agencies over their and others' constituencies is a case in point. Hence, these religious communities are focused on, or affected by, global as well as local concerns. In fact, there is an interplay between these two levels, when religious communities are situated in ways that blend both levels together. Thus, globalising policies do not necessarily follow isomorphic processes but can effect localisation and cause de-coupling, yet with strikingly similar homogenising tendencies. In the final analysis, these differences are systemic parts of the continuous religious vitality of Muslim cultures, and all the more in South Asia. And they should be understood as different facets of cultural praxis embedded in culturally conditioned symbol-systems, that is in lived religions, in all of their contextual richness.

SELECT BIBLIOGRAPHY

Titles quoted more than once or used as general reference have been listed in the select bibliography. Other titles refered to are to be found in the respective chapters.

Map 1 has been redrawn on the basis of the image provided in
- Jamal Malik: *Islamische Gelehrtenkultur in Nordindien. Entwicklungsgeschichte und Tendenzen am Beispiel von Lucknow*, Leiden 1997

Maps 2–8 have been redrawn on the basis of the images provided in
- Jane Hussain: *An Illustrated History of Pakistan, Book 2*, Karachi 1983, pp. 9, 14, 31, 42, 55, 58, 66

Maps 9–11 have been anglicised on the basis of the images provided in
- Jamal Malik: "Islam in Südasien", in: A. Noth & J. Paul (eds.): *Der islamische Orient—Grundzüge seiner Geschichte*, Würzburg 1998, pp. 544–546

General titles

Abu al-Fazl: *Akbar Namah, I–III*, Calcutta: Baptist Mission Press 1886, transl. H. Beveridge, New Delhi: Atlantic Publishers 1989 (repr.)

——: The A'in-i Akbari, I–III, Calcutta 1867–1877, transl. by H. Blochmann and ed. by D.C. Phillott, Calcutta 1927, New Delhi 2001 (repr.)

Badauni, 'Abdul Qadir: *Muntakhab al-Tawarikh, I–III*, Calcutta 1865; transl. by G.S.A. Ranking/W.H. Lowe/S.W. Haig, Patna 1973

Delval, Raymond (ed.): *A Map of the Muslims of the World*, Leiden 1984

Elliot, H.M./Dawson, J.: *The History of India as told by its own Historians. I ff*, Calcutta 1959(3) (first 1867)

Elliot, H.M.: *Encyclopaedia of castes, customs, rites and superstitions of the Races of North India, I–II*, 1st Indian reprint, Delhi 1985, first published 1870

Embree, A.T. (ed.): *Sources of Indian Tradition, Vol. I: From the Beginning to 1800*, New Delhi 1991 (2)

Encyclopaedia Iranica (EnI), ed. Ehsan Yarshater, London 1985ff.

Encyclopedia of Islam, English edition [*EI(2)*], ed. H.A.R. Gibb/J.H. Kramers/E. Lévi-Provencal, J. Schacht, Leiden 1960ff.

Esposito, J.L. et al. (eds.): *The Oxford Encyclopedia of the Modern Islamic World*, Vols. I–IV, New York and Oxford 1995

Habib, Irfan: *An Atlas of the Mughal Empire: Political and Economic Maps with Detailed Notes, Bibliography and Index*, Delhi 1982

Ikram, S.M.: *Modern Muslim India and the Birth of Pakistan*, Lahore 1977(3)

Markovits, Claude (ed.): *Histoire de l'Inde moderne*, Paris 1994

Martin, Richard (ed.): *Encyclopedia of Islam and the Muslim World*, New York 2004, Vols. I–II

Mujeeb, Mohammed: *The Indian Muslims*, Delhi 1965

Muthiah, S. (ed.): *An Atlas of India*, Delhi 1990

Platts, J.T.: *A Dictionary of Urdu, Classical Hindi and English*, Lahore 1983 (first 1911)

Qureshi, Ishtiaq Husain: *The Muslim Community of the Indo-Pakistan Subcontinent (610–1947). A brief analysis*, Gravenhage 1962

Robinson, Francis (ed.): *Cambridge Encyclopedia of India, Pakistan, Bangladesh, Sri Lanka, Nepal, Bhutan and the Maldives*, Cambridge 1989

——: *Islam and Muslim History in South Asia*, New Delhi 2000
Russell, R.: *The Pursuit of Urdu Literature; A Select History*, London 1992
Schimmel, Annemarie: *Islam in the Indian Subcontinent*, Leiden 1980
Schwartzberg, J.E.: *An Historical Atlas of South Asia*, Chicago and London 1978
Storey, C.A.: *Persian Literature. A bio-bibliographical survey*, 2 vols., London 1927–1971
Voll, Klaus and Doreen Beierlein (eds.): *Rising India—Europe's Partner?*, Berlin 2006
Wilson, H.H.: *A Glossary of Judicial and Revenue Terms of British India*, London 1875, repr. ed. Delhi 1968
Yule, Henry/Burnell, A.C.: *Hobson-Jobson, A Glossary of Colloquial Anglo-Indian Words and Phrases*, ed. by William Crooke, London 1903, reprint ed. Delhi 1984(4)

Individual works

ʿAli, Rahman: *Tadhkirah-ye ʿUlamaʾ-ye Hind*, Lucknow 1914
——: *Tadhkirah-ye ʿUlamaʾ-ye Hind*, Urdu with annotations by Muhammad Ayyub Qadiri, Karachi 1964
Abbas, Shemeem Burney: *The Female Voice in Sufi Ritual: Devotional Practices of Pakistan and India*, Austin 2002
Abu Daʾud: *Sahih Sunan Abi Daʾud*, al-Kuwait 2002
Abu-Rabiʾ, Ibrahim M. (ed.): *The Blackwell Companion to Contemporary Islamic Thought*, Malden—Oxford 2006
Ahmad, A. and G.E. v. Grunebaum (eds.): *Muslim Self-statement in India and Pakistan 1857–1968*, Wiesbaden 1970
Ahmad, Aijauddin: *Muslims in India, Vols. I–III*, New Delhi 1993–95
Ahmad, Aziz: *An Intellectual History of Islam in India*, Edinburgh 1969
——: *Islamic Modernism in India and Pakistan*, Oxford 1967
——: *Studies in Islamic Culture in the Indian Environment*, Oxford 1964
Ahmad, Imtiaz (ed.): *Ritual and Religion among Muslims of the Subcontinent*, Lahore 1985
Ahmad, Imtiaz and Helmut Reifeld (eds.): *Lived Islam in South Asia. Adaptation, Accommodation and Conflict*, New Delhi 2004
Ahmad, Imtiaz: "The Ashraf-Ajlaf Dichotomy in Muslim Social Structure in Indian", in: *The Indian Economic and Social History Review* 3 (1966), pp. 268–278
Ahmad, Mohiuddin: *Sayyid Ahmad Shahid: His Life and Mission*, Lucknow 1975
Ahmad, Nazir: *Mirat al-ʿUrus*, transl. *The Bride's Mirror*, Delhi 2001
——: *The Son of the Moment*, translated by Mohammed Zakir, Haydarabad 2002
Ahmad, Q.: *The Wahhabi Movement in India*, Calcutta 1966
Ahmed, R. (ed.): *Religion, Nationalism and Politics in Bangladesh*, New Delhi 1990
Ahmed, Rashid: *Taliban: Militant Islam, Oil and Fundamentalism in Central Asia*, New Haven 2000
Alam, Muzaffar and Sanjay Subrahmanyam (eds.): *The Mughal State*, New Delhi 1998
Alam, Muzaffar et alii. (eds.): *The Making of the Indo-Persian Culture: Indian and French Studies*, Delhi 2000
Alam, Muzaffar: *The Crisis of Empire in Mughal North India*, Delhi 1986
——: "Some Aspects of the Changes in the Position of the Madad Ma'ash Holders in Awadh, 1676–1722", in: S. Chandra (ed.): *Essays in Medieval Indian Economic History*, Delhi 1987, pp. 72–80
——: "Akhlaqui Norms in Mughal Governance" in: Alam et alii. (eds.): *The Making of the Indo-Persian Culture*
——: "Shariʿa and Governance in the Indo-Islamic Context", in: Gilmartin and Lawrence (eds.): *Beyond Turk and Hindu*, pp. 216–245

——: "The Culture and Politics of Persian in Precolonial Hindustan", in: Pollock (ed.): *Literary Cultures*, pp. 131–198

——: "The Pursuit of Persian: Language in Mughal Politics", in: *Modern Asian Studies* 32/2 (1989), pp. 317–349

——: *The Languages of Political Islam in India: 1200–1800*, New Delhi 2004

Alavi, Seema: *The Sepoys and the Company. Tradition and Transition in Northern India 1770–1830*, New Delhi 1995

Ali, A.K.M. Ayyub: *History of traditional Education in Bangladesh* (down to A.D. 1980), Dhaka 1983

Ali, M. Athar: *The Apparatus of Empire: Awards of Ranks, offices and Titles to the Mughal Nobility (1574–1658)*, Delhi 1985

——: *The Mughal Nobility under Aurangzeb*, Bombay 1970(2)

Ali, Meer Hasan: *Observations on the Musalmans of India, I–II*, London 1832

Ali, Rahmat: *Now or Never: Are we to Live or Perish For Ever?* Cambridge 1933

Anderson, Benedict: *Imagined Communities: Reflections on the Origin and Spread of Nationalism*, London 1983

Ansari, Sara F.D.: *Sufi Saints and State Power. The Pirs of Sind, 1843–1947*, Cambridge 1992

——: "Partition, migration and refugees: responses to the arrival of Muhajirs in Sind", in: *South Asia* 18 (1995), pp. 95–108

Appadurai, A.: "Number in the Colonial Imagination", in: Breckenridge et al. (eds.): *Orientalism*, pp. 314–340

Arnold, Thomas W.: *The Caliphate*, Oxford 1924

Asani, Ali S.: *Ecstasy and Enlightenment—The Ismaili Devotional Literature in South Asia*, London 2002

Asher, Catherine B. and Cynthia Talbot: *India before Europe*, Cambridge 2006

Asher, Catherine B.: *Architecture of Mughal India (The New Cambridge History of India, I:4)*, Cambridge 1992

Askari, S.H.: *Maktub & Malfuz Literature. As a Source of Socio-Political History*, Patna 1981

Assmann, Jan: *Das kulturelle Gedächtnis: Schrift, Erinnerung und politische Identität in frühen Hochkulturen*, München 1992

Ayalon, David: *The Mamluk military society*, London 1979

Azeez, A.M.A.: "Ceylon", in: EI(2), II, pp. 26b

Aziz, K.K.: *Rahmat Ali, a Biography*, Lahore 1987

——: *The Pakistani Historian*, Delhi 1994

Baladhuri, Ahmad b. Yahya ibn Jabir al-: *Kitab futuh al-buldan*, ed. M.J. de Goeje, Leiden 1866

Baljon, J.M.S: *Modern Muslim Koran Interpretation 1880–1960*, Leiden 1961

Baloch, N.A.: "Kandabil", in: *EI(2), IV*, pp. 534ff.

Barani, Ziya al-Din: *Fatawa-ye Jahandari*, ed. A. Salim Khan, Lahore 1972

Barnett, Richard B.: *North India Between Empires: Awadh, the Mughals, and the British, 1720–1801*, Berkeley 1980

Barth, Fredrik: *Political Leadership among Swat Pathans*, London 1959

Basu, Helene and Pnina Werbner (eds.): *Embodying Charisma: Modernity, Locality and the Performance of Emotion In Sufi Cults*, London 1998

Bayly, C.A.: "The Small Town and Islamic Gentry in North India: the Case of Kara", in: K. Ballhatchet and J. Harrison (eds.): *The City in South Asia*, London 1980, pp. 20–48

——: "Pre-colonial Indian Merchants and Rationality", in: Mushirul Hasan and Narayani Gupta (eds.): *Indian's Colonial Encounter*, Delhi 1993, pp. 3–24

——: "The Pre-history of 'Communalism'? Religious Conflict in India, 1700–1860", in: *Modern Asian Studies* 19/2 (1985), pp. 177–203

——: *Empire and Information. Intelligence gathering and social communication in India, 1780–1870*, Cambridge 1997
——: *Indian Society and the Making of the British Empire*, Delhi 1990 (reprint)
——: *Origins of Nationality in South Asia. Patriotism and Ethical Government in the Making of Modern India*, New Delhi 1998
——: *Rulers, Townsmen and Bazaars: North Indian Society in the Age of British Expansion, 1770–1870*, Cambridge 1983
Bayly, Susan: *Saints, Goddesses and Kings—Muslims and Christians in South Indian society 1700—1900*, Cambridge 1989
Bazmee Ansari, A.S.: "al-Fatâwa al-ʿAlamgîriyya", in: *EI(2), II*, pp. 836f.
——: "Daybûl", in: *EI(2), II*, pp. 188f.
——: "Djât", in: *EI(2), II*, pp. 488f.
Berkemer G., T. Frasch, H. Kulke, J. Lütt (eds.): *Explorations in the History of SOUTH ASIA. Essays in Honour of Dietmar Rothermund*, New Delhi 2001
Bhattacharya, Neeladri: "Myth, History and the Politics of Ramjanmabhoomi", in: Gopal (ed.): *Anatomy of a Confrontation*, pp. 122–140
Bilgrami, Ghulam ʿAli Azad: *Ma'athir al-Kiram*, Agrah 1910
——: *Subhat al-marjan fi athar Hindustan*, Urdu by Shams al-Din, Lucknow 1878
Bilgrami, Rafat M.: *Religious and Quasi-Religious Departments of the Mughal Period (1556–1707)*, New Delhi 1984
Binder, L.: *Religion and Politics in Pakistan*, Berkeley 1961
Biruni, al-: *Kitab fi al-Hind; Alberuni's India*, Engl. transl. and ed. by Ed. Sahan, Lisbon 1978 (repr.)
Bitterli, Urs: *Cultures in Conflict: Encounters Between European and Non-European Cultures, 1492–1800*, Stanford 1989
Bitterli, Urs: *Die "Wilden" und die "Zivilisierten"; Grundzüge einer Geistes- und Kulturgeschichte der europäischen-überseeischen Begegnung*, München 1976
Blake, Stephen P.: *Shahjahanabad. The Sovereign City in Mughal India 1639–1739*, Cambridge 1991
Bose, S. and A. Jalal (eds.): *Nationalism, Democracy and Development. State and Politics in India*, Delhi 1997
Bosworth, C.E.: "Ghaznawids", in: *EI(2), II*, p. 1050
——: "Muhammad b. Mahmûd", in: *EI(2), VII*, pp. 406f.
——: "Ucch", in: *EI(2), X*, p. 767
——: *The Ghaznavids*, Edinburgh 1964
——: *The later Ghaznavids*, Edinburgh 1977
Bourdieu, P. and Passeron, J.-C.: *Reproduction in education, Society and Culture*, transl. Richard Nice, London 1990
Bourdieu, Pierre: "The forms of capital" in: John G. Richardson (ed.): *Handbook of Theory and Research for the Sociology of Education*. Westport, CT 1986, pp. 242–258
Boyle, J.A.: "Čingiz-Khân", in: *EI(2), II*, pp. 41ff.
Brand, Michael and Lowry, Glenn D.: *Akbar and Fatehpur Sikri*, Bombay 1987
Brass, Paul: *Language, Religion and Politics*, Cambridge 1974
——: *The Production of Hindu-Muslim Violence in Contemporary India*, Seattle 2003
Braudel, Fernand: *Civilization and Capitalism. 15th–18th Century*, Vol. III, New York 1986
Brown, Daniel: *Rethinking tradition in modern Islamic thought*, Cambridge 1999
Bukhari, Muhammad ibn Ismaʿil al-: *al-Jamiʿa al-Sahih*, al-Riyad 1998
Bulliet, Richard W.: *The Patricians of Nishapur: A Study in Medieval Islamic Social History*, Cambridge 1972
Burki, S.J.: *Pakistan under Bhutto*, New York 1979
Burton-Page, J.: "Hind", in: *EI(2), III*, p. 415
——: "Karnatak", in: *EI(2), IV*, pp. 666f.

——: "Lôdîs", in: *EI(2), V*, pp. 782ff.
——: "Djawnpûr", in: *EI(2), II*, pp. 498f.
——: "Gudjarât", in: *EI(2), II*, pp. 1123ff.
Canfield, Robert L. (ed.): *Turco-Persia in Historical Perspective*, New York 1991
Chandra, Bipan: *Communalism in Modern India*, Delhi 1984
Chandra, Satish: "Jizya and the State in India during the Seventeenth Century", in: Eaton (ed.): *India's Islamic Traditions*, pp. 132–149
——: *Parties and Politics at the Mughal Court 1707–1740*, New Delhi 1972(2)
Chatterjee, Partha: *Nation and its Fragments. Colonial and Postcolonial Histories*, Princeton 1993
Chattopadhyaya, Brajadulal: *Representing the Other? Sanskrit Sources and The Muslims (Eighth to Fourteenth Century)*, New Delhi 1998
Chaudhuri, K.N.: *Trade and Civilization in the Indian Ocean, An Economic History from the Rise of Islam to 1750*, Cambridge 1985
Chiragh-e Dehli, Mahmud Nasir al-Din: *Khair al-majalis*, ed. and annotated by Khaliq Ahmad Nizami, 'Aligarh 1959
Chittick, William: "Notes on Ibn al-'Arabi's Influence in the Indian Sub-Continent", in: *Muslim World* 82 (1992), pp. 218–241
Cohn, B.S.: "Representing Authority in Victorian India", in: Ranger and Hobsbawm. (eds.): *The Invention of Tradition*, pp. 165–209
——: "The Command of Language and the Language of Command", in: R. Guha (ed.): *Subaltern Studies IV*, Delhi 1985, pp. 276ff.
Cole, J.R.: *Roots of North Indian Shi'ism in Iran and Iraq; Religion and State in Awadh, 1722–1859*, Berkeley 1988
Conermann, Stephan (ed.): *Die muslimische Sicht (13.–18. Jahrhundert). Geschichtsdenken der Kulturen*, Frankfurt/M. 2002
——: *Die Beschreibung Indiens in der "Rihla" des Ibn Battuta; Aspekte einer herrschaftssoziologischen Einordnung des Delhi-Sultanates unter Muhammad Ibn Tughluq*, Berlin 1993
Copley, Anthony: *Religions in Conflict. Ideology, Cultural Contact and Conversion in late-colonial India*, Delhi 1997
Coppola, Carlo (ed.): *Marxist Influences in South Asian Literature*, Vols. 1–2, Michigan 1974
Corbridge, Stuart and Harriss, John: *Reinventing India: Liberalization, Hindu Nationalism and Popular Democracy*, Cambridge 2000
Cowasjee, S. and Duggal, K.S. (eds.): *Orphans of the Storm: Stories on the Partition of India*, Delhi 1995
Currie, P.M.: *The Shrine and Cult of Mu'in al-din Chishti of Ajmer*, New Delhi 1989
Daftary, Farhad: *A Short History of the Isma'ilis. Traditions of a Muslim Community*, Edinburgh 1998
Dale, Stephen F.: *The Garden of the Eight Paradises. Babur and the Culture of Empire in Central Asia, Afghanistan and India, 1483–1527*, Leiden 2004
——: *The Mappillas of Malabar, 1498–1922: Islamic Society on the South Asian Frontier*, Oxford 1980
Dallapiccola, A.L. and Lallemant, S. Zingel-Avé (eds.): *Islam and Indian Regions*, Wiesbaden 1993
Dalmia, V., A. Malinar, M. Christof-Fuechsle (eds.): *Charisma and Canon: The formation of religious identity in South Asia: Festschrift for Professor Heinrich von Stietencron*, Delhi 2001
Dalmia, Vasudha: *The Nationalization of Hindu Traditions. Bharatendu Harishchandra and Nineteeth-Century Banaras*, New Delhi 1996
Dalrymple, William: *White Mughals. Love and Betrayal in 18th century India*, London 2002
Damrel, David W.: "The 'Naqshbandi Reaction' Reconsidered", in: Gilmartin and Lawrence (eds.): *Beyond Turk and Hindu*, pp. 176–198

Dani, A.H.: "Bangala", in: *EI(2), I*, p. 1014

Davis, Richard H.: *Lives of Indian Images*, Princeton 1997

Day, Upendra N.: *Medieval Malwa. A Political and Cultural History, 1401–1562*, Delhi 1965

Desai, Z.A. and Begley, W.E. (eds.): *The Shah Jahan Nama of 'Inayat Khan'*, New Delhi 1990

Desai, Z.A.: *Malfuz Literature: As a source of Political, Social, and Cultural History of Gujarat and Rajasthan*, Patna 1991

Dietrich, A.: "al-Hadjdjâdj", in: *EI(2), III*, pp. 39ff.

Digby, Simon: "Abd al-Haqq Gangohi (1456–1537 A.D.): The Personality and Attitudes of a Medieval Indian Sufi", in: *Medieval India—a Miscellany*, Vol. 3 (1975)

——: "The Sufi Shaikh as a source of authority in Medieval India", in: *Purusartha, Islam et Societe en Asie du Sud* 9 (1986), pp. 57–77

——: "The Sufi shaykh and the sultan: a conflict of claims to authority in Medieval India", in: *Iran* 28 (1990), pp. 71–81

Dirks, Nicholas B.: "Colonial Histories and Native Informants: Biography of an Archive", in: Breckenridge et al. (eds.): *Orientalism*, pp. 279–313

——: *Castes of Mind. Colonialism and the Making of Modern India*, Delhi 2002

Dittmer, K.: *Die indischen Muslims und die Hindi-Urdu-Kontroverse in den United Provinces*, Wiesbaden 1972

Donner, F.M.: *The Early Islamic Conquests*, Princeton 1981

Dostal, Walter: "Die Arber in vorislamischer Zeit", in: Noth and Paul (eds.): *Der islamische Orient*, pp. 25–44

Douglas, I.H.: *Abul Kalam Azad. An Intellectual and Religious Biography*, Delhi 1988

Dumont, Louis: *Homo hierarchicus. The Caste System and its Implications*, Transl.: Mark Sainsbury, Chicago 1970

Eaton, Richard M.: "Sufi Folk Literature and the Expansion of Indian Islam", in: *History of Religions* 14/2 (1974), pp. 117–127

—— (ed.): *India's Islamic Traditions, 711–1750*, Oxford 2003

——: *Sufis of Bijapur 1300–1700*, New Jersey 1978

——: *The Rise of Islam and the Bengal Frontier, 1204–1760*, Berkeley 1993

Edwards, Michael: *The Nabobs at Home*, London 1991

Ehlers, Eckart and Krafft, Thomas (eds.): *Shâhjahânâbâd/Old Delhi. Islamic Tradition and Colonial Change*, Stuttgart 1993, and New Delhi 2003

Eickelman, Dale and James Piscatori (eds.): *Muslim Travellers: Pilgrimage, Migration, and the Religious Imagination*, London 1990

——: *Muslim Politics*, Princeton 1996

Engineer, Asghar Ali: *Lifting the Veil: Communal Violence and Communal Harmony in Contemporary India*, Bombay 1995

Ernst, Carl W. and Bruce B. Lawrence: *Sufi Martyrs of Love: The Chishti Order in South Asia and Beyond*, Basingstoke 2002

Ernst, Carl W.: 'An Indo-Persian Guide to Sufi Shrine Pilgrimage', in: Smith and Ernst (eds.): *Manifestations of Sainthood*, pp. 43–67

——: "Muslim Studies of Hinduism? A Reconsideration of Persian and Arabic Translations from Sanskrit", in: *Iranian Studies* 36 (2003), pp. 173–195

——: "Persecution and Circumspection in Shattari Sufism", in: Fred De Jong and Berndt Radtke (eds.): *Islamic Mysticism Contested: Thirteen Centuries of Debate and Conflict*, Leiden 1999

——: *Eternal Garden: Mysticism, History and Politics at a South Asian Sufi Centre*, Albany 1992

——: "Ellora Temples as Viewed by Indo-Muslim Authors", in: Gilmartin and Lawrence (eds.): *Beyond Turk and Hindu*, pp. 98–120

Ewans M.: *Afghanistan: A new history*, London 2002

Ewing, K.: "The Politics of Sufism: Redefining the Saints of Pakistan", in: *Journal of Asian Studies* XLII/2 (1983), pp. 251–269

——: "*The Modern Businessman and the Pakistani Saint: The Interpenetration of Worlds*", in: Smith and Ernst (eds.): *Manifestations of Sainthood*, pp. 69–84

Farooqi, N.R.: *Mughul-Ottoman Relations*, Delhi 1989

Faruqi, Shamsur Rahman: "A Long History of Urdu Literary Culture, Part 1. Naming and Placing a Literary Culture", in: Pollock (ed.): *Literary Cultures in History*, pp. 805–863

——: "A Stranger in The City: The Poetics of *Sabk-e Hindi*", in: *The Annual of Urdu Studies* 19 (2004)

——: *Early Urdu. Literary Culture and History*, Delhi 2001

Faruqi, Ziya-ul-Hassan: *The Deoband School and the Demand for Pakistan*, Lahore 1963

Findly, Ellison Banks: *Nur Jahan: Empress of Mughal India*, New Delhi 2001

Fisch, Jörg: *Die europäische Expansion und das Völkerrecht*, Stuttgart 1984

Fisher, Michael H.: *A Clash of Cultures: Awadh. The British, and the Mughals*, New Delhi 1987

——: *Indirect Rule in India: Residents and the Residency System 1764–1857*, New Delhi 1991

Fleischer, Cornell H.: *Bureaucrat and Intellectual in the Ottoman Empire: The Historian Mustafa Ali (1541–1600)*, Princeton 1986

Flemming, Leslie A.: *Another Lonely Voice: The Life and Works of Saadat Hasan Manto*, Lahore 1985

Forbes, A.D.W.: "Maʿbar", in: *EI(2), V*, pp. 937f.

——: "Malabar", in: *EI(2), VI*, pp. 206f.

Fragner, Bert G.: *Die "Persophonie". Regionalität, Identität und Sprachkontakt in der Geschichte Asiens*, Halle & Berlin 1999

Franke, Heike: *Akbar und Ǧahangir. Untersuchungen zur politischen und religiösen Legitimation in Text und Bild*, Schenefeld 2005

Freitag, S.B.: *Collective Action and Community, Public Arenas and the Emergence of Communalism in North India*, Delhi 1990

Freitag, Ulrike and William G. Clarence-Smith (eds.): *Hadhrami Traders, Scholars and Statesmen in the Indian Ocean 1750s–1960s*, Leiden 1997

Frey, H.: *Der Indisch-Pakistanische Konflikt in den Jahren 1957–1968*, Wiesbaden 1978

Friedmann, Y. and D. Shulman: "Mêd", in: *EI(2), VI*, 967a

Friedman, Yohanan: *Prophecy Continuous: Aspects of' Ahmadi Religious Thought and Its Medieval Background*, Berkeley 1988

——: "A Contribution to the early History of Islam in India" in: M. Rosen-Ayalon (ed.): *Studies in Memory of Gaston Wiet*, Jerusalem 1977

——: "al-Mansura", in: *EI(2), VI*, pp. 439f.

——: "Islamic thought in relation to the Indian context", in: Marc Gaborieau (ed.): *Islam et Société en Asie du Sud*, Paris 1986, pp. 79–92

——: "Medieval Muslim Views of Indian religions", in: *Journal of the American Oriental Society* 95/2 (1975), pp. 214–221

——: "The Naqshbandis and Awrangzêb: a reconsideration", in: M. Gaborieau, A. Popovic, Th. Zarcone (eds.): *Naqshbandis; Historical Developments and Present Situation of a Muslim Mystical Order*, Istanbul 1990

——: "The Origins and Significance of the Chach Nama", in: *Islam in Asia, Vol. I: South Asia*, Jerusalem 1984, pp. 23–37

——: "The temple of Multan", in: *Israel Oriental Studies* 2 (1972), pp. 176–182

——: *Shaykh Ahmad Sirhindi. An Outline of His Thought and a Study of His Image in the Eyes of Posterity*, Montreal 1971

——: *Tolerance and Coercion in Islam*, Cambridge 2003

Frykenberg, Robert E. (ed.): *Delhi through the Ages. Essays in Urban History, Culture and Society*, Delhi 1986

Fusfeld, W.E.: "Communal Conflict in Delhi, 1803–1930", in: *The Indian Economic and Social History Review* 19 (1982), pp. 181–200

Fusfeld, W.E.: *The Shaping of Sufi Leadership in Delhi: The Naqshbandiyya Mujaddidiyya, 1750–1920*, Ph.D. dissertation, Pennsylvania 1981

Gaborieau, Marc: "A Nineteenth-Century Indian 'Wahhabi' Tract Against the Cult of Muslim Saints: *Al-Balagh al-Mubin*", in: Troll (ed.): *Muslim Shrines in India*

——: "Late Persian, Early Urdu: The Case of 'Wahhabi' Literature (1818–1857)", in: F.N. Delvoye (ed.): *Confluence of Cultures: French Contributions to Indo-Persian Studies*, New Delhi 1995, pp. 170–191

——: "Muslim Saints, Faquirs and Pilgrims in 1831 according to Garcin de Tassy", in: Malik (ed.): *Perspectives of Mutual Encounters*

——: *Traditional Pattern of Dominance among South Asian Muslims*, Paris: Centre National de la Recherche Scientifique 1979

Ghalib, Mirza Asadullah Khan: *Dastanbuy: A Diary of the Indian Revolt of 1857*, transl. and ed. by K.A. Faruqi, Delhi 1970

Ghose, Indira (ed.): *Memsahibs Abroad; Writings by Women Travellers in Nineteenth Century India*, Delhi 1998

Gilmartin, David and Bruce Lawrence (eds.): *Beyond Turk and Hindu: Rethinking Religious Identities in Islamicate South Asia*, New Delhi 2002

Gilmartin, David: "Partition, Pakistan, and South Asian History: In Search of a Narrative", in: *Journal of Asian Studies* 57, 4 (1998), pp. 1068–1095

——: "Religious Leadership and the Pakistan Movement in the Punjab", in: *Modern Asian Studies* 13/3 (1979), pp. 485–517

——: *Empire and Islam: Punjab and the Making of Pakistan*, Berkeley 1988

Golden, P.B.: *An Introduction to the History of the Turkic Peoples*, Wiesbaden 1992

Göle, Nilüfer: *The Forbidden Modern. Civilization and Veiling*, Michigan 1997

Golwalkar, M.S.: *We, or our nationhood defined*, Nagpur 1939

Gopal, S. (ed.): *Anatomy of a Confrontation*, New Delhi 1991

Gottlob, Michael (ed.): *Historical Thinking in South Asia. A Handbook of Sources from Colonial Times to the Present*, New Delhi 2003

Gran, Peter: *Islamic Roots of Capitalism: Egypt, 1760–1840*, Texas and London 1979

Green, Nile: "Geography, empire and sainthood in the eighteenth-century Muslim Deccan", in: *Bulletin of the School of Oriental and African Studies* 67/2 (2004), pp. 207–225

Grewal, J.S.: *The Sikhs of the Punjab*, Cambridge 1990

Guenther, Alan M.: "Hanafi Fiqh in Mughal India: The Fatawá-i ʿAlamgiri", in: Eaton (ed.): *India's Islamic Traditions*, pp. 209–230

Gupta, Raghuraj: "Changing Role and Status of the Muslim Minority in India: A Point of View", in: *Journal; Institute of Muslim Minority Affairs* 5/1 (1984)

Haar, J.G.J. ter: *Follower and heir of the Prophet. Shaykh Ahmad Sirhindi (1564–1624) as Mystic*, Leiden 1992

Habib, Irfan (ed.): *Medieval India 1. Researches in the History of India 1200–1750*, Delhi 1992

——: The *Agrarian System of Mughal India (1556–1707)*, Bombay 1963

Hai, S. Abdul: *India during Muslim Rule*, Lucknow 1977

Haig, T.W. and Riazul Islam: "Malwa", in: *EI(2), VI*, pp. 309f.

Halbfass, Wilhelm: *India and Europe. An Essay in Philosophical Understanding*, Delhi 1990

——: *Indien und Europa: Perspektiven ihrer geistigen Begegnung*, Basel/Stuttgart 1981

Hali, Altaf Husain: *Musaddas. The Flow and Ebb of Islam*, translated and with a critical introduction by Christopher Shackle and Javed Majeed, Delhi 1997

Hallaq, Wael B.: "Was the Gate of Ijtihad Closed?", in: *International Journal of Middle Eastern Studies* 16 (1984), pp. 3–41

Halm, Heinz: *Shiʿism*, transl. by Janet Watson, new Material translated by Marian Hill, New York 2004 (2)

——: *The empire of the Mahdi: The Rise of the Fatimids*, Translated from German by Michael Bonner, Leiden 1996

Hamawi, Yaqut al-: *Mu'jam al-buldan*, Vol. 1, ed. Ferdinand Wüstenfeld, Leipzig 1866

Hamilton, Charles (transl.): *Hedaya, or Guide; A Commentary on the Musalman Laws, 4 Vols.*, London 1791

Hansen, Thomas B.: *The Saffron Wave. Democracy and Hindu Nationalism in Modern India*, New Delhi 1999

Haq, S. Moinul: "The Story of the War of Independence (being an English translation of Allamah Fadl-i-Haqq's Risalah on the War", in: *Journal of Pakistan Historical Society* V/1 (1957), pp. 23–57

——: "Rise of the Naqshbandi and Qadiri Silsilahs in the Subcontinent", in: *Journal of Pakistan Historical Society* XXV (1977), pp. 1–33

Haqq, 'Abd al-: *Marhum Dihli College*, Delhi 1989 (reprint)

Hardy, Peter in: A.T. Embree (ed.): *Sources of Indian Tradition*

Hardy, Peter: "Abu'l Fazl's Portrait of the Perfect Padshah: a political Philosophy for Mughal India—or a personal puff for a pale", in: Troll (ed.): *Islam in India*

——: "Modern Muslim and European Explanations of Conversion to Islam in South Asia: A Preliminary Survey of the Literature", in: N. Levtzion (ed.): *Conversion to Islam*, New York 1979, pp. 68–99

——: "Is the Chach Nama Intelligible as Political Theory?," in: Hamida Khuro (ed.): *Sind Through the Centuries*, Oxford 1982, pp. 111–117

——: "Islamischer Patrimonialimus: Die Moghulherrschaft", in: Wolfgang Schluchter (ed.): *Max Webers Sicht des Islam*, Frankfurt a.M. 1987, pp. 190–216

——: "The Growth of Authority over a Conquered Political Elite: The Early Delhi Sultanate as a Possible Case Study," in: Richards (ed.): *Kingship and Authority*

——: *Historians of Medieval India, Studies in Muslim-Historical Writing*, London 1960

——: *Partners in Freedom and true Muslims. Political Thought of some Muslim Scholars in British India 1912–1947*, Lund 1971

——: *The Muslims of British India*, Cambridge 1972

Hartung, Jan-Peter: "The Land, the Mosque, the Temple. More than 145 Years of Dispute over Ayodhya", in: Richard Bonney (ed.): *Ayodhya 1992–2003. The Assertion of Cultural and Religious Hegemony*, Leicester 2003, pp. 31–44

——: *Viele Wege und ein Ziel. Leben und Wirken von Sayyid Abu l-Hasan 'Ali al-Hasani Nadwi (1914–1999)*, Würzburg 2004

Hasan, Mohibbul: "Kashmir", in: *EI(2), IV*, pp. 706f.

Hasan, Mushirul (ed.): *Communal and Pan-Islamic Trends in Colonial India*, Delhi 1985

—— (ed.): *Inventing Boundaries: Gender, Politics and the Partition of India*, Delhi 2000

Hasan, Mushirul and Margrit Pernau (eds.): *Regionalizing Pan-Islamism. Documents on the Khilafat Movement*, Delhi 2005

Hasan, Mushirul: "Sectarianism in Indian Islam: The Shia-Sunni divide in the United Provinces", in: *The Indian Economic and Social History Review* 27/2 (1990), pp. 209–228

——: "The Communal Divide: A Study of the Delhi Proposals", in: Hasan (ed.): *Communal and Pan-Islamic Trends*, pp. 281ff.

——: *A Nationalist Conscience: M.A. Ansari, the Congress and the Raj*, Delhi 1987

——: *From Pluralism to Separatism. Qasbas in Colonial Awadh*, New Delhi 2004

——: *Legacy of a Divided Nation; India's Muslims Since Independence*, Delhi 1997

——: *Nationalism and Communal Politics in India, 1885–1930*, Delhi 1991

Hasan, Zoya (ed.): *Forging Identities. Gender, Communities and the State*, Delhi 1994

Hayy, Sayyid 'Abd al-: *Al-Thaqafa al-Islamiyya fi al-Hind*, Dimashq 1958

——: *Nuzhat al-khawatir wa bahjat al-masami' wa al-Nawazir, I–VIII*, ed. S. Abu al-Hasan 'Ali al-Hasani al-Nadwi, Haydarabad/Deccan, 1956ff.

Hermansen, Marcia: *The Conclusive Argument from God. Shah Wali Allah of Delhi's Hujjat Allah al-Baligha*, Leiden 1996

Hodgson, Marshall: *Venture of Islam. Conscience and History in a World Civilization*, Vols. 1–3, Chicago 1975

Hoexter, M., Sh. N. Eisenstadt, N. Levtzion (eds.): *The Public Sphere in Muslim Societies*, New York 2002

Hollister, J.N.: *The Shi'a of India*, London 1953

Hujwiri, 'Ali Ibn 'Uthman al-Jullabi al-: *Kashf al-Mahjub. The oldest Persian Treatise on Sufiism*, transl. by R.A. Nicholson, Lahore 1953

Humphreys, R. Stephen: *Islamic History. A Framework for Inquiry*, London 1991 (revised Ed.)

Ikram, Shaikh Muhammad: *Ab-e kawthar*, Lahore 1984(10)

——: *Mawj-e kawthar*, Lahore 1984(12)

——: *Rawd-e kawthar*, Lahore 1984(9)

Imam, Zafar (ed.): *The Musalmaans of the Subcontinent*, Lahore 1980

Inalcik, Halil: *The Ottoman Empire; the classical age 1300–1600*, New York 1973

Inden, Ronald: "Orientalist Constructions of India," in: *Modern Asian Studies* 20 (1986), pp. 401–46

——: *Imagining India*, London 1990

International Crisis Group, Asia Report N° 95, 18 April 2005: http://www.crisisgroup.org/library/documents/asia/south_asia/095_the_state_of_sectarianism_in_pakistan.pdf (accessed 19 April 2005)

Iqbal, Afzal: *Islamization in Pakistan*, Lahore: Vanguard Books 1986

Iqbal, Muhammad: 'Presidential Address', in: *Speeches and Statements of Iqbal*, Lahore: Al-Manar Academy 1948(2), pp. 3–36

——: *Shikwa & Jawab-i-Shikwa; Complaint and Answer; Iqbal's Dialogue with Allah*, transl. with intro. by Khushwant Singh, Delhi 1992(2)

Ishaque, K.M.: "Role of history in the growth of national consciousness", *Journal of the Pakistan Historical Society* 17 (1969), pp. 25–39

Iskandar, Kai Kaus ibn: *Qabus Nama* (A Mirror for Princes), transl. Reuben Levy, New York 1951

Islam, Riazul: *Sufism in South Asia. Impact on Fourteenth Century Muslim Society*, New Delhi 2003

Islam, Zafarul: "Origin and Development of *Fatawa*-Compilation in Medieval India", in: *Hamdard Islamicus* XX/1 (1997), pp. 7–18

Ismail, Shah Muhammad: *Support of Faith*, transl. by Mir Shahamat Ali, Lahore 1969

Jackson, Paul (transl.): *Letters from Maneri; Sufi Saint of Medieval India*, New Delhi 1990

Jackson, Peter: *The Delhi Sultanate. A Political and Military History*, Cambridge 1999

Jaffrelot, Chr.: "The BJP in Madhya Pradesh: Networks, Strategies and Power", in: Pandey (ed.): *Hindus and Others*, pp. 110–137

Jahan, R.: *Pakistan: Failure in National Integration*, New York 1972

Jalal, Ayesha: "The Convenience of Subservience: Women and the State of Pakistan", in: D. Kandiyoti (ed.): *Women, Islam and the State*, London 1991, pp. 77–114

——: *The Sole Spokesman; Jinnah, the Muslim League and the Demand for Pakistan*, Cambridge 1985

Jehlumi, Muhammad: *Hada'iq al-Hanafiyyah*, Lucknow 1906

Johansen, Baber: *Contingency in a Sacred Law: Legal and Ethical Norms in the Muslim Fiqh*, Leiden 1999

Jones, K.W.: *Socio-Religious Reform Movements in British India (The New Cambridge History of India)*, Cambridge 1989

Jordens, J.T.F.: "Reconversion to Hinduism: The Shuddhi of the Arya Samaj", in: G.A. Oddie (ed.): *Religion in South Asia*, pp. 215–230

Joshi, Sanjay: *Fractured Modernity. Making of a Middle Class in North India*, Delhi 2001

Juergensmeyer, Mark: *Religious Nationalism Confronts the National State*, Delhi 1996
Juneja, Monica (ed.): *Architecture in Medieval India. Forms, Contexts, Histories*, New Delhi 2001, pp. 1–105
——: "On the Margins of Utopia—One more look at Mughal Painting", in: *The Medieval History Journal* 4/2 (2001), pp. 203–240
Juynboll, G.H.A.: *Muslim Tradition: Studies in Chronology, provenance and authorship of early hadith*, Cambridge 1983
Kabir, B.M. Monoar: "The Politics of Religion: The Jamaat-i-Islami in Bangladesh", in: Ahmed (ed.): *Religion, Nationalism and Politics in Bangladesh*, pp. 118–136
Kabir, M.G.: "Religion, Language and Politics in Bangladesh", in: Ahmed (ed.): *Religion, Nationalism and Politics in Bangladesh*, pp. 35–49
Kakar, Sudhir: *The Colours of Violence*, New Delhi 1995
Kaul, S. (ed.): *The Partitions of Memory: The Afterlife of the Division of India*, Delhi 2001
Kaur, Kuldip: *Madrasa Education in India; a study of its past and present*, Chandigarh: Centre for Rural and Industrial Development 1990
Keddie, Nikki R.: *An Islamic Response to Imperialism: Political and Religious Writing of Sayyid Jamal al-Din "al-Afghani"*, Berkeley 1968
——: *Sayyid Jamal ad-Din 'al Afghani'; a political biography*, Berkeley 1972
Kepel, Gilles: *Jihad. Expansion et decline de l'Islamisme*, Paris 2000
Khaldun, Ibn: *The Muqaddimah. An introduction to History*, translated by F. Rosenthal, in three volumes, London 1967(2)
Khalfaoui, Moez: *Le pluralisme et l'anti-pluralism en Asie du sud au XIIe siècle. Le Cas d'al-Fatawa al-Hindiyya al-'Alamjīriyya*, Erfurt (Ph.D. Islamic Studies) 2007
Khan, A.U., Saqib, M. and Anjum, Zafar H.: *To Kill the Mockingbird. Madarsah* (sic!) *System in India: Past, Present, and Future*, http://www.indiachinacentre.org/bazaarchintan/pdfs/madarsas.pdf (accessed 20 Feb. 2004)
Khan, Dominique Sila: *Crossing the Threshold: Understanding Religious Identities in South Asia*, London 2004
——: *Conversions and Shifting Identities. Ramdev Pir and the Ismailis in Rajasthan*, Manohar 1997
Khan, M.D.: *Fara'idi Movement*, Karachi 1965
Khan, M.I.: "The Impact of Islam on Kashmir in the Sultanate Period (1320–1586)", in: *The Indian Economic and Social History Review* 23 (1986), pp. 187–205
——: *Kashmir's Transition to Islam—The Role of Muslim Rishis*, New Delhi 1994
Khan, N.A.: *A History of Urdu Journalism*, Delhi 1991
Khan, S. Ahmad: *Athar al-Sanadid*, vols. I–III, ed. by Khaliq Anjum, Dilli 1990
Khan, Shah Nawaz: *Ma'athir al-umara', I–III*, Engl. translation by H. Beveridge, Delhi: Mehra Offset Press 1979(2)
Khan, Yasmin: "Asking New Questions about Partition of the Indian Subcontinent", in: *History Compass*, http://www.history-compass.com/popups/print.asp?items=7554 (accessed 25 April 2005)
King, A.D.: *Colonial urban development: culture, social power and environment*, Boston/London 1976
King, Christopher R.: *One Language Two Scripts: The Hindi Movement in Nineteenth Century North India*, Bombay 1994
King, Richard: *Orientalism and Religion: Postcolonial Theory, India, and 'The Mystic East'*, London 1999
Knysh, Alexander D.: *Islamic Mysticism: A Short History*, Leiden 2000
Kolff, D.D.A.: "A Warlord's Fresh Attempt at Empire", in: M. Alam and S. Subrahmanyam (eds.): *The Mughal State*, pp. 75–114
Kopf, David: *The British Orientalism and the Bengal Renaissance*, Calcutta 1969

Kozlowski, Gregory C.: "Imperial Authority, Benefactions and Endowments (Awqaf) in Mughal India", in: *International Journal of Middle Eastern Studies* 38 (1995), pp. 355–370

——: *Muslim endowments and society in British India*, Cambridge 1985

Krishna, Gopal: "Piety and Politics in Indian Islam", in: T.N. Madan (ed.): *Muslim communities in South Asia*

Kulke, Hermann and Dietmar Rothermund: *A History of India*, New York 1990(2)

Kumar, Sunil: "Assertions of Authority: A Study of the Discursive Statements of Two Sultans of Delhi", in: M. Alam et alii. (eds.): *The Making of Indo-Persian Culture*, pp. 37–65

——: *The emergence of the Delhi Sultanate, 588–685/1192–1286*, unpublished Ph.D., Duke University 1992

Lal, Ruby: "Historicizing the Harem: The Challenge of a Princess's Memoir", in: *Feminist Studies* 30 (2004), pp. 590–616

——: "Mughal India: 15th to Mid-18th Century", in: *Encyclopedia of Women in Islamic Cultures*, Leiden 2003, pp. 64–69

Lalji: *Mir'at al-Auda'* (Pers. mss in A.M.U. Library; Tarikh No. 60)

Lapidus, Ira M.: "Muslim Cities as Plural Societies: The Politics of Intermediary Bodies", in: Takeshi Yukawa (ed.): *Proceedings of the International Conference on Urbanism in Islam*, I, Tokyo 1989, pp. 134–163

Lawrence, Bruce B. (trans. and ed.): *Nizam al-din Awliya: Morals for the Heart*, New York 1992

——: "Early Indo-Muslim Saints and Conversion", in: Y. Friedman (ed.): *Islam in Asia, Vol. I, South Asia*, Boulder 1984, pp. 109–145

——: "Islam. South Asian", in: Esposito et al. (eds.): *The Oxford Encyclopedia of the Modern Islamic World*, Vol. II

——: *Defenders of God. The Fundamentalist Revolt against the Modern Age*, University of South Carolina 1995

Lelyveld, David: "The fate of Hindustani: Colonial Knowledge and the Project of a National Language", in: Breckenridge et al. (eds.): *Orientalism*, pp. 189–214

——: *Aligarh's first Generation*, Princeton 1978

Leonard, Karen: "The 'Great Firm' Theory of the Decline of the Mughal Empire", in: *Comparative Studies in Society and History* 21/2 (1979), pp. 161–167

——: "Hyderabad: The Mulki-Non-Mulki Conflict", in: V.K. Bawa: *The Last Nizam*, New Delhi 1992, pp. 54–62

Lokhandwalla, S.T. (ed.): *India and Contemporary Islam*, Simla 1971

Ludden, David: "Orientalist Empiricism: Transformations of Colonial Knowledge", in: Breckenridge et al. (eds.): *Orientalism*, pp. 250–276

——: *An Agrarian History of South Asia*, Cambridge 1999

MacLean, D.N.: *Religion and Society in Arab Sind*, Leiden 1989

——: "Real Men and false Men at the Court of Akbar. The Majalis of Shaykh Mustafa Gujarati", in: Gilmartin and Lawrence (eds.): *Beyond Turk and Hindu*

——: "The Sociology of Political Engagement: The Mahdawiyah and the State", in: Eaton (ed.): *India's Islamic Traditions*, pp. 150–166

Madan, T.N. (ed.): *Muslim Communities of South Asia*, New Delhi 2001(3)

——: "Religious Ideology in a Plural Society: The Muslims and Hindus of Kashmir", in: *Contribution to Indian Sociology* 6 (1972), pp. 106–41

Madani, Maulana Hussain Ahmad: *Composite Nationalism and Islam*, transl. from Urdu into English by Mohammad Anwer Hussain and Hasan Imam, Delhi 2005

Mahmood, Tahir: "The Dargah of Sayyid Salar Mas'ud in Bahraich: Legend, Tradition and Reality", in: Troll (ed.): *Muslim Shrines in India*, pp. 24–43

Majeed, Javed: *Ungoverned Imaginings: James Mill's* The History of British India *and Orientalism*, Oxford 1992

Makdisi, George: *The Rise of Colleges. Institutions of Learning in Islam and the West*, Edinburgh 1981
Malieckal, Bindu: "Muslims, Matriliny, and *A Midsummer Night's Dream*: European Encounters with the Mappilas of Malabar, India", in: *The Muslim World* 95/2 (2005), pp. 297–316
Malik, Jamal (ed.): *Madrasas in South Asia. Teaching Terror?* London 2008
—— (ed.): *Perspectives of Mutual Encounters in South Asian History, 1760–1860*, Leiden 1997
Malik, Jamal and John Hinnells (eds.): *Sufism in the West*, London 2006
Malik, Jamal and Helmut Reifeld (eds.): *Religious Pluralism in South Asia and Europe*, New Delhi 2004
Malik, Jamal: "Islamic Institutions and Infrastructure in Shahjahanabad", in: Ehlers and Krafft (eds.): *Shahjahanabad*
——: "Letters, prison sketches and autobiographical literature: The case of Fadl-e-Haqq Khairabadi in the Andaman Penal Colony", in: *The Indian Economic and Social History Review* 43, 1 (2006), pp. 77–100
——: "Muslim Culture and Reform in 18th Century South Asia", in: *Journal of the Royal Asiatic Society* 13/2 (2003), pp. 227–243
——: *Colonialization of Islam. Dissolution of Traditional Institutions in Pakistan*, New Delhi 1996
——: *Islamische Gelehrtenkultur in Nordindien. Entwicklungsgeschichte und Tendenzen am Beispiel von Lucknow*, Leiden 1997
Mamdani, Mahmood: *Good Muslim, Bad Muslim. Islam, the USA, and the Global War Against Terror*, New Delhi 2004
Manto, S.H.: *Kingdom's End and other Short Stories*, transl. by Khalid Hasan, London 1989
Marshall, P.J. (ed.): *The Eighteenth Century in Indian History: Evolution or Revolution?* New Delhi 2003
Marty, Martin E. and R. Scott Appleby (eds.): *Accounting for Fundamentalisms. The Dynamic Character of Movements*, Chicago 1994
—— (eds.): *Fundamentalism Observed*, Chicago 1991
Masud, Muhammad Khalid (ed.): *Travellers in Faith. Studies of the Tablighi Jama'at as a Transnational Islamic Movement for Faith Renewal*, Leiden 2000
——: "The World of Shah 'Abd al-'Aziz (1746–1824)", in: Malik (ed.): *Perspectives of mutual encounters*
——: "Religious Identity and Mass Education", in: J. Meuleman (ed.): *Islam in the Era of Globalization*
——: *Fatawa Alamgiri*: Mughal Patronage of Islamic law (Draft paper for discussion)
Matthews, D.J. and Chr. Shackle, Sh. Husain (eds.): *Urdu Literature*, London 1985
Matthews, D.J. and Chr. Shackle (eds.): *An Anthology of Classical Urdu Love Lyrics, text and translations*, London 1972
Maududi, A.A.: *The Islamic Law and Constitution*, Lahore 1969 [1955]
Maududi, Syed Abul-Ala: *Four Basic Quranic Terms*, Engl. transl. by Abu Asad, Lahore 1996 (4)
Mayaram, Shail: "Rethinking Meo Identity: Cultural Faultlines, Syncretism, Hybridity or Liminality?" in: Mushirul Hasan (ed.): *Islam, Communities and the Nation. Muslim Identities in South Asia and Beyond*, Delhi 1998, pp. 283–307
McCrindle, John W. (transl. and ed.): *Ancient India as Described by Megasthenes and Arrian*, Calcutta and Bombay 1877
Memon, M.U.: "Partition Literature: A Study of Intizār Husain", in: *Modern Asian Studies* 14 (1980), pp. 377–410
Memon, M.U.: "Pakistani Urdu Creative Writing on National Disintegration: The Case of Bangladesh", in: *Journal of Asian Studies* 43 (1983/84), pp. 105–127

Memon, Moojan: *An Introduction to Shi'i Islam. The History and Doctrines of Twelver Shi'ism*, New Haven 1985
Menon, R. and K. Bhasin (eds.): *Borders and Boundaries*, New Delhi 1998
Metcalf B.D. and Th.R. Metcalf: *A Concise History of India*, Cambridge 2002
Metcalf, B.D. (ed.): *Moral Conduct and Authority: The Place of Adab*, Berkeley 1984
——: "Living Hadith in Tablighi Jama'at", in: *Journal of Asian Studies* 52 (1993), pp. 584–608
——: *Islamic Revival in British India: Deoband 1860–1900*, Princeton 1982
——: *Perfecting Women: Maulana Ashraf 'Ali Thanawi's Bihishti Zewar*, Berkeley 1990
Metcalf, Th.R.: *The Aftermath of Revolt: India, 1857–70*, Princeton 1965
Meuleman, Johan (ed.): *Islam in the Era of Globalization*, London 2002
Mian, Syed Mohammad: *The Prisoners of Malta*, transl. from Urdu into English by Mohammad Anwer Hussain and Imam Manak, Delhi 2004
Michell, George and Richard Eaton: *Firuzabad: Palace City of the Deccan*, Oxford 1992
Michell, George and S. Shah (eds.): *Ahmadabad*, Bombay 1988
Miller, Roland E.: *Mappila Muslims of Kerala: A Study in Islamic Trends*, Madras: Orient Longman 1992
Minault, Gail and David Lelyveld: "The campaign for a Muslim University, 1898—1920", in: *Modern Asian Studies* 8 (1974), pp. 145–188
Minault, Gail: "Urdu Political poetry during the Khilafat Movement," in: *Modern Asian Studies* 8 (1974), pp. 459–71
——: *Secluded Scholars. Women's Education and Muslim Social Reform in Colonial India*, Delhi 1998
——: *The Khilafat-Movement: Religious Symbolism and Political Mobilization in India*, New York 1982
——: "Other Voices, Other Rooms. The View from the Zenana', in: Nita Kumar (ed.): *Women as Subjects. South Asian Histories*, Calcutta, Stree, 1994, pp. 108–125
Misra, Salil: "Transition from the Syncretic to the Plural. The World of Hindi and Urdu", in: Malik and Reifeld (eds.): *Religious Pluralism*, pp. 268–298
Mitchell, Timothy: *Colonising Egypt*, Cambridge 1988
Miyan, Sayyid Muhammad: *'Ulama-ye Haqq awr un ke mujahidanah Karname*, Delhi 1975
Mojtaba'i, Fath Allah: "Dabistan-i Madaheb," in: *Encyclopaedia Iranica*, VI, pp. 532–534
Monzavi, Ahmad (compl.): *A comprehensive catalogue of Persian Manuscripts in Pakistan*, Islamabad 1983
Mubarikpuri, Qadi Athar: *Islami Hind ki 'azmat-e raftah*, Dehli 1969
Mukherjee, R.: *Awadh in Revolt, 1857–1858. A study in popular resistance*, Delhi 1984
Mukhia, Harbans: *The Mughals of India*, Pondicherry 2004
Muslim, Ibn al-Hajjaj al-Qushairi: *Sahih Muslim*, Bairut 1955
Nadwi, Abul Hasan Ali: *Appreciation and Interpretation of Religion in the Modern Age*. Lucknow 1982
Naim, C.M.: "Poet-audience interaction at Urdu musha'iras", in: C. Shackle (ed.): *Urdu and Muslim South Asia; Studies in the honour of Ralph Russell*, London 1989, pp. 167–173
Nandy, Ashis: "The Politics of Secularism and the Recovery of Religious Tolerance," in: Veena Das (ed.): *Mirrors of Violence: Communities, Riots and Survivors in South Asia*, Delhi 1990, pp. 69–93
Narayanan, Vasudha: "Religious Vocabulary and Regional Identity: A Study of the Tamil *Cirappuranam* (Life of the Prophet')", in: Eaton (ed.): *India's Islamic Traditions*, pp. 393–410
Nasa'i, Abu 'Abd al-Rahman Ahmad al-: *al-Sunan al-Sughra*, Cairo n.d.

Nasr, S.H.: "The Traditional Texts Used in the Persian Madrasahs", in: S.H. Nasr: *Traditional Islam in the Modern World*, London 1987

Nasr, Seyyed Vali Reeza: "The Rise of Sunni Militancy in Pakistan: The Changing Role of Islamism and the Ulama in Society and Politics", in: *Modern Asian Studies* 34 (2000), pp. 139–180

——: *Mawdudi and the Making of Islamic Revivalism*, New York 1996

——: *The Vanguard of Islamic Revolution: The Jama'at-i Islami of Pakistan*, London 1994

Newman, Andrew J.: "The nature of the Akhbari/Usuli dispute in late Safawid Iran. Part 1 and 2", in: *Bulletin of the School of Oriental and African Studies* LV (1992), pp. 22ff and pp. 250ff.

Nielsen, J.: *Muslims in Western Europe*, Edinburgh 1992

Nizami, K.A.: *Religion and Politics in India during the 13th century*, Delhi 2002

——: *Secular Tradition at AMU*, Aligarh 1992

——: *Some Aspects of Religion and Politics in India During the Thirteenth Century*, New Delhi 1961

Noth, Albrecht and Jürgen Paul (eds.): *Der islamische Orient—Grundzüge seiner Geschichte*, Würzburg 1998

Noth, Albrecht: "Früher Islam", in: Ulrich Haarmann (ed.): *Geschichte der arabischen Welt*, München 1991, pp. 11–100

——: "Von der medinensischen 'Umma' zu einer muslimischen Ökumene", in: Noth and Paul (eds.): *Der islamische Orient*, pp. 81ff.

——: *The Early Arabic Historical Tradition. A source-critical study. (Studies in Late Antiquity and Islam 3)* 2nd. ed. in collaboration with Lawrence I. Conrad., Transl. from the German by Michael Bonner, Princeton 1994

Nu'mani, 'Abd al-Hamid: *Maslah-ye kufw aur isha'at-e Islam*, New Delhi 2002

Nu'mani, Shibli: *Omar the Great*, Lahore 1981 (written in Urdu in 1898)

Oddie, G.A. (ed.): *Religion in South Asia—Religious Conversion and Revival Movements in South Asia in Medieval and Modern Times*, Delhi 1991

O'Fahey, R.S. and B. Radtke: "Neo-Sufism Reconsidered", in: *Der Islam* 70 (1993), pp. 52–87

Oldenburg, V.T.: "Lifestyle as Resistance: The Case of the Courtesans of Lucknow", in: D. Haynes and G. Prakash (eds.): *Contesting Power: Resistance and Everyday Social Relations in South Asia*, Delhi 1991, pp. 23–61

——: *The making of colonial Lucknow, 1857–1877*, Princeton 1984

Osterhammel, Jürgen: *Die Entzauberung Asiens. Europa und die asiatischen Reiche*, München 1998

Pandey, G. (ed.): *Hindus and Others; The question of identity in India today*, New Delhi Viking 1993

——: *The Construction of Communalism in Colonial India*, Delhi 1990

Panikkar, K.N.: *Against Lord and State: Religion and Peasant Uprisings in Malabar, 1836–1921*, Delhi 1989

Paul, Jürgen: "Hagiographische Texte als historische Quelle", in: *Saeculum* 41/1 (1990), pp. 17–43

Pearson, H.O.: *Islamic Reform and Revival in the Nineteenth Century India: The 'Tariqah-i Muhammadiyah'*, Ph.D., Duke University 1979 (unpublished)

Pearson, M.N.: "Shivaji and the Decline of the Mughal Empire", in: *Journal of Asian Studies* 35 (1976), pp. 221–235

Pedersen, J. and Makdisi, G.: "Madrasa", in: *EI(2), V*, pp. 1123ff.

Pernau, Margit: *Bürger im Turban. Muslime in Delhi im 19. Jahrhundert*, Göttingen 2008

—— (ed.): *The Delhi College. Traditional Elites, the Colonial State, and Education before 1857*, Delhi 2006

——: "Introduction", in: C.F. Andrews: *Zaka Ullah of Delhi*, reprint with introductions by Mushirul Hasan and Margrit Pernau, Delhi 2003, pp. xlvii–lxxv

——: *The Passing of Partimonialism: Politics and Political Culture in Hyderabad 1911–1948*, New Delhi 2000

——: *Verfassung und politische Kultur im Wandel. Der indische Fürstenstaat Hyderabad 1911–48*, Stuttgart 1992

Peters, Rudolph: "Idjtihad and Taqlid in 18th and 19th Century Islam", in: *Die Welt des Islams* 20 (1980), pp. 131–145

——: *Islam and Colonialism: The Doctrin of Jihad in Modern History*, The Hague 1979

Petievich, Carla: "*Rekhti.* Impersonating the Feminine in Urdu Poetry", in: *South Asia. The Journal of South Asian Studies*, Special Issue, XXIV (2001), pp. 75–90

——: *Assembly of Rivals. Delhi, Lucknow and the Urdu Ghazal*, New Delhi 1992

Petruccioli, Attillio: "The Geometry of Power: The City's Planning", in: Michael Brand and Glenn D. Lowry (eds.): *Akbar and Fatehpur Sikri*, Bombay 1987, pp. 49–64

Philips C.H. (ed.): *Historians of India, Pakistan and Ceylon*, London 1961

—— (ed.): *Select Documents on the History of India and Pakistan, 1858–1947*, vol. 4, London 1972

Pinault, David: *The Shi'ites. Ritual and Popular Piety in a Muslim Community*, New York 1993

Pollock, Sheldon (ed.): *Literary Cultures in History. Reconstructions from South Asia*, New Delhi 2004

——: "Deep Orientalism? Notes on Sanskrit and Power Beyond the Raj", in Breckenridge et al. (eds.): *Orientalism*, pp. 76–133

——: "India in the Vernacular Millennium", in: *Daedalus* 127(3) 1998, pp. 41–74

Popp, Stephan: *Muhammad Iqbal's Romanticism of Power. A Post-Structural Approach to His Persian Lyrical Poetry*, Wiesbaden 2004

Powell, A.A.: *Muslims and Missionaries in Pre-Mutiny India*, London 1993

Preckel, Claudia: *Begums of Bhopal*, New Delhi 2000

——: *Islamische Bildungsnetzwerke und Gelehrtenkultur im Indien des 19. Jahrhunderts: Muhammad Siddiq Hasan Khan (st. 1890) und die Entstehung der Ahl-e hadit Bewegung*, Bochum/Erfurt (Ph.D. Islamic Studies) 2005

Pritchett, Frances W.: "A Long History of Urdu Literary Culture, Part 2. Histories, Performances and Masters", in: Pollock (ed.): *Literary Cultures in History*, pp. 864–911

Qadiri, Muhammad Ayyub: *Hindustan men muslim fi rqah wariyat*, Karachi 1982

——: *Urdu Nathr ke irteqa' men 'ulama' ka hissah*, Lahore 1988

Qureshi, I.H.: *Ulama in Politics*, Karachi 1974

Qureshi, Ishtiaq Husain: *The Administration of the Sultanate of Dehli*, Karachi 1958(4)

Qureshi, Naeem M.: *Pan-Islam in British Indian Politics. A Study of the Khilafat Movement 1918–1924*, Leiden 1999

Qureshi, Saleem: 'The Politics of the Shia Minority in Pakistan: Context and Development', in: Dh. Vajpeyi and Y.K. Malik (eds.): *Religious and Ethnic Minority Politics in South Asia*, Delhi 1989, pp. 109–138

Rahim, Enayetur: "Bengali Muslims and Islamic Fundamentalism: The Jama'at-i-Islami in Bangladesh", in: Rafiuddin Ahmed (ed.): *Understanding the Bengal Muslims*, Dhaka 2001

Rai, Amrit: *A House Divided. The Origin and Development of Hindi/Hindavi*, Delhi 1984

Rai, Mridu: *Hindu Rulers, Muslim Subjects: Islam, Rights, and the History of Kashmir*, Princeton 2004

Ranger, T. and E.J. Hobsbawm (eds.): *The Invention of Tradition*, Cambridge 1983

Rao, Velcheru Narayan; David Shulman, Sanjay Subrahmanyam: *Textures of Time. Writing History in South India 1600–1800*, New Delhi 2001

Ray, Rajat Kanta: *The Felt Community. Commonality and Mentality before the Emergence of Indian Nationalism*, Delhi 2003

Reetz, Dietrich: *Islam in the public sphere: Religious Groups in India (1900–1947)*, Delhi 2006

Richards, J.: "The Formulation of Imperial Authority under Akbar and Jahangir", in: Troll (ed.): *Islam in India*
Richards, J.F. (ed.): *Kingship and Authority in South Asia*, Madison 1978
——: "Norms of Comportment among Imperial Mughal Officers", in: B. Metcalf (ed.): *Moral conduct and authority*, pp. 255–289
——: "The Islamic frontier in the east: expansion into South Asia", in: *South Asia* 4 (1974), pp. 94ff.
——: *Mughal Administration in Golconda*, Oxford 1975
——: *The Mughal Empire*, Cambridge 1995 (reprint)
Rixinger, Martin: *Sanā'ullāh Amritsari (1868–1948) und die Ahl-i-Hadis im Punjab unter britischer Herrschaft*, Würzburg 2004
Rizvi, S.A.A.: "Islamic Proselytisation: Seventh to Sixteenth Centuries", in G.A. Oddie (ed.): *Religion in South Asia*, pp. 19–37
——: *A History of Sufism in India. Vols I–II*, New Delhi 1978
——: *A Socio-Intellectual History of the Isna 'Ashari Shi'is in India* Vols. 1–2, New Delhi 1986
——: *Religion and Intellectual History of the Muslims in Akbar's Reign, with special reference to Abu'l Fazl (1556–1605)*, New Delhi 1975
——: *Shah 'Abd al 'Aziz: Puritanism, Sectarian Polemics, and Jihad*, New Delhi 1982
Rizvi, Sayyid Mahbub: *History of the Dar al-Ulum Deoband*, Allahabad 1980
Robb, Peter (ed.): *Rural India: Land, Power and Society under British Rule*, London 1983
——: *A History of India*, Basingstoke 2002
Robinson, F.: "Perso-Islamic Culture in India from the seventeenth to the early twentieth century", in: Robert L. Canfield (ed.):*Turco-Persia in Historical Perspective*, pp. 104–131
Robinson, Francis: "Technology and Religious Change: Islam and the Impact of Print", in: *Modern Asian Studies* 27/1 (1993), pp. 229–251
——: *Separatism among Indian Muslims; the politics of the United Provinces' Muslims 1860–1923*, Cambridge 1974
——: *The 'Ulama of Farangi Mahall and Islamic Culture in South Asia*, New Delhi 2001
Rocher, Rosane: "British Orientalism in the Eighteenth Century: The Dialectics of Knowledge and Government", in Breckenridge et al. (eds.): *Orientalism*, pp. 215–249
Rogers, A. and Beveridge, H. (transl. and ed.): *The Tuzuk-i-Jahangiri or the Memoirs of Jahangir*, Vols. 1–2, Delhi 1989 (reprint)
Rosenthal, Franz: *A History of Muslim Historiography*, Leiden 1968 (2. revised Ed.)
Rothermund, Dietmar: "Der Traditionalismus als Forschungsgegenstand für Historiker und Orientalisten", in: *Saeculum* 40/2 (1989), pp. 142–148
——: *Mahatma Gandhi. An Essay in Political Biography*, New Delhi 1991
Rouse, Shahnaz: "The Outsider(s) within", in: P. Jeffery and A. Basu (eds.): *Appropriation Gender: Women's Activism and Politicized Religion in South Asia*, London 1998
Roy, Asim: "The interface of Islamization, regionalization and syncretization: the Bengal paradigm", in: Dallapiccola and Zingel-Ave Lallemant (eds.): *Islam and Indian Regions*, pp. 95ff.
——: "The high politics of India's partition", in: *Modern Asian Studies* 24 (1990), pp. 385–415
——: *The Syncretistic Tradition in Bengal*, Princeton 1983
Roy, Olivier: *Globalised Islam: The Search for a New Ummah, London* 2004
——: *The Failure of Political Islam*, tr. by Carol Folk, Cambridge 1994
Rüsen, Jörn and Sebastian Manhart (eds.): *Geschichtsdenken der Kulturen, Südasien*, Frankfurt/M. 2002
Russell, R./Islam, K. (tr. and ed.): *Ghalib; 1797–1869; Vol. I: Life and Letters*, London 1969

Sadiq, Muhammad: *A History of Urdu Literature*, Delhi 1995

Said, Edward S.: *Orientalism*, London 1978

Sanyal, Usha: *Devotional Islam and Politics in British India: Ahmad Reza Khan Barelwi and his Movement 1870–1920*, Delhi 1996

Saqi, Must'ad Khan: *Maasir-i-ʿAlamgiri; A history of the Emperor Aurangzib-ʿAlamgir (Reign 1658–1707 A.D.)*, transl. and annotated by Jadunath Sarkar, Delhi 1986 (first 1947)

Sarkar, Sumit: *Modern India, 1885–1947*, Basingstoke 1989

——: *The Swadeshi Movement in Bengal, 1903–1908*, New Delhi 1977

Saxena, N.C.: "Historiography of Communalism in India", in: Hasan (ed.): *Communal and Pan-Islamic Trends*, pp. 302–313

Sayeed, K.B.: *Politics in Pakistan*, New York 1980

Schimmel, Annemarie: "Turk and Hindu", in: Speros Vryonis (ed.): *Islam and Cultural Change in the Middle Ages*, Wiesbaden 1975

——: *And Muhammad is His Messenger*, Chapel Hill, NC. 1985

——: *Gabriel's Wing. A Study into the Religious Ideas of Muhammad Iqbal*, Leiden 1963

——: *Mystical Dimensions of Islam*, Chapel Hill 1975

——: *Pain and Grace: a Study of Two Mystical Writers of Eighteenth-Century Muslim India*, Leiden 1976

Schirrmacher, Christine: *Mit den Waffen des Gegners*, Berlin 1992

Schulze, Reinhard: "Die islamische Welt in der Neuzeit (16.–19. Jahrhundert)", in: Noth and Paul (eds.): *Der islamische Orient*, pp. 384–386

——: "Schauspiel oder Nachahmung? Zum Theaterbegriff arabischer Reiseschriftsteller im 19. Jahrhundert", in: *Die Welt des Islams*, 34/1994, pp. 67–84

——: *Geschichte der Islamischen Welt im 20. Jahrhundert*, München 1994

——: *Islamischer Internationalismus im 20. Jahrhundert*, Leiden 1990

Seervai, H.M.: *Partition of India; Legend and Reality*, Bombay 1989

Shah ʿAbd al-ʿAziz: *Fatawa-ye ʿAzizi*, Karachi 1412 h. (reprint)

Shah, Sayed Wiqar Ali: *Ethnicity, Islam and Nationalism. Muslim Politics in the North-West Frontier Province 1937–1947*, Karachi 1999

Shaikh, F.: *Community and Consensus in India: Muslim Representation in Colonial India 1860–1947*, Cambridge 1989

Shakeb, M.Z.A.: "The role of the Sufis in the changing society of the Deccan, 1500–1750", in: L. Lewisohn and D. Morgan (eds.): *The Heritage of Sufis, Vol. III: Late Classical Persianate Sufism (1501–1750)*, Oxford 1999

Sharma, Sanjay: *Famine, Philanthropy and the Colonial State. North India in the Early Nineteenth Century*, Oxford 2001

Sherwani, H.K.: "Bahmanis", in: *EI(2), I*, pp. 923f.

——: "Golkonda", in: *EI(2), II*, pp. 1118f.

——: "Mahmûd Gawân", in: *EI(2), VI*, pp. 66ff.

Shokoohy, Mehrdad: "The town of Cochin and its Muslim heritage on the Malabar coast, South India", in: *Journal of the Royal Asiatic Society* series 3, 8, part 3 (1998), pp. 351–394

——: *Bhadresvar. The Oldest Islamic Monuments in India*, Leiden 1988

——: *Muslim Architecture of South India, the Sultanate of Maʿbar and the Traditions of the Maritime Settlers on the Malabar and Coromandel Coasts (Tamil Nadu, Kerala and Goa)*, London 2003

Siddiqui, Iqtidar H.: "Social Mobility in the Delhi Sultanate", in: Habib (ed.): *Medieval India 1*, pp. 22–48

——: "The Agrarian System of the Afghans", in: *Studies in Islam* 1965, pp. 229–253

——: *Perso-Arabic Sources of Information on the Life and Conditions in the Sultanate of Delhi*, Delhi 1992

Siddiqui, M.K.A. (ed.): *Marginal Muslim Communities in India*, New Delhi 2004

Siddiqui, M.Z.: "The Muhtasib Under Aurangzeb", in: *Medieval India Quarterly* 5 (1963), pp. 113–119

Sikand, Y.: *Islam, Dalit-Muslim Relations in India*, New Delhi 2004

——: *The Origins and Development of the Tablighi Jama'at*, New Delhi 2002

Sirriyeh, E.: *Sufis and Anti-Sufis. The Defence, Rethinking and Rejection of Sufism in the Modern World*, Richmond 1999

Smith, Grace Martin and Carl W. Ernst (eds.): *Manifestations of Sainthood in Islam*, Istanbul 1993

Smith, W.C.: *Modern Islam in India. A Social Analysis*, London 1946, (reprint) Lahore 1969

Spear, Percival: *The Nabobs: A Study of the Social Life of the English in Eighteenth Century India*, London 1963

Stahmann, Christian: *Islamische Menschenrechtskonzepte und das Problem sogenannter 'islamischer' Menschenrechtsverletzungen in Pakistan seit 1977*, Heidelberg 2005

Stanford, J.K. (ed.): *Ladies in the sun. The Memsahibs' India, 1790–1860*, London 1962

Stark, Ulrike: *An Empire of Books: The Naval Kishore Press and the Diffusion of the Printed Word in Colonial India, 1858–1895*, New Delhi 2008

Stein, Burton: *A history of India*, Oxford 1998

——: *Vijayanagar*, Cambridge 1989

Stewart, Gordon: "Maratha Patronage of Muslim Institutions in Burhanpur and Khandesh", in: Gilmartin and Lawrence (eds.): *Beyond Turk and Hindu*, pp. 327–338

——: *The Marathas 1600–1818*, Cambridge 1993

Stewart, Tony K.: "In Search of Equivalence: Conceiving the Muslim-Hindu Encounter Through Translation Theory", in: Eaton (ed.): *India's Islamic Traditions*, pp. 363–392

Stietencron, Heinrich von: "Religious Configurations in Pre-Muslim India and the Modern Concept of Hinduism", in: V. Dalmia and H. v. Stietencron (eds.): *Representing Hinduism. The Construction of Religious Traditions and National Identity*, New Delhi 1995, pp. 51–81

Stokes, Eric: *The English Utilitarians and India*, Delhi 1992(3)

——: *The Peasant Armed: The Indian Revolt of 1857*, ed. C.A. Bayly, Oxford 1986

Subrahmanyam, Sanjay, V. Narayana Rao and David Shulman (eds.): *Textures of Time: Writing History in South India, 1600–1800*, New Delhi 2003

Subrahmanyam, Sanjay: "Connected Histories: Notes towards a Reconfiguration of Early Modern Eurasia", in: *Modern Asian Studies* 31/3 (1997), pp. 735–762

——: *Explorations in Connected History. From the Tagus to the Ganges*, New Delhi 2005

——: *Explorations in Connected History. Mughals and Franks*, New Delhi 2005

Sufi, G.M.D.: *Al-Minhaj; evolution of curricula in the Muslim educational institutions*, Lahore 1981 (first 1941)

Syed, A.: *Pakistan: Islam, Politics and National Security*, Lahore 1984

Talbot, Ian: "Inscribing the Other, Inscribing the Self: Hind-Muslim Relations in Pre-Colonial India", in: *Comparative Studies in Society and History* 37 (1995), pp. 692–722

——: *Provincial Politics and the Pakistan Movement. The Growth of the Muslim League in North-West and North-East India 1937–47*, Karachi 1988

Tavakoli-Targhi, Mohamad: "Orientalism's Genesis Amnesia", in: *Comparative Studies of South Asia, Africa and the Middle East* XVI/1 (1996), pp. 1–14

Thapar, Romila et al.: *Communalism and the Writing of Indian History*, New Delhi 1977 (2)

Thapar, Romila: "A historical perspective on the story of Rama", in: S. Gopal (ed.): *Anatomy of a Confrontation*, pp. 141–163

——: *Somanatha. The Many Voices of a History*, New Delhi 2004

Tonki, S.M.: *Aligarh and Jamia; Fight for National Education System*, New Delhi 1983

Trimingham, J.S.: *The Sufi Orders in Islam*, Oxford 1971
Troll, Chr.W. (ed.): *Islam in India. Studies and Commentaries, II*, New Delhi 1985
—— (ed.): *Muslim Shrines in India*, New Delhi 1989
——: *Sayyid Ahmad Khan: A Reinterpretation of Muslim Theology*, Karachi 1979
Tusi, Nasir al-Din: *Akhlaq-e Nasiri (The Nasirean Ethics)*, trans. G.M. Wickens, London 1964
Umar, Muhammad: *Islam in Northern India During the Eighteenth Century*, New Delhi 1993
Vaikuntham, Y. (ed.): *People's Movements in the Princely States*, New Delhi 2004
Vassie, R.: "'Abd al-Rahman Chishti and the Bhagavadgita 'unity of religion' theory in practice", in: L. Lewisohn (ed.): *The Heritage of Sufism, Vol. II: The Legacy of medieval Persian Sufism (1150–1500)*, pp. 368–377
Veer, P. van der: *Religious Nationalism: Hindus and Muslims in India*, New Delhi 1996
Wagner, Christian: *Die Muslime Sri Lankas*, Freiburg 1990
Wagoner, Phillip B: "'Sultan among Hindu Kings': Dress, Titles, and the Islamicization of Hindu Culture at Vijayanagara", in: *Journal of Asian Studies* 55 (1996), pp. 851–880
Walter, C.: *The Warrior Saints in Byzantine Art and Tradition*, Oxford 2003
Washbrook, David: "South Asia, The World System, and World Capitalism", in: *Journal of Asian Studies* 49/3 (1990), pp. 479–508
Weber, Max: "Religionssoziologie, Typen religiöser Vergemeinschaftung", in: *Wirtschaft und Gesellschaft, Grundriss der verstehenden Soziologie*, Tübingen 1980(5)
Werbner, Pnina (ed.): *Person, Myth and Society in South Asian Islam*, Social Analysis 28, Adelaide 1990
——: "Factionalism and Violence in British Pakistani Politics", in: Donnan Hasting and Pnina Werbner (eds.): *Economy and Culture in Pakistan; Migrants and Cities in a Muslim Society*, London 1991, pp. 188–215
——: "Allegories of Sacred Imperfection: Magic, Hermeneutics, and Passion in 'The Satanic Verses'", in: *Current Anthropology* (Chicago) 37 (1996), Supplement
Wesseling, H.L. (ed.): *Expansion and Reaction. Essays on European Expansion and Reaction in Asia and Africa*, Leiden 1978
Wild, Anthony: *The East India Company: trade and conquest from 1600*, London 2000
Willmer, David: "Women as Participants in the Pakistan Movement: Modernization and the Promise of a Moral State", in: *Modern Asian Studies* 30 (1996), pp. 574–578
Wink, André: "Islamic society and culture in the Deccan", in: Dallapiccola et al. (eds.): *Islam and Indian Regions*, pp. 217–227
——: "Sovereignty and Universal Dominion in South Asia", in: *The Indian Economic and Social History Review* 21 (1984), pp. 265–92
——: *Al-Hind. The Making of the Indo-Islamic World; Vol. II: The Slave Kings and The Islamic Conquest. 11th–13th Centuries*, Leiden 1997
——: *Al-Hind. The Making of the Indo-Islamic World; Vol. I: Early Medieval India and the Expansion of Islam, Seventh to Eleventh Centuries*, Delhi 1990
Ya'qubi, Ahmad ibn Abi Ya'qub: *Kitab al-Buldan*, Leiden 1892
Young, Robert J.C.: *Colonial Desire: Hybridity in Theory, Culture, and Race*, London 1995
Zaidi, 'Ali Jawwad: *Tarikh-e musha'irah*, Dehli 1989
Zaman, M.Q.: "Commentaries, Print and Patronage: "Hadith" and the Madrasas in Modern South Asia", in: *Bulletin of the School of Oriental and African Studies* 62 (1999), pp. 60–81
——: *The Ulama in Contemporary Islam. Custodians of Change*, Karachi 2002
Zarcone, Thierry: "Central Asian Influences on the Early Development of the Chishtiyya Sufi Order in India", in: M. Alam et alii. (eds.): *The Making of Indo-Persian Culture*, pp. 99–116
Ziegler, Norman P: "Some Notes of Rajput Loyalties During the Mughal Period", in: Richards (ed.): *Kingship and Authority*

Zilfi, Madelaine C.: *The Politics of Piety: The Ottoman Ulema in the Postclassical Age, 1600–1800*, Minneapolis 1988
Ziring, L.: *Bangladesh. From Mujib to Ershad. An interpretative study*, Karachi 1992
Zutshi, Chitralekha: *Languages of Belonging: Islam, Regional Identity, and the Making of Kashmir*, New York 2004

GLOSSARY

ʿabd	slave, servant
ʿada, pl. ʿadat	customary practices of social interaction
adab	taste, proper behaviour, etiquette, order, also literature
afaqi	non-indigenous people, foreigners, esp. in Deccan
ahinsa	Hindu practice not to kill any living being, non-violent protest
Ahl al-dhimma, also dhimmi	people of the covenant, protected people living under Islamic rule and pay jizya
Ahl al-kitab	"people of the book", who are believed to have received a divine book
Ahl al-Sunna wa al-Jamaʿa	"People of (the Prophet's) custom and community"
Ahl-e Hadith	"the people of hadith" evolved in the second quarter of nineteenth century; they strictly follow Quran and Prophetic tradition and deny the authority of all schools of law
Ahmadiyya	millenarian movement established by Mirza Ghulam Ahmad (died 1908) whom his followers consider to have been endowed by prophethood. Since this belief contradicts the doctrine that Muhammad was the last prophet, Ahmadis are usually hereticised by other Muslims.
Ahrar	political party which emerged in the wake of the Khilafat movement, mainly based in Punjab
aʾimmahdar	revenue grant holder, usually religious scholar
ʿajam	"having no voice"; non-Arabs derogatory called by Arabs
ajlaf	"a body of any kind without a head upon it", unsound in intellect, lower classes, indigenous Indians converted to Islam
akhbar	discrete anecdotes and reports
akhlaq	conduct, ethics and morality
ʿaqaʾid	religious beliefs, creedal statements
ʿaql	reason, intelligence
amir, pl. umaraʾ	leader of a group of community, guide
amsar, sing. masr	garrison post
anjuman	association, usually not religious in the first place
ansar	"helpers", those tribes from Medina, who joined Muhammad's mission after his emigration from Mecca in 622
ardhal, also radhil, ridhalah	local converts, lower classes
ashraf, also sharif	Muslim nobility; usually descendants of the Prophet, and other important figures
avatar	epiphany, incarnation of a deity
awliyaʾ, see wali	
aya, pl. ayat	divine sign, verse of the Quran
baiʿa	pact, vow of alliance to a Sufi master

baraka	blessing, spiritual power
Barelwi	toponym of a North Indian (Bareilly) Hanafi movement which came into being in reaction to revivalist trends such as Deobandis and Ahl-e Hadith. They give great importance to the idea of a living Prophet Muhammad and emphasise devotional practices attached to shrines.
bhadralok	local Hindu elites of Bengal evolved in nineteenth century under British rule
bhakti	popular devotional trend in medieval Hindu traditions
bidʿa	unlawful innovation, even heresy
Bohra	predominately Shia trading community of western India
chilla	forty days of seclusion, in which pious people engage in prayer and meditation
Chishtiyya	Sufi order brought to South Asia by Hasan Muʿin al-Din (died 1236) from Chisht. It tends towards shared religious traditions with the tradition of samaʿ as a major vehicle of mystical experience
daʿi, pl. duʿat	one who invites, missionary
daʿwa	"missionary activity", call to religion, to proselytise
daʾira	"circle", congregation cell of the Mahdawiyya
dakhani	older settlers, mostly Sunni immigrants from North India
dar al-ʿulum	"house of sciences", institution of higher (religious) school
dar al-harb	"abode of war", territory not under Muslim sovereignty
dar al-Islam	"abode of Islam", territory under Islamic rule
dar al-sulh	"land of settlement"
dargah	sanctified space represented by sufi tombs and shrines
dars-e nizami	syllabus developed by Farangi Mahallis
Deobandis	Hanafi scholars who adhere to the scholarly tradition of the madrasa in Deoband in Northern India. They focused on rigorous training in transmitted sciences in order to reform as well as to conserve Islamic mores and identity
dharma	Hindu moral and societal order
dhikr	remembrance of God or the Prophet
dhimma	covenant of protection of the people of the book
dhimmi	Jews, Christians, and other non-Muslims paying special tax (jizya) in return of legal protection of their lives and property
din	religion, faith
diwan	revenue official; head of a shrine
diwani	revenue collection rights
faqih, pl. fuqahaʾ	a Muslim jurisprudent; expert in Islamic law (fiqh)
faqih, pl. fuqaha	scholar of law
faraʾid	religious duties of Muslims, rules of inheritance
Farangi Mahalli	Muslim scholarly tradition called so after the European quarter in Lucknow which was given by the emperor in 1694 as compensation. The Farangi Mahalli tradition generated a syllabus (dars-e nizami) with regional varieties, and later became quite active also in politics.
farman	written and sealed command issued by the court
farr-e izadi	"divine glory", derived from Iranian tradition to serve Akbar's splendour
fatwa, pl. fatawa	advisory legal opinion issued by a mufti
fiqh	"understanding", Islamic jurisprudence
fitna, pl. fitan	"temptation", treasury, disorder, civil war in early Islam
futuh	early Muslim expansions

ghair muqallid	those who do not adhere to a school of law and taqlid, commonly the Ahl-e Hadith
ghazal	brief poem in monorhyme
ghazi	someone who goes for a ghazwa, holy warrior
ghazwa	raid, attack, war, sometimes synonym for jihad
ghulam	slave
ginan	religious poetry of the Ismaili community
hadd, pl. hudud	"limit"; term for some few punishments prescribed in the Quran
hadith	sayings attributed to the Prophet Muhammad, compiled in several collections, with a normative character for the Muslims, second to the Quran. The elements of a hadith are the isnad (the chain of traditionarians) and the matn (the text).
hajj	pilgrimage to Mecca, which should be performed by every Muslim once in life; takes place at the beginning of the last month of the Islamic lunar calendar
Hanafi	someone adhering to one of four Sunni schools of law attributed to Abu Hanifa (699–767), which became widespread as in Ottoman and Mughal legal traditions
Hanbali	someone adhering to one of four Sunni schools of law attributed to Ahmad b. Hanbal (780–855), prominent in West Asia and the Arab Peninsula
hijra	migration of Muhammad from Mecca to Medina in 622; beginning of the Muslim era
hisba	state authority
hundi	bills of exchange, note of credit
ʿibada, pl. ʿibadat	obligation by human being to god, in contrast to muʿamalat, prescribing the social behaviour and conduct among humans
ijaza	"authorisation" to teach a particular (religious) text
ijmaʿ	"consensus", the method of arriving at a consensus in an Islamic judicial trial
ijtihad	"effort", independent judgement, based on the interpretation of sources of Islamic law, such as Quran, hadith, qiyas and ijmaʿ
ʿilm, pl. ʿulum	knowledge, science, scholarly discipline
imam, pl. aʾimmah	leader in prayer or of the community; in Shia tradition also the true successor of the Prophet
Imambargah	building in which the festival of Muharram is celebrated in where services are held in commemoration of the death of ʿAli and his sons Hasan and Husain
inʿam	revenue grant exempt from tax
iqtaʿ	transferable revenue assignment in lieu of salary for service
iqtaʿdar	holder of an iqtaʿ
islah	reform
isnad	chain of transmitters appended to a hadith
itaʿa	absolute obedience
Ithna ʿAsharis	Twelver Shiʿites; they consider twelve consecutive descendants of the Prophet Muhammad through his daughter Fatima and his son in law ʿAli their infallible spiritual and political guides
Jaʿfari	school of law of the Twelver Shiʿites named after the sixth Shiʿite imam, Jaʿfar al-Sadiq (d. 765)
jagir	temporary assignment of land-revenues in the Mughal system
jagirdar	in the Mughal system the holder of temporary revenue rights
jahiliyya	"age of ignorance", period of paganism before the advent of Islam, also used as metaphor for unbelief and apostasy in contemporary Islamist discourses

jama'a	community reached by consensus
jami'	congregational mosque
Jam'iyyat al-'ulama-ye Hind	Deobandi "Association of the Scholars of India" established in 1919
Jam'iyyat-e 'ulama-ye Islam	Deobandi pro-Pakistan "Association of Muslim scholars" founded in 1945
Jam'iyyat-e 'ulama-ye Pakistan	Barelwi "Association of Pakistani scholars" established in 1947
janapada	clan territory
Jat	major Hindu agricultural caste
Jati	type; usually endogamous group
jihad	"struggle", spiritual as well as armed struggle against evil, holy war
jizya	capitation tax for dhimmis as stipulated in Quran 9:29
kafir (pl. kuffar)	infidel, unbeliever
kalam	"word"; used for the discipline of dialectical theology
khalifa, pl. khulafa'	successor; title of those who presided the Islamic empire after the death of Muhammad. In mystical terminology the successor of a Sufi shaikh
khalisa	crown land, producing revenue for the emperor and central treasury
khan	honorific title for nobleman
khanaqah	Sufi hospice
khanazad	"son of the house" with hereditary family service
khanazadagi	system of old and established families, offspring of one kinship group
khatib, pl. khutaba',	preacher, delivering the friday sermon (khutba)
khilafa	succession, office of the caliph
khilafat movement	Indian movement in support of the Ottoman caliph from 1919 to 1924
Khojas	Ismaili trading community
khutba	friday sermon; at the end the name of the ruler is mentioned acknowledging his legitimate rule
kotwal	head of city police, castellan
kufr	infidelity
ma'qulat	the rational sciences
madad-e ma'ash	right to tax-free land revenue usually given for religious or scholarly purpose
madaris, see madrasa	
madhhab, pl. madhahib	school of Muslim religious law
madrasa, pl. madaris	place of learning, religious school
mahdi	"rightly guided", chiliastic figure of the expected and awaited one
majlis	meeting, session, convent
maktab	place of memorising and reading the Quran, school
maktab-e fikr, pl. makatib-e fikr	a school of thought. Some schools of thought do not differ from each other in a theological sense. In contrast to this one may mention the madhahib (sing. madhhab) (schools of law) with considerable differences in their principles of interpretation of the Islamic law
maktubat	didactical letters, usually of holy men

malfuzat	sayings of a sufi master, collected and recorded by his disciples
manaqib	miracle stories
manqulat	so-called transmitted sciences
mansab	status and position indicated by numerical rank
mansabdar	holder of civil or military appointment in Mughal imperial service
Mappila	a Malyali Muslim
marthiya	threnody, dirge, especially in commemoration of the martyrs of Kerbala
masha'ikh, sing. shaikh	Islamic mystic and leader of an order
masjid	"place of prostration", mosque
mawas	territory inaccessible to attack
mirza	title for a member of a royal family or aristocracy
mleccha	"impure", Muslims as perceived by Hindus
muʿamalat	social obligations
mufti	Islamic scholar, qualified to give legal opinions, jurisconsultant
muhaddith, pl. muhaddithun	scholars studying hadith and propagating its normative importance
muhajir, pl. muhajirun	"migrant", Muslims who accompanied Muhammad on his migration from Mecca to Medina; someone who left India for Pakistan. Today general expression for refugee
Muharram	preceded by the month of hajj this is the first lunar month of the Islamic calendar; ʿAli's son Husain was killed by Umayyad troops in the battle of Kerbala in 680. Therefore, Shiʿites commemorated Muharram with mourning and processions.
muhtasib	market supervisor, censor, overseer of public morality
mujaddid	renewer of religion who is supposed to appear at the beginning of every century
mujahid, pl. mujahidun	holy warrior; someone waging jihad
mujtahid	someone authorised to practise ijtihad
muqallid	one who adheres to one of the four schools of Islamic jurisprudence and thus practices taqlid
muqtaʿ	holder of an iqtaʿ
murid	disciple, usually of a mystical master
murshid	leader, usually of a mystical order, cf. also pir
musaddas	poem in six-lined strophes
muttahida qaumiyyat	composite nationalism; propagated by Indian Muslim Deobandi scholars against the idea of the Two-Nation-Plan
nabi (pl. anbiya)	prophet
nabobs	an epithet for Europeans returning with fortunes from India
Naqshbandiyya	mystical order attributed to Baha' al-Din Naqshband (d. 1388) emphasising Islamic pietist teachings
nasab	concept of holding kinship ties with the Prophet's family
nawa'it	descendants of an Arab tribe adhering to Shafiʿi school of law, predominantly in Gujarat
nizamat	"arrangement", administration of justice
padishah	master-king, highest rank

pir	Persian word for mystical leader, sufi master
purdah	veil; seclusion of woman
qadi	a qualified judge; in British time reduced to an officer of registrary
Qadiriyya	mystical order attributed to ʿAbd al-Qadir Jilani (died 1166), which strives toward traditionalist Hanbalite legalism with ecstatic mystic individualism
qanun	state or administrative law, in contrast to fiqh
qasbah	administrative, market and garrison town
qaum	people or nation affiliated by traditions, ethnicity, territory, language
qaumiyyat	national consciousness, nationalism
qayyum	the highest spiritual authority, in Sirhindi's theology
qiyas	reasoning by analogy in Islamic jurisprudence
radhil, also ardhal, ridhalah	"uncivilised", local converts, lower classes
raj	rule, kingdom; in particular British rule in India
Rajput	Hindu military and landholding caste
rasul	messenger
rekhta	"mixed", poetical form in which local languages and Persian intermingled
rekhti	subgenre of Urdu ghazal in which both the narrator and the narrative idiom is female
ridhalah, also ardhal, radhil	local converts, lower classes
sabiqa	concept of outstanding merits in the cause of Islam
sabk-e hindi	Indian-Persian literary diction known as the Indian style
sadr al-sudur	highest civil officer who was in charge of profane and religious law
sahaba	the companions of the Prophet Muhammad
sajjada-nashin	successor to the leadership of a pir
salaf	"pious ancestors", referring to earliest generations of Muslims religious scholars
salafiyya	Islamic reform movement founded by the end of nineteenth century
samaʿ	"hearing," mystical concert
sanad	degree, certificate
satyagraha	"truth force", non-violent resistance as taught by Gandhi
sayyid, pl. sadat	descendant of the Prophet
Shafiʿi	one adhering to the legal tradition attributed to al-Shafiʿi (died 820) and his legal dogmatism
shaikh, pl. shuyyukh	Muslim dignitary, an elder, often a Sufi master
shariʿa	Muslim law governing profane as well as a sacred law
sharif, pl. ashraf	"noble," claiming descent from the Prophet
Shia (Shiʿa)	Muslims who regard ʿAli, the son-in-law of the Prophet, and his descendants through Fatima the only divinely designated and legitimate leaders of the Muslim community. In course of history the Shia eventually spilt in several sub-divisions.
Shiʿite	adhering to Shia
shirk	"association", blasphemy by polytheism
shuddhi	"purification", movement aiming at reconverting Hindus from Islam

sijda	"prostration", extreme form of submission favored by Sufi disciples as well as some rulers such as Akbar
silsila	"chain", Sufi chain of spiritual authority
sira(t)	"biography," especially of the Prophet
siyasat	administration, political power and will
suba	province, dominion
Sufi	"wearer of wool", Muslim mystic
Sufism	mystical movement in Islam
sulh-e kull	Akbar's notion of peace with all, or universal peace
sunna	"custom," normative practice of the Prophet, embodied in hadith literature
Sunni, Sunnite	someone adhering to the sunna and mainstream Muslim norms and practices
swadeshi	"of one's own land"; boycott movement
swaraj	self-rule, independence
taʿalluqdar	one who collects land revenue in return for a commission from imperial treasury; one who holds estate or a division of a province
taʾrikh, tarikh	history, chronicles
tabligh	propagation; missionary activity
Tablighi Jamaʿat	A most popular proselytising movement which evolved near Delhi in Northern India a decade after the collapse of Khilafat movement
tadhkira	biographies recording lives and works of Muslim holy men and authors, hagiography
tafsir	exegesis, commentary of the Quran
Tahdhib al-Akhlaq	refinement of morals leading to intellectual revelation
tajdid	renewal of faith, reform
takhallus	pen name
taqiyya	concealing one's true religious beliefs, often practised by Shiʿites in order to escape from persecution
taqlid	"investing with authority", following the legal ideas of a recognised school of law; in contrast to ijtihad
tariqa, pl. turuq	way; mystical path, fraternity
Tariqah-ye Muhammadi or al-tariqa al-muhammadiyya	"the Muhammadan Path," mystical ethical concept in the eighteenth century. One century later this concept was radicalised in mystical movement which also had an anti-colonial stand.
tasawwuf	Arabic term for Sufism
tauhid	believe in the unity of god (monotheism) in contrast to shirk, polytheism
ʿulama, sing. ʿalim	"people of knowledge" usually holding authorisation in formal training in the field of Islamic learning
ʿulum-e ʿaqliyyah	the acquired or rational sciences
ʿulum-e naqliyyah	the transmitted sciences
umma	community of Muslims worldwide
ʿurf	customary law

ʿurs	"marriage"; celebration of the death anniversary of a Sufi
varna	order of traditional Hindu society
varna-sankara	mixing of caste
wahdat al-shuhud	"unity of vision", testimonial unity
wahdat al-wujud	"unity of being", existential unity
wali Allah	friend of god, Sufi holy person, who has particular relationship with god
waqf, pl. awqaf	tax-free pious, religious endowment
watan	ancestral country, abode, residence
wilayat	province, also spiritual territory or saintly realm of Sufis
zabt	system of land tax assessment and collection under the Mughals
zakat	"purification"; alms-tax on annual savings (2.5%) compulsory for Muslims, as stipulated in Quran 2:177
zamindar	landlord controlling the peasantry directly in contrast to taʿal-luqdar

ISLAM IN SOUTH ASIA—SELECT OVERVIEW

The Arabs

612	First Mosque in the Indian State of Kerala
630	Ships of Muslim travellers on Indian coast
644	Muslim Arabs forces enter Sind
661	Arab expeditions along the Indus
711	Muhammad Bin Qasim invades Sind
713	Multan conquered
738	al-Mansura founded
750	Abbasid expeditions
965	Ismaili state around Multan

The Ghaznawids

977–997	Sebüktigin
999–1027	Mahmud of Ghazni invaded India 17 times
1026	Mahmud at Somnath in Gujarat
1031–1041	Masʿud I
1041–1050	Maudud
1050	Masʿud II
1050	al-Biruni (973–1050)
1053–1059	Farrukhzad
1059–1099	Ibrahim
1071	al-Hujwiri (1009–1071)
1099–1115	Masʿud III
1115–1118	Arslan Shah
1118–1152	Bahram Shah
1152–1160	Khusraw Shah
1160–1187	Khusraw Malik

The Ghorids

1156–1160	Ghorids advance to and conquer Ghazni
1173	Ghorids advance eastwards.
1175	Muhammad Ghori occupies Multan and Uchh
1180	invasion of Gujarat
1186–1187	Lahore occupied by Muhammad Ghori
1191–92	Delhi and Ajmer invaded
1200	Ghorids conquer Bengal
1206	Muhammad Ghori assassinated

The Sultanate of Delhi

The Slave Dynasty

1206–1210	Qutb al-Din Aybak in Delhi
1210–1211	Aram Shah
1211–1236	Iltutmish
1235	death of Bakhtiyar Kaki Chishti
1236	death of Mu'in al-Din Chishti
1236–1240	Radiyya Sultana
1240–1242	Mu'izz al-Din Bahram
1242–1246	'Ala al-Din Mas'ud
1246–1266	Nasir al-Din Mahmud
1258	Mongols capture Baghdad
1262	death of Baha' al-Din Zakariyya Suhrawardi
1266–1286	Balaban
1266	death of Farid al-Din Ganj-e Shakar
1286–1290	Mu'izz al-Din Qaiqabad

The Khalajis

1290–1296	Jalal al-Din Khalaji
	Jizya imposed
1294	Conquest of Devagiri (Daulatabad)
1296–1306	Several Attacks by Mongol at Delhi
1296–1316	'Ala al-Din Khalaji
1297	Conquest of Gujarat
1305	Conquest of Malwa
1316–1320	Qutb al-Din

The Tughluqids

1320–1324	Ghiyath al-Din Tughluq Shah I
1324–1351	Muhammad Ibn Tughluq
1325	death of Nizam al-Din Auliya
1325	death of Amir Khusraw
1327	Capital shifted from Delhi to Daulatabad
1333–1345	Ibn Batutta (died 1377) in India
1335 and 1342	famines
1351–1388	Firoz Tughlaq
1388–1389	Tughluq II
1389–1390	Abu Bakr
1390–1393	Nasir al-Din Mahmud Shah
1393–1394	Sultan Mahmud II
1397	Timur (dies 1405) invades South Asia

The Sayyids

1414–1421	Khizr Khan
1421–1434	Mubarak Shah
1434–1448	'Alam Shah

The Lodhis

1451–1489	Bahlul Lodhi
1489–1517	Sikandar Lodhi
1517–1526	Ibrahim Lodhi
1440–1518	Kabir
1469–1539	Guri Nanak

Independent Muslim centres

1352–1576	Bengal
1381	death of Sharaf al-Din Yahya Maneri
1453	death of Shaikh Qutb-e ʿAlam
1339–1561	Kashmir
1385	death of Sayyid Ali Hamadani
1438	death of Nur al-Din
1420–1470	Zain al-ʿAbidin
1347–1527	Deccan (Bahmanids)
1422	death of Muhammad Gesudaraz
1370–1601	Deccan (Faruqids)
1490–1633	Ahmadnagar (Nizamshahis)
1490–1686	Bijapur (Adilshahis)
1512–1687	Golconda (Qutbshahis)
1394–1479	Jawnpur (Sharqis)
1445	death of Shihab al-Din Daulatabadi
1505	death of Sayyid Muhammad Kazimi in Khurasan
1406–1570	Malwa
1407–1572	Gujarat
1411	Ahmadabad
1431	death of ʿAla al-Din Mahaʾimi
1498	Vasco da Gama at the port of Calicut

The coming of the Mughals

1526	Babur defeats Ibrahim Lodhi at Panipat
1530–1539	Humayun succeeds his father Babur
1539	Humayun defeated by Surs

Sur interlude

1538–1545	Sher Shah
1545–1553	Islam Shah Suri
1553–1555	ʿAdil Shah

The return of the Mughals

1555–1556	Humayun second Mughal emperor
1556–1605	Akbar I (born 1542)
1564	jizya abolished
1560s–	Rawshaniyya Movement
1575	jizya reimposed
1580s–	Mahdawiyya Movement
1581	Akbar proclaims sulh-e kull
1605–1627	Jahangir

1624	death of Ahmad Sirhindi
1627–1658	Shahjahan
1631–1647	Taj Mahal and Shahjahanabad
1658	Aurangzeb succeeds Shahjahan
1659	Dara Shikoh executed
1666	death of Shahjahan
1668–1678	Fatawa-ye ʿAlamgiri
1663–1689	Shivaji and Shambhuji and the Maratha War
1678	great Rajput rebellion
1679	re-introduction of jizya
1680	death of Shivaji
1680–1689	Shambhaji
1681	Aurangzeb founds Aurangabad
1694	Farangi Mahall handed over to Muslim scholars
1698	British acquire zamindari rights over Calcutta
1707	death of Aurangzeb
1707–1712	Bahadur Shah I
1712	Jahandar Shah
1713–1719	Farrukh Siyar
1717	English East India Company allowed carrying out duty-free trade
1719	Shahjahan II
1719–1748	Muhammad Shah
1700s	independent movements
1716	Murshid Quli Khan in Bengal, Murshidabad capital
1722	Burhan al-Mulk in Awadh, Lucknow capital
1724	Nizam al-Mulk in Deccan, Haydarabad capital
1729	death of Shah Kalim Allah Chishti
1739	Nadir Shah invades Delhi
1748	death of Mulla Nizam al-Din
1748–1754	Ahmad Shah
1754–1759	ʿAziz al-Din ʿAlamgir II

The Colonial context

1757	Battle of Plassey
1759–1806	Shah ʿAlam II
1763	Peace of Paris
1761	Battle of Panipat
1762	death of Shah Wali Allah
1764	Battle of Buxar
1765	Diwani of Bengal to EIC
1761–1782	Haydar ʿAli in Mysore
1773	Warren Hastings first Governor General
1781	Madrasa Aliyya Kalkatta
1785–1793	Charles Cornwallis, Governor General of India
1793	Permanent Settlement
1798–1805	Lord Wellesley, Governor General of India
1801	Awadh partly annexed
1803	Delhi annexed
1803	fatwa by Shah ʿAbd al-ʿAziz (died 1824)
1806–1837	Akbar II
1813	East India Company's Charter; Christian missionaries
1815	Congress of Vienna
1818	East India Company establishes almost all-India rule

1818–1862	Faraidiyya in Bengal
1820–1857	Tariqah-ye Muhammadi in North West and later also in Bengal
1828–1835	William Bentinck Governor General of India
1829	Sati banned
1830s	Ahl-e Hadith movement
1831	Sayyid Ahmad of Rae Bareli and Shah Isma'il Dihlawi killed
1835	English and Hindustani replace Persian
1836	Education Minutes by Thomas B. Macauley (1800–1859)
1837–1857	Bahadur Shah II
1843	Punjab annexed
1849	Sind annexed
1848–1856	Dalhousie (1812–1860), Governor-General of India
1856	Annexation of Awadh
1857	Great Upheaval; Rebellion
1858	India becomes part of British Empire
1867	Seminary in Deoband
1870s	Barelwi movement
1875	Arya Samaj founded
1876	Mohammedan Anglo-Oriental College at Aligarh
1885	Indian National Congress founded
1889	Ahmadiyya founded by Mirza Ghulam Ahmad (1835–1908)
1892	Nadwat al-'Ulama inaugurated in Kanpur
1893	Muhammadan Anglo Oriental Defence Association
1898	death of Sayyid Ahmad Khan
1905	Partition of Bengal
1906	foundation of All India Muslim League
1916	Lucknow Pact
1919–1924	Khilafat Movement
1919	Killing at Jallianwala Bagh
1919	Foundation of Jam'iyyat al-'Ulama-ye Hind
1920	Aligarh Muslim University
1920	Jamia Millia Islamia, New Delhi established
1929	Khuda-ye Khidmatgar founded
1930	Iqbal's Address at Allahabad
1931	Khaksar movement founded
1934	Tablighi Jama'at founded
1938	death of Muhammad Iqbal
1940	Pakistan Resolution
1941	Jama'at-e-Islami founded

The nation states

1947	India and Pakistan (East and West) independent
1948	M.K. Gandhi assassinated, death of Muhammad 'Ali Jinnah
1948	War on Kashmir between India and Pakistan
1948–	Congress rule in India
1952–53	Anti-Ahmadiyya campaign in Pakistan
1958–69	martial law imposed by General Ayub Khan in Pakistan
1964	death of Jawaharlal Nehru
1965	War between India and Pakistan
1968	Green Revolution
1971	War between India and Pakistan
1971	Bangladesh independent
1972–1977	Zulfiqar 'Ali Bhutto (hanged 1979) Prime Minister of Pakistan

1974	Ahmadiyya declared un-Islamic in Pakistan
1975	Shaikh Mujib al-Rahman assassinated, coup d'etat by Zia al-Rahman
1975–1977	Emergency under Indira Gandhi
1977	coup d'etat by General Zia al-Haqq (killed 1988) in Pakistan
1979	Soviet occupation of Afghanistan followed by guerrilla war
1979	death of A.A. Maududi
1980s–	Kashmir militant movement
1982	General Irshad in power in Bangladesh
1984	Zia al-Haqq president of Pakistan
1984	Indira Gandhi assassinated
1985	Shah Bano case in India
1988–1990	Benazir Bhutto Prime Minister of Pakistan
1989	Rushdie affair
1990–1993	Nawaz Sharif Prime Minister of Pakistan
1991	Rajiv Gandhi assassinated
1992–1996	Mujahidun declare Islamic State in Afghanistan
1993	Benazir Bhutto Prime Minister of Pakistan
1991–96	Khalida Zia Prime Minister of Bangladesh
1992	Babri Mosque demolished in Ayodhya
1996–2001	Taliban control Afghanistan
1996–2001	Shaikh Hasina Prime Minister of Bangladesh
1997–1999	Nawaz Sharif Prime Minister of Pakistan
1998–2004	Bharatiyya Janata Party in India
1999	nuclear crisis between India and Pakistan
1999	coup d'etat by Pervez Musharraf in Pakistan
2001	attack on WTC
2002	Godhra train incident in Gujarat

INDEX OF NAMES

INDEX OF PLACES, RIVERS AND REGIONS

INDEX OF KEYWORDS

Themes in Islamic Studies

ISSN 1389-823X

1. Knysh, A. *Islamic Mysticism*. A Short History. 2000. ISBN 90 04 10717 7
2. Stillman, Y.K. and Stillman, N.A. (ed.) *Arab Dress, A Short History*. From the Dawn of Islam to Modern Times. 2003. ISBN 90 04 11373 8
3. El-Ashker, A. and Wilson, R. *Islamic Economics*. A Short History. 2006. ISBN-10: 90 04 15134 6, ISBN-13: 978 90 04 15134 5
4. Malik, J. *Islam in South Asia*. A Short History. 2008. ISBN 978 90 04 16859 6